The Official Illustrated History of

LEEDS

The Official Illustrated History of

LEEDS

ANDREW MOURANT
1919–1997

Author's acknowledgements:

I am indebted to many people for their help with this book. Colin S. Jeffrey has been invaluable as advisor, proof reader and guide to researching the early years. I also thank Phil Shaw of the Independent for reading the text and providing the tickets and programmes which illustrate the book, Andrew Ward for his guidance and fellowship, and Mark Evans for his dedicated work on the statistical appendix.

Past players have helped greatly with information and anecdotes. Above all, thanks go to Tommy Burden, Jimmy Dunn, John Charles, Jim Storrie, Peter Lorimer, Eddie Gray, Joe Jordan, Terry Connor and Gordon Strachan.

The newspaper library of Leeds Central Library is an essential source of material relating to the early years. Much information has been gleaned from the *Yorkshire Post, Yorkshire Evening Post;* also back numbers of *The Times, Sunday Times, Guardian, Observer, Independent, Independent on Sunday, Daily Telegraph* and *Daily Mirror.* Thanks also to Bob Baldwin, commercial manager of Leeds United, for supplying printed and video material.

First published in Great Britain in 1996 by Hamlyn, an imprint of Reed International Books Ltd, Michelin House, 81 Fulham Road, London SW3 6RB and Auckland, Melbourne, Singapore and Toronto.

Produced by Butler and Tanner
Printed in Great Britain

Art Director: Keith Martin
Design Manager: Bryan Dunn
Original Design: Peter Burt
Jacket Design: Martin Topping
Design: Paul Webb
Picture Research: Maria Gibbs
Publishing Director: Laura Bamford
Editors: Adam Ward and Trevor Davies
Assistant Editor: Tarda Davison-Aitkins
Production: Mark Walker

Suggested further reading:

The Origin and Development of Football in Leeds by Mike Green (published by the author); *The Origins of Professional Football in the West Riding District* by A.J. Arnold (Thoresby Society pamphlet); *Leeds United: A Complete Record* by Malcolm MacDonald and Martin Jarred (Breedon); *The Leeds United Story* by MacDonald and Jarred (Breedon); *Leeds United: The Official History of the Club* by Don Warters (Wensum Books); *The Leeds United Book of Football nos 1, 2 and 3* (Souvenir Press); *The Leeds United Story* by Jason Tomas (Arthur Barker); *For Leeds and England* by Jackie Charlton (Stanley Paul); *Don Revie, Portrait of a Footballing Enigma* by Andrew Mourant (Mainstream); *Leeds United: Player by Player* by Andrew Mourant (Guinness).

Photographic acknowledgements:

Allsport 6, 134, /Shaun Botterill 139 right, /Clive Brunskill 163, /Ross Kinnaird 160, 162, /Ben Radford 155 below, 158 top, /Dave Rodgers 154/5.

British Library 9, 10, 13, 14, 15, 16, 18 below.

Colorsport 7, 18, 22, 25, 27, 28, 29, 30, 31, 33, 34, 35, 37, 41, 44, 52, 56 top, 60, 61, 69 top, 87 top, 87 below, 92 top, 94 top left, 96, 97, 99, 100, 101 top, 101 below, 104, 105, 107, 108 top, 110, 111 top, 112, 113, 115, 116, 117, 118, 119, 121, 123, 124, 125, 126, 127 below, 127 top, 128, 129 below, 129 top left, 129 top right, 130 top left, 130 below, 130 top right, 131 top left, 132 top right, 132 below, 133 top, 133 below, 135, 136, 137 top right, 137 top right, 138 top, 139 left, 140 left, 141 below, 141 top, 142, 143, 144, 145 top, 146 top, 146 below, 148 below, 149, 150, 151 below, 151 top, 152, 153 below, 153 top, 155 top, 156, 157, 161, 164 top, 164 below, 165

Hulton Getty Picture Collection 17, 21, 26, 32/3, 36, 39, 40, 45, 47, 49, 50, 51, 53, 54 below, 54 top, 55, 56 below, 57, 59, 62/3, 64, 65, 66, 68 below, 68 top, 69 right, 70 below, 73 below, 73 top left, 75, 78, 79, 80, 82, 83, 84 top, 85 top, 85 below, 86, 89 top, 89 below, 93, 95 below, 102/3, 103 below, 106, 109, 120, 122, /Reuters 147 top, /Sportsphoto 137 below.

Mirror Syndication International 114.

Press Association News /David Giles 159.

Ross Parry / Yorkshire Evening Post 11, 19, 24, 42/3, 48, 58, 71 below, 72, 74 top right, 75 below, 76, 77 left, 88 top left, 90, 91 left, 91 right, 95 top, 98.

Phil Shaw 63 right, 67, 70 top left, 71 top, 73 top right, 74 below, 74 left, 77 right, 81, 81 left, 81 centre, 84 below, 88 below left, 92 left, 94 below, 108 below, 111 below, 131 below right, 131 top right, 132 top left, 138 below, 140 inset, 145 below, 147 below, 147 below, 148 left, 154 below, 158 inset below, 158 below.

Contents

Foreword

By Gordon Strachan

WHEN I came to Elland Road from Manchester United in 1989, I knew I was joining a club with a great tradition. Leeds were in the second division yet determined to recapture past glories. That was what excited me most.

Leeds United's rise from obscurity to become Britain's most powerful team in the late 1960s and 1970s is an inspiring story. Helping them back to the top and winning the league championship in 1992 was a thrilling highlight in my career. Leeds United fans are among the most passionate in the land and have been starved of success for far too long. A return to the big time was the least they deserved.

Football in Leeds has had a chequered history, as this book amply records. Yet the determination of key figures who love the game has always won through. The rapid formation of Leeds United in 1919, after Leeds City's disastrous expulsion from the Football League, was clear proof that soccer had come of age in what had been a rugby-dominated city.

At times, the great days of the Revie era were like a millstone to successor managers. Revie built a team of legends, but after he went there was a tendency for fans to live in the past. Yet the awesome new Elland Road ground is a monument to success, 1990s-style. I am proud, and feel privileged, to have been involved in that part of the club's story. Leeds United will always be special to me: long may they remain a force in the land.

Football comes to Leeds

Leeds United, one of the great football clubs, was born in a die-hard rugby city and came of age only after decades of turbulence. Association football was slower to take root in Leeds than in any of the other Victorian conurbations: the city remains the largest in Britain with only one professional team. Long after soccer had gripped Lancashire and the Midlands, the game remained on the fringes of organised sport in Leeds.

Rugby dominated sport in the West Riding of Yorkshire: by 1880, there were an estimated 100 teams taking the field each week, many of which were attached to the principal churches. At the turn of the century, West Yorkshire was a soccer desert; whilst towns as modest as Burton and Glossop had professional teams, Leeds and Bradford had none. Despite being developed in the public schools and in many areas a preserve of the middle classes, rugby had become a sport of the people in the West Riding woollen towns.

As much as anything, this was a reflection of social cohesion. In his pamphlet *The Origins of Professional Football*, A. J. Arnold says that textile firms, the basis of West Yorkshire's industrial and commercial life, were generally specialised and small, and their owners remained in close contact with employees. Members of the Yorkshire business community were often educated locally rather than at distant public schools. 'Yorkshire (rugby) clubs were from the outset less socially exclusive than their counterparts in Lancashire and other parts of the country, and more accessible to working-class enthusiasts.'

Interest in rugby was further galvanised by the institution of a knockout cup competition in 1877, the year efforts were first made to introduce soccer to Leeds. The pioneer was Sam Gilbert, cricket professional at Hunslet cricket club, and a native of Sheffield where soccer was the main game. Gilbert formed the first Hunslet Association Football Club. It was through Gilbert's determination that the club kept going for five seasons, though it was a constant struggle to find fixtures. There were flickers of soccer activity in other parts of the city – between 1877 and 1883, Rothwell, Oulton, Hunslet Wesleyans and Meanwood all produced soccer teams – but in 1883 Hunslet AFC folded through lack of fixtures, finance and interest.

Hunslet's successors fared little better. By 1885 Leeds FC had emerged, playing on the Star and Garter ground at Kirkstall, yet the club failed to attract any top quality opposition or much support. The club disbanded only to reappear in 1888, the year the Football League was formed. This prompted new clubs to emerge locally – enough, in 1894–95, to form the West Riding Association Football League. Three years later, leading local clubs formed the Yorkshire League, encompassing teams from South Yorkshire and including the reserve sides of Sheffield Wednesday and Sheffield United.

At the turn of the century, a revived Hunslet was the strongest association football club in Leeds, but, without a ground of its own, the playing and financial future was always precarious. After losing the lease on its home at Nelson Street, Hunslet disbanded in 1902 to concentrate on fund-raising and planning.

Welcome to Elland Road

In 1903, when the ailing Bradford rugby club Manningham decided to abandon rugby for professional soccer, Hunslet only had promises of backing and commitment from players eager to join up. The demise of Holbeck rugby club in 1904, however, was the catalyst which gave Hunslet the chance of having their own home at Elland Road.

Holbeck had joined the Northern Union in 1896 and developed a football and athletics ground at Elland Road in 1897 opposite the Peacock Inn. But the club folded after failing to beat

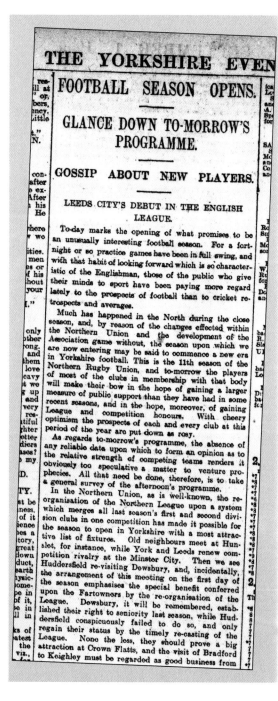

THE YORKSHIRE EVEN

FOOTBALL SEASON OPENS.

GLANCE DOWN TO-MORROW'S PROGRAMME.

GOSSIP ABOUT NEW PLAYERS.

LEEDS CITY'S DEBUT IN THE ENGLISH LEAGUE.

To-day marks the opening of what promises to be an unusually interesting football season. For a fortnight or so practice games have been in full swing, and with that habit of looking forward which is so characteristic of the Englishman, those of the public who give their minds to sport have been paying more regard lately to the prospects of football than to cricket retrospects and averages.

Much has happened in the North during the close season, and, by reason of the changes effected within the Northern Union and the development of the Association game without, the season upon which we are now entering may be said to commence a new era in Yorkshire football. This is the 11th season of the Northern Rugby Union, and to-morrow the players of most of the clubs in membership with that body will make their bow in the hope of gaining a larger measure of public support than they have had in some recent seasons, and in the hope, moreover, of gaining League and competition honours. With cheery optimism the prospects of each and every club at this period of the year are put down as rosy.

As regards to-morrow's programme, the absence of any reliable data upon which to form an opinion as to the relative strength of competing teams renders it obviously too speculative a matter to venture prophecies. All that need be done, therefore, is to take a general survey of the afternoon's programme.

In the Northern Union, as is well-known, the re-organisation of the Northern League upon a system which merges all last season's first and second division clubs in one competition has made it possible for the season to open in Yorkshire with a most attractive list of fixtures. Old neighbours meet at Hunslet, for instance, while York and Leeds renew competition rivalry at the Minster City. Then we see Huddersfield re-visiting Dewsbury, and, incidentally, the arrangement of this meeting on the first day of the season emphasises the special benefit conferred upon the Fartowners by the re-organisation of the League. Dewsbury, it will be remembered, established their right to seniority last season, while Huddersfield conspicuously failed to do so, and only regain their status by the timely re-casting of the League. None the less, they should prove a big attraction at Crown Flatts, and the visit of Bradford to Keighley must be regarded as good business from

St Helens in a play-off for a place in division one of the Northern Union in 1904. That August, Hunslet FC officials and other interested parties attended a meeting in the Griffin Hotel, Boar Lane, calling for the establishment of a 'good association club in Leeds', resolving that it be called Leeds City and that 'the action of renting Holbeck's ground for the season, with the option of purchase for a sum not exceeding £5,000, be endorsed'.

This was the birth of Leeds City. A team was assembled and joined the new West Yorkshire League. City's first game at Elland Road was played on 15 October 1904 against Hull City, and drew a crowd of some 3,000. City lost 2-0 and struggled throughout the season, finishing 11th. The club set great store by arranging friendly matches against top sides such as Preston North End and left the reserves to fulfil mundane league fixtures.

However, events off pitch were perhaps of greater importance. In April 1905, Leeds City AFC was incorporated with 15 directors including Norris Hepworth, a noted wholesale clothier, and Joseph Henry, a prominent iron founder who had been actively involved with the Holbeck club. The club was encouraged by a regular support of 2,000 and the potential for greater numbers. Hepworth was pleased to have a ground 'in the centre of the working classes.'

In applying for Football League status, Leeds City's viability and ambition were of far greater importance to the League than a season's indifferent results. On 29 May 1905, 25 votes saw City elected into the second division of the league which had expanded from 36 to 40 clubs.

Leeds City busied itself with establishing a ground that would match the club's aspirations. A new stand was built on the Elland Road side with a 30-foot high barrel wooden roof. Known to fans as the Scratching Shed, it lasted for 70 years. There was a further transformation in 1906 when the pitch was turned through 90 degrees end-on to Elland Road, a barrel-roofed main west grandstand built and more terracing added on.

Leeds City's first season in the West Yorkshire League had been marred by the club being reprimanded by the FA for paying players on a results-only basis, although the team's form had been so erratic that few would have got rich. Once they gained league status, the squad was transformed. Gilbert Gillies, formerly with Chesterfield, had been appointed secretary-manager in March 1905 on a three-year contract. He built up the side helped by trainer George Swift, formerly a full-back with Loughborough.

During the team's first campaign as Football League members, 23 players appeared in Leeds City's blue and gold colours. Their opening match against neighbours Bradford City, which Leeds lost 1-0, drew 15,000 to Valley Parade. The Leeds line-up that auspicious day consisted of Harry Bromage (formerly of Burton United), John McDonald (Blackburn Rovers), Dick Ray (Chesterfield), Charles Morgan (Tottenham Hotspur), Harry Stringfellow (Swindon), James Henderson (Bradford City), Fred Parnell (Derby County), Bob Watson (Woolwich Arsenal), Fred Hargraves (Burton United), Dickie Morris (Liverpool) and Harry Singleton (Queen's Park Rangers).

'Leeds City have no reason to feel disappointed with the first performance of their men,'

■ Rugby had long been the dominant sport in West Yorkshire but league football finally came to Leeds in 1905. City lost their first game at Bradford City but soon found their feet in the second division.

■ The *Yorkshire Post* celebrates Leeds City's first league victory, a 1-0 win at Leicester Fosse. Harry Singleton scored the goal.

'It was a somewhat lucky goal that gave them victory, but no less than they deserved.'

Yorkshire Post

wrote the *Yorkshire Post* soccer correspondent. 'Their greatest fault was to finish in front of goal. Had they taken advantage of the chances that came their way, a very different story would have to be told. Bromage more than once proved himself a capable defender of goal.'

As Gillies' newly-assembled team took time to find its feet, the Leeds public blew hot and cold. A week after the Bradford City defeat, West Bromwich Albion came to Elland Road and won 2-0 before a crowd of 6,802; yet two days later, on a Monday afternoon, just 3,000 turned up to watch City gain their first league point in a 2-2 draw against Lincoln. The following Saturday, Gillies' team won 1-0 at Leicester Fosse. 'It was a somewhat lucky goal that gave them victory, but no less than they deserved. They had throughout the better of the argument,' claimed the *Yorkshire Post* report.

Buoyed by this success, City managed to draw a crowd of 13,654 for their 3-1 home win against Hull on 23 September. The upbeat mood was recorded by the *Yorkshire Post*: 'The struggle to establish the dribbling code on a sound and attractive footing in Leeds has been an uphill one, but there were many smiling faces around the pioneers at the old Holbeck rugby enclosure. The game itself was full of incident and excitement...four goals were scored during the afternoon and all were brilliantly worked for. Singleton got through a tremendous amount of work...Leeds were clever and spirited throughout the game.'

The 2-2 draw with Lincoln was the first of a fruitful run during which City lost only once in nine games and gained 13 points out of a possible 18. The team had knitted together quickly and their attack was further strengthened by the arrival in December of David Wilson, signed from Hull City. Wilson, a Scotsman and former soldier with the Cameron Highlanders who had fought in the Boer War, made a forceful impact scoring 13 goals in 15 games. He might have done even better had he not been carried off with a knee injury in the first minute of the match at Grimsby on 17 March. A fortnight earlier Wilson had been uncontainable in City's 6-1 win at Clapton Orient where, undeterred by the greasy conditions underfoot, he scored four, had another goal disallowed and hit the bar.

A solid season in which City finished sixth was blemished by crowd trouble during the last home match against Manchester United. Whilst disorder among spectators was not yet endemic in the game, outbreaks of violence were quite frequent although the aggression tended to be channelled towards match officials rather than rival fans.

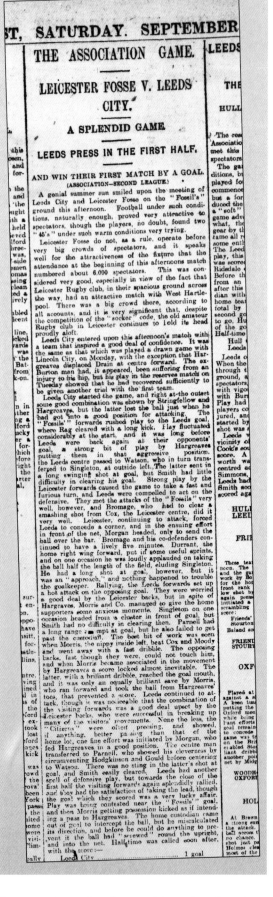

A succession of unfavourable refereeing decisions goaded a few in the Leeds crowd to hurl missiles onto the pitch. One of these hit the referee T. I. Campbell on the nose. Two weeks

1906–07
Gillies (Secretary & Manager), Morgan, Hargraves, Clark, Walker, Bromage, Freeborough, Ray, Kennedy, Swift (Trainer)
Whitley, Jefferson, Cubberley, Morris, D. Murray, Harwood, Lavery, Singleton, W. Murray
Parnell, George, Henderson

earlier, Campbell's handling of Bradford City's home game against Manchester United had provoked a near riot and caused the FA to order the temporary closure of Valley Parade.

The *Yorkshire Post* deplored such 'cowardly reprisals', saying, 'All the season, the spectators have been remarkably well-behaved...but on Saturday, owing to the blackguardly conduct of some half-a-dozen, this good character was sadly besmirched. The suspension of the Bradford ground...has apparently not acted as deterrent to the few hooligans who infest all football grounds.'

A tragedy on the pitch

Notwithstanding that unruly encounter, everyone connected with Leeds City had grounds for optimism in 1906–07. The team had made a wobbly start but recovered by October, recording successive wins against Burton United, Grimsby Town and Port Vale before their home match with Burnley on the 27th. That afternoon Leeds City's morale was dealt a shattering blow when David Wilson paid with his life for his dedication to the team's cause.

Wilson, a heavy smoker, who had missed several earlier games and not scored in the new season, had complained about a shortage of breath in the weeks before his death. At half-time, as if recognising that his performance was below par, he told colleagues that he should have scored twice. Soon after the restart Wilson left the pitch feeling ill but, against the doctor's advice, returned within a few minutes 'to a storm of cheers'.

'What that effort meant,' wrote the *Yorkshire Post*, 'was probably shown by the subsequent occurrence. He was only on the field a minute or two when, realising his helpless condition, he returned to the dressing room and had expired practically before any further assistance could be rendered to him, his untimely end in that fashion forming a tragedy unprecedented in English League football.'

The inquest jury returned a verdict of death by over-exertion. There emerged a striking picture of Wilson's courage: on first leaving the field, he had told club officials he could not remain in the dressing room with the team in such straits: City were 1-0 down and winger Harry Singleton was injured. Such spirit exacted a terrible price.

It knocked City off their stride. They lost their next five league matches; indeed, their form for the rest of the season remained as inconsistent as the level of support. The team finished tenth and crowds at Elland Road varied from 3,000 to

■ The men who saw Leeds City through their second season of league football. Leeds finished 10th, their form and morale badly affected in mid-season by the death of David Wilson.

20,000. There was, however, cause for celebration with the arrival of centre-forward Billy McLeod, signed from Lincoln City as a replacement for Wilson. McLeod became one of City's great mainstays and achieved a remarkable strike rate of 178 goals in 301 appearances.

New faces at Leeds

At the beginning of 1907–08, Gillies brought in a crop of new players of whom the one real success was left-winger Fred Croot, signed from Glossop. But for all the vibrancy that Croot and McLeod brought to the forward line, the lack of goals became an acute problem: between 21 December and 11 April, the team scored only 13 times in 18 matches.

By then, the Leeds board felt Gillies was unable to take the team any further. His three-year contact was not renewed at the end of March. The directors brought in Frank Scott-Walford, whom they lured away from Brighton and Hove Albion, with two years of his five-year contract still to run. Scott-Walford, aged 36 when appointed, had trained as an engineer before becoming immersed in football. He had kept goal as an amateur with Tottenham Hotspur and played subsequently for Lincoln, Small Heath and Aston Villa.

In the short-term Scott-Walford had a galvanising effect – 'Leeds on the up-grade', noted the *Yorkshire Post* of 20 April, after the team recorded successive home victories over Stockport (3-0) and Wolves (3-1). Of the latter match, the Post reporter declared, 'There have been better exhibitions on the Elland Road ground, but it is questionable whether spectators have ever enjoyed play to the same extent. Croot's runs along the touchline and accurate centres appealed forcibly to all. His flights held the spectators spell-bound, a hush of expectancy accompanying every movement.'

But any ambitions Scott-Walford might have had for the team were, like those of Gillies, impeded by lack of money. A clutch of players imported from Brighton made little immediate impact and the team's form lurched wildly throughout the 1908–09 season. City again finished 12th, but without a platform on which to build. Scott-Walford used 28 players in 1909–10 as he searched in vain for a winning combination, but the campaign was dogged more by humiliation than covered in glory, notably a record 7-0 defeat at Elland Road by Barnsley on 23 October.

By March, City were hovering just above the bottom of the second division. After the team's abject display in the second half at West Bromwich on 7 March, the *Yorkshire Post* was scathing. 'Five or six men who wore the club's colours need to be replaced if something like a sustained effort to bring Leeds City to the fore is to be made. McLeod, Roberts and Croot were well worth their places on the forward line...Affleck and White fell back to cover their goal with a fair amount of judgement but their efforts to turn defence into attack were not at all skilful.' The paper's mood was similarly waspish after a 3-0 defeat at Burnley 12 days later. 'The usual level of mediocrity was on display at Turf Moor. Surely the present (team) members have had a fair trial.'

Elland Road itself was on trial, having been selected to stage the FA Cup semi-final between Barnsley and Everton. The event was a fiasco, the stadium chokingly overcrowded. Said the *Yorkshire Post*, 'It was obvious there would be a record gate though the ground was so packed that the entrance gates had to be closed an hour before the match commenced. There certainly would have been a crowd of 50,000 or more if the ground could have held that number. It shows the possibilities of the Association game in this district and also the desirability of making the accommodation at Elland Road equal to occasions such as Saturday's.'

Financial problems loom

Leeds City finished 17th, with just four points more than bottom team Birmingham. They had made a disastrous start to 1910–11, losing their first four matches and by now the club was having to resolve its financial situation. Around 60 shareholders attended a special meeting in September and, according to the *Yorkshire Post*, 'pledged to use every endeavour to raise £4,000, which together with £8,000 pledged by a section of directors, will place the club in a secure financial position. There would then be £1,000–£1,500 working capital for development...so that if the directors saw any promising player, they would have a chance of purchasing.'

All Scott-Walford's buys were cheap – most came and went without making much impression. From his Brighton days, only centre-half Tom Morris had merited a regular place in the team. Full-back George Affleck, signed in autumn 1909 from junior football in Scotland, became an established partner, yet the defence, which also included Alec Creighton (ex-Distillery), Scotsman John Harkins and the long-serving Stan Cubberley, was often erratic: sound in the second half of 1910–11 as City fin-

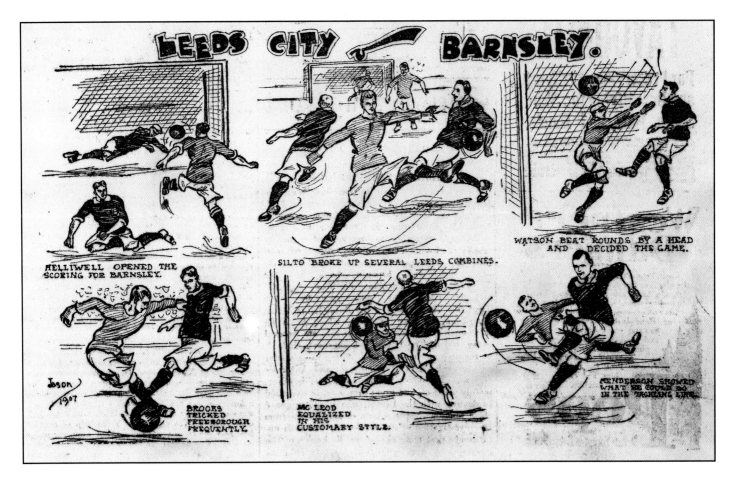

LEEDS CITY v BARNSLEY.

HELLIWELL OPENED THE SCORING FOR BARNSLEY.

SILTO BROKE UP SEVERAL LEEDS COMBINES.

WATSON BEAT ROUNDS BY A HEAD AND DECIDED THE GAME.

BROOKS TRICKED FREEBOROUGH FREQUENTLY

MC LEOD EQUALIZED IN HIS CUSTOMARY STYLE.

HENDERSON SHOWED WHAT HE COULD DO IN THE TACKLING LINE.

ished 11th, but frequently shambolic in 1911–12 as the team slumped to 19th, forcing the club to seek re-election.

A bad start to a bad season

Dismal images of past seasons haunted Leeds City in what turned out to be the most traumatic year of the club's brief history. The decline in standards of play had set in by December was roundly admonished by the *Yorkshire Post*. Of the 5-1 home defeat by Burnley it said, 'Leeds City are going from bad to worse. Saturday's defeat was almost a rout...no excuses can be advanced...a vein of incompetence ran through the Leeds team from goalkeeper to centre-forward. McLeod drifted back into slackness and mediocrity...though in justice to Gillespie it should be stated that he was the best forward in the City side.'

Yet Billy Gillespie, who had been signed from Derry in the close season, was to play only one more match for Leeds. A swift, adroit forward, Gillespie was transferred mid-season to Sheffield United where he prospered and won 25 caps for Northern Ireland in an international career that stretched from 1913 to 1931.

City could ill afford to squander the talents of good players who had been found cheaply. By March 1912, the club's finances were in such dis-

array that a receiver had to be called in. As it reflected on the bleak position, the *Yorkshire Post* was ready once more with unpalatable truths. 'The crisis...which has been expected for some time, has now been reached. In a playing sense, the position of the club is deplorably low...the club's indebtedness to the chairman Norris Hepworth is £10,713; the club's total indebtedness £13,297.' An appeal made at the start of the season for fresh capital had been largely ignored. Under the circumstances, Scott-Walford saw little future in staying and resigned.

During an FA Cup fourth round replay between Bradford City and Barnsley earlier in March, another crowd control debacle bore witness to maladminstration. A picture of infernal chaos was painted by the *Yorkshire Post*, which wrote, 'No such crowd (45,000) as assailed the gates at the Elland Road ground has ever been seen in the city or its environments. One of the large gates was rushed at noon...several hundred got in without paying. In the rush...turnstiles and pay boxes were smashed...the pressure and desire to see the game at all hazards caused thousands to jump the barriers and invade the field of play. Mounted and foot police forced the crowd back over the touchline.'

There were moments of farce amid the crush: as fans spilled repeatedly on to the pitch causing interruptions to the game of up to 11 minutes,

■ All the action from a local derby in comic strip form. Leeds were 2-1 winners of this lively encounter with Barnsley, played at Elland Road on 16 March 1907.

SUSPENSION OF THE LEEDS CITY CLUB.

LORD MAYOR INTERVENES.

CHARGE OF EXCESSIVE PAYMENT TO PLAYERS.

The alarmist rumours which have been bruited abroad regarding the Leeds City Football Club have come to a head. From to-day the club is virtually under suspension, though the Lord Mayor of Leeds (Mr. Joseph Henry) has intervened, and is hopeful of saving the club.

The exact position of affairs at the moment is that the directors, Messrs. J. Connor, J. C. Whiteman, S. Glover, and G. Sykes are prepared to resign the management of the club to Mr. Henry if the League and the Football Association will allow him to carry it on until a new company is formed.

There is a disposition in some quarters unfriendly to Leeds City to regard the club as already "down and out," but we have the authority of Mr. Henry for stating that he has great hopes of saving the club—and he is in a better position than anyone else at the moment to assess the club's prospects at their true value.

During the week-end Mr. Henry interviewed in Sheffield Mr. J. C. Clegg, the chairman of the Football Association Commission which has been holding the Leeds City Inquiry, and Mr. A. J. Dickinson, who is a member of the F.A. Council. Mr. Henry has persuaded Mr. Clegg to call a further sitting of the Commission, which is to meet in Sheffield on Wednesday afternoon.

"I have very great faith," he explained to a "Yorkshire Evening Post" representative to-day, "that as the outcome of the proposals which I shall then put forward the drastic step of causing the permanent suspension of the club will not be carried out."

Meanwhile, it is a fact that Leeds City stands suspended. That arises because of the non-compliance of the directors with an instruction to produce certain documents.

The history of the unhappy business which has brought the club so near to disaster that it can only be averted by the resignation of the active directors is soon told. C. Copeland, a Leeds City player, who was recently transferred to Coventry City, wrote to the Football Association in the summer making charges against the directors of making excessive payments to certain players who assisted Leeds City during the war-time period.

Later, Mr. J. W. Bromley, a former director of the club, brought certain facts to the notice of the Football Association, but it is believed to have been upon the information of Copeland chiefly that the Football Association acted in the first instance in appointing a Commission of Inquiry.

When the Commission sat in Manchester last Friday week, important conclusions turned upon the production of certain documents. Some of these documents had been in Mr. Bromley's possession, but, by agreement, they had been sealed up and handed to Alderman W. H. Clarke, the solicitor acting in the matter, to be kept in his strong room. The package was not to be opened except with the consent of all the parties concerned.

Much importance was attached to those documents, and they were ordered to be produced, failing which the club was to be suspended as from to-day. The documents in Ald. Clarke's possession had not been produced.

Meanwhile, however, the Lord Mayor of Leeds (Mr. Joseph Henry), who was a director of the Leeds City Club during the late Mr. Norris Hepworth's chairmanship, has consented, in consideration of his past interest in football, to find a way of continuing the club which it is hoped will be acceptable to the authorities of the Football Association and the Football League.

If the worst happens—if, for instance, the Football Association Commission persists in their suspension of the club notwithstanding the resignation of the directors—Leeds City will have completed its career in English League football with the sensational victory which was gained by the team in their match at Wolverhampton on Saturday.

IF THE WORST HAPPENS.

In this case, the vacancy in the Second Division would presumably be filled by the admission of Burslem Port Vale, who were only beaten by one vote in the election at the annual meeting of the League. There is a disposition in some quarters to take that for granted. Indeed, it is announced, with some show of authority, that Port Vale are prepared to take over Leeds City's fixtures.

The rules of the League provide that if Leeds City be permanently suspended, the transfer rights of the players will rest in the Football League. The players engaged in the club's service would not suffer any loss of wages, which would be guaranteed by the Football League out of the transfer fees.

goal and touchlines had to be freshly white-washed before play could resume. Leeds City's unfitness to manage a big occasion could not have been more graphically illustrated.

A 2-1 defeat at Leicester Fosse in the last game of the season confirmed City's need to seek re-election. A meagre haul of 28 points from 38 games along with 78 goals conceded – the worst defensive record in the division – bode badly. But in May came fresh hope. Norris Hepworth promised to give the club all the financial backing it might need and also announced Herbert Chapman, the Northampton Town manager, as Scott-Walford's successor.

Enter Herbert Chapman

Chapman became one of English football's most successful bosses, but his great years were still to come, after his time with Leeds City, when he took over first at Huddersfield and then Arsenal. Little in Chapman's playing background – he was a journeyman forward who had drifted around various clubs – hinted that one day he would become a soccer icon. But Chapman, under whom Northampton won the Southern League in 1908–09, had bags of energy which he poured into rebuilding Leeds City when the club won re-election, topping the poll with 33 votes. Chapman understood the need for players of proven achievement, rather than the hopefuls collected by Scott-Walford. Accordingly, his signings included the Everton and Ireland goalkeeper Billy Scott, Scottish international full-back George Law, former England centre-half Evelyn Lintott, who came from Bradford City and who was soon joined by team-mate and inside-left Jimmy Speirs, and inside-right Jimmy Roberston from Barrow.

Stalwarts such as Affleck, Croot and McLeod survived the Chapman revolution. His new combination was rocked by a 4-0 defeat at Fulham on the opening day of the 1912–13 season, but soon pulled itself together. While the defence proved alarmingly porous on occasions, as in the 6-2 defeat at Hull on 2 November and when City lost 6-0 at Stockport County on 15 February, generally the team gave as good as it got. Battle honours included a 5-1 home win over champions Preston, which made the drubbing a week later at Stockport – who were to finish second from bottom – all the more unsatisfactory.

Despite its inconsistency, the verve with which Leeds City played drew spectators back to Elland Road. When Chapman's team finished sixth, the average attendance rose from below 8,000 in 1911–12 to more than 13,000 the following year, enabling the club to record a small profit, a remarkable turn-around from the financial problems of the previous season. 'Chapman...has done a tremendous amount of good work for the club; he has gained the confidence of everybody,' wrote the *Yorkshire Post*.

With Speirs and Robertson pepping up the forward line, Billy McLeod rediscovered his most potent form, scoring 27 goals in 38 matches – form he sustained in 1913–14 as City played with

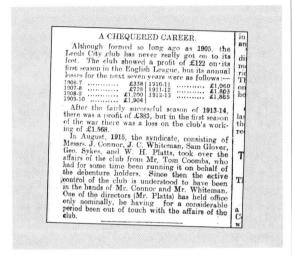

A CHEQUERED CAREER.

'Although formed so long ago as 1905, the Leeds City club has never really got on to its feet. The club showed a profit of £122 on its first season in the English League, but its annual losses for the next seven years were as follows:—

1906-7 .... £358 | 1910-11 .... £1,060
1907-8 .... £728 | 1911-12 .... £1,803
1908-9 .... £1,200 | 1912-13 .... £1,865
1909-10 .... £1,904 |

After the fairly successful season of 1913-14, there was a profit of £383, but in the first season of the war there was a loss on the club's working of £1,568.

In August, 1915, the syndicate, consisting of Messrs. J. Connor, J. C. Whiteman, Sam Glover, Geo. Sykes, and W. H. Platts, took over the affairs of the club from Mr. Tom Coombs, who had for some time been running it on behalf of the debenture holders. Since then the active control of the club is understood to have been in the hands of Mr. Connor and Mr. Whiteman. One of the directors (Mr. Platts) has held office only nominally, he having for a considerable period been out of touch with the affairs of the club.

a conviction that marked them out as potential first division material. The attack was enlivened further by the signing of amateur winger and professional journalist Ivan Sharpe from Derby County; and the defence stiffened by John Hampson, bought from Northampton to replace Lintott at centre-half. The *Yorkshire Evening Post* viewed Lintott, who was also a teacher and lay preacher, as 'a man of culture', and felt he had raised the status of the professional player.

Although some of their old fallibilities remained, City were no soft touch for opposing forward lines. One important defensive signing was that of full-back Fred Blackman from Huddersfield Town, regarded by the *Yorkshire Post* as 'possibly the most polished back in the second division'. Meanwhile McLeod and the team plundered frail defences such as that of Nottingham Forest, past which City ran up eight goals at Elland Road on 29 November. 'This score, a record for the City team, marks the grand advance they have made this season...hopes of supporters will naturally dwell all the more lovingly on promotion prospects,' wrote the *Yorkshire Post*. 'Speirs changed places with Price as the inside man...to the wonderment yet ultimate gratification of the club's followers.'

A brief but damaging loss of form during January, during which City lost three consecutive league matches and were defeated 2-0 at home by West Bromwich in the FA Cup second round,

probably cost them promotion. The campaign was further undermined by a farcical match at Clapton Orient on 2 March which the London team arranged to kick off at 4.30pm. In a pre-floodlights era it was inevitable that the game would finish in the semi-darkness of an early spring evening. Clapton Orient won 3-1, but City goalkeeper Billy Scott claimed he was unable to see the last two goals put past him. On those grounds, Leeds City appealed – without success – against the result.

Why was the match not abandoned? The explanation, according to the *Yorkshire Post*, was that 'the referee asked linesmen if they could follow the ball and, receiving an affirmative reply, the game was allowed to proceed. It was quite certain, however, that the players themselves could not follow the ball.'

Leeds City finished with six fewer points than champions Notts County, but only two behind runners-up Bradford Park Avenue. 'Promotion has been denied them but taking into account the resources of the club, fourth place should be considered satisfactory,' said the *Yorkshire Post*. 'Not only have the club attained a higher position than ever before but receipts and attendances have outstripped any previous record.' Much of the improvement could be attributed to Chapman's management style: he was a pioneer in introducing regular team talks and planned tactics in consultation with the players. He also believed it essential that they should relax, so introduced a weekly round of golf into the team's training routine.

War halts Leeds' progress

Chapman's team reached its peak in 1913–14, the last season before the onset of the First World War, although the 1914–15 programme was completed before the Football League suspended operations. In August 1914, a syndicate of businessmen bought the club from the receiver, but the team had lost its sure touch and lapsed into spluttering inconsistency, capable of beating the best, yet losing drastically to the worst. City slumped to 15th place, although McLeod, as ever, was a potent force, the scorer of 18 goals in 31 matches.

Despite the disruption of war, many clubs, Leeds City among them, continued to play organised football. League competitions were run regionally with Leeds taking part in the Midlands Section. As players were called up for military service, guest footballers weighed in and out of the teams – 34 wore Leeds City colours in 1915–16; 36 in 1918–19.

■ Immediately after the auction of City's assets, prominent local figures and supporters met to plan the revival of professional football in the city.

> 'Speirs changed places with Price as the inside man...to the wonderment yet ultimate gratification of the clubs followers.'
>
> *Yorkshire Post*

■ Fallout from the debacle: after City's expulsion from the League, Elland Road was let to Yorkshire Amateurs. But the Amateurs quickly offered to stand aside as moves began to form a new professional club, Leeds United.

Although attendances were drastically reduced and finances straitened, Leeds City prospered within this confined tournament. In 1917–18, they won the Midland Section principal tournament and then beat Lancashire league champions Stoke City 2-1 on aggregate over two matches. It meant Leeds City were entitled to be considered League Champions, although the achievement had no official status because of the disruption caused by the war.

But disharmony at Elland Road arose following Herbert Chapman's temporary departure in the summer of 1916 to take up a senior managerial position in the munitions factory at Barnbow. In his absence, assistant George Cripps took charge, first of administration then of team selection. Joseph Connor, City's chairman, who had first picked the team himself, had a poor relationship with Cripps whom he blamed for Leeds' parlous financial state. Yet despite failing to win the players' confidence, Cripps sued for wrongful dismissal when expected to resume his position of assistant after Chapman returned in 1918.

An ignominious ending for Leeds City

A curious aspect of the legal settlement was that Cripps – who engaged former Leeds City director James Bromley as his solicitor – was requested to hand over an assortment of letters and documents to club directors in the offices of City's solicitor, Alderman William Clarke. They almost certainly contained evidence of a potent scandal that the board dreaded Cripps making public: that Leeds City had made illegal payments to players, contravening a Football League rule that, during wartime, professionals should play for expenses only.

Cripps' silence may have been bought, but City had another mutineer, full-back Charlie Copeland. In the summer of 1919 Copeland, who had joined the club in 1912, demanded a pay rise, but was promised more only if he won a regular first team place. Such was his anger at being offered a basic £3.10.0d a week (£3.50) – a deal that Copeland claimed left him worse off than before the war – that he contacted the FA and blurted out all he knew about City's alleged illegal payments.

It is unclear quite how Copeland became aware of the payments, but like Cripps, he had engaged as his solicitor James Bromley. The effect of his whistle-blowing was that the FA and Football League initiated a joint inquiry. When it convened at the Grand Hotel in Manchester on 26 September 1919, there were ominous signs that the investigators would not be fobbed off

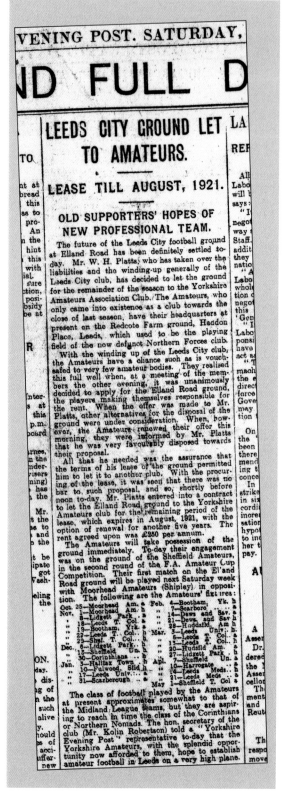

easily. 'We are awaiting documents,' said the FA chairman, J.C. Clegg – the ones deposited with City solicitor William Clarke, which the club was so anxious should never be revealed.

Leeds was rife with speculation as the club was given a week to produce the papers. On deadline day the *Yorkshire Post* conveyed an upbeat message, 'In view of the alarmist rumours being spread abroad concerning the future of Leeds City FC, supporters...will be gratified to know that there is every prospect of a satisfactory arrangement being made for the continuance of the club. The club's prospects are receiving attention in influential quarters of the city and it is confidently anticipated that the scheme which is to be submitted will yield satisfactory results.'

So much for confidence. The next day, 7 October, the *Yorkshire Post* was reporting on City's suspension by the FA commission for failing to deliver the goods. 'The documents in question...according to an agreement entered into by Mr J. Connor, chairman of directors and Mr J.W. Bromley, a former director...were some time ago sealed and handed over to Alderman W.H. Clarke, the solicitor acting in the matter, the understanding being that they should not be revealed without the consent of all concerned.'

In a last minute effort to appease the FA, City proposed that the club be run by the Lord Mayor of Leeds, Joseph Henry, also a former director, and that directors Connor, Whiteman, Glover and Sykes would all resign if the FA and Football League allowed Henry to carry on until a new company could be formed. This, the club hoped, was something the commission might consider when it reconvened at the Russell Hotel in London on 13 October.

But officials gave the scheme short shrift. Their final decision was damning and devastating: Leeds City was to be expelled from the Football League and the club to be suspended until all the books and papers were produced. Moreover, directors Connor, Whiteman, Glover, Sykes and Herbert Chapman and George Cripps (late officials of the club) were to be suspended *sine die* and not allowed to attend any further football matches.

Interviewed a few days later, the league chairman J. McKenna declared, 'The authorities of the game intend to keep it absolutely clean. We will have no nonsense. The League would not be denied in their inquiries. Every member of the Commission was heartily sorry that Leeds had to be dealt with at all. We recognised that they had gone through troublous times. Leeds were defiant and could only be defiant through one cause, fear of the papers giving away certain secrets.'

Leeds, robbed at a stroke of its football team, was in shock. 'The drastic way the Commission have exercised their authority will stagger the followers of Association Football in Leeds and the West Riding,' wrote the *Yorkshire Post*. 'For the time being, at any rate, it means the extinction of the club. Expulsion from the League was a step that could not have been contemplated. Meanwhile, the Association public of Leeds, numbering many thousands, will have to consider the possibility of making a fresh start. A general meeting of the club's supporters appears to be advisable.'

Everything must go

On 17 October at the Metropole Hotel in Leeds city centre, there occurred one of the saddest and most extraordinary events in the history of football's early years: the auction of Leeds City players to other clubs, arranged and administered by the Football Association commission. Reviewing what was advertised somewhat bizarrely as 'A Sale of Effects' the *Yorkshire Evening Post* later reported: 'The tragedy of the Leeds City FC reached its most poignant step this afternoon when the players, many of whom have been regarded with familiar and ever-increasing interest by the Leeds football public, were called upon to choose clubs from those desiring their services.'

'A melancholy spectacle' was the *Yorkshire Post* description, reporting the prices as if it were some livestock auction: Billy McLeod (to Notts County), Harry Millership (to Rotherham) and John Hampson (Aston Villa) each raised £1,000; Willis Walker (South Shields), Tommy Lamph (Manchester City) and John Edmonson (Sheffield Wednesday) went for £800; William Hopkins (South Shields) for £600; George Affleck (Grimsby), Ernest Goodwin (Manchester City) Billy Kirton (Aston Villa), William Ashurst (Lincoln City) for £500; Fred Linfoot (Lincoln City) and Herbert Lounds (Rotherham) for £250; Arthur Wainright (Grimsby) and William Short (Hartlepool United) for £200; Francis Chipperfield (Lincoln City) £100.

There was a separate auction of goal posts, nets, footballs, shower baths, billiard tables, jerseys, shirts, vests, knickers; anything that could raise a few more pounds was put up for sale. The remains of Leeds City Football Club were ignominiously scattered in all directions.

■ Herbert Chapman, City's manager, was banned from involvement in professional football after the scandal but successfully appealed on the grounds that he was absent from the club, managing a munitions factory, when the alleged illegal payments were made.

'A melancholy spectacle'

Yorkshire Post

Leeds United: The pre-War Years

Above: A new era for football in Leeds. Harry Duggan, a sharp and enthusiastic right-winger, joined Leeds United in 1925 and played almost 200 matches in the following decade.

Right: The newly-formed Leeds United's first match was played against Yorkshire Amateurs. United then joined the Midland League before gaining election to the second division in May 1920.

Their club was dead but the people of Leeds were determined that professional football should live on. If the auction of human beings on the afternoon of 17 October was the nadir of Leeds soccer history, a crowded meeting of passionate supporters and businessmen at Salem Hall a few hours later marked the start of its renaissance. The FA, whose hard line had brought about City's downfall, had nevertheless given its blessing to any new enterprise that might create a successor club.

The Salem Hall meeting was instigated by Leeds solicitor and former City vice-chairman Alf Masser. Joseph Henry junior, the Lord Mayor's son, was appointed chairman of a seven-man committee looking at ways of starting afresh. An immediate decision was taken to enrol members of a supporters club. Another committee member, former City full-back Dick Ray, was elected secretary-manager.

The new club was to be called Leeds United. Advertisements were placed in local newspapers to try to recruit a team: apart from the footballers who had been auctioned off, Leeds had lost the services of Jimmy Speirs and Evelyn Lintott, both killed in action. The war also claimed the lives of two other former City men, full-back David Murray and centre-half Gerald Kirk. Charlie

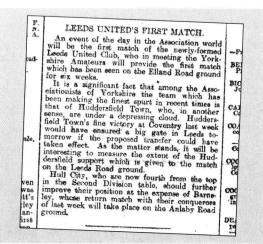

LEEDS UNITED'S FIRST MATCH.

An event of the day in the Association world will be the first match of the newly-formed Leeds United Club, who in meeting the Yorkshire Amateurs will provide the first match which has been seen on the Elland Road ground for six weeks.

It is a significant fact that among the Associationists of Yorkshire the team which has been making the finest spurt in recent times is that of Huddersfield Town, who, in another sense, are under a depressing cloud. Huddersfield Town's fine victory at Coventry last week would have ensured a big gate in Leeds to-morrow if the proposed transfer could have taken effect. As the matter stands, it will be interesting to measure the extent of the Huddersfield support which is given to the match on the Leeds Road ground.

Hull City, who are now fourth from the top in the Second Division table, should further improve their position at the expense of Barnsley, whose return match with their conquerors of last week will take place on the Anlaby Road ground.

Copeland had moved south to Coventry City on a free transfer.

Herbert Chapman successfully appealed against his suspension, claiming that as he had worked at the munitions factory during the time of the alleged illegal payments, he could not be held culpable. Meanwhile Leeds City's place in the Football League had been taken by Port Vale, whose intense lobbying was deplored by Joseph Henry senior. 'I am sure that they did not act in a very sportsmanlike way in pressing their claim before the final decision (regarding City's fate) was arrived at,' he said.

1920–21
M. Barker, Hilton Crowther, Duffield, Cooper, Hart, Brown, Jacklin, Downs, Coope
Walton, Jeffries, Stead (Ass. Trainer), Fairclough (Manager), D. Murrel (Trainer)
Frew, Spencer, Lyons, Elson, Thompson, Stuart, Goldthorpe, Reynolds
Armitage, Mason, Baker, Tillotson, Musgrove, McGee, Best

Crowther on board

Leeds United were confirmed as members of the Midland League on 31 October 1919, but suddenly found their affairs enmeshed with those of neighbouring Huddersfield Town. Huddersfield's wealthy chairman, J. Hilton Crowther despaired at the lack of public support for his club and felt that the city of Leeds had far greater potential. He proposed amalgamating the fledgling Leeds United with Huddersfield and moving the entire organization to Elland Road.

A majority of the Leeds board backed the scheme, but the threat of losing their football team whipped the Huddersfield public into action. Fans demanded a public meeting and a committee was established to devise ways of acquiring Crowther's stake in the club, estimated at £25,000.

Two months of fund-raising, legal manoeuvring and brinkmanship followed before Crowther was finally bought out in January 1920. The ramifications of this curious affair benefited both teams: Huddersfield Town were revitalised and they ended the season promoted to division one as runners-up. They also reached the FA Cup final. Meanwhile Crowther

decamped to Leeds, eager to invest part of his fortune in the club. He brought with him one other great asset: Arthur Fairclough, the Huddersfield secretary-manager who had been a close ally during the campaign for amalgamation.

Fairclough, an ebullient character and astute football man who had taken Barnsley to two FA Cup finals, succeeded Dick Ray in February 1920. Ray remained as assistant until 1923, when he left to manage Doncaster Rovers. Both Fairclough and Crowther were determined to drum up support for Leeds United's campaign to gain Football League status. They threw themselves into the task, at the same time attempting to shape a team that could successfully compete in second division football.

Their powers of persuasion were remarkable. On 31 May 1920, Leeds United were elected to the second division. 'The promoters are to be congratulated on the energy and determination they have shown,' commented the *Yorkshire Post*. 'Financial stability seems already to be assured and the nucleus of a thoroughly capable side has been secured. So good a case did Leeds United make, so effectively had claims been canvassed by Mr Hilton Crowther and Arthur Fairclough, that Leeds headed the poll with 31 votes.'

■ Leeds United's first league squad. The team made steady progress under the astute management of Arthur Fairclough.

■ Opposite: The Leeds defence is under pressure as West Ham attack at Upton Park in February 1921. United lost 3-0.

It is possible that the pair had drawn on sympathy for the plight of Leeds City. Nevertheless, the Football League was unlikely to dismiss any sensible application from a club representing England's fifth biggest city. If successful, Leeds United could become one of the division's biggest generators of money.

Up to the day of the election, an appeal for share capital from the growing numbers of Leeds supporters had raised £10,000. Meanwhile United had secured the option on buying Elland Road for £5,500. Further financial details emerged in the *Yorkshire Post*. 'This will be exercised co-jointly with the floating of a company with £25,000 nominal capital. Messrs Crowther and Platts (William Platts, a chartered accountant)...will presumably take debentures to the amount of the purchase price.'

'Steps are to be taken at once to put the ground and stands in a thorough state of repair...and it is likely that a scheme of extension will be embarked upon to give the ground a holding capacity for 60,000 spectators. Mr Arthur Fairclough, than whom there is probably no more astute team builder in the country, has been given a free hand in the signing on of players. Leeds United should, with ordinary luck, qualify for the first division within three years.'

It was just a hunch on the part of the *Yorkshire Post*, but, to within a season, one that came off. In buoyant mood Alf Masser predicted average gates of 25,000–30,000 for the new club. His hope was 'to find the name of Leeds inscribed indelibly on the rolls of the Football Association as the city which passed through fire, was cleansed, and was given a fair and sporting chance to rehabilitate itself.'

> 'Leeds United should, with ordinary luck, qualify for the first division within three years.'
>
> *Yorkshire Post*

Leeds United kick-off

Fairclough recruited numerous players from local junior football clubs, but also needed experienced professionals from whom they could learn. Two key defensive signings were centre-half Jim Baker, signed from Huddersfield, who was a robust, hard-tackling defender and became Leeds United's first captain, and full-back Jimmy Frew from Hearts.

The new era heralded a different look: Leeds United forsook the old City colours of blue and old gold for blue and white striped shirts and white shorts. The team that took the field for United's first league match at Port Vale on 28 August 1920 seemed disturbingly lacking in experience. The eleven were made up of Billy Down, goalkeeper (from Ashington); Bert Duffield, right-back (Castleford Town); Arthur Tillotson, left-back (Castleford Town); Robert Musgrove, right-half (Durham City); Jim Baker; Jimmy Walton, left-half (West Stanley); George Mason, outside-right; Ernie Goldthorpe, inside-right (Bradford City); Robert Thompson, centre-forward (Durham City); John Lyon, inside-left (Hull City) and Jerry Best outside-left (Newcastle United).

It would have been a glorious revenge for Leeds City's tribulations if United had overcome Port Vale, but, although Fairclough's team lost 2-0, there was, said the *Yorkshire Post*, 'evidence of potential success in that Leeds overplayed their opponents in the first half. The chief failing was among the forwards...Ernest Goldthorpe was the one success. The rear division...was undoubtedly efficient...Baker is a centre-half of experience, intelligence and enthusiasm.'

Leeds United's first home game against South Shields drew a crowd of 16,958 to Elland Road. They lost, 2-1, as John Lyons made history as the scorer of United's first goal in league football; yet on the evidence of two slender defeats, it seemed unlikely that Fairclough's team would be overwhelmed in second division company. Their third game, played before 15,000 at Elland Road, was one to savour: a 3-1 win against Port Vale with two goals from Matt Ellson, a signing from Frickley Colliery, and one from Jerry Best.

There were few outstanding teams in the division. Throughout the campaign Leeds, robbed of Goldthorpe's services early on by injury, had struggled for goals. The season's most emphatic victory, a 4-0 trouncing of Coventry on 1 December was, according to the *Yorkshire Post*, less notable for vibrant attacking play than for Baker's towering performance. Leeds finished 14th with 38 points from 42 matches but, to put this into perspective, only 16 points separated Bristol City, in third place, from Coventry, who were second from bottom.

For Leeds, survival was an achievement. Crowds averaged just under 16,000 which, though well below Alf Masser's blithe predictions, was evidence of solid interest. Baker was an indomitable figure and played in every league game, as he would do in 1921–22. By then, Leeds, fully acclimatised to league football, finished eighth, but while the defence held firm, the forwards laboured. Towards the end of 1920–21, Fairclough paid a club record of £1,750 for Bristol City centre-forward Tommy Howarth who, in his first full campaign, was top scorer with 13 goals in 28 games. But Howarth had scant support except from inside-left Jack Swan, signed mid-season from Huddersfield, and the only other player to reach double figures.

However, when on form, Leeds United could see off anyone. During an excellent run towards the end of the season, they beat Coventry 5-2 at Elland Road in what the *Yorkshire Post* described as 'a hurricane finish – four goals in ten minutes. Better forward play has not been seen on this ground for a long while.' Two weeks later, Leeds swept aside promotion candidates Barnsley, winning 4-0 at Elland Road in atrocious conditions...with turf soddened...almost the whole of the second half was played in a violent sleet storm. Leeds United triumphed over their surroundings in great style.'

United's passage through 1922–23 followed a similar pattern. The defence was meaner than ever with Baker and young Ernie Hart formidable twin pillars. Hart, one of United's earliest finds, had signed as an 18-year-old from junior football in Doncaster and evolved into a skilful, tenacious defender, serving for 16 years and winning eight England caps. The combination of Baker and Hart, alongside Fred Whalley in goal, full-backs Duffield and Frew and right-half Harry Sherwin, was a sound basis for a promotion team.

Leeds had finished seventh, but despite being enlivened by Percy Whipp, a mid-season buy from Sunderland and scorer of 19 goals in 25 games, their attack, like many others in the division, struggled for goals. Fairclough continued to rejig his forwards, gambling on Joe Richmond, a non-league signing from Durham at centre-forward. As the 1923–24 campaign got underway, it finally looked as though Leeds had found a winning formula.

Leeds on the up

Despite an inauspicious start, by November Leeds had surged to the top of the table with a dazzling streak of results that included seven successive victories. They faltered in December, losing twice to promotion rivals Bury, but on Boxing Day recovered enough to thrash Oldham 5-0 at Elland Road with goals from Swan (2), Richmond and Whipp (2). The *Yorkshire Post* celebrated 'a fine exhibition of aggressive play...Leeds would not have been flattered if they'd doubled the score. They had a very effective left-wing in Armand and Swan whose perfect combinations went a very long way to securing this victory.'

Six straight wins from January to March kept Leeds buoyant. Yet, despite being on the threshold of the first division, home attendances were dispiritingly low: only 11,000 saw the 3-1 home victory over Coventry on 9 February; just 8,000

the midweek 2-1 win against South Shields on 27 February. Leeds United were about to make history, but Elland Road, when only a quarter full, was a downbeat arena; its pulse rate low. The team, however, was full of fight and fire.

On 21 April Leeds clinched their promotion by beating Stockport 4-0 at Elland Road and for once there was a sense of occasion. 'The holiday crowd, officially returned at 22,145, was more demonstrative than perhaps any that has been assembled in this ground since the War,' reported the *Yorkshire Post*. 'Though cleverer teams have won promotion, no set of players has tried harder or trained more conscientiously. The extraordinary tenacity of the home players and their effective tackling was too much for Stockport in the second half.'

Five days later, Leeds became second division champions: a goal by Walter Coates three minutes from the end of their home match against Nelson sufficient to win the title. There had been more spectacular achievements in the division's history, but rarely had champions fashioned a triumph from such unpromising and hostile circumstances. In their low-key way, Fairclough and his team had performed a miracle.

Leeds in the First Division

On the opening day of their first division programme, Leeds United played host to footballing aristocracy. The difference between Fairclough's team and their opponents, Sunderland, could not have been more graphic. Leeds were the cut-price new boys, assembled for just a few hundred pounds. Sunderland, with 45 years of history and five league championships behind them, the most recent in 1922–23, had invested £8,000 in new blood during the summer.

Leeds had always suffered financial hardship and would do so for a further 40 years. But the club was adept at making the best of what it had and hoped that pride would spur on the players over some of the hurdles they would face.

There was no shortage of support for their first division debut: the crowd of 33,722 was a league record at Elland Road. 'A knowledge of the training methods led to the expectation that United players would lack nothing in physical fitness, but the speed and alertness of the whole side and the incisive methods of the forwards astonished even the most fervent admirer...the Sunderland half-backs...were overwhelmed by the whirlwind attacks,' the *Yorkshire Post* observed.

A header from Swan 'greeted with a wild celebration of enthusiasm' gave Leeds the lead. The celebration lasted only the two minutes it took

> ## 'a hurricane finish – four goals in ten minutes'
>
> *Yorkshire Post*

■ Opposite: A study in concentration: Ernie Hart displays the determination that made him such a formidable opponent.

1923–24

Murrell (Trainer), Bell, Coates, Robson, Armand, Menzies, Flood, Gordon, Noble, Duffield, Ure (A. Trainer)

Baker, Frew, Smith, Hart, Morris, Bell, Swan, Baker, Gascoigne, Harris

Whalle, Johnson, Sherwin, Poyntz, Norman (Team Manager), Crowther (Chairman), Fairclough (Manager), Richmond

Fullam, Down, Lambert, Mason, Baker (Captain), Allen, Whipp, Speak

■ Heading for the top: the squad of 1923–24 created history by taking Leeds United into the first division.

Sunderland to equalise, yet the 1-1 result, if not a cause for triumph, satisfied most Leeds fans. But even as the team savoured their first point in the top division, their underfunding was proving problematic. That Saturday evening, Leeds United supporters were urged to join the 'Lend us a Fiver' campaign to raise funds.

The problem was that J. Hilton Crowther, whom the club now owed £54,000, wanted £35,000 of his money back and to relinquish his position as chairman. 'He has acted as a sort of fairy godfather to this club...if 7,000 rank and file supporters interested in the maintenance of high class soccer subscribe a £5 note each, then the problem would disappear,' the meeting was told. Among those joining the appeal were the MP for Leeds South-East, James O'Grady, and Crowther's successor in waiting, Major Albert Braithwaite, who was in cajoling mood. 'Unfortunately many people appear to be oblivious to the obvious advantage of Leeds United retaining the position they have won,' he said.

It was a position the team was hard-pressed to cling to. Vulnerable away from Elland Road, Leeds' results were sometimes bizarrely inconsistent, as they had been in the second division, most notably in mid-season when they lost 6-1 at Arsenal on 20 December then on Christmas Day beat Aston Villa 6-0 at Elland Road. By the time

they had snapped out of a run of nine matches without a win by beating Liverpool 4-1 at Elland Road on 28 March, Fairclough had been forced to draft in new players.

Three of his recruits were destined to become key figures: wing-half Willis Edwards, centre-forward Tom Jennings and inside-left Russell Wainscoat. Edwards, signed from Chesterfield the previous week, became one of Leeds United's great servants. Without flamboyance, he nevertheless timed his tackles perfectly and passed the ball with superb precision, relying on technique rather than brute force. Edwards was never booked or sent off, his manner an illuminating contrast to that of defenders who bit legs for a pastime. Such was Edwards' talent that, a year after his debut for Leeds, he was called up by England to play against Wales, the first of a total of 16 caps.

Tom Jennings was bought from Raith Rovers and during his years at Leeds achieved a prodigious strike rate – 112 goals in 167 league appearances. Jennings was a sturdy determined striker, hard to knock off the ball and were it not for bouts of illness might have scored many more for Leeds.

Russell Wainscoat, whom Fairclough bought for £2,000 from Middlesbrough, was another rock throughout the late 1920s. A tall, broad-

■ Tom Jennings lets fly. Jennings, who joined Leeds in March 1925, was Leeds United's most prolific pre-war marksman, scoring 112 goals in 167 games.

shouldered inside-left, Wainscoat was a sharp, intelligent player, creator and goalscorer, whose abilities were recognised by England when he was capped against Scotland in 1929. Edwards, Jennings and Wainscoat all made an impact towards the end of an arduous season in which Leeds finished 18th.

Offside change

The offside law was altered at the start of 1925–26, so that a player could not be offside if two (rather than three) opponents were closer to their own goal line when the ball was last played. The effect was that, while goals became more plentiful, the Leeds defence, in common with others, was sometimes baffled by the new rule. Although they had gifted individuals, Leeds United endured another season of grim struggle,

and despite gaining two points more than in 1924–25, were sucked into a battle against relegation. They finished 19th with just a point to spare them from the drop.

Yet Leeds had occasionally confounded expectations. On 6 February, as they sent championship contenders Arsenal packing from Elland Road on the wrong end of a 4-2 scoreline, the *Yorkshire Post* marvelled at Leeds' inconsistency. 'The forwards gave an exhibition of skill...that made their supporters wonder why they had not won more matches this season. The result was a personal triumph for Jennings: his tally of three goals...indicates that he has come back to the form which made him such a formidable centre-forward in the early months of the season.'

Jim Baker, a stalwart who had made 208 appearances in league and cup, left Leeds during

'...a personal triumph for Jennings...'

Yorkshire Post

United found the first division hard work. Goalkeeper Bill Johnson saves as Tottenham attack at White Hart Lane on December 19 1925. Leeds lost the match 3-2.

the season. His commanding presence was hard to replace and, despite their attacking flair, defensive weakness brought about Leeds' downfall, and relegation, in 1926–27. Yet expectations had been high in early autumn when Jennings' goal salvos surpassed all records. On 9 October he plundered all four goals, a third consecutive hat-trick, as Leeds beat Blackburn 4-1 to record their fifth win in six games. 'A personal triumph for Jennings, but United had much the stronger half-back line, and Townsley was masterful in his straight and low passing up the field. Leeds showed good control in a high wind,' reported the *Yorkshire Post*.

Townsley, signed from Falkirk in December 1925, had begun his Leeds career by replacing Baker before converting to full-back. But although the half-back line had been strong against Blackburn, too often it came off second best. For all Jennings' marksmanship – 35 goals in 41 league matches – the defence was shipping goals faster than he could score them. Leeds finally lost their tenuous hold on the first division with a 4-1 defeat at Tottenham on 23 April.

It marked the end of Fairclough's time as manager. He resigned and was succeeded by

Dick Ray, who was determined to cling on to his star players. With all mainstays present at the start of 1927–28, the *Yorkshire Post* sensed optimism at Elland Road. 'The enforced return of Leeds United to the second division has awakened a new spirit among the management and players alike. There is a feeling that United's setback is only temporary...the utmost confidence is felt that a team which includes players of such outstanding merit as Townsley, Edwards, Jennings and White will make a bold strike for a return to the higher status.'

Inside-right John White had been Arthur Fairclough's last big money signing, bought for £5,600 from Hearts towards the end of 1926–27. He was an excellent ball player with a sharp turn of speed, who linked up well with Jennings, Edwards and outside-right Bobby Turnbull, a tricky darting winger Fairclough had signed from Bradford Park Avenue in May 1925.

With the left flank strengthened by Tom Mitchell, whose direct surging runs ruffled many defences, Leeds announced their intentions on the first day of the season as they ripped apart South Shields in a 5-1 away win. 'The effect on morale of such a victory is incalculable. With confidence restored, Leeds should stand out in the second division,' predicted the *Yorkshire Post*.

Yet Leeds showed some uncertainty in the autumn, before clicking into an irresistible winning rhythm in early December, their 5-0 home win over Chelsea the first of seven straight wins. Before the start of their home match with Southampton on 7 January 1928, the new Lowfields Road stand, which with other ground improvements had cost £30,000, was formally opened. In cheerful mood, Leeds embarked on the destruction of their guests, winning 4-1, with White and Wainscoat in sparkling form.

Although Tom Jennings was laid low intermittently through the effects of blood poisoning, Dick Ray maintained his team's momentum with the mid-season acquisition from non-league football of centre-forward Charlie Keetley. Keetley was one of five footballing brothers, the rest of whom played at various times for Doncaster Rovers. For Keetley, the higher standard in league football made no difference to his habits – he continued scoring as if for fun, running in 18 goals during Leeds' final 16 matches.

A 3-2 win at Stamford Bridge against promotion rivals Chelsea, delivered by two goals from Keetley and one from White, ensured United's immediate return to the first division. The match drew a crowd of 47,562 and was worthy of the occasion. In the *Yorkshire Post*'s view, 'the exchanges were extraordinarily fast and keen and reached a high standard of cleverness.' On their return to Midland Station in Leeds that night, United were greeted as heroes by hordes of supporters including the Lord Mayor and Mayoress.

Leeds gained 57 points from 42 matches but defeats in the last two games saw the championship snatched from them by Manchester City. City beat Ray's men 1-0 in an anti-climactic match at Elland Road which attracted 49,799, a ground record. But although unable to gild their promotion, Leeds United had made a noble revival. It was achieved by a settled team of honest players who occasionally conjured the spectacular. No more could have been asked of Dick Ray.

Success on a shoestring

Despite their unpredictability, Leeds remained in the first division for all but one of the next 11 seasons. It was success, of a sort, on a shoestring: the crowds at Elland Road were as variable as the team's performances and the club could never rely on substantial funding to further its footballing ambitions.

The impetus of promotion seemed to propel Leeds forward in the early weeks of 1928–29. By

the end of October they appeared potential contenders for the championship, having gained 18 out of a possible 24 points. In the event this fruitful start became insurance against relegation, for the team's form went haywire in mid-season. A poor sequence of results in February saw Leeds lose 8-2 at West Ham and 5-0 at Burnley in successive away matches. They finished modestly, in 13th place.

In 1929–30 there were significant changes to the squad which had carried Leeds through for so long. Jack Milburn, brother-in-law of goal

■ Half-back Willis Edwards relied on craft rather than muscle. He played 16 times for England and was a great servant for Leeds.

A talented inside-forward and occasionally a prolific scorer, Russell Wainscoat's excellent performances for Leeds earned him a call up for England against Scotland in 1929.

keeper Jimmy Potts and one of three Milburn brothers to play for Leeds, took over at left-back from the canny, slightly-built Bill Menzies. Potts himself was displaced for more than half the season by Bill Johnson, who spent most of his eight years at Elland Road in the reserves. David Magnall, a young centre-forward and prolific scorer in the Midland League scored six times in nine matches when he broke fleetingly into the first team before being transferred – prematurely, some felt – to Huddersfield where he continued to plunder defences.

Early season fortunes seemed to mirror those of the previous season's campaign: Leeds made another wonderful start, gaining 20 points from a possible 26 until they skewed off-course in November and December with a five-match losing run. Yet despite erratic play, Dick Ray's team harvested 46 points to finish fifth, their highest-ever placing. There was also the kudos of a league double over champions Sheffield Wednesday and the defence, although still prone to off-days, was much tighter conceding only 63 goals in contrast to 84 the previous season.

■ Inside-forward John White, who arrived in February 1927 from Hearts for £5,600, was a record signing for Leeds. A former Scottish international, he scored 36 goals in 102 games in three seasons at Elland Road.

The signs looked good for 1930–31. But Leeds United seemed fated never to have consecutive seasons of prosperity. The club was distracted once more by financial problems and undermined by injuries and loss of form. A damaged knee put left-half George Reed, a mainstay for three and a half years, out of the side before the season had started. His replacement, Barnsley-born Wilf Copping, who had been signed from non-league Middlecliffe Rovers, made an inauspicious start that gave little hint of the fearsome, indomitable defender that he was to become.

The new half-back line of Edwards, Hart and Copping that played in the first match of 1930–31, a 2-2 home draw with Portsmouth, were all to play for England. 'Copping, whilst displaying latent talent, has something to learn,' observed the *Yorkshire Post*, reflecting on the left-half's debut. The defence was now a much less solid unit, with Dick Ray forced to shuffle around his players. Jack Milburn's brother George was drafted in at right-back and played 22 matches, his first consistent run in the team.

The season yielded several eccentric results,

■ Bobby Turnbull was a lively presence on Leeds' right wing for six seasons.

including a record 7-3 win at Blackpool who, despite conceding 125 goals, secured a point in their final game to survive at Leeds United's expense. Dick Ray's team was too fallible too often, though defensively by no means the worst in the league – nine of Leeds' 23 defeats were by the margin of a single goal.

There was a shake-up of personnel after Leeds were relegated, but the Edwards, Hart, Copping backbone remained intact. Ray felt his team had been unlucky and knew from recent experience that descent into the second division was not a

disaster. Already new forwards had appeared when regulars Jennings and Keetley became injured or lost form: inside-left Billy Furness, from non-league Unsworth Colliery, played most of the season, Tom Cochrane had replaced Tom Mitchell on the left wing and Harry Duggan would take over from Bobby Turnbull on the right. Old hand Russell Wainscoat moved to Hull City having played just three matches in the 1931–32 campaign.

After an uncertain start, Leeds recorded nine straight league victories in the autumn and swept

Jack Milburn was one of three brothers from a great footballing dynasty to play for Leeds United.

to the top of the second division. Only a patch of stuttering form and a dynamic burst by Wolves over the final matches deprived Dick Ray's team of the championship – but they had done enough to clinch promotion. For once in their brief history Leeds United had excelled on their travels, winning ten and drawing five of their 21 away matches. It was the second time in five years that they had bounded back into the first division.

Leeds City alderman Eric Clarke succeeded Albert Braithwaite as chairman in August 1931, but did little to alleviate the club's financial prob-

lems. Despite the team's success, the only gate above 20,000 at Elland Road all season was a Boxing Day crowd of 34,005 for the derby with Bradford Park Avenue. Once again Leeds United had to live off their wits – and Ray's eye for a bargain, such as 20-year-old Arthur Hydes. Signed from non-league football in Barnsley in May 1930, Hydes was a sharp, aggressive forward of some calibre, the scorer of 20 league and cup goals in his new role as a first-choice striker.

In defence – particularly during the first half of 1932–33 – Leeds United held as firm as ever

■ Leeds attack the Queen's Park Rangers goal during the FA Cup tie at White City in January 1932. But United, notoriously poor performers in the Cup, lost 3-1.

they had in the first division with the Milburn brothers present at left and right-back throughout the campaign. A sustained run of good results up to Christmas had optimists dreaming of the league championship – all the more so when on Boxing Day, Leeds excelled themselves by winning 2-1 against Herbert Chapman's Arsenal side at Highbury.

The next day Leeds was seized by football fever. Every train, every tram, every taxi was overflowing and seemingly every living soul from miles around descended on Elland Road as United and Arsenal squared up for the return fixture. Spectators began arriving four hours before kick-off. Once, an influx of such a huge number of supporters would have caused bedlam, but the ground was bigger now and despite the intense crush as thousands were locked out, a semblance of order was maintained.

Biggest crowd in Leeds' history

The game attracted 56,988, much the biggest crowd in Leeds' history, but, the *Yorkshire Post* observed that the ground was not uncomfortably full. 'Had proper packing been possible, it could have held many more especially behind the goal at the Gelderd Road end.' Elsewhere however, 'the crowd overflowed on to the roof of the newly covered part of the popular side...scores were seen watching from the roof of an inn...so great was the crush that gates had to be opened to relieve some of the pressure.' The match was a 0-0 draw but no damp squib: 'a game worthy of the occasion, fought at a tremendous pace.' *The Times* reported that Leeds 'were only kept from success by the familiar concentration under pressure of eight members of the Arsenal side within or near their penalty area...the tackling of Hart and the brothers Milburn was too strong for the Arsenal men.'

But both the team and the city of Leeds soon sobered up. On 31 December, Dick Ray's men lost 5-1 at Derby County and for United's next home match against Blackburn Rovers on 7 January there was no crushing stampede but an orderly trickle. The crowd was only 14,043: 42,000 football fans had vanished, many never to be seen again.

Despite some aberrant defeats near the season's end, in no way had the Leeds team let their public down. Finishing in eighth place marked an honourable return to the top-class football of the first division; the wider world was coming to appreciate the sterling qualities of a team that Dick Ray had built with only meagre resources at his disposal. Their form was repeated in

'the crowd overflowed on to the roof...so great was the crush...'

Yorkshire Post

1933–34, with Leeds dropping just one place to ninth, yet without causing the stir they had previously. Once again they were away to Arsenal on Boxing Day, but while the champions were flying, Leeds were languishing in 17th place and lost 2-0, 'the score no indication as to the superiority of Arsenal,' commented *The Times*.

Nevertheless the Edwards, Hart, Copping half-back line was widely acclaimed. Edwards, capped sixteen times by England, featured in many a dream team of the day. 'An ideal half-back who could go forward or back at any time, and all the time,' said his Arsenal and England contemporary Eddie Hapgood. Glasgow Rangers and Scotland international Alan Morton, known popularly as the 'wee blue devil' viewed Edwards as 'a really grand all round player, so firm on the ball yet so light on his feet and accurate in his passing.'

Centre-half Ernie Hart was not only powerful and dominating, but also gifted with skill and great tactical sense. Copping, at left-half, was liable to unnerve the opposition with just one fixed stare from his craggy face. The harder the going, the more Copping liked it. Had football been war, he would have been first out of the trenches, bayonet fixed. For Hapgood, the sight of Copping dispensing his unique medicine during a rasping international match against Italy, was completely unforgettable: 'Wilf Copping

had been a regular guest full-back for Leeds City between 1917-19 and whose jobs included managing Carlisle after he retired as a player in 1930.

In Hampson's first season, Leeds United enjoyed a modest revival, finishing 11th. A bluff character, Hampson had a reputation for fair dealing, and continued grooming one of Dick Ray's notable protégés, right-back Bert Sproston, who had made his debut two seasons earlier and won the first of 11 England caps in 1937. Sproston was a versatile, stylish defender but chronic lack of funds forced Leeds to sell him to Tottenham in 1938 for £9,500. It was a depressingly familiar story.

By 1936–37, the defence lacked Hart – who had joined Mansfield after making 472 appearances for Leeds in league and cup – as well as Copping, and was regularly in disarray. Only good home form saved Leeds from relegation: they finished 19th with 34 points after losing all but two of their away games. Hampson experimented with new players, but injuries and loss of form disrupted the team pattern.

Towards the end of that difficult season, he made one key signing, centre-forward Gordon Hodgson from Aston Villa who, although nearly 34,

■ The Leeds defence was a Milburn family business. George (left) played 166 games for United while older brother Jack (right) played over 400 matches, missing only a handful of games through the 1930s.

enjoyed himself that afternoon. For the first time in their lives, the Italians were given a sample of real honest shoulder charging, and Wilf's famous double-footed tackle was causing them furiously to think.'

Yet Copping (his motto was 'Get stuck in') was more than just a bruiser. When he won the ball, he could deliver precise constructive passes that turned defence into attack. During 1933–34, Herbert Chapman, whose Arsenal team were on course for a second successive title, kept a close eye on the Leeds number 6. 'That's the man for me,' he is said to have remarked; and during the close season lured the Leeds iron man to Highbury for a fee of £6,000.

Copping was badly missed. In 1934–35 Leeds sank to 18th place, though with only four points fewer than in the previous campaign. But defensively there were some dreadful embarrassments: an 8-1 defeat at Stoke in the second match of the season, a 6-3 defeat at West Bromwich in November and a 7-1 thrashing at Chelsea in March – despite Leeds having taken a 10th-minute lead in the latter.

By then, Dick Ray had resigned as manager. With only slender resources at his disposal, he did much to enhance Leeds United's reputation, fostering the talents of several fine young players, but felt there was little more progress he could make. He was succeeded by Billy Hampson, who

United's leading scorer in the mid 1930s, Arthur Hydes was a bargain signing from Ardsley Recreation, a junior team near Barnsley.

gave new impetus to Leeds' attack. By 1937–38, Hampson had managed to stop the rot and a settled side had evolved. The defence looked more solid, with Sproston and Jack Milburn regular partners at full-back and Tom Holley, bought from Barnsley in July 1936, restoring some authority at centre-half. James Makinson and Bobby Browne were sturdy, if unspectacular, wing-halves. Replacing the injury-prone Arthur Hydes, South African-born Hodgson scored 25 goals in 36 games and was ably partnered at inside-left by the stylish Eric Stephenson, a rising

star who by the end of the season was called up to play for England.

There were no relegation scares: Leeds finished ninth, and before Christmas had been among the leaders until brought to earth by a run of poor form in the New Year. In 1938–39 they slipped to 13th, never threatening to make any impact on the title race. Crowds frequently dipped below 20,000 as Hampson tinkered with the team. The defence was shored up by the return in March of Wilf Copping, still full of bite, and Irish goalkeeper Jim Twomey, an excellent prospect signed the previous season. Two new wingers, David Cochrane on the right and Jack Hargreaves at outside-left had youth, pace and potential, but the forwards, save for Hodgson, often toiled vainly for goals. An exception was when, for the second time in five seasons, they ran eight past a hapless Leicester City side doomed to relegation.

World War Two intervenes

It was the last full season before the war intervened again. Hampson could be satisfied with keeping Leeds in the first division although, as Dick Ray had found, the club's horizons were limited by grinding debt. Leeds could always be outbid for the best talent and a need to balance the books forced the sale of some outstanding players to the richer clubs.

On 2 September, the day before Britain declared war against Germany, Hampson's men lost 1-0 at home to Sheffield United before a crowd of 9,799. With the war came an immediate suspension of the Football League programme and the return of regional league and knock-out competitions. Elland Road was requisitioned by the army for administrative purposes with the team allowed use of the premises for just two hours on match days. The challenge confronting the board, now chaired by Ernest Pullan, was to ensure the club's survival through the uncertainty of the war years.

As in the First World War, a bewildering number of guest players turned out in Leeds United colours, with team selection often sorted out at the last minute by Gordon Hodgson and Willis Edwards, acting as coaches-cum-secretaries. Results and performances were unpredictable and eccentric, and spectators, inevitably for wartime, often numbered just a thousand or two.

The war robbed Leeds of Eric Stephenson, killed in action in Burma during September 1944. Alan Fowler, who played 15 games at centre-forward in the 1932–33 and 1933–34 seasons before transferring to Swindon, died in France in June 1944. Jim Milburn was wounded in Belgium, but made a full recovery and returned to his place in the Leeds defence when League football resumed once more.

Although the war was over by August 1945, many footballers were still in uniform and most clubs unready to pick up the threads of a full Football League programme. In 1945–46 the Football League Northern Section ran its competition again, although the FA Cup was reinstated, operating on a two-legs basis.

With more than 40 players pulling on a Leeds United jersey, Hampson's team appeared in more disarray than most, finishing bottom of the league and conceding an 118 goals. Some results were dismal, with scorelines more suited to rugby than football: a 9-4 defeat at Bradford Park Avenue; losing 11-6 on aggregate to Middlesborough in the FA Cup third round. The Leeds public could only pray that serious competition might concentrate the players' minds and that with the return of a full league programme, the pantomime season would end.

■ 'First in't tackle don't get hurt.' So believed the indestructible Wilf Copping who won 20 England caps with Leeds and Arsenal and struck fear into opponents at home and abroad.

The Rise of Modern Leeds United

The public's appetite for football was enormous in 1946–47, one of a handful of pleasures that was not rationed. Had Billy Hampson's team done anything to encourage their supporters, Elland Road might well have seen record crowds. But while individual results were less dire than in the last season, Leeds United's habit of losing became even worse. After New Year, the team fell apart, winning only one of their last 21 matches – a 2-1 home victory over Chelsea that attracted 37,884, the highest crowd of the season.

The statistics made grim reading: Leeds' points tally of 18 was the lowest ever recorded in the first division and their away record – won 0, drawn 1, lost 21 – uniquely awful. Hampson had little money for new players and relied on those from pre-war days such as Tom Holley, Jim Twomey, David Cochrane, Bobby Browne, Welsh inside-forward Aubrey Powell, signed in 1936, a regular during 1938–39 and in wartime, and centre-forward George Ainsley, who also featured during the last two pre-war seasons.

With an ill-starred combination of youth and experience, Leeds plunged back into the second division and Billy Hampson resigned. Some players felt he did not need to fall on his sword. Rookie full-back Jimmy Dunn, whom Hampson had brought to Leeds from Scotland, said, 'He seemed a wonderful chap. It was a surprise when he went so quickly.'

As the problem of debt gnawed away, three new faces joined the board: Percy Woodward, Harold Marjason and Robert Wilkinson. Through the goodwill of some shareholders the club managed to reduce its debenture burden and Willis Edwards took on the task of team manager. He was a benign man with a wonderful playing pedigree, but lacked the brutish drive to dismantle and reconstruct a team that was in such poor shape. Dunn sensed in Edwards uncertainty and a lack of conviction. 'He seemed to be picking the team with the directors and trainer. I think he was just a figurehead; not management material. There was a sense of the club drifting.' The role was not for Edwards. Under his stewardship, Leeds sank to 18th in the second division and he resigned as April 1948, content to remain as assistant trainer. It was clear to new chairman Sam Bolton that Leeds United needed a firm, experienced hand. They were to find one in Major Frank Buckley, an idiosyncratic 64-year-old army officer, invariably accompanied by his small Welsh terrier.

Major Frank Buckley was one of football's legendary names. In the 1930s he transformed

Wolves from second division mediocrity to elite members of the first where they were championship runners-up in 1938 and 1939. A brilliant assessor of potentially great young players, Buckley also had a deep knowledge of tactical and psychological matters, combined with an intuitive feel for the game. Furthermore, he excelled in the transfer market, netting Wolves more than £100,000 in assorted deals.

In 1944 Buckley surprised many by leaving Wolves 'for personal and private reasons', coming to Leeds after spells at Notts County and Hull. His style was not to everyone's taste: some considered him autocratic and were disinclined to humour his whims and outlandish ideas.

He embarked on a clearout of old players. New blood had to be acquired cheaply: straitened finances governed all Buckley's actions and at his behest, admission prices at Elland Road were raised. His first season of revolution, 1948–49, arrested Leeds United's decline, but the team still only finished 15th. It was not a roaring success, but there were signs that Buckley's instinctive appraisal of talent was starting to bear fruit.

One excellent capture was wing-half Tommy Burden, whom Buckley had known as a teenager from Wolves days and signed from Chester on Willis Edwards' recommendation. Burden, who had played as a forward at Chester, was a reliable, intelligent, even-tempered player – though quite capable of standing up to Buckley – and an excellent passer of the ball. He became a popular captain. 'He had a nice way of encouraging people not by bollocking them, but through leading by example. He was a wonderful lad,' Jimmy Dunn recalls.

The Gentle Giant arrives

Meanwhile in South Wales, Leeds scout Jack Pickard began taking an interest in some juniors on the books of Swansea Town. Among these was a young man called John Charles, who had spent two years on the groundstaff but had never had a first team game. 'Mr Pickard asked some of us if we'd like to go for a trial,' Charles says. 'Three of us said yes. I first played in a friendly against Queen of the South when I was 17 and had a good game – well I think I did – and was then picked to play the following Saturday at Blackburn. I was never out of the team after that.'

Major Buckley had unearthed the discovery of a lifetime. Charles was a prodigy, the most enormous talent Leeds United had ever seen.

■ Major Frank Buckley, a man of sartorial elegance, stern discipline and unconventional ideas, did much to revive Leeds United's fortunes.

Moreover, he was a manager's dream: seemingly indestructible, yet without a hint of conceit or malice. At centre-half he could soak up endless pressure and launch swift counter-attacks; at centre-forward he was an uncontainable scoring machine. No player in the history of the English game had ever filled both positions with quite such ease.

'You could see he was marvellous when he arrived,' says Jimmy Dunn. 'So dainty for a big man and he wouldn't go in with a shoulder charge. Other players could pull him down and kick him but he never lost his temper.' For all the punishment that Charles took from opposing players, Tommy Burden recalls only one outburst from the Welshman. 'Someone was pulling at him as he was going down the by-line and John turned on him. I had to shout across. I've not seen the likes of him...he was superb in every way. He made things look so easy.'

In fact Charles worked hard to improve his technique. 'I didn't have it all there,'he said. 'I had to practise a lot, I can assure you. I used to go down the back of the big stand with Major Buckley and would keep hitting and hitting the ball. Throughout the three months summer break I was working every day at jumping. When I first came I only used to jump a foot off the ground. That's the way I improved it.'

Within a year, Charles became Wales's youngest international, winning his first cap against Northern Ireland. It was an uncharacteristically poor performance. The *Yorkshire Post* made no bones about it: 'Charles was a complete failure...he was prepared neither to go in and tackle nor stand off and wait...he was lost in helpless indecision.'

By 1949–50 the Leeds United team was more settled and assured. Charles, Jimmy Milburn, Dunn, Burden, right-half Jim McCabe and goal-keeper Harry Searson provided the cohesion that had long been lacking. But the attack, led by centre-forward Len Browning and Frank Dudley, did not always click. At 6'2", Browning had an imposing physical presence and Dudley, who packed a fierce shot, could unsettle defences, with surging runs on goal; but neither quite had the craft or consistency to be persistently threatening in front of goal.

But enough was stirring at Elland Road to whip up public interest. As Leeds pushed up the table in mid-season, Buckley's team played before an increasing number of huge crowds at Elland Road: 41,303 saw a 3-1 win against Preston on Christmas Eve; 47,817 a 1-0 victory over Barnsley on December 27; and 50,476 a 3-0 win against leaders Tottenham on 14 January, during

'So dainty for a big man and he wouldn't go in with a shoulder charge'

Jimmy Dunn on John Charles

which David Cochrane, in irrepressible form on the right wing, tore Spurs' defence to pieces.

For once Leeds kept going in the FA Cup. Their record in the competition was abysmal – they had never progressed beyond the fifth round and in 1948–49 had the humiliation of being dumped out in the third round, losing 3-1 at home to Newport County. Yet one good thing came out of that defeat; Buckley managed to sign the Newport winger Harold Williams, who had been a source of torment to Leeds throughout the afternoon.

The 1949–50 run of success did much to atone for past failures. The third round 5-2 win at Carlisle was straightforward, but Leeds then showed real metal by disposing of first division Bolton in the fourth round, digging into their mental and physical reserves on a quagmire of a pitch at Burnden Park to win 3-2 in extra time after the first match was drawn 1-1 at Elland Road. Playing with the confidence of a team that had won their last five league matches, Leeds swept Cardiff aside, winning 3-1 at Elland Road in the fifth round in front of 53,099 spectators.

There could be no more severe test of Leeds' recent progress than in the sixth round tie against Arsenal at Highbury. Buckley's men, by no means overawed by the occasion or by the 62,273 crowd, played superbly, defending in depth and counter-attacking effectively. But they were beaten by the only goal of the game, prodded in by Reg Lewis after 52 minutes. Despite a desperate late onslaught, Leeds could not fashion an equaliser.

Possibly hungover from the match in which they had given so much and dulled by a sense of anti-climax, Leeds lost some of their form towards the end of the season. Yet by finishing fifth with 47 points, just five fewer than promoted Sheffield Wednesday, Leeds United signified that the revival was underway.

Major Buckley's unusual methods

Buckley's methods had sharpened things up. 'At Leeds, there were never training sessions such as they had at Wolves where players would come in the morning and go out running in spiked shoes,' Tommy Burden recalls. 'In his last season, Tom Holley only used to train at night. Buckley was a shock to Leeds United. He couldn't bear a player who only had one foot. He felt that if you earned your living at football you should be able to use both feet. He had a go at me about it in front of the rest of the players. I remember him looking at his little Welsh terrier and saying, "You've got a better left foot than him, haven't you?".'

1954–55
Roxburgh (Trainer), Brook, Gibson, Dunn, Wood, Kerfoot, Hair
McCall, Nightingale, Charles (Captain), Forrest, Meek

Buckley had an abrasive side to his character and soon fell out with inside-forward Ken Chisholm, an assertive Scot who had served in the RAF as a fighter pilot and scored 17 goals in 40 league matches for Leeds. 'Ken was a character – a good goal-poacher who liked to go out with the lads for a drink. Buckley told him, "This city's not big enough for both of us and I'm not going",' Jimmy Dunn recalls. So ultimately Chisholm went – to Leicester City in an exchange deal that brought Ray Iggleden to Elland Road.

The Leeds manager, a pre-First World War centre-half of distinction who played for numerous clubs, cut an extraordinary figure. 'He spoke like an upper-class gentleman. I remember him bawling out Len Browning one day for not saying good morning,' says Tommy Burden. 'He always wore Oxford bags and his shoes were hand-welted, shining to perfection. You didn't call him Frank, you called him Major.' But not everyone saw Buckley as a martinet. 'He was very eccentric, but a lovely man and very good to me,' says John Charles.

Buckley's emphasis on fitness was conventional enough, but some of his other methods were outlandish. He introduced players to a mechanical kicking device which looked like a rocket launcher and released balls at varying heights. It was used for goalkeepers to practise shot-stopping and outfield players to improve their heading. Occasionally he held dancing sessions on the Elland Road pitch, with music blaring from the public address system, to try to enhance the players' balance and co-ordinate the movement of their feet.

The Major also administered extract of monkey gland to the players, the aim of which was to boost their mental and physical powers. This had been a hobbyhorse of Buckley's since 1935 and he had been depicted as something of a footballing witch doctor. But Tommy Burden was unimpressed. 'I said, "I'm not having it...I don't believe in it." Buckley said, "Oh, you must do... if you'll have it, they'll have it: you're the skipper, they'll follow you".' Burden held firm, though some of his team-mates did take the concoction. The effect, if any, was never studied scientifically.

■ United's class of 1954–55 were a lively team and only just missed out on promotion to the first division.

The 1950–51 season confirmed Leeds United's revival. They finished fifth once more, with 48 points, but there was less to fire the imagination; FA Cup interest ended early, with a 4-0 defeat at Manchester United in the fourth round, and Leeds' elevated position was due to a good late-season run. Injuries had taken an early toll; they were never strong contenders in the promotion race.

As he cast around for a number nine to play at Manchester City on Easter Saturday, Major Buckley's eye fell on John Charles. 'He told me, "There are two centre-forwards injured – you'll have to play there – I haven't got anyone else to put in",' Charles recalls. 'I went in the side and we got beaten 4-1. When he told me I'd have to play there again at home to Hull City on Easter Monday, I said, "You saw me, I didn't get a kick." Anyway I did play and I got two goals. Next day, the Major said, "Well done, lad, you'll stay at centre-forward." I don't know how I did it. Things just went right for me.'

Buckley had good cause to be delighted by his protégé's versatility, but Charles' absence on National Service for much of the 1951–52 season did nothing to help Leeds' cause. With David Cochrane having retired and Len Browning transferred to Sheffield United for £12,000, Buckley was forced to juggle the forward line, but

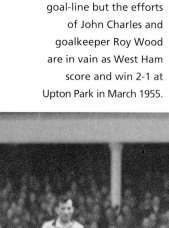

A melée on the Leeds goal-line but the efforts of John Charles and goalkeeper Roy Wood are in vain as West Ham score and win 2-1 at Upton Park in March 1955.

to no great effect. Too few goals and the lack of money to buy a proven scorer: they were the perennial problems.

But one inexpensive newcomer, Eric Kerfoot, proved a first-rate bargain. Signed for £3,000 from Stalybridge Celtic, he ousted Jim McCabe from right-half and went on to play 349 league and cup games for Leeds. Kerfoot was an enthusiastic team player, good on the ball and with the awareness that marked him out as a future captain. Save for the rare injury, he became an ever-present player and great servant for Leeds throughout the 1950s.

Charles returns...as a striker

Leeds finished sixth; the return of John Charles, in itself, was not enough to haul them to the top of the division. Only Ray Iggleden, enjoying his most effective season, managed a regular strike rate, scoring 19 goals in 41 league matches. But he could not shoulder the burden of striker alone. As Leeds made a shaky start to 1952–53, Buckley decided to throw John Charles up front as the centre-forward once more.

The effect was sensational. Through the autumn, Charles plundered defences, scoring 14 goals in ten games. Leeds shot up the table, but their promotion aspirations were undermined by

poor away form: despite 11 draws, they managed only one win away, at Plymouth on 3 January.

Jim McCabe was recalled to play at centre-half for much of the season and Grenville Hair, a debutant in March 1951, became the regular left-back in place of the veteran Jim Milburn. Two new faces in attack were winger George Meek and inside-forward Albert Nightingale and both became mainstays in the mid-1950s. Meek, although less tricky than Harold Williams, was tirelessly industrious, feeding John Charles with a liberal supply of swift, accurate crosses. Nightingale had in him a bit of the devil that Leeds sometimes lacked. 'You were pleased to have him on your side – he was a bugger when he was tackling,' says Tommy Burden. John Charles recalls Nightingale's opportunism in looking for a penalty – 'He'd get tackled on the halfway line and fall down in the area.'

Perhaps Leeds' real problem was that Charles could not be in two places at once – his 28 league matches in the forward line had brought 26 goals and they finished 10th with 43 points. But defensively, Leeds had become leaky, conceding 63 goals. Shortly before the season ended, Buckley decided that he could go no further with the limited means available to him and resigned.

John Charles would have fetched Leeds a small fortune. But, as yet, he was not keen to go,

and the directors had no desire to sell him. The Major however, had built his career on trading players. 'I remember when a lot of clubs were after him saying to Buckley, "You're not going to sell him, are you?" He said, "You watch me...I like money in the bank to cover my salary...he'll go if I get the right money for him",' Tommy Burden recalls.

Raich Carter takes over

The bountiful talents of Charles and the problem of running a football club on a shoestring were inherited by Raich Carter, the Hull City manager and one of England's finest inside-forwards in the 1930s and 1940s when he was with Derby and Sunderland. His first full season at Leeds, 1953–54, was a curious mirror image of Buckley's last: 10th position, 43 points, numerous absent-minded defensive performances, yet with Charles triumphant at centre-forward, breaking all club records as he scored 42 goals in 39 league matches. Leeds potential was enormous if the defence could be tightened up.

For all his ability Willis Edwards had lacked managerial authority, whereas Carter had a self-confidence that some felt bordered on arrogance. A dressing room row following a bungled free kick routine that cost Leeds a goal during the 5-3

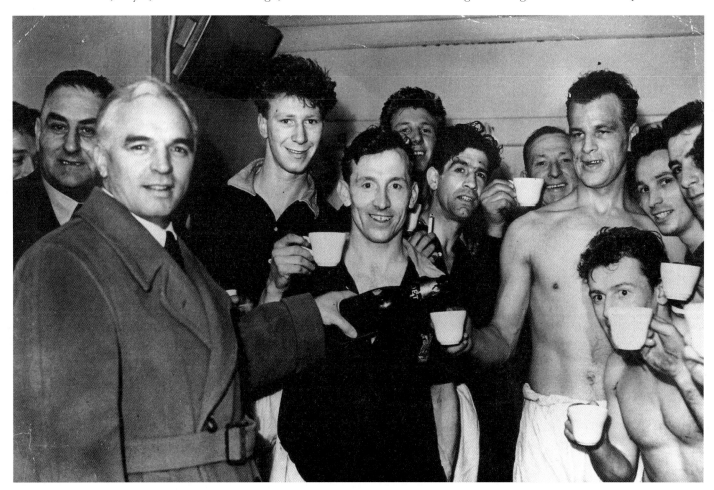

■ Champagne tastes good even out of teacups as Raich Carter's team celebrate promotion at the end of 1955–56 after a 4-1 win at Hull City.

defeat at Bury early in 1954–55 made Tommy Burden decide that he'd had enough. 'Carter was blaming the goalkeeper Jack Scott. I thought "This isn't fair..." so I turned round said, "You're the one who's bloody well to blame." We fell out... I think Raich suffered from thinking that there weren't many better players than he.'

Burden, who had been making the wearisome 500 mile round trip to matches at Elland Road from his home in Somerset, transferred to Bristol City. He was not alone in finding the Leeds manager hard going. 'Carter was very opinionated,' says John Charles. 'He had the view "I do it his way, so you do it this (not his) way, so you do it this way." He wouldn't let you argue. He was a nice man but he loved himself...he would take the credit for what you'd done.'

Yet Carter was astute enough to take pains to foster Charles' talent, encouraging him to rub shoulders with the best players. 'I played a lot with him – he took me to play charity matches with stars such as Finney and Matthews. On the field he would tell you what to do, where to run; getting you to move where he wanted you to. He was a good manager.'

Five defeats in their first six games – including the fiasco at Bury – gave no hint that Leeds would challenge for promotion. But in the tightest imaginable finish, the first three teams, Birmingham, Luton and Rotherham finished with 54 points and Leeds, storming home with six wins and two draws in their last eight matches, ended with 53. Their uncertain start had been compounded by doubts over Charles' future. Having finally decided that it was time he was playing first division football, the Welshman had made a written transfer request. Arsenal and Cardiff were anxious to sign him, but the Leeds board met to block the move. 'Our aim is to get United into the first division and we cannot do that by selling our star player,' Sam Bolton told the world.

For once, football ambition prevailed over the constant need to pump cash into the club. Charles accepted the situation equably and Leeds prospered. Although Charles was withdrawn to centre-half, a lively forward presence was sustained by Harold Brook, bought cheaply from Sheffield United as a replacement for Ray Iggleden. Brook scored 16 goals in 37 league matches and the attack was further galvanised in the spring by George Meek's return from National Service.

Carter made a few key adjustments for 1955–56, despatching Charles forward once more and feeding in Jack Charlton at centre-half. For Charlton, who had made his debut in April

1953, it was the start of a momentous career at Leeds United, although it was only after years of uneven performances and tantrums that he matured into a great defender. Wing-half Archie Gibson was another late developer, who had spent four years in the reserves. Gibson was highly thought of by Charles. 'I thought he should have got a Scottish cap – he was a mixture of Burden and Kerfoot – good on the ball, could pass and worked very hard.'

In for the injury-prone Harold Williams, Jack Overfield was a new face at left wing, recently returned from National Service. At his best, Overfield displayed intricate ball skills, though sometimes a lack of self-confidence made him anonymous. But he was a valuable component of the 1955–56 team and John Charles thrived on his fusillade of accurate crosses.

Again, Leeds' fortunes were uncannily similar to 1954–55. In a division of few outstanding sides, their start was unconvincing, but another late run of good form swept them upwards. On 21 April, with three games to go, Elland Road succumbed to football fever as 49,274 packed in for the clash against promotion rivals Bristol

Rovers. It was classic drama with a happy ending: Leeds fought back from losing a goal after three minutes to win 2-1, Charles and Overfield the scorers.

Top flight again

Having clawed their way into second place, Leeds were in no mood to let go. Two days later, goals from Nightingale, both created by Meek, secured a 2-0 win at Rotherham. Huge numbers of Leeds fans followed their team to Hull, who were already relegated, for the final match. There were no slip-ups after Hull equalised Charles' early goal: Carter's team kept running, worked openings, and ran in three second half goals. A 4-1 victory meant that their nine-year exile from the first division was over. Leeds were promoted back into top flight football, with 52 points, runners-up behind the league champions Sheffield Wednesday.

Without Charles, scorer of 29 goals, it is unlikely that Leeds would have made it. But although manifestly the finest footballer in the Leeds team, the second division and probably the

country, he was the last man to brag about his contribution. 'The four people in the middle, the wing-halves and inside-forwards did all the work; they were the bees,' Charles says. 'Raich Carter didn't change the system – most teams played the same way. We were all on the same money; nobody was any better than anyone else. We gelled...there was a good team spirit; we played a lot of games together. The spectators were behind us to a man. It convinced us we could win promotion.'

That spirit sustained Leeds throughout 1956–57. They began with a swagger, running rings around Everton, whom they beat 5-1 at Elland Road on opening day. It was an immediate triumph for Harold Brook, who scored a hat-trick, but there was a severe long-term cost for Leeds: Nightingale suffered a knee injury so serious that it ended his career.

West Stand in flames

But Leeds United's honourable return to the first division was overshadowed by a great fire that destroyed the West Stand on the night of 18 Sep-

■ United players tip-toe through the wreckage of the West Stand, destroyed by fire in September 1956.

■ Don Revie's best
playing days were
during the 1950's with
Manchester City. Bill
Lambton brought him to
Leeds unaware of the
revolution Revie would
later cause.

tember, the ramifications of which played a critical role in their fortunes during the all the following years.

The blaze consumed the entire structure, offices, kit and club records. All that remained was a charred steel skeleton. The alarm had been raised by Jimmy Dunn's father-in-law, Arnold Price, who ran a fish and chip shop nearby, but nothing could be saved. Damage was estimated at £100,000 and a public appeal was launched immediately. The stand had unfortunately been grossly under-insured.

Leeds rose to the occasion, making contingency arrangements to ensure that the home game scheduled against Aston Villa four days later could go ahead. Players changed at the sports ground of Petty's, a local printing firm, and were bussed to the ground. 'The atmosphere was very odd,' says John Charles. 'Running out was funny – you went into the car park then into nothing. We all had new boots and had to soak and wear them in the days before, kicking the ball like hell to get them ready in time.'

More than 35,000 turned up for the match against Aston Villa, eager to rally around the team. Leeds won 1-0 and from then on never looked uncomfortable in the first division, finishing 8th with 44 points. Charles was the indefatigable provider of goals – 38 in 40 league matches – proving he could do just as easily in the first division what he had done in the second.

Charles leaves for Juventus

At last Leeds received an offer for him that they could not refuse, not from England but Juventus of Italy, whose president, Signor Umberto Agnelli was a scion of the family that had made its fortune producing Fiat cars. Agnelli could afford any player he wanted: Juventus were struggling for goals; Charles seemed able to score at will. The Turin club was not alone in wanting Charles' services, as officials from Inter Milan had cast predatory eyes in Leeds' direction.

Never was there a more contented player than Charles. 'Leeds was my team – I loved the place,' he says. 'To be honest, I went for the money. The wages were less (a basic £60-70 a month) but if you beat Turin or Milan you got £500 bonuses.' Charles was also offered the huge sum of £10,000 for signing on. The riches were unimaginable to British players toiling away on an artisan's rate of pay.

No case could be made against the arithmetic of the deal. The new West Stand was costing Leeds £130,000 and only the sale of Charles could finance the shortfall. A fee of £65,000 was

agreed on condition that Juventus play a friendly match at Elland Road the following season. Meanwhile Charles gave Leeds his all up until the end, firing home two goals against Sunderland during a final emotional game at Elland Road on 22 April.

He was irreplaceable as a scorer: 157 goals in 327 matches; as a centre-half, stopper and creator; as a captain and talisman. In Italy, Charles was to win three championships, a cup medal and become Footballer of the Year. And Raich Carter was left with only half the transfer money to try to fill the breach.

The task proved impossible, though Carter could not fault new his new centre-forward Hugh Baird, bought from Airdrie for £12,000, who scored 20 goals in 39 league games during 1957–58. But Baird had neither Charles' presence nor his ability to make waves. Carter experimented with various inside-forwards:

Bobby Forrest, in and out of the team since 1954, managed only seven goals; Wilbur Cush, signed from Glenavon for £7,000 in November 1957, hit just three goals in 21 appearances; George O'Brien, signed from Dunfermline the previous March, scored only three in 19 outings. The team still had its backbone in Roy Wood, the first choice goalkeeper for three seasons, as well as Dunn, Hair, Gibson, Charlton and Kerfoot; but the heart had gone from the line-up.

The decline was steady rather than drastic. Leeds finished 17th, though with only seven fewer points than in Charles' final season. They were never enmeshed in a struggle against relegation, but the directors decided not to renew Carter's contract when it expired in March 1958. 'It could never be any more than a holding season once Charles had gone,' Carter reflected.

Lambton takes charge

The situation at Elland Road did not augur well for any successor. A firm, knowledgeable and imaginative hand was needed to restore confidence. With hindsight, the appointment of Bill Lambton, whom Carter had brought to the club as coach in December 1957, was ill-judged. Lambton's regime lasted less than a year and for most of that time, he only had the title of 'acting manager'.

A pre-war goalkeeper of only modest ability, who once had been on Nottingham Forest's books, Bill Lambton failed to win over the players with his methods. Jimmy Dunn viewed him as 'a bloody comedian.' 'He had no experience. I remember he once took his boot off on the Fullerton Park training ground and said, "You don't need boots when you're crossing a ball." Eventually, there was a players' meeting in protest. It was a rebellion. Eric (Kerfoot) and I had complained about him. I can't remember exactly what we said but it came down to the fact that he couldn't manage the club.'

Despite this discontent, Lambton was collecting players whom he hoped might dig Leeds out of their hole. Hughie Baird had returned to Scotland, joining Aberdeen. His replacement, Alan Shackleton signed from Burnley, did well in 1958–59, scoring 16 goals. But Don Revie, now 31, whose best days had been in the mid-1950s with Manchester City, was to have the profoundest influence on Leeds United and in ways that might have astonished even the most fanciful crystal ball gazer. Lambton had bought not so much a cultured forward as a revolutionary.

Part of Leeds United's problem was the dearth of young players coming through. Winger Chris

Crowe was an exception; his sharp performances were to be rewarded with England under-23 caps, and, when with Wolves in the early 1960s, full international honours. If Leeds were unsuccessful, Crowe was sometimes picked on by the crowd and his game suffered. In March 1960 he joined Blackburn Rovers for £25,000. Leeds could ill afford to lose such talent.

Shortly after Revie took over the captaincy from Wilbur Cush, discontent with Bill Lambton reached a peak. Hair and Overfield had both

■ Past his playing prime but the face of Leeds United's future. Don Revie's arrival from Sunderland was destined to make Leeds United into one of the world's great football teams.

demanded transfers. By March 1959, directors were expressing disquiet about Lambton and the beleaguered manager resigned, claiming there had been 'interference...in my training methods'. It was a poor testimony to the set-up at Leeds that the first choice replacement, Arthur Turner, preferred to stay at non-league Headington (later Oxford) United rather than run the first division club. Tommy Burden also turned down the post.

Despite the rebellious mood that had hung over Elland Road for much of 1958–59, three wins and a draw in their final four matches saw Leeds escape relegation quite comfortably, finishing 15th with 39 points. Lambton's eventual successor was Jack Taylor who had managed Queen's Park Rangers through the 1950s, though without conspicuous success. Somehow, with almost no money, he was expected to do better. It was almost impossible for anyone to envisage just how.

The close season saw the departure of two great stalwarts, Eric Kerfoot and Jimmy Dunn. Team-mates felt that Dunn had been unlucky not to play for Scotland. 'He was one of the best full-backs I played with, though I think he could have passed the ball better,' says John Charles, 'but he was very fit, strong and hard; and at covering, unbelievable.'

Bremner arrives at Elland Road

The maligned Lambton had begun work on a more structured policy on youth, poverty at Leeds forcing the pace. He discovered among others, Billy Bremner, destined to become one of Leeds United's greatest midfield players.

'The move to Leeds came out of the blue really,' Bremner recalls. 'I was 15 and had just played for Scotland schoolboys at Ibrox against England. I was destined for Celtic...that's who I always wanted to play for. Celtic came up, but Leeds had popped in before. Tommy Henderson, a friend of mine in the team, said he was going to sign for Leeds United. One of the directors, Harry Reynolds, said he wanted a word with me. He came up to the house, talked to my mum and convinced her Leeds was the place for me. To be perfectly honest I'd never heard of Leeds United.'

Nurturing new talent was a key responsibility of one of Jack Taylor's new appointees, coach Syd Owen, who had joined from Luton Town where he had briefly been manager. Owen insisted in bringing with him trainer Les Cocker, but for all their good work, Leeds drifted down the first division and towards relegation in 1959–60. Although young and inexperienced,

> ### 'To be perfectly honest I'd never heard of Leeds United.'
>
> *Billy Bremner*

Bremner was shocked by the ramshackle organisation at Leeds United. 'We went to play a crucial game towards the end of the season at Blackburn Rovers. I remember wondering where we were going to eat. In the end we stopped at a café and had beans on toast. It was all a bit of rush...yet this was the most important game of the season.'

John McCole, a powerful, confident striker signed from Bradford City, became Leeds' third centre-forward in three seasons after Alan Shackleton's sudden move to Everton in September 1959. One could not have asked for more than the 22 goals he scored in 33 matches, but he got scant support. Irish inside-forward Noel Peyton, with five, was next highest scorer. The old defensive guard of the 1950s, save for Hair and Charlton, was no longer in place. Taylor tried several unsuccessful combinations and the belated signing of Freddie Goodwin, a stern robust stopper from Manchester United, was not enough to save Leeds from the drop. They finished 21st, with 34 points.

As Leeds floundered in the second division, disillusionment and cynicism deepened amongst spectators. Sometimes the players were greeted with cries from the terraces of 'Here come the mugs'. Taylor shuffled his pack of players once more and brought in several new recruits of modest ability, few of whom seemed passionate about effecting a revival. Injuries also sabotaged his plans.

One newcomer, Eric Smith, a hard-tackling wing-half, who had signed from Celtic, was appalled by the apathy he found. 'The players were undisciplined,' Smith recalled. 'It wasn't their fault – Jack Taylor was the manager, but had let things go. I certainly didn't expect what I saw in the first three or four days. We would go on long training runs and players would walk in with ice lollies in their hands.'

Revie, however, did take training seriously, and was often exasperated by the laxity of some of his colleagues. His reflective approach had already come to the attention of Harry Reynolds, much the most dynamic figure on the board of directors, although not yet chairman. They drifted together as like-minded souls, sharing thoughts about the game, mulling over what might be best for Leeds United.

Their rise to power was imminent; and early in 1960–61, spectators were given a glimpse of the future – for the home game against Middlesbrough on 17 September 1960, the team appeared in what was basically an all white strip, though with blue and gold trimmings, instead of the blue shirts, white shorts and blue and gold

A cheeky-looking boy who evolved into one of the world's great midfield generals; but Billy Bremner's early career was threatened by an inability to control his temper.

socks. What was in a change of strip? In the mind of Revie, Leeds' manager-in-waiting, it meant everything. One of his first acts in charge was to claim the colours, without the trimmings, as his own, and make Leeds play in the unadorned all white of Real Madrid, Europe's most legendary club side. It was the visionary, the romantic, stirring in him.

By March 1961, with Leeds toiling in the lower reaches of division two, the Leeds board decided Taylor's time was up. His dismissal, on 13 March, coincided with Revie's own desire to leave the club and have a shot at management.

He had in mind the vacancy at Bournemouth and asked Harry Reynolds for a reference. There was plenty Reynolds could say about Revie's potential: so much that suddenly he halted when writing the letter and tore it up.

For there was a vacancy, too, at Leeds and Reynolds realised that the club's great thinker was in danger of slipping away from right under their nose. The board was persuaded that it could do worse than charge Revie with trying to revive the fortunes of their sickly club. Four days after Taylor's departure, Reynolds' protégé was crowned successor.

apathy, indifference and poor management, attitudes which Revie was not prepared to tolerate.

Among his contemporaries, Revie regarded Matt Busby of Manchester United as a mentor. Shortly after taking over at Elland Road, the Leeds manager called on Busby at Old Trafford for a tutorial on how to manage a sickly team on a shoestring budget. Look to youth and establish a consistent coaching pattern right through the club, Busby told him.

Boardroom backing

Revie drew most support from Harry Reynolds, the Leeds United director who in December 1961 would succeed Sam Bolton as chairman. Reynolds was a self-made millionaire who had gained his fortune through a steel stockholding business. He was born in Holbeck, a few minutes' walk from Elland Road, and had followed the club all his life. His daughter, Margaret Veitch, fondly recalls being swept along by her father's enthusiasm. 'When I was a little girl, he used to take me and we would stand on the terraces. He was a very good amateur footballer himself – he played for Leeds schoolboys and I don't know how many times the school he went to won their championship."

The Revie Revolution

1961–62 Work begins

There were no manuals on how to rescue an ailing football club. Everyone could see that Leeds United were impoverished by too little investment, a lack of strategy on the pitch and a surfeit of ill-assorted players; all symptoms of an enveloping malaise. But there could be no quick remedy.

Revie was shrewd, had a deep understanding of the game and a fascination for tactics, combined with a great sense of purpose. Already he cut a responsible, paternal figure. However, he had no managerial experience and needed to lean on others, father-figures who could give advice; there was no time to learn the job at a steady pace.

Of all the league managers he'd known in his playing career, Revie had greatest respect for his first, Johnny Duncan, for whom he played at Leicester in the late 1940s. Duncan, whose niece, Elsie, Revie eventually married, inspired a great sense of loyalty through dedication to the welfare of his players. Elsewhere on his travels, through Hull, Manchester City, Sunderland and at Leeds United itself, Revie, according to his own accounts, had encountered varying degrees of

■ A dynamic force and a man of the people, chairman Harry Reynolds' partnership with Don Revie stimulated the Leeds United revolution. A fan of the club all his life, Reynolds was chairman from 1961 to 1967, when he was forced to retire through ill health.

Reynolds believed in conducting business graciously. 'He had the attitude that everybody mattered from the cleaners to the top managers,' said Margaret Veitch. Moreover, Reynolds and Revie shared a sense of the importance of family relationships. Over the next three years, this belief helped Leeds United woo the best young talent from all over Britain, despite fierce competition – Revie had taken Matt Busby's advice to heart. 'But it was my father who said to Don, "You must go to see the families, not just leave it to the scouts",' said Margaret Veitch.

Reynolds frequently accompanied Revie on raiding missions to Scotland where their combination of charm, persuasiveness, and Revie's vision of a potentially brilliant future at Elland Road, made them a hard act to resist.

In the short term, Revie had a mess to sort out. The players he inherited from Jack Taylor, often pulled in different directions, if they pulled at all. Revie's first game in charge was on 18th March and Leeds lost 3-1 at Portsmouth. In the remaining matches, his charges recorded just one win, a 7-0 victory over Lincoln City who were doomed to relegation.

One experiment he made while shuffling around his pack was to introduce a 21-year-old black winger from South Africa, Albert Johanneson, who made his debut on 8 April in a 2-2 draw at Elland Road against Swansea. In time, Johanneson's talents would dazzle; but few players captured the imagination as Leeds went through the motions in their remaining matches. A change of manager failed to enthral the Leeds public; United's final home game of the season, a 2-2 draw against Scunthorpe, drew a crowd of just 6,975, the lowest gate at Elland Road for a league fixture since the war.

Harry Reynolds sensed that one reason for low morale was a lack of self-esteem – the club had habitually done things on the cheap. Soon that would change. 'Even though money was short initially,' said Margaret Veitch, 'he said, "We're going to go first class...we're going to stay at good hotels." His attitude was that if we were going to be a top club, we would do the things expected of a top club.'

But the money problem was always gnawing away. The only close season signing Revie could afford was right-winger Derek Mayers from Pre-

■ Albert Johanneson shows off his bewitching skills to team-mates. On his day, few defenders could contain the South African winger yet his confidence was often undermined, especially by racial abuse.

'We're going to go first class...'

Margaret Veitch quoting Harry Reynolds

ston North End. There was youthful talent at Elland Road, but mostly too raw to be pitched into the regular toil of the second division. The only exception was 18 year-old Billy Bremner, who had played 31 league matches during 1960–61, mostly at inside-forward, and would become an automatic first team choice for the next 14 seasons.

The team of tomorrow

In programme notes for the home match against Southampton on 28 October, Revie wrote proudly of his protégés playing in the Northern Intermediate League, 'Their average age is 16, but in this tough competition, our young team can more than hold its own. Here are some of our lads: Gareth Sprake, goalkeeper, 16, from Swansea Schoolboys...right-half Jimmy Greenhoff 15, star of the Barnsley Boys team which won the Yorkshire Cup and English Schools' Shield last year...Paul Reaney, captain and centre-half, a Leeds lad from the Leeds City Boys team...Norman Hunter, inside-forward from Newcastle district. We think we have a young team well worth watching – take a look and judge for yourselves.'

A fortnight later, before the home game against Leyton Orient, the Leeds manager was again beating the drum for his youth squad: 'Terry Cooper, a 17 year-old outside-left is another apprentice of great promise. But to get the best out of them, they must be brought along gradually. It is of course frustrating to a football supporter to be asked repeatedly to be patient but I am afraid that is what is required,' Revie astutely said.

Hard times

The first team was struggling again. Victories at home to Charlton and at Brighton in the first games of the campaign gave a false impression of success. Soon Leeds were showing their usual shaky form and gates quickly slumped to below 10,000. Revie, who still felt compelled to play, had a constant battle to make the best of what he had and, with the wilful Jack Charlton, to impose his authority. 'Either go on doing it your way and get out of the game, or do it my way and play for England,' Revie told him. Charlton, whose career was at a crossroads, eventually decided to do as he was told.

The inability or unwillingness of members of the first team to give their best brought about an ill-disguised frustration on Revie's part. Writing of Leeds' 'financial and playing depression', he tried publicly to gee-up former England youth international winger John Hawksby, who had failed to produce a goal since scoring in his first two games the previous season. 'John has yet to make his position in the club secure. In Central League matches and in training, he is outstanding but on the field in the cut-and-thrust of the Football League, his skill is not as apparent,' Revie said.

Meanwhile, crucial changes were taking place in the boardroom. When Harry Reynolds succeeded Sam Bolton as chairman, two other businessmen, Manny Cussins and Albert Morris were appointed to the board. Each director agreed to lend an equal amount of money to the club and share financial commitments. 'Encourage them, they are shouldering a big responsibility,' wrote Sam Bolton in his valedictory message to supporters.

Before the home match against Liverpool on 23 December, Harry Reynolds revealed that Revie now had more 'sinews of war – what we Yorkshiremen call brass at his disposal than his predecessors had. How much more must remain our secret – the soccer market is as tricky a field of business to operate in as you will find,' he said. There were, however, seven board members and, Margaret Veitch recalls, Reynolds himself put up £50,000.

In a desperate bid for goals, Revie had signed Belfast-born centre-forward Billy McAdams from Bolton Wanderers. The Leeds manager had been unprepared for the sudden departure in October of John McCole, scorer of 20 goals in 35 league matches the previous season, who also caused a local sensation by bagging four when Leeds beat Brentford 4-1 at Elland Road in the League Cup during September. A confident, fearless striker who excelled in the air, McCole's sudden return to Bradford City was as unexpected as it was disruptive.

McAdams had been Revie's team-mate at Manchester City and a consistent scorer – 62 goals in 127 league games. But at Leeds, form deserted him and the Ulsterman's performances were conspicuous more for chances missed – 'so many it wasn't true,' according to Leeds winghalf Eric Smith – rather than the four goals he managed in 13 matches.

In the New Year, the meagre ration of goals was becoming a famine – the Leeds attack squeezed out just four in seven league games. In desperation, Revie moved Jack Charlton to centre-forward. But Charlton was no John Charles, nor was there a high-revving midfield to constantly supply him.

As March and the transfer deadline quickly approached, Leeds fortunes slumped and the club sank deeper and deeper into trouble. For the first time in the United's history, the unthinkable was fast becoming a reality, and relegation to the third division beckoned. 'It was a desperate situation,' said Syd Owen. 'We knew that with good quality players we could develop a team that

■ Opposite: Once a skinny young player without the strength to kick the ball where he wanted, Norman Hunter became one of the most feared defenders in football. Although remembered as a hard man, he was a superb passer of the ball with a surprisingly delicate touch.

■ Don Revie takes a snapshot of team captain Bobby Collins, the catalyst for Leeds' great revival. Experience at the top level allied to a passion for the game made Collins an invaluable asset.

might last up to ten years. We were trying to develop the young ones as quickly as possible, but to stabilise the position, we had to get some mature professionals.'

The team needed strengthening almost everywhere, though one success, unexpected in the eyes of many, was former Scottish international goalkeeper Tommy Younger, signed from Stoke at the end of September 1961. Younger's reputation as a slacker proved ill-founded: he brought some authority to the defence, gave Don Revie sage advice, and played an invaluable role in coaching Gary Sprake.

In March, three new faces arrived at Elland Road: left-back Cliff Mason, signed from Sheffield United for £10,000, centre-forward Ian Lawson, who cost £20,000 from Burnley, and inside-left Bobby Collins from Everton for a fee of £25,000. Mason and Lawson were sound, honest players, but Bobby Collins was a miraculous investment: the dynamic, indefatigable footballer for which Leeds United had been desperately searching.

New arrivals

Collins felt bewildered and slighted when, at 31, he suddenly found himself out of favour with Everton manager Harry Catterick. This was a golden opportunity for Revie to snap up a player who still had so much to offer. Immediately, the Leeds recruitment team swung into action. 'When I came home from training, Don, Harry Reynolds and Manny Cussins were waiting for me on the doorstep. We got talking and then I agreed to sign. I was impressed by how badly Revie wanted me. I was bought to teach and inspire,' Collins said.

A near miracle was being asked of Collins, who had won 28 Scotland caps with Celtic and Everton. He was a wonderful ally but a fiendish opponent, his game an amalgam of craft, vision and fearsome tackling. Although only 5ft 4ins tall, Collins was the last footballer in the world to be pushed around. At Leeds, his job was to grab a drifting team by the scruff of its neck, to instil passion and order – to be the embodiment of Revie on the field.

Flirting with the drop

With 11 games still to go, time was running out. All augured well in Collins' first match: he was a scorer in the 2-0 home win against Swansea on 10 March, a game which attracted a gate of 17,314, more than double the attendance for Leeds' 3-2 defeat by Plymouth Argyle at Elland

Road a fortnight earlier.

It was Leeds United's first win in seven matches. But although the defence was becoming a tighter unit, it was blown apart early the following Saturday when, hours before the match at Southampton, Tommy Younger was suddenly taken ill. Sixteen year-old Gary Sprake was summoned from his bed and flown as an emergency replacement to Southampton by chartered aircraft. Leeds lost 4-1, their heaviest defeat since Boxing Day; but the goals could be blamed more on collective uncertainty than errors made by the debutant goalkeeper.

Proof that the collapse at Southampton was an aberration came in the last nine games. Suddenly the porous Leeds defence found the cohesion it had been lacking and became the meanest in the league. Cliff Mason, a former captain at Sheffield United, by no means the hardest left-back in the division, proved invaluable as an intelligent, calming influence on the team. His greatest asset was anticipation: few were more adept at spotting the intentions of opposing forwards and nipping trouble in the bud. In those final nine matches, Leeds conceded only four goals.

Despite Collins' promptings, however, goal-scoring was as big a problem as ever. The nine-match run-in, now a desperate relegation battle, yielded only ten goals, of which three were scored by the opposition. Ian Lawson scored just once in 11 outings, in the debacle at Southampton. Revie's team had mastered the art of shutting out other teams, but not the ability to break them down.

The dogfight at the bottom included two rasping encounters against fellow-strugglers Bury. When the Shakers came to Elland Road on 24 April for the penultimate match of the season, they had scrambled clear of relegation, yet still fought as if their lives depended on it, denying Leeds victory in a 0-0 draw. Habitual draws had now become Leeds' problem – this was the fifth in a sequence that included a 1-1 at Gigg Lane four days earlier.

Much was at stake – Leeds United's second division future and possibly Revie's job – in the final match at Newcastle on 28 April. Defeat, and victory for Bristol Rovers at Luton would banish Leeds to the third division. But Revie and Reynolds had the tenacity of driven men. 'I don't think they ever thought of failure, and even if they did go down, it would be a little hiccup,' said Margaret Veitch. The thought of third division football provided a powerful incentive for the players.

On the day, Newcastle were swept away by

Leeds United's fearsome will to win. The 3-0 victory was probably their best performance of the season, although Bobby Collins recalls: 'It was a funny game...Newcastle weren't up to much that day'; and memorable for a grotesque own goal by Newcastle defender Dick Keith, who steered a back-pass into his own net 15 minutes before the final whistle.

But by then, Johanneson and McAdams had put Leeds 2-0 up. The famous victory was not due just to Newcastle's inadequacies: Leeds had mastered a bumpy pitch and stiff wind, with Collins and Johanneson outstanding in a disciplined team display. The sense of relief gave rise to celebrations as joyful as if Leeds had won the championship. Revie had bought the time to continue his revolution.

■ Above: Portrait of the genius as a young man. In time Bremner, who began life as a forward, assumed Bobby Collins' mantle as midfield captain and inspiration.

■ Opposite: Jim Storrie's arrival from Airdrie for £15,000 caused little excitement at the time. However, he proved to be an effective replacement for the great John Charles.

1962–63 Out with the old…

At the start of 1962–63, the 'Cinderella' club was suddenly starting to make a big impression. Billy McAdams, Derek Mayers and Bobby Cameron were all sold, and, in an extravagant gesture, Don Revie brought John Charles back to Elland Road from Juventus for a club record fee of £53,000. More than 27,000 flocked to Stoke City for Leeds' opening game, expecting great things from the leading man.

Yet the winning goal was scored by Revie's other close season recruit, Jim Storrie, acquired from Airdrie for £15,000, whose arrival caused much less excitement. Perceived as a bread-and-butter forward from a workaday club, Storrie was to deliver the goods expected of Charles who, after five years in Italy, was unable to fulfil the role of returned Messiah.

Revie clearly saw something in Storrie, who had been playing only part-time at Airdrie, that others had missed. 'I didn't fancy Leeds at all at first…I thought they were heading for the third division,' Storrie said. 'Then later Don Revie and Harry Reynolds came up to our house. My wife said I was at work, so they came to the works. They were very persuasive.'

After his team's doughty finish the previous season, Revie was dismayed at the erratic start Leeds made in 1962–63. Following a 2-1 defeat at home to Bury on 5 September, the third in six league matches, he lost patience. Drastic changes were ordered for the next match, away to Swansea Town. It was time, Revie decided, to expose his striving young reserves to life in the second division. The Leeds manager also had to replace Eric Smith, his hard-tackling right-half, whose football career was ended when he broke his leg in a tackle during the 2-0 home win over Chelsea on 15 September.

In came Gary Sprake, recommended to Revie by Jack Pickard, the scout who discovered John Charles, Paul Reaney (now converted to right-back), Norman Hunter (no longer an inside-forward but a left-half) and Rod Johnson (centre-forward). Out went Tommy Younger, Grenville Hair, Willie Bell and John Charles. Johnson scored in the 2-0 win, but injury prevented his career from gaining any momentum. The others became part of the bedrock of Leeds United for the next decade and even beyond that.

Revie's trawl of Scotland had also netted Peter Lorimer, a young forward from Dundee with a fiendish shot, whose seasonal goals tally in junior football resembled the stuff of fantasy. Injury to Billy Bremner pressed Lorimer into first-team service for the home game with Southampton on 29 September. At the age of 15 years and 289 days, Lorimer was not overawed at being the

youngest debutant in Leeds United's history – he was blessed with a remarkably phlegmatic temperament.

'We wanted to bring on these boys as quickly as possible and entered them in tournaments abroad where we knew they would be extended and tested,' explained Syd Owen. 'It was almost one of the first things we did. Teams from Brazil would be in some of the competitions we played in. We knew that if they could perform against those kind of people, there was a great chance of their coming through in English football.'

The pastoral side received meticulous attention. Syd Owen recalls: 'There was a lot of competition for the boys, so we invited the parents to come down to the club as well. We put them up in hotels and let them stay a short time. We took them to see the people who looked after the boys in digs. We even had a church minister come down to the ground every Thursday to walk round the dressing room and ask the young players if they had any problems.'

Revie offered his youngsters spiritual and financial advice. 'He would always tell us to say our prayers before the game,' Gary Sprake said, 'and he advised us about pension schemes. I took one out when I was 16 and saved half my wages.'

Charles bound for Rome

Whilst the young players were quickly learning their trade – and how to conduct themselves – it soon became apparent that the John Charles experiment had failed. 'John just didn't fancy it at Leeds when he came back from Italy,' said Jim Storrie. 'He and Les Cocker didn't get on. He wouldn't train as rigorously as they wanted – in Italy he was used to flicking the ball about and wandering around the park. It led to conflict.'

Charles' own recollections are different. 'I was very happy to come back, but things never went right. It wasn't the training – I got on with Syd Owen and Les Cocker alright. I had a bit of personal trouble at the time and that worried me. It was just myself – I couldn't settle back into it. Some people had said never to go back to a club that you've been to before – people expect too much of you. At the end, I thought it was no good staying on. I was very sorry actually – I would have loved to play in the Revie side.'

Charles' best performance had been against Southampton on 29 September, when he was switched to centre-half after an injury to Jack Charlton forced Revie to rejig the team. But by then, another Italian club, Roma, was making overtures about signing him. After 11 games and three goals – a shadow of his former strike rate –

Charles returned to Italy, sold for £65,000. 'Don Revie said, "We don't want you to go really", but I took the chance, though I didn't really like it. I didn't care for Rome,' Charles said.

So a potentially expensive mistake turned into a good piece of business – more so than the decision of the Leeds board to exploit Charles' return by doubling admission prices. The first two home games of the season, against Rotherham and Sunderland, had attracted crowds of 14,119 and 17,753, well below expectation. After the experiment was abandoned, the next home match against Bury drew 28,313.

But Leeds' early form had been inconsistent. Although Jim Storrie was scoring regularly, he found his new role as target man a shock. 'Really, I was an old-fashioned inside-forward carrying the ball through, playing one-twos,' he said. 'In Scotland, no-one bothered how you played and I always seemed to be looking for people to play off. But when I was the target man, I had the goalkeeper behind me. Individually, I think I became a worse player. My wife Nancy told Revie this at a function one night, but he just laughed and said, "you may be right but they are a very successful team". That was true. The success glossed over a million deficiencies. I adapted because I was caught up in all the enthusiasm.'

■ Striding out purposefully: Jack Charlton, now a highly effective centre-half, and a youthful Gary Sprake, were key figures in an ever-meaner defence.

> 'In Scotland, no-one bothered how you played.'
>
> *Jim Storrie*

In December, to beef up the attack further, Revie signed Don Weston from Rotherham United. Although not the most stylish centre-forward, Weston had terrific pace, fitness and a tendency to unsettle defences with rapid surges towards goal from a deep position. Storrie, was strong, brave, and an intuitive goal-scorer.

Weston made a dramatic entry into the Leeds team, scoring a hat-trick on his debut during the 3-1 home victory over Stoke City on 15 December. But the forward partnership did not establish itself until March 1963, after the winter freeze wiped out more than two months of league football. Few teams were readier for action than Revie's Leeds team once the pitches had thawed. With almost half a season's fixtures crammed into two-and-a-half months, the demands on fitness and stamina were intense. But Les Cocker's draconian training sessions had made Leeds into one of the most robust teams in the league.

'We were a ball-winning side, free of injuries, and champing at the bit to go,' remembers Storrie. 'We played a method game, high pressure football. Bobby Collins would get hold of the ball and spray passes all over the park for people to chase after. The forwards would hustle, cutting off the supply of back passes to the goalkeeper. I reckon we scored about 10-15 goals a season through forced errors that way.'

Leeds hit their best run of form since 1956–67 and, for the first time since 1951–52, progressed to the fifth round of the FA Cup before losing 3-0 at

Nottingham Forest. During a hectic April, Revie's men won six, drew one and lost only two league matches, scoring 19 goals. They became unexpected outsiders for promotion before their form deserted them in May, when they lost three of their four remaining fixtures before finally finishing fifthin the league.

But the team had learned a great deal and there was now the backbone of a side that would not flinch and had the potential to go far. For once, no-one in Leeds was looking fearfully at the relegation trapdoor.

Fit for anything: Don Revie and Jack Charlton lead the way in training. Stamina and hard-running were trademarks of the new look Leeds who were destined to take the second divsion by storm.

1963–64 Leeds on the up

Through the summer Revie pondered how best to make an eager hustling side into something more rounded and capable of regaining first division status. Again, he made an inspired signing, paying Manchester United £32,000 for their disaffected right-winger Johnny Giles.

For many, the surprise was that Giles wanted to leave at all. He had played in Manchester's FA Cup-winning team and in almost all the league games. Still only 23, his prospects, superficially, appeared to be much better at Old Trafford. But Giles felt the team contained too many ill-matched personalities and decided to move. 'I'd been there since I was 15 and was maybe not appreciated,' he said. 'There was a feeling about Leeds; that they were trying to do something and were on the up-and-up.'

Besides Revie's well-rehearsed persuasiveness, the presence of Bobby Collins helped to make up Giles' mind. Meanwhile, the younger players were maturing fast. Reaney and Hunter were already rock solid defenders; Billy Bremner, for whom Revie had fended off bids from Everton and Hibernian, seemed settled and started 1963–64 season at right-half, the position he was to make his own. The friction of earlier seasons, when Revie forced Bremner against his will to play on the right wing, was forgotten. The remodelled team was a coherent and efficient unit: there was a sense of Leeds being as united as ever they had been.

Among the senior players, Willie Bell, signed by Jack Taylor in 1960 and who had once toiled away as a mediocre wing-half, improved so dramatically that within two years of replacing Grenville Hair at left-back, he was twice capped for Scotland. Despite the occasional lapse, Jack Charlton was overcoming his rebellious streak and evolving into one of England's most effective centre-halves.

There had been a watershed the previous season during the 2-2 draw at Luton. 'We lost a goal after an awful tangle in defence,' Jim Storrie recalls. 'We were meant to get an offside, but Jack didn't come. He was used to slipshod methods...standing in the penalty area and hoping the ball would arrive. Afterwards Revie told him to mark the centre-forward, tackle, win the ball and make the simplest available pass.'

At first, Johnny Giles found Leeds tactically naive, yet they carried over their newly found good form and made a fine start, winning five, drawing four and losing only one of their first ten games, a 3-2 defeat at Manchester City. It was

the only occasion throughout the campaign that Leeds conceded three league goals, although they were also to lose 3-1 at Maine Road in the third round of the League Cup when lacking five first team regulars.

The Reynolds roar

In the home game against Derby County on 19 October, Revie's team lapsed into an unfamiliar meek style of football, finding themselves 2-0

■ Johnny Giles' disillusionment with Manchester United was Leeds' good fortune. His move to Elland Road in 1963–64 gave Revie's team the cunning it had lacked.

After being promoted in 1963–64, Leeds United's quality and power took the first division by storm. Pipped by Manchester United for the League Championship and beaten in the FA Cup final by Liverpool in extra time, Revie's men still received a hero's welcome on their return from Wembley.

down at half-time. As the Leeds manager castigated his players in the dressing room, Harry Reynolds assumed the role of cheerleader. Addressing the crowd on the public address system, he outlined an extravagant vision of the future: Leeds would win promotion, then the first division championship and the FA Cup, to say nothing of European trophies. But first the fans must get behind the team or risk losing the match against Derby. With players and crowd suitably fired up, Leeds fought back to draw 2-2.

Away from Elland Road, there was an unswerving reliance on a hustling method football that relied on sweat, toil and everyone fighting and working for each other. 'We were very defensive and invited teams to come on to us. When we scored, we put up the shutters,' said Jim Storrie. 'Some of the games we played weren't too enjoyable.'

Systematic success

Organization and planning were taken to new heights. Revie's obsession with tactics had its

roots in his teenage days when he played for Middlesbrough Swifts. On Sundays, Swifts' manager Bill Sanderson conducted a thorough post-mortem and analysis of his team's performance on a model pitch using corks as players. At Leicester, Revie's first league club, Sep Smith, the former England inside-forward, began producing intelligence and scouting reports for the club manager Johnny Duncan.

When Revie reached Manchester City in 1951, he was steeped in theories and stratagems. In the mid-1950s, he became the key figure in a style of play that required a centre-forward to play deep, roaming the field as provider and receiver of balls played to feet.

During 1963–64, Syd Owen was despatched to examine and report on a young player in whom Revie was interested. The thoroughness of his breakdown delighted the Leeds manager. It led to the beginning of the renowned dossiers cataloguing the strengths and weaknesses of the opposition in minute detail, becoming part of Leeds United's preparation for each match.

Although unpopular and notoriously hard to

play against, Leeds had flair when they chose to show it. On the left wing, Albert Johanneson was having a fine season, playing with the pace and skill that often made him uncontainable. 'He was always a little bit apprehensive and never had a great deal of inner confidence,' said Syd Owen, 'but eventually he became more relaxed and some of the things he could do were amazing. I think he must have lived with the ball when he was a junior.'

The rigid structure of the side meant that, despite the loss through injury of Jack Charlton and Jim Storrie for much of the season, Freddie Goodwin and Ian Lawson could slot in and a successful pattern of play be maintained. But the desire to win regardless gave rise to some furious matches. In the 1-1 draw against promotion rivals Preston at Elland Road in November, the game grew so fractious that referee Eric Jennings called a halt and lectured both teams about their bad behaviour.

The clash at Sunderland on 28 December, which Leeds lost 2-0, was just as vengeful. Jim Storrie was carried off with a leg injury that kept him out of the game for almost the rest of the season. 'Johnny Crossan was antagonising Billy Bremner from the beginning, but both were having a dunk at each other off the ball,' Storrie recalls. 'Crossan said, "You're mad, you Leeds." When I was carried off, the fans were spitting at me. But Bobby Collins went out and sought retribution – later Len Ashurst was carried off, too.'

A week later, during a 1-0 victory against Cardiff at Ninian Park in round three of the FA Cup, Leeds also lost Freddie Goodwin because of a broken leg. The hapless Goodwin had collided with John Charles, whose short spell with Roma had not been a success. The injury marked the end of Goodwin's career at Leeds.

Suddenly Revie's squad looked threadbare. The master plan was foundering for want of a powerful forward to disrupt defences and score goals. In February, the Leeds manager moved quickly to sign Alan Peacock, Middlesbrough's England international centre-forward, for £53,000. Brave, sometimes recklessly so, Peacock, like Goodwin, was prone to injury, but fit enough to harass defences and use his aerial strength to help reignite Leeds United's season. Since December, the Leeds attack had scored only a trickle of goals. In March, they finally started to flow again: Peacock's tally of eight in fourteen matches gave Leeds' promotion campaign its crucial impetus.

By Easter, Leeds had closed in on the first division. Although susceptible to nerves on a big occasion, Johanneson had a magnificent match in the 2-1 home win over Newcastle, which attracted United's second 40,000 crowd of the season. Promotion finally came at Swansea Town, where three first-half goals, two from Peacock and one from Giles, brought deliverance from the second division. Two weeks later, a 2-0 victory at Charlton gave Leeds United the championship – with a club record of 63 points – and the final word in their battle at the top with Sunderland, who had also been promoted. Yet Don Revie's ambition was unsated. He wanted to climb mountains, but so far had only scaled the foothills.

1964–65 Back in the big time

Leeds United had never conquered the first division. Occasionally they managed to look comfortable – fifth in 1929–30, eighth in 1932–33 and again in 1956–57 – but seasons of toil and pessimism were never far off, whether through ill-fortune, mismanagement or the onset of yet another financial crisis.

However, the club had never before been run as Revie ran it. He was the most driven manager in Leeds United's history. At the outset, he set impossible targets for the squad, of whom only a handful had first division experience. The psychology was unsophisticated but effective. 'Revie

■ Another Revie protege: Jimmy Greenhoff, a midfielder converted to centre-forward had immense talent and was unlucky never to win a full England cap. Yet he never quite fitted in at Leeds and had his finest years at Stoke City.

A party piece from Bremner. This time Chelsea are on the receiving end as his overhead kick flies into the goal, the final act of a 7-0 rout.

> ## 'we are going to be the best team in the league.'
>
> *Jim Storrie*

never spoke of consolidation,' Jim Storrie recalls. 'He said, "I'll be very disappointed if you don't finish in the top four. You will come up against world-class individuals – Greaves, Law and Charlton – but we are going to be the best team in the league".'

The message was clear. For Leeds to survive in exalted company, they would have to carry on fighting for each other with equal, if not greater, tenacity than when winning promotion. But they also needed to learn self-control. Lessons had been learned from last season's battle at Roker Park. 'Don Revie told us there was no point in having Billy Bremner suspended and sitting in the stand. If picked on, he was to walk away, and then we would go over to the referee and point out a few things,' said Storrie.

Victories in the first three games, including a 4-2 win against champions Liverpool, gave Leeds more confidence than could ever have come from Revie's words alone. They badly needed the points as various injuries to Bell, Giles, and Weston, and the prolonged absence of Alan Pea-

cock caused their form to falter. They lost four of the next eight games. The striker's burden was once more thrust upon Jim Storrie: Leeds had not taken the opportunity to strengthen the squad during the close season.

The team was emerging from its slump when a newspaper story appeared in October saying that Revie was about to leave Elland Road for Sunderland because he felt undervalued by the terms of the three-year contract he had signed in May 1963. At the home game against Tottenham on 17 October, Leeds fans gave vent to their dismay. 'They chanted and shouted at the directors, "We want Revie". My father was rather pleased at the demo. It backed him up – he certainly didn't want Don to go,' said Margaret Veitch.

Battling with the best

With their manager having agreed new terms, Leeds' recovery built up a head of steam. But at Goodison Park on 7 November, it boiled over into a game of frightening violence. When Jack Charlton was fouled in the first minute, it seemed clear that Everton, aware of Leeds' reputation, had decided to rough them up. Within five minutes, Sandy Brown was sent off for fouling Johnny Giles. A goal – the winning goal, a rare score from Willie Bell who headed in a Collins free kick – inflamed the atmosphere. A shuddering clash between Bell and Everton's Derek Temple in the 35th minute caused such a furore that referee Roger Stokes was forced to take both teams off as supporters hurled cushions from the stands onto the pitch.

Bobby Collins, revisiting his old club, was in the thick of it. 'When Sandy Brown was sent off, it was like a fuse on a bomb. It really got a bit nasty and brutal. But the referee is meant to control the game. You can't turn the other cheek or the other team will kill you,' he said. But whatever their wounds, Leeds' powers of recovery were remarkable: the same team was ready in time to beat Arsenal 3-1 at Elland Road just four days later.

Peacock's long-term injury had forced Revie to employ auxiliary centre-forwards Rod Belfitt and Rod Johnson in mid-season. At West Ham on 21 November, the depleted attack was further weakened by the absence of Albert Johanneson, and Leeds suffered their first league defeat in nine matches, although the team had earlier been despatched from the League Cup by Aston Villa, 3-2 winners at Elland Road on 14 October.

Defensive discipline sustained Leeds in December when they won four out of five matches and conceded only one goal, in the 1-1 draw with Blackburn Rovers at Elland Road on Boxing Day. The brash newcomers, with Chelsea and Manchester United, looked serious contenders for the first division championship. The run included a 1-0 win against Manchester United at Old Trafford on December 5 where fog, rather than the Manchester attack, had threatened to deny them success.

Yet against some artful players, Leeds still looked naive. 'For years, Billy Bremner was given a role as a man-to-man marker, but he didn't always get away with it,' Jim Storrie reminisced. 'He had the reputation of being a great tackler, but when we played Arsenal at Highbury, he was exposed by George Eastham. Eastham wouldn't stay still – he'd just slip past Billy and play little balls off. We were 1-0 down, but Norman Hunter was put on Eastham in the second half. Norman was much better at timing his tackles and after that Billy had a freer role.'

Leeds' harassment of the subtle Arsenal midfielder did not endear them to the home fans or the media. 'When we went after George Eastham and stopped him playing, we got the worst press ever,' said Bobby Collins. 'Nobody liked playing us. We wanted to win.'

Winning habits were carried into the FA Cup. Victories over Southport, Everton (after a replay) and Shrewsbury took Leeds to the quarter finals, their best run since 1950. In March, with an increasing burden of matches, the team was galvanised by the return of Alan Peacock. Goal-scoring suddenly became much easier.

Efforts to thwart Leeds by strong-arm tactics alone were doomed to failure. Crystal Palace, their sixth round opponents, had orders from manager Dick Graham to be as 'hard' as Revie's men. They also sought to create confusion by taking the field with the numbers on their team jerseys all mixed up. The first half was fierce and goalless, but on the hour, a long run and defence-

■ The move from left-wing to left-back ignited the career of Terry Cooper, the most effective overlapping defender of his generation and, despite his deep position, a splendidly creative figure.

splitting pass by Paul Reaney set up Alan Peacock to score. 'It was like a pin going into a balloon,' Jim Storrie remembers. Leeds took control and won 3-0, with Peacock and Storrie each scoring from opportunities created by left-winger Terry Cooper.

Cooper was to have a wonderful career at Leeds, but as an attacking left-back rather than as a winger. His defensive qualities helped Leeds vanquish Manchester United, their semi-final opponents, and eventually propel the Yorkshire team to their first FA Cup final.

For all the skills of George Best, Denis Law and Bobby Charlton, Leeds saw Manchester's midfield player, Pat Crerand, as the greatest threat. 'Terry Cooper played at number 11, but had to mark Crerand,' said Jim Storrie. 'Crerand was a great passer...could land the ball on a beer mat from 40 yds. So we cut off his supply. It was like starving a deep-sea diver of oxygen and meant that Stiles and Foulkes, who were less gifted, had to put balls through. And instead of the goalkeeper being able to find Crerand, he had to kick it upfield where Jack Charlton would

■ Leeds' attacking flair deserted them and they were constantly under pressure against Liverpool in the 1964–65 FA Cup final.

win it in the air. Best, Law and Charlton were locked in their own half of the field.'

The match, played at Hillsborough on 31 March, was an acerbic goalless draw littered with fouls and yielding few chances. The replay, held four days later at the City Ground, Nottingham, was no less intense but blessed with some fine football. In the first half, Manchester broke free of Leeds' shackles and played the fluid football for which they were renowned. But Gary Sprake appeared unbeatable. As the second half wore on, Revie's team wrested control. Five minutes remained when Billy Bremner, who had joined the marauding Leeds attack, leaped up unmarked to head home Johnny Giles's free kick. For the first time in their 45-year history, Leeds had reached Wembley.

Race for the title

By mid-April, as Chelsea's form wavered, the title became a two-horse race involving the Uniteds of Leeds and Manchester. The Yorkshire team, which had won nothing save for a second

division championship, was on the threshold of winning the League and Cup double, a far cry from their second division days. On 17 April, 52,368 people packed Elland Road for the most momentous league match in Leeds' history. But with Bremner replacing the injured Storrie at inside-right and Jimmy Greenhoff drafted in at number four, Leeds' swaggering home form (four successive wins with 14 goals scored) deserted them when it mattered most.

For Jim Storrie, watching in the stand, the frustration was enormous. 'We lost 1-0 to a daisy cutter scored by John Connelly from outside the box. It was a dour game but enough to give Manchester the championship,' he said. With four matches and eight points still to play for, the morale of Revie's men had been shot to pieces, and they still appeared in shock two days later, losing 3-0 at Sheffield Wednesday. Their defiance in fighting back from 3-0 down at Birmingham to draw the final match of the season 3-3 was not enough. Both Uniteds finished with 61 points, but Manchester's goal average was far superior.

Wembley woe

Five days after completing their league programme, Leeds faced Liverpool in the FA Cup final. On 1 May, a murky Saturday afternoon, Revie's young players were forced to realise that they had grown up less quickly than everyone thought. 'It was a new experience for the lads, with radio and TV wanting them,' said Jim Storrie, 'but to play at Wembley, you need experience at winning and to be single-minded.'

'Revie said, "Don't let the occasion become bigger than you – you've made the occasion..." But we did. So many of our youngsters were sidetracked from the purpose of the event, and Revie didn't help – he told us earlier in the Cup run that a fortune teller – it may have been one of his relations – had said we'd reach the final, but lose. Some of the guys believed it.'

The soothsayer was right. Leeds' opponents, Liverpool, champions the previous season, were too experienced, despite being handicapped by an injury to Gerry Byrne, who played almost the entire match and extra time with a broken collarbone. But Leeds were too overawed to exploit the advantage: Storrie himself was far from fit; Albert Johanneson, as unnerved as anyone, was an anonymous figure; Alan Peacock's authority in the air was cancelled out by the gigantic Liverpool centre-half Ron Yeats. Leeds' creative players were forced to become auxiliary defenders.

A tedious stalemate continued into extra time before Liverpool took a deserved lead with Roger Hunt's headed goal. Leeds enjoyed one glorious spirited moment eight minutes later when Bremner burst through the Liverpool defence and smashed home an equaliser. But it did not banish the timidity that infected Revie's team throughout the afternoon. Ian St John's headed winner for Liverpool nine minutes from time seemed as inevitable as it was unwelcome. Achieving the double was a reverie from which Leeds had been rudely awoken. Yet for those who had known only the club's faltering past, the progress made by Revie was the stuff of fantasy. Leeds were welcomed home as heroes.

> 'It was a new experience for the lads, with radio and TV wanting them...'
>
> *Jim Storrie*

1965–66 European adventures begin

Although the two great prizes eluded Leeds in 1964–65, their strenuous campaign had its consolations. At the age of 34, Bobby Collins, whose cunning, commitment and stamina made him such a potent force, was voted Footballer of the Year. Collins' vigorous captaincy had helped the club reach new heights. Finishing runners-up was a passport to European competition, the Inter-Cities Fairs Cup. Foreign expeditions, many of them turbulent, became woven into Leeds United's seasons for the next decade.

New faces appeared. Peter Lorimer, who had made only three appearances since being pressed into service against Southampton as a 15-year-old in September 1962, was preferred to Don Weston at inside-right. Mike O'Grady, signed from local rivals Huddersfield in October 1965 for £30,000, became a familiar figure on both wings as Albert Johanneson suffered injuries and loss of form. Terry Cooper broke into the team, yet remained unsettled. Revie still didn't know how best to use him: for all his sparky talent and excellent control, Cooper was too slow to be a persistent menace on the flanks.

Leeds' winning form did not desert them. Sometimes unexciting when playing away, at Elland Road they attacked constantly, smashing in goals from all angles. Following the loss of Bobby Collins with a broken leg in October, it was remarkable that they managed to remain a force almost all season.

United's place in Europe owed much to Collins' leadership, but he was fated to remain a bystander for most of the Fairs Cup campaign. On 6 October 1965, Leeds, who had drawn Torino in the first round, travelled to Italy for the second leg of the tie defending a 2-1 lead. With 50 minutes gone and the score 0-0, Collins surged towards the Torino penalty area, but was clattered to the ground by full-back Poletti. It was a fearsome collision. The impact of Poletti's kick broke Collins thigh, and though he recovered to play a smattering of games, effectively his brilliant career at Leeds was over.

Reduced to ten men, Leeds defended with a tenacity that must have gladdened Collins' heart. Revie considered the 2-1 aggregate victory one of the greatest performances he had seen from his team. They made further progress in the competition before Christmas, knocking out the East German team SC Leipzig, also 2-1 on aggregate.

The loss of his captain forced Revie to switch Johnny Giles from outside right to Collins's position. Giles a stronger, more aggressive player

■ Jack Charlton keeps watch. Charlton's career blossomed when Revie forced him to improve his positional play. Few were more adept than the Leeds centre-half at man-marking.

than he was when signed from Manchester United, relished the move and became the perfect foil to Bremner in midfield. There was no-one quicker thinking or with more football cunning than Giles. He rarely wasted a pass, long or short, and could sniff out defensive weakness in the opposition like a shark scenting blood. Also, like Collins, Giles was not averse to putting in a strong tackle on anyone he felt needed it.

Up until the Christmas programme, Leeds were again strong contenders for the league championship. When they won at Anfield on 27 December with an early goal scored by Peter Lorimer, morale soared. 'We played superbly well,' said Jim Storrie. 'Revie was hugging all the boys and then went into their dressing room to look for Bill Shankly.'

But despite his friendship with Revie, Shankly did not appear until the Leeds team bus had departed. Then, with the return fixture at Elland Road the following day, he began to apply the psychology that had allowed Liverpool to surmount so many obstacles. It entailed belittling their conquerors. 'Shankly went into their dressing room and said that they (Leeds) were a rugby team, and they came here and won. He com-pared us to Hull Kingston Rovers, and said that they'd beat us at Elland Road. They did. Afterwards Shankly was saying to his team, "Leeds are the best team in the league – they hadn't lost at home and you beat them".'

Domestic disappointments

Following the 1-0 defeat, Leeds' title challenge faded. Liverpool set a pace that no-one could compete with, winning seven and drawing one of their next eight matches. Meanwhile, having lost in the League Cup 4-2 at Elland Road to West Bromwich in October, and been unrewarded for a vibrant performance when losing 1-0 to Chelsea at Stamford Bridge in the FA Cup fourth round, interest at Leeds became more focused on Europe.

European education

The first leg of their Fairs Cup third round tie against Valencia, played at Elland Road on 2 February 1966, created uproar. The flashpoint occurred 15 minutes from time with the score at 1-1 and the Spaniards, their first half lead erased

■ There was no finer passer than Johnny Giles, a grand master at probing weak spots and unlocking defences.

by a Peter Lorimer goal, defending like desperate men. When Jack Charlton, now team captain, was kicked and punched supporting a Leeds attack, he went berserk. 'I had completely lost control myself and neither the Spaniards nor my team-mates could prevent my pursuit of vengeance,' he said.

Within seconds a mass brawl erupted. As police intervened, Dutch referee Leo Horn was forced to take off both sets of players. Charlton and Valencia left-back Vidagany were sent off, and inside-forward Sanchez-Lage was later dismissed for kicking Jim Storrie. But feverish talk of banning both teams from the competition came to nothing. In the second leg, Leeds recovered their composure, defended with great discipline, and won the game with a single goal by Mike O'Grady.

Their fourth round tie against the Hungarians, Ujpest Dozsa, was less rancorous. In the first leg, the crowd was entertained both by Leeds' masterful attacking performance in a 4-1 victory and a dog that invaded the Elland Road pitch defying all efforts to catch it for some ten minutes. Leeds may have thought their work was done and relaxed for the return match, but in the second leg they were given a footballing lesson, with the 1-1 score scant reflection of the extent of their inferiority.

In the semi-final, Leeds' luck finally ran out and they were outgunned. Although Real Zaragoza could be as vicious as their compatriots from Valencia, they were also undoubtedly a fine footballing side. The first leg was played in Spain, and once more both sides finished with ten men when Giles and Zaragoza right-half Violeta were sent off after a clash four minutes from time. By then, Zaragoza had taken the lead with a penalty goal and managed to defend their 1-0 advantage for the whole of the second leg at Elland Road.

It was as full-blooded a match as any seen at Elland Road, much influenced by Jack Charlton's forward incursions. He made Leeds' first goal, thumping the ball forward for Johanneson to add the final touch, and headed home Norman Hunter's cross for the second. But between times, Zaragoza had scored. With the aggregate scores level at 2-2, a play-off was needed. Charlton won the toss to ensure the game would be played at Elland Road but home advantage counted for nothing as Zaragoza's forward line of Canario, Santos, Marcellino, Villa and Lapetra – christened by Revie 'The Magnificent Five' – tore Leeds to pieces. Within 13 minutes Leeds were 3-0 down, and out. Charlton's goal ten minutes' from time was merely a flicker of defiance.

Again, Leeds finished the season empty-handed. But their European campaign had had an epic quality. Much had been learned – and football education was rarely wasted on Revie and his team. The lessons could soon be applied, for in finishing runners-up to Liverpool, Leeds had earned the chance of another assault on Europe.

1966–67 ...In with the new

Youthful talent continued to blossom in 1966–67. Few players breaking into the Leeds side had more natural ability than winger Eddie Gray who, despite being wooed by almost 30 other clubs, had been lured to Elland Road by Revie in 1963. Gray could have picked any top club – Arsenal and Celtic were among those courting him – rather than an obscure team finding its feet in the second division. 'Leeds were unglamorous, but it was the character of Revie that did it. I liked the feel of the place,' he said.

Revie beat a path to Gray's school and whisked the 15 year-old prodigy away from beneath the noses of other scouts. Eddie Gray was to have a brilliant career, but only intermittently. His ability to operate at peak fitness was compromised by a thigh injury sustained shortly after arriving and more than a year before he made his first team debut. 'It happened when I was 16 and playing for the reserves against Sheffield Wednesday. Since then, I never played the game when I was 100 per cent fit.'

Outwardly, it appeared not to inhibit him. Gray made his debut against Sheffield Wednesday on 1 January 1966, and scored in Leeds' 3-0

'Leeds were unglamorous, ...but I liked the feel of the place.'

Eddie Gray

■ Opposite: Muscling in: Peter Lorimer puts Chelsea's Peter Bonetti under pressure at Stamford Bridge. Intense rivalry built up between the two sides during the late 1960s and early 1970s.

Such humiliations, unprecedented during his reign as manager, infuriated Revie. Chastened by his harsh words, the team tightened up, winning five and drawing three of the next eight league matches. This improvement coincided with the brief return of Bobby Collins, recalled following an injury to Johnny Giles. 'But then I was dropped. I didn't particularly like that – in fact, I couldn't understand it,' Collins said. Although his appetite for the game was undimmed, it was evident that Collins did not figure in Revie's plans, and in March 1967 he went to Bury on a free transfer after making his last appearance in Leeds' 3-0 home win over Stoke City on 11 February.

Double cup run

Leeds were never serious contenders for the league title, but the season was pepped up by the FA Cup and Inter-Cities Fairs Cup. Leeds had learned much – perhaps too much – from battles abroad in the previous campaign, but by Febru-

■ Above: Elegance and economy of effort characterised Paul Madeley's game. His versatility made him an essential component of the Leeds team.

■ Right: By 1967, Hunter's rugged talents were recognised by England manager Alf Ramsey. Only the pre-eminence of Bobby Moore prevented him from getting more than 28 international caps.

victory. Few were surprised that the youth who had made such an impact playing for Scotland schoolboys settled so quickly. 'From the moment I got into the team, I never felt out of place,' he said later.

Along with other protégés Jimmy Greenhoff, a wing-half converted to striker, and Paul Madeley, among the most adaptable players ever to grace the first division, Gray became a regular as injuries and loss of form among experienced players forced Revie to experiment. The team made a spluttering start – the worst since 1962–63 – and by November was adrift in mid-table. Two numbing defeats – 7-0 at West Ham in round four of the League Cup and 5-0 at Liverpool in the league 12 days later – suggested that Leeds' fearsome defence had suddenly gone completely soft.

ary had disposed of DWS Amsterdam (8-2 on aggregate) and Valencia (3-1 on aggregate). The 2-0 victory in Spain, achieved against the odds by a makeshift team with Billy Bremner starring as an emergency centre-half, was among the most composed and professional of any Leeds team which, on the night, had been deprived of Reaney, Cooper, Greenhoff, Johanneson and O'Grady, all injured.

Critics however deplored some of the continental traits Leeds had imported. The team was frequently accused of gamesmanship. 'But we didn't classify it as such – we looked upon it as

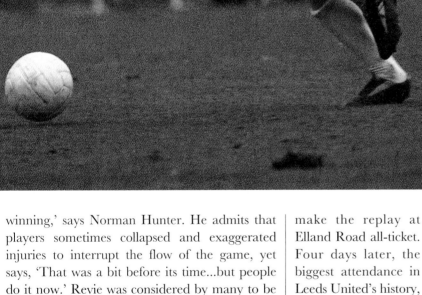

■ Talent ran in the Gray family...Eddie was to be joined by younger brother Frank who made the game look easy.

winning,' says Norman Hunter. He admits that players sometimes collapsed and exaggerated injuries to interrupt the flow of the game, yet says, 'That was a bit before its time...but people do it now.' Revie was considered by many to be the arch-villain, but Billy Bremner claimed, 'I never knew the gaffer say to us to go out and kick them, or to waste time. What was called cynical in this country was called professional when the Italians played it. We picked it up off them... walking out to take a corner...or, if the game was getting a bit heated, someone would feign an injury.'

In March, the season began to boil. After FA Cup victories over Crystal Palace and West Bromwich Albion, Leeds needed three attempts to dispose of Sunderland in the fifth round. Following a 1-1 draw at Roker Park, there was no time to make the replay at Elland Road all-ticket. Four days later, the biggest attendance in Leeds United's history, 57,892 fans swarmed into a ground ill-prepared for the influx. A crush barrier on the Lowfields Road terracing collapsed and several people were injured as spectators spilled onto the pitch.

After another 1-1 draw, the saga continued at Boothferry Park, Hull. Old hostilities exploded two minutes from time when, with the scores at 1-1, Jimmy Greenhoff was felled as he advanced on the Sunderland goal. So furious were the Sunderland remonstrations when a penalty kick was awarded that George Herd and George Mulhall were sent off. Johnny Giles, apparently unmoved by the furore, stroked the ball into the net and put Leeds into the sixth round of the FA Cup.

Within hours, Leeds were on the plane to Italy for their Inter-Cities Fairs Cup quarter final tie against Bologna. It was a stern test of mental and physical strength, and under the circumstances a 1-0 defeat was excusable. As March drew to a close, the demands on Revie's squad intensified with Leeds forced to play four league games in seven days. With a show of bravado, they won the lot, their best sequence of the season.

April was less frenetic, but much was at stake. In their FA Cup quarter-final against Manchester City at Elland Road, Leeds were constantly pushed back, yet against the run of play stole the match with a headed goal from Jack Charlton. After beating Bologna 1-0 at Elland Road in the second leg of the Fairs Cup quarter-final, under the absurd rules of the time – a toss of a disc – the outcome was determined in Leeds' favour, and they were given

■ The selfless hustler: Mick Jones was everything a target man should be: brave, strong and more interested in the team's success than in personal glory.

right of passage to play the Scottish team, Kilmarnock, in the semi-final.

The season appeared to stretch on without end. The Kilmarnock games would not be played until May, and fixture congestion meant that the Fairs Cup final was suspended until the start of 1967–68. Meanwhile, Leeds' FA Cup semi-final against Chelsea did not take place until 29 April, a melodramatic game that left Revie's team feeling as if the gods had started to conspire against them.

From the ebb and flow of an impassioned match, two incidents stand out: for Chelsea fans, the meandering dribble by Charlie Cooke, who delivered a perfect cross for Tony Hateley to despatch a flying header past Gary Sprake – the classic centre-forward's goal; but Leeds supporters, who watched their team besiege the Chelsea goal after half-time, still rue the goal that never was. It came two minutes from the end. Awarded a free kick outside the Chelsea penalty area, Giles paused briefly while Chelsea defenders began to form a wall, then he rolled the ball sideways to Lorimer who then thumped the ball into the net with a shot of tremendous power.

But the triumph of this great moment was undone when referee Ken Burns disallowed Lorimer's strike because Giles had taken the kick too quickly. The Leeds players were so stunned that they had no time to be angry. 'I was amazed when afterwards the referee said he had told us to wait,' says Lorimer. 'I didn't hear him and nor did Johnny.'

The knack of winning had deserted Revie's team when it mattered most. Yet their league form, only one defeat in the last 13 matches, gave them 55 points, fourth place and re-entry to Europe, even as they were still trudging forward in the Fairs Cup.

They looked a good bet. An unexpected star of the semi-final against Kilmarnock was reserve centre-forward Rod Belfitt, scorer of an incredible hat-trick within 30 minutes of the first leg at Elland Road, which Leeds won 4-2. In the second leg, held on 22 May, Leeds' defensive know-how was enough to hold off the Scottish team and achieve a goalless draw. A date with the Yugoslavian side, Dinamo Zagreb, and an early chance of glory and silverware the following season, awaited them.

1967–68 **Winners at last**

Revie's team showed little sign of rejuvenation after the short summer break, beginning 1967–68 with a draw and two defeats. The side was already in disarray through injuries when the Fairs Cup final date with Dinamo Zagreb was upon them. Terry Cooper was pressed into service at left-back, Mick Bates drafted in for Johnny Giles and Rod Belfitt led the attack. Their mission in Yugoslavia was to defend, but under Zagreb's onslaught Leeds buckled twice and despite a late rally were unable to claw a goal back.

At Elland Road, 2-0 down, they needed to go for broke. But Revie continued to brood on the threat posed by Zagreb. He was so bereft of attacking options that Paul Reaney was put on the right wing. Such stultifying caution exasperated Mike O'Grady, playing on the left. 'Revie was really defensive although we had been beaten away. He filled our heads with the opposition. I was being warned about the other winger and expected to cover defensively as well. It was hard work,' O'Grady said later on.

Leeds toiled fruitlessly, unable to find a way through. The match ended 0-0; the cup was lost. Supporters became increasingly preoccupied by the team's lack of punch. 'There will be no panic buying,' fans were told in the programme before the home match with Leicester on 23 September. But even as it was going to print, Revie, after much casting around, finally got his man: the burly 22-year-old Sheffield United centre-forward Mick Jones.

Jones came at a transitional time for Leeds United. At first he appeared ungainly and awkward, yet, with improved ball control, became the ideal target man – as brave as Peacock, as willing to chase any cause but, in his first years at least, less injury-prone.

Even before Jones' arrival, the team was snapping out of its sluggish start, having won three and drawn one of the previous four matches. Terry Cooper had found his true position at left-back from where he could make threatening sorties down the wing. His ascendancy marked the end of Willie Bell's career at Leeds, who was

■ Leeds' first Inter Cities Fairs Cup final ended in disappointment. Two goals scored by Dinamo Zabgreb in the away leg were enough to sink them.

At Elland Road, Revie's team battles in vain to wipe out the two goal deficit against Dinamo Zagreb. But the match was goalless and on the night Leeds showed little imagination.

> 'In the mid-1960's there used to be trouble on the supporters' trains.
>
> *Colin Jeffrey*

transferred to Leicester City for £45,000. Bell, now 30, lacked Cooper's flair, but was a sound defender with an excellent temperament, effective if not eye-catching,

Changing chairmen

Meanwhile, there were changes in the boardroom. Albert Morris replaced Harry Reynolds as club chairman, forced to retire through ill-health. For all his preoccupation with building the new Leeds United, Reynolds never became detached from the fans on the terraces. Colin S. Jeffrey, author of Twelve at The Top, a survey of the Don Revie era at Leeds, recalls his direct if unconventional approach.

'In the mid-1960s there used to be trouble on the supporters' trains. Sometimes the team travelled in the same train and Don Revie was getting fed up with the disruption. So Harry Reynolds went off and addressed the supporters in each coach, telling them they were damaging the image of the club. I couldn't imagine the chairman of any other club doing that, walking the full length of a ten-coach train,' says Jeffrey.

'He had a rapport with supporters. I was once in a queue outside the West Stand when he came out and asked if we'd like to buy or sell club lottery tickets. He went right down the line, approaching everyone.'

Morris's chairmanship was short-lived. A prominent member of the local Jewish community, he died within eight months of succeeding Reynolds and was replaced by Percy Woodward who, like Reynolds, had supported Leeds United from the terraces as a boy.

The world remained ambivalent about Leeds United's claims to excellence, but on 7 October, they sent warning to all-comers of their fearsome potency, demolishing managerless Chelsea by seven goals to nil at Elland Road. Successive 5-0 victories in January at Fulham and over Southampton at Elland Road confirmed that, when the mood took them, Leeds would devour the weak and the mediocre.

Barely had Leeds lost the Inter-Cities Fairs Cup final to Dynamo Zagreb than they were tramping over European fields again. They used part-timers Spora Luxembourg for target practice, winning 16-0 on aggregate, and overcame provocation with skill in Yugoslavia to earn a 3-2 aggregate win over Partisan Belgrade. Confined to Britain thereafter, Leeds then edged past Hibernian (2-1), dismissed Glasgow Rangers (2-0) and beat Dundee (2-1) en route to a second successive Fairs Cup final.

League Cup final

One tournament for which Leeds United never showed any appetite was the League Cup. But since becoming a Wembley showpiece the previous year, the final had acquired some glamour. Leeds' addictive winning habit saw them make stealthy progress. After mundane victories against Luton Town, Bury, Sunderland and Stoke City, they were in the semi-finals facing Derby County. Always too knowing and powerful for their second division opponents, Leeds won the two-legged contest 4-2 on aggregate.

For the second time in four years, Revie's team was at Wembley. Their opponents, Arsenal, were a less formidable prospect than Liverpool had been in the 1965 FA Cup Final, but unlikely to give Leeds an easy ride. Bertie Mee, who had more the air of a benign headmaster than a football manager, camouflaged a rasping team.

But Leeds United's hunger was intense. Victory mattered above all, even more than atoning for their dreary display three years before. 'It was a game that had to be won,' says Eddie Gray. His words convey the single-minded, sometimes ruthless approach Leeds adopted in a mauling match that had few moments of grandeur. For Leeds fans however, no wonder of the world could compare with Terry Cooper's volleyed

goal in the 18th minute that won the trophy. But it was symptomatic of the game that there was furious controversy – Arsenal claiming that Jack Charlton had balked goalkeeper Jim Furnell who was trying to deal with Eddie Gray's corner.

There were excuses for a poor show: Greenhoff and Giles were only half fit. Revie was unabashed by the poverty of the football. 'We would have been foolish to play attractively with nine fully fit men,' he said, adding that under normal circumstances he would have played neither Greenhoff nor Giles. 'It meant a lot to both clubs – but more to this club,' says Eddie Gray. 'It was the first major trophy and a great lift to the morale of the supporters in the city.'

Season's end

Leeds' passage in the FA Cup was another saga of hard knocks. They beat Derby, Nottingham Forest, Bristol City – a match in which Gary Sprake was sent off – and Sheffield United. But by late April, after a prodigious run of success, Revie's men were showing battle fatigue. Hopes of winning the League Championship began to cave in after a 3-2 defeat at Stoke on April 23, and when Leeds faced Everton in the FA Cup semi-final at Old Trafford four days later, they were in an edgy mood.

A horrible error by Gary Sprake three min-utes from half-time led to the knock-out blow. Nursing an injured shoulder, and under pressure from Joe Royle in the penalty area, Sprake's feeble kick dropped at the feet of Jimmy Husband. Jack Charlton handled his goal-bound kick; Johnny Morrissey scored from the penalty.

Leeds lost their final three league matches for which Revie sent out experimental sides packed with reserves, few of whom were to make the grade. But between times, the regulars had shown the strength and wit to beat Dundee in the Fairs Cup semi-final 2-1 on aggregate. Delight at winning the League Cup had long since evaporated, but prospects of another European final buoyed up the spirits.

■ Above, top: No marks for artistry but the result was all important. During an afternoon of attrition, Leeds beat Arsenal 1-0 to win the 1968 League Cup final and their first trophy.

■ Above: The joy of finally having some silverware: Gary Sprake and Paul Madeley lead the victory parade around Wembley.

1968–69 Record breakers

Injuries and a surfeit of fixtures had done much to undermine Leeds' campaign. In all competitions they had played 66 matches and used 25 players. Yet if to win four trophies meant scaling four different mountains, Leeds United would strive to climb the lot, such was the players' response to Revie's voracious ambition.

The risk, as they knew only too well, was ending up with little or nothing. Although victory in the League Cup released Leeds from the morbid belief that they were doomed to fail at the final hurdle, confidence was always fragile at Elland Road: Revie was a mass of superstitions, as were many of his players.

Soon they were on the treadmill again. Leeds' close season lasted less than two months. It was still almost high summer when they played the first leg of the Fairs Cup final against the Hungarian team, Ferencvaros. For all its importance, the match had the air of a non-event: live television coverage and a clash with the peak holiday season reduced the crowd at Elland Road to 25,000.

Leeds won a scrappy match with an inelegant goal. Charlton was once more a key figure, heading down Lorimer's corner for Mick Jones to force the ball over the line. Later, as the match grew increasingly violent, Jones was carried off injured after being flattened by a crude challenge from goalkeeper Geczi.

It was the first game played before the newly-constructed covered Kop, the most significant ground development since the rebuilding of the West Stand in 1956. Part of Harry Reynolds' vision was to create an arena fit for champions and, while Leeds United were not yet rich, success had wiped out a £250,000 overdraft and put the club into the black. The new Kop was a monument to this financial transformation.

Yet the Ferencvaros game conveyed scant sense of being a milestone. Five weeks elapsed before the Fairs Cup final second leg was played in Budapest, and supporters became diverted by Leeds' formidable start in the league, six victories and a draw. But the emphasis was on results rather than entertainment; the absence of Giles through injury impoverished the team. Some of the brightest performances in an often arid winning sequence came from reserve left-winger Terry Hibbitt.

However, many fans were dismayed that Revie was reluctant to accommodate Jimmy Greenhoff, one of his shining young talents, who had played in most matches the previous season.

'He was a great centre-forward,' says Syd Owen. 'A lovely mover, who always looked the part. When he first came he was a midfield player, but we felt he would be better as a forward where his first touch, skill and distribution would be an asset. He had very good self-control: he never got over-excited irrespective of any abuse bestowed on him.'

Greenhoff's £70,000 transfer to Birmingham was widely lamented. He then moved to Stoke where he had his finest years. Meanwhile in Budapest on 11 September, an examination of resilience and character awaited Revie's team, only 90 minutes away from winning the Inter-Cities Fairs Cup.

Gary Sprake and Bobby Gould clash at Highbury. Though often critcised by the media, Sprake was well regarded by his team-mates at Leeds.

The feeling was that Mick Jones' lone goal might not carry them through. But the lessons learned in Turin, Valencia and other hothouses were never put to better use. For all their skill and passion, and the frenzied support of a 76,000 crowd, Ferencvaros could not pierce the masterful Leeds defence in which Gary Sprake shone out above all.

While Sprake had made costly blunders in the past, and would do so again, he frequently held the fort when all seemed lost. 'I was always a great fan of Gary Sprake,' says Eddie Gray. 'I think he suffered through exposure on television and found that hard to handle. On form, he was marvellous – a natural – with great hands, great at stopping shots, on crosses, and he had great distribution. But he did one or two unfortunate things. When Gary was younger, I've not seen a better goalkeeper. Remember, he played for Wales when he was only 18.'

A clash of the Titans. Encounters betwen Liverpool and Leeds, the two outstanding teams of their generation, usually produced stirring matches. Paul Madeley squares up to the ball in this 1969 encounter at Elland Road, a 1-1 draw.

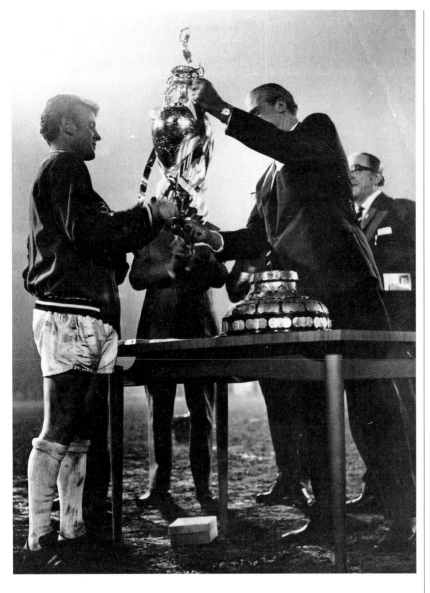

■ The greatest prize of all. A glorious moment for all connected with Leeds United as Billy Bremner receives the League Championship trophy.

The home front

The goalless draw in Hungary gave Leeds their second trophy in six months, yet their league form remained scratchy. A 3-1 defeat against Manchester City on 28 September ended the nine-match unbeaten run and three weeks later Leeds were thrashed 5-1 at Burnley. There could be no hard luck stories: both times they were torn apart. But critics who scented a collapse in form had perhaps forgotten that two years ago the same team braced up immediately after the humiliations suffered at West Ham and Liverpool.

No team managed by Don Revie came apart easily at the seams. Leeds steadied themselves with three goalless draws, then recovered winning ways with a 1-0 victory at Coventry. As Christmas approached, the championship shook down into a three-horse race involving Leeds, Liverpool and Everton. On 21 December, Burnley, out of sorts and hit by injury, came to Elland and were repaid for the embarrassment suffered at Turf Moor as Leeds beat them 6-1.

In January Leeds got lucky. The referee intervened on their behalf against Manchester United at Elland Road by ruling out what seemed a perfectly good goal from George Best. It allowed Leeds to recuperate and score a winning goal 15 minutes from time. Two weeks later, Leeds travelled to Loftus Road, where Queen's Park Rangers, fighting for their first division lives, bombarded Sprake's goal for much of the game. But Revie's men clung on to the second-minute lead given them by Mick Jones in their longest, most desperate rearguard action of the season.

Leeds concentrate on the league

Defeat in the League Cup fourth round by Crystal Palace, and in the FA Cup third round after a replay against Sheffield Wednesday, helped to clear the decks for a drive towards the league title. But the Inter-Cities Fairs Cup continued to interfere. After a barbarous encounter with Napoli in the second round, the Leeds board threatened to withdraw the club from European competition altogether. 'The revenue is important, but the safety of the players far more so,' said club chairman Percy Woodward. 'We were lucky that no-one received an injury that could have him out of the game for several weeks.'

In the event, old adversaries Ujpest Dozsa ended Leeds' involvement, winning the fourth round tie 3-0 on aggregate. But in the league, Leeds were undefeated since the debacle at Burnley in October. In January they overhauled Liverpool at the top. By April, with the league championship tantalisingly close, the unbearable importance of each game set nerves on edge. On 5 April, grim determination kept Manchester City at bay before Leeds broke out and Giles put the Elland Road crowd out of its agony, scoring the only goal from a ball that had bounced off City goalkeeper Joe Corrigan.

A week later at Highbury on a bright chilly afternoon, there was an ominous sense of unease. In an abrupt, violent exchange, Arsenal centre-forward Bobby Gould clipped Gary Sprake with his heel while challenging for the ball. Sprake's instant response was a punch that left the Arsenal dazed and on the floor. Again, Leeds' luck held in astonishing fashion; against all odds, the Leeds goalkeeper was allowed to stay on the pitch. 'Gary realised his flash of temper could have cost us the championship, let alone the match,' said Billy Bremner. Leeds made the most of their let-off and won 2-1, Jones and Giles pouncing on mistakes to which they knew the Arsenal defenders were prone.

The destiny of the league championship was

1969–70 A footballing marathon

Winning the championship had shorn Leeds United of many inhibitions; although Revie and Syd Owen continued to plan for every match with military attention to detail. Yet once in their stride, the team established a wonderful winning rhythm with some excellent performances in 1969–70. Revie, however, was always insistent that 'it would have been suicidal to allow much freedom of expression during our first few seasons in division one due to their lack of experience'.

Not all his players agreed – Mike O'Grady for one, who, despite making an inspired contribution to the championship campaign on the wing, was released by Revie and sold to Wolves for £80,000 – had cursed his manager's over-caution in the Fairs Cup final against Dynamo Zagreb. And Revie himself admitted that points were squandered by timidity away from home before the championship was won.

Reflects Norman Hunter: 'We had a weakness whereby we could have gone and beaten teams better than we did...but we used to have battles on our hands against teams that we had outplayed. We'd score, then sit back and invite them on to us.'

However, the close season signing of Allan Clarke from Leicester City for a record £165,000 fee showed that Revie intended taking a bolder direction. He needed a stronger squad with which to pursue the European Cup – his new great ambition now the title had been won.

Clarke, a striker, who had also played in midfield had the sharpest reflexes of any forward in the country. At Fulham, Clarke's second club, Johnny Haynes had taught him the art of passing, but Clarke seemed to be born with the nerveless self-assurance to create and devour goal-scoring opportunities. His partnership with Mick Jones was to create havoc among opposition defences. As Johnny Giles says, 'Mick was a straightforward, no-frills player. Clarke read the game. One was the bludgeon, the other the sword.' The sword's impact was immediate: Clarke made a scoring league debut for Leeds in their 3-1 win against Tottenham, the first match of the new campaign.

Everton, pretenders to the championship throne the previous season, began 1969–70 with

now in Leeds United's hands, while Liverpool could only hope for a last minute loss of nerve; and third placed Everton for a freakish collapse in form by both clubs. But on April 22 at Goodison Park, Leeds surrendered nothing, fending off all Everton's pressure and prising out a priceless point from a 0-0 draw.

The biggest test came last. Leeds had to play Liverpool at Anfield. Another goalless draw would do them. Liverpool, who had to win or surrender hopes of the title, attacked with the fervour of crusaders, a battery of red shirts beating constantly against a white wall. But on the rare occasions they breached the Leeds defence, they squandered openings amid the frenzy. At Ferencvaros, Queen's Park Rangers, Everton and now finally at Liverpool, Revie's team showed themselves supreme exponents of the rearguard action. Harried to the last, they held firm and grasped the title on the soil of their old adversaries.

'Go and take yourselves off to the Kop,' the Leeds manager told his delighted players. And the crowd that had howled for the Liverpudlian cause minutes earlier, roared generous approval of the new champions. Two days later, in the home game against Nottingham Forest, Leeds embellished the achievement with a 1-0 victory, so breaking the record for the number of points gained (67), the fewest defeats (two) and fewest goals conceded (26) in a 42-match season.

Revie, however, wanted to create the greatest club in Europe – if not the world. There would be no standing still. As long as he was in charge, Leeds United would be driven forever upwards.

■ Dressing up the image. Leeds strove for glamour as well as for success. Stocking tags, which were thrown into the crowd, became part of their act in the early 1970s.

'One was the bludgeon, the other the sword'

Johnny Giles

Allan Clarke profited handsomely from the waves made by Mick Jones in enemy territory. A predator of startling assurance, there was no more menacing sight for the opposition than that of Clarke homing in on goal.

a swagger, their fluid play based on the harmonised midfield talents of Alan Ball, Howard Kendall and Colin Harvey. Leeds' visit to Goodison on 30 August promised a mighty spectacle. Revie's men were unbeaten in 34 league matches, yet groping for form: four of their first six games had been drawn in an unconvincing, sometimes irascible fashion.

Although without Kendall that day, Everton had the talent to inflict damage from all sides. Centre-forward Joe Royle thrived on the excellent service and after 50 minutes Leeds were 3-0 down. The Everton crowd was euphoric. But thanks largely to Bremner's fighting spirit, Leeds rallied, scored twice and caused panic in the home defence as full-time approached. Defeat was no disgrace; the second half revival was something from which Leeds could draw considerable comfort.

All comers defeated

By September, things were looking up. In the European Cup, part-time opponents Lyn Oslo served as cannon fodder for Leeds, as had Spora Luxembourg in the Fairs Cup. Leeds' 16-0 aggregate win created a competition record, but much more impressive was the way they crushed Ferencvaros in November, winning 3-0 in both legs, and inflicting crucial damage during the rampant opening half hour of the first game at Elland Road. A goal from Giles and two from Mick Jones, fashioned by electrifying football in driving rain, put the Hungarians down and out.

Said Don Revie, 'I don't think any team could have lived with Leeds on that performance.' Few disagreed. Geoffrey Green, football correspondent of *The Times* wrote: 'I would not have believed a Ferencvaros side full of such talented players could have been so ground down.' For Russian referee Makhramov, it was 'the best exhibition of football I have ever seen in Europe'. But at home, Leeds were flaying teams in a similar fashion: they had warmed up for Ferencvaros by beating

Nottingham Forest 6-1 and Ipswich 4-0 in consecutive home matches, combining craft and passion to devastating effect.

By Christmas Leeds had reeled in Everton's lead at the top and although their unbeaten run

Dressed for the outback: Peter Lorimer and Billy Bremner head for Gander Green Lane, the home of Sutton United, Leeds' fourth round opponents in the 1970 FA Cup. Leeds won at a canter, 6-0.

of 18 league matches was interrupted by a 2-1 defeat in a fractious game at Newcastle on Boxing Day, the team were as resolute as ever when Everton visited Elland Road the following day.

The biggest crowd of the season, 46,770, poured into Elland Road. Yet a bemused Revie had found himself having to drum up support. Leeds, playing some of the best football in their history, were once again championship contenders, yet attendances had dipped. The 2-0 home win over Sunderland on 16 November drew fewer than 26,000. If Revie was to realise his dream of building a colossal club that might rival or even eclipse the likes of Liverpool and

Manchester United, he needed much more fervent backing from the Leeds public.

But there was no lack of fervour for the Everton match. On the day, the visitors abandoned their flowing style for strong-arm tactics but found, as had others, that it was impossible to intimidate Leeds United. After a bruising first 45 minutes, Revie's men were 2-0 up thanks to the bravery and energy of Mick Jones. Everton's second half goal from Alan Whittle and late rally could not save the game.

Once more Leeds were at the top of the first division. On 12 January they travelled to Chelsea, the league's form team, and performed albeit with the help of frail goalkeeping by stand-in Tommy Hughes, Bremner and co. transformed a 2-1 half-time deficit into a 5-2 lead, strutting about the pitch with insolent confidence, pulling Chelsea apart with lethally sophisticated moves and goals from Cooper, a Giles penalty, Lorimer and Jones. By the end, Chelsea were dazed. Leeds had picked a televised match at London's trendiest football venue to proclaim themselves the finest club team in the English League.

Cup campaigns

Leeds showed little inclination to cling on to the League Cup, losing 2-0 to Chelsea in a third round replay during October. But in the FA Cup, after a stuttering 2-1 win over Swansea, Leeds began to flatten all-comers. As a souvenir of their 6-0 fourth round demolition of Isthmian League Sutton United, Don Revie signed centre-half John Faulkner who had done a valiant man-marking job on Mick Jones. It was Faulkner's misfortune to break a kneecap in his second match for the club, and although his career never took off at Leeds, he made the grade after being transferred to Luton.

While fifth round opponents Mansfield Town proved almost as obdurate as Swansea – Leeds laboured to a 2-0 win – Revie's men were in an imperious mood for the quarter-final at Swindon which highlighted the Jones/Clarke partnership's ability to rip apart defences. Clarke's two goals before half-time had the match neatly stitched up and Leeds squatted on their lead, running the show without any superfluous effort.

Winning the league championship eased traumatic memories of 1967–68, when prolonged involvement in every competition caused Leeds to buckle at the last. But by March, the 1969–70 season threatened to oppress them in a similar fashion. The games were becoming bigger, with players picking up niggling injuries. European Cup quarter-final matches against Standard Liège became mixed up with the FA Cup semi-final confrontation with Manchester United – the latter a gruelling marathon that had fatal consequences for Leeds' high ambitions.

Fixture congestion

Yet the month was young and Leeds still at full throttle when they travelled to Liège. Once more, their expertise in defence and sharp counter-attack served them well. A brilliant move involving Giles, Madeley and Cooper carved open a chance for Lorimer who rifled home the ball from a narrow angle. It was as well that Leeds had the insurance of a 1-0 lead, for two weeks later at Elland Road they were jumpy,

The pitch was terrible and Leeds had endured a gruelling season. Yet the 1970 FA Cup final against Chelsea was a classic, and the first draw since that between Barnsley and West Bromwich Albion in 1912.

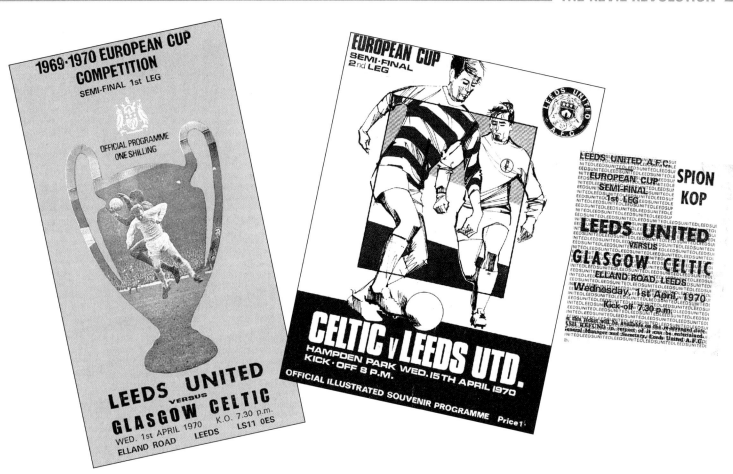

struggling to master a swirling wind and unsettled by a Liège team still full of fight. A Giles penalty 12 minutes from time finally saw Leeds into the next round.

Unfinished business with Manchester United took its toll. Four days earlier, on 14 March, the two sides fought out a titanic but goalless draw at Hillsborough, with Leeds soaking up waves of pressure before launching a late onslaught. Five days after Revie's team had disposed of Standard Liège and also beaten Wolves 2-1 at Molineux, the two Uniteds were locked in conflict again, at Villa Park. Rain lashed down, the pitch was sodden and the pattern resumed: Manchester driving against the Leeds defence; Leeds breaking out; drama at both ends – but even after extra time, no goals.

There were three days respite before the second replay, at Burnden Park. Bremner for one, still had a spring in his step. 'I had just been told I'd won the Footballer of the Year award. It meant a great deal and I was determined to celebrate by leading Leeds to victory,' he said. Within the first ten minutes, he did just that. A high ball knocked down by Allan Clarke bounced off Mick Jones' legs and the Leeds captain blazed the ball past Alex Stepney with a left-footed shot. Bremner's solitary goal in 300 minutes of football had settled the issue. Leeds were back at Wembley.

Yet Leeds' programme was so frenetic that two days later they were facing Southampton at Elland Road in the league. Several hardy players were either injured or exhausted: Reaney, Cooper, Bremner, Hunter, Giles and Jones. Yet even with a patched-up side, Leeds took the lead after an hour thanks to Peter Lorimer. But there was still time enough for a succession of disastrous mishaps to turn the match against Leeds. At full-time, own goals by Charlton, Yorath, and a hotly disputed penalty given against Hibbitt gave the game to Southampton 3-1. It was Leeds' first home defeat of the season.

Revie decided to cut his losses, and effectively handed Everton the championship by fielding an entire team of reserves for the Easter Monday fixture at Derby. The episode cost the club a £5,000 fine for flouting League regulations, but Revie was unapologetic. 'I would do the same again...I can't describe how much those Manchester United games took out of the Leeds players,' he said.

Two days later, a patched-up first team squared up for the battle at Elland Road against Celtic in the European Cup semi-final. The absence of Norman Hunter to buttress the defence left Terry Cooper exposed to the wiles of Celtic right-winger Jimmy Johnstone. Leeds had no time to feel their way into the game. Within a minute the rearguard was sliced open and cen-

> 'I can't describe how much those Manchester United games took out of the Leeds players.'
>
> *Don Revie*

■ Eddie Gray sets out to tease Chelsea right-back David Webb once more. But for all his virtuosity, Leeds, despite dominating, could not keep Chelsea down.

tre-forward Willie Wallace controlled a high through ball, feeding George Connelly who thrashed it past Gary Sprake.

It seemed to confirm Revie's claim that the players were drained, that their sharpness had gone. Billy Bremner recalled that 'most of the guys – a good 70 per cent – have played with injuries in games where they shouldn't have done.' But for Eddie Gray, who came closest to equalising with a shot that hit the crossbar, there was nothing to grumble about. 'Celtic had played a lot of games that season – they were involved in everything. We were confident enough we could win the game. I think it surprised a lot of people, the strength and ability in the Celtic team. I wouldn't look for any excuses.'

A day after their 1-0 defeat by Celtic, Leeds were forced to play at West Ham. It was in keeping with their run of bad luck that Paul Reaney broke a leg after an accidental collision during an inessential fixture. There was no fitter, faster or tighter marking full-back than Reaney. It was another grievous reduction of Leeds' options for the FA Cup final and the European Cup away game with Celtic. Reaney would miss England's World Cup campaign in Mexico and half the 1970–71 season.

Wembley once more

A week's respite made a huge difference to the walking wounded. Revie's men appeared rejuvenated for the FA Cup final against Chelsea, even if the pitch, which had been churned up by horses, appeared a cross between a mudflat and a cabbage patch. Billy Bremner was scathing. 'It was in a terrible state. You found yourself almost ankle deep in mud at times. It destroyed the energy of the players as the game wore on. The ball came at you from awkward angles, bouncing and bobbling about.'

Yet on this unpromising surface, one of the best Wembley Cup finals of modern times was played. Leeds had the game in their clutches, but allowed it to wriggle away with a lapse of concentration when leading 2-1 with only four minutes left. By then, the pitch had already influenced events. At 20 minutes, Jack Charlton's close-range header failed to bounce as the Chelsea defence expected and dribbled into the goal. Shortly before half-time, Sprake was deceived by a low shot from Peter Houseman

that squeezed beneath the his body for the equaliser.

The best performance came from Eddie Gray, who created havoc down the left flank. It was a day of embarrassment for right-back David Webb. 'But,' says Johnny Giles, 'Chelsea were to blame for allowing Webb to be exposed. Tommy Baldwin was in an unfamiliar right-wing role and gave little cover.'

Gray does not dwell on his star performance. 'In the end, it was a 2-2 draw and I would have gladly given up my so-called finest hour for a Cup winner's medal, for that's something we had never won and we were much the better team. We just went to sleep when they got the free kick near the end.' From that fateful kick, Ian Hutchinson leaped up to equalise what everyone thought had been Mick Jones's winning goal four minutes earlier.

Extra time was a cruel slog. It was a miracle that both teams kept their shape and concentration. 'We were done but we had to go on and on. Players were going down with cramp and the game became a slow motion sort of affair,' says Bremner. The deadlock could not be broken, so Leeds faced Chelsea in the first FA Cup final replay since 1912 – the last thing Revie's exhausted team needed.

European disappointment north of the border

Leeds travelled uncertainly to Hampden Park for the European Cup semi-final second leg against Celtic and, despite stout resistance and a brilliant breakaway goal by Bremner, were blown away by Celtic's vibrant play and the madhouse din

■ It's first blood to Leeds as Bonetti is fooled by the bounce of Jack Charlton's header.

Bonetti under pressure again, this time in the Cup final replay at Old Trafford. But although once more the better side, Leeds fans were stricken with despair as Chelsea wore down Revie's men in extra time and won 2-1.

whipped up by 136,000 supporters, the biggest crowd in European Cup history.

Once more tormented by Jimmy Johnstone, the Leeds defence was twice breached in the second half. Centre-forward John Hughes inflicted the crucial damage, scoring the first goal and then colliding with Gary Sprake as he bore down again on goal. With his leg too badly injured for Sprake to continue, on came stand-in goalkeeper David Harvey. Within seconds Harvey was picking a shot from Bobby Murdoch out of the net. Recalling the hectic night in which the Leeds defence was so often in turmoil, Terry Cooper said, 'I don't recall an occasion when I have been given so much trouble. If I live to be a hundred, I'll never forget the wizardry of Johnstone and what hard work it was to contain him.'

Leeds v Chelsea part II

All hopes now rested on the Cup Final replay at Old Trafford on April 29. A fortnight's rest appeared to restore Leeds' edge. They needed all their energy and courage: the match was fierce, yet moments of brilliance prevented it becoming a dogfight. After half-an-hour, Leeds scored a stupendous goal. Running from midfield, Allan Clarke swept past three defenders before releasing the ball to Mick Jones. Jones continued the forward surge then, at full momentum, crashed the ball past Bonetti to put Leeds a goal up.

But it was easier to outplay Chelsea than to outfight them. In Reaney's absence, Paul Madeley had dropped to right-back. With the Leeds midfield less solid, Chelsea clawed their way into the game as the second half ticked

away. Just as Jimmy Johnstone had tormented Leeds on the right at Hampden, so Charlie Cooke did on the left at Old Trafford. The Chelsea equaliser eight minutes from time was a masterpiece of muscular elegance: Cooke's teasing run and a perfect cross for Peter Osgood to send an angled header whipping past David Harvey in the Leeds goal.

Once more there was the distress of extra time. Leeds had simply played too many games. They were, perhaps without knowing it, punch-drunk by recent reverses and strangely vulnerable. In extra time, one minute before the interval, came the blow that turned their season of great ambition into a tragedy. A long throw in from Ian Hutchinson sailed high into the Leeds penalty area. Flicked on by John Dempsey, it reached David Webb at the far post and he bundled home the header. The Leeds players could not reply.

So Chelsea had won the Cup. For all their genius, Leeds had nothing. In the dressing room the players were numbed. 'If ever we felt crushed and disappointed, this was it,' says Eddie Gray. 'But footballers can't feel sorry for themselves. People will never feel sorry for you if you're not performing – you're getting paid to bring success to the club.' Don Revie said, 'Go and enjoy your holiday, and we'll start all over again.'

But despite Gray's modest and unsentimental view, the world did feel sorry for them. 'Robbery with Violence' screamed the headline in the *Daily Mirror*, referring to Chelsea's pugilistic methods. Yet at least Leeds' talent and courage had been universally recognised and acclaimed. They finally had people on their side. That was their real achievement.

1970–71 Highs and lows

Pride, ability and team spirit kept Leeds United rolling forwards. An insatiable lust for victory had made them one of the most formidable teams in history. The players had matured together and were approaching their peak. They were well-paid, well-managed and well-motivated and the competitive spirit in Leeds' sharp five-a-side matches was legendary. 'I used to love training,' says Peter Lorimer. 'Don Revie had created this little fortress in which everyone was friendly – people appreciated everybody's play.'

'The boss treated us like human beings,' agrees Billy Bremner. 'He knew we had flaws in our make-up; he knew certain guys wanted a bevvy and sometimes a few guys had a few too many. But as long as we were down on the ground training and it didn't affect the performance, he was alright. He didn't interfere if we didn't disturb other people.'

Player scandals were notable for their absence throughout Revie's management as Lord Harewood, the Leeds United president since 1961, recalls. 'He got them out of one scrape after another – drunken high jinks, that sort of thing. He was very good at keeping things low key.'

Revie's best XI

Whereas in his early days, Revie cast around desperately among two dozen players for a winning combination, by 1970–71 the team picked itself – Sprake, Reaney, Cooper, Bremner, Charlton, Hunter, Lorimer, Clarke, Jones, Giles and Gray were the first eleven specialists. Yet there was always a place for Madeley, a star without a position, who missed only one game in all the competitions throughout the season, slotting in for whomever was injured. 'I don't think he had a single weakness,' says Syd Owen. 'He was always thinking about what was going to happen; an elegant mover. You knew what you were going to get out of him before the game started. He took pride in his performance.'

Leeds' uneven displays early in the 1970–71 campaign mostly coincided with Giles' injury-enforced absence. But only once before Christmas did Leeds let their defences down badly, in the 3-0 defeat at Stoke on 12 September. By New Year, they were in their accustomed position at the top. Sometimes they played it rough; at other times they were serene – a side for all seasons. In the 1-0 home win over Manchester City on 28 November, *Sunday Times* reporter James Wilson wrote, 'there was pre-

sent...the touch of inspiration which turns a good team into a great one'.

Before Christmas, Leeds had dismissed Sarpsborg (6-0) on aggregate, Dynamo Dresden (2-2, winning on away goals) and Sparta Prague (9-2) from the European Fairs Cup. But whereas league attendances had risen, Elland Road was frequently half-empty for European games. The fans had become blasé and expected their team to progress. 'There used to be a saying in Leeds when we played in the Fairs Cup, "We'll wait until the semi-finals",' says Johnny Giles.

By April when the semi-final arrived, the public appetite had suddenly been revived. For one

■ Time to uncork the champagne as Jack Charlton, the grand old man of Revie's team, is presented with a salver to mark his 600th appearance for the club.

'I don't think he had a single weakness...'

Syd Owen on Paul Madeley

■ Sparta Prague are put to the sword, demolished by Leeds over two legs on their way to another European triumph in the Fairs Cup final. Terry Yorath, on as substitute for Hunter, makes an aerial challenge during Leeds 3-2 victory in Czechoslovakia.

■ Leeds were in disarray when visiting fourth division Colchester in the 1971 FA Cup fifth round. Their 3-2 defeat was the greatest Cup shock in modern times.

thing the opponents were Liverpool, and for another, Leeds' seemingly inexorable progress in both League and FA Cups received two severe and unexpected jolts. The Fairs Cup became valuable currency again, more so than the League Cup from which Leeds had been dismissed at the outset, losing 2-0 at Sheffield United in the second round.

Colchester catastrophe

Having despatched Rotherham, after a replay, and then Swindon from the FA Cup, Leeds' fifth round assignment was at Layer Road, the home of Colchester United. Revie had professed some unease, and his disquiet had a habit of being transmitted to players. Whereas Leeds United's expedition to Sutton the previous season had had the air of a state visit, fourth division Colchester turned out to be startlingly disrespectful.

The lack of Gray and Bremner was no explanation for why things went so wrong. On a cramped pitch and hemmed in by a partisan crowd, Leeds were 3-0 down after 54 minutes, outplayed and in disarray. Veteran centre-for-

ward Ray Crawford scored twice and gave Jack Charlton a terrible time. Hunter, Leeds' one tower of strength, led a late rally, his goal the first of two retaliatory strikes so that by full-time, Colchester hardly knew how to cling on.

But Leeds had woken up too late. Neutrals rejoiced to see them humbled. 'Although Don used to try to make us concentrate before every game, we were slack at the start,' explains Peter Lorimer. 'They had one or two good players and threw them forward. Gary Sprake didn't have one of his better games and was at fault for two of the goals. They were running twice as hard as they had ever run before and knocked us out of our stride. After the game, Don was, to say the least, very annoyed.'

Yet Leeds responded in typical fashion with four consecutive league wins and by drumming Vitoria Setubal out of the Fairs Cup quarter-final 3-2 on aggregate. Sporadic setbacks did not affect their form. The 3-1 defeat at Chelsea on 27 March was followed by a 4-0 home win over Burnley. Clarke, who had tormented the frail defence pitilessly, scored all the goals.

In most seasons, Leeds' consistency would

have seen off all challengers. But Arsenal were in tenacious pursuit. Revie's men could ill afford an off-day, yet on 17 April, with the Londoners having won all their three games in hand, were to have one that cost them dearly.

Nine months wasted

The home game against West Bromwich Albion, who had not won away for 16 months, appeared unthreatening. Yet Leeds seemed brittle and Albion unexpectedly confident; the more so after taking a 19th minute lead. As Leeds groped for a way back into the game, after 70 minutes Albion scored a second goal that brought uproar to Elland Road. It hinged on referee Ray Tinkler's decision to overrule a linesman who had flagged Colin Suggett offside when Albion intercepted a pass and broke out of defence. Tony Brown, as bemused as anyone, carried on towards goal, and squared the ball to Jeff Astle who sidefooted it home to put Albion in the lead.

A handful of furious fans ran on to the pitch to protest. After the disturbance had been quelled, Clarke scored, but too late to retrieve the match. Arsenal took over at the top of the league; yet for all the furore fuelled by Revie's bitter condemnation of Tinkler, whom he accused of ruining nine months' hard work, Leeds were still in the race.

The following week, on form once again, they won 3-0 at Southampton. When Arsenal came to Elland Road two days later, Leeds were in mean and determined mood, and as the match wore on, their bombardment of Bob Wilson's goal became fearsomely intense. A minute from the end, amid furious Arsenal protests that he was offside, Jack Charlton scrambled the ball home. The goal stood: luck had not completely deserted Revie's team.

In previous tight finishes, Leeds had thrown away championships. Overburdened by commitments, their form deserted them. The 1970–71 race was won by Arsenal's unrelenting late run of victories, interrupted only by the 1-0 defeat at Leeds. Revie's men finished with a flourish, brimming with creative energy as they beat Nottingham Forest 2-0 at Elland Road. But Arsenal won first at home to Stoke then at Tottenham to clinch the title. They had 65 points to Leeds' 64 – the highest points tally ever for runners-up.

As Arsenal captain Frank McLintock received his award as Footballer of the Year, he said, 'We have copied the Leeds style...the way they fight for every ball...the way they never give up. I have no great feeling for them...other than a tremendous admiration for their professionalism.'

Leeds fans could only rue that Arsenal had copied them too well. But there was compensation in the Fairs Cup. A headed goal by Bremner, who had played only 25 minutes competitive football in the previous three months, conquered Liverpool at Anfield and was the only score in two hard-fought matches.

Fairs Cup final

In the final against Juventus, Leeds were still full of life, unperturbed by a false start in Turin where the first match was washed out by torrential rain after 52 minutes. Two days later, Leeds achieved a thrilling 2-2 draw in what was the high point of

■ Above, top: Bremner remonstrates with Tinkler as police restrain outraged supporters. Leeds were banned from playing their first four home matches of 1971–72 at Elland Road.

■ Above: Mick Bates looks the epitome of grace in the Fairs Cup final against Juventus.

1971–72 A bad start to the campaign

There was a price to pay for the riotous scenes against West Bromwich – Leeds were forced to stage their first four 'home' matches away from Elland Road, and Don Revie was fined £500 by an FA disciplinary hearing for his acerbic remarks about referee Ray Tinkler. But being nomadic for a month did not seem not to worry the team unduly. Playing at Huddersfield, Hull and Sheffield Wednesday, they won twice and drew twice.

Yet by early October, Leeds had lost four away games, twice as many as in the entire 1970–71 campaign. This was their worst start for five years. Meanwhile, Manchester United had established a commanding position at the top. By the end of the month, however, Leeds had found their touch and travelled to Old Trafford in high feather. 'Leeds United at their best are a team of organisation, skill and inspiration to such a degree that their opponents are to be pitied. They have the extra ability to tailor their brilliance to their needs at any given time,' wrote Paul Wilcox in the Guardian.

There would be many more eulogies before the season's end. A speculative long range shot from Peter Lorimer in the fourth minute was enough to win the match. Leeds' ability to exert almost complete control was remarkable and when the going got rough in the first half, they could match Manchester kick for kick.

Early exit from Europe

For once, Leeds were not bogged down in Europe, having lost 4-2 on aggregate to SK Lierse in the first round of the UEFA Cup. The approach had been undeniably half-hearted: Leeds threw away a 2-0 advantage from the away leg by fielding a side full of reserves at Elland Road. Their hold on the trophy, which had been achieved with such style, lasted just three months. Interest in the League Cup did not survive the third round when Leeds lost a replay at Elland Road 1-0 to West Ham.

Although they began climbing the table, consistency still eluded Leeds through the early months. Anxious to inject new energy and provide cover for Eddie Gray and Johnny Giles, Revie moved to sign Asa Hartford from West Bromwich Albion. But a rigorous medical conducted before the player signed revealed that the ebullient midfielder had a hitherto undiscovered heart defect. At the last minute, Revie pulled out of the deal.

utility player Mick Bates' career. Bates, on as substitute and playing superbly in midfield, scored the second equaliser as he seized on a feeble punch by goalkeeper Piloni and swept in the ball from close range.

With away goals counting double in the tie, Bates' strike proved decisive. Yet Juventus remained dangerous at Elland Road, swiftly drawing level after Clarke gave Leeds a 12th minute lead. Thereafter it was a stern encounter, rich in good football and excitement, with Cooper a source of torment to the Juventus right flank. But the scoring was over. Revie was overjoyed. 'Juventus played well, but Leeds were superb and had by far the better of the play. We spent 80 of the 90 minutes looking for goals,' he said.

It was 3 June, the close season shorter than ever. But Leeds' morale was high; the confidence reinforced. Few would bet against them in 1971–72.

■ Above: The double act: Allan Clarke, scorer in Leeds 1-1 draw against Juventus at Elland Road, celebrates with striking partner Mick Jones.

Left: By the end of 1971–72, David Harvey supplanted Gary Sprake as first choice goalkeeper. Bravery was one of his great assets: Harvey never shrank from diving at an attacker's feet.

Below: With an elegant swing of a dainty foot, Peter Lorimer despatches a corner kick. Apart from the deadly power of his shooting, Lorimer delivered superb service with accurate crosses and corners.

Confounding the critics

Watching Leeds gain a point from a scratchy 0-0 draw at Chelsea on 11 December, Brian Glanville of *The Sunday Times* wrote: 'If last season they looked a team about to go gracefully over the hill, yesterday they looked one which has arrested the process but is scarcely on the brink of great things.' Moreover, the collapse of the Hartford deal meant that there would be no big signing to help pep things up.

Yet three weeks later, Leeds' New Year's Day performance at Liverpool, who were unbeaten at Anfield for 34 matches, had critics making a swift reassessment. With two superb second-half strikes from Clarke and Jones, Leeds plundered Liverpool's proud home record. Great things were much nearer than some had anticipated.

In the New Year, Leeds embarked on their FA Cup trail with swaggering assurance. Having brushed aside Bristol Rovers 4-1 in the third round, the draw took Leeds to Anfield once again. The match was typical of those between the first division titans – 'the second half, one continuous climax,' wrote Brian James in *The Sunday Times*. But the Liverpool gale could not blow down the Leeds defence. Bill Shankly's men failed to seize the moment. A goalless draw meant a replay at Elland Road in which Leeds were, according to Eric Todd of the Guardian, 'blessed with a mutual understanding given to very few'. Two superb goals from Clarke, the second a masterpiece of team play, settled the issue.

By February, Leeds were at full throttle. 'We were a settled side, all fit, all at the top of our game,' says Peter Lorimer. On 19 February, Manchester United, by now plunging down the table, were torn to pieces as Leeds destroyed their defence from all angles and won 5-1. 'They had good players, but we absolutely murdered them,' Lorimer says.

In the FA Cup fifth round tie at Ninian Park, Cardiff City flexed every muscle to keep Leeds at

■ Liverpool on the rack at Elland Road. In 1971–72, Leeds' mastery of their close rivals was absolute: a league double and a 2-0 victory, after a replay, in the FA Cup fourth round.

bay, but endeavour alone wasn't enough. Leeds always knew too much and outclassed them in speed and control. Goals in each half from Johnny Giles settled the issue.

The following week, on 4 March, it was Southampton's lot to visit Elland Road. Struggling and short of confidence, they were first annihilated then tortured as Leeds, 7-0 up, played an insolent game of keep-ball, once more flaunting their talents before a television audience of millions.

'We were flying at the time, and in our pomp,' says Peter Lorimer. 'They were charging around trying to get a kick. When we'd put about twelve passes together the crowd started chanting olé, so the lads thought they'd give them a bit of entertainment. They'd seen us putting the ball into the net, so we thought we'd keep it for a change. Don Revie loved that. He felt it was a great way of answering the public who in the past had accused us of being negative.'

Leeds' sixth round cup tie against Tottenham was a far more rigorous test of talent. But although the winning margin, 2-1, was slender, some critics regarded the Leeds display as peerless. Goalkeeper Pat Jennings, who had seen Leeds at uncomfortably close quarters and made a string of superlative saves, considered Revie's team the best club side he had faced. 'In all essences of the game, except courage, Tottenham were outclassed,' wrote Hugh McIlvaney in the Observer. Of Leeds, he said that there was scarcely a weakness to be seen and excellence was everywhere.

The style of victory befitted the pre-match theatricals: Leeds players trotting out with names emblazoned on track suits, wearing fancy stocking tags and performing a choreographed warm-up routine. They were the talk of the country and fulfilling Revie's most extravagant dreams; being spoken of in the same breath as Real Madrid.

Yet pitfalls awaited them in a title race that no-one had led with authority. The first team squad was still quite small and injuries to key players left them exposed. Without Jones and

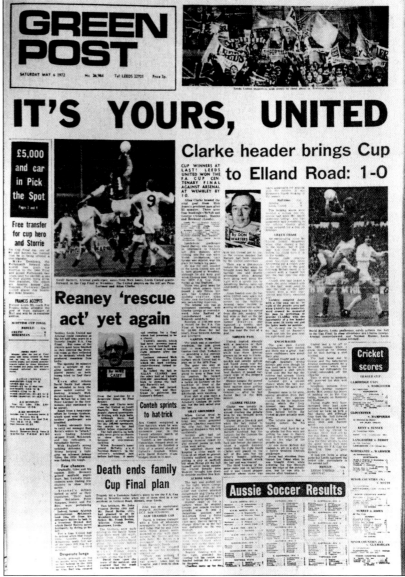

Giles on Easter Saturday, they were well beaten in the 2-0 defeat at Derby. A 3-0 victory at Stoke one week later exacted a terrible price: Cooper was carried off with a broken leg, never to regain a regular place in the Leeds team.

By 1 May, Leeds' season, as ever, was bubbling furiously. Two weeks earlier and full of strutting arrogance, they had brushed aside second division Birmingham City in the FA Cup semi-final at Hillsborough, winning 3-0. A 2-0 home victory over Chelsea in the penultimate match of the season counted out their requirements for a place in history: beat Arsenal in the FA Cup final then draw at Wolves two nights later to become perhaps the greatest double winning side.

Arsenal, pedestrian double-winners the previous season, had never looked like retaining the league championship. Self-professed copyists of Leeds they may have been, but in a manner that suggested the role model was the raw United of the mid-60s rather than the sophisticated machine into which Revie's team had evolved.

FA Cup winners at last

The Centenary Cup Final began with some horrible tackles. 'Arsenal tried to upset us physically, knock us out of our stride and Bob McNab brought me down a couple of times early on which was a bit out of order,' said Peter Lorimer. They were the wrong tactics with the wrong man: Lorimer was neither frightened nor easily riled. Hunter and his team meted out their own

punishment, but amid the conflict Leeds began to play powerful rippling football and push Arsenal on to the defensive.

On 53 minutes the goal came that won the Cup. A ball from Lorimer found Jones on the right wing, who scurried to the by-line and then whipped over a perfect cross. Clarke, moving in at full pelt, sent a flying header past Geoff Barnett. It was a goal drawn in bold colours by assured hands.

While Arsenal had their moments – Charlie George hit the bar – Barnett's goal had many more desperate escapes. Clarke and Lorimer had been deadly throughout. Yet just as Leeds were about to grasp the prize, melodrama unfolded in the last minute. Mick Jones, bearing down on the Arsenal goal in pursuit of Hunter's pass, collided with Barnett and fell awkwardly, dislocating his elbow. Amid all his team-mates' celebrations at full-time, Jones was a picture of agony.

Shepherded by Norman Hunter, it was all Mick Jones could do to stagger up to the royal box

■ Above, left: Up for the Cup once more: a Wembley steward models the official Leeds United team jacket before the centenary Cup final against Arsenal.

■ Above, right: The front page says it all: Leeds' local sports paper rejoices in United's FA Cup final victory over Arsenal.

■ Joy at Wembley as Jack Charlton, Allan Clarke – scorer of the only goal – and David Harvey celebrate.

FOOTBALL ASSOCIATION CHALLENGE CUP COMPETITION
CENTENARY YEAR
1872   1972
FINAL
SATURDAY 6th MAY 1972 ...... KICK-OFF 3 p.m.

ARSENAL v LEEDS UNITED
EMPIRE WEMBLEY STADIUM
Official Souvenir Programme 15p

and receive his winner's medal from the Queen. Afterwards, as the Leeds centre-forward lay nursing his injured arm in the dressing room, Allan Clarke walked over to show off his man-of-the-match trophy. 'I wanted Jonesy to see it first. I got the credit for the goal, but it was as much due to his running,' he said.

Eddie Gray recalls a post-match mood of quiet reflection rather than euphoria. 'The usual thing is to have a Cup final banquet but it was straight out of Wembley and onto the bus. A few minutes saying hello to people, then away.'

> 'It's just too much, we should have had three clear penalties...'
>
> *Don Revie*

The final hurdle

Within 48 hours, the Leeds United bandwagon decamped to Wolverhampton. There were 53,000 people shoehorned into Molineux, Wolves supporters as feverish as if their own team's title hopes were at stake. Leeds were carrying walking wounded, Gray and Clarke; and Jones was unable to make the match at all.

For all their valour, hard work and application, Leeds could not quite paper over the cracks when confronted by opponents who played as if their lives depended on it. Wolverhampton goals after 42 and 67 minutes were enough to sink Leeds. But not without a fight: no team containing Billy Bremner ever accepted defeat, and within a minute of his team going two goals down, the Leeds captain scored to put his side back in the hunt.

Revie's men battled with magnificent ferocity. Their prize was heroic failure. After an enthralling title race, 58 points gave Derby County the title with Leeds, Liverpool and Manchester City each on 57. Revie was distraught. 'It's just too much,' he said, 'we should have had three clear penalties. But I was proud of the team. I don't know where they got the energy from in the second half.' Yet Wolves, perhaps intoxicated by the prospect of denying Leeds their place in history, had fended them off. 'They were up for it that night,' says Eddie Gray. 'One or two crucial decisions went against us. They became known for stopping us doing the double and made a name for themselves.'

Beat Leeds and make a name for yourself. For years that maxim had been an inspiration to less gifted opposition. Revie's exhausted players may have lost the league by the width of a goal post, but remained the giants that every club wanted to topple.

1972–73
Runners-up at home and in Europe

Suspensions and injuries forced changes at the start of 1972–73. With Cooper injured long term and 37-year-old Jack Charlton past his best, the Leeds defence, which had selected itself during the last five years, needed reshaping. David Harvey had already ousted Gary Sprake. Trevor Cherry and Roy Ellam were bought from Huddersfield Town for £100,000 and £30,000 respectively as cover for Cooper and Charlton.

There were immediate signs that all might not

go smoothly. Harvey was hurt and had to be carried off in Leeds' first game at Chelsea. Peter Lorimer was forced to take over in goal and Leeds lost 4-0. The entire defence had looked makeshift and Hunter, suspended, was sorely missed. With Jones also injured, Leeds played over an hour with only ten men.

New blood

During this transitional season, two new young players forced their way into the side: midfielder Terry Yorath and centre-forward Joe Jordan. Yorath began his sporting life as a rugby union

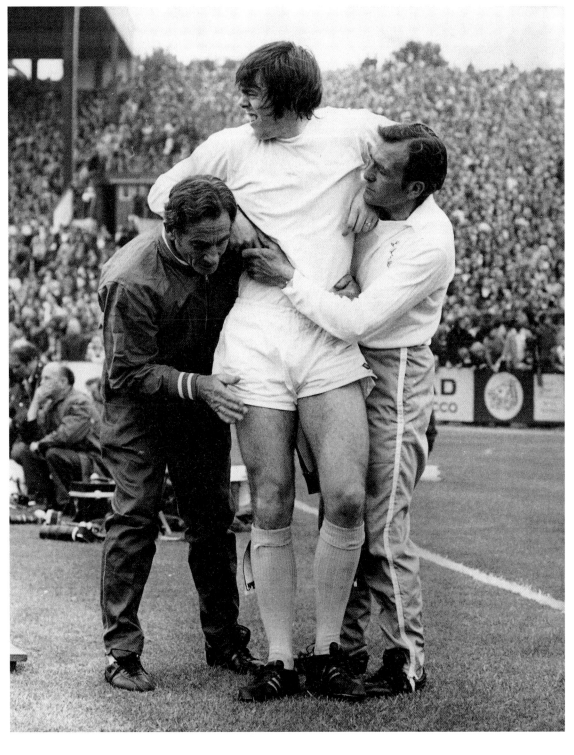

Dismay for Leeds as Harvey is carried off with concussion during the first game of 1972–73 at Stamford Bridge. Peter Lorimer went in goal and Leeds lost 4-0.

When no-one else could find a way through, interventions by Bremner were usually decisive. It's another goal for the ingenious Leeds captain who clutches the net in triumph.

scrum-half in South Wales. After switching to soccer, he was spotted by Jack Pickard and served a long apprenticeship at Elland Road learning the arts of hustle and tackling from Norman Hunter.

Bobby Collins, now coaching at Morton, did his former boss a favour by recommending that Joe Jordan, an 18-year-old centre-forward, move from Cappielow to Leeds. Jordan arrived in October 1970 and played occasionally in 1971–72, but the speed at which he matured thereafter astonished almost everyone. 'It was down to the people all around me,' says Jordan. 'If I didn't listen to them, I was wasting my time and theirs. These guys had done it all. Though it wasn't an easy place with all the micky-taking and banter that goes on in the dressing room. If I could survive that, I could survive anything that

happened on a Saturday. From the day I arrived, it was a battle of wits. It could be cruel, though it was good-humoured.'

Battles on the pitch were not all going Leeds United's way. Almost a third of the season passed before the team hit anything like consistent form. In the home game against Liverpool on 30 September, they appeared jaded as they surrendered a 1-0 lead and lost 2-1. The retort, however, was instant – a 5-0 demolition of champions Derby County at Elland Road the following week.

But defeat by Liverpool was a portent. While Leeds never abandoned their quest for league points, they no longer had an aura of invincibility. Liverpool kept their noses in front and Arsenal were once more jostling at the top. Leeds had much else on their plate: the European Cup Winners Cup and FA Cup, although they bowed out of the League Cup losing 1-0 to Liverpool after a fourth round replay.

The Cup trail

Their passage to the other cup finals was sometimes bumpy but often exhilarating. Yet indiscipline often left the team poorer; by mid-March, Hunter and Cherry had each been cautioned eight times. Leeds' 3-2 league win at Derby on 3 March, in which centre-half Gordon McQueen made his league debut, was blighted by almost 50 fouls.

Revie's men had reached the FA Cup final by beating Norwich (5-0 after two replays), Plymouth Argyle (2-1), West Bromwich Albion (2-0) and Wolves (1-0). In disposing of Albion and in their eventual demolition of Norwich, Leeds looked as formidable as ever. The semi-final with Wolves was a rousing encounter, settled yet again by a single goal from Billy Bremner and given much of its zip by a keen marauding performance from Jordan, who came on as substitute for Jack Charlton in the first half.

In Europe, Leeds laboured to beat the Turkish side Ankaragucu (2-1 on aggregate) and Carl Zeiss Jena (2-0) before unleashing their best form against Rapid Bucharest in the quarter-final, whom they beat 8-1. Their win at Elland Road moved Eric Todd to write in the Guardian: 'Keeping cool in the face of much evil tackling, they ran in five without reply and if it had not been for Raducanu's brilliant goalkeeping must have reached double figures. It was one of United's greatest performances in a European competition.' The same could not be said of the sullen, aggressive semi-final encounters against Hajduk Split. Leeds squeezed through to the next round, thanks to an Allan Clarke goal in the first leg at Elland Road.

Unpopular favourites for the Cup

By this time, Revie's team was contemplating an FA Cup final against second division Sunderland. 'After the Wolves game, when we heard that they'd beaten Arsenal, I thought it would be a formality,' says Peter Lorimer. But as 5 May approached, the unease emanating from the Leeds manager had taken root. 'I could sense in the build-up during the week that there wasn't a relaxed atmosphere,' says Eddie Gray. 'Don Revie was more uptight than I'd ever seen him... certainly so on the morning of the game.'

While Leeds were the bookmakers' favourites,

the rest of the world rallied behind the underdogs. The Sunderland camp appeared hilariously at ease, relishing the occasion as the day out of a lifetime, while Leeds looked stiff and apprehensive. Wembley stadium was awash with Sunderland colours. For Revie's men, it was like an away game.

Yet they thrived on adversity, and almost everyone beyond Wearside believed them able to cope with whatever Sunderland could muster. But Revie's pre-match tension appeared to be an omen. After 32 minutes, Ian Porterfield scored for Sunderland from a corner. Leeds, urged on especially by the athletic promptings of Madeley, came back breathing fire and on 65 minutes believed they had saved the game. But Sunderland goalkeeper Jim Montgomery, who earlier

■ Above: Few would have though the season would turn out so sour as Bremner, arms aloft, celebrates his goal against Wolves that put Leeds into the 1973 FA Cup final.

■ Below: The championship was sweet after losing to Sunderland in the 1973 Cup final. Trevor Cherry scored but the effort was disallowed.

■ A wretched end to 1972–73 as Leeds lose 1-0 to AC Milan in the European Cup Winners' Cup final. Chiarugi's shot squeezes through the wall, and Milan, aided by the referee, survived after desperate defending for almost all of the game.

had handled the ball as fearfully as if it were a live coal, redeemed himself with a stupendous double stop, first beating away a Cherry header and then, hurling himself off the ground to flip Lorimer's goal-bound shot against the underside of the bar.

This, the most famous save in Cup final history, broke Leeds' hearts. As his team-mates sat dazed and morose in the dressing room afterwards, Peter Lorimer still couldn't believe that he was on the losing side. 'I had all the time in the world, all the goal to shoot at. When I swung my foot, the keeper was the wrong side of goal. Don't ask me how he got back,' he said. A few yards away, Stoke was uncontainably jubilant. 'That TV panel – a couple of second division managers aren't they – wrote us off. We watched them and that was the extra kick we needed. What a marvellous day.'

Leeds v AC Milan...a nightmare in Greece

For Leeds, with a European Cup Winners Cup Final date against AC Milan in Greece ten days later, it was like a kick in the teeth. Another awaited them; there were rumours, gathering in substance, that Revie was preparing to abandon ship at Elland Road and manage Everton. The Leeds party arrived in Salonika with ranks depleted and morale low. Jack Charlton, who had been a grand presence during his latter ten years at Leeds, was leaving to manage Middlesbrough. Suspensions and injuries had ripped the heart out of the side: no Bremner, Clarke, Giles or Eddie Gray. Mick Bates, Joe Jordan, Eddie's

> ## 'I had all the time in the world, all the goal to shoot at.'
>
> *Peter Lorimer*

younger brother Frank, and Terry Yorath were drafted in as replacements.

Yet had AC Milan not been so flagrantly assisted by the referee Christos Michas, Leeds might still have triumphed. It was with Michas' help that Milan took the lead after four minutes, when he penalised Madeley's innocuous challenge with an indirect free kick. Chiarugi's shot was deflected on to the post and squirmed past Harvey into the Leeds net.

For the rest of the game, Leeds besieged the Milan goal yet could find no way through. Three times Michas turned down what seemed irrefutable claims for penalties. Near the end, Hunter, goaded beyond endurance by fouls and injustices, was sent off for retaliation, along with the Italian, Sogliano. At full-time the Greek spectators were chanting 'shame' in recognition of Leeds' plight, as victims of injustice. They cheered the losers as victors. By contrast, the Milan team bus was spat upon and stoned.

Michas was promptly suspended by UEFA. 'It was horrendous...a disgrace,' says Joe Jordan. 'That referee was shocking – it was never going to be easy, but we had none of the breaks – three penalty decisions turned down. It was a terrible disappointment to arrive at the final of a major European competition and see it handled that way.'

Revie though, for whatever reason, had changed his mind about leaving. The season had been ruined, but there remained the promise of continuity; of Leeds doing things in their familiar old style. But, wondered the critics, were the old warhorses finally past their prime? Did they still have the energy?

1973–74 Super Leeds

As long ago as 1971, doubts had been expressed about Leeds' ability to keep going with the same bunch of ageing players. After the debacle against AC Milan, many were convinced that their time was up, that the great engineers, Giles, Hunter and, above all, Bremner, could not physically sustain the performance they had given in recent seasons.

Around them, Revie had begun a stealthy reconstruction. By Leeds' standards, Roy Ellam had not been a success at centre-half and Revie decided to gamble on young Gordon McQueen, signed from St Mirren for £30,000 in September 1972, as replacement for Jack Charlton. Charlton's place in history and folklore was secure; a miraculous career of downs, then ups, which added up to 772 appearances and 95 goals for Leeds, 35 caps for England and being voted Footballer of the Year in 1967.

Gary Sprake also departed, sold to Birmingham City for £100,000 after 506 appearances. But a back injury soon brought his career to a premature end. David Harvey had proved a fine replacement, less erratic than Sprake, whom supporters with selective memories blamed for Leeds' failure to win several crucial games.

If the team's luck had been bad in 1972–73, so, on occasions, had been the behaviour of some players. An FA disciplinary commission imposed a suspended £3,000 fine on the club, to be activated only if Leeds did not mend their ways. Already they were working on their image. They appointed Peter Fay as the club's first public relations officer, and Don Revie decided Leeds' cause may be better served by conveying a less paranoid image to the media. He also began writing a statesmanlike column in each match programme.

Setting the pace

Those who believed that Leeds United were a spent force were once more confounded. Revie's men made a miraculous start to the 1973–74 campaign: victorious, elegant and demure with a mastery of their peers that invoked once more the superlatives used in 1972. Successive victories in their second and third games at Arsenal (2-1) and Tottenham (3-0) were a splendid advertisement for the new refined, mild-mannered Leeds. 'It meant that in London we were getting the publicity,' says Joe Jordan. 'That mattered – we'd made our mark. I think then that people were looking very closely at Leeds.' Reviewing their 3-0 win at Spurs, Brian Glanville wrote, 'How sad it is that Leeds United should not be our representatives in the European Cup, for they are indisputably the finest club team we have.'

The rookie centre-half Gordon McQueen was learning his trade quickly. 'It was the one place

It's celebration time for a team who confounded critics with the quality of their football in 1973–74, and were worthy champions.

Billy Bremner light-heartedly accepts flowers on one knee. Leeds' midfield inspiration was a great character throughout the whole of his career.

on the field which we feared wasn't going to be put right,' Jordan recalls. 'But he was playing with Norman Hunter, who had great experience and could coach Gordon through the game. In front there were Giles and Bremner. All Gordon really had to do was head the ball away.'

Leeds cruised serenely through their first seven games, winning the lot and leaving the rest of the division amazed. In the eighth, Leeds dropped their first point in a goalless draw at Elland Road against a Manchester United team seemingly intent on unarmed combat. Eddie

Gray was a long-term casualty of the clash and played only one more match all season.

Although jolted out of their immaculate rhythm, Leeds' style continued to illuminate the division. It seemed fitting that new floodlights, beaming down from the tallest pylons in the country, had been installed to shine on this particular team. When the unbeaten record went at Ipswich, in a 2-0 League Cup defeat, few cared. The championship campaign continued regardless. Of Leeds' 4-1 win against West Ham at Elland Road on 3 November, Keith Botsford wrote in *The Sunday Times* that there was no evidence that Leeds were anything other than super-Leeds, superior to any in England and to most in Europe.

But the burden of expectation became oppressive. With Giles becoming another long-term casualty, the creative department was severely depleted, for all that Bates and Yorath strove to plug the gap. Greater demands than ever fell on Bremner. In early December, a half-strength team bowed out of the UEFA Cup, beaten by Vitoria Setubal 3-2 on aggregate. After the New Year, victories became fewer and less emphatic; draws, for which Leeds were sometimes made to hang on grimly, more frequent.

Already they were in uncharted territory, the 2-1 win against Chelsea at Stamford Bridge on 15 December meant that Revie's men had gone 21 league matches unbeaten from the start of a season, breaking the record set by Liverpool. Leeds were playing to packed houses everywhere: everyone wanted to be first to knock down the champions-elect. Two weeks later, Leeds' visit to Birmingham City pulled in more than 50,000. Joe Jordan has vivid memories of a day in which Leeds were run ragged by the opposition, yet survived.

'I had had a fitness test that morning in a local park and passed. We were 1-0 down and time was running out. Then right near the end, Peter Lorimer crossed the ball to me and I thought "Christ, this is an easy one; I can't miss it." There was a fraction of a second to think. I hit the target, kept it low and it went in. Seconds after that, the whistle blew.'

Jordan, his team-mates and the Leeds fans were almost delirious with relief. The result left Revie's team eight points ahead of Liverpool: Leeds had 39 points to Liverpool's 31, and both had played 23 matches. Few envisaged the championship going anywhere other than to Elland Road, even though Leeds' form was markedly less glorious than in the autumn.

FA Cup defeat raises questions

But any ideas of making a stately procession to the finishing line were shattered in February. A warning that all was not well came in the fifth round of the FA Cup when, to the astonishment of everyone, Leeds lost their fifth round replay against Bristol City 1-0 at Elland Road. Four days later at Stoke, in their 30th league match, Leeds' weaknesses finally caught up with them.

Although lacking Jones, McQueen and Reaney, Leeds at first did not appear handicapped. After 17 minutes they were leading 2-0,

■ With Mick Jones frequently absent through injury, centre-forward Joe Jordan provided a new aggressive dimension to the Leeds attack.

but an injury to Giles soon afterwards disrupted the midfield, and Cooper, on as substitute and seeking restoration to the team after 21 months, could not fill the breach. Stoke rallied, charged and after 67 minutes, Revie's team were 3-2 down. They were beaten.

Some Leeds players still remain bemused by this turn of events. 'At 2-0 up we were cruising, all over them,' says Peter Lorimer. 'We had this capability of playing in second gear and still winning. I don't know how it happened. Then on the Monday we had a team meeting and Don Revie

Worse was in store the following week. Leeds lost their shape, composure and heads as Burnley, early championship contenders who had long since faded from the race, revived their form of the autumn and beat Leeds 4-1 at Elland Road. Losing 3-1 at West Ham the following Saturday made Revie's men jumpier than ever. 'If some of the Leeds players cannot master their temperaments better than they did in the last 20 minutes, then they lack the requisite qualities of champions and their supporters must prepare themselves for the worst,' wrote the *Guardian's* John Samuel.

It was their darkest hour. For the first time, Leeds could now be overtaken by Liverpool. Yet their torments were coming to an end. Though still out of sorts, the points began to stop haemorrhaging away. Liverpool's martial tread had been halted by defeat at Sheffield United on 8 April, and Leeds, 2-0 winners over Derby at Elland Road two days earlier, once more had a little breathing space.

The race for the title changed irrevocably in their favour on 16 April on a turbulent night at Bramall Lane. After a goalless first half against Sheffield United, news reached the Leeds camp that Liverpool were 4-0 up at Anfield against Manchester City. The occasion demanded that Leeds ransack their reserves of character and resilience. They did so. Jones, far from being fully fit, together with Lorimer harried the Blades to distraction and finally dismantled their defence. Lorimer scoring twice, once from the penalty spot. For all their first-half fireworks, Liverpool had not advanced.

Expectancy was high, nerves raw and Eddie Gray was playing his first game since September as Leeds lined up for their penultimate match against Ipswich at Elland Road. 'This was not so much a game as an emotional explosion,' wrote Ken Jones in the *Sunday Mirror*. For Leeds fans had to endure watching their team let slip a two goal lead given to them by Lorimer and Bremner. There were horrible echoes of the match at Stoke. But this time Leeds, holding their nerve and discipline, sharpened up; and in the 69th minute Clarke scored. Ipswich players protested that the Leeds striker controlled the ball with his hand, but the goal was allowed to stand.

There was pandemonium at full-time. Not only had Leeds won, but also a rumour swept the ground that Everton were leading at Anfield. It was wishful thinking, but in drawing 0-0, Everton did Leeds a grand service. Clarke's controversial strike was to give Leeds the championship. Divine intervention appeared in the unlikely form of Arsenal who, becalmed in mid-table,

■ Norman Hunter, one of Leeds greatest servants, is presented with an award by Leeds chairman Manny Cussins following his 600th first team appearance. Hunter was voted PFA Player of the Year in 1972–73.

said that if we weren't prepared to do the business, he'd bring in some players who would. He really had a go at us.'

The team did not easily shrug off the blow. In successive draws at Elland Road with Leicester and Newcastle, Leeds looked sickly and only an undeserved penalty allowed them to squeeze a 1-0 home victory over Manchester City. Meanwhile, as Liverpool were closing, an away fixture at Anfield beckoned. It was no place to recuperate.

On the day, Leeds played better than for some time in a match that was stern but never vicious. But their stout rearguard action was all in vain, for Liverpool scored seven minutes from time. Defeat left Billy Bremner in a black, hypercritical mood. 'We played like a bunch of bloody nancies most of the time. Then just as it looked as if we were going to start putting it together a bit, we have to give them a soft goal.'

astounded all by travelling to Anfield four days later to snatch Liverpool's unbeaten home record and snuff out their flickering hopes of the title.

For Don Revie the moment was sublime. 'This is the greatest moment of my life,' he said. 'Deep down, I thought our chance had gone after three defeats on the trot before Easter. All credit to Billy Bremner and the lads for coming back. That is the mark of true champions.' His words conveyed only a hint of the strain that the players could see he was under. 'During those last couple of months he looked as if he'd aged about five years,' Peter Lorimer recalled

Without a care in the world, the champions went out to celebrate. Hordes of Leeds camp followers swelled the gate to 35,353, a ground record, for their final match against Queen's Park Rangers at Loftus Road. Clarke's solitary goal decided the game and gilded the occasion. 'It was a proud crowning ceremony...and gave time for reminiscences about the brilliant way Leeds commanded the first division until their recent totterings towards the finishing line,' wrote Peter Corrigan in the *Observer*.

No-one then knew that a great era was about to end and Leeds fans would find themselves living on those reminiscences for more years than they could ever have dreamed.

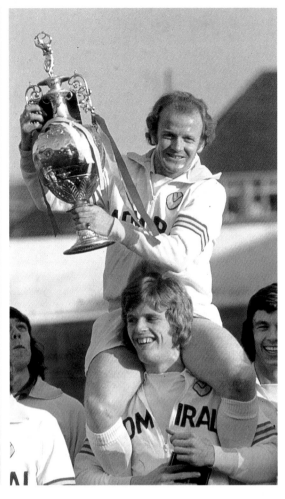

■ Left: Bremner in familar triumphant pose after Leeds win the League Championship in 1973–74. He is born aloft by Gordon McQueen, who matured rapidly at centre-half.

■ Below: Terry Yorath, who frequently filled in when injury forced Giles out of the team, celebrates one of his rare goals in Leeds' championship campaign.

The Search for a Successor

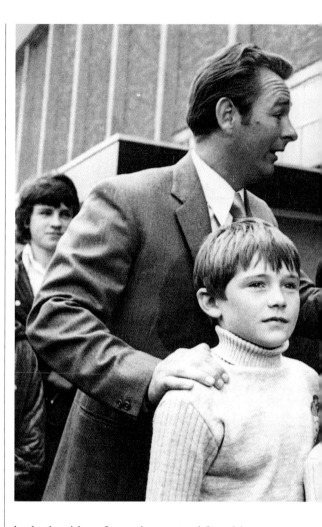

1974–75 Clough's 44 days

A second championship seemed finally to have sated Revie's ambitions at club level. He was also unsure of his abilitiy to reconstruct the team whilst maintaining standards. Revie could be ruthless yet, as Lord Harewood recalls, would shrink from telling the likes of Bremner and Hunter that their time was up. 'The agony of having to replace them was something he was glad not to face...it was a fundamental reason for his leaving.'

For Revie, even the prospect of a second tilt at the European Cup could not compete with the allure of managing England. With Joe Mercer's caretaker managership coming to a close, Revie had already contacted Ted Croker, the FA secretary. Events moved rapidly – FA officials were impressed by Revie's plans and a deal was struck with the Leeds board accepting an offer of money to assist in appointing a new manager. The day after his appointment was announced, Revie cleared his desk at Elland Road and Les Cocker went with him.

Revie recommended that Johnny Giles should be his successor; Giles was tough, shrewd and understood the game, but the Leeds directors had other ideas. In casting around for a big name they hooked Brian Clough, then in charge of Brighton and Hove Albion, who in recent years had been heard loudly castigating the means and methods of Revie's Leeds. The appointment was viewed variously as bold, bizarre or perverse.

Of all Clough's mistakes at Elland Road, his greatest was to tell Revie's old guard that the medals they had won in the past were the fruits of cheating. 'The atmosphere was terrible at the club with him meeting the players and telling them they could throw their medals in the bin...criticising them all the time,' says Eddie Gray. 'I think if things had continued, the club would have struggled to survive that year.'

Behind all the bluster, Clough was unsure of himself. Elsewhere, he had moulded and shaped teams in a brilliant if somewhat authoritarian manner, but at Leeds he had inherited league champions. Yet Clough could not bring himself to be deferential: abrasion was his natural style. He rued the absence of Peter Taylor, his long-time partner and assistant, who had elected to stay at Brighton. They were a double act from which Clough, for all his individual flair, derived much strength.

Clough's first chilly encounter with Syd Owen would have done little to raise his spirits. 'He

brought his two sons with him...and asked if I could get one of the apprentices to take them down to the gymnasium and entertain them,' Owen recalls. 'I told him apprentices were here to develop their capabilities as professional footballers and not look after the manager's boys.'

Clough's men join

At least Clough had the moral support of former Derby trainer Jimmy Gordon and had signed two players who served him well at Derby County, midfielder John McGovern and centre-forward John O'Hare. Clough also paid £250,000 for the mercurial Nottingham Forest inside-forward Duncan McKenzie. With these players at the core, he hoped to start building a team of his own.

For McGovern, it was an especially miserable time. He was expected to fill in for the absent Billy Bremner, who had been suspended for eight matches following a fracas at Wembley with Kevin Keegan during the FA Charity Shield match against Liverpool. As Leeds made a feeble start, winning only one of their first seven league matches, McGovern became a scapegoat for the Leeds crowd, a symbol for everything that was going wrong. He was, in Eddie Gray's view, 'a

■ Goodwill was conspicuous by its absence in the 1974 FA Charity shield match against Liverpool. Billy Bremner and Kevin Keegan were sent off after a running feud though Clough blamed the Leeds captain for provoking the trouble.

■ John McGovern had a wretched time at Leeds, blamed by the fans for the team's poor start in 1974–75. But his career was resurrected by Brian Clough at Nottingham Forest.

Joe Jordan. 'I think that proved that it wasn't the right marriage.' Clough had also refused to pay the fine imposed on Bremner following his brawl with Keegan. It came as an unpleasant shock for the Leeds captain who was used to Revie settling disciplinary fines out of a club kitty which had been set up for the purpose.

Clough was often absent. 'I never really got to know him; he used to turn up late for training when we were running round the park with Jimmy Gordon,' Gray says. Yet when he did arrive, he struggled to impose his presence. Colin Jeffrey recalls watching a seven-a-side game on the training ground. 'Clough was supposedly playing, but I watched for a good ten minutes and he hardly touched the ball. Play was going on all around, but somehow the ball always by-passed him. The players were enjoying it, but as far as they were concerned, Clough just didn't exist.'

By mid-September, growls of discontent had reached the boardroom. There followed an extraordinary meeting of players and directors engineered by two anti-Clough members of the board, Sam Bolton and Percy Woodward, in which team members were invited to air their grievances. Clough himself was there, briefly, until Johnny Giles said he didn't feel it right for the manager to be present when under discussion. Many of the Leeds team remain evasive about their contributions, but the outcome hastened Clough's departure from Elland Road. Two days later, after a special board meeting, he was fired. 'A sad day for Leeds,' he declared, departing after 44 days if not wiser, certainly £25,000 richer and having exacted a commitment from the club to pay his income tax for the next three years.

Armfield takes over

There was an urgent need to restore stability. Leeds chairman Manny Cussins wanted to act on Revie's recommendation and go for Johnny Giles. 'When Clough had been and gone and it was up for grabs again, I was assured I would get it by a 3-2 vote on the board,' Giles recalls. 'But I thought about it long and hard and rang the secretary to tell her to take my name out of the hat. If I won by 3-2, it would mean I had two directors against me. I didn't need the job in those circumstances.'

Assistant manager Maurice Lindley took over as caretaker until, after a prolonged deliberation, the board appointed Jimmy Armfield. A former full-back who had served Blackpool and England with distinction, Armfield had also achieved

neat and tidy player with a good knowledge of the game but not the ability of Giles or Bremner...I think he was unfortunate with the time he came. He was very loyal to Brian Clough.'

Bremner and Clough got off on the wrong foot almost immediately. 'After he was appointed, he went on holiday and asked Billy to go out and meet him but Billy wouldn't go,' says managerial success at Bolton, winning the third division championship in 1972–73. An equable temperament may also have helped sway the board. The Leeds directors did not want any more upheavals.

In his first season, Armfield was content to use the players already at his disposal, although McGovern and O'Hare were quickly sold. His arrival also marked the revival of Eddie Gray's career. 'When Jimmy came, I was just waiting to get Football League insurance and pack the game in,' Gray said. 'Because I couldn't play, Jim asked me if I'd take the kids' team. Then I started to join in the training and the reserves and Jimmy said, "Do you want to give it another go?" My first game back was against Cardiff in the FA Cup, and I scored.' After this stealthy fight-back, Gray played over 200 more matches in the following nine seasons for Leeds.

United recovered some form in mid-season, though not enough to suggest they could retain the championship. Moreover they were distracted by the FA Cup and, above all, the European Cup – their exploits in both thrust them centre stage once more.

The team played eight FA Cup matches – enough to win the trophy with a couple to spare – yet only reached the quarter finals. In round four, Southern League Wimbledon had threatened an enormous upset, drawing 0-0 at Elland Road after goalkeeper Dickie Guy saved a Peter Lorimer penalty. It took an own-goal from Dave Bassett in the replay at Selhurst Park for Leeds to stumble through.

They were more fluent against first division opposition, but in the sixth round found their passage blocked by Bobby Robson's Ipswich Town, rising stars and championship contenders. It took four tough matches to determine the winner. The first, a 0-0 draw, attracted 38,010 to Portman Road, Ipswich's largest-ever gate. The first replay drew 50,074 to Elland Road, 7,000 of whom had comparatively civilised accommodation in the newly-opened South Stand which had replaced the Scratching Shed, a relic of Leeds City days. The game was a 1-1 draw. After another 0-0 match at Filbert Street, Leicester, the sides were finally separated in a scintillatingly open third replay, also at Filbert Street, with Leeds losing 3-2.

European adventures

By then, Armfield's men had reached the semi-final of the European Cup, the point at which, five years earlier, Revie's ambitions had foundered, his drained and over-stretched side

cut to pieces by Glasgow Celtic. This time there were concerns about the ages of such linchpins as Bremner 32, Hunter 31, and Reaney, 30, who depended not only on technique but also vigour and speed for effectiveness. Yet their guile and experience was unmatched; their hunger for the trophy enough to sweep aside most obstacles.

In the first round, Leeds had played two low-

■ A box of tricks. Duncan McKenzie was blessed with the skills to unlock any defence yet was sometimes disinclined to toil for the common cause.

■ After the upheaval caused by the Clough affair, Jimmy Armfield brought much-needed stability to Leeds but lacked the drive to build a team that would return to the top.

key games against FC Zurich, winning 5-3 on aggregate. The second round against Ujpest Dozsa recalled ferocious battles of old. McKenzie, making his European debut, was sent off after 15 minutes of the away leg for retaliation after having been fouled. With the scores at 1-1, and reduced to ten men, Leeds responded seven minutes later by scoring a second goal through Gordon McQueen. At the end of a hostile encounter, Ujpest had also had a man sent off and Lorimer missed a penalty. Leeds' determination gave them a decisive advantage for the leg at

Elland Road which was settled by goals from McQueen, Bremner and Yorath.

Against Anderlecht, their quarter-final opponents, Leeds had to battle through fog at Elland Road, but they overran Anderlecht with goals from Jordan, McQueen and Lorimer. Away in Belgium they played a canny containing game in torrential rain struggling to keep their feet on a sodden pitch covered in pools of water and sealing victory through a lobbed goal from Bremner.

Barcelona provided imperious opposition in the semi-final. Their line-up included Johan

Cruyff, universally regarded as Europe's most accomplished footballer. But Bremner, a genius for conjuring up goals on the big occasion, was not far behind, and in the first leg at Elland Road, struck quickly, hammering home the ball after only ten minutes and sending the 50,393 crowd into a state of rare euphoria.

Barcelona equalised after 66 minutes through Asensi, but Leeds were the more enterprising and inventive side, and their reward came when Clarke drove home a second goal 11 minutes from time. It was, however, a meagre lead to take to the Nou Camp stadium where Barcelona would surely come at Leeds hammer and tongs, egged on by the gale of noise whipped up by 110,000 supporters.

But few were more adept at withstanding a siege than Bremner, Hunter and co. The task was made easier when a ferocious early strike from Peter Lorimer gave Leeds a lead, and breathing space, after just seven minutes. Leeds were able to fend off Barcelona's increasingly feverish challenge until the 70th minute when Clares equalised. Soon after, following a tussle with Clares, McQueen threw a wild punch and was sent off. Leeds withstood a twenty minute bombardment as Trevor Cherry and stand-in goalkeeper David Stewart performed near miracles to protect the Leeds goal.

The Bayern debacle

In the final, Leeds met Bayern Munich at the Parc des Princes stadium, Paris. Don Revie was among the spectators, surveying the fortunes of his old team as part of a BBC commentary team. What he was to witness on the evening of 28 May 1975 stirred memories of all the ill-fortune that had long stalked Leeds, who would surely have won many more trophies if it had not been for perverse refereeing.

It was the last chance for the old stalwarts to win Europe's great prize. They were Revie men, all: Stewart, Reaney, Frank Gray, Bremner,

■ Although a persistent thigh injury stifled his development into a world class player, the revival of Eddie Gray's career was a legacy of the Armfield era.

Madeley, Hunter, Lorimer, Clarke, Jordan, Giles, Yorath. Leeds were near their best, bearing down on Bayern's goal with a series of stylish sweeping moves, Hunter smiting the bar with a mighty shot, and only the adroit goalkeeping of Sepp Maier keeping Bayern alive. But the fortunes of the game turned on a scene horribly familiar to Leeds United fans, that of the seemingly good goal disallowed at a crucial time.

On 67 minutes, Lorimer's thunderous kick left the Bayern keeper stranded. Leeds players and supporters began to celebrate. The linesman ran back to the halfway line fully expecting the goal to be given, but the French referee, Marcel Kitabdjian, judged Bremner offside and interfering with play. For Leeds, who in the first half had had two loud penalty appeals turned down against the Bayern captain Beckenbauer – one for handball, the other for fouling Clarke – the decision was a fatal blow to morale. The inevitable followed: Bayern Munich, having ridden their luck for so long, found their rhythm and with lethal counter-attacks scored twice through Roth and Muller.

For the second time in three seasons, Leeds felt they had been mugged by officialdom just as they were on the threshold of a great European prize. 'It was a disgrace... maybe more of a disgrace than what happened in Salonika,' says Joe Jordan. 'For the older players it was the last chance of a crack at Europe. They had played, suffered, but also achieved. It was the finish for that team. They should have won to stamp their name in history. It was taken away from them. I don't think the decision should have been allowed to stand... it was a travesty. That was the one game that would have given the team a cup to show the world how good they were. They deserved it... for it to be taken away from them by bad decisions was unjust.'

The misery was compounded by the riotous behaviour of a section of Leeds fans, some of whom had been a drunken nuisance before the game had started. Drink, the sense of having been cheated, bitter frustration and poor crowd control by ill-trained stewards caused terrible scenes, with ripped out seats hurled on to the pitch during the final minutes. What should have been Leeds United's greatest night became a violent debacle; and an ominous warning of what lay ahead.

1975–76 Revie's team dismantled

The time had come to dismantle Revie's old team, which Armfield managed with the minimum of rancour. Some things sorted themselves out: Johnny Giles left to become player-manager of West Bromwich Albion, and the injury-plagued Mick Jones, who had not played throughout 1974–75, was forced to retire. In March 1975, Terry Cooper had been sold to Middlesbrough for £50,000. His was another great career jolted by injury; he never quite recaptured his coruscating form after breaking a leg at Stoke in 1972.

Frank Gray became the new choice at left-back. Although lacking brother Eddie's mesmeric skills, he had the natural talent to make the game look easy. The burden of replacing Johnny Giles fell to Terry Yorath, who always suffered unflattering comparison with the Irishman. Giles was a unique figure, his game a mix of high intelligence, craft and menace that few opponents mastered. Yorath could tackle, chase, make surging runs and shoot powerfully – Leeds had few more willing servants, but he was never the equal of Giles as a plotter and schemer.

The 1975–76 campaign was the last season for Bremner and Hunter, and saw the departure of Syd Owen to coach Birmingham City. But there was nothing to suggest that Leeds were in decline. Although falling early in both League and FA Cup, they finished fifth; and an inspired mid-season run in which they won eight matches, drew one and lost two, conceding only six goals, hinted at championship potential. A BBC radio commentator watching the 4-0 rout of Leicester City at Elland Road on 27 December described Leeds' display as the finest he had seen in years.

Duncan McKenzie had scored twice and been at his fizzing best: one day he was a sorcerer, the next his presence was scarcely felt and by the end of the season he had left Elland Road to try his luck in Belgium with Anderlecht. In his two seasons with Leeds, McKenzie had entertained and exasperated in equal measure. 'He was an exhibitionist on the park and it was a pity he didn't use his ability better in certain areas of the field,' says Eddie Gray. 'You could never tell him how to play the game; he was a law unto himself. He would drive you crazy, but did well in games that seemed to matter.'

When dealing with players, Armfield's gentle manners were sometimes construed as indecision, but his diplomacy had influenced the decision to treat Leeds more leniently after the European Cup final riot in Paris. As a result of his reasoned intervention, a four-year ban from competition in Europe imposed by UEFA was reduced to two.

By October 1976, Armfield had managed to wean his Leeds team off Bremner and Hunter. They had both been rocks for 14 years; the two players Revie relied on most. Bremner played his last match for Leeds on 18 September in a brisk 2-2 draw against Newcastle, and moved to Hull City. His international career had ended in September 1975, following a fracas at a Copenhagen nightclub after Scotland's 1-0 win over Denmark in the European Championships. A life ban imposed by the Scottish FA on Bremner and four others was later rescinded, but the Leeds captain, who had won 54 caps and whose leadership helped make Scotland a force in Europe, was never picked for his country again.

Hunter's last appearance

Norman Hunter's final appearance for Leeds came three weeks later in a 3-1 win at West Ham. The holder of 28 England caps, the last gained in 1975, Hunter moved to Bristol City, where he played more than 100 games and became a folk hero. Forever the hearty and often fearsome player, Hunter was the last man to play the role of indolent ageing star, jogging about the pitch and picking up his money. Like Allan Clarke, he finished his playing days at Barnsley.

Bremner and Hunter had each played more than 700 matches for Leeds; their like would not

■ A rising star: Norman Hunter gifts were indisputable but sometimes his application did not match his talents.

■ Flamboyance
personified. Tony
Currie's cavalier skills
enlightened many Leeds
performances. For all his
inconsistency, Currie was
a great favourite among
supporters.

be seen again. By now Armfield's side was in transition and there was much juggling around to fill vacancies and gaps caused through injury. Trevor Cherry, vigorous, stern and sometimes unforgiving in the Revie tradition, moved to number four; Frank Gray's elegant versatility was exploited in various positions as Peter Hampton, a product of the youth team, was tried at left-back; and Paul Madeley spent most of the season in Norman Hunter's old position.

The disillusioned Terry Yorath was sold to Coventry for £125,000. He had been ousted by Armfield's first major signing, Tony Currie, bought from Sheffield United for £240,000. A pivotal figure the like of which had never been accommodated in any Revie team, much, sometimes too much, depended on Currie's mood. He was an abundantly gifted midfielder; few sights at Elland Road have been more enthralling than that of Currie cantering about the pitch, spraying passes in all directions and indulging in his speciality of spectacular long-range goals. But sometimes he appeared maddeningly languid; the authoritarian gang of three, Bremner, Giles and Hunter who might have chivvied him along, had gone. A hard-running game was not Currie's favoured style and when he was disinclined to play, Leeds looked pedestrian.

1976–77 League lows

They showed no consistency in the league, finishing 10th, the lowest since returning to the first division 12 seasons earlier. Most of the excitement in 1976–77 came in the FA Cup: Leeds now performed better in one-off encounters. In the third round, they had swept Norwich aside, scoring five in the first half en route to a 5-2 victory. A fourth round 2-1 victory at Birmingham coaxed a virtuoso performance from Frank Gray that suggested he favoured the big occasion over the bread-and-butter diet of a league season.

As at St Andrews, there was an electrifying atmosphere at Elland Road for the fifth round meeting with Manchester City. Few, if any, matches in the Armfield era generated more intensity and passion. It was settled by Trevor Cherry three minutes from time: a slightly stumbling run, then a half-hit shot past Joe Corrigan triggered delirious celebrations among most of the 47,731 crowd. The sixth round match at Wolverhampton was of a different complexion, Leeds stealing it through a headed goal from Eddie Gray in the first half and successfully shutting out Wolves thereafter.

But in the semi-final against Manchester United at Hillsborough, Armfield's team came apart at the seams. A mix-up over ticket distribution at Leeds, which resulted in Manchester having overwhelmingly more support, was a bad omen. Before Leeds had a chance to pick up the pace of the game, the Reds had twice sliced them open, Jimmy Greenhoff and Steve Coppell scoring in the first ten minutes. Although Leeds scored through an Allan Clarke penalty, Manchester's opening salvo had blown away hopes of a trip to Wembley.

The season finished in muted anti-climax. But even before defeat at Hillsborough, there were signs that supporters were deserting. Only 18,700 watched the 3-2 home win over Norwich on 23 March 1977, the lowest gate for a league match at Elland Road since the club's return to the first division in 1964. The team had able individuals, but the old Leeds will to fight their corner and rough up those who stood in their way had gone.

The Battle of the Roses

The Football Association Challenge Cup Semi-Final at Hillsborough, Sheffield on Saturday, April 23rd 1977. Kick-off 3pm
LEEDS UNITED v MANCHESTER UNITED
OFFICIAL MATCH MAGAZINE 25p

■ Caught on the hop: Leeds never fully recovered from Manchester United's scorching start in the 1977 FA Cup semi-final.

1977–78 An indifferent season

For all his experience and ability, Armfield, unlike Revie, was never driven by insatiable ambition. 'Jimmy knew the game, but I always got the impression that he never enjoyed the job,' says Eddie Gray. 'You see a lot of managers and they all enthuse all the time. They love it, but I don't think Jimmy did. I don't think he liked laying down the law; and at football clubs people need upsetting. The hassle is part and parcel of the job. When players grumbled about being left out, I think he just let it go over him.'

Injuries to Allan Clarke had blunted the attack, which scored only 48 league goals. Two newcomers enlivened things in 1977–78: outside-left Arthur Graham, signed from Aberdeen for

> 'Jimmy knew the game, but I always got the impression that he never enjoyed the job'
>
> *Eddie Gray*

■ Battering ram: Ray Hankin's physical style created mayhem in many defences. He is congratulated after scoring by Byron Stevenson and Gordon McQueen.

£125,000 and centre-forward Ray Hankin, who cost £170,000 from Burnley. In November, Hankin's former teammate Brian Flynn, a diminutive midfielder who played in an energetic scurrying manner redolent of Billy Bremner, also joined Leeds for a fee of £175,000.

All had their moments. Graham, a Scottish international, was a darting direct winger, hard to shrug off the ball and able to throw defences either by beating men on the outside and whipping in crosses from the by-line, or by cutting inside then shooting on sight. He supplied plentiful ammunition for Hankin who, although sometimes relying more on brute force than finesse, caused plenty of turbulence in the opposition penalty area and scored 20 goals in 33 league matches.

As the season unfolded, Hankin replaced Joe Jordan, who had become increasingly restless. 'Leeds had an offer for me from Bayern Munich after the European Cup Final and I wanted to go,' says Jordan. 'After that team was broken up, I thought that was it. I wanted to play in Europe – nothing against Leeds. But they wouldn't let me and I was annoyed at that. I was a bit disillusioned, as a lot of people were. I wanted to try and win things and I really didn't think we were going to do that.'

Jordan and McQueen depart

In January 1978, Jordan's wish to go was granted. He joined Manchester United for £350,000 en route to achieving his dream of playing abroad with AC Milan. But although he had long been unsettled, Jordan respected Armfield's achievements. 'He came in at a most delicate time, replacing Don Revie who had been more than a manager. It was a thankless task. There was a lot to be steadied. I think he did quite well with the difficulties and problems facing him. After Brian Clough had been and gone, a lot of managers might not have even taken that chair. There had to be a lull.'

Gordon McQueen, Jordan's closest friend at the club, was also discontented. His last match for Leeds was on 7 January 1978 in a shambles of a third round FA Cup tie against Manchester City. McQueen's dispiriting scuffle with David Harvey, evidence of a deep malaise, was overshadowed by mob violence triggered midway through the second half when a rogue fan attacked City goalkeeper Joe Corrigan just as his team had gone 2-0 up. Play was halted for 15 minutes as mounted police restored order. Leeds lost the match 2-1, the right to play FA Cup matches at home the following season, and Gor-

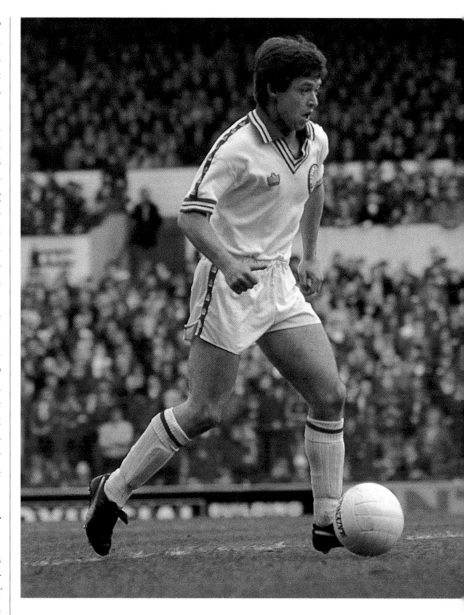

don McQueen who followed Joe Jordan to Old Trafford, transferred for a club record £450,000.

The sale of Jordan and McQueen was an emotive issue. The fact that both players had defected to Leeds' bitter rivals was, by some fans, considered treachery; that they should have been transferred at all seemed as if the club was telling the world that it had resigned from the elite and would settle for second best.

Supporters' hopes of glory lasted for another six weeks, until Nottingham Forest knocked Leeds out of the League Cup semi-final. Forest ripped them apart at Elland Road, winning 3-1 and, for good measure, beat them 4-2 at the City Ground. For Jimmy Armfield, it was the beginning of the end. Though Leeds finished the season in ninth position in the league, the fans and directors demanded more than just a respectable position. In the summer Armfield was dismissed, a victim not so much of failure, more of partial success, and perhaps his own benign leadership.

■ The latest in a succession of Leeds United midfield dynamos, Brian Flynn's direct rushing style complemented Tony Currie's more graceful game.

1978–79 The arrival of Adamson

As Armfield's successor, Jock Stein appeared to be the ideal appointment: a legendary figure who had achieved fabulous success with Celtic; forever associated with the Glasgow club's finest hour when, in 1967, they became the first British club to win the European Cup. Stein was charismatic and a great tactician; and dismayed to have been pushed aside at Parkhead in favour of Billy McNeill.

It was hard to imagine a more popular appointment, though how Stein might have rebuilt the team can only be guessed at, for after 44 days he walked out on Leeds United to become Scotland team manager. With hindsight there had been signs that his true ambitions lay elsewhere. 'I don't really know what Jock came for,' says Eddie Gray. 'I think in the end it may have been to force the SFA into a corner. He had no intention of moving here – his family stayed up in Scotland and he stayed in a hotel. We never really got to know him. I always got the feeling that coming here was just a stop-gap and that he was waiting for the phone call from Scotland.'

Maurice Lindley once more became caretaker manager until, in October 1978, the Leeds board persuaded Jimmy Adamson to move from Sunderland. Although lacking Stein's credentials, Adamson was viewed as a sound choice. He spent all his playing career at Burnley, was Footballer of the Year in 1962, and considered unlucky never to have received a full England cap. He had also managed Burnley, but became frustrated at being forced to sell promising young players so that the club could survive. In 1976–77, when taking over at Sunderland, Adamson had almost managed to stave off relegation when in mid-season the team appeared certain to drop to the second division.

At Leeds his first task was to re-establish stability; the team he inherited had won only three of its first ten league matches. Two of the great names of the Revie era had departed: Paul Reaney, who made over 700 appearances for Leeds, went to Bradford City, and Allan Clarke transferred to Barnsley as player manager.

Reaney, although only rewarded with three full international caps, had been one of England's great defenders. To be marked by the speedy Leeds defender was to be shut out of the game: he was probably the defender that George Best most dreaded playing against. As a last-line of defence Reaney was superb, with theatrical goal-line clearances his speciality.

Without the vigorous support of Mick Jones and Joe Jordan, Allan Clarke was less effective in the latter part of his career which had been interrupted by injury, but at his best there had been no more complete striker. Rarely had someone who had broken the British transfer record – £165,000 in summer 1969 – proved himself cheap at the price so quickly.

Before he left, Jimmy Armfield's last two major buys had been centre-half Paul Hart, signed from Blackpool for £330,000 in March and, in the close season, John Hawley, from Hull City for £80,000. By the time Adamson took over, Hart had found his feet, imposing his rugged presence after some traumatic early games which were marked by a mini-epidemic of own-goals or gifting the opposition penalty kicks. Hawley, of whom many supporters had only modest expectations, was a revelation, an unfancy swift-running centre-forward with a clear eye for goal.

■ The task of reviving Leeds United's fortunes defeated Jimmy Adamson who was driven out by a hostile crowd following a run of poor results.

■ Despite early mishaps, Paul Hart became a commanding figure in the Leeds defence, a committed player in a declining team.

Leeds recover

In late October came signs of a Leeds recovery. A 2-2 draw at Norwich marked the start of a splendid run in which Adamson's team lost only twice in 23 league matches. On 4 November Leeds travelled to Liverpool, startling Bob Paisley's team with a performance of fluid conviction, and gaining a 1-1 draw, only to see victory wrested from them by a late penalty. Liverpool were eventually runaway champions with a record points total of 68.

By mid-season, Leeds were serving up superlative entertainment. Their FA Cup fourth round tie against West Bromwich Albion, who also were in resplendent form, was a feast, a 3-3 draw all the more satisfying as Leeds, orchestrated by Tony Currie, came back from 3-1 down. Yet an extended FA Cup run was always against the odds with Leeds having been made to forfeit home advantage by the FA. They succumbed in the replay, losing 2-0 after extra time.

By then, interest in the League Cup had ended. Yet a Wembley appearance had been on

■ Injuries and loss of form thwarted defender Brian Greenhoff's career following his move from Manchester United.

The close season had another shock in store for Leeds fans. Tony Currie, who had become unsettled for personal reasons, was transferred to Queen's Park Rangers for £400,000. Few, if any, in the English game could match his flamboyant skills. How he might be replaced was unclear.

1979–80 New faces appear

Adamson began importing new faces. In March 1979 he had bought defender-cum-midfielder Kevin Hird from Blackburn Rovers for £354,000. Though Hird's dedication was unquestionable, his performances were erratic and sometimes undermined by a lack of self-belief. During the close season Adamson paid £400,000 for Alan Curtis, the stylish Swansea City striker in whom several clubs had been interested. The ranks were further swollen by Manchester United defender Brian Greenhoff (brother of Jimmy) for £350,000; Gary Hamson, a combative midfielder from Sheffield United (£140,000), centre-forward Wayne Entwistle (£80,000) and midfielder/winger Jeff Chandler from Blackpool (£100,000).

It was hard to imagine them gelling or to fathom Adamson's strategy. The scheme was sabotaged by injuries; of the outfield players, only Hird, Hart, Cherry and Eddie Gray managed 30 or more league appearances. The team suffered humiliating exits from all the cup competitions: a 7-0 thrashing at Arsenal in a second round League Cup tie; a 4-0 aggregate defeat at the hands of Universitatea Craiova in round two of the UEFA Cup; another drubbing from Nottingham Forest, 4-1 winners at Elland Road in round three of the FA Cup.

'It was a strange period for the club, with a lot of people coming and going – decent players, but not of the highest level,' Eddie Gray recalls. 'Jimmy Adamson very rarely came on to the training park; Dave Merrington, his assistant did it all. When Jimmy was talking to us on Saturday, at times I got the impression he never really knew what had been going on in the week; watching players and knowing how they react to situations. Even if somebody else is taking them, you've got to be there, to see if players are taking it on board. He was a lovely man, but I think that was a fault. He was so laid back, it made him appear as if he wasn't interested. But he was – he wanted things to go well.'

By mid-autumn, the Leeds supporters were mutinous and staged vehement post-match demonstrations against Adamson after successive

the cards when, in the home leg of the semi-finals, Adamson's men raced into a 2-0 half-time lead against Southampton. But they were no longer sufficiently forceful or wily to hang on when it mattered. For all Leeds' skills, the word formidable, used so often of them in the Revie era, no longer applied. Southampton equalised and won through to the final with an early goal at the Dell.

Despite finishing fifth and qualifying for Europe, defeats by Nottingham Forest and Liverpool in the last two home games were cause for unease. Liverpool's 3-0 victory was embarrassingly comprehensive and, as a result, they amassed their 68th point. It eclipsed Leeds' record of 67 which, depite being treasured by the fans, Adamson's men had surrendered meekly.

home defeats by Tottenham and Bristol City. Goals were scarce – Adamson had sold John Hawley to Sunderland for £200,000 – and performances drab. Yet the season was briefly and unexpectedly rejuvenated in one of its darkest hours. As Leeds, watched by a meagre crowd of 17,481, were toiling against West Bromwich at Elland Road on November 17, Adamson unleashed Terry Connor, a 17-year-old coloured centre-forward for his first game. Substituting for the injured Paul Madeley, Connor became the scourge of West Bromwich's defence, and seven minutes from time bundled home Kevin Hird's centre to give Leeds their second victory in only six league matches.

It was a rapid and startling propulsion to fame for the young striker. 'I'd come out of school aged 16 and was trying to learn an apprenticeship,' Connor recalls. 'I was just beginning to cope with morning and afternoon training and all the odd jobs we had to do when I was called into the first team. I was petrified. There I was, running alongside Madeley and Gray. I had watched them from the terraces. To my mind, they were idols.'

Almost overnight, Connor found himself the target of high hopes. The six goals he scored in his first 11 matches made waves well beyond Leeds. Yet the week before his debut, Adamson's management had been condemned by Johnny Giles, now managing the Republic of Ireland. Writing in the *Irish Sunday Independent*, Giles declared, 'Adamson was the wrong appointment from the start...notoriously indecisive in regard to team selection, and then getting rid of players not because it was the right thing for the club, but rather because it seemed to offer him a quiet life.'

The mood had changed entirely; the *Sunday Express* was at its most fulsome after Connor's display in Leeds' 3-0 home win over Wolves on December 15. 'A determined teenager with a voracious appetite for goals yesterday sent Leeds marching purposefully out of their long tun-

nel of despair and mediocrity,' it said. 'Terry Connor, big, strong and just 17, again emphasised his rich potential with a mature performance liberally laced with purpose and skill...and completely overshadowed his costly counterpart, Wolves' £1,500,000 Andy Gray.'

However, as Connor, recalls, life could not always remain so sweet. "Nobody knew me...I was quicker than they thought. But then the hard part began. You have to add more to your game. That's possibly when I should have come out of the side, learned a bit more about the game and then come back in. But there wasn't the money to go out and buy a finished centre-forward to give me a breather. I had to play. I couldn't get on a learning curve. I did find things hard, and struggled.'

Lukic replaces Harvey

Few young players breaking into the Leeds team showed the quality that marked them out for a future at the top. An exception was goalkeeper John Lukic, who replaced David Harvey, and for whom the first of a run of 146 consecutive appearances began two days before his 19th birthday in Leeds' 0-0 draw at Brighton on 13 October. Lukic, 6ft 4in, soon cut a reassuring figure, dominating his territory and showing remarkable composure for one so young.

As Connor's goals began to peter out, Adamson cast around for striking reinforcements. In March 1980, he signed Derek Parlane from

■ Below: Leeds men past and present: Derek Parlane comes away with the ball with Gordon McQueen, now wearing Manchester United colours in close attendance.

> **'I was just beginning to cope...when I was called into the first team.'**
>
> *Terry Connor*

Rangers, who had scored 80 goals in 200 games for the Glasgow club. But Parlane rarely got going at Elland Road except in Leeds' final home game of the season, a 2–0 victory over Manchester United, when he produced a stirring performance as if galvanised by the crowd's yearning to see the Lancashire club denied the league championship.

Adamson could have wished for no better finale after a tough season, but although the victory helped sustain morale through the summer break, it could not mask the side's deficiencies. Seeking to restore flair in midfield, Adamson made a bold move into the transfer market – buying the Argentinian Alex Sabella from Sheffield United. Sabella was a dashing footballer with excellent close control and awareness, but at Leeds, he would have little chance to show what he could do.

The reprieve that Connor's early burst of form gave Adamson was short-lived. In 1980–81, Leeds made another feeble start to their league campaign, losing six of their first seven matches. Much reviled, Adamson resigned as manager in September. Trying to rebuild a club where expectations exceeded resources had been a traumatic experience – finishing 11th the previous season, Leeds average home gate had been only 22,992. It was Adamson's final job in football management.

His plight touched Terry Connor, who recalls Adamson's good nature. 'He was a thoroughly nice fellow...I never heard him shout. Sometimes he used to give me a lift home even though I wanted to catch the bus...I didn't really want to be seen in the manager's car. Then he'd talk about the game. Dave Merrington was the one who used to scream and shout at the players; and try to bully them to do the right thing. If Jimmy Adamson could have added that to his personality and not wait for someone else to tell you, he would have gained the players' respect more.'

1980–81 Clarke back at Elland Road

Maurice Lindley undertook another brief spell as caretaker manager before the Leeds board appointed Allan Clarke. With a secure place in Leeds United's history as scorer of the goal that won the FA Cup in 1972, Clarke was bound to be popular with the fans at the outset, despite concerns about his inexperience. But he had guided Barnsley from the third to the second division and arrived at Leeds full of ambition, vowing that within three years he would bring a major trophy to the club. He brought from Barnsley his assistant Martin Wilkinson and Barry Murphy as coach. Dave Merrington had departed with Adamson.

Clarke the player had been full of incisive attacking flair, the scorer of 151 goals for Leeds. But Clarke the manager decided that if his team were to survive in the first division, defence – albeit at the expense of entertainment – was essential. Following a shambolic 5-0 home defeat by Arsenal on 8 November, he switched Eddie Gray to left-back. It was an inspired move; Gray no longer had great pace, but his positional sense and vision was a key to the defence becoming much meaner: only 19 goals conceded in the remaining 26 league matches.

■ Opposite: Managerial upheavals meant that Argentinian midfielder Alex Sabella had little chance to prove himself though he impressed team-mates with his skills and dedication.

■ The outlook is grim. Allan Clarke, tight-lipped and looking drawn, watches from the dug out as his players toil for goals and points.

Fading memories of Leeds United's great past. Paul Madeley, seen here in an aerial duel with Alan Sunderland, was soon to retire. The team around him had begun to fall apart.

'I thought Alex was brilliant... as good as any player, but didn't hit it off with the staff'

Eddie Gray

For Paul Madeley, another veteran of more than 700 matches, who had served Leeds with distinction in every outfield position, the fiasco against Arsenal was a sorry finale. Shortly afterwards he announced his retirement. Grace, style and intelligence were the hallmarks of Madeley's game, though latterly he seemed uncomfortable during the club's upheavals on and off the field.

With Trevor Cherry still going strong, and Hart and Greenhoff free of injury, Clarke established the defensive stability that eluded Jimmy Adamson who, in August, had sold Peter Hampton to Stoke City for £175,000. Clarke slowly began to do his own deals, an early one of which was selling Alan Curtis back to Swansea City for £165,000. Leeds had enjoyed few glimpses of Curtis at his best: he had recovered from injury, but not in time to find favour with Allan Clarke.

Nor was Alex Sabella to figure in Clarke's plans. The following season he returned to Argentina. 'I thought Alex was brilliant – he could have been as good as any player, but didn't seem to hit it off with the staff,' says Eddie Gray. 'He had a good temperament and was popular; he knew about the game and at one time had a good spell. But he never did what he should have done at Leeds. Perhaps he was in the wrong place at the wrong time.'

Clarke could ill-afford to squander players who had flair, for even though the defence was sound, the team managed only 39 league goals all season. Watching Leeds claw up the table into ninth place was a grim spectacle; crowds were commonly below 20,000 and the only player to manage double figures was the Welsh international winger Carl Harris, who scored ten goals.

Harris had signed for Leeds as a 17-year-old in 1973, making his debut in 1975 but only breaking into the first team squad as a regular in 1978/79 after Peter Lorimer had left for Toronto Blizzard. A player of moods, Harris, who won 24 caps for Wales, could cause havoc when at his best with speedy runs on goal, but sometimes appeared not to be on the same wavelength as those around him.

1981–82 Relegation looms

During the close season, Allan Clarke gambled with Leeds United's limited finances, investing £930,000 in the England and West Bromwich winger Peter Barnes. For all Barnes' enthralling talents, it was an expensive misjudgement. Barnes had the skill to win matches but was a peripheral player who sought the luxury of having balls delivered to him. Leeds still remained deficient in midfield and there was little money left to do anything about it.

Clarke had bought back Frank Gray, whom Jimmy Adamson had sold to Nottingham Forest two seasons earlier for £500,000 and where he had won a European Cup medal. Gray's brief interlude away from Elland Road brought him more success than at any time in his career, yet he had never sought to leave Leeds and was happy to return. Clarke deployed Gray at left-back – wastefully so, in the view of brother Eddie. 'I think it was easier for Frank to play there...he should have pushed himself...been harder on himself. I found it ridiculously easy to play at left-back compared with the middle of the field.'

In their first game of 1981–82, Leeds were mauled by newly-promoted Swansea City, losing 5-1 at the Vetch Field on a sweltering August day. Among Swansea's chief tormentors was Alan Curtis, his old form rediscovered. The result appeared to make Leeds fall apart. By mid-October they were relegation candidates with only one win from ten games. The attack managed only seven goals and the defence, disrupted by injury, had gone to pieces, conceding 21.

There seemed to be a lack of heart. The combative Gary Hamson was frequently absent, sometimes through suspension – he had been banned for a record nine matches in 1981 – but more often through injuries, which were to continue to blight his career. While the next nine league matches brought some improvement – Leeds won five, drew two and lost only two, an abysmal run from 30 January to 13 March saw them fail to score as they lost six and drew one of the next seven matches.

Clarke's forays into the transfer market smacked of desperation. By March, he had recruited Kenny Burns from Nottingham Forest to stiffen the central defence and midfield, and Frank Worthington from Birmingham to score goals. Worthington, exchanged for Welsh international Byron Stevenson who had filled various defensive and midfield positions in seven seasons at Leeds, was a wizard, combining cheek and technique to make fools of defenders. But at 33, he was past his best and tended to ration his performances. Leeds needed more than his occasional flourishes of footballing wit.

A lack of fighting spirit

A glance at the league table showed that Leeds were in danger of losing their 18-year

■ Carl Harris' sharp raids down the flanks and powerful shooting were rare highlights as Allan Clarke's team became enmeshed in a dour battle against relegation.

■ Opposite: As a striker and central defender, Kenny Burns had excelled earlier in his career but when he joined Leeds from Nottingham Forest, his best days were behind him.

■ Below: A vital young player of whom too much was expected: Terry Connor made a dazzling impact in his early games but then lost form and confidence.

membership of the first division. But, as Eddie Gray recalls, a few of his team-mates seemed oblivious. 'I remember having conversations and them saying "We're too good to go down". I would say, "Hold on a minute. You're not too good to go down. It happened to Man United." Some players didn't care enough about getting beaten. There was a different type of attitude to the one the club had before. Then there was a meaner streak; they wouldn't lie down – they'd fight and scrap for everything.'

Terry Connor agrees. 'I really did feel that Frank Worthington and Kenny Burns didn't offer anything to the cause. And with Frank Gray, I felt he was only playing half-cock. The number of occasions you would see him and think, "Come on, Frank". He could do it but I felt that he didn't have that hunger to play.'

There was no lack of effort on Clarke's part. 'Allan worked tremendously hard on the training park. But he could have done with one or two people around him who really knew the game,' says Eddie Gray. Terry Connor became increas-ingly dispirited with training. 'We used to do the same things then just go and play,' he says. 'It needed someone to come and sort a few things out, but Martin Wilkinson was less experienced than Allan Clarke, so the manager couldn't go to his assistant. The same old things in training became the same old things on the pitch... losing. Allan became more and more withdrawn, and possibly let too many senior players have too much of a say. He'd say one thing, but you'd get the feeling they weren't pulling in that direction.'

Leeds go down

In their penultimate match of the season, Leeds recovered a goal deficit to beat Brighton with late goals from Hamson and Hird. After their fraught afternoon, Leeds supporters celebrated their teams victory as maniacally as if the league championship had been won, and travelled in force for their crucial last match at West Bromwich Albion three days later. A win would ensure Leeds' survival in the first division. Defeat meant almost certain relegation to the second division.

And defeat there was, amid scenes as ugly as any ever contrived by Leeds' hard core of trucu-lent support. Second-half goals from Cyrille Regis and Steve MacKenzie effectively con-signed Clarke's team, which had played with muddled anxiety rather than passion, to the sec-ond division. At full-time the seething phalanx of Leeds supporters penned in the Smethwick End attempted to invade the pitch and it took a police baton charge to drive them back. They wreaked destruction outside the ground instead, terroris-ing the neighbourhood.

For Terry Connor, who had lost much of the confidence he had displayed when he broke into the first team, defeat was unbearable. 'I was cry-ing, bawling,' he recalls. 'I took it as a personal thing...that I wasn't good enough to play...that I'd let the club, the city and all my mates down. But towards the end, we just didn't have enough to stay up. By then, Allan Clarke really did look ill for a guy who had waltzed into the club and said 'I'm going to change things round'. To look at him, you'd think, 'There's no way he's going to be able to carry on like this.''

A draw two nights later at the Victoria Ground between Stoke City and West Bromwich Albion, both of whom had also been involved in the relegation dogfight, confirmed Leeds' relegation to the second division. The trophies and glory of Revie's tenure seemed a lifetime ago. A great era had come to an end with a dis-heartening struggle and shameful scenes.

The Second Division Years

1982–83
Eddie Gray takes over the hot seat

It was also the end for Allan Clarke and Martin Wilkinson, both of whom were sacked in the summer. Eddie Gray, who had shown a sure touch in guiding young players, was appointed player/manager for 1982–83. He brought in as assistant an old friend from his schooldays and former reserve team player Jimmy Lumsden, who had been on the staff at Celtic. Gray also persuaded Syd Owen to return as chief scout.

There was a belief among some fans that Leeds would bounce straight back into the first division as if by divine right. But such conviction was misguided: relegation had not been the result of an isolated season's misfortune but of steady decline: no coherent strategy, too many ill assorted players, a shortage of home-produced talent and supporters deserting in their thousands. The club had enormous debts, reputedly running to more than £1 million. Gray was appointed, in the words of former chief executive Peter Nash, 'as a cheap but hopeful option'.

It meant no money for big transfers. Players would have to be bought cheaply, swapped and borrowed. With Gary Hamson injured long-term, Gray had tried mid-season to stiffen the midfield with the energetic Neil McNab. 'He came on loan, but we couldn't afford to sign him. We didn't have any money to pay wages,' Gray recalls. Leeds' loss was Manchester City's gain: McNab proved an excellent servant at Maine Road during the mid-1980s.

The second division was a tougher school than anticipated. Yet Leeds started brightly, winning six and losing only one of the first twelve league matches. Worthington was scoring regularly alongside a new striking partner, Aidan Butterworth. Butterworth was a locally-produced young player whose direct style was similar to that of Terry Connor. But after winning only one league match throughout November and December, it became clear that Gray's team would not escape easily.

The violent mob that had attached itself to the club did not help matters. There had been trouble at Grimsby on the opening day, at Chelsea on 9 October and at Elland Road three weeks later when, during Leeds' 3-1 win over Newcastle, Kevin Keegan was struck by a ball-bearing hurled from the terraces. An editorial on the programme cover for the next home match against Charlton warned: 'The future of Leeds

United...hangs in the balance...the mindless actions of a minority of the club's so-called supporters have placed an enormous degree of uncertainty over this great club.'

The FA ordered closure of the Kop for two matches. Gates for the home matches against Queen's Park Rangers and Shrewsbury were depressed to 11,528 and 8,741; but the hooligans carried on, most notoriously during the 3-3 draw at Derby on 22 Jan 1983, after Leeds had lost a 3-1 lead. A month later, with the team still conceding goals and losing points, Gray dropped John Lukic in favour of a comfortingly familiar face, David Harvey, returned from Vancouver Whitecaps. In time Lukic too would return, but Gray was able to profit from the younger goal-keeper's discontent by selling him to Arsenal for £125,000 in the close season.

Terry Connor was a Leeds man to the core, yet Gray felt he was a marketable commodity and in March 1983 exchanged him for Brighton's centre-forward Andy Ritchie. It proved a good piece of business but caused Connor a great deal of anguish. 'It was made clear to me that if I didn't play for Brighton, I wouldn't play for Leeds,' Connor says. 'Eddie thought Aidan Butterworth and I were too similar...we both wanted to chase the ball into channels... and run through a lot of things. My game was power and pace but he wanted someone of Andy Ritchie's quality who could lay the ball off and be happy doing that. It hurt me an awful lot...

■ Andy Ritchie, traded for Terry Connor, had all the attributes of a top class striker, but sometimes lacked aggression.

125

■ A fine sight when on the ball, John Sheridan matured rapidly and became a pivotal figure. Many considered him the best midfield player in the second division.

'I suppose it could be taken as a sad reflection of the game, having to recall a man who has been abroad for three years…'

Peter Lorimer

■ Opposite, top: The slightly-built Scott Sellars was another Gray protege blessed with the ability to strike superb passes.

■ Opposite, bottom: A tall yet mobile defender, Andy Linighan, like many of Gray's youngsters, moved on to better things, though was perhaps too diffident to make the most of his ability.

yet I think it was the making of me as a person.'

Gray could be satisfied with some astute deals and, having guided Leeds to eighth place, with stopping the rot. Moreover the club had made some money from a protracted fourth round FA Cup tie against Arsenal which ran to three matches, with Leeds coming to within seconds of winning in the first replay at Elland Road.

As with Don Revie 20 years earlier, circumstances compelled Gray to gamble on junior players. One, 18-year-old midfielder, John Sheridan, showed sufficient promise to keep Brian Flynn out of the side and cause his move to Burnley the following season. However, the close season departure to Nottingham Forest of Paul Hart, who was impatient to resume a first division career, deprived Leeds of an authoritative defender and a key figure around whom a promotion team might have been built.

1983–84 Home gates slump

Leeds' frailty became apparent in the opening weeks of 1983–84 wherein they lost six and won only two of their first nine matches. The 5-1 defeat at Shrewsbury in balmy weather on 1 October was faintly surreal, with Leeds fallen

giants, who ten years earlier had taken English football to rare heights, now stumbling around as if befuddled by their pastoral surroundings. There was more to follow: a 4-1 drubbing in the replayed third round League Cup tie at Oxford United; ignominious defeat at Scunthorpe, 4–2, in the FA Cup third round second replay.

Yet if the flurry of imports bought to stiffen the defence and midfield made little impact, the core of young players brought on by Gray in the second half of the season were a source of hope. They had as mentor 37-year-old Peter Lorimer who, after spells in Toronto and Vancouver, had returned at Eddie Gray's request to provide cover in midfield. Of his move, Lorimer said at the time, 'I suppose it could be taken as a sad reflection of the game, having to recall a man who has been abroad for three years, but most successful teams have one or two old pros. My role is now to help settle down the pace of the game and control players who want to rush in here, there and everywhere.'

Leeds finished tenth, never contenders for promotion, and the poorer for having lost John Sheridan with a broken leg in the 2-0 win at Barnsley on 22 October. 1983–84 was the last season Peter Barnes, Kenny Burns and Kevin Hird would appear for Leeds. Gray had seen enough from his younger players to persevere with them. And it was on these young players that the responsibility of luring back the Leeds public fell: home gates had dipped to below 10,000 for less appealing opposition.

1984–85 Promotion hopes slip away

The core team for 1984–85 included 18-year-old Irishman Denis Irwin at right-back; 22-year-old centre-half Andy Linighan who had cost £20,000 from Hartlepool; 19-year-old defender Neil Aspin, midfielders John Sheridan and 18-year-old Scott Sellars, and 18-year-old striker Tommy Wright. They were bound together by older hands such as David Harvey, Frank Gray, Peter Lorimer – the latter having made his debut for Leeds before most of the youngsters were born – Andy Ritchie and, now playing left-back, Gary Hamson.

It was an intriguing blend. Playing sweet football, Leeds won their first four matches, but skill and delicacy alone could not sustain their winning run. The next three league games were lost; although frequently the most stylish team in the division, Leeds were all too easily knocked out of their stride. This vulnerability was wickedly exposed in November by Oxford United, who snatched away Leeds' early 2-0 lead as if it were some flimsy veil and retorted with five goals. It was the performance of champions against also-rans.

The afternoon was blighted once again by hooliganism: the Leeds mob, enraged by so swift an about turn, began demolishing a TV gantry in the Cuckoo Lane End, hurling down lances of wood and metal on to the pitch. It was the harbinger of worse to come, for an excellent late-season run left Gray's team with a slender chance of gaining promotion on the last day of the season.

Leeds travelled to Birmingham City, who already had been promoted, followed by hordes of supporters determined to make their mark. They were hemmed into a ludicrously small section of the Tilton Road End and trouble brewed before the game kicked-off. When Martin Kuhl scored for Birmingham in the first half, it was the signal for a riot and pitch invasion that took police more than half an hour to quell. The game thereafter was abnormally tentative; the atmosphere eerily subdued.

At full-time as the Leeds mob piled out, a supporting wall collapsed beneath their weight, killing a teenage boy. Meanwhile what should have been a day of celebration at Bradford City

became instead one of the worst disasters of modern times, as fire swept through the main stand at Valley Parade killing 56 people. 11 May 1985 marked the most wretched end of a football season in the game's history.

1985–86 Bremner's team

Eddie Gray had deserved better. His was a well-mannered team, although he gave it a more abrasive edge by signing centre-forward Ian Baird from Southampton for £50,000 towards the end of the season. Baird's goals had helped push Leeds to the threshold of promotion before the ill-fated trip to Birmingham.

The young players had done him proud. Irwin was a tidy, unflappable footballer who rarely betrayed his inexperience. Aspin, although less accomplished, had great determination and would chase any cause. Linighan was an undemonstrative centre-half, good in the air, with a neat touch for one so tall. Sheridan, so quick to learn, showed the awareness and passing skills of a top midfielder. Sellars, who also had a wonderful touch, was less assertive and, though stronger than his slight appearance suggested, was played on the left flank for his own protection. Tommy Wright was a small, sharp striker with great acceleration, adept at outwitting advancing goalkeepers.

History would show this to be an impressive roll call of talent. Eddie Gray had sufficient confidence in his squad to sell brother Frank to Sunderland for £100,000. But the Leeds manager, and much of his side, was soon to be swept away. After a poor start to the 1985–86 campaign, most of the directors lost patience and in October, Gray was sacked along with Jimmy Lumsden. The fans, and several players, were outraged as was one board member: Brian Woodward, son of former chairman Percy, resigned in protest.

During the home game against Middlesborough, supporters called for the head of chairman Leslie Silver. But Silver and his colleagues were quick to mollify fans by appointing Billy Bremner as Gray's successor. Although Bremner's managerial achievements with Doncaster Rovers had been modest, there was, in the eyes of Leeds fans, no greater playing hero.

Bremner's method of reconstruction was to pack the side with journeyman professionals, many of whom served the side well. Money was still tight: average attendances had slumped to 15,000 from a high of 39,472 in 1970–71. At the end of 1985–86, the figure dipped to 13,265 – the second lowest in the club's history and only fractionally more than in 1922–23. To put the club on a sounder financial footing, Leeds United sold the Elland Road ground to the city council for £2.5 million in return for a 125-year lease.

Lorimer and Harvey leave

With Bremner's arrival, Peter Lorimer's time was up. He and David Harvey, whom Eddie Gray had replaced in goal with Mervyn Day the previous season, had had extraordinary two-part careers at Elland Road: as young men making their way to the top and then as paternal guiding hands. They had been great servants.

■ Passionate player; passionate manager. Billy Bremner roars on his team. During his reign, Leeds began to rediscover self-belief and the crowds started to return.

Gray's final, most lavish deal, was to sign the England under-21 midfielder Ian Snodin for £200,000 from Bremner's old club Doncaster Rovers. Although a fourth division player, Snodin's combination of aggression and technical ability had aroused much interest among big clubs. Bremner made Snodin captain, but the following season, under pressure from the club's directors, sold him to Everton for £800,000. It was the highest price Leeds had received for any player. Once viewed as a potential England captain, a string of injuries were to arrest the development of Snodin's career at the Merseyside club.

With the team in a state of flux, performances suffered. Bremner was disinclined to persevere with Gray's protégés. Linighan (for £55,000) and Tommy Wright (£60,000) were sold cheaply to Oldham Athletic and eventually Irwin left on a free transfer (also to Oldham), followed by Sellars (£20,000) to Blackburn. Left-back Terry Phelan, given his debut in the 3-1 win at Shrewsbury on 7 September 1985, had shown startling pace, but after 14 games was dropped and eventually joined Swansea City on a free transfer. It seemed a grievous haemorrhaging of talent.

Brendan Ormsby, from Aston Villa, and David Rennie, from Leicester, were bought to shore up the defence. Ritchie and Baird continued to be the most effective strikers; other Bremner combinations, some enforced by injury, yielded little. It was a grim season which included a humbling FA Cup exit in the third round as Leeds lost 1-0 at fourth division Peterborough. Only after beating Millwall 3-1 at Elland Road on 12 April could Leeds feel safe from the threat of relegation. They finished 14th: Eddie Gray was entitled to believe he might have fared better with his young charges. The spectre of crowd disorder continually haunted the club even though the FA had ordered Leeds away matches to be all-ticket after the riot at Birmingham.

■ Top left: Brendan Ormsby, signed from Aston Villa, was a brave defender willing to take hard knocks, and epitomised Bremner's more forceful approach.

■ Top right: Signed from Leicester by Bremner, David Rennie played in defence and midfield. Rennie's finest moment was his headed goal against Coventry in the 1987 FA Cup semi-final, which had Leeds fans dreaming of Wembley.

■ Left: Few expected great things of Jack Ashurst but the central defender, signed from Carlisle, proved a reliable partner for Ormsby.

1986–87 FA Cup run

The first half of 1986–87 saw little evidence of improvement; there was no hint of high drama in the offing. Until January, the team played in fits and starts. Bremner had already brought in new

■ Top left: Peter Haddock was another first-rate defensive signing. Although his career was undermined by injury, he was an assured figure throughout Leeds' promotion season.

■ Top right: Keith Edwards was never the prolific scorer at Leeds he had been at Sheffield United, yet retained the knack of delivering crucial goals in key matches.

■ Right: Leeds were further toughened by the introduction of Mark Aizlewood who could play in defence or midfield. But the abrasive Welsh international was stripped of his captaincy and sold after falling foul of Howard Wilkinson.

faces: defenders Jack Ashurst from Carlisle for £35,000; Peter Haddock from Newcastle, £45,000; youth team midfielder John Stiles, son of England World Cup hero Nobby; and high-scoring Sheffield United striker Keith Edwards for £125,000, but such was the team's inconsistency, Bremner was driven to prop up the side with another clutch of recruits in the New Year.

The Leeds manager had been reluctant to sell Ian Snodin, yet felt he could build a side around John Sheridan, who had evolved into the division's best midfielder. Money from Snodin's sale paid for left-back/winger Micky Adams (£110,000 from Coventry), full-back Bobby McDonald (£25,000 from Oxford), midfielder Mark Aizlewood (£200,000 from Charlton) and centre-forward John Pearson (also from Charlton, £72,000).

Leeds' season began to stir on a freezing Sunday afternoon at West Bromwich, the venue for their third round FA Cup tie against Telford United. The oppressive police presence might have been designed to quell an invasion of Visigoths rather than manage 2,000 Leeds United fans subdued by the intense cold. Another cup embarrassment threatened as the non-league side took the lead, but two goals from Ian Baird rescued the tie.

Hillsborough, was like some old heroic legend: full of endeavour and fluctuating fortunes; a match that teased the emotions, the result of which was perpetually uncertain. Leeds led early on when David Rennie headed in a corner, but surrendered the initiative in the second half after an elementary error from Ormsby who, under

■ Holding on: centre-forward John Pearson, helping out in defence, and goalkeeper Mervyn Day struggle to contain Coventry's Brian Kilcline in the 1987 FA Cup semi-final.

In the fourth round game at Swindon, Leeds showed enough technique and composure to ease through, winning 2-1, and were much enlivened by Adams's forceful display. The club's first fifth round appearance for ten years was marked with a home tie against first division Queen's Park Rangers. It was like old times: 31,324 inside Elland Road and a potent atmosphere that flared into violence when Rangers equalised Baird's early goal. Yet Leeds' response provided a platform for the rest of the season; a stirring rally and victory snatched almost on full-time, with a goal bravely headed in at the far post by Brendan Ormsby.

The Coventry semi-final

Leeds had grown sterner; become better organised. Of the next ten league matches, they won six, drew three and lost only once. They also knocked Wigan Athletic out of the FA Cup in the sixth round and set up an FA Cup semi-final against Coventry City. While semi-finals have an ignoble tradition of being tension-ridden, spoiling and dull, this encounter, played at

pressure from Coventry winger Dave Bennett, conceded possession on the by-line. Bennett crossed: Micky Gynn scored the equaliser; Keith Houchen scored Coventry's second soon afterwards, and Leeds had to retrieve a 2-1 deficit.

It was time for Keith Edwards, whose goal touch hitherto had deserted him, to make a leading man's late entrance. On as substitute, he found unaccustomed space in the Coventry defence and headed the equaliser with five minutes of normal time remaining. During extra time, the balance of power continued to sway, but Leeds, who had poured in all their passion and energy, began to wilt and were finally undone by Dave Bennett's goal. The Leeds supporters, too, had been impassioned but orderly. A semi-final had been lost but to great acclaim. As a public relations exercise, the match was a triumph; as an opportunity for reinforcing self-belief, invaluable.

The play-offs

After their fruitful league run, Leeds finished fourth and qualified to play off for the third pro-

■ Right: A deft, nimble winger, Vince Hilaire lacked the aggression to make a great impact at Leeds after his move from Portsmouth.

■ Below: Gary Williams, another signing from Aston Villa, was a neat defender capable of overlapping and joining the attack. But his career was blighted by injury.

motion place. Edwards had emerged from hibernation with a sharp appetite for scoring decisive late goals, the scourge of Oldham Athletic in both legs of the semi-final as he destroyed the Latics' first division hopes with wicked, unanswerable last-gasp strikes.

Matches against Coventry and Queen's Park Rangers had taught Bremner's team about the first division. Charlton Athletic, their opponents in the play-off final were in the lower reaches, fighting to survive. They were obdurate opponents over both legs: 1-0 victors over Leeds at Selhurst Park, and beaten 1-0 at Elland Road by a goal from Brendan Ormsby. But for all their fervour, Leeds could not quite deliver the knock-out blow.

On 29 May, with midsummer only three weeks away, the teams met for a third time, at Birmingham. By now the contest had become laborious, grinding into extra time. Charlton were the first to crack as, in the first period, John Sheridan scored from a superb curled free kick. But the absence of Brendan Ormsby, injured earlier in the match, had weakened the Leeds defence. Charlton summoned reserves of energy to push forward and score twice in the final throes through Peter Shirtliff. For the Londoners, it was the reward for dogged determination. For Leeds, whose supporters had overwhelmingly outnumbered those of Charlton, it was a melodramatic near-miss redolent of the Revie years.

1987–88 The crowds return

The sense of revival at Elland Road survived a dour start to 1987–88: just two victories and three goals in the first nine matches. Leeds were no longer served by Andy Ritchie's elegant skills. He had been sold by Billy Bremner to Oldham Athletic – resting place for several not-so-old Leeds boys – for £50,000 in August. Keith Edwards was dropped, and eventually sold to Hull for £50,000 in March 1988, after failing to score in eight matches. With Baird injured, much of the scoring burden fell on Bob Taylor, a 19-year-old centre-forward signed from non-league Hordern Colliery Welfare. Other newcomers included Glynn Snodin, brother of Ian, who could play either at left-back or in midfield, signed from Sheffield Wednesday for £150,000, and full-back Gary Williams, a £230,000 signing from Aston Villa.

In October, Taylor started to find his form, scoring four times in five matches, but, although

Bremner had sustained the revival of support: Leeds' average crowd, 20,284, was their best since relegation.

But just as a near-miss followed by a poor start in the new season led to Eddie Gray's demise, so it did for Billy Bremner. After only one league win in the first six matches of 1988–89, Bremner was sacked. Said Leslie Silver, 'Leeds United has often been labelled a sleeping giant...and we must now find the right man to arouse that sleeping giant and take the club back to its rightful place among the elite.' Another era had come to an end – that of the Revie old boys striving to emulate their mentor's achievements. Enter the outsider.

■ Left: Strong, resourceful and with an excellent eye for goal: Bobby Davison, often underrated, was a vibrant presence at centre-forward.

■ Below: David Batty's juvenile appearance was deceptive: he never flinched from taking on the hard men.

Bremner was to find him support when he bought the Derby centre-forward Bobby Davison for £350,000, the Leeds attack struggled for goals. Sheridan was to be top scorer, yet seven out of his 12 goals were penalties.

Leeds' most fruitful run came in December and with it the recurring belief that they might be on the verge of great things. Their run of six successive victories, played before ever-increasing crowds, coincided with the arrival of 18-year-old midfielder David Batty, whose snappy, hard-tackling game belied his boyish appearance. Batty had been at the club since the age of 13, and his ability to win the ball, then execute a telling pass or drive forward with surging runs, was to have a profound influence.

Expectations became feverish on New Year's Day 1988 as Leeds beat Bradford City 2-0 at Elland Road watched by 36,004, their highest league gate for seven seasons. But there was no inexorable charge to the first division; the old inconsistencies returned, and Leeds finished seventh. Even though there was disappointment,

The Glory Years Return

1988–89 The outsider arrives

As career moves go, Howard Wilkinson's decision to become the new Leeds United manager seemed curious. He abandoned Sheffield Wednesday, a club in the top half of the first division, for a team at the foot of the second. Yet, as he later explained, he felt that Leeds had the greater ambition. The club had a proud history, though Wilkinson deplored its tendency to continue living in the past. Soon after taking charge, he banished pictorial mementoes of the Revie era from the foyer and, in a shake-up of staff, sacked Norman Hunter from the coaching team.

A winger of moderate ability, first with Sheffield Wednesday then Brighton, Wilkinson had made his name as a coach, thinker and strategist. He had gained a degree in physical education at Sheffield University and spent two years teaching. After qualifying as an FA coach, he held various posts, becoming manager of the England Under-21 squad in 1982. As a league manager, he had won promotion with Notts County and Sheffield Wednesday.

A lucrative four-year contract, the promise of money for players and the notion of Leeds

■ Above, right: No more Revie old boys: following Bremner's dismissal in 1988, Howard Wilkinson was appointed manager. His brief was clear and simple: to get Leeds back into the first division.

United as sleeping giant combined to lure Wilkinson. He brought Mick Hennigan with him from Hillsborough as coach. To begin with, there was no drastic reconstruction of Bremner's team. 'I cannot complain about the commitment of the players. My inclination is that there are areas where improvements can be made, but rash and hasty decisions...are not the answer in my experience, and I see no reason to panic,' he told supporters after Leeds had gained only one league victory from their first 12 matches.

A good mid-season run took them up the table. Essentially, this was still Bremner's team: the former Leeds manager had re-signed Ian Baird having sold him to Portsmouth, from where he had also acquired centre-half Noel Blake on a free transfer and winger Vince Hilaire, whose fee was fixed by tribunal at £175,000. Wilkinson's own early recruits, winger/full-back Mike Whitlow, from Witton Albion and midfielder Andy Williams, a £170,000 signing from Rotherham United, were in and out of the team.

Strachan joins Leeds

With Leeds neither in danger of relegation nor candidates for promotion, Wilkinson sprang into

■ Steady and composed, Chris Fairclough was one of Wilkinson's most astute signings. In his first full season (1989–90) at Leeds, he was voted supporters' player of the year, scoring eight league goals during the successful promotion campaign.

action as the transfer deadline approached, buying three experienced players: centre-half Chris Fairclough from Spurs (£500,000), Carl Shutt from Bristol City (in an exchange deal involving Bob Taylor) and Gordon Strachan from Manchester United (£300,000). The Strachan deal caused general astonishment. What would a 32-year-old winger, seemingly isolated and disaffected at Old Trafford, want from Leeds – or have to offer them? Similar questions had been asked 26 years earlier of Bobby Collins; yet he became the catalyst for a playing revolution. Strachan was destined to play the same role.

'Once people left Manchester United, everyone used to think you went away, curled up and died...I didn't fancy that, dying a death at 32,' Strachan says. 'My stamina and fitness were still good but I'd lost my appetite for the game. I'd been with Alex Ferguson too long and it wasn't working. I met Howard Wilkinson and Bill Fotherby (the managing director). They were very determined...they knew where they wanted to go; there was a long-term plan. They told me they wanted me for a specific job and were confident I could do it...basically to lead Leeds out of the second division. It was the first time for a long

tively. Mark Aizlewood, latterly team captain, fell foul of Howard Wilkinson when, having been barracked by the crowd for a poor performance, gesticulated rudely after scoring the winner against Walsall. Within weeks, he was transferred to Bradford City for £200,000.

In came Mel Sterland, the former Sheffield Wednesday and Glasgow Rangers full-back, bought for £650,000, winger John Hendrie from Newcastle for £500,000 and centre-half John McClelland from Watford for £150,000. But Wilkinson's most extraordinary gesture was the £600,000 purchase of midfielder Vinnie Jones from Wimbledon. There wasn't a player in the country with a more uncouth image. Cynics believed that Jones had found his true niche at a club notorious for its hooligan followers. Leeds fans were either dumbfounded, delighted or dismayed.

Gordon Strachan was on holiday when he heard the news that Jones had signed. 'The kids came through from the swimming pool and said that Leeds had signed Vinnie Jones. I started laughing and they said no, it was serious. I leapt into the pool, but thought, "There's no point in drowning yourself, you're getting well paid." But then we got together, Vinnie and myself, and I found out we were on the same wavelength – he had got a buzz from meeting Howard. We ended up being the best of mates.'

Jones soon received a sharp warning about his excesses. 'We didn't want him to be a monster...once we had seen him play, we knew he could actually pass the ball,' says Strachan. 'I didn't like the things he got up to at Wimbledon. We put him right in a pre-season game. Something happened...we were playing Anderlecht and one of their players ended up with a bloody nose. Vinnie thought that was what he was here for. I had to pull him aside and say, "No, you're not here for that. By all means put the fear of death into people by talking to them, but don't try injuring anybody."'

■ Carl Shutt, signed in an exchange deal that saw Bob Taylor go to Bristol City, scored a hat-trick on his league debut. Often a substitute, he nevertheless scored some vital goals for Leeds.

time that I felt someone really believed in me as a player. I got a great buzz from that. And I was offered a lot of money.'

The 1988–89 campaign petered out with Leeds finishing tenth. With the death during the close season of Don Revie, who for three years had been suffering from the incurable muscle-wasting illness motor neurone disease, Leeds fans once more had cause to reminisce on the club's heyday. Revie's career as England manager may have ended in disgrace, but his achievements at Elland Road were never disparaged.

More arrivals

During the summer, Howard Wilkinson continued to startle with his transfer dealings. John Sheridan and Neil Aspin, the last of Eddie Gray's protégés, were sold to Nottingham Forest for £650,000 and Port Vale for £140,000 respec-

1989–90 High hopes

For all the high pre-season hopes, Leeds crashed heavily in their first league game of 1989–90, beaten 5-2 at Newcastle. But it was a false alarm. Fairclough and Jones had been out injured and their return coincided with a 15-match unbeaten run. A 2-0 win at Middlesbrough on 9 December put Leeds top, yet Wilkinson was still driven to change the team, most significantly by selling Ian Baird to Middlesbrough for £500,000 and recruiting as target man Lee Chapman for

£400,000 from Nottingham Forest. The mid-field, already gingered up by Vinnie Jones, became even more ferocious when Chris Kamara joined the ranks, signed from Stoke City for £150,000.

Most of Wilkinson's big buys were inspired. Strachan was the hub of Leeds' creativity, darting about the pitch with inexhaustible energy; Sterland at right-back, was a driving force in defence and as an overlapping attacker provided much ammunition for Leeds' forwards; Fairclough at centre-half was highly efficient, with a knack of scoring timely goals; and Jones, tamed but not neutered, proved a decent footballer – still a hustler but now more likely to cause damage through his powerful shooting or parabolic long throw-ins than by inflicting grievous bodily harm.

Batty had sustained his early promise; Mervyn Day, for the most part, kept splendidly in goal; and Peter Haddock was a steady partner for Fairclough, reading the game well and skilful enough to extricate himself from danger. But the arrival of Lee Chapman from Nottingham Forest divided Leeds supporters: Baird had been a popular figure and loyal servant, whereas Chapman had drifted around numerous clubs and, moreover, appeared awkward and ungainly.

However Wilkinson, who had managed Chapman for four seasons at Sheffield Wednesday, knew the nomadic centre-forward better than most. 'He's never let me down,' was Wilkinson's terse summary. Chapman was also held in high esteem by Brian Clough, who claimed much of the credit for improving his game. 'We gave him the ball below the level of

■ Mervyn Day's career had many ups and downs but in Leeds' promotion season, he was always dependable.

his forehead. He received it to his feet 90 per cent more than at any time in his career.'

Once more, Wilkinson's judgement proved sound; Chapman was to score crucial goals as the promotion struggle, a three-horse race involving Leeds, Sheffield United and Newcastle, boiled up. The run-in became excruciatingly tense, with savage twists of misfortune spreading insecurity on all sides; for if Leeds believed that their 4-0 rout of Sheffield United on Easter Monday had put first division football within their grasp, losing their unbeaten home record to Barnsley nine days later invoked the dread of another failure at the final hurdle.

Tension builds

'There was a oneness with the team and supporters...'

Gordon Strachan

Two games of monumental importance remained: the final home match against Leicester City and an away game at Bournemouth, who were fighting a relegation battle. The Leicester game generated unbearable tension. 'I've been in stadiums all over the world and that day there was an atmosphere that I don't think I'll ever feel again,' says Gordon Strachan. 'There was a oneness with the team and supporters...you get that once or twice in a career...they're in there with you, making the pass, feeling every tackle, feeling the hurt.'

Mel Sterland gave Leeds the lead with a fierce low diagonal shot from the right, but the outcome hinged on the contributions of two midfielders, Leicester's Gary McAllister and Strachan himself. McAllister had been a constant menace, and while Day kept out one of his sharp volleys, another screamed past him into the net. Few goals had ever caused such despair at Elland Road.

With time running out, and Leeds in frenetic search of a winner, McAllister, for once, misdirected a pass. It landed at Strachan's feet and as the Leeds captain advanced, he smashed home a shot that outdid even McAllister's. The Leeds crowd was exultant, but their travails were not yet over. Newcastle had beaten West Ham, and for Leeds to clinch promotion and the championship, they had to win at Bournemouth.

Promotion at last

Dean Court, a compact ground with a capacity of 10,000, was ill-favoured for a match of such importance. Only 2,000 Leeds fans had been allocated tickets, yet hordes more travelled down

hoping to find a way in. Dorset's chief constable had been apprehensive about the implications for public order long before it transpired that the fate of both sides depended on the outcome.

His worst fears were justified. There was trouble throughout the weekend, culminating in a pre-match riot as drunken Leeds fans made abortive efforts to storm the ground. Inside everyone was hot, bothered and on edge. But Bournemouth, for all that this was their last stand against relegation, were muted, and as time elapsed, a sense grew in the Leeds camp that the match was there to be won.

The two new boys delivered victory. Early in the second half, Kamara broke down the right and his accurate centre found Chapman who, unmarked, headed the goal that won Leeds the match, the championship and ended eight years exile from the first division. Unruly celebrations

spread along the south coast. For Wilkinson, Strachan and co., it had all happened more quickly than they had dreamed; and a miraculous pattern had been set where, for the next two seasons, expectations were destined to be outstripped by actual success.

1990–91 Wilkinson builds his team

Wilkinson could have asked no more of his team, yet was unsentimental about the players who had returned Leeds to the first division. In the close season he paid £1 million to bring back John Lukic from Arsenal, £450,000 for centre-half Chris Whyte from West Bromwich Albion, and £1 million for Leicester City's Gary McAllister, so recently a tormentor. Overnight, Mervyn Day found himself second choice in goal and Whyte

was to supplant the injury-prone Haddock.

The arrival of McAllister, who had also been courted by Nottingham Forest, made the most waves. It posed an immediate question over Vinnie Jones' future. Jones had become a folk hero at Leeds, obeying orders to stay out of trouble and channel his aggression constructively, yet before the season was a month old, and with only one match behind him, he was off-loaded, sold to Sheffield United for £650,000.

McAllister was the final component of an impressive midfield that featured Batty and Strachan on the right and Gary Speed on the left. Speed, a versatile, athletic young player full of endeavour and with great aerial ability, had matured rapidly after forcing his way into the side near the end of the promotion campaign.

Yet McAllister was slow to settle at Leeds and was sometimes abrasive about the technical

■ Top left: The hordes descend on Bournemouth. Leeds' 1-0 victory in May 1990 marked a return to the first division after eight years but was marred by hooliganism.

■ Top right: Building for the future. Gary McAllister became the final component of a Leeds midfield which became the best in Britain. McAllister's arrival saw Vinnie Jones move to Sheffield United.

■ The versatile Gary Speed was another member of the midfield quartet but lost form and confidence in the mid 1990s. At the end of 1995–96, he was transferred to Everton for £3.5 million.

deficiencies of his team-mates'. 'Verbally he used to abuse players quite a lot,' says Strachan. 'That had to be put right. And it was – it was a simple thing. Once he did that, he got all the respect from the players that he wanted. But to begin with, he couldn't understand why people couldn't read his flick round the corner, pass or one-two. All he could do to be a good pro was to try to teach them to come to the same level as him.'

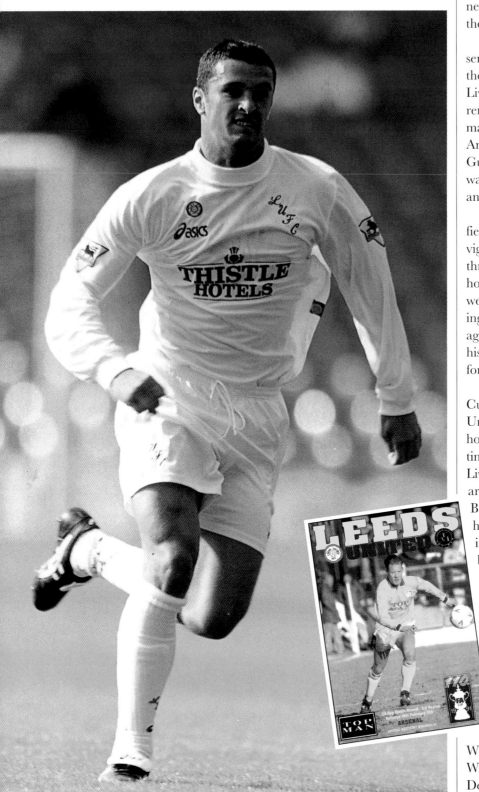

Leeds make an impact

In the first game of 1990–91, Leeds supporters had a sense of being in dreamland as they saw the team go 3-0 up against Everton at Goodison Park. Although Everton pulled back two goals, the victory fortified morale; there was a sense that the first division might not be such a trial. Leeds' league form was uneven until November, but they then won eight and drew two of their next ten matches, an emphatic declaration that the rest had better look out.

Throughout January and February came a series of searching tests in league and cup against the cream of the division. A 3-0 defeat against Liverpool at Anfield on New Year's Day removed a few delusions of grandeur, but Leeds' marathon fourth round FA Cup encounter with Arsenal, which ran to three replays before the Gunners won through 2-1, showed that there was little to choose between the champions-elect and Wilkinson's newcomers.

Leeds were making an impact. Their midfield, a harmonious combination of craft and vigour, looked the best in the division. Chapman thrived on the service and was a tireless chaser, holding up the ball, flicking-on, laying-off. There were few braver centre-forwards; after nose-diving into the cinder track during Leeds 0-0 draw against Tottenham in February 1991, he forced his way, scar-faced, back into the side too quickly for his own good.

A sparkling run in the Rumbelows League Cup was ended in the semi-final by Manchester United, who won 3-1 on aggregate. The last hope of a trophy had disappeared, yet Leeds continued to play brisk inventive football. Against Liverpool at Elland Road on 13 April, half-time arrived with Leeds 4-0 down, carved to pieces by Barnes, Beardsley, Rush et al. In the second half, Wilkinson's men were hell-bent on rescuing an apparently lost cause. Liverpool won 5-4 but were left reeling from Leeds' explosive recovery. Chapman had played a majestic part, scoring three and having what would have been an equaliser disallowed.

Dorigo joins from Chelsea

Leeds finished fourth and appeared settled everywhere save at left-back, a slot seemingly cursed by injury. Peter Haddock, Chris Kamara, Glynn Snodin and Mike Whitlow all took a turn but in the close season, Wilkinson signed England international Tony Dorigo from Chelsea for £1.3 million. Fans at Stamford Bridge were aghast at the loss of their

stylish defender – Dorigo was greeted with bitter taunts of 'Judas' when he returned to his old stamping ground.

Gordon Strachan marvelled at the apparent ease with which Dorigo performed. 'He gave us extra pace at the back, among a lot of other things. He could play anywhere: he should have won a lot more caps with his talent. Because he ran so quickly, so effortlessly, the game was too easy for him. Maybe it was just the way he looked...his hair was immaculate, he never seemed to be dirty. I was more than happy with what he was giving us. But for himself, I thought he had another ten per cent.'

One of Leeds' rare ineffectual performances had been at Southampton in March. Strachan, injured, was a helpless on-looker as his team-mates stumbled to a 2-0 defeat, the defence plagued constantly by Rod Wallace's incisive play. In the close season, Howard Wilkinson decided it was safer to have Wallace among the Leeds ranks than as a foe, and signed him for £1.6 million along with brother Ray, a full-back valued at £100,000. To add further depth, Steve Hodge, who had won 24 England caps, was signed from Nottingham Forest for £900,000.

■ Above: Stretching to the limit: central defender David Wetherall wins the ball from Arsenal's Paul Merson as Tony Dorigo looks on.

■ Left: At his best, Rod Wallace was irrepressible, a scorer of spectacular goals and with the control to waltz past defences.

■ Steve Hodge, signed at the beginning of Leeds' championship season, strengthened the squad but often languished on the substitute's bench.

'...without doubt we were the hardest-working team in Britain.'

Gordon Strachan

■ Opposite: study of a great captain in action: Gordon Strachan was always running, watching and thinking ahead.

1991–92 The waiting ends

Hodge was to appear fitfully in 1991–92, somewhat disgruntled by his role as perennial substitute. Yet on 21 September, in his first full game, he struck a goal of monumental importance: it sank Liverpool at Elland Road and meant that Leeds had beaten the dominant force in English football. There were more than the usual celebrations; the exultant crowd now believed that anything was possible.

Leeds won five and drew four of their first nine league matches, and thereafter never dropped out of the top two places. The league became a duel between Wilkinson's men and Manchester United, long demonized by Leeds fans as the great enemy. Wilkinson's men continued to enhance their reputations with televised extravagant victories away from home; 6-1 win against flu-stricken Sheffield Wednesday on 12 January and, to greater acclaim, 4-1 at Aston Villa six weeks earlier.

'I didn't think the team would do so well,' said Strachan. 'But then, I didn't realise how good the players were that we'd bought. The nicest thing said about us was that without doubt we were the hardest-working team in Britain. I think that's wonderful. We were also disciplined and well-organised. That was down to Howard; the hard work he put in during training. He made us understand the game better.'

Devotion to the work ethic was a key to Strachan's game. In February 1992, he turned 35, but while other midfielders his age trotted around in leisurely fashion the Leeds captain was irrepressibly energetic, sprinting up and down the pitch, chivvying, trying tricks and ideas, the antithesis of complacency.

Wilkinson snaps up Cantona

Wilkinson, too, was hard to satisfy, still not quite convinced that his team was championship material. Although a disciplinarian, he was undeterred by headstrong characters if he believed they could offer a new dimension – few could have imagined Vinnie Jones knuckling down so well. Now Wilkinson had become interested in another maverick, French international Eric Cantona who had walked out on his club, Nimes, vowing never to play football again – the latest chapter in a rancorous career.

In the event, Cantona came to England and had a trial with Sheffield Wednesday. Wednesday could not make up their minds, but Wilkinson had seen film of Cantona in action. Whatever the Frenchman's temperamental flaws, he had skills that were rare in the English game, enough for the Leeds manager to make a snap decision and sign him on loan.

Cantona's debut at Oldham Athletic on 8 February 1992 was inauspicious: Leeds lost only their second league match of the season, the start of a stuttering run in which they won just three games out of twelve. Many Leeds supporters gave up hope on 4 April when the team was crushed 4-0 at Manchester City. It left Manchester United on top with three games in hand.

But City still had a mischievous role to play. The following Wednesday, and in defiance of everything loaded against them, they thwarted their rivals in the Manchester derby at Old Trafford. For United, leading 1-0 at half-time and playing against only ten men after Neil Pointon had been sent off, victory seemed inevitable. Instead City dug in, rallied and equalised. A draw for them was a matter of pride, little more; but for Leeds, it meant that the leaders had been reined in just as they were threatening to run away with the race.

All Leeds could do was to keep winning. The following Saturday, their 3-0 win over Chelsea finished with a crescendo of celebration as Cantona contrived one of his dazzling party pieces,

controlling the ball on his chest, flicking it up, then smashing home a thunderous volley. Yet Wilkinson still had doubts about using him for a full game. There were elements of genius in the Frenchman's play, but Cantona's individualism had the Leeds manager on his guard. He did not want the team destabilized. There were also questions about Cantona's fitness.

Yet three weeks earlier, the goalless draw against West Ham at Elland Road showed Cantona to be much more than just an alchemist. While Leeds had been kept at bay by West Ham's Czech goalkeeper Ludek Miklosko, the team seemed pedestrian save for the Frenchman. His was a substantial performance, full of runs, prompting, flicks, guidance by example and, despite his reputation as a trickster, invariably for the good of the team; a hint that if he could be accommodated, Cantona had it in him to be a pivotal figure.

His talent was indisputable. 'The sign of a great player is if he can do simple things well,' says Strachan. 'Cantona's very brave on the ball and does simple things brilliantly. If he's not got a move on, he lays the ball off. When he passed me the ball it was to my right foot, knowing that I wanted to hit it first time. Lots of players don't appreciate that.'

Yet in Leeds' run-in, Cantona remained on the fringe of things. After victory over Chelsea, Leeds travelled to Liverpool and played a patient, containing game, resisting the temptation to make the sort of headstrong dash for victory that might result in defeat. Wilkinson's team got their reward with a goalless draw.

Manchester United collapse

But strange things were happening to Manchester United. They seemed terrified by the need to satisfy the club's great obsession, that of winning the League Championship for the first time in 25 years. Their flowing football had congealed and on Easter Monday, they suffered a shattering blow as Nottingham Forest avenged their Rumbelows League Cup final defeat by winning 2-1 at Old Trafford.

Suddenly the luck seemed to flow Leeds' way. Manchester had played at lunchtime; the demands of television coverage put back the

■ Once beloved of the fans, Eric Cantona, whose flair gave Leeds a new dimension during the championship run-in, became a bête noire when sold by Howard Wilkinson to Manchester United in November 1992.

Leeds game against Coventry to mid-afternoon. There could be no greater incentive to win a game, yet Leeds too were faltering and unsure, settling down only in the second half when goals from Chris Fairclough and a penalty from McAllister delivered victory. The style of the win, was less important than the message it transmitted to Manchester: that Leeds were keeping their nerve to the end.

Two days later, Alex Ferguson's inhibited team travelled to bottom-of-the-table West Ham and lost 1-0 – full-back Kenny Brown getting the all important goal. All their games in hand were squandered and Leeds were left with a one-point lead. Both teams had two matches to play. It was conceivable, though improbable, that Wilkinson's men might just snatch the championship four days later if they won at Sheffield United and Manchester lost at Liverpool.

Leeds win Championship

Manchester United's capacity for self-destruction had introduced a bizarre element into the race, and a crazy game of football between Leeds and Sheffield United at Bramall Lane on Sunday 26 April compounded their agony. This time, Leeds kicked off at noon while Manchester had to hang on until 3.00pm for the questionable pleasure of starting at Anfield.

It was a bright blustery day; pitches almost everywhere were inhospitably hard. The conditions were designed to sabotage decent football. At times, the ball swirled and bobbled about Bramall Lane as if it had a will of its own, but Sheffield were quicker getting to grips with it, taking a 28th minute lead through Alan Cork. As Leeds pressed, just on half-time they were rewarded with a freakish goal: from Strachan's quick free-kick, Brian Gayle's attempted clearance bounced first off Gary Speed, then Rod Wallace, and into the net.

There was more to come in this vein, though Leeds, the wind now at their backs, improved in the second half and with 25 minutes to go, scored the best goal of the game through Jon Newsome, playing out of position at right-back in favour of the injured Mel Sterland. McAllister's free kick found Newsome unmarked by the far post and the young defender's low stooping header flashed past goalkeeper Mel Rees. Leeds' joy lasted precisely two minutes, when the defence failed to clear a Sheffield corner and Lee Chapman turned John Pemberton's shot over his own goal-line.

The final goal was the final madness. With 13 minutes left, the Blades' full-back, David Barnes,

■ Above: The Elland Road party begins as Leeds receive the championship trophy before their final game of 1991–92 against Norwich City.

■ Right: David Rocastle was signed from Arsenal to boost Leeds' bid for the European Cup. But despite some vigorous displays, he was unable to oust a fully-fit Strachan from the team.

lofted a high ball towards his own goal. Cantona, on as substitute, and Rod Wallace chased after it, but the three-man race was won by Gayle who, with Rees standing just behind, looped a header over him and into the net. For all its absurdity, Gayle's own goal was destined to deliver Leeds United their third championship. Three hours later, Manchester United lost 2-0 at Liverpool.

There was a sense of wonderment. Wilkinson himself had been unprepared to see his team crowned champions so soon. He was however irritated by critics who had compared the side unfavourably with that of Revie. But in many ways the class of 1992 was more popular, their achievements untainted by accusations of gamesmanship or foul play. 'It was down to organisation. We were willing to work with each other,' says Strachan. 'That side played to their maximum; they gave it their best shot. We just kept on doing what we thought we were good at.'

1992–93 Back in Europe

Pessimism rarely follows a championship win. The feeling was that Leeds were back where they belonged, that they might do as well again, and that the European Cup would be a great adventure. Wilkinson had strengthened the side primarily in midfield, paying Arsenal £2 million for David Rocastle and Blackburn £900,000 to bring Scott Sellars back to Elland Road.

There were concerns about Gordon Strachan, who during the summer had had three operations for a back injury. Yet the season started with an exuberant 4-3 Charity Shield victory over Liverpool at Wembley in which Cantona scored a hat-trick. With the Leeds captain absent, Cantona found a regular place in the Leeds starting line-up, but only until Strachan bounced back to fitness in mid-September. Sterland had become a longer-term casualty, so Newsome, impressively solid in his few games during the climax to the championship, began the season at right-back.

German games

Two wins, three draws and two defeats in their first seven league matches meant that Leeds travelled to Germany for their encounter with Stuttgart in the European Cup without having established a consistent rhythm. In this, his first start, Rocastle missed Leeds' best chance during a goalless first half. It was symptomatic of a frustrating and short career at Leeds: Rocastle's inability to command a regular place puzzled fans and player alike.

During the second half, Leeds went to pieces. Shortly after Fritz Walter gave Stuttgart the lead on the hour, Cantona, who seconds earlier had pulled up and was hobbling about the pitch with an injury, played a dreadful cross-field ball from the left. In a flash, Walter was through for his second. Few gave Leeds a chance of retrieving the tie after Andreas Buck scored a third eight minutes from time.

Just 20,457 turned up at Elland Road for the second leg but the atmosphere was intense, almost feverish, as Leeds put on their most virile performance for months. They attacked incessantly and with ten minutes to go, goals from Speed, a McAllister penalty, Cantona and Chapman put them 4-1 up on the night. But the Germans managed to fend off Leeds until the final whistle, a 34th minute goal from Buck seemingly enough to take them through to the next round. Yet much as in their 4-5 defeat against Liverpool two seasons earlier, Leeds were acclaimed conquerors.

'We played unbelievable football that night,' says Gordon Strachan. 'I get the feeling we could have scored any time we wanted. We took on the German champions and really hammered them. People pontificate about the English game

being behind that of other countries, but I can't remember anyone saying when we hammered Stuttgart "that's how far the Germans are behind England". That cliché is only used when we get beaten.'

As things turned out, it was not the end for Leeds. Stuttgart had broken UEFA rules by fielding too many foreign players, and after fierce representations from both clubs, UEFA ordered that there should be a play-off at the Nou Camp stadium, Barcelona. There were just 7,400 fans in small clusters scattered around a ground that could hold 110,000, but the Leeds contingent was vociferous and in buoyant mood. The team carried on as if at Elland Road, the hero of their 2-1 victory Carl Shutt who, within a minute of coming on as substitute for Eric Cantona, broke clear, advanced on the Stuttgart goal and slotted the ball into the net.

■ Above: An athlete in action: Gary Speed's overhead kick is an arresting sight.

For Leeds, this was to be the finest moment of the 1992–93 season. All consistency had gone in the league; by the end of November they were adrift in the race for the championship. Howard Wilkinson himself was among those who found it incomprehensible.

Beaten by Rangers

Despite the joy of beating Stuttgart in the European Cup and the excitement generated by drawing Glasgow Rangers in the second round, Leeds departed from the competition in anti-climactic fashion. At Ibrox, a mirac- ulous volley from Gary McAllister in the second minute promised to give Leeds the momentum that might carry them through. But midway through the first half when John Lukic, dazzled by the floodlights, lost sight of an in-swinging corner and punched the ball into his own net, Leeds surrendered the initiative. Rangers won 2-1; and, just as McAllister had at Ibrox, striker Mark Hateley hit a magnificent shot in the second minute of the return leg at Elland Road that made the Glaswegians' advantage unassailable. McCoist's headed goal on the hour was icing on the cake; Cantona's close-range angled shot five minutes from time, irrelevant.

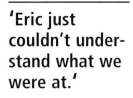

'Eric just couldn't under- stand what we were at.'

Gordon Strachan

■ Tension in the European Cup second round as Chris Fairclough, Rangers' Mark Hateley and Jon Newsome challenge for the ball. Hateley's early strike at Elland Road killed off Leeds' hopes of further progress.

By February 1993, the champions had nowhere to go and nothing to fight for except survival in the newly-fashioned FA Premier League. There had been early exits from both the Coca-Cola League Cup and the FA Cup. A season that had been eagerly anticipated brought little but trauma, most of all in November when Eric Cantona was transferred to Manchester United for a mere £1.2 million.

Cantona leaves

The Leeds fans had adored Cantona. 'But Eric had made up his mind that he couldn't relate to big Lee Chapman as a player,' says Gordon Strachan. 'He found it hard to understand how Chappy played and Chappy found it difficult to understand him. We had to play a certain style...it was very hard...we didn't have megabucks to change the whole side just to suit Eric Cantona. Hard work made us tick – and no lack of skill, but sometimes when we went away from home, Eric just couldn't understand what we were at. It frustrated him, there's no doubt about that.'

'When we went to Rangers, he just didn't produce a performance. There were a lot of places he didn't produce. We needed a bit of help...we needed to be met a wee bit. It might have bought some time for him to meet us, and we might have been able to bring in some better players to play with him. He had just made up his mind he wanted to leave; there was no way he wanted to stay. Nobody had anything against him personally. He wasn't a problem to get on with.'

Strachan believes that a change in the rules whereby goalkeepers could no longer handle back-passes had created unease in the Leeds defence. 'That's what killed the side,' he says. 'The game became longer and the defenders had to be able to pass and play. People like Chris Whyte had been magnificent for us but they found the change difficult. They would have to play a bit more and got stretched in the middle of the park. That meant the strikers had to hold the ball up longer and that wasn't Chappy's game. He needed the ball played up to him and people around him quickly. The players found the new ruling difficult. That's what changed us. Man United had better players when the rules changed and they took over. They had Pallister and Bruce at the back who could play the ball better than Chris Fairclough and Chris Whyte.'

Often in 1992–93, Leeds lost games or points through conceding late goals. An alarming inability to win away from home saw the team become preoccupied with staving off relegation.

In January, Wilkinson paid IK Staart £250,000 for the Norwegian striker Frank Strandli, a Leeds supporter since boyhood, but whatever passion Strandli had for the club, it could not disguise his limitations. The following season he returned to Scandinavia with few memories to cherish of his short time at Elland Road.

■ Chris Whyte had two splendid seasons at Leeds but, along with his defensive partners, struggled with the new back-pass law and lost form in 1992–93.

The New East Stand

Leeds' return to top class football had been a catalyst for Elland Road's most monumental development, the 17,000 seater East Stand. Ground capacity had fluctuated in recent years

■ A monument to the Leeds revival: the massive 17,000-seater East Stand opened in 1993.

as work was carried out to comply with the Taylor report. The towering new structure was the centrepiece of Elland Road's metamorphosis into a 40,000 all-seater stadium and international venue. Yet unease about whether or not Leeds fans would see Premier League football in such grand surroundings was to last almost all season. The team finished 17th, without an away win in the league all season, leaving manager and supporters perplexed.

Despite the failure at senior level, the campaign had a celebratory footnote. For the first time, Leeds United's young players won the FA Youth Cup, 4-1 aggregate winners over Manchester United. Each leg of the final drew more than 30,000 spectators; the Elland Road crowd were as impassioned as if they were watching the old enemy's first team. Manchester, containing names such as Scholes and the Neville brothers Gary and Phillip, were favourites, but Leeds, coached by former centre-half Paul Hart, ran them into the ground. They also trumped Manchester for flair with Jamie Forrester's spectacular overhead kick in the second leg at Elland Road.

1993–94 More team rebuilding

There was a less euphoric mood as the 1993–94 campaign began, and some substantial rebuilding of the team. Mel Sterland's injury forced him out of the game, his place taken by Irish teenager Gary Kelly. Kelly was a revelation, a player of boundless energy, pace and with an appetite for attack. Once in the side, he was immovable and developed so rapidly that at the end of his first full season, he was representing the Republic of Ireland in the World Cup finals. Kelly made defender David Kerslake, signed from Swindon for £500,000 in March 1993, redundant almost immediately, and within months, Kerslake was sold to Tottenham.

It was also the end for Chris Whyte and Lee Chapman, both of whom perhaps had stayed a season too long. Whyte's lack of pace had been exposed in 1992–93, and, constantly at full stretch, he had been booked numerous times for tackling from behind. Yet he had had two distinguished seasons and, like Sterland, was valued as a good-natured colleague. Whyte moved to

Birmingham City. Chapman, thwarted by the absence of a reliable striking partner, had toiled for less reward than in the championship season, and was transferred to Portsmouth for £200,000.

Having tried unsuccessfully to sign the Dundee United centre-forward Duncan Ferguson, Howard Wilkinson moved in on Sheffield United's Brian Deane, paying £2.7 million for the Leeds-born striker. As part of a defensive reconstruction, Wilkinson acquired the Arsenal veteran David O'Leary, a belated career move that was to be aborted by injury. However, Deane had arrived to stay; a sometimes puzzling figure whose touch and control alternated between being delicate and clumsy. For a tall striker, he appeared to be less than commanding in the air, seemingly more at ease when playing down the flanks. Few, however, could fault his effort or temperament.

Out of the cups

As cover and competition for John Lukic, Wilkinson had bought goalkeeper Mark Beeney from Brighton for £350,000. After Leeds' poor start to

1993–94, which included a 4-0 home defeat by Norwich on 21 August, Beeney got his chance, and had a run of 27 games before he in turn was dropped, paying the penalty for indifferent form after Leeds' dismal exit from the FA Cup when they were beaten 3-2 by Oxford United at Elland Road in a fourth round replay.

Leeds had also lost 4-2 on aggregate to Sunderland in the second round of the Coca Cola League Cup. It was as if the team had some deep-rooted aversion to knockout competition which they could only conquer once every ten years or so. But, after a shaky start, Leeds put much more beef into their league campaign, the turning point a 2-0 victory at Southampton in September. It was Leeds' first league win away from home since the extraordinary success at Sheffield United that had secured the championship in 1992.

A stable partnership had yet to establish itself in central defence, but for all their flaws and cup embarrassments, Leeds recovered their equilibrium in 1993–94, finishing fifth. Rod Wallace was the sparky figure of old, his revived confidence crystallised in what was to be voted BBC Match of the Day's goal of the season: a long and swift dribble from the left flank, finished by a shot

bent artfully into the net, the second of his two goals in Leeds' home victory over Tottenham on 17 April. Wallace finished the season as top scorer with 17 league goals.

Howard Wilkinson had retained his capacity to shock in the transfer market with the sale of David Batty to Blackburn Rovers for £2.7 million. There were, however, signs that Batty had grown disenchanted with the defensive aspect of his role. 'He was a great tackler but more, he was a ball winner,' says Gordon Strachan. 'Often you see people tackle but they don't win the ball. Batts would win the ball and could make good passes afterwards. But sometimes you need to move on; you need the change.' Less surprising was David Rocastle's move to Manchester City in a £1 million exchange deal that brought striker David White to Leeds. Despite the occasional stirring performance, Rocastle proved not to be Wilkinson's kind of player.

1994–95 Farewell to Strachan

At the start of 1994–95 Strachan was still being picked for the first team although not through choice. Already, his career was starting to take a new direction. 'I was really enjoying myself taking the Leeds youngsters...playing in the reserves with them. I got a kick from playing with the lads...they were good to work with. I had a run of 14 games with them and I think we won 13...I loved it. But because of the circumstances, I ended up playing in the first team again. I really didn't want to do it.'

Strachan eventually departed mid-season to become assistant manager of Coventry City. In a team largely comprising six-footers, he felt he had increasingly little influence, but his had been one of the most remarkable of all Indian summers. Bought simply to help take Leeds out

■ South African striker Phil Masinga is first to the ball in this clash against Coventry City and races away from former Leeds man David Rennie.

Mansfield humiliation

For the first half of 1994–95, Leeds were frustrating in their inconsistency. Humiliation in the Coca-Cola League Cup had become almost an annual ritual; they were scalped in the second round by third division Mansfield Town, losing 1-0 on aggregate. 'You don't have to delve through the statistics too closely to know that our cup record in recent times has not had supporters dancing the conga down the Headrow,' said Wilkinson dryly.

In the FA Cup third round, Walsall had threatened to do the same. David Wetherall was Leeds' saviour, heading home a McAllister free-kick four minutes from time. But Walsall continued making nuisances of themselves at Elland Road, and with the scores 2-2 at full-time, it took the introduction of Phil Masinga, on as substitute for Rod Wallace, to settle matters. His hat-trick, scored in just nine minutes, was as timely as it was unexpected.

Beset by the need for a top-class striker, Wilkinson cast around once more, and in January 1995 persuaded Ghanaian international Tony Yeboah to join Leeds at a cost of £3.4 million. As with Cantona, Wilkinson had only ever seen Yeboah play on film. Yeboah had spent five

■ Left: Studs flying, another Leeds old boy David Batty launches into a tackle with Carlton Palmer who, with McAllister, assumed the role of motivator.

■ Below: A new face in defence: John Pemberton's assets were pace and stern tackling.

of the second division, Strachan had finished up with a championship medal, being recalled by Scotland, voted the Footballer of the Year in 1991 and awarded the OBE.

There were more striking changes in 1994–95: two recruits arrived from South African clubs, Philomen Masinga, a striker, and defender Lucas Radebe. Sheffield Wednesday left-back Nigel Worthington was signed as cover for Tony Dorigo. Wilkinson's biggest financial deal pre-season was the signing of Carlton Palmer, also from Sheffield Wednesday, for £2.7 million. As with Deane, Palmer's commitment was absolute, but opinions divided about his ability. A tall, gangling figure whom Wilkinson intended playing in central defence, some believed his forceful unsophisticated style might be put to better and safer use in midfield.

The central defence continued to see changes after Jon Newsome was sold to Norwich for £1 million. David Wetherall, a first-class honours graduate in chemistry who had arrived from Sheffield Wednesday with Newsome three years earlier, as the second component of a £275,000 deal, became the preferred choice at number five. Later in the season he was partnered by John Pemberton, signed for £250,000 from Sheffield United in November 1993.

Right: Brian Deane drives forwards against A.S. Monaco. Leeds' accomplished performance in the away leg of their UEFA Cup tie was a highlight of 1995–96.

Opposite, top: Quick, muscular, with explosive finishing, Ghanaian international striker Tony Yeboah proved one of the most exciting talents ever seen at Elland Road.

contented years in Germany with Eintracht Frankfurt, where he had been captain and scored 68 goals in 123 games before falling out of favour with the new management. His morale was low but his talent explosive; he was the most exotic figure to pull on a Leeds shirt since Eric Cantona had departed for Old Trafford.

Yeboah's first goal for Leeds came in a torrid FA Cup fifth round match at Manchester United on 19 February which Leeds lost 3-1 – a half-hit shot that dribbled across the goal-line. Short of match fitness, he did not look then what he would prove to be, namely the most ferocious striker of a football in Britain. Six months later, Yeboah had the measured Wilkinson groping for superlatives. 'The best striker I've worked with...clinical, cool and calm.'

In the spring, and coinciding with Yeboah's adjustment to the frenetic English game, possibilities began to open up for Leeds in what had seemed destined to be an irredeemably mediocre season. The revival began on 11 March when Leeds travelled to Chelsea and astonished almost everyone with the flair and gusto of their play: Yeboah scoring twice and McAllister getting the other goal in a 3-0 victory.

A place in Europe

'The best striker I've worked with ...clinical, cool and calm.'

Howard Wilkinson

Suddenly, as if all their self-confidence had been restored, Leeds set about the rest of the campaign, their minds fixed on gaining a place in Europe. Of their last 13 matches, they recorded nine victories and lost only at Nottingham Forest. They beat Liverpool 1-0 at Anfield, took a point in a goalless draw from defending champions Manchester United, and delivered a lethal blow to Newcastle's European aspirations with a 2-1 win at St James' Park.

Needing only a point to qualify for the UEFA Cup, Wilkinson's men gained it at Tottenham on the last Sunday of the season. Yeboah, who had fired 12 goals in 16 matches had been the catalyst of Leeds' surge but Deane, who had persevered through bad times, was now enjoying the good. With a splendid run and thumping shot, he scored to give his team a 1–1 draw, their UEFA place and great cause for optimism.

Opposite, bottom: Gary Kelly has possession but Leeds were humiliated by PSV Eindhoven in the UEFA Cup second round.

1995–96 Uneven league form

Three successive victories at the start of 1995–96 and a volleyed goal of stupendous ferocity from Tony Yeboah against Liverpool in their first home match kept Leeds' spirits primed. Might there be an assault on the championship? fans

wondered. It looked as if the swelling confidence with which Howard Wilkinson's team finished the previous campaign had been sustained and could drive them back to the top.

Those were indeed nine precious points. But few people could have imagined that their value would act as insurance against relegation rather than a platform from which to challenge for the

title. The season was destined to go horribly wrong, though until Christmas Leeds showed occasional flashes of brilliance. It was not until March that Wilkinson's injury-hit team suffered a shocking collapse of morale.

Leeds' league form became uneven. Yet in September, they were still playing incisive, breezy football. Their first game in the UEFA Cup for 17 seasons was at Monaco, who were no mugs, but on the night incapable of dealing with Leeds, especially the disruptive power of Yeboah, who scored a hat-trick. Eleven days later, Yeboah was at it again in Leeds' 4-2 win at Wimbledon, juggling with the ball before scoring a goal that combined impudence and thunderous power.

Persuading the 29-year-old Ghanaian to sign on for three years had been Wilkinson's top priority in the close season. His only other signing had been central defender Paul Beesley, bought from Sheffield United for £250,000. But Yeboah, for all his talents, could not make a team. Increasingly Leeds were starting to appear lacklustre; their home performance against Monaco, which they lost 1-0, was a pale shadow of the sparkling football they had produced away.

A 3-0 home defeat by Arsenal on 14 October was poor preparation for the UEFA Cup second round tie with PSV Eindhoven. Three days

Swedish striker Tomas Brolin, Leeds' record signing, appears deceptively carefree. Though doubts about his fitness and application persisted, Brolin was unhappy at not being a first team regular.

later, the Dutch team cut Wilkinson's frail side to pieces at Elland Road. Losing 5-3, Leeds had looked naive and technically inferior, despite a show of defiance in the second half when they had managed to get on terms at 3-3. A miracle was required for Leeds to salvage the tie away from home. Instead they capitulated without fuss, losing 3-0.

Brolin's record transfer

With the team looking stretched, and the role of creator falling heavily on Gary McAllister, Wilkinson realised the need for reinforcements. In November, he paid £4.5 million for Swedish international Tomas Brolin, a stocky striker with an excellent touch. It was a protracted deal, but from the outset manager and player seemed equivocal about the future, for Brolin's contract contained a clause allowing him to leave in the summer if things did not work out.

Interviewed a few months later by Ken Jones in the *Independent*, Wilkinson admitted his mistake. 'What I failed to see was that it implied a doubt in commitment both on his part and mine. Buying him when we did meant there was no time to get him properly fit and into the rhythm of the Premiership. I played Brolin too soon, instead of working hard with him for six or seven weeks as I did with Tony Yeboah. Brolin wanted to be in and foolishly I went along with it.'

Brolin did look unfit, yet on Christmas Eve bestirred himself to play superbly in Leeds' 3-1 win over Manchester United. This was to be the highlight of their league season, an impassioned performance that reduced the old adversary to a shambles. It seemed unimaginable that eight days earlier, Leeds had lost 6-2 at Sheffield Wednesday, as a result of which John Lukic again temporarily lost his place to Mark Beeney.

League Cup progress

Yet Leeds had made stealthy, if low-key progress in the Coca-Cola League Cup, beating Notts County, Derby, Blackburn and Reading before arriving in the semi-finals for the first time since 1979. Their opponents, Birmingham, were difficult to fathom, a club full of ambitious noise, yet in a state of perpetual revolution with manager Barry Fry buying job-lots of new players and fielding substitutes three at a time. It was almost impossible for Wilkinson to predict the team his opposite number would select for the match.

Their talisman was Kevin Francis, a 6ft 7in centre-forward, and in the first leg at St Andrew's it was Francis who thumped a superb shot past the reinstated Lukic to give Birmingham a 25th minute lead. But for all Birmingham's scurrying, Leeds remained unruffled and grasped the game in the second half. A goal from Yeboah and an own-goal from former Leeds defender Chris Whyte buoyed them up for the second leg at Elland Road and the prospect of a first

appearance in a Wembley cup final since 1973.

At Elland Road, Leeds were rarely under pressure, picking off the visitors with goals from Masinga, Yeboah and Deane. Long before full-time, supporters were rejoicing at the prospect of a trip to Wembley. Their passage had never been spectacular, but at least they had not lumbered into an elephant trap set by the likes of Mansfield Town. Yet it was success at a price: Kelly and Dorigo had been carried off injured, the latter, who had pulled a hamstring, destined to miss the rest of the season.

The Coca-Cola League Cup helped banish gloomy memories of January. To the puzzlement of many Leeds fans, Wilkinson had sold striker Noel Whelan, one of the club's brightest prospects, to Coventry for £2 million. With Yeboah and Masinga absent playing in the African Nations' Cup, the forward line was left threadbare. Few would have put their money on Wilkinson turning to Lee Chapman as temporary cover. It seemed an eccentric gesture and ended in bathos: in the 2-0 home win over West

Ham on 13 January, the first of his two games, Chapman was sent off for elbowing an opponent.

The defence was also causing problems. Richard Jobson, signed from Oldham for £800,000 in November, had picked up a long-term injury. For all that Pemberton, Beesley and Worthington were honest, swift-running professionals, there was a lack of a commanding presence. They were not the most adept at holding the ball and bringing it out from the back. Lacking a dynamic creative force in right midfield, the team was looking increasingly fragile.

Yet until March, there was still the prospect of Leeds reaching two cup finals. They had shown character in fighting back from two goals down to win 4-2 at Derby County in the FA Cup third round, but subsequent progress, a 1-0 win at Bolton in round four, and a 2-1 fifth round replay victory over Port Vale, in which McAllister's individual brilliance transcended a laboured performance did not inspire team confidence.

The season was soon to blow up. Leeds' FA Cup sixth-round draw against Liverpool should

A Leeds man at heart, yet Noel Whelan would soon be wearing Coventry colours. There was widespread dismay when the enthusiastic young striker was sold to the Sky Blues.

■ John Lukic shouts out his orders. But for Lukic, 1995–96 was an unsettling season during which he temporarily lost his place to understudy Mark Beeney.

> **'I agree it was a horrible match, but there isn't anything in my contract to say we must look good on television.'**
>
> *Howard Wilkinson*

have been a classic match of old rivals, but a combination of high ticket prices, live television coverage and a disenchantment with recent poor league form meant that the ground was half empty. Leeds played like the away team, intent only on containment and achieving their end in a miserable goalless draw.

Wilkinson, mindful of the 5-0 drubbing his team had suffered at Anfield on 20 January, was defiant. 'I agree that it was a horrible match, but there isn't anything in my contract to say we must look good on television. I felt our best chance was to keep things tight and try to expose the flaws we had spotted. It didn't work out and we were outplayed in the replay.' That was an understatement: after a bright first ten minutes, Leeds offered little except desperate defence, and in losing 3-0 had escaped lightly.

Coca-Cola Cup final

It did not augur well for the Coca-Cola Cup final four days later against Aston Villa, though the Leeds hordes descending on Wembley could take comfort from knowing that a team's recent form did not dictate how they might perform. But in the event, the match echoed all the season's disappointments. Villa were potent and adventurous, worthy 3-0 winners, and Leeds were

timid, tentative and bereft of ideas, save from 18-year-old winger Andy Gray. Gray, the son of former Leeds star Frank, had just broken into the team and glided about the pitch with grace, making the game look easy.

Howard Wilkinson had looked forward to the final as much as the most ardent fan. The failure of his team to make a fight of it was a shattering blow. 'I was gutted. I couldn't believe the way some of our players performed,' he later told the *Independent*. 'I almost wished that one of them would take a swing at the referee or they would start fighting among themselves. Anything to show they were actually interested. What should have been a marvellous experience, win or lose, turned into a nightmare. I was emotionally disembowelled, close to walking away from it all.'

It was understandable. Club managers rarely leave Wembley with jeers and catcalls ringing in their ears. The fans' mood became increasingly grim as Leeds lost six of their last seven matches, pausing only in mid-collapse to give Manchester United, who were closing in on the championship, a traumatic night at Old Trafford. Leeds lost 1-0 but, although forced to field Lucas Radebe in goal when Beeney was sent off for handling outside the penalty area, rediscovered their pride and fought like tigers. Andy Gray once more had been a menace; swift, inventive and unafraid.

The youngsters emerge

The emergence of Gray and other young players such as Mark Ford, Andy Couzens and Mark Tinkler, were Wilkinson's one source of encouragement. 'Too many too soon can cause problems, but there is no doubt they bring vitality,' he said. Vitality, above all, was the side's great deficiency towards the end of 1995–96. The season ended with Elland Road affected by uncertainty after Leslie Silver, Leeds United's chairman for 14 years, resigned from the board in April.

Silver had left, he said, on medical grounds. 'The job is getting more and more involved, and with the development of the premier league, substantially more demanding,' he said. When he joined the board in April 1981, the club had no money and needed 'a lot of pump priming'. 'But you can't do that today...in those days you were talking of £200,000 making a big difference. Now you are talking of millions not making a difference. The chairmanship needs professionalism and high quality management.'

It was a reminder of where the club had been, what it had become, and what football had become; a reminder also that had not Silver and Wilkinson joined forces in 1988, Leeds United might have been forever excluded from soccer's plutocracy. At the end of the season, Wilkinson signed Ian Rush, one of Britain's finest post-war strikers, on a free transfer from Liverpool. At 34, the popular belief was that Rush must be past his best. But Wilkinson had signed him mindful that many great moments in Leeds United's history have been fashioned by older maestros galvanising the bright and the young.

■ New hope from an old master. Howard Wilkinson sought inspiration as well as goals from striker Ian Rush.

1996–97 A season of change

Leslie Silver's departure created turmoil at Elland Road throughout the summer. It resulted in the advent of corporate management at Leeds; the era of paternalist chairmen, such as Harry Reynolds, Manny Cussins and Silver, was swept away. Football had become a business in which it was unlikely that individuals could carry on buying and sustaining success.

The struggle for control of Leeds United became an acrimonious saga. The contenders were the London-based media group Caspian and Conrad, a sports and leisure company whose finance director Ian Townsend was a long-standing Leeds United fan. In the wings lurked another plutocratic Leeds supporter Barry Rubery, owner of a substantial stake in Pace Microtechnology, producers of satellite decoders.

Of the three principal shareholders, two, Silver and managing director Bill Fotherby, favoured Caspian's bid. The third, Peter Gilman, was implacably opposed. On 3 July the club announced that Caspian had bought Leeds United for £35 million and that Howard Wilkinson would have £12 million to spend on players. But Gilman declared: 'It stinks for the fans and under-values the club.' Moreover, he claimed, it breached an agreement made by the three major shareholders that any sale would have to be approved unanimously.

Gilman began High Court proceedings, litigation that paralysed Howard Wilkinson's efforts to reconstruct the team. The Leeds manager saw many fine foreign players – some of whom had performed at Elland Road during Euro '96 –

picked off by rival clubs. Most of Wilkinson's transfer activity was confined to offloading: in June, Gary Speed was sold to Everton for £3.5 million and Phil Masinga, unable to get his work permit renewed, departed to the Swiss club St Gallen for £500,000.

When in early July, Wilkinson was promised funds by Caspian 'beyond people's wildest imaginings', he swiftly invested £2.6 million in Charlton midfielder Lee Bowyer who, at 19, became Britain's most expensive teenage footballer. But within a week, Gilman's legal action brought the Leeds manager's spending to an abrupt halt.

Wilkinson's uncertainties were compounded by Tomas Brolin's failure to report for pre-season training. So public and prolonged had been the Swedish striker's disenchantment, few were surprised. But the departure of Gary McAllister to Coventry City for £3.5 million – just a week after he had publicly promised to remain at Elland Road – left fans aghast and feeling betrayed.

The Yorkshire Evening Post spoke for many supporters when it declared: 'Leeds are in a sorry state – other clubs must be laughing'. Hamstrung by legal action and deserted by his only creative midfield player, Wilkinson's frustrations intensified. The new season was less than a month away when, after a four-day hearing, Mr Justice Rattee finally approved Caspian's takeover. Gilman had hoped that the judge would force Fotherby and Silver to sell their shares to him, or else prevent any sale to Caspian.

It left Leeds United ill-prepared for the new season though Wilkinson moved as quickly as possible to strengthen the team. On 29 July, as Caspian finally took control, he spent £2.25 million on Crystal Palace goalkeeper Nigel Martyn. This was to prove a brilliant investment. A week before kick-off, Wilkinson tried to plug the hole in left midfield, paying Manchester United £4.5 million for Lee Sharpe. While Sharpe's consistency and application were open to debate, his ability and experience were proven.

Four new faces, Rush, Bowyer, Martyn and Sharpe were cause for modest optimism. But the rebuilding was only half done. There was no commanding presence in right midfield and, with Tony Yeboah's injured knee slow to heal, the attack looked lightweight. There was another hole in the team: Tony Dorigo had yet to recover from the hamstring injury sustained during the Coca-Cola Cup semi-final.

In the final frenetic week of the close season, Manchester United's financial director Robin Launders, credited with fashioning much of the Old Trafford club's commercial success, was

■ It was an unhappy reunion for Lee Sharpe, Howard Wilkinson's last signing, with his former Manchester United team-mates. Leeds were routed; and the debacle precipitated Wilkinson's dismissal.

appointed Leeds United chief executive. Ian Rush had become club captain and Carlton Palmer team captain. 'Team spirit is the best it has been,' Palmer declared on the eve of Leeds' first game at promoted Derby, where twice they were to squander a lead through defensive howlers, and drew 3–3.

While Lee Bowyer's energetic display, which was crowned with a goal, was a good omen, such lapses against a moderate attack were cause for alarm. Three days later, Leeds were outplayed and outrun by Sheffield Wednesday at Elland Road and when the following week they limped to a dreary 1–0 home victory over Wimbledon, disgruntled supporters called for Wilkinson's head and chanted for Kenny Dalglish.

Wilkinson sacked

In times of crisis, Wilkinson was wont to cast around for old warhorses: David O'Leary, Lee Chapman, Ian Rush; and now Mark Hateley. Hateley knew the game inside out but, at 35, was a shadow of the player who four seasons earlier had torpedoed Leeds' campaign in the European Cup. During his short spell on loan, Hateley, like Rush, was forced to toil in an abortive search for scraps.

Yet the mood in the camp improved as Leeds won at Blackburn on 4 September. Despite the abuse heaped upon him, Wilkinson vowed to stick to a passing game – in contrast to his dismal and direct approach of 1995–96 – and Blackburn, shockingly ineffectual on the night, let Leeds knock the ball daintily around Ewood Park. Ian Harte's header brought a 1–0 victory and appeared to fortify Leeds for their encounter with Manchester United at Elland Road four days later.

In the same fixture nine months earlier, Leeds had crushed the old enemy. Manchester were to repay them with interest: Wilkinson's fragile team was routed. When Eric Cantona, who once wore Leeds colours and was released for a song, scored Manchester's fourth and then preened himself mocking in front of the Gelderd End, the game was up for the Leeds manager. It was, as former Leeds favourite Frank Worthington said, one insult too many: 'The fans were really hurt to see the likes of Manchester United...winning so easily and Cantona, a fantastic player who they let go, rubbing it in,'.

Wilkinson's record over the preceding six months convinced the new regime at Elland Road that he should be made a sacrifice. Yet despite rumblings from the crowd and murmurs in the press, the Leeds manager seemed taken

■ Energy and aggression characterised Lee Bowyer's performances in midfield where, despite his youth, he grew up quickly and made a successful transition from First Division to Premiership.

aback. After his dismissal, he said: 'I'm very disappointed, sad, and shocked...I don't see the last eight years as a failure.' Nor were they; but the ability to motivate players, so manifest when Leeds won the championship in 1992, seemed to have deserted him.

'The hardest decision of my life – it was like tearing a piece of my body away,' declared Bill Fotherby, now installed as Leeds United's chairman. But a replacement was quickly found. The shadow of George Graham, emerging from his period of disgrace following an FA ban from the game, hovered around Elland Road; and rumours that he was the anointed successor intensified when he rejected the vacancy at Manchester City.

The arrival of George Graham

Graham had been out of football for 18 months, sacked from Arsenal in February 1995 after receiving monies from transfer deals that brought John Jensen and Pal Lydersen to Highbury. When the affair was exposed, Graham repaid the money to Arsenal; but while confessing he had been stupid and greedy, claimed that the payments were unsolicited gifts. The Leeds board cared little for such trifles: what mattered was that Graham had brought Arsenal two league championships, the FA Cup, the League Cup twice and the European Cup Winners' Cup.

He arrived at Elland Road on 10 September 1996 promising 'total commitment...hard work

> 'The hardest decision of my life – it was like tearing a piece of my body away'
>
> *Bill Fotherby on Wilkinson's dismissal.*

■ Arsenal old boys in charge. Soon after his arrival, George Graham made David O'Leary his assistant. O'Leary had been signed by Howard Wilkinson as defensive cover but injury restricted him to a handful of appearances.

and passion'; and swiftly chose David O'Leary as his assistant. 'I don't know how long it will take but the fans are going to see a committed Leeds team. I will be working with the defence first…all the great sides have a good defence,' Graham said. His appointment instantly caused Caspian shares, which on 2 August had been issued at 18.5 pence, to rise to 30 pence.

Much of the money promised to Wilkinson for buying new players remained unspent. But the season was underway: most wheeling and dealing had been done. Graham, thrifty by nature, would not make a splash for the sake of it. 'I'm quite well known for my canny buying and selling – I don't think it would be right to dash off into the transfer market straight away,' he said.

Graham's preferred method was to take stock of his inheritance and see how much players could improve. But injuries continually distorted the team. The midfield, at best bereft of quality, went into the match at Coventry on 14 September threadbare: no Sharpe, no Bowyer; and Andy Couzens' first-minute goal was not enough to prevent Leeds being overrun. Noel Whelan, whose performances in a Leeds shirt Graham had once admired, scored Coventry's second-half winner.

The 2–1 defeat at Highfield Road provided Graham with a thorough introduction to Leeds United's frailties. The defending, though less supine than against Manchester United, remained erratic; and much depended on Nigel Martyn's skill and bravery in goal. Yeboah, Dorigo, Deane and Pemberton all had long-term

injuries, so Graham was forced to send out patched-up sides and hope for the best.

It was a month before the new Leeds manager tasted a league victory. On 12 October, adroit finishing by Rod Wallace gave Leeds a 2–0 win over fellow strugglers Nottingham Forest. There was relief rather than euphoria: for long periods Forest had dominated midfield. But the quality of the win mattered little; the points were priceless.

After the Manchester United debacle, expectations sank so low that any successor to Howard Wilkinson could consider his job done if Leeds hung on in the Premiership. No-one expected a challenge for trophies. Dreadful defeats at home against Aston Villa – marked by Hateley's last game on loan and Rush's 35th birthday – and against Arsenal at Highbury emphasised that survival could not be taken for granted. In an oblique criticism of the former regime, Graham said: 'The kids we have are good but nowhere near good enough for the Premiership. Frankly, I've been very surprised by the lack of numbers and experience in the first-team squad at Leeds – for a club of our size, it is not good enough.'

But Leeds developed a knack of snatching victory against other teams in peril. A week after the Arsenal defeat, Deane and Bowyer returned for the home match against Sunderland. The outcome hinged on another prodigious goalkeeping display by Nigel Martyn: once he had fended off the visitors, Leeds seized victory with goals from Mark Ford, his first in senior football, Brian Deane and Lee Sharpe.

It took Leeds until 1 December to produce an authoritative performance against stern opposition. Their robust 2–0 victory over Chelsea, who man for man were abundantly more talented, gave George Graham's team a third victory in four matches. Chelsea were unable to recover from Leeds' storming start: goals from Deane and Rush after ten minutes buoyed up the team for the rest of the match.

Few enjoyed the day more than Rush, who scored his first goal in Leeds colours. Once the greatest striker of his generation, such was the paucity of talent at Leeds that the former Liverpool man was forced to play wide right, hustle in midfield and sometimes help out in defence: alien work, yet he did it uncomplainingly.

A tighter defence

Graham was starting to discover what his players were made of. Amid the disappointments, there were some good signs: Martyn's poise and confidence in goal; Bowyer, for one so slight and young, was a forceful presence on the left of midfield; and Lucas Radebe had learned the craft of dogged man-marking, able to snuff out the threat from sorcerers such as Liverpool's Steve MacManaman and Gianfranco Zola of Chelsea.

In early December, Graham sought to buttress his defence further. After failing to sign John Scales from Liverpool, who had a last-minute change of mind and joined Tottenham, Graham indulged his thrifty instincts by paying Oldham Athletic £400,000 for Gunnar Halle little more than a tenth of the fee Scales commanded. Yet, with his acute positional sense and awareness, Halle proved to be a bargain buy; vindication, perhaps, of George Graham's reluctance to join the paper-chase for big-name players.

Successive defeats by Coventry, Manchester United and Newcastle over the Christmas and New Year period awoke old insecurities. A defence that had gone five matches without conceding a goal suddenly leaked seven in three; though six points reaped from fellow strugglers Leicester and West Ham helped stabilise things by the time people's thoughts were turning towards the FA Cup.

Many big name teams crashed out early. When the reverberations subsided and the fifth round draw was made, Leeds found themselves joint favourites. They had disposed first of Crystal Palace, after a replay, and stolen victory in the fourth round at Arsenal, slamming shut the defence and withstanding a siege after Rod Wallace gave them an early lead.

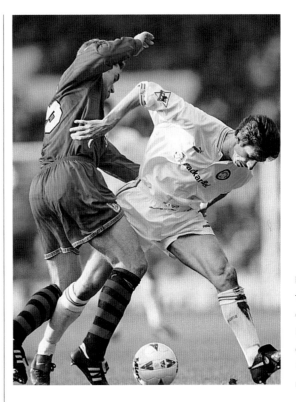

■ Although no longer the striker who terrorised defences all over Europe, Ian Rush continued to give his all for Leeds United, willing to chase many a lost cause.

Such miracles as Leeds produced were usually defensive ones: at Highbury, Halle and Kelly had been outstanding. Up front, where there was little over which to enthuse, Wallace, injury-prone and bafflingly inconsistent, still had it in him to be one of the finest sights in the Premiership, bewitching opponents with his speed and close control. His goals had taken Leeds to the fifth round, and a tie at Elland Road against first division Portsmouth. Optimistic fans saw the road to Wembley opening up before them.

Too often though Leeds served up dismal football. Some supporters took to creating their own entertainment, ritually stripping to the waist at half-time, singing and chanting while waving aloft their shirts. Even in the freezing midwinter, it gave more pleasure than sitting in silence through abominable spectacles such as the 0–0 home draw with Derby on 29 January.

An attack that had scored only twice in its last four games held few terrors for Portsmouth. In the event, they dumped Leeds out of the Cup by outplaying George Graham's men in every department, the 3–2 scoreline was scant reflection of Pompey's superiority. Yet Graham stuck with the same sickly eleven for the game at Liverpool four days later. Mulling over Leeds United's abject 4–0 defeat, *The Yorkshire Evening Post*, normally a model of restraint, described Leeds as 'woefully inept'.

The days when Tony Yeboah's power and wizardry had thrilled supporters and catalysed the Leeds attack were becoming a distant memory. Yeboah's relationship with George Graham

■ Circumstances forced Lucas Radebe to play in defence and midfield. But he grew in stature throughout 1996–97, becoming less erratic and evolving into an unyielding man-marker. His improvement was rewarded by being appointed captain of South Africa.

'Nigel Martyn has kept us in the Premiership and that could be worth £6–8 million,'

Bill Fotherby

had grown strained; quarrels about his fitness, commitment and other grievances were conducted in the glare of the media. But after Leeds' humiliating capitulation away to Liverpool, George Graham appeared to concede that those clamouring for Yeboah's return might have a case; and on 22 February recalled the Ghanaian for the trip to Sunderland.

He missed two sitters, yet almost scored with an extravagant drive from 35 yards. Such was Yeboah's style. But while on another afternoon his profligacy could have been costly, a goal from Lee Bowyer brought victory: the first of three successive 1–0 wins that kept Leeds above the relegation mire.

Save for the lapses at Liverpool and against Portsmouth, Graham had gone a long way towards fashioning a stout defence. 'You know me – I want it to be watertight: the goalkeeper to be redundant,' he said. In January, with this mission in mind, he paid the Dutch team FC Volendam £1.1 million for Robert Molenaar, a rugged, beefy defender, though one capable of working the ball tidily out of defence.

Graham was to spend ever more time trawling the continent for unsung talent. The likes of Molenaar and Halle had proved a point: it was hard to imagine how John Scales could have performed more effectively. But finding creative players and goalscorers cheaply was a taller order. Meanwhile Tomas Brolin remained in exile, having been farmed out on loan first to FC Zurich, then to his old club, Parma. The prospects of any reconciliation with Leeds looked forlorn.

Before the transfer deadline, two more recruits were drafted in by Leeds from the bargain basement: Derek Lilley, a 24-year-old striker from Morton valued at £700,000, and Pierre Laurent, 26, a winger signed from the French league club, Bastia, for £250,000. Neither had much opportunity to shine as the team's performances became numbingly sterile. 'So much money, so little talent' lamented *The Yorkshire Evening Post* after Leeds players, some of them earning several thousands of pounds a week, bored fans to tears with a 0–0 draw at Elland Road against Blackburn Rovers.

■ Clearing his lines: Nigel Martyn, an invaluable part of Howard Wilkinson's legacy to George Graham, may well have kept Leeds in the Premiership. The outcome of several key matches turned on Martyn's ability to thwart the opposition; and earned him an England recall for the match against South Africa in May 1997.

Yeboah was again in cold storage. Although no more culpable than most of his colleagues for the 1–0 defeat at Tottenham on 15 March, he responded to being substituted by ripping off his shirt and hurling it towards the Leeds dugout. Such petulance, which endeared him neither to the management nor the fans who campaigned for his restoration, signified a deeper malaise. With his confidence shot to pieces, Yeboah, banished to reserve team football, confessed: 'I'm too nervous for the first-team. In the reserves, I am relaxed; I can try my tricks. Without them, I'm nothing.'

Amid the miserable performances, there was a sparkling 2–2 draw at Sheffield Wednesday in which George Graham's team showed more enterprise and fewer inhibitions than at any time in the season. Some may have found a strand of irony in the manager's post-match reflections. 'Everyone in football knows it's not my style to be dour and functional,' Graham said. 'What the fans saw from Leeds at Hillsborough is what I really stand for.'

Young talent

Yet what stylish football had been played in Leeds colours came principally from the juniors: FA Youth Cup winners for the second time in four seasons and Northern Intermediate League champions. The consensus was that the class of 1996–97, moulded by Paul Hart and Eddie Gray, was technically superior to that of 1992–93, from which only Noel Whelan had graduated with any distinction.

Andy Gray, the most confident and mature young player to break into the first team, missed much of 1996–97 through injury, but some fans were mystified that after regaining fitness, he remained peripheral. A palpable exception to Graham's mantra that British football produced too few talented youngsters, doses of Gray's flair might have enlivened the last rites of what *The Yorkshire Evening Post* described as 'A tedious campaign: the fans have been the true heroes, digging deep into their pockets.'

It was a season in which Leeds never retrieved a deficit in League matches: once a goal down, they were invariably out. Off the field, dissatisfaction over the club's commercial operation led to the sacking of Robin Launders. Business and football considerations were woven into Bill Fotherby's review of 1996–97. 'Nigel Martyn has kept us in the Premiership; and that could be worth between £6–8 million,' he said.

Martyn had been outstanding in a year that Leeds' miserable tally of 28 League goals made them the ugliest team in the Premiership. After the final match, a 1–1 draw at Elland Road that condemned Middlesbrough to relegation, George Graham resumed moulding Leeds United in his own image, paying Glasgow Rangers £800,000 for Scottish international left-back David Robertson. He remained true to his dictum: get the defence right first. The fireworks would have to wait.

The shape of things to come? Hopes for the future were high at Elland Road after the youth team's magnificent double: Northern Intermediate League champions and FA Youth Cup winners. Here they celebrate at Selhurst Park after their Cup victory over Crystal Palace.

Facts and Figures

This section contains all of Leeds United's results, team line-ups and goalscorers between 1920 and 1996 in the League, the FA Cup, the League Cup and in European competitions. There are no statistics for the years from 1939-1946 – no League or Cup fixtures took place during those seasons. Opponents' name in capitals denotes a home fixture.

DIVISION TWO 1920-21

			1	2	3	4	5	6	7	8	9	10	11
Aug 28	Port Vale	0-2	Down	Duffield	Tillotson	Musgrove	Baker	Walton	Mason	Goldthorpe	Thompson	Lyon	Best
Sep 1	SOUTH SHIELDS	1-2	Down	Duffield	Tillotson	Musgrove	Baker	Walton	Mason	Ellson	Armitage 1	Lyon	Best
Sep 4	PORT VALE	3-1	Down	Duffield	Frew	Musgrove	Baker	Walton	Mason	Ellson 2	Armitage	Lyon	Best 1
Sep 8	South Shields	0-3	Down	Duffield	Frew	Musgrove	Baker	Walton	Hill	Ellson	Goldthorpe	Lyon	Best
Sep 11	Leicester City	1-1	Down	Duffield	Frew	Musgrove	Baker	Walton	Hill	Ellson 1	Goldthorpe	Lyon	Best
Sep 18	LEICESTER CITY	3-1	Down	Duffield	Frew	Musgrove	Baker	Walton	Mason	Ellson 1	Goldthorpe 2	Lyon	Best
Sep 25	Blackpool	0-1	Down	Duffield	Frew	Musgrove	Baker	Walton	Mason	Ellson	Goldthorpe	Lyon	Best
Oct 2	BLACKPOOL	2-0	Down	Duffield	Frew	Musgrove	Baker	Walton 1	Mason 1	Ellson	Goldthorpe	Lyon	Best
Oct 9	Sheffield Wednesday	0-2	Down	Duffield	Frew	Musgrove	Baker	Walton	Mason	Ellson	Armitage	Lyon	Best
Oct 16	SHEFFIELD WEDNESDAY	2-0	Down	Duffield	Frew	Musgrove	Baker	Walton	Mason	Ellson 1	Thompson 1	Lyon	Brook
Oct 23	Hull City	1-0	Down	Duffield	Frew	Musgrove	Baker	Walton	Mason	Ellson	Thompson 1	Lyon	Best
Oct 30	HULL CITY	1-1	Down	Duffield	Frew	Musgrove	Baker	Walton	Mason	Ellson 1	Armitage	Lyon	Best
Nov 6	Stoke	0-4	Down	Duffield	Frew	Musgrove	Baker	Walton	Mason	Ellson	Armitage	Lyon	Boardman
Nov 13	STOKE	0-0	Down	Duffield	Frew	Musgrove	Baker	Walton	Mason	Ellson	Thompson	Lyon	Boardman
Nov 27	Coventry City	1-1	Down	Duffield	Frew	Musgrove	Baker	Walton	Mason	Ellson	Thompson	Lyon 1	Hill
Dec 1	COVENTRY CITY	4-0	Down	Duffield	Frew	Musgrove	Baker	Walton	Mason 1	Ellson 1	Thompson 2	Lyon	Sharpe
Dec 4	Notts County	2-1	Down	Duffield	Frew	Musgrove	Baker	Walton	Mason	Ellson	Thompson	Lyon 2	Hill
Dec 11	NOTTS COUNTY	3-0	Down	Duffield	Frew	Musgrove	Baker	Walton	Mason	Ellson	Thompson 3	Lyon	Hill
Dec 18	Birmingham	0-1	Down	Duffield	Frew	Musgrove	Baker	Walton	Mason	Ellson	Thompson	Lyon	Hill
Dec 25	FULHAM	0-0	Down	Duffield	Frew	Musgrove	Baker	Walton	Mason	Ellson	Thompson	Lyon	Wood
Dec 27	Fulham	0-1	Down	Duffield	Frew	Musgrove	Baker	Walton	Mason	Ellson	Thompson	Lyon	Hill
Jan 1	BIRMINGHAM	1-0	Down	Duffield	Frew	Musgrove	Baker 1	Walton	Mason	Ellson	Thompson	Lyon	Wood
Jan 8	ROTHERHAM	1-0	Down	Duffield	Frew	Musgrove	Baker	Walton	Mason	Ellson 1	Thompson	Lyon	Wood
Jan 15	Wolverhampton Wans	0-3	Down	Duffield	Frew	Musgrove	Baker	Walton	Mason	Ellson	Thompson	Lyon	Wood
Jan 22	WOLVERHAMPTON WANS	3-0	Down	Duffield	Frew	Musgrove	Baker	Walton	Mason	Ellson	Thompson 2	Lyon 1	Wood
Jan 29	WEST HAM UNITED	1-2	Down	Duffield	Frew	Musgrove	Baker	Walton	Brock	Ellson	Thompson 1	Lyon	Wood
Feb 5	West Ham United	0-3	Down	Duffield	Frew	Musgrove	Baker	Walton	Brock	Boardman	Thompson	Lyon	Wood
Feb 12	Stockport County	1-3	Down	Duffield	Smelt	Musgrove	Baker	Walton	Brock	Boardman	Thompson 1	Lyon	Wood
Feb 19	STOCKPORT COUNTY	0-2	Down	Duffield	Frew	Baker	Hart	Stuart	Mason	Ellson	Thompson	Butler	Wood
Feb 26	Clapton Orient	0-1	Down	Duffield	Frew	Lamph	Baker	Walton	Mason	Musgrove	Thompson	Ellson	Wood
Mar 5	CLAPTON ORIENT	2-1	Down	Duffield	Frew	Lamph	Baker 1	Walton	Mason	Musgrove 1	Thompson	Ellson	Wood
Mar 12	Bury	1-1	Down	Duffield	Frew	Lamph	Baker	Walton	Thompson	Musgrove	Howarth 1	Ellson	Wood
Mar 19	BURY	1-0	Down	Duffield	Frew	Lamph	Baker	Walton	Thompson	Musgrove 1	Howarth	Ellson	Wood
Mar 26	BRISTOL CITY	0-1	Down	Duffield	Frew	Lamph	Baker	Walton	Mason	Brock	Howarth	Ellson	Wood
Mar 28	Cardiff City	0-1	Down	Duffield	Frew	Lamph	Baker	Walton	Mason	Brock	Howarth	Ellson	Wood
Mar 29	CARDIFF CITY	1-2	Down	Duffield	Frew	Musgrove	Baker	Walton	Mason	Powell	Howarth 1	Lyon	Wood
Apr 2	Bristol City	0-0	Down	Duffield	Baker	Musgrove	Hart	Walton	Mason	Powell	Howarth	Lyon	Wood
Apr 9	BARNSLEY	0-0	Down	Duffield	Frew	Musgrove	Baker	Walton	Mason	Ellson	Howarth	Lyon	Wood
Apr 16	Barnsley	1-1	Down	Duffield	Frew	Musgrove	Baker	Walton	Mason	Ellson	Howarth 1	Lyon	Wood
Apr 23	NOTTINGHAM FOREST	1-1	Down	Duffield	Rodgerson	Hart	Baker	Walton	Mason	Ellson	Howarth 1	Lyon	Wood
Apr 30	Nottingham Forest	0-1	Down	Frew	Rodgerson	Musgrove	Hart	Walton	Mason	Duffield	Howarth	Ellson	Wood
May 7	Rotherham	2-0	Down	Duffield	Rodgerson	Musgrove	Hart	Walton	Mason	Armitage	Howarth 2	Powell	Wood

F.A. CUP

Sep 11	BOOTH TOWN	Qrd 1 5-2	Jacklin	Coope	McGee	Stuart	Hart	Cooper	Waterhouse	O'Doherty 3	Armitage 2	Butler	Thompson
Sep 25	Leeds Steelworks (At Elland Road)	Qrd 2 7-0	Jacklin	Coope	Smelt	Stuart	Hart 1	Cooper	Waterhouse 1	O'Doherty 1	Thompson 1	Butler 3	Hill

After defeating Leeds Steelworks, the club then withdrew from the F.A. Cup.

DIVISION TWO 1921-22

Aug 27	PORT VALE	2-1	Whalley	Duffield	Rodgerson	Baker	Sherwin	Walton 1	Clark	Armitage	Howarth 1	Moore	Wood
Aug 29	Bristol City	0-0	Whalley	Duffield	Rodgerson	Baker	Sherwin	Walton	Clark	Armitage	Howarth	Moore	Wood
Sep 3	Port Vale	1-0	Whalley	Duffield	Rodgerson	Baker	Sherwin	Walton	Clark	Armitage	Howarth 1	Moore	Wood
Sep 5	BRISTOL CITY	3-0	Whalley	Duffield	Rodgerson	Baker	Hart	Walton	Mason	Armitage	Howarth 2	Moore 1	Wood
Sep 10	BLACKPOOL	0-0	Whalley	Duffield	Rodgerson	Baker	Hart	Walton	Mason	Armitage	Howarth	Moore	Wood
Sep 17	Blackpool	3-1	Whalley	Duffield	Rodgerson	Baker	Hart	Walton	Mason 1	Armitage	Howarth 1	Moore	Wood 1
Sep 24	CLAPTON ORIENT	2-0	Whalley	Duffield	Rodgerson	Baker	Hart	Walton	Coates	Armitage	Howarth 1	Moore	Wood 1
Oct 1	Clapton Orient	2-4	Whalley	Frew	Rodgerson	Baker	Hart	Walton	Coates	Armitage	Howarth 1	Moore 1	Wood
Oct 8	SOUTH SHIELDS	0-0	Whalley	Duffield	Rodgerson	Baker	Hart	Walton	Coates	Armitage	Howarth	Moore	Wood
Oct 15	South Shields	1-0	Whalley	Duffield	Rodgerson	Baker	Hart	Walton	Coates	Armitage	Howarth 1	Moore	Wood
Oct 22	STOKE CITY	1-2	Whalley	Duffield	Rodgerson	Baker	Hart	Walton	Coates	Armitage	Howarth 1	Moore	Wood
Oct 29	Stoke City	0-3	Whalley	Duffield	Rodgerson	Sherwin	Hart	Baker	Mason	Armitage	Poyntz	Moore	Wood
Nov 5	BRADFORD	3-0	Whalley	Duffield	Frew	Sherwin	Hart	Baker	Mason 1	Armitage 1	Howarth 1	Moore	Wood
Nov 12	Bradford	1-0	Whalley	Duffield	Frew	Sherwin	Hart	Baker	Mason	Armitage	Howarth 1	Moore	Wood
Nov 19	Hull City	0-1	Whalley	Duffield	Frew	Sherwin	Hart	Baker	Mason	Moore	Howarth	Swan	Wood
Nov 26	HULL CITY	0-2	Whalley	Frew	Rodgerson	Sherwin	Hart	Baker	Mason	Armitage	Howarth	Moore	Wood
Dec 3	Notts County	1-4	Down	Duffield	Frew	Sherwin	Hart	Baker	Mason	Armitage	Howarth 1	Moore	Wood
Dec 10	NOTTS COUNTY	1-1	Jacklin	Duffield	Frew	Gascoigne	Sherwin	Baker	Mason	Moore 1	Howarth	Ellson	Wood
Dec 17	CRYSTAL PALACE	0-0	Jacklin	Duffield	Potts	Gascoigne	Baker	Walton	Mason	Moore	Poyntz	Powell	Clark
Dec 24	Crystal Palace	2-1	Jacklin	Duffield	Rodgerson	Gascoigne	Baker	Walton	Mason	Moore 1	Howarth	Swan 1	Wood
Dec 26	SHEFFIELD WEDNESDAY	1-1	Whalley	Duffield	Rodgerson	Gascoigne	Baker	Walton	Mason	Moore	Howarth	Swan 1	Wood
Dec 27	Sheffield Wednesday	1-2	Whalley	Frew	Rodgerson	Gascoigne	Hart	Baker	Mason	Armitage	Howarth 1	Swan	Wood
Dec 31	ROTHERHAM	0-2	Whalley	Duffield	Rodgerson	Gascoigne	Baker	Frew	Mason	Moore	Howarth	Swan	Wood
Jan 14	Rotherham	0-1	Whalley	Duffield	Rodgerson	Sherwin	Baker	Walton	Mason	Armitage	Howarth	Swan	Wood
Jan 21	WEST HAM UNITED	0-0	Whalley	Duffield	Rodgerson	Sherwin	Baker	Walton	Coates	Poyntz	Howarth	Swan	Wood
Jan 28	West Ham United	1-1	Whalley	Duffield	Rodgerson	Sherwin	Hart	Baker	Coates	Poyntz	Armitage 1	Swan	Wood
Feb 4	BURY	2-0	Whalley	Duffield	Rodgerson	Sherwin	Hart	Baker	Coates	Poyntz 1	Armitage 1	Swan	Wood
Feb 11	Bury	1-2	Whalley	Duffield	Rodgerson	Sherwin	Hart	Baker	Coates	Poyntz	Armitage 1	Swan	Wood
Feb 20	LEICESTER CITY	3-0	Whalley	Duffield	Rodgerson	Sherwin	Hart	Baker	Coates	Poyntz 3	Armitage	Swan	Moore
Feb 25	Leicester City	0-0	Whalley	Duffield	Rodgerson	Sherwin	Hart	Baker	Coates	Poyntz	Armitage	Moore	Wood
Mar 4	DERBY COUNTY	2-1	Whalley	Duffield	Rodgerson	Sherwin	Hart	Baker	Coates	Howarth	Armitage	Swan 2	Moore
Mar 11	Derby County	0-2	Whalley	Duffield	Rodgerson	Sherwin	Hart	Baker	Coates	Moore	Howarth	Swan	Wood
Mar 18	Coventry City	0-1	Whalley	Duffield	Frew	Walton	Hart	Baker	Coates	Robson	Howarth	Swan	Wood
Mar 25	COVENTRY CITY	5-2	Whalley	Duffield	Frew	Sherwin	Hart	Baker	Coates	Robson	Armitage 2	Swan 3	Wood
Apr 1	Barnsley	2-2	Whalley	Duffield	Frew	Sherwin	Hart	Baker	Coates	Poyntz	Armitage 1	Swan 1	Clark
Apr 8	BARNSLEY	(o.g.) 4-0	Whalley	Duffield	Frew	Sherwin	Hart	Baker	Coates	Poyntz 1	Armitage	Swan 2	Clark
Apr 14	FULHAM	2-0	Whalley	Duffield	Frew	Sherwin	Hart	Baker	Coates 1	Poyntz 1	Armitage	Swan	Clark
Apr 15	Wolverhampton Wans	0-0	Whalley	Duffield	Frew	Sherwin	Hart	Baker	Coates	Poyntz	Armitage	Swan	Clark
Apr 17	Fulham	1-0	Whalley	Duffield	Frew	Sherwin	Hart	Baker	Coates	Poyntz	Armitage 1	Swan	Clark
Apr 22	WOLVERHAMPTON WANS	0-0	Whalley	Duffield	Frew	Sherwin	Hart	Baker	Wood	Poyntz	Armitage	Swan	Clark
Apr 29	Nottingham Forest	0-1	Whalley	Rodgerson	Frew	Sherwin	Hart	Baker	Mason	Moore	Howarth	Swan	Wood
May 6	NOTTINGHAM FOREST	0-0	Whalley	Duffield	Frew	Sherwin	Hart	Baker	Robson	Poyntz	Howarth	Powell	Wood

F.A. CUP

Jan 7	Swindon Town	Rd 1 1-2	Whalley	Duffield	Rodgerson	Sherwin	Baker	Walton	Mason	Armitage	Howarth	Swan 1	Moore

DIVISION TWO 1922-23

Aug 26	BLACKPOOL	1-1	Whalley	Duffield	Frew	Sherwin	Hart	Baker	Mason	Poyntz	Howarth	Swan 1	Harris
Aug 28	Southampton	1-0	Whalley	Duffield	Frew	Sherwin	Hart	Baker	Mason	Poyntz	Howarth	Swan 1	Harris
Sep 2	Blackpool	0-1	Whalley	Duffield	Frew	Sherwin	Hart	Baker	Mason	Poyntz	Howarth	Swan	Harris
Sep 4	SOUTHAMPTON	1-0	Whalley	Duffield	Frew	Sherwin	Hart	Baker	Mason	Robson	Howarth	Armitage	Harris 1
Sep 9	STOCKPORT COUNTY	2-0	Whalley	Duffield	Frew	Sherwin	Hart	Baker	Mason	Walton 1	Armitage 1	Powell	Harris
Sep 16	Stockport County	1-2	Whalley	Duffield	Frew	Gascoigne	Hart	Baker	Mason	Walton	Armitage 1	Powell	Harris
Sep 23	BRADFORD CITY	1-0	Whalley	Duffield	Frew	Sherwin	Hart	Baker	Mason	Poyntz	Armitage	Swan	Harris 1
Sep 30	Bradford City	2-0	Whalley	Duffield	Frew	Sherwin	Hart	Baker	Mason	Poyntz	Armitage	Swan 1	Harris 1
Oct 7	Clapton Orient	0-3	Whalley	Duffield	Frew	Sherwin	Hart	Baker	Mason	Poyntz	Armitage	Swan	Clark

DIVISION TWO 1922-23 continued

			1	2	3	4	5	6	7	8	9	10	11
Oct 14	CLAPTON ORIENT	0-0	Whalley	Duffield	Potts	Gascoigne	Hart	Baker	Mason	Poyntz	Howarth	Swan	Harris
Oct 21	LEICESTER CITY	0-0	Whalley	Duffield	Potts	Sherwin	Hart	Baker	Mason	Poyntz	Howarth	Swan	Harris
Oct 28	Leicester City	1-2	Whalley	Duffield	Potts	Sherwin	Hart	Baker	Mason	Dark	Poyntz	Swan	Harris 1
Nov 4	WEST HAM UNITED	3-1	Whalley	Duffield	Potts	Sherwin	Hart	Baker	Noble	Whipp 3	Poyntz	Swan	Harris
Nov 11	West Ham United	0-0	Whalley	Duffield	Potts	Sherwin	Hart	Baker	Noble	Whipp	Poyntz	Swan	Harris
Nov 18	SOUTH SHIELDS	0-1	Whalley	Duffield	Potts	Sherwin	Hart	Baker	Noble	Whipp	Poyntz	Swan	Harris
Nov 25	South Shields	2-0	Whalley	Duffield	Potts	Sherwin	Hart	Baker	Noble	Whipp 1	Poyntz 1	Walton	Harris
Dec 2	WOLVERHAMPTON WANS	1-0	Whalley	Duffield	Potts	Sherwin	Hart	Baker	Noble	Whipp	Poyntz	Walton 1	Harris
Dec 9	Wolverhampton Wans	1-0	Whalley	Duffield	Frew	Sherwin	Hart 1	Baker	Noble	Whipp	Richmond	Walton	Harris
Dec 16	Coventry City	2-1	Whalley	Duffield	Frew	Sherwin	Hart	Baker	Noble	Whipp	Richmond 2	Walton	Clark
Dec 23	COVENTRY CITY	1-0	Whalley	Duffield	Frew	Sherwin	Hart	Baker	Noble	Whipp 1	Richmond	Walton	Clark
Dec 25	Bury	1-1	Whalley	Duffield	Bell T.	Sherwin	Hart	Baker	Noble	Whipp 1	Armitage	Walton	Harris
Dec 26	BURY	0-0	Whalley	Duffield	Frew	Sherwin	Hart	Baker	Mason	Whipp	Richmond	Walton	Harris
Dec 30	Port Vale	2-1	Whalley	Duffield	Frew	Sherwin	Hart	Baker	Noble	Whipp 2	Armitage	Walton	Harris
Jan 6	PORT VALE	2-1	Whalley	Duffield	Frew	Sherwin	Hart	Baker	Noble	Whipp 2	Armitage	Walton	Harris
Jan 20	Manchester United	0-0	Whalley	Duffield	Frew	Gascoigne	Hart	Baker	Noble	Whipp	Armitage	Swan	Harris
Jan 27	MANCHESTER UNITED	0-1	Whalley	Duffield	Frew	Sherwin	Hart	Baker	Noble	Whipp	Armand	Swan	Harris
Feb 10	Barnsley	0-1	Whalley	Duffield	Frew	Gascoigne	Hart	Baker	Noble	Whipp	Armitage	Swan	Harris
Feb 17	SHEFFIELD WEDNESDAY	0-0	Whalley	Duffield	Frew	Gascoigne	Hart	Baker	Noble	Whipp	Richmond	Armand	Harris
Feb 24	BARNSLEY	1-1	Whalley	Duffield	Frew	Gascoigne	Hart	Baker	Noble	Whipp	Armand	Swan 1	Harris
Mar 3	HULL CITY	2-2	Whalley	Duffield	Frew	Sherwin	Baker	Gascoigne	Noble	Whipp	Armand	Swan 2	Harris
Mar 10	Hull City	1-3	Whalley	Duffield	Frew	Gascoigne	Hart	Baker	Noble	Whipp	Swan 1	Armand	Harris
Mar 17	Crystal Palace	0-1	Whalley	Duffield	Frew	Gascoigne	Hart	Baker	Noble	Whipp	Armand	Swan	Harris
Mar 19	Sheffield Wednesday	1-3	Whalley	Duffield	Frew	Gascoigne	Hart	Baker	Noble	Robson	Powell 1	Armand	Harris
Mar 24	CRYSTAL PALACE	4-1	Whalley	Duffield	Frew	Sherwin 1	Hart	Baker	Noble	Whipp 1	Powell 1	Swan 1	Harris
Mar 30	ROTHERHAM	2-0	Whalley	Duffield	Frew	Sherwin	Hart	Baker	Noble	Whipp 1	Powell 1	Swan	Harris
Mar 31	Fulham	0-3	Whalley	Duffield	Frew	Gascoigne	Hart	Baker	Coates	Whipp	Powell	Swan	Harris
Apr 2	Rotherham	1-3	Whalley	Potts	Frew	Dark	Hart	Baker	Noble	Whipp	Powell	Swan	Harris 1
Apr 7	FULHAM	1-1	Whalley	Duffield	Frew	Dark	Hart	Baker	Noble	Robson	Powell	Whipp 1	Harris
Apr 14	Notts County	0-1	Whalley	Duffield	Frew	Sherwin	Hart	Baker	Noble	Robson	Powell	Whipp	Harris
Apr 21	NOTTS COUNTY	3-0	Whalley	Duffield	Frew	Sherwin	Hart	Baker	Noble	Robson	Powell 1	Whipp 2	Harris
Apr 28	Derby County	1-0	Whalley	Duffield	Frew	Smith	Hart	Baker	Noble 1	Robson	Powell	Whipp	Harris
May 5	DERBY COUNTY	1-0	Whalley	Duffield	Frew	Smith	Hart	Baker	Noble	Robson	Powell 1	Whipp	Harris

F.A. CUP

Jan 13	Portsmouth	Rd 1 0-0	Whalley	Duffield	Frew	Sherwin	Hart	Baker	Noble	Whipp	Armitage	Walton	Harris
Jan 17	PORTSMOUTH	Rd 1 R 3-1	Whalley	Duffield	Frew	Sherwin	Hart	Baker	Noble	Whipp 1	Armitage 1	Swan 1	Harris
Feb 3	Bolton Wanderers	Rd 2 1-3	Whalley	Duffield	Frew	Sherwin	Hart	Baker	Noble	Whipp	Armitage	Swan 1	Harris

DIVISION TWO 1923-24

Aug 25	Stoke City	1-1	Whalley	Duffield	Speak	Sherwin	Mason	JW Baker	Noble 1	Whipp	Richmond	Fullam	Harris
Aug 27	CRYSTAL PALACE	3-0	Whalley	Duffield	Speak	Sherwin	Mason	JW Baker	Noble 1	Whipp 1	Richmond	Fullam 1	Harris
Sep 1	STOKE CITY	0-0	Whalley	Duffield	Speak	Sherwin	Mason	JW Baker	Noble	Whipp	Powell	Fullam	Harris
Sep 5	Crystal Palace	1-1	Whalley	Duffield	Speak	Sherwin	Mason	JW Baker	Noble	Whipp 1	Richmond	Fullam	Harris
Sep 8	Leicester City	0-2	Whalley	Duffield	Frew	Sherwin	Mason	JW Baker	Noble	Lambert	Powell	Whipp	Harris
Sep 15	LEICESTER CITY	1-2	Whalley	Duffield	Speak	Sherwin	Mason	JW Baker	Noble	Whipp	Richmond	Swan 1	Harris
Sep 22	Hull City	2-1	Down	Duffield	Speak	Sherwin	L Baker	JW Baker	Noble	Whipp	Richmond	Swan 2	Harris
Sep 29	HULL CITY	5-2	Down	Duffield	Speak	Sherwin	L Baker	JW Baker	Noble	Whipp	Richmond 3	Swan 1	Harris 1
Oct 6	Clapton Orient	1-0	Down	Duffield	Speak	Gascoigne	L Baker	JW Baker	Noble	Whipp	Richmond 1	Swan	Harris
Oct 13	CLAPTON ORIENT	1-0	Down	Duffield	Speak	Gascoigne	L Baker	JW Baker	Coates	Whipp	Richmond	Swan	Harris 1
Oct 20	Port Vale	1-0	Down	Duffield	Speak	Sherwin	Hart	JW Baker	Coates	Whipp	Richmond 1	Swan	Harris
Oct 27	PORT VALE	3-0	Down	Duffield	Frew	Sherwin	Hart	JW Baker	Coates	Whipp	Richmond 1	Swan 2	Harris
Nov 3	BRADFORD CITY	1-0	Down	Duffield	Frew	Sherwin	Hart	JW Baker	Coates	Whipp 1	Richmond	Swan	Harris
Nov 10	Bradford City	0-0	Down	Duffield	Speak	Sherwin	Hart	JW Baker	Coates	Whipp	Richmond	Swan	Harris
Nov 17	BARNSLEY	3-1	Down	Duffield	Speak	Sherwin	Hart	JW Baker	Coates	Whipp 1	Richmond	Swan 2	Harris
Nov 24	Barnsley	3-1	Down	Duffield	Speak	Sherwin	Hart	JW Baker	Coates	Whipp	Richmond 2	Swan	Harris 1
Dec 1	MANCHESTER UNITED	0-0	Down	Duffield	Speak	Sherwin	Hart	JW Baker	Coates	Whipp	Richmond	Swan	Harris
Dec 8	Manchester United	1-3	Down	Duffield	Speak	Sherwin	Hart	JW Baker	Coates	Whipp 1	Richmond	Swan	Harris
Dec 15	BURY	1-2	Down	Duffield	Speak	Sherwin	Hart	JW Baker	Coates	Whipp 1	Richmond	Swan	Harris
Dec 22	Bury	0-3	Down	Duffield	Speak	Mason	Hart	L Baker	Noble	Armand	Powell	Swan	Harris
Dec 25	Oldham Athletic	2-2	Down	Duffield	Menzies	Sherwin	Hart	L Baker	Noble	Armand	Richmond 2	Swan	Harris
Dec 26	OLDHAM ATHLETIC	5-0	Down	Duffield	Speak	JW Baker	Hart	L Baker	Noble	Whipp 2	Richmond 1	Swan 2	Armand
Jan 5	South Shields	0-2	Down	Duffield	Speak	JW Baker	Hart	L Baker	Noble	Whipp	Richmond	Swan	Harris
Jan 19	Sheffield Wednesday	0-0	Down	Duffield	Menzies	Sherwin	Mason	L Baker	Armand	Whipp	Richmond	Swan	Harris
Jan 26	SHEFFIELD WEDNESDAY	1-0	Down	Duffield	Menzies	Sherwin	Hart	JW Baker	Noble	Whipp	Powell	Swan 1	Harris
Feb 9	COVENTRY CITY	3-1	Down	Duffield	Frew	Gascoigne	Mason	JW Baker	Coates	Armand 1	Richmond 1	Swan	Harris 1
Feb 16	Bristol City	1-0	Down	Duffield	Menzies	Sherwin	Hart	JW Baker	Coates	Whipp	Richmond	Swan 1	Harris
Feb 27	SOUTH SHIELDS	2-1	Whalley	Duffield	Menzies	Sherwin	Hart	JW Baker	Noble	Whipp 1	Armand 1	Swan	Harris
Mar 1	Southampton	(o.g.) 1-0	Johnson	A Bell	Menzies	Sherwin	Hart 1	JW Baker	Noble	Whipp	Armand	Swan	Harris
Mar 8	SOUTHAMPTON	(o.g.) 3-0	Down	Duffield	Speak	Sherwin	Hart	JW Baker	Noble	Whipp	Richmond	Swan 1	Harris 1
Mar 10	Coventry City	1-2	Down	Duffield	Menzies	Sherwin 1	Hart	JW Baker	Noble	Whipp	Richmond	Swan	Harris
Mar 15	FULHAM	3-0	Johnson	Duffield	Menzies	Sherwin	Hart	JW Baker	Coates 1	Whipp	Richmond	Swan 2	Harris
Mar 19	BRISTOL CITY	0-0	Down	Duffield	Menzies	Sherwin	Hart	JW Baker	Coates	Whipp	Richmond	Swan	Harris
Mar 22	Fulham	2-0	Down	Duffield	Speak	L Baker	Mason	Smith	Harris	Whipp 1	Swan	Fullam 1	Allen
Mar 29	BLACKPOOL	0-0	Down	Duffield	Menzies	JW Baker	Hart	Smith	Harris	Whipp	Swan	Fullam	Allen
Apr 5	Blackpool	1-1	Down	Duffield	Menzies	JW Baker	Hart	Smith	Noble	Whipp	Richmond 1	Swan	Harris
Apr 12	DERBY COUNTY	1-1	Down	JW Baker	Menzies	Sherwin	Hart	Smith	Noble	Whipp 1	Richmond	Swan	Harris
Apr 18	Stockport County	1-1	Down	Menzies	Speak	JW Baker	Hart	Smith	Noble	Whipp	Richmond 1	Swan	Harris
Apr 19	Derby County	0-2	Johnson	Menzies	Speak	Sherwin	Hart	Smith	Coates	Whipp	Richmond	Fullam	Harris
Apr 21	STOCKPORT COUNTY	4-0	Down	Duffield	Menzies	JW Baker	Hart	Smith	Coates	Whipp	Richmond 1	Swan 2	Harris 1
Apr 26	NELSON	1-0	Down	Duffield	Menzies	JW Baker	Hart	Smith	Coates 1	Whipp	Richmond	Swan	Harris
May 3	Nelson	1-3	Down	Duffield	Menzies	Sherwin	Hart	Smith	Coates	Whipp	Richmond	Swan 1	Harris

F.A. CUP

Jan 12	STOKE CITY	Rd 1 1-0	Down	Duffield	Speak	Sherwin	Hart	JW Baker	Armand	Whipp 1	Richmond	Swan	Harris
Feb 2	West Ham United	Rd 2 1-1	Down	Duffield	Speak	Sherwin	Hart	JW Baker	Coates 1	Whipp	Richmond	Swan	Harris
Feb 6	WEST HAM UNITED	Rd 2 R 1-0	Down	Duffield	Speak	Sherwin	Hart	JW Baker	Coates	Whipp 1	Richmond	Swan	Harris
Feb 23	Aston Villa	Rd 3 0-3	Down	Duffield	Menzies	Sherwin	Hart	JW Baker	Coates	Whipp	Richmond	Swan	Harris

DIVISION ONE 1924-25

Aug 30	SUNDERLAND	1-1	Down	Duffield	Menzies	Sherwin	Hart	JW Baker	Noble	Whipp	Richmond	Swan 1	Harris
Sep 1	Notts County	0-1	Down	Duffield	Menzies	Duxbury	Hart	JW Baker	Harris	Thom	Graver	Swan	Clark
Sep 6	Cardiff City	0-3	Down	Duffield	Menzies	Duxbury	Hart	JW Baker	Coates	Whipp	Richmond	Swan	Harris
Sep 10	NOTTS COUNTY	1-1	Down	Duffield	Menzies	Sherwin	Hart	JW Baker	Coates	Whipp	Richmond	Swan 1	Harris
Sep 13	PRESTON NORTH END	4-0	Down	Duffield	Menzies	Sherwin	Hart	JW Baker	Coates	Whipp	Thom 1	Swan 2	Harris 1
Sep 17	EVERTON	1-0	Down	Duffield	Menzies	Sherwin	Hart	JW Baker	Coates	Whipp	Thom 1	Swan	Harris
Sep 20	Burnley	1-1	Down	Duffield	Menzies	Sherwin	Hart	JW Baker	Coates	Whipp	Thom 1	Swan	Harris
Sep 27	HUDDERSFIELD TOWN	1-1	Down	Duffield	Menzies	Sherwin	Hart	JW Baker	Coates	Whipp	Thom	Swan 1	Harris
Oct 4	BIRMINGHAM	0-1	Johnson	Duffield	Menzies	Sherwin	Hart	JW Baker	Coates	Whipp	Thom	Swan	Harris
Oct 11	West Bromwich Albion	1-3	Johnson	Duffield	Speak	Duxbury	Hart	JW Baker	Robson 1	Whipp	Richmond	Swan	Harris
Oct 18	TOTTENHAM HOTSPUR	1-0	Johnson	Duffield	Menzies	Sherwin	Hart	JW Baker	Robson	Whipp 1	Thom	Swan	Harris
Oct 25	Blackburn Rovers	3-2	Johnson	Duffield	Menzies	JW Baker	Hart	Smith	Robson 2	Whipp	Richmond	Swan 1	Harris
Nov 1	WEST HAM UNITED	2-1	Johnson	Duffield	Menzies	JW Baker	Hart	Smith	Robson	Whipp	Richmond 1	Swan 1	Harris
Nov 8	Sheffield United	1-1	Johnson	Duffield	Menzies	JW Baker	Hart	Smith	Robson	Whipp	Richmond	Swan 1	Harris
Nov 15	NEWCASTLE UNITED	1-1	Moore	Duffield	Menzies	JW Baker	Hart	Smith	Robson	Whipp 1	Richmond	Swan	Harris
Nov 22	Liverpool	0-1	Moore	Duffield	Menzies	JW Baker	Hart	Smith	Robson	Whipp	Richmond	Swan	Harris
Nov 29	NOTTINGHAM FOREST	1-1	Down	Duffield	Menzies	Sherwin	Hart	Smith	Robson 1	Whipp	Richmond	Swan	Harris
Dec 6	Bury	0-1	Down	Duffield	Menzies	JW Baker	Hart	Smith	Noble	Whipp	Richmond	Swan	Harris
Dec 13	MANCHESTER CITY	0-3	Down	Duffield	Menzies	JW Baker	Hart	Smith	Robson	Whipp	Armand	Swan	Harris
Dec 20	Arsenal	1-6	Down	Duffield	Menzies	Mason	Hart	JW Baker	Robson	Armand	Whipp 1	Swan	Harris
Dec 25	ASTON VILLA	6-0	Moore	Duffield	Menzies	Sherwin	Hart 1	Smith	Robson	Armand	Whipp 3	Swan 2	Harris
Dec 26	Aston Villa	1-2	Moore	Menzies	Speak	JW Baker	L Baker	Smith	Robson	Armand	Powell	Swan 1	Harris
Dec 27	Sunderland	1-2	Moore	Duffield	Speak	Sherwin	Hart	Smith	Robson	Graver	Richmond 1	Swan	Harris
Jan 3	CARDIFF CITY	0-0	Moore	Duffield	Menzies	Sherwin	Hart	Smith	Robson	Whipp	Richmond	Swan	Harris
Jan 17	Preston North End	4-1	Down	Duffield	Menzies	JW Baker	Hart	Smith	Robson	Whipp 2	Richmond	Powell 2	Harris
Jan 24	BURNLEY	0-2	Down	Duffield	Menzies	JW Baker	Mason	Smith	Robson	Whipp	Richmond	Powell	Harris
Jan 31	Huddersfield Town	0-2	Russell	Duffield	Menzies	JW Baker	Hart	Atkinson	Coates	Whipp	Powell	Swan	Harris
Feb 7	Birmingham	0-0	Russell	Menzies	Speak	JW Baker	Hart	Atkinson	Noble	Whipp	Graver	Powell	Harris
Feb 14	WEST BROMWICH ALBION	0-1	Down	Menzies	Speak	JW Baker	Hart	Atkinson	Noble	Whipp	Swan	Powell	Harris
Feb 28	BLACKBURN ROVERS	1-1	Down	Duffield	Menzies	JW Baker	Hart	Atkinson	Noble 1	Armand	Whipp	Swan	Harris

DIVISION ONE 1924-25 continued

			1	2	3	4	5	6	7	8	9	10	11
Mar 7	West Ham United	0-0	Down	Duffield	Menzies	Noble	Mason	JW Baker	Harris	Armand	Richmond	Graver	Martin
Mar 9	Tottenham Hotspur	1-2	Down	Duffield	Menzies	Noble	Mason	JW Baker	Harris	Armand 1	Richmond	Graver	Martin
Mar 14	SHEFFIELD UNITED	1-1	Down	Duffield	Menzies	JW Baker	Mason	Smith	Noble	Armand	Jennings	Powell	Harris 1
Mar 21	Newcastle United	1-4	Down	Duffield	Menzies	Edwards	Hart	Atkinson	Robson	Armand	Jennings	Wainscoat 1	Harris
Mar 28	LIVERPOOL	4-1	Russell	Duffield	Menzies	Edwards	Hart	Atkinson	Whipp	Armand 1	Jennings 1	Wainscoat 1	Harris 1
Apr 4	Nottingham Forest	0-4	Russell	Duffield	Menzies	Edwards	Hart	Atkinson	Whipp	Armand	Jennings	Wainscoat	Harris
Apr 10	Bolton Wanderers	0-1	Russell	Duffield	Menzies	Edwards	Hart	Atkinson	Whipp	Armand	Jennings	Wainscoat	Harris
Apr 11	BURY	1-0	Russell	Duffield	Menzies	Edwards	Hart	Atkinson	Noble	Whipp	Jennings 1	Wainscoat	Harris
Apr 14	BOLTON WANDERERS	2-1	Russell	Duffield	Menzies	Edwards	Hart	Atkinson	Noble	Whipp	Jennings 1	Wainscoat 1	Harris
Apr 18	Manchester City	2-4	Russell	Duffield	Menzies	Edwards	Hart	Atkinson	Noble	Whipp 1	Jennings	Wainscoat 1	Harris
Apr 25	ARSENAL	1-0	Russell	Duffield	Menzies	Edwards	Hart	Atkinson	Armand	Whipp 1	Jennings	Wainscoat	Harris
May 2	Everton	0-1	Down	Duffield	Menzies	Edwards	Hart	Atkinson	Armand	Whipp	Jennings	Wainscoat	Harris

F.A. CUP

Jan 10	Liverpool	0-3	Down	Menzies	Speak	Sherwin	Hart	Smith	Robson	Armand	Whipp	Swan	Harris

DIVISION ONE 1925-26

Aug 29	Notts County	0-1	Johnson	Duffield	Menzies	Edwards	Hart	Atkinson	Turnbull	Whipp	Jennings	Wainscoat	Harris
Aug 31	BOLTON WANDERERS	2-1	Johnson	Duffield	Menzies	Edwards	Hart	Atkinson	Turnbull	Whipp	Jennings 1	Wainscoat	Harris 1
Sep 5	ASTON VILLA	2-2	Johnson	Duffield	Menzies	Edwards	Hart	Atkinson	Turnbull	Whipp	Jennings 2	Wainscoat	Harris
Sep 7	Bolton Wanderers	0-1	Johnson	Allan	Menzies	Edwards	Hart	Baker	Harris	Whipp	Jennings	Wainscoat	Jackson
Sep 12	Leicester City	3-1	Johnson	Duffield	Menzies	Edwards	Hart	Baker	Turnbull 2	Whipp	Jennings 1	Wainscoat	Jackson
Sep 16	NEWCASTLE UNITED	2-0	Johnson	Duffield	Menzies	Edwards	Hart	Baker	Turnbull	Whipp	Jennings 1	Wainscoat	Jackson 1
Sep 19	WEST HAM UNITED	5-2	Johnson	Allan	Menzies	Edwards	Hart	Smith	Turnbull	Whipp 1	Jennings 2	Wainscoat 2	Jackson
Sep 26	Arsenal	1-4	Johnson	Allan	Menzies	Edwards	Hart	Smith	Turnbull	Whipp	Jennings	Wainscoat 1	Jackson
Oct 3	MANCHESTER UNITED	2-0	Johnson	Allan	Menzies	Edwards	Hart	Baker	Turnbull	Whipp	Jennings 1	Wainscoat 1	Jackson
Oct 10	Liverpool	1-1	Johnson	Allan	Menzies	Edwards	Hart	Baker	Turnbull	Whipp	Jennings	Wainscoat 1	Jackson
Oct 17	HUDDERSFIELD TOWN	0-4	Johnson	Duffield	Menzies	Edwards	Hart	Baker	Armand	Whipp	Jennings	Wainscoat	Jackson
Oct 24	Everton	2-4	Johnson	Allan	Menzies	Edwards	Hart	Baker	Turnbull	Armand	Jennings 1	Wainscoat 1	Jackson
Oct 31	BURY	2-3	Johnson	Allan	Menzies	Edwards	Hart 1	Atkinson	Sissons	Armand	Jennings	Mears	Jackson 1
Nov 7	Blackburn Rovers	2-2	Johnson	Allan	Menzies	Edwards	Hart 1	Atkinson	Sissons	Whipp	Jennings 1	Turnbull	Jackson
Nov 14	CARDIFF CITY	1-0	Johnson	Allan	Kirkpatrick	Edwards	Hart	Atkinson	Sissons	Whipp	Jennings	Turnbull 1	Jackson
Nov 21	Sheffield United	0-2	Johnson	Allan	Kirkpatrick	Edwards	Hart	Atkinson	Sissons	Whipp	Jennings	Chadwick	Turnbull
Nov 28	WEST BROMWICH ALBION	0-1	Johnson	Allan	Kirkpatrick	Edwards	Hart	Atkinson	Turnbull	Whipp	Jennings	Chadwick	Jackson
Dec 5	Birmingham	1-2	Johnson	Allan	Kirkpatrick	Edwards	Hart	Atkinson	Turnbull	Whipp	Jennings 1	Chadwick	Jackson
Dec 12	MANCHESTER CITY	3-4	Johnson	Allan	Menzies	Edwards	Hart	Atkinson	Turnbull	Armand 2	Jennings	Chadwick 1	Jackson
Dec 19	Tottenham Hotspur	2-3	Johnson	Allan	Kirkpatrick	Edwards	Atkinson	Smith	Turnbull	Whipp	Jennings	Armand 2	Jackson
Dec 25	BURNLEY	2-2	Johnson	Allan	Kirkpatrick	Edwards	Townsley	Atkinson	Turnbull 1	Whipp 1	Jennings	Armand	Jackson
Dec 26	Burnley	3-6	Thornton	Atkinson	Kirkpatrick	Edwards	Townsley	Smith	Turnbull	Whipp 1	Jennings 1	Armand 1	Jackson
Jan 1	Sunderland	3-1	Johnson	Allan	Menzies	Edwards	Townsley 1	Atkinson	Turnbull	Whipp	Jennings 1	Armand 1	Jackson
Jan 2	NOTTS COUNTY	2-1	Johnson	Allan	Menzies	Edwards	Townsley	Atkinson	Turnbull	Whipp 1	Jennings	Armand 1	Jackson
Jan 23	LEICESTER CITY	1-0	Johnson	Allan	Menzies	Edwards	Hart	Atkinson	Turnbull	Armand	Jennings	Chadwick 1	Jackson
Jan 30	West Ham United	2-4	Johnson	Allan	Menzies	Edwards	Townsley	Atkinson	Turnbull	Chadwick	Jennings 2	Wainscoat	Jackson
Feb 3	Aston Villa	1-3	Johnson	Allan	Menzies	Edwards	Townsley	Atkinson	Turnbull	Chadwick	Jennings 1	Wainscoat	Jackson
Feb 6	ARSENAL	4-2	Johnson	Allan	Menzies	Edwards	Townsley	Atkinson	Turnbull	Chadwick 1	Jennings 3	Wainscoat	Jackson
Feb 13	Manchester United	1-2	Johnson	Allan	Menzies	Edwards	Townsley	Atkinson	Turnbull	Chadwick	Jennings 1	Wainscoat	Fell
Feb 20	LIVERPOOL	1-1	Johnson	Allan	Menzies	Edwards	Townsley	Smith	Turnbull	Armand	Jennings 1	Wainscoat	Jackson
Feb 27	Huddersfield Town	1-3	Potts	Allan	Menzies	Edwards	Townsley	Baker	Sissons	Whipp	Jennings	Wainscoat 1	Jackson
Mar 6	EVERTON	1-1	Potts	Allan	Menzies	Edwards	Townsley	Baker	Sissons	Whipp	Jennings	Wainscoat 1	Jackson
Mar 13	Bury	2-0	Potts	Roberts	Allan	Townsley	Hart	Menzies	Turnbull	Armand 1	Jennings 1	Wainscoat	Fell
Mar 20	BLACKBURN ROVERS	2-1	Potts	Allan	Menzies	Edwards	Hart	Townsley	Turnbull	Armand 1	Jennings	Wainscoat	Fell 1
Mar 27	Cardiff City	0-0	Potts	Allan	Menzies	Edwards	Hart	Townsley	Turnbull	Armand	Jennings	Wainscoat	Fell
Apr 3	SHEFFIELD UNITED	2-0	Potts	Allan	Menzies	Edwards	Hart	Townsley	Turnbull 1	Armand	Jennings 1	Wainscoat	Fell
Apr 5	Newcastle United	0-3	Potts	Allan	Menzies	Edwards	Hart	Townsley	Turnbull	Armand	Jennings	Wainscoat	Fell
Apr 6	SUNDERLAND	0-2	Potts	Allan	Menzies	Edwards	Townsley	Reed	Turnbull	Chadwick	Jennings	Wainscoat	Armand
Apr 10	West Bromwich Albion	0-3	Potts	Allan	Menzies	Edwards	Hart	Townsley	Turnbull	Whipp	Jennings	Chadwick	Fell
Apr 17	BIRMINGHAM	0-0	Potts	Allan	Menzies	Atkinson	Townsley	Smith	Turnbull	Whipp	Jennings	Chadwick	Jackson
Apr 27	Manchester City	1-2	Potts	Allan	Menzies	Edwards	Townsley	Atkinson	Turnbull	Whipp	Jennings 1	Chadwick	Jackson
May 1	TOTTENHAM HOTSPUR	4-1	Potts	Allan	Menzies	Edwards	Townsley	Atkinson	Turnbull 1	Whipp 1	Jennings 2	Chadwick	Jackson

F.A. CUP

Jan 9	Middlesbrough	Rd 3	1-5	Johnson	Allan	Menzies	Edwards	Townsley	Atkinson	Turnbull	Jennings	Whipp	Armand 1	Jackson

DIVISION ONE 1926-27

Aug 28	BOLTON WANDERERS	2-5	Potts	Allan	Menzies	Edwards	Townsley	Atkinson	Turnbull 1	Chadwick	Jennings	Wainscoat 1	Jackson
Aug 30	CARDIFF CITY	0-0	Potts	Allan	Menzies	Edwards	Townsley	Atkinson	Turnbull	Chadwick	Jennings	Wainscoat	Jackson
Sep 4	Manchester United	2-2	Potts	Allan	Menzies	Edwards	Hart	Townsley	Sissons	Whipp	Jennings 1	Wainscoat 1	Jackson
Sep 6	Cardiff City	1-3	Potts	Allan	Menzies	Edwards	Hart	Townsley	Sissons	Whipp 1	Jennings	Wainscoat	Fell
Sep 11	DERBY COUNTY	1-0	Potts	Allan	Menzies	Edwards	Hart	Townsley	Sissons	Whipp	Jennings 1	Armand	Fell
Sep 15	ASTON VILLA	3-1	Potts	Allan	Kirkpatrick	Edwards	Townsley	Menzies	Sissons 1	Whipp	Jennings 1	Armand 1	Fell
Sep 18	Sheffield United	0-1	Potts	Allan	Kirkpatrick	Edwards	Townsley	Menzies	Sissons	Whipp	Jennings	Armand	Turnbull
Sep 25	ARSENAL	4-1	Potts	Allan	Kirkpatrick	Edwards	Townsley	Menzies	Sissons	Armand	Jennings 3	Wainscoat 1	Turnbull
Oct 2	Liverpool	4-2	Potts	Roberts	Allan	Edwards	Townsley	Menzies	Sissons	Whipp	Jennings 4	Duggan	Fell
Oct 9	BLACKBURN ROVERS	4-1	Potts	Roberts	Robinson	Atkinson	Townsley	Menzies	Sissons	Duggan	Jennings 4	Wainscoat	Turnbull
Oct 16	Leicester City	2-3	Potts	Roberts	Allan	Edwards	Townsley	Menzies	Sissons	Duggan	Jennings 2	Wainscoat	Turnbull
Oct 23	EVERTON	1-3	Potts	Roberts	Allan	Edwards	Townsley	Menzies	Sissons	Duggan	Jennings 1	Wainscoat	Turnbull
Oct 30	Huddersfield Town	1-4	Potts	Roberts	Allan	Edwards	Townsley	Menzies	Turnbull	Duggan	Jennings 1	Wainscoat	Fell
Nov 6	SUNDERLAND	2-2	Potts	Roberts	Allan	Edwards	Townsley	Menzies	Turnbull	Duggan 1	Jennings 1	Wainscoat	Mitchell
Nov 13	West Bromwich Albion	4-2	Potts	Roberts	Menzies	Edwards	Townsley	Atkinson	Sissons	Whipp 1	Jennings	Armand 1	Mitchell 2
Nov 20	BURY	4-1	Potts	Roberts	Menzies	Edwards	Townsley	Atkinson	Sissons	Whipp	Jennings 3	Armand	Mitchell 1
Nov 27	Birmingham	0-2	Potts	Roberts	Menzies	Hart	Townsley	Atkinson	Sissons	Whipp	Jennings	Armand	Mitchell
Dec 4	TOTTENHAM HOTSPUR	1-1	Potts	Roberts	Menzies	Edwards	Townsley	Atkinson	Sissons	Whipp	Jennings	Armand 1	Mitchell
Dec 11	West Ham United	2-3	Potts	Roberts	Menzies 1	Edwards	Townsley	Atkinson	Sissons	Whipp	Jennings	Armand 1	Mitchell
Dec 18	SHEFFIELD WEDNESDAY	4-1	Potts	Roberts	Menzies	Edwards 1	Townsley	Reed	Turnbull	Whipp 1	Jennings 1	Armand	Mitchell 1
Dec 27	NEWCASTLE UNITED	1-2	Potts	Roberts	Menzies	Edwards	Townsley	Reed	Turnbull	Whipp	Jennings 1	Armand	Mitchell
Dec 28	Aston Villa	1-5	Potts	Roberts	Allan	Edwards	Townsley	Reed	Turnbull	Whipp	Jennings	Armand 1	Mitchell
Jan 1	Newcastle United	0-1	Potts	Roberts	Allan	Edwards	Townsley	Reed	Turnbull	Whipp	Jennings	Armand	Mitchell
Jan 15	Bolton Wanderers	0-3	Potts	Roberts	Allan	Edwards	Townsley	Reed	Turnbull	Duggan	Jennings	Armand	Mitchell
Jan 22	MANCHESTER UNITED	2-3	Potts	Roberts	Menzies	Edwards	Townsley	Reed	Sissons	Duggan	Jennings 2	Armand	Mitchell
Feb 5	SHEFFIELD UNITED	1-1	Potts	Roberts	Menzies	Edwards	Townsley	Reed	Turnbull	Armand	Jennings 1	Wainscoat	Mitchell
Feb 12	Arsenal	0-1	Potts	Roberts	Menzies	Townsley	Hart	Reed	Turnbull	White	Jennings	Wainscoat	Mitchell
Feb 19	Derby County	0-1	Potts	Roberts	Menzies	Edwards	Townsley	Reed	Turnbull	White	Jennings	Wainscoat	Mitchell
Feb 23	LIVERPOOL	0-0	Potts	Roberts	Robinson	Edwards	Townsley	Atkinson	Turnbull	White	Jennings	Armand	Fell
Feb 26	Blackburn Rovers	1-4	Potts	Roberts	Robinson	Edwards	Townsley	Reed	Turnbull	White 1	Mears	Armand	Mitchell
Mar 5	LEICESTER CITY	1-1	Potts	Roberts	Robinson	Edwards	Townsley	Reed	Turnbull	White	Jennings 1	Wainscoat	Mitchell
Mar 12	Everton	1-2	Potts	Roberts	Menzies	Edwards	Townsley	Reed	Turnbull	White	Jennings 1	Wainscoat	Mitchell
Mar 19	HUDDERSFIELD TOWN	1-1	Potts	Roberts	Menzies	Atkinson	Townsley	Reed	Turnbull 1	White	Jennings	Wainscoat	Mitchell
Mar 26	Sunderland	2-6	Potts	Roberts	Menzies	Edwards	Townsley	Reed	Turnbull	White	Jennings	Wainscoat 2	Mitchell
Apr 2	WEST BROMWICH ALBION	3-1	Potts	Roberts	Allan	Atkinson	Townsley	Reed	Turnbull	White	Jennings 2	Wainscoat 1	Jackson
Apr 9	Bury	2-4	Potts	Roberts	Allan	Edwards	Townsley	Reed	Turnbull	White	Jennings 1	Wainscoat 1	Jackson
Apr 15	Burnley	2-3	Potts	Roberts	Allan	Edwards	Townsley	Reed	Turnbull 1	White	Jennings 1	Wainscoat	Jackson
Apr 16	BIRMINGHAM	2-1	Potts	Roberts	Allan	Edwards	Townsley	Reed	Turnbull 1	White	Jennings 1	Wainscoat 1	Jackson
Apr 19	BURNLEY	0-2	Potts	Roberts	Menzies	Edwards	Townsley	Reed	Turnbull	White	Jennings	Wainscoat	Jackson
Apr 23	Tottenham Hotspur	1-4	Potts	Roberts	Menzies	Edwards	Townsley	Reed	Turnbull	White	Jennings 1	Wainscoat	Mitchell
Apr 30	WEST HAM UNITED	6-3	Potts	Roberts	Allan	Edwards	Townsley	Reed	Turnbull 1	White 1	Jennings	Wainscoat 4	Mitchell
May 7	Sheffield Wednesday	0-1	Potts	Roberts	Allan	Edwards	Townsley	Reed	Turnbull	White	Jennings	Wainscoat	Mitchell

F.A. CUP

Jan 8	SUNDERLAND	Rd 3	3-2	Potts	Roberts	Menzies	Edwards	Townsley	Reed	Turnbull	Duggan 1	Jennings 2	Armand	Mitchell
Jan 29	BOLTON WANDERERS	Rd 4	0-0	Potts	Roberts	Menzies	Edwards	Townsley	Reed	Sissons	Wainscoat	Jennings	Armand	Mitchell
Feb 2	Bolton Wanderers	Rd 4 R	0-3	Potts	Allan	Roberts	Edwards	Townsley	Reed	Mears	White	Jennings	Wainscoat	Mitchell

DIVISION TWO 1927-28

Aug 27	South Shields	5-1	Potts	Roberts	Menzies	Edwards	Townsley	Reed	Turnbull	White 2	Jennings 1	Wainscoat 1	Mitchell 1
Aug 29	BARNSLEY	2-2	Potts	Roberts	Menzies	Edwards	Townsley	Reed	Turnbull	White 1	Jennings 1	Wainscoat	Mitchell
Sep 3	SOUTHAMPTON	2-0	Potts	Townsley	Menzies	Edwards	Hart	Reed	Turnbull	White	Jennings	Wainscoat 2	Mitchell
Sep 10	NOTTINGHAM FOREST	4-0	Potts	Townsley	Menzies	Edwards	Hart	Reed	Turnbull 1	White	Jennings 1	Wainscoat 1	Mitchell 1

DIVISION TWO 1927-28 continued

			1	2	3	4	5	6	7	8	9	10	11
Sep 17	Manchester City	1-2	Potts	Townsley	Menzies	Edwards	Hart	Reed	Turnbull	White	Jennings 1	Wainscoat	Mitchell
Sep 24	HULL CITY	2-0	Potts	Townsley	Menzies	Edwards	Hart	Reed	Sissons	White	Jennings 1	Wainscoat 1	Mitchell
Sep 26	Barnsley	1-2	Potts	Roberts	Menzies	Edwards	Townsley	Reed	Turnbull	White	Jennings	Wainscoat	Mitchell 1
Oct 1	Preston North End	1-5	Potts	Roberts	Allan	Edwards	Townsley	Reed	Turnbull	White 1	Jennings	Wainscoat	Mitchell
Oct 8	SWANSEA TOWN	5-0	Potts	Roberts	Allan	Baker	Townsley	Reed	Turnbull 1	White 2	Jennings 2	Wainscoat	Mitchell
Oct 15	Fulham	1-1	Potts	Roberts	Allan	Baker	Townsley	Reed	Turnbull	White 1	Jennings	Wainscoat	Mitchell
Oct 22	Grimsby Town	2-3	Potts	Roberts	Allan	Coutts	Townsley	Reed	Turnbull	White	Jennings 1	Wainscoat 1	Mitchell
Oct 29	OLDHAM ATHLETIC	1-0	Potts	Allan	Menzies	Atkinson	Townsley	Reed	Turnbull	White	Jennings	Wainscoat	Mitchell 1
Nov 5	Notts County	2-2	Potts	Allan	Menzies	Atkinson	Townsley	Reed	Turnbull	White	Jennings 2	Wainscoat	Mitchell
Nov 12	READING	6-2	Potts	Allan	Menzies	Atkinson	Townsley	Reed	Turnbull 2	White 2	Jennings 1	Wainscoat 1	Mitchell
Nov 19	Blackpool	2-0	Potts	Allan	Menzies	Atkinson	Townsley	Reed	Turnbull	White	Jennings	Wainscoat	Mitchell 2
Nov 26	WEST BROMWICH ALBION	1-2	Potts	Allan	Menzies	Atkinson	Townsley 1	Reed	Turnbull	White	Jennings	Wainscoat	Mitchell
Dec 3	Clapton Orient	1-2	Potts	Townsley	Allan	Edwards	Hart	Reed	Turnbull	White	Jennings	Wainscoat	Mitchell 1
Dec 10	CHELSEA	5-0	Potts	Townsley	Allan	Edwards	Hart	Reed	Turnbull	White 1	Jennings 4	Wainscoat	Mitchell
Dec 17	Bristol City	2-1	Potts	Townsley	Allan	Edwards	Hart	Reed	Turnbull	White 1	Jennings	Wainscoat 1	Mitchell
Dec 24	STOKE CITY	5-1	Potts	Townsley	Menzies	Edwards	Hart 1	Reed	Turnbull 1	White 1	Jennings 2	Wainscoat	Mitchell
Dec 26	Port Vale	2-1	Potts	Townsley	Menzies	Edwards	Hart	Reed	Turnbull	White 1	Jennings	Wainscoat 1	Mitchell
Dec 27	PORT VALE	3-0	Potts	Townsley	Menzies	Edwards	Hart	Reed	Turnbull	White	Jennings 2	Wainscoat 1	Mitchell
Dec 31	SOUTH SHIELDS	3-0	Potts	Townsley	Menzies	Edwards	Hart	Reed	Turnbull 1	White	Keetley 1	Wainscoat 1	Mitchell
Jan 7	Southampton	4-1	Potts	Townsley	Menzies	Edwards	Hart	Reed	Sissons	White 2	Keetley 1	Wainscoat 1	Mitchell
Jan 21	Nottingham Forest	2-2	Potts	Townsley	Menzies	Edwards	Hart	Reed	Sissons	White 1	Keetley 1	Wainscoat	Mitchell
Jan 28	BRISTOL CITY	3-2	Potts	Townsley	Robinson	Edwards	Hart	Reed	Turnbull	White	Keetley 3	Wainscoat	Mitchell
Feb 4	Hull City	1-3	Potts	Townsley	Allan	Edwards	Hart	Reed	Sissons	White	Jennings 1	Wainscoat	Mitchell
Feb 11	PRESTON NORTH END	2-4	Johnson	Townsley	Menzies	Edwards	Hart	Reed	Sissons	White	Keetley	Wainscoat 2	Mitchell
Feb 18	Swansea Town	1-1	Johnson	Townsley	Menzies	Edwards	Hart	Reed	Sissons	White	Jennings 1	Wainscoat	Mitchell
Feb 25	FULHAM	2-1	Johnson	Townsley	Menzies	Edwards	Hart	Reed	Sissons	White 1	Jennings	Wainscoat 1	Mitchell
Mar 3	GRIMSBY TOWN	0-0	Johnson	Townsley	Menzies	Edwards	Hart	Reed	Sissons	White	Jennings	Wainscoat	Mitchell
Mar 10	Oldham Athletic	1-0	Potts	Townsley	Menzies	Stacey	Hart	Reed	Turnbull	White	Keetley 1	Wainscoat	Mitchell
Mar 17	NOTTS COUNTY	6-0	Potts	Townsley	Menzies	Edwards	Hart	Reed	Turnbull 1	White 1	Keetley 3	Armand 1	Mitchell
Mar 24	Reading	1-0	Potts	Townsley	Menzies	Edwards	Hart	Reed	Turnbull	White	Keetley 1	Wainscoat	Mitchell
Mar 31	BLACKPOOL	4-0	Potts	Townsley	Menzies	Stacey	Hart	Reed	Turnbull	Armand 1	Keetley	Wainscoat 2	Mitchell 1
Apr 7	West Bromwich Albion	1-0	Potts	Townsley	Menzies	Edwards	Hart	Reed	Turnbull 1	White	Keetley	Wainscoat	Mitchell
Apr 9	Wolverhampton Wans	0-0	Potts	Townsley	Menzies	Edwards	Hart	Reed	Turnbull	White	Keetley	Wainscoat	Mitchell
Apr 10	WOLVERHAMPTON WANS	3-0	Potts	Townsley	Menzies	Edwards	Hart	Reed	Turnbull	White 1	Keetley 2	Wainscoat	Mitchell
Apr 14	CLAPTON ORIENT	4-0	Potts	Townsley	Menzies	Edwards	Hart	Reed	Turnbull	White 1	Keetley 3	Wainscoat	Mitchell
Apr 21	Chelsea	3-2	Potts	Townsley	Menzies	Edwards	Hart	Reed	Turnbull	White 1	Keetley 2	Wainscoat	Mitchell
Apr 25	MANCHESTER CITY	0-1	Potts	Townsley	Menzies	Edwards	Hart	Reed	Turnbull	White	Keetley	Wainscoat	Mitchell
May 5	Stoke City	1-5	Potts	Townsley	Menzies	Edwards	Hart	Reed	Turnbull	White	Keetley	Wainscoat 1	Mitchell

F.A. CUP

Jan 14	Manchester City	Rd 3 0-1	Potts	Townsley	Menzies	Edwards	Hart	Reed	Turnbull	White	Jennings	Wainscoat	Mitchell

DIVISION ONE 1928-29

Aug 25	ASTON VILLA	4-1	Potts	Townsley	Menzies	Edwards	Hart	Reed	Turnbull	Armand	Keetley 3	Wainscoat 1	Mitchell
Aug 27	BURY	3-1	Potts	Townsley	Menzies	Edwards	Hart	Reed	Turnbull	Armand 1	Keetley	Wainscoat 2	Mitchell
Sep 1	Leicester City	4-4	Potts	Townsley	Menzies	Edwards	Hart	Reed	Turnbull 1	Armand 1	Keetley 2	Wainscoat	Mitchell
Sep 8	MANCHESTER UNITED	3-2	Potts	Townsley	Menzies	Edwards	Hart	Reed	Turnbull	Armand 1	Keetley 1	Wainscoat 1	Mitchell
Sep 15	Huddersfield Town	1-6	Potts	Roberts	Menzies	Townsley	Hart	Reed	Turnbull	Armand	Jennings	Wainscoat 1	Mitchell
Sep 22	Liverpool	1-1	Potts	Townsley	Menzies	Buck	Hart	Reed	Turnbull	White	Jennings	Wainscoat 1	Mitchell
Sep 29	WEST HAM UNITED	4-1	Potts	Townsley	Menzies	Edwards	Hart	Reed	Turnbull	White 1	Jennings 2	Wainscoat 1	Mitchell
Oct 6	Newcastle United	2-3	Potts	Townsley	Menzies	Edwards	Hart	Reed	Turnbull	White	Jennings 1	Wainscoat 1	Mitchell
Oct 13	BURNLEY	2-1	Potts	Townsley	Menzies	Edwards	Hart	Reed	Turnbull	White 1	Jennings 1	Wainscoat	Mitchell
Oct 20	MANCHESTER CITY	4-1	Potts	Townsley	Menzies	Edwards	Hart	Buck	Turnbull	White 3	Jennings	Wainscoat 1	Cochrane
Oct 27	Everton	1-0	Potts	Townsley	Menzies	Edwards	Hart	Reed	Turnbull	White	Jennings	Wainscoat 1	Cochrane
Nov 3	PORTSMOUTH	3-2	Potts	Townsley	Menzies	Edwards	Hart	Reed	Turnbull	White 1	Jennings 1	Wainscoat 1	Cochrane
Nov 10	Bolton Wanderers	1-4	Potts	Townsley	Menzies	Edwards	Hart	Reed	Turnbull 1	White	Jennings	Armand	Cochrane
Nov 17	SHEFFIELD WEDNESDAY	0-2	Potts	G. Milburn	Menzies	Buck	Townsley	Reed	Turnbull	White	Jennings	Armand	Cochrane
Nov 24	Derby County	4-3	Potts	Townsley	Menzies	Edwards	Hart	Reed	Turnbull	White 1	Keetley 1	Wainscoat 1	Mitchell 1
Dec 1	SUNDERLAND	0-3	Potts	Townsley	Menzies	Edwards	Hart	Reed	Turnbull	White	Keetley	Wainscoat	Mitchell
Dec 8	Blackburn Rovers	1-0	Potts	Townsley	Menzies	Stacey	Gribben	Reed	McNestry	White	Keetley 1	Wainscoat	Mitchell
Dec 15	ARSENAL	1-1	Potts	Townsley	Menzies	Stacey	Gribben	Reed	Turnbull	White	Keetley 1	Wainscoat	Mitchell
Dec 22	Birmingham	1-5	Potts	Townsley	Menzies	Stacey	Hart	Reed	Turnbull 1	White	Keetley	Wainscoat	Mitchell
Dec 25	CARDIFF CITY	3-0	Potts	Townsley	Menzies	Stacey	Hart 1	Reed	Turnbull	White 1	Keetley 1	Wainscoat	Mitchell
Dec 26	Cardiff City	1-2	Potts	Townsley	Menzies	Buck	Hart	Reed	Turnbull 1	White	Keetley	Wainscoat	Mitchell
Dec 29	Aston Villa	0-1	Potts	Townsley	Menzies	Buck	Hart	Reed	Turnbull	White	Keetley	Wainscoat	Cochrane
Jan 1	Bury	2-2	J Wilson	Townsley	Menzies	Buck	Hart	Reed	Turnbull 1	White	Keetley	Wainscoat 1	Cochrane
Jan 5	LEICESTER CITY	4-3	Potts	Townsley	Menzies	Buck	Hart	Reed	Turnbull 1	White	Keetley 3	Wainscoat	Mitchell
Jan 19	Manchester United	2-1	Potts	Townsley	Menzies	Edwards	Hart 1	Reed	Turnbull	White	Keetley 1	Wainscoat	Cochrane
Feb 2	LIVERPOOL	(o.g.) 2-2	J Wilson	Townsley	Menzies	Edwards	Hart	Reed	Turnbull	Keetley	Jennings 1	Wainscoat	Cochrane
Feb 9	West Ham United	2-8	J Wilson	Townsley	Roberts	Edwards	Hart	Reed	Turnbull	Keetley	Jennings 1	Wainscoat 1	Mitchell
Feb 16	NEWCASTLE UNITED	0-0	Potts	Townsley	G Milburn	Edwards	Hart	Reed	Turnbull	Keetley	Jennings	Wainscoat	Armand
Feb 23	Burnley	0-5	Potts	G Milburn	Menzies	Edwards	Townsley	Reed	Turnbull	Keetley	Jennings	Wainscoat	Mitchell
Mar 2	Manchester City	0-3	Potts	Townsley	Menzies	Edwards	Gribben	Reed	Turnbull	Armand	Keetley	Wainscoat	Mitchell
Mar 9	EVERTON	3-1	Potts	Townsley	Menzies	Edwards	Hart	Reed	Turnbull	White	Keetley 3	Wainscoat	Mitchell
Mar 16	Portsmouth	2-0	Potts	Townsley	Menzies	Edwards	Hart	Reed	Turnbull	White	Keetley	Wainscoat 1	Mitchell 1
Mar 30	Sheffield Wednesday	2-4	Potts	Townsley	Menzies	Edwards	Hart	Reed	Turnbull	White	Keetley 1	Wainscoat 1	Mitchell
Apr 1	Sheffield United	1-1	Potts	Roberts	G Milburn	Edwards	Longden	Buck	McNestry	White	Keetley 1	Wainscoat	Cochrane
Apr 2	SHEFFIELD UNITED	2-0	Potts	Roberts	Menzies	Edwards	Hart	Reed	Turnbull	White 1	Jennings 1	Wainscoat	Mitchell
Apr 6	DERBY COUNTY	1-1	Potts	Roberts	Menzies	Edwards	Hart	Reed	Turnbull	White	Keetley	Wainscoat	Mitchell 1
Apr 13	Sunderland	1-2	Potts	Townsley	Menzies	Stacey	Hart	Reed	Turnbull	White	Keetley 1	Longden	Mitchell
Apr 20	BLACKBURN ROVERS	0-1	Potts	Townsley	Menzies	Edwards	Hart	Reed	Turnbull	White	Keetley	Wainscoat	Mitchell
Apr 27	Arsenal	0-1	Potts	Townsley	Menzies	Edwards	Hart	Reed	Turnbull	G Wilson	Keetley	Wainscoat	Mitchell
Apr 29	BOLTON WANDERERS	2-2	Potts	Townsley	Menzies	Edwards	Hart	Reed	Turnbull	G Wilson	Jennings	Wainscoat 2	Mitchell
May 1	HUDDERSFIELD TOWN	1-2	Potts	Townsley	Menzies	Edwards	Hart	Reed	Turnbull	G Wilson	Jennings 1	Wainscoat	Mitchell
May 4	BIRMINGHAM	0-1	Potts	Roberts	G Milburn	Stacey	Longden	Underwood	McNestry	Firth	Keetley	Wainscoat	Cochrane

F.A. CUP

Jan 12	Exeter City	Rd 3 2-2	Potts	Townsley	Menzies 1	Edwards	Hart	Reed	Turnbull	White	Keetley 1	Wainscoat	Mitchell
Jan 16	EXETER CITY	(o.g.) Rd 3 R 5-1	Potts	Townsley	Menzies	Edwards	Hart	Reed 1	Turnbull	White	Keetley 1	Wainscoat 1	Cochrane 1
Jan 26	Huddersfield Town	Rd 4 0-3	J Wilson	Townsley	Menzies	Edwards	Hart	Reed	Turnbull	White	Keetley	Wainscoat	Cochrane

DIVISION ONE 1929-30

Aug 31	Arsenal	0-4	Potts	Roberts	Menzies	Edwards	Hart	Underwood	Turnbull	Longden	Jennings	Wainscoat	Mitchell
Sep 7	ASTON VILLA	4-1	Johnson	Roberts 2	Menzies	Edwards	Hart	Underwood	Turnbull	Longden 1	Jennings 1	Wainscoat	Mitchell
Sep 11	Everton	1-1	Johnson	Roberts	Menzies	Edwards	Hart	Underwood	Turnbull 1	Longden	Jennings	Wainscoat	Mitchell
Sep 14	Huddersfield Town	0-1	Johnson	Roberts	Menzies	Edwards	Hart	Reed	Turnbull	Longden	White	Wainscoat	Mitchell
Sep 16	EVERTON	2-1	Johnson	Roberts	J Milburn	Edwards	Hart	Reed	Turnbull	White	Jennings 1	Wainscoat 1	Mitchell
Sep 21	Sheffield Wednesday	2-1	Johnson	Roberts	J Milburn	Edwards	Hart	Reed	Turnbull 1	White	Jennings	Wainscoat 1	Mitchell
Sep 23	PORTSMOUTH	1-0	Johnson	Roberts	J Milburn	Edwards	Hart	Reed	Turnbull	White 1	Jennings	Wainscoat	Mitchell
Sep 28	BURNLEY	3-0	Johnson	Roberts	J Milburn	Edwards	Hart 1	Reed	Turnbull	White 1	Mangnall	Wainscoat 1	Mitchell
Oct 5	Sunderland	4-1	Johnson	Roberts	J Milburn	Edwards	Hart	Reed	Turnbull 1	White	Mangnall 2	Wainscoat 1	Mitchell
Oct 12	BOLTON WANDERERS	2-1	Johnson	Roberts	J Milburn	Edwards	Hart	Reed	Turnbull 1	White	Mangnall 1	Wainscoat	Mitchell
Oct 19	BIRMINGHAM	1-0	Johnson	Roberts	J Milburn	Stacey	Townsley	Reed	Turnbull 1	White	Mangnall	Wainscoat	Mitchell
Oct 26	Leicester City	2-2	Johnson	Roberts	J Milburn	Edwards	Hart	Reed	Turnbull	White	Mangnall 1	Wainscoat	Mitchell 1
Nov 2	GRIMSBY TOWN	6-0	Johnson	Roberts	J Milburn	Stacey	Townsley	Reed 1	Turnbull 1	White 1	Mangnall 1	Wainscoat 2	Mitchell
Nov 9	Sheffield United	2-3	Johnson	Roberts	J Milburn	Edwards	Hart	Reed	Turnbull 1	White	Mangnall 1	Wainscoat	Mitchell
Nov 16	WEST HAM UNITED	1-3	Johnson	Roberts	J Milburn	Edwards	Hart	Reed	Turnbull	White	Mangnall	Wainscoat 1	Mitchell
Nov 23	Liverpool	0-1	Johnson	Roberts	J Milburn	Edwards	Hart	Reed	Turnbull	White	Mangnall	Wainscoat	Mitchell
Nov 30	MIDDLESBROUGH	1-2	Potts	Roberts	J Milburn	Edwards	Hart	Reed 1	Turnbull	White	Jennings	Furness	Mitchell
Dec 7	Blackburn Rovers	1-2	Potts	Roberts	J Milburn	Edwards	Hart	Reed	Turnbull	Longden	Jennings	Wainscoat	Mitchell 1
Dec 14	NEWCASTLE UNITED	5-2	Potts	Roberts	J Milburn	Edwards	Hart	Reed	Turnbull	Longden 2	Jennings 2	Wainscoat 1	Mitchell
Dec 21	Manchester United	1-3	Potts	Roberts	J Milburn	Edwards	Hart	Reed	Turnbull	Longden 1	Jennings	Wainscoat	Mitchell
Dec 25	DERBY COUNTY	2-1	Potts	Roberts	J Milburn	Edwards	Hart	Reed	Turnbull	Longden 1	Keetley	Wainscoat 1	Mitchell
Dec 26	Derby County	0-3	Potts	Roberts	J Milburn	Stacey	Townsley	Underwood	Turnbull	Longden	Jennings	Wainscoat	Mitchell
Dec 28	ARSENAL	2-0	Potts	Roberts	J Milburn	Edwards	Townsley	Reed	Turnbull	White	Jennings 2	Wainscoat	Mitchell
Jan 4	Aston Villa	4-3	Potts	Roberts	J Milburn	Edwards	Hart	Reed	Turnbull	White 1	Jennings 2	Wainscoat 1	Mitchell
Jan 18	HUDDERSFIELD TOWN	0-1	Potts	Roberts	J Milburn	Edwards	Hart	Reed	Turnbull	White	Jennings	Wainscoat	Mitchell
Feb 1	Burnley	3-0	Potts	J Milburn	Menzies	Edwards	Townsley	Reed	Duggan 1	Longden	Jennings 2	Wainscoat	Cochrane
Feb 8	SUNDERLAND	5-0	Potts	J Milburn	Menzies	Edwards	Townsley	Reed	Duggan	Longden 1	Jennings 1	Wainscoat 2	Cochrane 1

DIVISION ONE 1929-30 continued

			1	2	3	4	5	6	7	8	9	10	11
Feb 15	Bolton Wanderers	2-4	Potts	J Milburn	Menzies	Edwards	Townsley	Reed	Duggan 1	Longden	Jennings 1	Wainscoat	Cochrane
Feb 22	Birmingham	0-1	Johnson	J Milburn	Menzies	Edwards	Hart	Reed	Turnbull	Longden	Jennings	Wainscoat	Mitchell
Mar 1	LEICESTER CITY	1-2	Johnson	Roberts	J Milburn	Edwards	Townsley	Reed	Turnbull	Firth	Jennings 1	Furness	Mitchell
Mar 8	Grimsby Town	2-1	Johnson	Roberts	J Milburn	Edwards	Longden	Reed	Turnbull	Firth 1	Jennings 1	Wainscoat	Mitchell
Mar 15	SHEFFIELD UNITED	2-2	Johnson	Roberts	J Milburn	Edwards	Longden	Reed	Turnbull 1	Firth	Jennings	Wainscoat 1	Cochrane
Mar 22	West Ham United	0-3	Johnson	Roberts	J Milburn	Edwards	Townsley	Reed	Turnbull	Longden	Jennings	Wainscoat	Cochrane
Mar 29	LIVERPOOL	1-1	Johnson	J Milburn	Menzies	Edwards	Longden	Reed	Turnbull	Furness	Jennings	Wainscoat 1	Cochrane
Apr 5	Middlesbrough	1-1	Johnson	J Milburn	Menzies	Edwards	Hart	Reed	Mitchell	Longden	Keetley 1	Wainscoat	Cochrane
Apr 9	SHEFFIELD WEDNESDAY	3-0	Johnson	J Milburn	Menzies	Edwards	Hart	Reed	Duggan	Longden	Keetley 3	Wainscoat	Mitchell
Apr 12	BLACKBURN ROVERS	4-2	Johnson	J Milburn	Menzies	Edwards	Hart 1	Reed	Duggan	Longden 1	Keetley 1	Wainscoat	Mitchell 1
Apr 19	Newcastle United	1-2	Johnson	J Milburn	Menzies	Edwards	Hart	Reed	Duggan	Longden	Keetley 1	Wainscoat	Mitchell
Apr 21	Manchester City	1-4	Johnson	J Milburn	Menzies	Edwards	Hart	Reed	Turnbull	Longden	Keetley 1	Wainscoat	Mitchell
Apr 22	MANCHESTER CITY	3-2	Potts	Roberts	J Milburn	Edwards	Hart	Reed	Turnbull 1	Firth	Keetley 1	Wainscoat 1	Cochrane
Apr 26	MANCHESTER UNITED	3-1	Potts	Roberts	J Milburn	Edwards	Hart	Reed	Turnbull	Firth 1	Keetley 2	Wainscoat	Cochrane
May 3	Portsmouth	0-0	Potts	G Milburn	J Milburn	Edwards	Hart	Longden	Turnbull	Firth	Keetley	Wainscoat	Cochrane

F.A. CUP

Jan 11	CRYSTAL PALACE	Rd 3 8-1	Potts	Roberts	J Milburn	Edwards	Hart	Reed	Turnbull 1	White 2	Jennings 2	Wainscoat 3	Mitchell
Jan 25	West Ham United	Rd 4 1-4	Potts	Roberts	J Milburn	Edwards	Hart	Reed	Turnbull	White	Jennings 1	Wainscoat	Mitchell

DIVISION ONE 1930-31

Aug 30	PORTSMOUTH	2-2	Johnson	Roberts	J Milburn	Edwards	Hart	Copping	Turnbull 1	Longden	Keetley 1	Wainscoat	Cochrane
Sep 3	Derby County	1-4	Johnson	Roberts	J Milburn	Edwards	Hart	Copping	Turnbull	Longden	Keetley	Wainscoat 1	Mitchell
Sep 6	Arsenal	1-3	Potts	G Milburn	J Milburn	Edwards	Hart	Copping	Duggan	Firth	Jennings	Furness 1	Cochrane
Sep 8	MANCHESTER CITY	4-2	Potts	G Milburn	J Milburn	Edwards	Townsley	Copping	Duggan	Firth	Keetley 3	Furness	Cochrane 1
Sep 13	BLACKBURN ROVERS	4-2	Potts	G Milburn	J Milburn	Edwards	Townsley	Copping	Duggan 1	Furness 1	Keetley 1	Wainscoat 1	Cochrane
Sep 17	Manchester City	0-1	Potts	G Milburn	J Milburn	Edwards	Townsley	Copping	Duggan	Furness	Keetley	Wainscoat	Cochrane
Sep 20	Blackpool	7-3	Potts	G Milburn	J Milburn	Edwards	Hart	Copping	Turnbull 1	Furness 2	Keetley 2	Wainscoat	Cochrane 2
Sep 27	HUDDERSFIELD TOWN	1-2	Potts	G Milburn	J Milburn	Edwards	Hart	Copping	Turnbull	Furness	Keetley	Wainscoat 1	Cochrane
Oct 4	SUNDERLAND	0-3	Potts	Townsley	J Milburn	Edwards	Hart	Copping	Turnbull	Furness	Keetley	Wainscoat	Cochrane
Oct 11	Leicester City	0-4	Potts	G Milburn	J Milburn	Edwards	Hart	Copping	Duggan	Hornby	Keetley	Furness	Mitchell
Oct 18	Liverpool	0-2	Potts	Townsley	J Milburn	Edwards	Hart	Copping	Duggan	Hornby	Keetley	Furness	Mitchell
Oct 25	MIDDLESBROUGH	7-0	Potts	Roberts	J Milburn	Edwards	Hart	Copping	Duggan 2	Furness	Jennings 2	Wainscoat 2	Mitchell 1
Nov 1	Newcastle United	1-4	Potts	Roberts	J Milburn	Edwards	Hart	Copping	Duggan	Furness	Jennings 1	Wainscoat	Mitchell
Nov 8	SHEFFIELD WEDNESDAY	2-3	Potts	Roberts	J Milburn	Edwards	Hart 1	Copping	Duggan	Furness	Jennings 1	Wainscoat	Cochrane
Nov 15	West Ham United	1-1	Johnson	G Milburn	J Milburn	Edwards	Hart	Copping	Duggan	Furness	Jennings	Wainscoat 1	Cochrane
Nov 22	CHELSEA	2-3	Johnson	G Milburn	J Milburn	Edwards	Hart	Copping	Duggan 1	Furness	Jennings	Wainscoat 1	Cochrane
Nov 29	Grimsby Town	0-2	Potts	G Milburn	J Milburn	Edwards	Hart	Copping	Turnbull	Furness	Keetley	Wainscoat	Cochrane
Dec 6	BOLTON WANDERERS	3-1	Potts	G Milburn	J Milburn	Edwards	Hart	Copping	Turnbull 1	Furness	Keetley 1	Wainscoat 1	Mitchell
Dec 13	Aston Villa	3-4	Potts	G Milburn	J Milburn	Edwards	Hart	Copping	Turnbull 1	Furness	Keetley 2	Wainscoat	Mitchell
Dec 20	MANCHESTER UNITED	5-0	Potts	G Milburn	J Milburn	Edwards	Hart	Copping	Turnbull 3	Furness 1	Keetley	Wainscoat 1	Mitchell
Dec 25	Birmingham	1-0	Potts	G Milburn	J Milburn	Edwards	Hart	Copping	Turnbull	Furness 1	Keetley	Wainscoat	Mitchell
Dec 26	BIRMINGHAM	3-1	Potts	G Milburn	J Milburn	Edwards	Hart	Copping	Turnbull	Furness 2	Keetley 1	Wainscoat	Mitchell
Dec 27	Portsmouth	1-1	Potts	G Milburn	J Milburn	Underwood	Townsley	Copping	Turnbull	Furness	Keetley 1	Hornby	Cochrane
Jan 1	Manchester United	0-0	Potts	G Milburn	J Milburn	Edwards	Hart	Copping	Turnbull	Furness	Jennings	Wainscoat	Mitchell
Jan 17	Blackburn Rovers	1-3	Potts	G Milburn	J Milburn	Edwards	Hart	Copping	Turnbull	Furness	Hydes 1	Wainscoat	Mitchell
Jan 28	BLACKPOOL	2-2	Potts	G Milburn	J Milburn	Edwards	Hart 1	Copping	Turnbull 1	Furness	Keetley	Wainscoat	Mitchell
Jan 31	Huddersfield Town	0-3	Potts	G Milburn	J Milburn	Hornby	Hart	Copping	Turnbull	Furness	Keetley	Wainscoat	Mitchell
Feb 7	Sunderland	0-4	Potts	G Milburn	J Milburn	Edwards	Hart	Copping	Green	Furness	Keetley	Hornby	Cochrane
Feb 18	LEICESTER CITY	1-3	Potts	Brown	J Milburn	Edwards	Townsley	Copping	Duggan 1	Hornby	Hydes	Wainscoat	Cochrane
Feb 21	LIVERPOOL	1-2	Potts	J Milburn	Menzies	Edwards	Hart	Copping	Turnbull	Furness	Jennings	Wainscoat 1	Cochrane
Feb 28	Middlesbrough	0-5	Potts	J Milburn	Menzies	Edwards	Hart	Copping	Green	Hornby	Keetley	Furness	Cochrane
Mar 7	NEWCASTLE UNITED	1-0	Potts	J Milburn	Menzies	Edwards	Hart	Copping	Turnbull 1	Hornby	Keetley	Furness	Cochrane
Mar 11	ARSENAL	1-2	Potts	J Milburn	Menzies	Edwards	Hart	Copping	Turnbull 1	Hornby	Keetley	Wainscoat	Cochrane
Mar 14	Sheffield Wednesday	1-2	Potts	J Milburn	Menzies	Edwards	Hart	Copping	Turnbull	Furness	Keetley	Wainscoat 1	Cochrane
Mar 21	WEST HAM UNITED	3-0	Potts	J Milburn	Menzies	Edwards	Hart	Copping	Turnbull 1	Furness	Alderson 2	Wainscoat	Cochrane
Mar 28	Chelsea	0-1	Potts	J Milburn	Menzies	Edwards	Hart	Copping	Turnbull	Furness	Alderson	Wainscoat	Cochrane
Apr 4	GRIMSBY TOWN	0-0	Potts	J Milburn	Menzies	Edwards	Hart	Copping	Turnbull	Furness	Alderson	Wainscoat	Cochrane
Apr 6	Sheffield United	1-1	Potts	J Milburn	Menzies	Edwards	Hart	Copping 1	Turnbull	Furness	Keetley	Wainscoat	Cochrane
Apr 7	SHEFFIELD UNITED	(o.g.) 4-0	Potts	J Milburn	Menzies	Edwards	Hart	Copping	Turnbull	Alderson	Keetley 2	Wainscoat 1	Cochrane
Apr 11	Bolton Wanderers	0-2	Potts	J Milburn	Menzies	Edwards	Hart	Copping	Turnbull	Furness	Keetley	Wainscoat	Cochrane
Apr 18	ASTON VILLA	0-2	Potts	J Milburn	Menzies	Edwards	Hart	Copping	Turnbull	Furness	Keetley	Wainscoat	Cochrane
May 2	DERBY COUNTY	3-1	Potts	G Milburn	Menzies	Edwards	Danskin	Copping	Green 1	Hornby	Keetley 2	Furness	Cochrane

F.A. CUP

Jan 10	HUDDERSFIELD TOWN	Rd 3 2-0	Potts	G Milburn	J Milburn	Edwards	Hart	Copping	Turnbull	Furness 1	Hydes 1	Wainscoat	Cochrane
Jan 24	NEWCASTLE UNITED	Rd 4 4-1	Potts	G Milburn	J Milburn	Edwards	Hart	Copping	Turnbull	Furness 1	Keetley 1	Wainscoat 2	Cochrane
Feb 14	Exeter City	Rd 5 1-3	Potts	G Milburn	J Milburn	Edwards	Hart	Copping	Turnbull	Furness	Hydes	Wainscoat	Cochrane 1

DIVISION TWO 1931-32

Aug 29	Swansea Town	2-0	Potts	J Milburn	Menzies	Edwards	Hart	Copping	Green 1	Firth 1	Keetley	Wainscoat	Cochrane
Aug 31	Port Vale	2-1	Potts	J Milburn	Menzies	Stacey	Danskin	Copping	Green 1	Firth	Keetley	Wainscoat 1	Cochrane
Sep 5	BARNSLEY	0-1	Potts	J Milburn	Menzies	Edwards	Hart	Copping	Green	Firth	Keetley	Wainscoat	Cochrane
Sep 7	MILLWALL	0-1	Potts	G Milburn	J Milburn	Edwards	Danskin	Copping	Green	Firth	Hydes	Furness	Cochrane
Sep 12	Notts County	1-1	Potts	G Milburn	J Milburn	Edwards	Hart	Copping	Duggan	Firth	Keetley	Furness	Cochrane 1
Sep 14	Millwall	3-2	Potts	G Milburn	J Milburn	Edwards	Hart	Copping	Duggan	Firth	Keetley 1	Furness 1	Cochrane 1
Sep 19	PLYMOUTH ARGYLE	0-0	Potts	J Milburn	Menzies	Edwards	Hart	Copping	Duggan	Firth	Keetley	Furness	Cochrane
Sep 26	Bristol City	2-0	Potts	J Milburn	Menzies	Edwards	Hart	Copping	Duggan	Firth	Keetley 1	Furness 1	Cochrane
Oct 3	OLDHAM ATHLETIC	5-0	Potts	J Milburn	Menzies	Edwards	Hart	Copping	Duggan	Firth	Keetley 3	Furness	Cochrane 2
Oct 10	Bury	4-0	Potts	J Milburn	Menzies	Edwards	Hart 1	Copping	Duggan 1	Firth 1	Keetley 1	Furness	Cochrane
Oct 17	WOLVERHAMPTON WANS	2-1	Potts	J Milburn	Menzies	Stacey	Hart	Copping	Duggan	Firth	Keetley 1	Furness 1	Cochrane
Oct 24	Charlton Athletic	1-0	Potts	J Milburn	Menzies	Edwards	Hart	Copping	Duggan	Firth	Keetley	Furness 1	Cochrane
Oct 31	STOKE CITY	2-0	Potts	J Milburn	Menzies	Edwards	Hart	Copping	Duggan	Firth	Keetley	Furness 1	Cochrane 1
Nov 7	Manchester United	5-2	Potts	J Milburn	Menzies	Stacey	Hart	Copping	Duggan 1	Firth 2	Keetley 1	Furness 1	Cochrane
Nov 14	PRESTON NORTH END	4-1	Potts	J Milburn	Menzies	Edwards	Hart	Copping	Duggan	Firth 2	Keetley 1	Furness 1	Cochrane
Nov 21	Burnley	5-0	Potts	J Milburn	Menzies	Edwards	Hart	Copping	Duggan	Firth 2	Keetley	Furness 1	Cochrane 2
Nov 28	CHESTERFIELD	3-3	Potts	J Milburn	Menzies	Edwards	Hart	Copping	Turnbull	Firth	Keetley 2	Furness 1	Cochrane
Dec 5	Nottingham Forest	3-3	Potts	J Milburn	Menzies	Edwards	Hart	Copping	Duggan	Firth	Keetley 2	Furness 1	Cochrane
Dec 12	Tottenham Hotspur	1-0	Potts	J Milburn	Menzies	Edwards	Hart	Copping	Green 1	Firth	Keetley	Furness	Cochrane
Dec 19	Southampton	1-2	Potts	J Milburn	Menzies	Edwards	Hart	Copping	Duggan 1	Firth	Keetley	Furness	Cochrane
Dec 25	Bradford	0-3	Potts	G Milburn	J Milburn	Stacey	Hart	Copping	Duggan	Firth	Hydes	Furness	Cochrane
Dec 26	BRADFORD	3-2	Potts	J Milburn	Menzies	Hornby	Hart	Copping	Duggan 1	Firth	Keetley 2	Bennett	Cochrane
Jan 2	SWANSEA TOWN	3-2	Potts	G Milburn	J Milburn	Edwards	Danskin 1	Copping	Duggan	Firth 1	Keetley 1	Bennett	Cochrane
Jan 16	Barnsley	2-0	Moore	G Milburn	J Milburn	Edwards	Hart	Copping	Duggan	Firth 1	Keetley 1	Bennett	Cochrane
Jan 23	NOTTS COUNTY	2-2	Moore	G Milburn	J Milburn	Edwards	Hart	Copping	Duggan	Firth	Keetley 2	Hydes	Cochrane
Jan 30	Plymouth Argyle	2-3	Moore	G Milburn	J Milburn	Hornby	Hart	Copping	Green	Firth 1	Keetley	Hydes 1	Wilkinson
Feb 6	BRISTOL CITY	1-0	Moore	J Milburn	Menzies	Hornby	Hart	Copping	Duggan	Firth 1	Keetley	Hydes	Cochrane
Feb 13	Oldham Athletic	1-2	Moore	J Milburn	Menzies	Hornby	Hart	Copping	Duggan	Firth	Keetley 1	Bennett	Cochrane
Feb 20	BURY	1-0	Moore	J Milburn	Menzies	Hornby	Hart	Copping	Duggan	Firth 1	Keetley	Bennett	Cochrane
Feb 27	Wolverhampton Wans	1-1	Moore	G Milburn	J Milburn	Stacey	Hart	Copping	Duggan	Hornby	Keetley	Bennett	Cochrane 1
Mar 5	CHARLTON ATHLETIC	2-0	Moore	G Milburn	J Milburn	Stacey	Hart	Copping	Duggan	Firth 1	Keetley 1	Bennett	Cochrane
Mar 12	Stoke City	4-3	Moore	G Milburn	J Milburn	Edwards	Hart	Copping	Duggan	Hornby 1	Keetley 1	Bennett 2	Cochrane
Mar 19	MANCHESTER UNITED	1-4	Moore	G Milburn	J Milburn	Stacey	Hart	Copping	Duggan	Hornby	Keetley	Bennett 1	Cochrane
Mar 26	Preston North End	0-0	Potts	J Milburn	Menzies	Edwards	Hart	Copping	Duggan	Hornby	Keetley	Furness	Cochrane
Mar 28	Bradford City	1-4	Potts	J Milburn	Menzies	Stacey	Hart	Copping	Duggan	Hornby	Keetley	Bennett 1	Cochrane
Mar 29	BRADFORD CITY	1-1	Potts	J Milburn	Menzies	Edwards	Hart	Copping	Duggan	Hornby	Hydes 1	Cochrane	Wilkinson
Apr 2	Burnley	3-1	Potts	J Milburn	Menzies	Edwards	Hart	Neal	Green	Duggan	Hydes 1	Furness 1	Cochrane 1
Apr 9	Chesterfield	1-1	Potts	J Milburn	Menzies	Stacey	Hart	Neal	Green	Duggan 1	Keetley	Furness	Cochrane
Apr 16	NOTTINGHAM FOREST	1-1	Potts	J Milburn 1	Menzies	Edwards	Hart	Copping	Green	Duggan	Keetley	Furness	Cochrane
Apr 23	Tottenham Hotspur	1-3	Potts	J Milburn	Menzies	Edwards	Hart	Copping	Duggan	Firth	Hydes	Furness 1	Cochrane
Apr 30	SOUTHAMPTON	1-0	Potts	J Milburn	Menzies	Edwards	Hart	Copping	Duggan	Firth	Keetley 1	Furness	Cochrane
May 7	PORT VALE	0-2	Potts	J Milburn	Menzies	Edwards	Danskin	Copping	Duggan	Firth	Keetley	Furness	Cochrane

F.A. CUP

Jan 9	Queen's Park Rangers	1-3	Moore	J Milburn 1	Menzies	Edwards	Danskin	Copping	Duggan	Firth	Keetley	Bennett	Cochrane

DIVISION ONE 1932-33

			1	2	3	4	5	6	7	8	9	10	11
Aug 27	DERBY COUNTY	0-2	Potts	G Milburn	J Milburn	Edwards	Hart	Copping	Green	Firth	Hydes	Furness	Mallon
Aug 29	Blackpool	1-2	Potts	G Milburn	J Milburn	Stacey	Hart	Copping	Green	Roper 1	Hydes	Furness	Cochrane
Sep 3	Blackburn Rovers	1-1	Potts	G Milburn	J Milburn	Stacey	Hart	Copping	Green	Firth	Keetley	Furness	Cochrane 1
Sep 5	BLACKPOOL	3-1	Potts	G Milburn	J Milburn	Stacey	Hart	Copping 1	Duggan	Hydes	Keetley 1	Furness 1	Cochrane
Sep 10	HUDDERSFIELD TOWN	1-1	Potts	G Milburn	J Milburn	Stacey	Hart	Copping	Duggan	Hydes	Keetley 1	Furness	Cochrane
Sep 17	SHEFFIELD WEDNESDAY	3-2	Potts	G Milburn	J Milburn	Stacey	Hart	Copping	Duggan 1	Hydes	Keetley 2	Furness	Cochrane
Sep 24	West Bromwich Albion	1-0	Potts	G Milburn	J Milburn	Stacey	Hart	Copping	Duggan	Hydes	Keetley 1	Furness	Cochrane
Oct 1	BIRMINGHAM	1-1	Potts	G Milburn	J Milburn	Stacey	Hart	Copping	Green	Hydes	Duggan 1	Furness	Cochrane
Oct 8	Sunderland	0-0	Potts	G Milburn	J Milburn	Stacey	Hart	Copping	Duggan	Hydes	Keetley	Furness	Cochrane
Oct 15	MANCHESTER CITY	2-1	Potts	G Milburn	J Milburn 1	Stacey	Hart	Copping	Duggan	Hydes 1	Keetley	Furness	Cochrane
Oct 22	Sheffield United	0-0	Potts	G Milburn	J Milburn	Stacey	Hart	Copping	Duggan	Hydes	Keetley	Furness	Cochrane
Oct 29	WOLVERHAMPTON WANS	2-0	Potts	G Milburn	J Milburn	Stacey	Hart	Copping	Duggan	O'Grady 1	Hydes 1	Furness	Cochrane
Nov 5	Liverpool	1-0	Potts	G Milburn	J Milburn	Stacey	Hart	Copping	Duggan 1	O'Grady	Hydes	Furness	Cochrane
Nov 12	LEICESTER CITY	1-1	Potts	G Milburn	J Milburn	Stacey	Hart	Copping	Duggan	O'Grady	Hydes 1	Furness	Cochrane
Nov 19	Portsmouth	3-3	Potts	G Milburn	J Milburn 1	Stacey	Hart	Copping	Duggan	O'Grady	Hydes	Furness 1	Cochrane 1
Nov 26	CHELSEA	2-0	Potts	G Milburn	J Milburn	Stacey	Hart	Copping	Duggan	O'Grady	Hydes 2	Furness	Cochrane
Dec 3	Newcastle United	1-3	Potts	G Milburn	J Milburn	Stacey	Hart	Copping	Duggan	Hydes 1	Keetley	Furness	Cochrane
Dec 10	ASTON VILLA	1-1	Potts	G Milburn	J Milburn	Edwards	Hart	Copping	Green	Hydes 1	Keetley	Furness	Cochrane
Dec 17	Middlesbrough	1-0	Potts	G Milburn	J Milburn	Stacey	Hart	Copping	Mahon	Hydes	Keetley 1	Furness	Cochrane
Dec 24	BOLTON WANDERERS	4-3	Potts	G Milburn	J Milburn	Stacey	Hart	Copping	Mahon	Hydes 2	Keetley 1	Furness 1	Cochrane
Dec 26	Arsenal	2-1	Potts	G Milburn	J Milburn	Stacey	Hart	Copping	Mahon	Hydes	Keetley 2	Furness	Cochrane
Dec 27	ARSENAL	0-0	Potts	G Milburn	J Milburn	Edwards	Hart	Copping	Duggan	Hydes	Keetley	Furness	Cochrane
Dec 31	Derby County	1-5	Potts	G Milburn	J Milburn	Edwards	Hart	Copping	Mahon	Hydes	Keetley 1	Furness	Cochrane
Jan 7	BLACKBURN ROVERS	3-1	Potts	G Milburn	J Milburn	Edwards	Hart	Copping	Mahon 1	Hydes	Keetley 1	Furness 1	Cochrane
Jan 21	Huddersfield Town	2-2	Potts	G Milburn	J Milburn	Edwards	Hart	Copping	Mahon	O'Grady 1	Keetley	Furness 1	Cochrane
Feb 4	WEST BROMWICH ALBION	1-1	Potts	G Milburn	J Milburn	Edwards	Hart	Neal	Mahon	O'Grady	Hydes 1	Furness	Cochrane
Feb 8	Sheffield Wednesday	0-2	Potts	G Milburn	J Milburn	Edwards	Hornby	Neal	Mahon	O'Grady	Hydes	Furness	Cochrane
Feb 11	Birmingham	1-2	Potts	G Milburn	J Milburn	Edwards	Hart	Neal	Mahon	Hydes 1	Fowler	Furness	Cochrane
Feb 22	SUNDERLAND	2-3	Potts	G Milburn	J Milburn	Edwards	Hart	Copping	Duggan 1	Firth	Hydes 1	Furness	Cochrane
Mar 4	SHEFFIELD UNITED	1-3	Potts	G Milburn	J Milburn	Edwards	Hart	Copping	Duggan	Firth	Hydes 1	Furness	Cochrane
Mar 11	Wolverhampton Wans	3-3	Moore	G Milburn	J Milburn	Edwards	Hart	Copping	Duggan	Hydes	Keetley 3	Furness	Cochrane
Mar 18	LIVERPOOL	(o.g.) 5-0	Moore	G Milburn	J Milburn	Edwards	Hart	Copping	Duggan 1	Hydes 1	Keetley	Furness	Mahon 2
Mar 25	Leicester City	1-3	Moore	G Milburn	J Milburn	Edwards	Hart	Copping	Duggan	Hydes	Keetley	Furness 1	Mahon
Apr 1	PORTSMOUTH	0-1	Moore	G Milburn	J Milburn	Edwards	Hornby	Copping	Duggan	Firth	Keetley	Furness	Mahon
Apr 5	Manchester City	0-0	Moore	G Milburn	J Milburn	Edwards	Hart	Copping	Duggan	Hydes	Keetley	Furness	Mahon
Apr 8	Chelsea	0-6	Moore	G Milburn	J Milburn	Edwards	Hart	Copping	Duggan	Hydes	Keetley	Furness	Mahon
Apr 15	NEWCASTLE UNITED	6-1	Moore	G Milburn	J Milburn	Edwards	Hart	Copping 1	Duggan	Hydes 1	Fowler 2	Furness	Mahon 2
Apr 17	Everton	1-0	Moore	G Milburn	J Milburn	Edwards	Hart	Copping	Duggan	Hydes 1	Fowler	Furness	Mahon
Apr 18	EVERTON	1-0	Moore	G Milburn	J Milburn	Edwards	Hart	Copping	Duggan 1	Hydes	Fowler	Furness	Mahon
Apr 22	Aston Villa	0-0	Moore	G Milburn	J Milburn	Edwards	Hart	Copping	Duggan	Hydes	Fowler	Furness	Mahon
Apr 29	MIDDLESBROUGH	0-1	Moore	G Milburn	J Milburn	Edwards	Hart	Copping	Duggan	Hydes	Fowler	Furness	Mahon
May 6	Bolton Wanderers	0-5	Moore	G Milburn	J Milburn	Edwards	Hornby	Copping	Duggan	Hydes	Keetley	Furness	Mahon

F.A. CUP

Jan 14	Newcastle United	Rd 3 3-0	Potts	G Milburn	J Milburn	Edwards	Hart	Copping	Mahon	Hydes 3	Keetley	Furness	Cochrane
Jan 28	Tranmere Rovers	Rd 4 0-0	Potts	G Milburn	J Milburn	Edwards	Hart	Copping	Mahon	Hydes	Keetley	Furness	Cochrane
Feb 1	TRANMERE ROVERS	Rd 4 R 4-0	Potts	G Milburn	J Milburn 1	Edwards	Hart	Copping	Mahon 1	O'Grady	Hydes 1	Furness	Cochrane 1
Feb 18	Everton	Rd 5 0-2	Potts	G Milburn	J Milburn	Edwards	Hart	Copping	Duggan	Hydes	Keetley	Furness	Cochrane

DIVISION ONE 1933-34

Aug 26	Blackburn Rovers	2-4	Moore	G Milburn	J Milburn	Stacey	Edwards	Copping	Duggan	Roper	Hydes 1	Furness	Cochrane 1
Aug 28	MIDDLESBROUGH	5-2	Moore	G Milburn	Wilkinson	Stacey	Turner	Copping	Duggan	Roper 1	Hydes 4	Furness	Cochrane
Sep 2	NEWCASTLE UNITED	3-0	Moore	G Milburn	J Milburn 1	Stacey	Turner	Copping	Duggan	Roper	Hydes 1	Furness	Cochrane 1
Sep 9	Huddersfield Town	0-0	Moore	G Milburn	J Milburn	Stacey	Turner	Copping	Duggan	Roper	Hydes	Furness	Cochrane
Sep 16	Derby County	1-3	Moore	G Milburn	J Milburn	Stacey	Turner	Copping	Duggan	Roper	Hydes 1	Furness	Cochrane
Sep 23	WEST BROMWICH ALBION	(o.g.) 3-0	Moore	G Milburn	J Milburn	Stacey	Hart	Copping	Duggan	Roper	Hydes 2	Furness	Cochrane
Sep 30	Birmingham	0-4	Moore	G Milburn	J Milburn	Stacey	Hart	Copping	Duggan	Roper	Hydes	Furness	Cochrane
Oct 7	SHEFFIELD WEDNESDAY	2-1	Moore	G Milburn	J Milburn	Stacey	Hart	Copping	Duggan	Roper	Fowler 2	Furness	Cochrane
Oct 14	Manchester City	1-0	Moore	G Milburn	J Milburn	Stacey	Hart	Neal	Green	Roper	Fowler 1	Furness	Cochrane
Oct 21	PORTSMOUTH	1-0	Moore	G Milburn	J Milburn	Stacey	Hart	Copping	Duggan	Roper	Fowler 1	Furness	Cochrane
Oct 28	Sunderland	2-4	Moore	G Milburn	J Milburn	Stacey	Hart	Copping	Duggan	Keetley 1	Fowler 1	Furness	Cochrane
Nov 4	ASTON VILLA	2-4	Moore	G Milburn	J Milburn	Stacey	Hart	Copping	Duggan	Hornby 1	Fowler	Furness 1	Cochrane
Nov 11	Liverpool	3-4	Moore	G Milburn	J Milburn	Edwards	Hart	Copping	Duggan 1	Hydes 1	Fowler 1	Furness	Cochrane
Nov 18	TOTTENHAM HOTSPUR	0-0	Moore	G Milburn	J Milburn	Edwards	Hart	Copping	Duggan	Hydes	Fowler	Furness	Cochrane
Nov 25	Leicester City	2-2	Moore	G Milburn	J Milburn	Edwards	Hart	Copping	Duggan 1	Keetley	Hydes 1	Furness	Cochrane
Dec 2	STOKE CITY	2-0	Moore	G Milburn	J Milburn	Edwards	Hart	Copping	Duggan	Keetley 1	Hydes 1	Furness	Cochrane
Dec 9	Sheffield United	1-2	Moore	G Milburn	J Milburn	Edwards	Hart	Copping	Duggan	Keetley	Hydes	Furness 1	Cochrane
Dec 16	WOLVERHAMPTON WANS	3-3	Moore	G Milburn	J Milburn	Edwards	Hart	Copping	Duggan 1	Keetley 2	Hydes	Furness	Cochrane
Dec 23	Chelsea	1-1	Moore	Sproston	J Milburn	Edwards	Hart	Copping	Duggan	Keetley 1	Hydes	Furness	Cochrane
Dec 25	ARSENAL	0-1	Moore	Sproston	J Milburn	Edwards	Hart	Copping	Duggan	Keetley	Hydes	Furness	Cochrane
Dec 26	Arsenal	0-2	Moore	Sproston	J Milburn	Hornby	Turner	Copping	Duggan	Firth	Hydes	Furness	Cochrane
Dec 30	BLACKBURN ROVERS	4-0	Moore	Sproston	J Milburn	Hornby	Hart	Copping	Duggan	Firth	Hydes 3	Furness 1	Cochrane
Jan 1	Middlesbrough	1-2	Moore	Sproston	J Milburn	Hornby	Hart	Copping	Duggan	Firth	Hydes 1	Furness	Cochrane
Jan 6	Newcastle United	0-2	Moore	G Milburn	J Milburn	Hornby	Hart	Copping	Duggan	Firth	Hydes	Furness	Cochrane
Jan 20	HUDDERSFIELD TOWN	1-1	Moore	G Milburn	J Milburn 1	Hornby	Turner	Copping	Green	Roper	Fowler	Furness	Mahon
Jan 31	DERBY COUNTY	0-2	Moore	G Milburn	J Milburn	Hornby	Turner	Copping	Mahon	Roper	Fowler	Furness	Cochrane
Feb 3	West Bromwich Albion	3-0	Moore	G Milburn	J Milburn	Hornby	Hart	Copping	Mahon 2	Roper 1	Keetley	Furness	Cochrane
Feb 10	BIRMINGHAM	1-0	Moore	G Milburn	J Milburn	Hornby	Hart	Firth	Mahon	Roper	Keetley	Furness 1	Cochrane
Feb 24	MANCHESTER CITY	3-1	Moore	G Milburn	J Milburn	Hornby	Hart	Copping	Mahon 1	Firth 1	Keetley	Furness 1	Cochrane
Feb 26	Sheffield Wednesday	2-0	Moore	G Milburn	J Milburn	Hornby	Hart	Copping	Mahon	Firth 1	Keetley 1	Furness	Cochrane
Mar 7	Portsmouth	1-2	Moore	G Milburn	J Milburn	Hornby	Hart	Copping 1	Mahon	Firth	Keetley	Furness	Cochrane
Mar 10	SUNDERLAND	3-1	Moore	G Milburn	J Milburn	Hornby	Hart	Copping	Mahon	Firth	Duggan 1	Furness 1	Cochrane 1
Mar 24	LIVERPOOL	5-1	Moore	G Milburn	J Milburn	Hornby	Hart	Copping	Mahon 1	Firth 2	Duggan 2	Furness	Cochrane
Mar 30	EVERTON	2-2	Moore	G Milburn	J Milburn	Hornby	Hart	Copping	Mahon	Firth	Duggan 2	Furness	Cochrane
Mar 31	Tottenham Hotspur	1-5	Moore	G Milburn	J Milburn	Hornby	Hart	Copping	Mahon	Firth	Duggan	Keetley 1	Cochrane
Apr 2	Everton	0-2	Moore	G Milburn	J Milburn	Hornby	Hart	Copping	Mahon	Keetley	Duggan	Furness	Cochrane
Apr 7	LEICESTER CITY	8-0	Moore	G Milburn	J Milburn	Edwards	Hart	Copping	Mahon 2	Firth 2	Duggan 2	Furness 2	Cochrane
Apr 14	Stoke City	2-1	Moore	G Milburn	J Milburn	Edwards	Turner	Hornby	Mahon	Firth 1	Duggan 1	Furness	Cochrane
Apr 21	SHEFFIELD UNITED	(o.g.) 1-1	Moore	G Milburn	J Milburn	Edwards	Hart	Copping	Mahon	Firth	Duggan	Furness	Cochrane
Apr 28	Wolverhampton Wans	0-2	Moore	G Milburn	J Milburn	Edwards	Hart	Copping	Mahon	Firth	Duggan	Furness	Cochrane
Apr 30	Aston Villa	0-3	Moore	G Milburn	J Milburn	Edwards	Hart	Copping	Mahon	Firth	Keetley	Furness	Cochrane
May 5	CHELSEA	3-1	Moore	G Milburn	J Milburn	Edwards	Hart	Hornby	Mahon 1	Firth 1	Duggan	Furness	Cochrane 1

F.A. CUP

Jan 13	PRESTON NORTH END	0-1	Moore	G Milburn	J Milburn	Hornby	Hart	Copping	Duggan	Firth	Keetley	Furness	Cochrane

DIVISION ONE 1934-35

Aug 25	MIDDLESBROUGH	2-4	Moore	G Milburn	J Milburn	Edwards	Hart	Hornby	Duggan	Firth	Mills 2	Furness	Cochrane
Aug 27	Stoke City	1-8	Moore	G Milburn	J Milburn	Edwards	Hart	Hornby 1	Worsley	Firth	Mills	Furness	Cochrane
Sep 1	Blackburn Rovers	1-1	Savage	G Milburn	J Milburn 1	Mills	Hart	Hornby	Worsley	Firth	Keetley	Furness	Cochrane
Sep 3	STOKE CITY	4-2	Savage	G Milburn	J Milburn	Mills	Hart	Neal	Mahon 1	JM Kelly	Duggan 1	Furness 1	Cochrane 1
Sep 8	ARSENAL	1-1	Savage	Sproston	J Milburn	Mills	Hart	Neal	Mahon	Wilkinson	Duggan	Furness 1	Cochrane
Sep 15	Portsmouth	0-0	Savage	Sproston	J Milburn	Mills	Hart	Neal	Mahon	Wilkinson	Duggan	Furness	Cochrane
Sep 22	LIVERPOOL	0-3	Savage	Sproston	J Milburn	Mills	Hart	Hornby	Mahon	Wilkinson	Duggan	Furness	Cochrane
Sep 29	HUDDERSFIELD TOWN	2-0	Savage	Sproston	J Milburn	Mills	Hart	Neal	Mahon	Hornby	Duggan 2	Furness	Cochrane
Oct 6	West Bromwich Albion	3-6	Savage	Sproston	J Milburn 1	Mills	Hart	Neal	Mahon 1	Hornby	Duggan 1	Furness	Cochrane
Oct 13	SHEFFIELD WEDNESDAY	0-0	Savage	Sproston	J Milburn	Mills	Hart	Neal	Mahon	Roper	Duggan	Furness	Cochrane
Oct 20	EVERTON	2-0	Savage	Sproston	J Milburn	Mills	Hart	Hornby	Mahon	Roper	Hydes 1	Furness 1	Cochrane
Oct 27	Grimsby Town	2-3	Savage	Sproston	J Milburn	Mills	Hart	Hornby	Mahon	Duggan	Hydes 2	Furness	Cochrane
Nov 3	CHELSEA	(o.g.) 5-2	Savage	Sproston	J Milburn	Mills	Hart	Hornby	Mahon 1	Duggan	Hydes 2	Furness 1	Cochrane
Nov 10	Wolverhampton Wans	2-1	Savage	Sproston	J Milburn 1	Mills	Turner	Hornby	Mahon 1	Duggan	Hydes	Furness	Cochrane
Nov 17	SUNDERLAND	2-4	Savage	Sproston	J Milburn	Mills	Turner	Hornby	Mahon	Duggan 1	Hydes	Furness 1	Cochrane
Nov 24	Leicester City	0-1	Moore	Sproston	J Milburn	Mills	McDougall	Wilkinson	Mahon	Duggan	Hydes	Furness	Cochrane
Dec 1	DERBY COUNTY	4-2	Moore	Sproston	J Milburn	Edwards	McDougall	Hornby	Mahon	Duggan	Hydes 2	Furness 2	Cochrane
Dec 8	Aston Villa	1-1	Moore	Sproston	J Milburn	Edwards	Turner	Hornby	Mahon	Duggan	Hydes 1	Furness	Cochrane
Dec 15	PRESTON NORTH END	3-3	Moore	Sproston	J Milburn	Edwards	Turner	Hornby 1	Mahon	Duggan 2	Hydes	Furness	Cochrane
Dec 22	Tottenham Hotspur	1-1	Moore	Sproston	J Milburn	Edwards	Turner	Hornby	Mahon	Duggan	Hydes	Furness 1	Cochrane
Dec 25	MANCHESTER CITY	1-2	Moore	Sproston	J Milburn 1	Edwards	McDougall	Hornby	Mahon	Duggan	Hydes	Furness	Cochrane
Dec 26	Manchester City	0-3	Moore	Sproston	J Milburn	Edwards	McDougall	Hornby	Mahon	Duggan	JM Kelly	Furness	Cochrane
Dec 29	Middlesbrough	3-3	Moore	Sproston	J Milburn	Edwards	McDougall	Neal	Mahon 1	Duggan	Hydes 2	Furness	Cochrane
Jan 5	BLACKBURN ROVERS	5-1	Moore	Sproston	J Milburn	Edwards	McDougall	Neal	Mahon	Firth 1	Hydes 3	Furness 1	Cochrane

DIVISION ONE 1934-35 continued

			1	2	3	4	5	6	7	8	9	10	11
Jan 19	Arsenal	0-3	Moore	Sproston	J Milburn	Edwards	Hart	Neal	Mahon	Firth	Hydes	Furness	Cochrane
Feb 2	Liverpool	2-4	Moore	G Milburn	J Milburn	Edwards	Hart	Hornby	Mahon	Firth	Hydes 2	Roper	Cochrane
Feb 9	Huddersfield Town	1-3	Moore	G Milburn	J Milburn	Edwards	Hart	Hornby	Mahon 1	Duggan	J Kelly	Firth	Cochrane
Feb 20	WEST BROMWICH ALBION	4-1	Savage	G Milburn	J Milburn 1	Edwards	Hart	Hornby	Duggan 1	J Kelly	Hydes	Cochrane	Mahon 2
Feb 23	Sheffield Wednesday	0-1	Savage	G Milburn	J Milburn	Edwards	Hart	Hornby	Duggan	J Kelly	Hydes	Cochrane	Mahon
Mar 2	PORTSMOUTH	3-1	Savage	G Milburn 1	J Milburn	Edwards	Hart	Hornby	Duggan	J Kelly	Hydes 2	Stephenson	Mahon
Mar 6	Everton	4-4	Savage	Sproston	J Milburn	Edwards	Hart	Hornby	Worsley	J Kelly	Hydes 2	Stephenson 2	Cochrane
Mar 9	GRIMSBY TOWN	(o.g.) 3-1	Savage	G Milburn	J Milburn 1	Edwards	Turner	Hornby	Duggan	J Kelly	Hydes 1	Stephenson	Cochrane
Mar 16	Chelsea	1-7	Daniels	G Milburn	J Milburn	Edwards	Hart	Hornby	Duggan	J Kelly 1	Hydes	Furness	Cochrane
Mar 23	WOLVERHAMPTON WANS	1-1	Savage	G Milburn	J Milburn	Edwards	Hart	Hornby 1	Duggan	J Kelly	Hydes	Stephenson	Cochrane
Mar 30	Sunderland	0-3	Savage	Sproston	J Milburn	Edwards	McDougall	Hornby	Duggan	J Kelly	Hydes	Furness	Cochrane
Apr 6	LEICESTER CITY	0-2	Savage	Sproston	J Milburn	Edwards	McDougall	Hornby	Duggan	J Kelly	Hydes	Furness	Cochrane
Apr 13	Derby County	2-1	Savage	G Milburn	J Milburn	Edwards	Hart	Hornby	Mahon	Duggan	Hydes	Furness 2	Cochrane
Apr 19	BIRMINGHAM	1-1	Savage	G Milburn	J Milburn	Edwards	Hart	Hornby	Mahon	Duggan	Hydes	Furness 1	Cochrane
Apr 20	ASTON VILLA	1-1	Savage	Sproston	Abel	Edwards	McDougall	Hornby	Mahon	Duggan	Hydes	Furness 1	Cochrane
Apr 22	Birmingham	1-3	Savage	G Milburn	J Milburn	Edwards	McDougall	Hornby	Duggan	Hydes	Hart	Furness 1	Cochrane
Apr 27	Preston North End	2-0	Savage	G Milburn	J Milburn	Edwards	Hart	Hornby	Mahon	Duggan 1	Hydes 1	Furness	Cochrane
May 4	TOTTENHAM HOTSPUR	4-3	Savage	G Milburn	J Milburn	Edwards	Hart 1	Hornby	Mahon	Duggan	Hydes 1	Furness 2	Cochrane

F.A. CUP

Jan 12	BRADFORD	Rd 3 4-1	Moore	Sproston	J Milburn	Edwards	McDougall	Neal	Mahon 1	Duggan	Hydes 2	Furness 1	Cochrane
Jan 26	Norwich City	Rd 4 3-3	Moore	Sproston	J Milburn	Hart	McDougall	Neal	Mahon 1	Duggan 1	Hydes	Furness	Cochrane 1
Jan 30	NORWICH CITY	Rd 4 R 1-2	Moore	Sproston	J Milburn	Edwards	McDougall	Neal	Mahon	Firth	Hydes 1	J Kelly	Cochrane

DIVISION ONE 1935-36

Aug 31	Stoke City	1-3	McInroy	G Milburn	J Milburn 1	Edwards	Hart	Hornby	Duggan	J Kelly	Hydes	Furness	Cochrane
Sep 4	BIRMINGHAM	0-0	McInroy	Sproston	J Milburn	Edwards	McDougall	Hornby	Duggan	Stephenson	Hydes	Furness	Cochrane
Sep 7	BLACKBURN ROVERS	1-4	McInroy	Sproston	J Milburn	Edwards	Hart	Hornby	Duggan	Stephenson	Hydes 1	Furness	Cochrane
Sep 11	Birmingham	0-2	Savage	Sproston	J Milburn	Edwards	McDougall	Neal	Mahon	Duggan	JM Kelly	Stephenson	Cochrane
Sep 14	Chelsea	0-1	McInroy	Sproston	J Milburn	Edwards	McDougall	Hornby	Mahon	Brown	JM Kelly	Stephenson	Cochrane
Sep 18	ARSENAL	1-1	McInroy	Sproston	J Milburn	Edwards	McDougall	Hornby	Mahon	Brown	J Kelly 1	Stephenson	Cochrane
Sep 21	LIVERPOOL	1-0	McInroy	Sproston	J Milburn 1	Edwards	McDougall	Hornby	Mahon	Brown	J Kelly	Stephenson	Cochrane
Sep 28	Grimsby Town	1-0	McInroy	Sproston	J Milburn	Edwards	McDougall	Hornby	Duggan	Brown	J Kelly 1	Stephenson	Cochrane
Oct 5	HUDDERSFIELD TOWN	2-2	McInroy	Sproston	J Milburn 1	Edwards	McDougall	Hornby	Duggan	Brown 1	J Kelly	Stephenson	Cochrane
Oct 12	WEST BROMWICH ALBION	1-1	McInroy	Sproston	J Milburn 1	Edwards	McDougall	Hornby	Duggan	Brown	J Kelly	Furness	Cochrane
Oct 19	Middlesbrough	1-1	McInroy	Sproston	J Milburn 1	Edwards	McDougall	Hornby	Duggan	Brown	J Kelly	Furness	Cochrane
Oct 26	ASTON VILLA	4-2	McInroy	Sproston	J Milburn	Edwards	McDougall	Browne	Duggan	Brown 2	J Kelly 2	Furness	Cochrane
Nov 2	Wolverhampton Wans	0-3	McInroy	Sproston	J Milburn	Edwards	McDougall	Browne	Duggan	Brown	J Kelly	Furness	Cochrane
Nov 9	SHEFFIELD WEDNESDAY	7-2	McInroy	Sproston	J Milburn 1	Edwards 1	McDougall	Browne	Duggan 3	Brown	J Kelly 1	Furness	Cochrane 1
Nov 16	Portsmouth	2-2	McInroy	Sproston	J Milburn	Edwards	McDougall	Browne	Duggan 1	Brown	J Kelly	Furness 1	Cochrane
Nov 23	BOLTON WANDERERS	5-2	McInroy	Sproston	J Milburn	Edwards	McDougall	Browne	Duggan 1	Brown 2	J Kelly 1	Furness 1	Cochrane
Nov 30	Brentford	2-2	McInroy	Sproston	J Milburn	Edwards	McDougall	Browne	Duggan	Brown 1	J Kelly	Furness	Cochrane 1
Dec 7	DERBY COUNTY	1-0	McInroy	Sproston	J Milburn	Edwards	McDougall	Browne	Duggan	Brown 1	J Kelly	Furness	Cochrane
Dec 14	Everton	0-0	McInroy	Sproston	J Milburn	Edwards	McDougall	Browne	Duggan	Brown	Hydes	Furness	Cochrane
Dec 21	PRESTON NORTH END	0-1	McInroy	Sproston	J Milburn	Edwards	McDougall	Browne	Duggan	Brown	J Kelly	Furness	Cochrane
Dec 26	Sunderland	1-2	McInroy	Sproston	J Milburn 1	Edwards	McDougall	Browne	Duggan	Brown	J Kelly	Furness	Cochrane
Dec 28	STOKE CITY	4-1	McInroy	Sproston	J Milburn 1	Edwards	McDougall	Browne	Duggan	Brown 2	J Kelly 1	Furness	Cochrane
Jan 4	Blackburn Rovers	3-0	McInroy	Sproston	J Milburn	Edwards	McDougall	Browne	Duggan	Brown	J Kelly	Furness	Cochrane
Jan 18	CHELSEA	2-0	McInroy	Sproston	J Milburn	Edwards	McDougall	Browne	Duggan	Brown	J Kelly	Furness	Cochrane
Feb 1	GRIMSBY TOWN	(o.g.) 1-2	McInroy	Sproston	J Milburn	Edwards	Hart	Hornby	Armes	Brown	J Kelly	Furness	Cochrane
Feb 8	Huddersfield Town	2-1	McInroy	Sproston	J Milburn	Edwards	Kane	Browne	Armes	Brown 1	J Kelly 1	Furness	Cochrane
Feb 19	West Bromwich Albion	2-3	McInroy	Sproston	J Milburn	Makinson	Kane	Browne	Armes	Furness 1	J Kelly	Stephenson 1	Cochrane
Feb 22	MIDDLESBROUGH	0-1	McInroy	Sproston	J Milburn	Makinson	Kane	Neal	Armes	Brown	J Kelly	Furness	Cochrane
Feb 29	Sheffield Wednesday	0-3	McInroy	Sproston	J Milburn	Edwards	McDougall	Browne	Armes	Brown	J Kelly	Furness	Hargreaves
Mar 7	BRENTFORD	1-2	McInroy	Sproston	J Milburn	Edwards	McDougall	Neal	Armes	Brown 1	J Kelly	Stephenson	Hargreaves
Mar 14	Aston Villa	3-3	McInroy	G Milburn	J Milburn	Edwards	McDougall	Browne	Turner	Brown 1	J Kelly 1	Furness 1	Cochrane
Mar 18	Liverpool	1-2	McInroy	Sproston	J Milburn	Edwards	McDougall	Neal	Turner	Brown 1	J Kelly	Furness	Cochrane
Mar 21	PORTSMOUTH	1-0	McInroy	Sproston	J Milburn 1	Edwards	Kane	Browne	Duggan	Brown	Carr	Furness	Cochrane
Mar 28	Bolton Wanderers	0-3	McInroy	Sproston	J Milburn	Edwards	Kane	Browne	Duggan	Brown	Carr	Furness	Cochrane
Apr 4	WOLVERHAMPTON WANS	2-0	McInroy	Sproston	J Milburn	Edwards	Kane	Browne	Duggan	Hydes 1	J Kelly 1	Furness	Cochrane
Apr 10	Manchester City	3-1	McInroy	Sproston	J Milburn	Edwards	Kane	Neal	Duggan	Hydes 2	J Kelly 1	Furness	Cochrane
Apr 11	Derby County	1-2	McInroy	Sproston	J Milburn	Makinson	McDougall	Hart	Turner	Hydes	J Kelly 1	Brown	Cochrane
Apr 13	MANCHESTER CITY	1-1	McInroy	Sproston	J Milburn	Edwards	Kane	Browne	Duggan	Hydes	J Kelly	Furness 1	Cochrane
Apr 18	EVERTON	3-1	McInroy	Sproston	J Milburn	Edwards	Kane	Browne	Duggan	Brown 2	J Kelly 1	Furness	Cochrane
Apr 22	SUNDERLAND	3-0	McInroy	Sproston	G Milburn	Edwards	McDougall	Browne	Duggan	Brown 1	J Kelly 1	Furness	Cochrane 1
Apr 25	Preston North End	0-5	McInroy	Sproston	G Milburn	Edwards	Kane	Browne	Duggan	Brown	Hydes	Furness	Cochrane
May 2	Arsenal	2-2	McInroy	Sproston	G Milburn	Edwards	McDougall	Browne	Armes	Hydes 1	J Kelly	Furness 1	Cochrane

F.A. CUP

Jan 11	Wolverhampton Wans	Rd 3 1-1	McInroy	Sproston	J Milburn	Edwards	McDougall 1	Browne	Duggan	Brown	J Kelly	Furness	Cochrane
Jan 15	WOLVERHAMPTON WANS	Rd 3 R 3-1	McInroy	Sproston	J Milburn	Edwards	McDougall	Browne	Duggan 1	Brown	J Kelly 1	Furness	Cochrane 1
Jan 28	BURY	Rd 4 3-2	McInroy	Sproston	J Milburn	Edwards	McDougall	Browne	Duggan 1	Brown 2	J Kelly	Furness	Cochrane
Feb 15	Sheffield United	Rd 5 1-3	McInroy	Sproston	J Milburn	Edwards	McDougall	Browne	Armes	Brown	J Kelly	Furness 1	Cochrane

DIVISION ONE 1936-37

Aug 29	CHELSEA	2-3	McInroy	Sproston	J Milburn 2	Edwards	McDougall	Browne	Duggan	Brown	J Kelly	Furness	Cochrane
Sep 2	Manchester City	0-4	McInroy	G Milburn	J Milburn	Edwards	McDougall	Browne	Armes	Furness	J Kelly	Stephenson	Hargreaves
Sep 5	Stoke City	1-2	McInroy	G Milburn	J Milburn	Edwards	Kane	Holley	Armes	Furness	J Kelly	Stephenson 1	Hargreaves
Sep 9	MANCHESTER CITY	1-1	McInroy	G Milburn	J Milburn	Howey	Kane	Browne	Armes	Furness	J Kelly	Stephenson	Hargreaves 1
Sep 12	CHARLTON ATHLETIC	2-0	McInroy	G Milburn	J Milburn	Edwards 1	Kane	Browne	Armes	Furness	Brown 1	Stephenson	Hargreaves
Sep 16	Portsmouth	0-3	McInroy	G Milburn	J Milburn	Edwards	Kane	Browne	Armes	Furness	Brown	Stephenson	Hargreaves
Sep 19	Grimsby Town	(o.g.) 1-4	McInroy	G Milburn	J Milburn	Edwards	Kane	Holley	Armes	Furness	Brown	Stephenson	Hargreaves
Sep 26	LIVERPOOL	2-0	McInroy	G Milburn	J Milburn	Edwards	Kane	Browne	Armes	Furness 1	J Kelly	Stephenson	Hargreaves 1
Oct 3	Huddersfield Town	0-3	McInroy	Sproston	J Milburn	Edwards	Kane	Browne	Armes	Furness	J Kelly	Stephenson	Cochrane
Oct 10	Birmingham	1-2	McInroy	Sproston	J Milburn	Edwards	McDougall	Browne	Armes	Stephenson	Hydes 1	Furness	Buckley
Oct 17	EVERTON	3-0	McInroy	G Milburn	J Milburn	Edwards	McDougall	Mills	Turner	Thomson 1	Hydes 1	Stephenson	Buckley
Oct 24	Bolton Wanderers	1-2	McInroy	Sproston	J Milburn	Edwards	McDougall	Mills	Turner	Thomson 1	Hydes	Stephenson	Buckley
Oct 31	BRENTFORD	3-1	McInroy	Sproston	J Milburn	Edwards	McDougall	Mills	Armes 1	Thomson	Hydes 1	Stephenson 1	Buckley
Nov 7	Arsenal	1-4	McInroy	Sproston	J Milburn	Edwards	McDougall	Mills	Armes	Thomson 1	Hydes	Stephenson	Buckley
Nov 14	PRESTON NORTH END	1-0	McInroy	Sproston	J Milburn	Edwards	McDougall	Mills	Armes	Thomson	Hydes 1	Stephenson	Buckley
Nov 21	Sheffield Wednesday	2-1	McInroy	Sproston	J Milburn	Edwards	McDougall	Mills	Armes	Thomson	Hydes 2	Stephenson	Buckley
Nov 28	MANCHESTER UNITED	2-1	McInroy	Sproston	J Milburn	Edwards	McDougall	Mills	Armes	Thomson 1	Hydes	Stephenson 1	Buckley
Dec 5	Derby County	3-5	McInroy	Sproston	J Milburn	Edwards	McDougall	Mills	Armes	Thomson	Hydes 1	Stephenson	Buckley 2
Dec 19	Sunderland	1-2	McInroy	Sproston	J Milburn	Edwards	McDougall	Mills	Turner	Ainsley 1	Hydes	Furness	Buckley
Dec 25	MIDDLESBROUGH	(o.g.) 5-0	Savage	Sproston	J Milburn	Makinson	Kane	Mills	Powell	Ainsley 2	Hydes 1	Furness	Buckley 1
Dec 26	Chelsea	1-2	Savage	Sproston	J Milburn	Makinson	Kane	Mills	Powell	Ainsley	Hydes 1	Furness	Buckley
Dec 28	Middlesbrough	2-4	Savage	Sproston	G Milburn	Edwards	Kane	Mills	Powell 1	Ainsley	Hydes 1	Furness	Buckley
Jan 2	STOKE CITY	2-1	Savage	Sproston	G Milburn	Edwards	Kane	Mills	Powell	Ainsley 1	Trainor	Furness	Buckley 1
Jan 9	Charlton Athletic	0-1	Savage	Sproston	G Milburn	Makinson	Kane	Mills	Powell	Ainsley	Trainor	Hydes	Buckley
Jan 23	GRIMSBY TOWN	2-0	McInroy	Sproston	J Milburn	Edwards	Kane	Mills	Armes	Ainsley	Hydes 1	Furness 1	Buckley
Jan 30	Liverpool	0-3	McInroy	Sproston	J Milburn	Edwards	Kane	Browne	Armes	Ainsley	Hydes	Furness	Buckley
Feb 6	HUDDERSFIELD TOWN	(o.g.) 2-1	McInroy	Sproston	J Milburn	Edwards 1	Kane	Mills	Powell	Ainsley	Hydes	Furness	Buckley
Feb 13	BIRMINGHAM	0-2	McInroy	Sproston	J Milburn	Edwards	Kane	Mills	Powell	Ainsley	Hydes	Furness	Hargreaves
Feb 27	BOLTON WANDERERS	2-2	McInroy	Sproston	J Milburn	Edwards 1	Kane	Mills	Armes	Ainsley	J Kelly	Furness 1	Buckley
Mar 3	Everton	1-7	McInroy	Sproston	Gadsby	Edwards	Holley	Mills	Powell	Ainsley	Hodgson 1	Furness	Buckley
Mar 6	Brentford	1-4	McInroy	G Milburn	J Milburn	Edwards	Holley	Mills	Powell 1	J Kelly	Hodgson	Furness	Buckley
Mar 13	ARSENAL	3-4	Savage	G Milburn	J Milburn	Edwards	Kane	Mills	Powell	Thomson 1	Hodgson 1	Furness	Buckley 1
Mar 20	Preston North End	0-1	Savage	G Milburn	J Milburn	Edwards	Kane	Mills	Powell	Thomson	Hodgson	Furness	Buckley
Mar 27	SHEFFIELD WEDNESDAY	1-1	Savage	G Milburn	J Milburn	Edwards	Kane	Browne	Mills	Ainsley 1	Hodgson	Furness	Buckley
Mar 29	West Bromwich Albion	0-3	Savage	G Milburn	J Milburn	Mills	Kane	Browne	Turner	Thomson	Hodgson	Stephenson	Buckley
Mar 30	WEST BROMWICH ALBION	3-1	Savage	Mills	J Milburn	Edwards	Kane	Browne	Turner	Thomson	Hodgson 2	Stephenson 1	Buckley
Apr 3	Manchester United	0-0	Savage	Mills	J Milburn	Edwards	Kane	Browne	Turner	Thomson	Hodgson	Stephenson	Buckley
Apr 10	DERBY COUNTY	2-0	Savage	Mills	J Milburn	Edwards	Kane	Browne	Turner	Thomson	Hodgson 1	Stephenson 1	Buckley
Apr 17	Wolverhampton Wans	0-3	Savage	Mills	J Milburn	Edwards	Kane	Holley	Turner	Thomson	Hodgson	Stephenson	Buckley
Apr 21	WOLVERHAMPTON WANS	0-1	Savage	Sproston	J Milburn	Edwards	Kane	Mills	Turner	Hydes	Hodgson	Thomson	Buckley
Apr 24	SUNDERLAND	3-0	Savage	Mills	J Milburn 1	Makinson	Kane	Browne	Armes	J Kelly	Hodgson 1	Furness 1	Hargreaves
May 1	PORTSMOUTH	3-1	Savage	Mills	J Milburn 1	Makinson	Holley	Browne	Armes	J Kelly 1	Hodgson	Furness 1	Hargreaves

F.A. CUP

Jan 16	Chelsea	Rd 3 0-4	Savage	Sproston	G Milburn	Edwards	Kane	Mills	Powell	Ainsley	Trainor	Hydes	Buckley

DIVISION ONE 1937-38

			1	2	3	4	5	6	7	8	9	10	11
Aug 28	Charlton Athletic	1-1	Savage	Sproston	Jack Milburn	Makinson	Holley	Browne	Armes	Ainsley	Hodgson 1	Stephenson	Buckley
Sep 1	CHELSEA	(o.g.) 2-0	Savage	Sproston	Jack Milburn	Makinson	Holley	Browne	Armes 1	Ainsley	Hodgson	Stephenson	Buckley
Sep 4	PRESTON NORTH END	0-0	Savage	Sproston	Jack Milburn	Makinson	Holley	Browne	Armes	Ainsley	Hodgson	Stephenson	Buckley
Sep 8	Chelsea	1-4	Savage	Sproston	Jack Milburn	Makinson	Holley	Browne	Armes	Ainsley	Hodgson 1	Stephenson	Buckley
Sep 11	Grimsby Town	1-1	Savage	Sproston	Jack Milburn	Makinson	Holley	Browne	Armes	Ainsley	Hodgson 1	Stephenson	Buckley
Sep 15	PORTSMOUTH	3-1	Savage	Sproston	Jack Milburn	Makinson	Holley	Browne	Armes	Ainsley 1	Hodgson 2	Stephenson	Buckley
Sep 18	HUDDERSFIELD TOWN	2-1	Savage	Sproston	Jack Milburn 1	Makinson	Holley	Browne	Armes 1	Ainsley	Hodgson	Stephenson	Buckley
Sep 25	LIVERPOOL	2-0	Savage	Sproston	Jack Milburn	Makinson	Holley	Browne	Armes 1	Ainsley 1	Hodgson	Stephenson	Buckley
Oct 2	West Bromwich Albion	1-2	Savage	Sproston	Jack Milburn 1	Makinson	Holley	Browne	Armes	Ainsley	J Kelly	Stephenson	Buckley
Oct 9	BIRMINGHAM CITY	1-0	Savage	Sproston	Jack Milburn	Makinson	Holley	Browne	Armes	Ainsley 1	J Kelly	Stephenson	Buckley
Oct 16	Everton	1-1	Savage	Sproston	Jack Milburn	Makinson	Holley	Mills	Armes 1	Ainsley	J Kelly	Thomson	Buckley
Oct 23	WOLVERHAMPTON WANS	1-2	Savage	Mills	Jack Milburn	Edwards	Holley	Makinson	Armes	Ainsley	J Kelly	Thomson	Buckley 1
Oct 30	Leicester City	4-2	Savage	Sproston	Jack Milburn 1	Makinson	Holley	Browne	Turner	Ainsley	Hodgson 2	Stephenson	Buckley 1
Nov 6	BLACKPOOL	1-1	Savage	Sproston	Jack Milburn	Makinson	Holley	Browne	Turner	J Kelly	Hodgson	Stephenson	Buckley 1
Nov 13	Derby County	2-2	Savage	Sproston	Jack Milburn	Makinson	Holley	Browne	Armes	Thomson 1	Hodgson 1	Stephenson	Buckley
Nov 20	BOLTON WANDERERS	1-1	Savage	Mills	Jack Milburn	Makinson	Kane	Browne	Armes	Thomson	Hodgson 1	Stephenson	Buckley
Nov 27	Arsenal	1-4	Savage	Sproston	Jack Milburn	Makinson	Holley	Mills	Armes	Thomson	Hodgson	Stephenson 1	Buckley
Dec 4	SUNDERLAND	4-3	Savage	Goldberg	Jack Milburn	Makinson	Kane	Mills	Armes	Thomson	Hodgson 1	Stephenson 3	Buckley
Dec 11	Brentford	1-1	Savage	Goldberg	Jack Milburn	Makinson	Kane	Mills	Armes	Thomson	Hodgson 1	Stephenson	Buckley
Dec 18	MANCHESTER CITY	2-1	Savage	Sproston	Jack Milburn	Makinson	Kane	Mills	Armes	Thomson	Hodgson	Stephenson 1	Buckley 1
Dec 25	MIDDLESBROUGH	5-3	Savage	Sproston	Jack Milburn	Makinson	Kane	Mills	Armes	Thomson 1	Hodgson 2	Stephenson 1	Buckley 1
Dec 27	Middlesbrough	0-2	Savage	Sproston	Jack Milburn	Makinson	Kane	Mills	Armes	Thomson	Trainor	Stephenson	Hargreaves
Jan 1	CHARLTON ATHLETIC	2-2	Savage	Sproston	Jack Milburn	Makinson	Kane	Mills	Armes	Thomson	Hodgson	Stephenson 1	Buckley 1
Jan 15	Preston North End	1-3	Savage	Sproston	Jack Milburn	Makinson	Kane	Browne	Armes	Ainsley	Hodgson	Thomson 1	Buckley
Jan 26	GRIMSBY TOWN	1-1	Savage	Sproston	Jack Milburn	Makinson	Kane	Mills	Armes	Ainsley	Hodgson	Stephenson	Buckley 1
Jan 29	Huddersfield Town	3-0	Savage	Sproston	Jack Milburn	Makinson	Holley	Browne	Armes 1	Thomson 1	Hodgson	Stephenson	Buckley 1
Feb 5	Liverpool	1-1	Savage	Sproston	Jack Milburn	Makinson	Holley	Browne	Armes	Thomson	Hodgson 1	Stephenson	Hargreaves
Feb 12	WEST BROMWICH ALBION	1-0	Savage	Sproston	Jack Milburn	Makinson	Holley	Browne	Armes	Thomson	Hodgson 1	Stephenson	Buckley
Feb 19	Birmingham City	2-3	Savage	Sproston	Jack Milburn	Makinson	Holley	Browne	Armes	Thomson 1	Hodgson 1	Stephenson	Hargreaves
Feb 26	EVERTON	4-4	Savage	Sproston	Jack Milburn	Makinson	Holley	Browne	Armes	Thomson	Hodgson 4	Stephenson	Hargreaves
Mar 5	Wolverhampton Wans	1-1	Savage	Sproston 1	Jack Milburn	Makinson	Holley	Browne	Armes	Thomson	Hodgson	Stephenson	Hargreaves
Mar 12	LEICESTER CITY	0-2	Savage	Sproston	Jack Milburn	Makinson	Kane	Browne	Armes	Thomson	Ainsley	Stephenson	Hargreaves
Mar 19	Blackpool	2-5	Twomey	Sproston	Jack Milburn	Makinson	Holley	Browne	Armes	Ainsley 1	Hodgson 1	Stephenson	Hargreaves
Mar 26	DERBY COUNTY	0-2	Twomey	Sproston	Jack Milburn	Makinson	Holley	Mills	Cochrane	Ainsley	Hodgson	Stephenson	Buckley
Apr 2	Bolton Wanderers	0-0	Twomey	Sproston	Jack Milburn	Edwards	D Kelly	Browne	Armes	Ainsley	Hodgson	Stephenson	Buckley
Apr 9	ARSENAL	0-1	Twomey	Goldberg	Jack Milburn	Edwards	D Kelly	Browne	Armes	Ainsley	Hodgson	Francis	Buckley
Apr 16	Sunderland	0-0	Twomey	Sproston	Jack Milburn	Makinson	Kane	Browne	Armes	Ainsley	Hodgson	Stephenson	Buckley
Apr 18	Stoke City	(o.g.) 1-0	Twomey	Sproston	Jack Milburn	Makinson	Kane	Browne	Armes	Ainsley	Hodgson	Stephenson	Buckley
Apr 19	STOKE CITY	2-1	Twomey	Sproston	Jack Milburn	Makinson	Kane	Browne	Armes	Ainsley 1	Hodgson 1	Stephenson 1	Buckley
Apr 23	BRENTFORD	4-0	Twomey	Sproston	Jack Milburn	Makinson	Kane	Browne	Armes	Ainsley 1	Hodgson 3	Stephenson	Buckley
Apr 30	Manchester City	2-6	Twomey	Sproston	Jack Milburn	Makinson	D Kelly	Browne	Armes	Ainsley	Hodgson 1	Stephenson	Buckley 1
May 7	Portsmouth	0-4	Twomey	Sproston	Jack Milburn	Makinson	D Kelly	Browne	Armes	Ainsley	Hodgson	Stephenson	Buckley

F.A. CUP

Jan 8	CHESTER	Rd 3	3-1	Savage	Sproston	Jack Milburn	Makinson	Kane	Mills	Armes 1	Ainsley	Hodgson	Stephenson	Buckley 2
Jan 22	Charlton Athletic	Rd 4	1-2	Savage	Sproston	Jack Milburn	Makinson	Kane	Mills	Armes	Ainsley	Hodgson 1	Stephenson	Buckley

DIVISION ONE 1938-39

Aug 27	PRESTON NORTH END	2-1	Twomey	John Milburn	Gadsby	Makinson	Holley	Browne	Armes	Ainsley	Hodgson 1	Stephenson	Buckley 1
Aug 31	BIRMINGHAM CITY	2-0	Twomey	John Milburn	Gadsby	Makinson	Holley	Browne	Armes	Ainsley 1	Hodgson	Stephenson	Buckley 1
Sep 3	Charlton Athletic	0-2	Twomey	John Milburn	Gadsby	Makinson	Holley	Browne	Armes	Ainsley	Hodgson	Stephenson	Buckley
Sep 5	Stoke City	1-1	Twomey	Goldberg	John Milburn	Edwards	Kane	Makinson	Cochrane	Ainsley	Hodgson 1	Stephenson	Buckley
Sep 10	BOLTON WANDERERS	1-2	Twomey	Goldberg	John Milburn	Edwards	Kane	Browne	Armes	Ainsley	Hodgson 1	Stephenson	Buckley
Sep 17	Huddersfield Town	1-0	Twomey	John Milburn	Gadsby	Makinson	Holley	Browne	Armes	Thomson	Hodgson 1	Stephenson	Buckley
Sep 24	Liverpool	0-3	Twomey	John Milburn	Gadsby	Makinson	Holley	Browne	Armes	Thomson	Hodgson	Powell	Buckley
Oct 1	LEICESTER CITY	8-2	Twomey	John Milburn 1	Gadsby	Makinson	Holley	Browne	Cochrane 1	Thomson	Hodgson 5	Powell	Hargreaves 1
Oct 8	Middlesbrough	2-1	Twomey	John Milburn	Gadsby	Edwards	Holley	Mills	Armes 1	Thomson	Hodgson 1	Powell	Hargreaves
Oct 15	WOLVERHAMPTON WANS	1-0	Twomey	John Milburn	Gadsby	Edwards	Holley	Mills	Cochrane	Thomson 1	Hodgson	Powell	Hargreaves
Oct 22	Everton	0-4	Twomey	John Milburn	Gadsby	Edwards	Holley	Mills	Cochrane	Thomson	Hodgson	Powell	Hargreaves
Oct 29	PORTSMOUTH	(o.g.) 2-2	Twomey	John Milburn	Gadsby	Edwards	Holley	Browne	Armes	Powell	Ainsley 1	Stephenson	Buckley
Nov 5	Arsenal	3-2	Twomey	John Milburn	Gadsby	Edwards	Holley	Browne	Cochrane	Powell	Ainsley	Stephenson 2	Buckley 1
Nov 12	BRENTFORD	3-2	Twomey	John Milburn	Gadsby	Edwards	Holley	Browne	Cochrane	Ainsley	Hodgson 2	Stephenson	Buckley 1
Nov 19	Blackpool	2-1	Twomey	John Milburn	Gadsby	Edwards	Holley	Browne	Armes	Powell	Hodgson 1	Stephenson	Hargreaves 1
Nov 26	DERBY COUNTY	1-4	Twomey	John Milburn	Gadsby	Edwards	Holley	Browne	Cochrane	Powell	Hodgson	Stephenson	Buckley 1
Dec 3	Grimsby Town	2-3	Twomey	John Milburn	Gadsby	Edwards	Holley	Browne	Armes 1	Powell 1	Hodgson	Stephenson	Buckley
Dec 10	SUNDERLAND	3-3	Twomey	John Milburn	Gadsby	Edwards	Holley	Mills	Cochrane	Powell 1	Ainsley 1	Stephenson	Hargreaves 1
Dec 17	Aston Villa	1-2	Twomey	John Milburn	Gadsby	Edwards	Holley	Browne	Cochrane	Ainsley	Hodgson	Stephenson	Hargreaves 1
Dec 24	Preston North End	0-2	Twomey	John Milburn	Gadsby	Edwards	Holley	Browne	Cochrane	Ainsley	Hodgson	Stephenson	Hargreaves
Dec 26	CHELSEA	1-1	Twomey	Goldberg	Gadsby	Edwards 1	Holley	Parry	Cochrane	Powell	Ainsley	Stephenson	Hargreaves
Dec 27	Chelsea	2-2	Twomey	Goldberg	Gadsby	Hampson	Holley	Parry	Armes	Powell	Hodgson 1	Stephenson 1	Hargreaves
Dec 31	CHARLTON ATHLETIC	2-1	Twomey	Goldberg	Gadsby	Edwards	Holley	Parry	Cochrane 1	Powell	Hodgson 1	Stephenson	Hargreaves
Jan 14	Bolton Wanderers	(o.g.) 2-2	Savage	John Milburn	Gadsby	Makinson	Holley	Parry	Armes	Ainsley	Hodgson 1	Stephenson	Hargreaves
Jan 28	LIVERPOOL	1-1	Twomey	Goldberg	Gadsby	Edwards	Holley	Mills	Armes	Powell	Hodgson 1	Stephenson	Hargreaves
Feb 4	Leicester City	0-2	Twomey	Goldberg	Gadsby	Edwards	Holley	Parry	Cochrane	Ainsley	Hodgson	Stephenson	Hargreaves
Feb 11	MIDDLESBROUGH	0-1	Twomey	John Milburn	Gadsby	Mills	Kane	Parry	Cochrane	Powell	Hodgson	Stephenson	Hargreaves
Feb 18	Wolverhampton Wans	1-4	Twomey	Goldberg	Gadsby	Mills	Kane	Parry	Cochrane	Powell	Sutherland 1	Stephenson	Hargreaves
Feb 23	EVERTON	1-2	Savage	Goldberg	Gadsby	Makinson	Kane	Mills	Cochrane	Ainsley 1	Sutherland	Stephenson	Hargreaves
Mar 8	Portsmouth	0-2	Twomey	Goldberg	Gadsby	Makinson	Holley	Copping	Cochrane	Ainsley	Sutherland	Stephenson	Hargreaves
Mar 11	ARSENAL	4-2	Twomey	Scaife	Gadsby	Makinson	Holley	Copping	Cochrane	Powell 1	Hodgson 1	Stephenson 1	Hargreaves 1
Mar 18	Brentford	1-0	Twomey	Goldberg	Scaife	Makinson	Holley	Copping	Cochrane	Powell	Hodgson	Stephenson	Hargreaves 1
Mar 25	BLACKPOOL	1-0	Twomey	Goldberg	Scaife	Makinson	Holley	Copping	Cochrane 1	Powell	Dunderdale	Stephenson	Hargreaves
Apr 1	Derby County	0-1	Twomey	Goldberg	Scaife	Edwards	Holley	Copping	Cochrane	Powell	Dunderdale	Stephenson	Hargreaves
Apr 7	Manchester United	0-0	Twomey	Scaife	Gadsby	Makinson	Holley	Copping	Henry	Ainsley	Dunderdale	Stephenson	Hargreaves
Apr 8	GRIMSBY TOWN	0-1	Savage	Scaife	Gadsby	Edwards	Holley	Copping	Cochrane	Ainsley	Hodgson	Powell	Hargreaves
Apr 10	MANCHESTER UNITED	3-1	Twomey	Scaife	Gadsby	Makinson	Holley	Copping	Cochrane	Powell	Hodgson 1	Ainsley 1	Buckley 1
Apr 15	Sunderland	1-2	Twomey	Goldberg	Gadsby	Makinson	Holley	Browne	Cochrane	Powell	Hodgson	Ainsley 1	Buckley
Apr 19	HUDDERSFIELD TOWN	2-1	Twomey	Goldberg	Gadsby	Makinson	Holley	Copping	Cochrane	Powell 1	Hodgson 1	Stephenson	Buckley
Apr 22	ASTON VILLA	2-0	Twomey	Scaife	Gadsby	Makinson	Holley	Copping	Cochrane	Powell	Hodgson	Stephenson	Hargreaves 2
Apr 29	Birmingham City	0-4	Twomey	Scaife	Gadsby	Makinson	Holley	Copping	Cochrane	Powell	Hodgson	Stephenson	Hargreaves
May 6	STOKE CITY	0-0	Twomey	Goldberg	Gadsby	Edwards	Holley	Copping	Henry	Powell	Hodgson	Stephenson	Buckley

F.A. CUP

Jan 17	BOURNEMOUTH	Rd 3	3-1	Savage	John Milburn	Gadsby	Edwards	Holley	Parry	Cochrane 1	Powell	Hodgson	Stephenson 1	Hargreaves 1
Jan 21	HUDDERSFIELD TOWN	Rd 4	2-4	Savage	John Milburn	Gadsby	Edwards	Holley	Parry	Cochrane 1	Powell	Hodgson 1	Stephenson	Hargreaves

DIVISION ONE 1946-47

Aug 31	Preston North End	2-3	Hodgson	Goldberg	James Milburn	Price	Holley	Batey	Cochrane	Powell	Henry	Short	Grainger 2
Sep 4	CHARLTON ATHLETIC	0-2	Hodgson	Goldberg	James Milburn	Price	Holley	Batey	Cochrane	Powell	Henry	Short	Grainger
Sep 7	SHEFFIELD UNITED	2-2	Hodgson	Goldberg	James Milburn	Price	Holley	Batey	Cochrane	Powell 1	Henry 1	Short	Grainger
Sep 14	Chelsea	0-3	Hodgson	Goldberg	James Milburn	Price	Holley	Batey	Cochrane	Powell	Ainsley	Short	Grainger
Sep 16	Stoke City	2-5	Hodgson	Bannister	James Milburn	Price	Kane	Batey	Cochrane	Powell	Ainsley 2	Hindle	Grainger
Sep 21	BOLTON WANDERERS	4-0	Hodgson	Bannister	James Milburn	Henry	Batey	Browne	Cochrane 1	Powell	Ainsley 1	Short 2	Grainger
Sep 25	Charlton Athletic	0-5	Hodgson	Bannister	James Milburn	Henry	Batey	Browne	Cochrane	Powell	Browning	Short	Grainger
Sep 28	Liverpool	0-2	Hodgson	Bannister	James Milburn	Henry	Holley	Price	Grainger	Powell	Short	Hindle	Heaton
Oct 5	HUDDERSFIELD TOWN	5-0	Fearnley	Bannister	James Milburn	Henry	Holley	Browne	Cochrane	Powell 1	Ainsley 3	Short 1	Grainger
Oct 12	GRIMSBY TOWN	1-0	Fearnley	Bannister	James Milburn	Henry	Holley	Browne	Cochrane	Powell 1	Ainsley	Short	Grainger
Oct 19	Wolverhampton Wans	0-1	Fearnley	Bannister	James Milburn	Henry	Holley	Browne	Cochrane	Short	Ainsley	Hindle	Grainger
Oct 26	BLACKBURN ROVERS	0-1	Fearnley	Bannister	James Milburn	Henry	Holley	Batey	Cochrane	Powell	Ainsley	Short	Grainger
Nov 2	Portsmouth	1-4	Fearnley	Bannister	James Milburn	Henry	Holley	Browne	Cochrane	Powell	Ainsley 1	Short	Grainger
Nov 9	EVERTON	2-1	Fearnley	Bannister	James Milburn	Henry	Holley	Browne	Cochrane	Powell 1	Ainsley	Short 1	Grainger
Nov 16	Arsenal	2-4	Fearnley	Bannister	James Milburn	Henry	Holley	Browne	Cochrane	Powell	Ainsley 2	Short	Grainger
Nov 23	BLACKPOOL	4-2	Twomey	Goldberg	Gadsby	Henry	Holley	Browne	Cochrane	Powell 2	Ainsley 1	Short	Grainger 1
Nov 30	Brentford	1-1	Twomey	Goldberg	Gadsby	Henry	Holley	Heaton	Cochrane 1	Powell	Ainsley	Short	Grainger
Dec 7	SUNDERLAND	1-1	Twomey	Goldberg	Gadsby	Henry	Holley	Browne	Cochrane 1	Powell	Ainsley	Short	Grainger
Dec 14	Aston Villa	1-2	Twomey	Goldberg	Gadsby	Henry	Holley	Browne	Cochrane	Powell 1	Ainsley	Short	Grainger
Dec 21	DERBY COUNTY	1-2	Twomey	Goldberg	Gadsby	Henry 1	Holley	Browne	Cochrane	Short	Ainsley	Hindle	Heaton
Dec 25	MIDDLESBROUGH	3-3	Twomey	Goldberg	Gadsby	James Milburn 1	Holley	Browne	Cochrane 1	Powell	Ainsley	Short 1	Grainger
Dec 26	Middlesbrough	0-3	Fearnley	Goldberg	Gadsby	James Milburn	Holley	Browne	Cochrane	Short	Ainsley	Hindle	Grainger
Dec 28	PRESTON NORTH END	0-3	Fearnley	James Milburn	Gadsby	Bannister	Holley	Browne	Cochrane	Powell	Short	Hindle	Grainger
Jan 4	Sheffield United	2-6	Twomey	Goldberg	Gadsby	James Milburn	Holley	Browne	Cochrane 1	Powell	Ainsley 1	Short	Grainger

DIVISION ONE 1946-47 continued

			1	2	3	4	5	6	7	8	9	10	11
Jan 18	CHELSEA	2-1	Hodgson	James Milburn	Bannister	Henry 1	Holley	Gadsby	Cochrane 1	Powell	Ainsley	Short	Grainger
Feb 1	LIVERPOOL	1-2	Hodgson	James Milburn	Bannister	Henry	Holley	Martin	Cochrane	Powell	Ainsley	Short	Grainger 1
Feb 3	Bolton Wanderers	0-2	Hodgson	James Milburn	Bannister	Henry	Holley	Browne	Cochrane	Powell	Ainsley	Short	Grainger
Feb 22	WOLVERHAMPTON WANS	0-1	Hodgson	James Milburn	Bannister	Henry	Holley	Martin	Cochrane	Powell	Clarke	Short	Grainger
Mar 1	Blackburn Rovers	0-1	Hodgson	James Milburn	Bannister	Henry	Holley	Martin	Cochrane	Ainsley	Clarke	Hindle	Grainger
Mar 22	ARSENAL	1-1	Hodgson	James Milburn	Bannister	Willingham	Holley	Martin	Cochrane	Powell	Clarke	Henry	Grainger 1
Mar 29	Blackpool	0-3	Hodgson	James Milburn	Bannister	Henry	Holley	Martin	Cochrane	Ainsley	Clarke	Hindle	Grainger
Apr 5	BRENTFORD	1-2	Hodgson	James Milburn	Bannister	Willingham	Holley	Martin	Cochrane	Ainsley	Clarke	Henry 1	Heaton
Apr 7	Manchester United	1-3	Hodgson	James Milburn	Bannister	Willingham	Holley	Henry	Cochrane 1	Ainsley	Clarke	Hindle	Heaton
Apr 8	MANCHESTER UNITED	0-2	Hodgson	James Milburn	Bannister	Willingham	Holley	Henry	Cochrane	Ainsley	Clarke	Hindle	Heaton
Apr 12	Sunderland	0-1	Hodgson	James Milburn	Gadsby	Willingham	Holley	Henry	Cochrane	Powell	Clarke	Hindle	Heaton
Apr 19	ASTON VILLA	1-1	Twomey	James Milburn	Gadsby	Willingham	Holley	Browne	Cochrane	Powell	Clarke 1	Henry	Heaton
Apr 26	Derby County	1-2	Twomey	James Milburn	Gadsby	Willingham	Holley	Browne	Cochrane	Powell 1	Clarke	Henry	Heaton
May 3	STOKE CITY	1-2	Twomey	James Milburn	Gadsby	Willingham	Holley	Henry	Grainger	Powell	Clarke	Short 1	Heaton
May 10	Huddersfield Town	0-1	Twomey	James Milburn	Gadsby	Willingham	Holley	Henry	Cochrane	Powell	Clarke	Short	Heaton
May 17	Grimsby Town	1-4	Twomey	James Milburn	Gadsby	Willingham	Holley	Henry	Cochrane	Powell	Clarke	Short 1	Heaton
May 24	PORTSMOUTH	0-1	Twomey	James Milburn	Gadsby	Willingham	Holley	Henry	Grainger	Powell	Ainsley	Short	Heaton
May 26	Everton	1-4	Twomey	Bannister	Gadsby	Hodgkinson	Holley	Henry	Powell 1	Clarke	Ainsley	Short	Heaton

F.A. CUP

Jan 11	West Bromwich Albion	1-2	Twomey	James Milburn	Gadsby	Henry	Holley	Martin	Cochrane	Powell	Ainsley 1	Short	Grainger

DIVISION TWO 1947-48

Aug 23	LEICESTER CITY	3-1	Twomey	Milburn	Gadsby	Henry	Holley	Martin	Cochrane	Powell	Ainsley 2	Short 1	Heaton
Aug 27	Barnsley	0-3	Twomey	Milburn	Gadsby	Henry	Holley	Martin	Cochrane	Powell	Ainsley	Short	Heaton
Aug 30	Southampton	(o.g.) 2-1	Twomey	Milburn	Gadsby	Henry	Holley	Martin	Cochrane	Short	Wakefield 1	Hindle	Heaton
Sep 3	BARNSLEY	4-1	Twomey	Milburn	Gadsby	Henry	Holley	Martin	Cochrane 1	Powell	Wakefield 2	Short 1	Heaton
Sep 6	Fulham	2-3	Twomey	Milburn	Gadsby	Henry	Holley	Martin	Cochrane	Powell	Wakefield 1	Short 1	Heaton
Sep 10	PLYMOUTH ARGYLE	5-0	Twomey	Milburn	Gadsby	Willingham	Holley	Martin	Cochrane	Powell 3	Wakefield	Short 1	Heaton 1
Sep 13	COVENTRY CITY	2-1	Twomey	Milburn	Gadsby	Willingham	Holley	Martin	Cochrane	Powell 2	Wakefield	Short	Heaton
Sep 17	Plymouth Argyle	0-1	Twomey	Milburn	Gadsby	Willingham	Holley	Martin	Cochrane	Powell	Wakefield	Short	Heaton
Sep 20	Newcastle United	2-4	Twomey	Milburn	Gadsby	Willingham	Holley	Martin	Cochrane 1	Powell	Wakefield 1	Short	Heaton
Sep 27	BIRMINGHAM CITY	0-1	Twomey	Milburn	Gadsby	Willingham	Holley	Martin	Cochrane	Short	Wakefield	Hindle	Heaton
Oct 4	West Bromwich Albion	2-3	Twomey	Milburn	Gadsby	Willingham	Ingham	Kirby	Grainger	Powell	Wakefield 1	Short	Heaton 1
Oct 11	DONCASTER ROVERS	0-0	Twomey	Milburn	Gadsby	Willingham	Holley	Martin	Cochrane	Powell	Wakefield	Short	Heaton
Oct 18	Nottingham Forest	0-1	Twomey	Milburn	Gadsby	Willingham	Holley	Kirby	Cochrane	Short	Wakefield	Martin	Heaton
Oct 25	BRADFORD	2-0	Twomey	Milburn	Gadsby	Willingham	Martin	Kirby	Cochrane	Powell	Wakefield 2	Heaton	Grainger
Nov 1	Cardiff City	0-0	Twomey	Dunn	Gadsby	Willingham	Martin	Kirby	Cochrane	Powell	Wakefield	Heaton	Grainger
Nov 8	SHEFFIELD WEDNESDAY	2-2	Twomey	Dunn	Gadsby	Willingham	Martin	Kirby	Cochrane	Powell	Wakefield 2	Heaton	Grainger
Nov 15	Tottenham Hotspur	1-3	Twomey	Dunn	Gadsby	Henry	Martin	Kirby	Cochrane 1	Powell	Wakefield	Heaton	Grainger
Nov 22	MILLWALL	2-1	Twomey	Dunn	Milburn	Hodgkinson	Holley	Martin	Cochrane	Powell 2	Wakefield	Heaton	Windle
Nov 29	Chesterfield	0-3	Twomey	Dunn	Milburn	Bullions	Holley	Martin	Cochrane	Powell	Wakefield	Short	Heaton
Dec 6	WEST HAM UNITED	2-1	Twomey	Dunn	Gadsby	Bullions	Holley	Martin 1	Cochrane	Powell	Wakefield	Short 1	Heaton
Dec 13	Bury	1-1	Twomey	Dunn	Gadsby	Bullions	Holley	Kirby	Powell	Short	Wakefield 1	Martin	Heaton
Dec 20	Leicester City	0-2	Twomey	Dunn	Gadsby	Bullions	Holley	Martin	Cochrane	Powell	Wakefield	Short	Heaton
Dec 26	LUTON TOWN	0-2	Twomey	Dunn	Milburn	Bullions	Holley	Martin	Cochrane	Powell	Wakefield	Hindle	Windle
Dec 27	Luton Town	1-6	Twomey	Milburn	Gadsby	Bullions	Holley	Kirby	Cochrane 1	Powell	Morton	Martin	Hindle
Jan 3	SOUTHAMPTON	0-0	Twomey	Milburn	Gadsby	Bullions	Martin	Willingham	Cochrane	Powell	Wakefield	Heaton	Hindle
Jan 17	FULHAM	0-1	Twomey	Milburn	Bannister	Bullions	Martin	Willingham	Cochrane	Powell	Wakefield	Chisholm	Hindle
Jan 24	NEWCASTLE UNITED	3-1	Twomey	Milburn	Bannister	Bullions	Martin	Willingham	Cochrane 1	Powell	Wakefield 2	Chisholm	Hindle
Jan 31	Coventry City	2-1	Twomey	Milburn	Bannister	Bullions	Martin	Willingham	Cochrane	Powell	Wakefield 2	Chisholm	Hindle
Feb 14	Birmingham City	1-5	Twomey	Milburn	Bannister	Bullions	Martin	Willingham	Cochrane	Powell	Wakefield	Chisholm 1	Hindle
Feb 21	WEST BROMWICH ALBION	(o.g.) 3-1	Hodgson	Milburn	Bannister	Bullions	Martin	Willingham	Cochrane	Powell	Wakefield	Chisholm 1	Hindle 1
Feb 28	Doncaster Rovers	0-3	Twomey	Milburn	Bannister	Bullions	Martin	Willingham	Cochrane	Powell	Wakefield	Chisholm	Hindle
Mar 6	NOTTINGHAM FOREST	2-2	Twomey	Milburn	Bannister	Bullions	Martin	Willingham	Cochrane	Powell 1	Wakefield 1	Chisholm	Hindle
Mar 13	Bradford	1-3	Twomey	Milburn	Gadsby	Bullions	Martin	McCabe	Cochrane	Powell 1	Wakefield	Chisholm	Hindle
Mar 20	CARDIFF CITY	4-0	Twomey	Milburn	Martin	Bullions	McCabe	Willingham	Cochrane	Powell 1	Short 1	Chisholm 2	Hindle
Mar 26	Brentford	0-3	Twomey	Milburn	Martin	Bullions	McCabe	Willingham	Wakefield	Powell	Short	Chisholm	Hindle
Mar 27	Sheffield Wednesday	1-3	Twomey	Dunn	Martin	Bullions	McCabe	Willingham	Wakefield	Powell	Short 1	Chisholm	Hindle
Mar 29	BRENTFORD	1-1	Fearnley	Dunn	Bannister 1	Bullions	McCabe	Willingham	Cochrane	Powell	Short	Chisholm	Hindle
Apr 3	TOTTENHAM HOTSPUR	1-3	Fearnley	Milburn	Gadsby	Bullions	McCabe	Willingham	Cochrane	Powell	Wakefield 1	Chisholm	Hindle
Apr 10	Millwall	1-1	Fearnley	Dunn	Millburn	Bullions	Holley	McCabe	Cochrane	Powell	Wakefield	Chisholm 1	Hindle
Apr 17	CHESTERFIELD	3-0	Fearnley	Dunn	Millburn	Bullions	Holley	McCabe	Cochrane	Powell	Wakefield 1	Chisholm 1	Hindle 1
Apr 24	West Ham United	1-2	Fearnley	Dunn	Millburn	Bullions	Holley	McCabe	Cochrane	Powell	Wakefield	Chisholm 1	Hindle
May 1	BURY	5-1	Fearnley	Dunn	Millburn	Bullions	Holley	McCabe	Cochrane 2	Powell	Wakefield 3	Chisholm	Heaton

F.A. CUP

Jan 10	Blackpool	Rd 3 0-4	Twomey	Milburn	Gadsby	Bullions	Martin	Willingham	Cochrane	Powell	Holley	Wakefield	Hindle

DIVISION TWO 1948-49

Aug 21	Leicester City	2-6	Twomey	Dunn	Millburn	Bullions	Holley	McCabe	Hindle	Short 1	Wakefield	Chisholm 1	Heaton
Aug 25	BRENTFORD	0-0	Twomey	Dunn	Millburn	Bullions	Holley	McCabe	Hindle	Short	Wakefield	Chisholm	Heaton
Aug 28	LUTON TOWN	2-0	Twomey	Dunn	Millburn	Bullions	Holley	McCabe	Hindle	Short	Wakefield	Chisholm 2	Heaton
Sep 1	Brentford	3-1	Twomey	Dunn	Millburn 1	McCabe	Holley	Martin	Cochrane	Short 1	Wakefield	Chisholm 1	Hindle
Sep 4	COVENTRY CITY	4-1	Twomey	Dunn	Millburn	McCabe	Holley	Martin	Cochrane	Short 2	Wakefield	Chisholm 2	Hindle
Sep 8	TOTTENHAM HOTSPUR	0-0	Twomey	Dunn	Millburn	McCabe	Holley	Martin	Cochrane	Short	Wakefield	Chisholm	Hindle
Sep 11	Sheffield Wednesday	1-3	Twomey	Dunn	Millburn	McCabe	Holley	Martin	Cochrane 1	Burden	Short	Chisholm	Hindle
Sep 13	Tottenham Hotspur	2-2	Twomey	Dunn	Millburn 1	McCabe	Holley	McAdam	Cochrane 1	Burden	Wakefield	Chisholm	Hindle
Sep 18	LINCOLN CITY	3-1	Twomey	Dunn	Millburn 1	McCabe	Holley	McAdam	Cochrane 1	Burden	Wakefield 1	Chisholm	Hindle
Sep 25	Chesterfield	1-3	Twomey	Dunn	Millburn	McCabe	Holley	McAdam	Cochrane	Burden	Wakefield 1	Chisholm	Hindle
Oct 2	WEST BROMWICH ALBION	1-3	Lomas	Dunn	Millburn	McCabe	Holley	McAdam	Cochrane	Marsh 1	Burden	Chisholm	Heaton
Oct 9	Bradford	1-1	Fearnley	Dunn	Millburn	McCabe	Holley	McAdam	Hindle	Burden	Wakefield	Chisholm 1	Heaton
Oct 16	SOUTHAMPTON	1-1	Fearnley	Dunn	Millburn	McCabe	Holley	McAdam	Cochrane 1	Burden	Wakefield	Chisholm	Heaton
Oct 23	Barnsley	1-1	Fearnley	Dunn	Millburn	McCabe	Holley	McAdam	Cochrane	Burden	Browning 1	Chisholm	Heaton
Oct 30	GRIMSBY TOWN	6-3	Fearnley	Dunn	Millburn 1	McCabe	Holley	McAdam	Cochrane	Burden 2	Browning 1	Chisholm 1	Heaton 1
Nov 6	Nottingham Forest	0-0	Fearnley	Dunn	Millburn	McCabe	Holley	McAdam	Cochrane	Burden	Browning	Chisholm	Heaton
Nov 13	FULHAM	1-1	Fearnley	Dunn	Millburn	McCabe	Holley	McAdam	Cochrane	Burden	Browning 1	Chisholm	Heaton
Nov 20	Plymouth Argyle	1-2	Fearnley	Dunn	Millburn	McCabe	Holley	McAdam	Cochrane	Burden	Browning	Chisholm	Heaton 1
Dec 4	Cardiff City	1-2	Fearnley	Dunn	Millburn	McCabe	Holley	McAdam	Cochrane	Burden	Browning 1	Chisholm	Heaton
Dec 11	QUEEN'S PARK RANGERS	1-2	Fearnley	Dunn	Millburn	McCabe	Holley	McAdam	Cochrane	Burden 1	Wakefield	Chisholm	Heaton
Dec 18	LEICESTER CITY	3-1	Fearnley	Dunn	Millburn	McAdam	Depear	McCabe	Cochrane	Burden	Browning	Chisholm 1	Heaton 2
Dec 25	West Ham United	2-3	Fearnley	Dunn	Millburn	McAdam	Holley 1	McCabe	Cochrane	Burden	Browning 1	Chisholm	Heaton
Dec 26	WEST HAM UNITED	1-3	Fearnley	J Williams	Millburn	McAdam	Depear	Dunn	Cochrane	Burden	Browning	Chisholm 1	Heaton
Jan 1	Luton Town	0-0	Fearnley	Dunn	Millburn	Bullions	Depear	McAdam	Cochrane	Iggleden	Browning	Marsh	Heaton
Jan 15	Coventry City	1-4	Searson	Dunn	Millburn	McCabe	Depear	McAdam	Cochrane	Iggleden	Browning 1	Burden	Heaton
Jan 22	SHEFFIELD WEDNESDAY	1-1	Searson	Dunn	Millburn	McCabe	Holley	McAdam	Cochrane 1	Burden	McMorran	Iggleden	Heaton
Jan 29	BLACKBURN ROVERS	1-0	Searson	Dunn	Millburn	McCabe	Holley	McAdam	Cochrane	Burden	McMorran 1	Iggleden	Heaton
Feb 5	Lincoln City	0-0	Searson	Dunn	Millburn	McCabe	Holley	Burden	Cochrane	Moss	McMorran	Iggleden	Heaton
Feb 12	BURY	0-1	Searson	Dunn	Millburn	McCabe	Holley	Burden	Cochrane	Moss	Iggleden	Rudd	McMorran
Feb 19	CHESTERFIELD	1-0	Searson	Dunn	Millburn	McCabe	Holley	Burden	Cochrane	Browning 1	McMorran	Iggleden	Rudd
Mar 5	BRADFORD	4-2	Searson	Dunn	Millburn	McCabe	Holley	Burden	Cochrane 1	McMorran	Browning 2	Iggleden 1	Rudd
Mar 12	Southampton	(o.g.) 1-2	Searson	Dunn	Millburn	Bullions	Holley	Burden	Cochrane	Marsh	Browning	Iggleden	Rudd
Mar 19	BARNSLEY	4-1	Searson	Dunn	Millburn	Bullions	Holley	Burden	Cochrane	McMorran 1	Browning 2	Moss 1	Rudd
Mar 26	Grimsby Town	1-5	Searson	Dunn	Millburn	Burden	Holley	Bullions	Edwards	Iggleden	Browning 1	Moss	Rudd
Apr 2	NOTTINGHAM FOREST	1-0	Searson	Dunn	Millburn	Bullions	Holley	Burden	Cochrane	McCabe	Browning	Iggleden 1	Rudd
Apr 6	West Bromwich Albion	0-1	Searson	Bannister	Millburn	McCabe	Holley	Burden	Cochrane	Iggleden	Browning	Moss	Edwards
Apr 9	Fulham	0-1	Searson	Bannister	Millburn	Ingham	McCabe	Burden	Cochrane	McMorran	Browning	Moss	Iggleden
Apr 16	PLYMOUTH ARGYLE	1-0	Searson	Dunn	Millburn	Bullions	McCabe	Burden	Cochrane	McMorran	Browning 1	Iggleden	Rudd
Apr 18	Bury	1-3	Searson	Dunn	Millburn	Bullions	McCabe	Burden	Cochrane	McMorran 1	Browning	Iggleden	Rudd
Apr 23	Blackburn Rovers	0-0	Searson	Bannister	Millburn	McCabe	Charles	Burden	Cochrane	McMorran	Browning	Iggleden	Rudd
Apr 30	CARDIFF CITY	0-0	Searson	Bannister	Millburn	McCabe	Charles	Burden	Cochrane	McMorran	Browning	Moss	Rudd
May 7	Queen's Park Rangers	0-2	Searson	Bannister	Millburn	McCabe	Charles	Burden	Cochrane	Marsh	Browning	Moss	Rudd

F.A. CUP

Jan 8	NEWPORT COUNTY	Rd 3 1-3	Fearnley	Dunn	Millburn	Bullions	Depear	McCabe	Cochrane	Burden	Browning 1	Marsh	Heaton

DIVISION TWO 1949-50

			1	2	3	4	5	6	7	8	9	10	11
Aug 20	QUEEN'S PARK RANGERS	1-1	Searson	Dunn	Millburn 1	McCabe	Charles	Burden	HT Williams	McMorran	Browning	Moss	Rudd
Aug 22	West Ham United	1-3	Searson	Dunn	Millburn	McCabe	Charles	Burden	HT Williams	McMorran	Browning	Dudley	Rudd 1
Aug 27	Preston North End	1-1	Searson	Dunn	Millburn	McCabe	Charles	Casey	Cochrane	Burden 1	Dudley	Moss	Rudd
Aug 31	WEST HAM UNITED	2-2	Searson	Dunn	Millburn	McCabe	Charles	Casey	Cochrane 1	Burden	Dudley 1	Moss	HT Williams
Sep 3	SWANSEA TOWN	1-2	Searson	Dunn	Millburn	McCabe	Charles	Casey	Cochrane	Burden	Dudley 1	Hilton	Rudd
Sep 5	Sheffield United	1-0	Searson	Dunn	Millburn	Burden	Charles	McAdam	Cochrane	Browning 1	Dudley	Moss	Rudd
Sep 10	Tottenham Hotspur	0-2	Searson	Dunn	Millburn	Burden	Charles	McAdam	Cochrane	Dudley	Browning	Moss	R Harrison
Sep 14	SHEFFIELD UNITED	0-1	Searson	Dunn	Millburn	Burden	Charles	Ingham	Cochrane	Dudley	Browning	Iggleden	R Harrison
Sep 17	Southampton	1-2	Searson	Dunn	Millburn	Burden	Charles	McAdam	Cochrane	Frost	Dudley	Wilkins	P Harrison 1
Sep 24	COVENTRY CITY	3-3	Searson	Dunn	Millburn	McAdam	Charles	Burden	Cochrane 1	McMorran 1	Dudley 1	Wilkins	P Harrison
Oct 1	Luton Town	0-1	Searson	Dunn	Millburn	McCabe	Charles	Burden	HT Williams	McMorran	Dudley	Wilkins	Rudd
Oct 8	CARDIFF CITY	2-0	Searson	Dunn	Bannister	McCabe	Charles	Burden	Cochrane	McMorran	Browning 1	Dudley 1	HT Williams
Oct 15	Blackburn Rovers	1-0	Searson	Dunn	Bannister	McCabe	Charles	Burden	Cochrane	McMorran	Browning	Dudley 1	HT Williams
Oct 22	BRENTFORD	1-0	Searson	Dunn	Bannister	McCabe	Charles	Burden	Cochrane	McMorran	Browning	Dudley 1	HT Williams
Oct 29	Hull City	0-1	Searson	Dunn	Bannister	McCabe	Charles	Burden	Cochrane	McMorran	Browning	Dudley	HT Williams
Nov 5	SHEFFIELD WEDNESDAY	1-1	Searson	Dunn	Bannister	McCabe	Charles	Burden	Cochrane	McMorran	Browning	Dudley	HT Williams 1
Nov 12	Plymouth Argyle	2-1	Searson	Dunn	Bannister	McCabe	Charles 1	Burden	Cochrane	McMorran	Browning	Frost 1	Dudley
Nov 19	CHESTERFIELD	0-0	Searson	Dunn	Milburn	McCabe	Charles	Burden	Cochrane	McMorran	Browning	Frost	Dudley
Nov 26	Bradford	2-1	Searson	Dunn	Milburn	McCabe	Charles	Burden	Cochrane	McMorran	Frost 1	Dudley 1	HT Williams
Dec 3	LEICESTER CITY	1-1	Searson	Dunn	Milburn	McCabe	Charles	Burden	P Harrison 1	McMorran	Frost	Dudley	HT Williams
Dec 10	Bury	0-2	Searson	Dunn	Milburn	Kerfoot	Charles	Burden	HT Williams	McMorran	Browning	Frost	Dudley
Dec 17	Queen's Park Rangers	1-1	Searson	Dunn	Milburn	Kerfoot	Charles	Burden	P Harrison	McMorran	Browning	Dudley 1	HT Williams
Dec 24	PRESTON NORTH END	(o.g.) 3-1	Searson	Dunn	Milburn	Kerfoot	Charles	Burden	HT Williams	McMorran	Browning 1	Dudley 1	Taylor
Dec 26	Barnsley	1-1	Searson	Dunn	Milburn 1	Kerfoot	Charles	Burden	HT Williams	Iggleden	Browning	Dudley	Taylor
Dec 27	BARNSLEY	1-0	Searson	Dunn	Milburn	Kerfoot	Charles	Burden	Cochrane	McMorran	Browning	Dudley	HT Williams 1
Dec 31	Swansea Town	2-1	Searson	Dunn	Milburn	Kerfoot	Charles	Burden	Cochrane	McMorran	Browning 1	Dudley	HT Williams 1
Jan 14	TOTTENHAM HOTSPUR	3-0	Searson	Dunn	Milburn	Kerfoot	Charles	Burden	Cochrane 2	Iggleden 1	Browning	Dudley	HT Williams
Jan 21	Southampton	1-0	Searson	Dunn	Milburn	Kerfoot	Charles	Burden	Cochrane	Iggleden	Browning	Dudley	HT Williams 1
Feb 4	Coventry City	4-0	Searson	Dunn	Milburn	McCabe	Charles	Burden	Cochrane	Iggleden 1	Browning 1	Dudley	HT Williams 2
Feb 18	LUTON TOWN	2-1	Searson	Dunn	Milburn	McCabe	Charles	Burden	Cochrane	Iggleden 1	Browning 1	Dudley	HT Williams
Feb 25	Cardiff City	0-1	Searson	Dunn	Milburn	McCabe	Charles	Burden	Cochrane	Iggleden	Browning	Dudley	HT Williams
Mar 11	Brentford	0-0	Searson	Dunn	Milburn	McCabe	Charles	Burden	Dudley	McMorran	Browning	Iggleden	HT Williams
Mar 18	HULL CITY	3-0	Searson	Dunn	Milburn 1	McCabe	Charles	Burden	Dudley	McMorran 1	Browning	Iggleden	HT Williams 1
Mar 25	Sheffield Wednesday	2-5	Searson	Dunn	Milburn	McCabe	Charles	Burden	Cochrane	McMorran	Browning 1	Iggleden	HT Williams 1
Apr 1	BRADFORD	0-0	Searson	Dunn	Milburn	McCabe	Charles	Burden	Cochrane	Iggleden	Browning	Dudley	HT Williams
Apr 7	Grimsby Town	0-2	Searson	Dunn	Milburn	McCabe	Charles	Burden	HT Williams	Iggleden	Browning	Frost	Casey
Apr 8	Leicester City	1-1	Searson	Bannister	Milburn	McCabe	Charles	Burden	Frost	Iggleden	Browning	McMorran 1	Taylor
Apr 10	GRIMSBY TOWN	1-0	Searson	Bannister	Milburn 1	McCabe	Charles	Burden	HT Williams	Iggleden	McMorran	Frost	Dudley
Apr 15	PLYMOUTH ARGYLE	1-1	Searson	Dunn	Milburn	McCabe	Charles	Burden	Cochrane	Iggleden	McMorran	Dudley	HT Williams 1
Apr 22	Chesterfield	1-3	Searson	Dunn	Milburn	McCabe	Charles	Burden	Cochrane	Iggleden	Dudley 1	Moss	HT Williams
Apr 26	BLACKBURN ROVERS	2-1	Searson	Dunn 1	Milburn	Kerfoot	Charles	Burden	Cochrane	McMorran	Dudley	Moss	HT Williams 1
Apr 29	BURY	4-1	Searson	Dunn	Milburn	Kerfoot	Charles	Burden	Cochrane 1	McMorran	Dudley 2	Moss 1	HT Williams

F.A. CUP

Jan 7	Carlisle United	Rd 3 5-2	Searson	Dunn	Milburn	McCabe	Charles	Burden	Cochrane 1	McMorran	Browning 1	Dudley 2	HT Williams 1
Jan 28	BOLTON WANDERERS	Rd 4 1-1	Searson	Dunn	Milburn	McCabe	Charles	Burden	Cochrane	McMorran	Browning 1	Dudley	HT Williams 1
Feb 1	Bolton Wanderers	Rd 4 R 3-2 (AET)	Searson	Dunn	Milburn	McCabe	Charles	Burden	Cochrane	Iggleden	Browning 1	Dudley 2	HT Williams
Feb 11	CARDIFF CITY	Rd 5 3-1	Searson	Dunn	Milburn	McCabe	Charles	Burden	Cochrane 1	Iggleden 1	Browning	Dudley	HT Williams 1
Mar 4	Arsenal	Rd 6 0-1	Searson	Dunn	Milburn	McCabe	Charles	Burden	Cochrane	Iggleden	Browning	Dudley	HT Williams

DIVISION TWO 1950-51

Aug 19	DONCASTER ROVERS	3-1	Searson	Dunn	Milburn	Kerfoot	Charles	Burden	Cochrane	Iggleden	Browning 1	Dudley 2	Williams
Aug 21	Coventry City	0-1	Searson	Dunn	Milburn	Kerfoot	Charles	Burden	Cochrane	Moss	Browning	Dudley	Williams
Aug 26	Brentford	2-1	Searson	Dunn	Milburn	Kerfoot	McCabe	Burden 1	Harrison	Moss	Browning	Dudley	Williams 1
Aug 30	COVENTRY CITY	1-0	Searson	Dunn	Milburn	Kerfoot	McCabe	Burden	Harrison	Frost	Browning 1	Dudley	Williams
Sep 2	BLACKBURN ROVERS	0-1	Searson	Dunn	Milburn	Kerfoot	Charles	McCabe	Harrison	Burden	Browning	Dudley	Williams
Sep 7	Swansea Town	2-4	Searson	Dunn	Milburn	Kerfoot	Charles	Burden	Harrison	Moss	Browning 1	Dudley 1	Williams
Sep 9	Southampton	0-2	Searson	Dunn	Milburn	Kerfoot	Charles	Burden	Harrison	Moss	Browning	Dudley	Williams
Sep 16	BARNSLEY	2-2	Searson	Dunn	Milburn	Kerfoot	Charles	Burden	Williams 1	Iggleden	Browning 1	Dudley	Hughes
Sep 23	Sheffield United	2-2	Searson	Dunn	Milburn	Kerfoot	Charles	Burden	Williams	Iggleden	Browning	Dudley 1	Hughes 1
Sep 30	LUTON TOWN	2-1	Searson	Dunn	Milburn	Kerfoot	Charles	Burden	Harrison	Iggleden	Browning 1	Dudley 1	Hughes
Oct 7	BURY	1-1	Searson	Dunn	Milburn	Kerfoot	Charles	Burden	Williams 1	Iggleden	Browning	Dudley	Hughes
Oct 14	Preston North End	0-2	Searson	Dunn	Milburn	Kerfoot	Charles	Burden	Williams	Iggleden	Dudley	Moss	Hughes
Oct 21	CHESTERFIELD	2-0	Searson	Dunn	Milburn	Kerfoot	Charles	Burden	Harrison	Iggleden 1	Browning 1	Moss	Dudley
Oct 28	Queen's Park Rangers	0-3	Searson	Dunn	Milburn	Kerfoot	Charles	Burden	Williams	Iggleden	Browning	Moss	Dudley
Nov 4	MANCHESTER CITY	1-1	Scott	Dunn	Milburn	McCabe	Charles	Kerfoot	Harrison	Burden	Browning	Dudley 1	Hughes
Nov 11	Leicester City	5-1	Scott	Dunn	Milburn	McCabe	Charles	Kerfoot	Harrison	Burden 1	Browning	Dudley 3	Williams 1
Nov 18	NOTTS COUNTY	0-1	Scott	Dunn	Milburn	McCabe	Charles	Kerfoot	Harrison	Burden	Browning	Dudley	Williams
Nov 25	Grimsby Town	2-2	Scott	Dunn	Milburn	McCabe	Charles	Kerfoot	Dudley	Iggleden	Browning 2	Burden	Williams
Dec 2	BIRMINGHAM CITY	3-0	Scott	Dunn	Milburn 1	McCabe	Charles	Kerfoot	Williams	Burden 1	Browning 1	Iggleden	Dudley
Dec 9	Cardiff City	0-1	Scott	Dunn	Milburn	McCabe	Charles	Kerfoot	Williams	Burden	Browning	Iggleden	Dudley
Dec 16	Doncaster Rovers	4-4	Searson	Dunn	Milburn	McCabe	Charles	Burden	Harrison 2	Miller	Browning 1	Dudley 1	Williams
Dec 23	BRENTFORD	1-0	Scott	Dunn	Milburn	McCabe	Charles	Burden	Harrison	Miller	Browning	Dudley 1	Williams
Dec 25	West Ham United	1-3	Scott	Dunn	Milburn	McCabe	Charles	Burden	Harrison 1	Miller	Browning	Dudley	Williams
Dec 26	WEST HAM UNITED	2-0	Searson	Dunn	Milburn	McCabe	Charles	Burden	Harrison	Miller	Browning 2	Dudley	Williams
Jan 13	SOUTHAMPTON	5-3	Searson	Dunn	Milburn	McCabe	Charles	Burden 1	Harrison	Miller	Browning 3	Dudley	Williams 1
Jan 20	Barnsley	(o.g.) 2-1	Searson	Dunn	Milburn 1	McCabe	Charles	Burden	Harrison	Miller	Browning	Dudley	Williams
Feb 3	SHEFFIELD UNITED	1-0	Scott	Dunn	Milburn	McCabe	Charles	Kerfoot	Harrison	Iggleden	Browning 1	Stevenson	Williams
Feb 10	Blackburn Rovers	1-2	Scott	Dunn	Milburn	McCabe	Kirk	Burden	Harrison 1	Iggleden	Browning	Stevenson	Williams
Feb 17	Luton Town	3-2	Scott	Dunn	Milburn	McCabe	Kirk	Burden	Harrison	Iggleden 1	Browning 1	Stevenson 1	Hughes
Feb 24	Bury	1-0	Scott	Dunn	Milburn	McCabe	Charles	Kerfoot	Harrison	Iggleden	Browning	Stevenson 1	Hughes
Mar 3	PRESTON NORTH END	0-3	Scott	Dunn	Milburn	McCabe	Charles	Burden	Williams	Iggleden	Browning	Stevenson	Hughes
Mar 10	Chesterfield	0-1	Scott	Dunn	Milburn	McCabe	Charles	Burden	Harrison	Miller	Browning	Stevenson	Williams
Mar 17	QUEEN'S PARK RANGERS	2-2	Scott	Dunn	Milburn 1	Kerfoot	Charles	Burden	Williams	Miller	Browning 1	Vickers	Hughes
Mar 23	Hull City	0-2	Scott	Dunn	Milburn	Kerfoot	Charles	Burden	Harrison	Miller	Browning	Vickers	Hughes
Mar 24	Manchester City	1-4	Scott	Dunn	Milburn	McCabe	Kirk	Kerfoot	Harrison 1	Burden	Charles	McNeish	Williams
Mar 26	HULL CITY	3-0	Searson	Dunn	Milburn	Kerfoot	Kirk	Burden	Harrison	Iggleden	Charles 2	Stevenson 1	Williams
Mar 31	LEICESTER CITY	2-1	Searson	Milburn	Hair	McCabe	Kirk	Kerfoot	Harrison	Iggleden	Burden 2	Stevenson	Williams
Apr 7	Notts County	0-0	Searson	Milburn	Hair	McCabe	Charles	Kerfoot	Harrison	Iggleden	Burden	Stevenson	Williams
Apr 14	GRIMSBY TOWN	1-0	Searson	Dunn	Milburn	McCabe	Kirk	Kerfoot	Harrison	Iggleden	Charles 1	Stevenson	Williams
Apr 21	Birmingham City	1-0	Searson	Dunn	Milburn	McCabe	Kirk	Kerfoot	Harrison	Iggleden	Burden	Stevenson 1	Williams
Apr 28	CARDIFF CITY	(o.g.) 2-0	Searson	Dunn	Milburn	McCabe	Kirk	Kerfoot	Harrison	Iggleden 1	Burden	Stevenson	Williams
May 5	SWANSEA TOWN	2-0	Searson	Dunn	Milburn	McCabe	Kirk	Burden	Harrison	Iggleden 1	Browning 1	Stevenson	Williams

F.A. CUP

Jan 6	MIDDLESBROUGH	Rd 3 1-0	Searson	Dunn	Milburn	McCabe	Charles	Burden	Harrison	Miller	Browning 1	Dudley	Williams
Jan 27	Manchester United	Rd 4 0-4	Searson	Dunn	Milburn	McCabe	Charles	Burden	Harrison	Iggleden	Browning	Dudley	Williams

FESTIVAL OF BRITAIN GAMES

May 9	RAPID VIENNA	2-2	Searson	Dunn	Milburn	McCabe	Kirk	Burden	Harrison	Iggleden 1	Charles	Hughes 1	Williams
May 14	F.C. HAARLEM	2-0	Scott	Ross	Hair	Kerfoot	Charles	Burden	Harrison 1	Miller 1	Browning	Hughes	Williams

DIVISION TWO 1951-52

Aug 18	BRENTFORD	1-1	Scott	Dunn	Milburn	McCabe	Kirk	Burden	Williams	Iggleden	Browning 1	Stevenson	Hughes
Aug 22	Birmingham City	1-1	Taylor	Dunn	Milburn	McCabe	Kirk	Burden	Harrison	Iggleden	Browning	Stevenson 1	Williams
Aug 25	Doncaster Rovers	0-2	Taylor	Dunn	Milburn	McCabe	Kirk	Burden	Finlay	Iggleden	Barritt	Stevenson	Harrison
Aug 29	BIRMINGHAM CITY	1-1	Taylor	Dunn	Milburn	McCabe	Kirk	Burden	Harrison	Iggleden 1	Barritt	Miller	Williams
Sep 1	EVERTON	1-2	Taylor	Dunn	Milburn	Kerfoot	McCabe	Burden	Harrison	Iggleden	Kirk	Miller 1	Williams
Sep 8	Southampton	0-0	Taylor	Dunn	Milburn	Mollatt	Kirk	Burden	Williams	Iggleden	Browning	Hughes	Tyrer
Sep 12	CARDIFF CITY	2-1	Taylor	Dunn	Milburn 1	Mollatt	Kirk	Burden	Hudson	Iggleden	Browning	Hughes 1	Tyrer
Sep 15	SHEFFIELD WEDNESDAY	3-2	Taylor	Dunn	Milburn	Mollatt	Kirk	Burden	Hudson	Iggleden	Browning 2	Hughes	Tyrer 1
Sep 22	West Ham United	0-2	Taylor	Dunn	Milburn	Mollatt	Kirk	Burden	Hudson	Iggleden	Browning	Hughes	Tyrer
Sep 29	Rotherham United	2-4	Taylor	Dunn	Milburn	Kerfoot	Kirk	Burden	Williams	Iggleden 2	Browning	Mills	Tyrer
Oct 6	SHEFFIELD UNITED	3-1	Taylor	Dunn	Ross	Kerfoot	Kirk	Burden	Harrison	Mills 1	Browning	Iggleden 2	Williams
Oct 13	Barnsley	1-3	Taylor	Dunn	Ross	Kerfoot	Kirk	Burden	Harrison	Mills	Browning	Iggleden 1	Williams
Oct 20	HULL CITY	2-0	Searson	Ross	Hair	Kerfoot	Kirk	Burden	Harrison 1	Mills	Barritt	Iggleden 1	Williams
Oct 27	Blackburn Rovers	3-2	Searson	Ross	Hair	Kerfoot	Kirk	Burden	Harrison 1	Mills	Fidler 1	Iggleden 1	Williams
Nov 3	QUEEN'S PARK RANGERS	3-1	Searson	Ross	Hair	Kerfoot	Kirk	Burden	Harrison	Mills	Fidler 1	Iggleden 1	Williams 1
Nov 10	Notts County	2-1	Searson	Dunn	Hair	Kerfoot 1	Kirk	Burden	Harrison	Mills	Fidler 1	Iggleden	Williams
Nov 17	LUTON TOWN	1-1	Searson	Dunn	Hair	Kerfoot	Kirk	Burden	Harrison	Mills	Fidler	Iggleden 1	Williams

DIVISION TWO 1951-52 continued

			1	2	3	4	5	6	7	8	9	10	11
Nov 24	Bury	2-1	Searson	Dunn	Hair	Kerfoot	Kirk	Burden	Harrison	Mills	Fidler 1	Iggleden 1	Williams
Dec 1	SWANSEA TOWN	1-1	Searson	Dunn	Hair	Kerfoot	Charles	Burden	Harrison	Mills 1	Fidler	Iggleden	Williams
Dec 8	Coventry City	2-4	Searson	Dunn	Hair	Kirk	Charles	Kerfoot 1	Harrison	Mills	Fidler	Iggleden	Williams 1
Dec 15	Brentford	1-2	Searson	Dunn	Hair	McCabe	Charles	Kerfoot	Harrison	Mills 1	Fidler	Iggleden	Williams
Dec 22	DONCASTER ROVERS	0-0	Searson	Dunn	Hair	Kerfoot	Charles	Burden	Harrison	Mills	Fidler	Iggleden	Williams
Dec 25	Leicester City	2-1	Searson	Dunn	Hair	Kerfoot	Charles	Burden	Harrison	Mills 1	Fidler	Iggleden 1	Williams
Dec 26	LEICESTER CITY	2-1	Searson	Dunn	Hair	Kerfoot	Charles	Burden	Harrison	Mills	Fidler 2	Miller	Williams
Dec 29	Everton	0-2	Searson	Dunn	Hair	Kerfoot	Charles	Burden	Harrison	Mills	Fidler	Iggleden	Williams
Jan 5	SOUTHAMPTON	1-1	Searson	Dunn	Hair	Kerfoot	Charles	Burden	Harrison	Mills	Fidler 1	Iggleden	Williams
Jan 19	Sheffield Wednesday	2-1	Searson	Dunn	Hair	Kerfoot	Charles	Burden	Kirk	Miller	Barritt	Iggleden 2	Williams
Jan 26	WEST HAM UNITED	3-1	Searson	Dunn	Hair	Kerfoot	Charles	Burden	Kirk 1	Stewart	Milburn 1	Iggleden 1	Williams
Feb 9	Rotherham United	3-0	Searson	Dunn	Hair	Kerfoot	Charles	Burden	Kirk	Stewart 1	Milburn 1	Iggleden 1	Williams
Feb 16	SHEFFIELD UNITED	0-3	Searson	Dunn	Hair	Kerfoot	Charles	Burden	Kirk	Stewart	Milburn	Iggleden	Williams
Mar 1	BARNSLEY	1-0	Searson	Dunn	Hair	Kerfoot	Charles	Burden	Williams	Mills 1	Kirk	Iggleden	Hughes
Mar 8	Hull City	2-3	Scott	Dunn	Hair	Kerfoot	Kirk	Burden	Harrison	Stewart 1	Milburn	Iggleden	Williams 1
Mar 15	BLACKBURN ROVERS	1-0	Scott	Dunn	Hughes	Kerfoot	McCabe	Burden	Harrison	Stewart	Fidler	Iggleden 1	Williams
Mar 22	Queen's Park Rangers	0-0	Scott	Dunn	Hughes	Kerfoot	Charles	Burden	Harrison	Stewart	Fidler	Iggleden	Hudson
Mar 29	NOTTS COUNTY	1-0	Scott	Dunn	Hughes	Kerfoot	McCabe	Burden	Harrison	Mills	Barritt	Iggleden	Williams
Apr 5	Luton Town	1-2	Scott	Dunn	Hair	Kerfoot	Charles	Burden	Harrison	Mills	Barritt	Iggleden 1	Williams
Apr 11	Nottingham Forest	1-1	Scott	Dunn	Hair	Kerfoot	McCabe	Burden	Harrison	Mills	Charles	Iggleden	Williams 1
Apr 12	BURY	2-1	Scott	Dunn	Hair	Kerfoot	McCabe	Burden	Harrison	Mills 2	Charles	Iggleden	Williams
Apr 14	NOTTINGHAM FOREST	0-0	Scott	Dunn	Hair	Kerfoot	McCabe	Burden	Harrison	Stewart	Charles	Iggleden	Williams
Apr 19	Swansea Town	1-4	Scott	Hair	Hughes	Kerfoot	McCabe	Burden	Harrison	Mills	Milburn	Iggleden	Williams 1
Apr 26	COVENTRY CITY	(o.g.) 3-1	Scott	Milburn	Hair	Kerfoot 1	McCabe	Burden	Harrison	Mills	Fidler 1	Iggleden	Williams
May 3	Cardiff City	1-3	Scott	Milburn	Hair	Kerfoot	McCabe	Burden	Harrison	Mills	Fidler	Iggleden 1	Williams

F.A. CUP

			1	2	3	4	5	6	7	8	9	10	11
Jan 12	Rochdale	Rd 3 2-0	Searson	Dunn	Hair	Kerfoot	Charles	Burden	Kirk 2	Mills	Fidler	Iggleden	Williams
Feb 2	BRADFORD CITY	Rd 4 2-0	Searson	Dunn	Hair	Kerfoot	Charles	Burden	Kirk	Stewart	Milburn 1	Iggleden 1	Williams
Feb 23	CHELSEA	Rd 5 1-1	Searson	Dunn	Hair	Kerfoot	Charles	Burden	Kirk	Mills	Milburn 1	Iggleden	Williams
Feb 27	Chelsea	Rd 5 R 1-1 (AET)	Searson	Dunn	Hair	Kerfoot	Charles	Burden	Williams	Stewart	Kirk 1	Iggleden	Hughes
Mar 3	Chelsea (At Villa Park)	Rd 5 2/R 1-5	Searson	Dunn	Hair	Kerfoot	Charles	Burden	Williams	Mills 1	Kirk	Iggleden	Hughes

DIVISION TWO 1952-53

			1	2	3	4	5	6	7	8	9	10	11
Aug 23	Huddersfield Town	0-1	Scott	Dunn	Hair	Kerfoot	Charles	Burden	Williams	Iggleden	Mills	McCall	Tyrer
Aug 28	Bury	2-2	Scott	Dunn	Hair	Kerfoot	Charles	Burden	Williams	McCall	Fidler	Iggleden 1	Langley 1
Aug 30	PLYMOUTH ARGYLE	(o.g.) 1-1	Scott	Dunn	Hair	Kerfoot	Charles	Burden	Williams	McCall	Fidler	Iggleden	Langley
Sep 3	BURY	2-0	Scott	Dunn	Hair	Kerfoot	Charles	Burden	Williams	McCall	Fidler	Iggleden 1	Langley 1
Sep 6	Rotherham United	1-3	Scott	Dunn	Hair	Kerfoot	Charles	Burden	Williams	McCall	Fidler	Iggleden 1	Langley
Sep 10	BIRMINGHAM CITY	0-1	Scott	Dunn	Hair	Kerfoot	Charles	Burden	Williams	Mills	Fidler	Iggleden	Langley
Sep 13	FULHAM	2-0	Scott	Dunn	Hair	Kerfoot	Charles	Burden	Williams	Mills 1	Smith 1	Iggleden	Tyrer
Sep 17	Birmingham City	2-2	Scott	Dunn	Hair	Kerfoot	Charles	Burden	Williams	Mills	Hastie 2	Iggleden	Tyrer
Sep 20	West Ham United	2-2	Scott	Dunn	Hair	Kerfoot	Charles	Burden	Williams	Mills	Hastie	Iggleden 1	Tyrer 1
Sep 24	SOUTHAMPTON	1-1	Scott	Dunn	Hair	Kerfoot	Charles	Burden	Williams	Mills	Hastie	Iggleden 1	Tyrer
Sep 27	LEICESTER CITY	0-1	Scott	Dunn	Hair	Kerfoot	Charles	Burden	Williams	Mills	Smith	Iggleden	Tyrer
Oct 4	Notts County	(o.g.) 2-3	Scott	Dunn	Hair	Kerfoot	Charles	Burden	Williams	Stewart	Hastie	Iggleden 1	Tyrer
Oct 11	Sheffield United	1-2	Scott	Dunn	Hair	Kerfoot	McCabe	Burden	Meek	Nightingale 1	Charles	Iggleden	Williams
Oct 18	BARNSLEY	4-1	Scott	Dunn	Hair	Kerfoot	McCabe	Burden	Williams	Mills 1	Charles 1	Nightingale 2	Tyrer
Oct 25	Lincoln City	1-1	Scott	Dunn	Hair	Kerfoot	McCabe	Burden	Williams	Mills	Charles 1	Nightingale	Tyrer
Nov 1	HULL CITY	3-1	Scott	Dunn	Hair	Kerfoot	McCabe	Burden	Meek	Nightingale	Charles 3	Iggleden	Williams
Nov 8	Blackburn Rovers	1-1	Scott	Dunn	Hair	Kerfoot	McCabe	Burden	Meek	Nightingale	Charles 1	Iggleden	Williams
Nov 22	Everton	2-2	Scott	Dunn	Hair	Kerfoot	McCabe	Burden	Meek	Nightingale	Charles 2	Iggleden	Williams
Nov 29	BRENTFORD	3-2	Scott	Dunn	Hair	Kerfoot	McCabe	Burden	Meek	Nightingale	Charles 3	Iggleden	Tyrer
Dec 6	Doncaster Rovers	0-0	Scott	Dunn	Hair	Kerfoot	McCabe	Burden	Meek	Nightingale	Charles	Iggleden	Tyrer
Dec 13	SWANSEA TOWN	5-1	Scott	Dunn	Hair	Kerfoot	McCabe	Burden	Meek	Nightingale 1	Charles 2	Iggleden 2	Tyrer
Dec 20	HUDDERSFIELD TOWN	2-1	Scott	Dunn	Hair	Kerfoot	McCabe	Burden	Meek	Nightingale	Charles 1	Iggleden 1	Tyrer
Dec 26	Luton Town	0-2	Scott	Dunn	Hair	Kerfoot	McCabe	Burden	Meek	Nightingale	Charles	Iggleden	Tyrer
Dec 27	LUTON TOWN	2-2	Scott	Dunn	Hair	Kerfoot	McCabe	Burden	Meek	Nightingale	Charles 1	Iggleden	Langley 1
Jan 3	Plymouth Argyle	1-0	Scott	Dunn	Hair	Kerfoot	McCabe	Burden	Meek	Nightingale	Charles	Iggleden 1	Tyrer
Jan 17	ROTHERHAM UNITED	4-0	Scott	Dunn	Hair	Kerfoot	McCabe	Burden	Meek	Nightingale 1	Charles 3	Iggleden	Tyrer
Jan 24	Fulham	1-2	Scott	Dunn	Hair	Kerfoot	McCabe	Burden	Meek	Nightingale	Charles	Iggleden	Tyrer 1
Feb 7	WEST HAM UNITED	3-2	Scott	Dunn	Hair	Kerfoot	McCabe	Burden	Meek	Nightingale	Charles 2	Iggleden 1	Tyrer
Feb 14	Lincoln City	3-3	Scott	Dunn	Hair	Kerfoot	McCabe	Burden	Meek 1	McCall	Charles 2	Iggleden	Tyrer
Feb 21	NOTTS COUNTY	3-1	Scott	Dunn	Langley	Kerfoot	McCabe	Burden 1	Meek	McCall 1	Charles	Iggleden 1	Tyrer
Feb 28	SHEFFIELD UNITED	0-3	Scott	Dunn	Langley	Kerfoot	McCabe	Burden	Meek	McCall	Charles	Iggleden	Tyrer
Mar 7	Barnsley	2-2	Scott	Dunn	Hair	Burden	McCabe	Mollatt	Meek	McCall 1	Charles 1	Iggleden	Langley
Mar 14	LEICESTER CITY	2-1	Scott	Dunn	Hair	Mollatt	Marsden	Burden	McCall	Nightingale	Charles	Iggleden	Meek 2
Mar 21	Hull City	0-1	Scott	Dunn	Hair	Mollatt	Marsden	Burden	McCall	Nightingale	Charles	Iggleden	Meek
Mar 28	BLACKBURN ROVERS	0-3	Scott	Dunn	Hair	Kerfoot	Marsden	Burden	Iggleden	Nightingale	Charles	Stewart	Meek
Apr 4	Nottingham Forest	1-2	Scott	Dunn	Hair	Kerfoot	Marsden	Burden	McCall	Nightingale 1	Forrest	Iggleden	Meek
Apr 6	Southampton	2-2	Scott	Dunn	Hair	Kerfoot	Marsden	Burden	McCall	Nightingale 2	Forrest	Iggleden	Meek
Apr 11	EVERTON	2-0	Scott	Dunn	Hair	Kerfoot	Marsden	Burden	McCall	Charles	Forrest 1	Nightingale	Meek 1
Apr 16	Swansea Town	2-3	Scott	Dunn	Hair	Kerfoot	Marsden	Burden	McCall	Nightingale	Charles 1	Forrest	Meek 1
Apr 18	Brentford	3-3	Scott	Dunn	Hair	Kerfoot	McCabe	Burden	Iggleden	Charles 2	Forrest 1	Nightingale	Meek
Apr 22	NOTTINGHAM FOREST	2-1	Scott	Dunn	Hair	Kerfoot 1	McCabe	Burden 1	Iggleden	Charles	Forrest	Nightingale	Meek
Apr 25	DONCASTER ROVERS	1-1	Scott	Dunn	Hair	Kerfoot 1	Charlton	Burden	McCall	Nightingale	Charles	Iggleden	Meek

F.A. CUP

			1	2	3	4	5	6	7	8	9	10	11
Jan 10	Brentford	1-2	Scott	Dunn	Hair	Kerfoot	McCabe	Burden	Meek	Nightingale	Charles 1	Iggleden	Tyrer

DIVISION TWO 1953-54

			1	2	3	4	5	6	7	8	9	10	11
Aug 19	NOTTS COUNTY	6-0	Scott	Dunn	Hair	Kerfoot	McCabe	Burden	Williams 1	Nightingale 1	Charles 4	Iggleden	Burbanks
Aug 22	ROTHERHAM UNITED	4-2	Scott	Dunn	Hair	Kerfoot	McCabe	Burden	Williams	Nightingale 1	Charles 3	Iggleden	Burbanks
Aug 27	Swansea Town	3-4	Scott	Dunn	Hair	Kerfoot	Charles 1	Burden	Williams	Nightingale 1	Burbanks 1	Iggleden	McCabe
Aug 29	Leicester City	0-5	Scott	Dunn	Hair	Kerfoot	McCabe	Burden	Williams	Nightingale	Charles	Iggleden	Burbanks
Sep 2	SWANSEA TOWN	3-2	Wheatley	Dunn	Hair	Kerfoot	McCabe	Burden	Burbanks	Nightingale 1	Charles 2	Iggleden	Williams
Sep 5	STOKE CITY	1-1	Wheatley	Dunn	Hair	Kerfoot	McCabe	Burden	Williams	Nightingale	Charles 1	Iggleden	Burbanks
Sep 7	Plymouth Argyle	1-1	Wheatley	Dunn	Hair	Kerfoot	McCabe	Burden	Williams	Nightingale	Charles 1	Iggleden	Burbanks
Sep 12	Fulham	3-1	Wheatley	Dunn	Hair	Kerfoot	McCabe	Burden	Williams 1	Nightingale	Charles 2	McCall	Burbanks
Sep 16	PLYMOUTH ARGYLE	1-1	Wheatley	Dunn	Hair	Kerfoot	McCabe	Burden	Williams 1	Nightingale	Charles	McCall	Burbanks
Sep 19	WEST HAM UNITED	1-2	Wheatley	Dunn	Hair	Kerfoot	McCabe	Burden	Williams	Nightingale	Charles 1	McCall	Burbanks
Sep 26	Lincoln City	0-2	Scott	Dunn	Hair	Kerfoot	McCabe	Mollatt	Williams	Nightingale	Charles	McCall	Burbanks
Oct 3	Birmingham City	3-3	Scott	Dunn	Hair	Kerfoot 1	Marsden	Mollatt	Nightingale	Burden	Charles 1	Iggleden 1	Willis
Oct 10	BRISTOL ROVERS	3-3	Scott	Dunn	Hair	Kerfoot	McCabe	Mollatt	Nightingale	Burden	Forrest 3	Iggleden	Willis
Oct 17	Brentford	1-2	Scott	Dunn	Hair	Kerfoot	McCabe	Mollatt	Nightingale	Forrest	Charles 1	Burden	Willis
Oct 24	DERBY COUNTY	3-1	Wood	Dunn	Hair	Kerfoot	Marsden	Burden	Williams	Nightingale 1	Charles 2	Iggleden	Tyrer
Oct 31	Blackburn Rovers	2-2	Wood	Dunn	Hair	Kerfoot	Marsden	Burden	Williams 1	Nightingale 1	Charles	Iggleden	Tyrer
Nov 7	DONCASTER ROVERS	3-1	Wood	Dunn	Hair	Kerfoot	Marsden	Burden	Williams	Nightingale 3	Charles	Iggleden	Tyrer
Nov 14	Bury	4-4	Wood	Dunn	Hair	Kerfoot	Marsden	Burden	Williams	Nightingale 1	Charles 3	Iggleden	Tyrer
Nov 21	OLDHAM ATHLETIC	2-1	Wood	Dunn	Hair	Kerfoot	Marsden	Burden	Williams	Nightingale 1	Forrest 1	Iggleden	Tyrer
Nov 28	Everton	1-2	Wood	Dunn	Hair	Kerfoot	Marsden	Burden	Williams	Nightingale	Charles 1	Iggleden	Tyrer
Dec 5	HULL CITY	0-0	Wood	Dunn	Hair	Kerfoot	Marsden	Burden	Williams	Nightingale	Charles	Iggleden	Tyrer
Dec 12	Notts County	0-2	Wood	Dunn	Hair	Kerfoot	Marsden	Burden	Williams	Nightingale	Charles	Iggleden	Tyrer
Dec 19	Rotherham United	4-2	Wood	Dunn	Hair	Kerfoot	Marsden	Burden	Williams	Nightingale	Charles 3	Iggleden 1	Tyrer
Dec 25	Nottingham Forest	2-5	Wood	Dunn	Hair	Kerfoot	Marsden	Burden	Williams	Nightingale 1	Charles 1	Iggleden	Tyrer
Dec 26	NOTTINGHAM FOREST	0-2	Scott	Dunn	Hair	Kerfoot	Marsden	Burden	Williams	Nightingale	Charles	Iggleden	Burbanks
Jan 2	LEICESTER CITY	7-1	Scott	Dunn	Hair	Kerfoot	Marsden	Burden	Williams 1	Nightingale 1	Charles 1	Iggleden 3	Tyrer 1
Jan 16	Stoke City	0-4	Scott	Dunn	Hair	Kerfoot	Marsden	Burden	Williams	McCall	Charles	Iggleden	Tyrer
Jan 23	FULHAM	1-2	Scott	Dunn	Hair	Kerfoot	Marsden	Burden	Williams	Flynn	Charles 1	Iggleden	Tyrer
Feb 6	West Ham United	2-5	Scott	Dunn	Hair	McCabe	Marsden	Burden	McCall 1	Kerfoot	Charles	Iggleden 1	Williams
Feb 13	LINCOLN CITY	5-2	Scott	Dunn	Hair	Kerfoot	Marsden	Burden	McCall	Nightingale 1	Charles 3	Iggleden 1	Williams
Feb 20	BIRMINGHAM CITY	1-1	Scott	Dunn	Hair	Kerfoot	Marsden	Burden 1	McCall	Nightingale	Charles	Iggleden	Williams
Feb 27	Bristol Rovers	1-1	Scott	Dunn	Hair	Kerfoot	Marsden	Burden	McCall	Nightingale 1	Charles	Iggleden	Williams
Mar 6	BRENTFORD	4-0	Scott	Dunn	Hair	Kerfoot	Marsden	Burden	McCall	Nightingale 1	Charles 2	Webb	Williams 1
Mar 13	Derby County	2-0	Scott	Dunn	Hair	Kerfoot	Marsden	Burden	McCall	Nightingale	Forrest 2	Webb	Williams
Mar 20	BLACKBURN ROVERS	3-2	Scott	Dunn	Hair	Kerfoot	Marsden	Burden	McCall 1	Nightingale 1	Charles 1	Forrest	Williams
Mar 27	Oldham Athletic	2-4	Scott	Dunn	Hair	Kerfoot	Marsden	Burden	McCall	Nightingale	Charles 1	Forrest	Williams 1
Apr 3	EVERTON	3-1	Scott	Dunn	Hair	Kerfoot 1	Marsden	Burden	Iggleden	Nightingale	Charles	Forrest 1	Williams 1
Apr 10	Doncaster Rovers	0-0	Scott	Dunn	Hair	Kerfoot	Marsden	Burden	Iggleden	Nightingale	Charles	Forrest	Williams

DIVISION TWO 1953-54 continued

			1	2	3	4	5	6	7	8	9	10	11
Apr 16	Luton Town	1-1	Scott	Dunn	Hair	Kerfoot	Marsden	Burden	McCall	Nightingale	Charles 1	Forrest	Williams
Apr 17	BURY	3-4	Scott	Dunn	Hair	Kerfoot	Marsden	Burden	McCall	Nightingale	Charles 2	Forrest 1	Iggleden
Apr 19	LUTON TOWN	2-1	Scott	Dunn	Hair	Kerfoot	Davies	Burden	McCall	Nightingale	Charles 2	Iggleden	Williams
Apr 24	Hull City	1-1	Scott	Dawson	Hair	Kerfoot	Marsden	Mollatt	McCall	Nightingale	Charles 1	Iggleden	Burbanks

F.A. CUP

Jan 9	TOTTENHAM HOTSPUR (o.g.) Rd 3	3-3	Scott	Dunn	Hair	Kerfoot	Marsden	Burden	Williams	Nightingale	Charles 1	Iggleden 1	Tyrer
Jan 13	Tottenham Hotspur Rd 3 R	0-1	Scott	Dunn	Hair	Kerfoot	Marsden	Burden	Williams	Nightingale	Charles	Iggleden	Tyrer

DIVISION TWO 1954-55

Aug 21	Hull City	2-0	Scott	Dunn	Hair	Kerfoot	Marsden	Burden	Toner	Nightingale	Charles 1	Brook 1	McCall
Aug 25	ROTHERHAM UNITED	2-4	Scott	Dunn	Hair	Kerfoot	Marsden	Burden	Williams	Nightingale	Charles 2	Toner	McCall
Aug 28	LINCOLN CITY	2-3	Scott	Dunn	Hair	Kerfoot	Charlton	Burden	Toner 1	Nightingale	Charles	Vickers 1	Williams
Aug 30	Rotherham United	0-3	Scott	Dunn	Hair	Kerfoot	Marsden	Burden	Williams	Nightingale	Charles	Vickers	McCall
Sep 4	Bury (o.g.)	3-5	Scott	Dunn	Hair	Kerfoot	Marsden	Burden	Toner	Forrest	Charles 1	Vickers	McCall 1
Sep 8	STOKE CITY	0-1	Scott	Dunn	Hair	Ripley	Charles	Kerfoot	Nightingale	Brook	Forrest	Vickers	McCall
Sep 11	SWANSEA TOWN	5-2	Scott	Dunn	Hair	Ripley	Charles	Kerfoot 1	Williams	Nightingale 3	Forrest	Brook 1	McCall
Sep 13	Stoke City	1-0	Scott	Dunn	Hair	Ripley	Charles	Kerfoot	Williams	Nightingale	Forrest 1	Brook	McCall
Sep 18	NOTTINGHAM FOREST	1-1	Scott	Dunn	Hair	Ripley	Charles	Kerfoot	Williams	Nightingale	Forrest 1	Brook	McCall
Sep 25	Ipswich Town	2-1	Scott	Dunn	Hair	Ripley	Marsden	Kerfoot	Williams 1	Nightingale 1	Forrest	Brook	McCall
Oct 2	BIRMINGHAM CITY	1-0	Scott	Dunn	Hair	Ripley	Charles	Kerfoot	Williams	Nightingale	Forrest 1	Brook	McCall
Oct 9	Derby County	4-2	Scott	Dunn	Hair	Ripley	Charles	Kerfoot	Williams	Nightingale	Forrest	Brook 2	McCall 2
Oct 16	WEST HAM UNITED	2-1	Scott	Dunn	Hair	Ripley 1	Marsden	Kerfoot	Williams	Nightingale	Forrest 1	Brook	McCall
Oct 23	Bristol Rovers	1-5	Scott	Dunn	Hair	Ripley	Marsden	Kerfoot	Williams	Nightingale	Charles	Brook 1	McCall
Oct 30	PLYMOUTH ARGYLE	3-2	Wood	Dunn	Hair	Ripley	Charles	Kerfoot	Williams 1	Nightingale 1	Forrest	Brook	McCall 1
Nov 6	Port Vale	1-0	Wood	Dunn	Hair	Ripley	Charles	Kerfoot	Williams	Nightingale 1	Forrest	Brook	McCall
Nov 13	DONCASTER ROVERS	1-0	Wood	Dunn	Hair	Kerfoot	Charles	Ripley 1	Williams	Nightingale	Forrest	Brook	McCall
Nov 20	Notts County	2-1	Wood	Dunn	Hair	Ripley	Charles	Kerfoot	Williams	Nightingale 2	Forrest	Brook	McCall
Nov 27	LIVERPOOL	2-2	Wood	Dunn	Hair	Ripley	Charles 1	Kerfoot	Williams	Nightingale	Forrest 1	Brook	McCall
Dec 4	Blackburn Rovers	2-1	Wood	Dunn	Hair	Ripley	Charles	Kerfoot	Williams	Nightingale 2	Forrest	Brook	McCall
Dec 11	FULHAM	1-1	Wood	Dunn	Hair	Ripley	Charles 1	Kerfoot	Toner	Nightingale	Forrest	Vickers	McCall
Dec 18	HULL CITY	3-0	Wood	Dunn	Hair	Ripley	Charles	Kerfoot	Williams	Nightingale 1	Forrest 1	Brook 1	McCall
Dec 25	MIDDLESBROUGH	1-1	Wood	Dunn	Hair	Ripley	Charles	Mollatt	Williams	Nightingale	Forrest 1	Brook	McCall
Dec 27	Middlesbrough	0-1	Wood	Dunn	Hair	Ripley	Charles	Mollatt	Williams	Nightingale	Forrest	Brook	McCall
Jan 1	Lincoln City	0-2	Wood	Dunn	Hair	Ripley	Charles	Mollatt	Williams	Nightingale	Forrest	Brook	McCall
Jan 15	BURY	1-0	Wood	Dunn	Hair	Mollatt	Charles	Kerfoot	Toner	Iggleden	Forrest	Brook	Lydon 1
Jan 22	Swansea Town	0-2	Wood	Dunn	Hair	Mollatt	Charles	Kerfoot	Toner	Iggleden	Forrest	Brook	Lydon
Feb 5	Nottingham Forest	1-1	Wood	Dunn	Hair	Ripley	Charles 1	Kerfoot	Williams	Vickers	Forrest	Brook	McCall
Feb 12	IPSWICH TOWN	4-1	Wood	Dunn	Hair	Ripley	Charles	Kerfoot	Williams	Nightingale	Brook 2	Vickers 2	McCall
Feb 26	DERBY COUNTY	1-0	Wood	Dunn	Hair	Ripley	Charles 1	Kerfoot	Williams	Nightingale	Brook	Iggleden	Lydon
Mar 2	Birmingham City	0-2	Wood	Dunn	Hair	Gibson	Charles	Kerfoot	Williams	Nightingale	Brook	Iggleden	Lydon
Mar 5	West Ham United	1-2	Wood	Dunn	Hair	Gibson	Charles	Kerfoot	Webb	Nightingale	Brook	Forrest 1	McCall
Mar 12	BRISTOL ROVERS	2-0	Wood	Dunn	Hair	Gibson	Charles	Kerfoot	McCall	Nightingale	Brook 1	Forrest 1	Meek
Mar 19	Plymouth Argyle	1-3	Wood	Dunn	Hair	Gibson	Charles	Kerfoot	Williams	Nightingale	Brook 1	Henderson	Meek
Mar 26	PORT VALE	3-0	Wood	Dunn	Hair	Gibson	Charles 1	Kerfoot	Nightingale	Ripley 1	Brook	Henderson 1	Meek
Apr 2	Doncaster Rovers	1-0	Wood	Dunn	Hair	Gibson	Charles	Kerfoot	Nightingale	Ripley	Brook 1	Henderson	Meek
Apr 8	Luton Town	0-0	Wood	Dunn	Hair	Gibson	Charles	Kerfoot	Williams	Nightingale	Brook	Henderson	Meek
Apr 9	NOTTS COUNTY	2-0	Wood	Dunn	Hair	Gibson	Charles	Kerfoot	Williams	Nightingale 1	Brook 1	Henderson	Meek
Apr 11	LUTON TOWN	4-0	Wood	Dunn	Hair	Gibson	Charles 2	Kerfoot	Williams	Nightingale	Brook 1	Henderson 1	Meek
Apr 23	Liverpool	2-2	Wood	Dunn	Hair	Gibson	Charles	Kerfoot	Williams	Nightingale	Brook 1	Henderson	Meek 1
Apr 26	BLACKBURN ROVERS	2-0	Wood	Dunn	Hair	Gibson	Charles	Kerfoot	Williams	Nightingale	Brook 2	Henderson	Meek
Apr 30	Fulham (o.g.)	3-1	Wood	Dunn	Hair	Gibson	Charles	Kerfoot	Williams	Nightingale 1	Brook	Henderson 1	Meek

F.A. CUP

Jan 8	TORQUAY UNITED Rd 3	2-2	Wood	Dunn	Hair	Ripley	Marsden	Kerfoot	Williams	Charles	Brook	Nightingale	McCall
Jan 12	Torquay United Rd 3 R	0-4	Wood	Dunn	Hair	Ripley	Marsden	Kerfoot	Williams	Charles	Brook	Nightingale	McCall

DIVISION TWO 1955-56

Aug 20	Barnsley	1-2	Wood	Dunn	Hair	Gibson	Charles	Kerfoot	Williams	Nightingale	Brook 1	Henderson	Meek
Aug 22	BURY	1-0	Wood	Dunn	Hair	Gibson	Charles	Kerfoot	Williams	Nightingale	Brook	Henderson 1	Meek
Aug 27	MIDDLESBROUGH	2-0	Wood	Dunn	Hair	Gibson	Charles	Kerfoot	Williams	Nightingale 1	Brook 1	Henderson	Meek
Aug 30	Bury	0-1	Wood	Dunn	Hair	Gibson	Charles	Kerfoot	Williams	Nightingale	Brook	Henderson	Meek
Sep 3	Bristol City	1-0	Wood	Dunn	Hair	Gibson	Charles	Kerfoot	Williams	Ripley	Brook	Forrest 1	Meek
Sep 5	HULL CITY	1-0	Wood	Dunn	Hair	Gibson	Charles	Kerfoot	Nightingale	Ripley 1	Brook	Forrest	Meek
Sep 10	WEST HAM UNITED	3-3	Wood	Dunn	Hair	Gibson	Charles	Kerfoot	Williams	Ripley 1	Brook	Nightingale 1	Meek 1
Sep 17	Port Vale	0-2	Wood	Dunn	Hair	Gibson	Charles	Kerfoot	Williams	Ripley	Brook	Nightingale	Meek
Sep 24	ROTHERHAM UNITED	4-1	Wood	Dunn	Hair	Charles	Charlton	Kerfoot	Williams	Ripley 3	Brook	Nightingale 1	Meek
Oct 1	Swansea Town	1-1	Wood	Dunn	Ashall	Charles	Charlton	Kerfoot	Nightingale	Ripley	Brook 1	Henderson	Williams
Oct 8	NOTTINGHAM FOREST	3-0	Wood	Dunn	Marsden	Charles 1	Charlton	Kerfoot	Meek	Ripley 1	Brook 1	Nightingale	Overfield
Oct 15	Sheffield Wednesday	0-4	Wood	Dunn	Marsden	Charles	Charlton	Kerfoot	Meek	Ripley	Brook	Nightingale	Overfield
Oct 22	LINCOLN CITY	1-0	Wood	Dunn	Hair	Ripley	Charlton	Kerfoot	Meek	Nightingale	Brook	Forrest	Overfield 1
Oct 29	Bristol Rovers	1-4	Wood	Dunn	Hair	Ripley	Charlton	Kerfoot	Meek	Henderson	Charles	Brook 1	Overfield
Nov 5	STOKE CITY	1-0	Wood	Dunn	Hair	Ripley	Charlton	Kerfoot	Meek	Nightingale	Charles 1	Forrest	Overfield
Nov 12	Plymouth Argyle (o.g.)	3-4	Wood	Dunn	Hair	Ripley	Charlton	Kerfoot	Williams 1	Nightingale	Charles 1	Forrest	Overfield
Nov 19	LIVERPOOL	4-2	Wood	Dunn	Hair	Ripley	Charlton	Kerfoot	Williams	Brook 1	Charles 2	Vickers	Overfield 1
Nov 26	Leicester City	2-5	Wood	Dunn	Hair	Ripley	Charlton	Kerfoot	Williams	Forrest	Charles 2	Vickers	Overfield
Dec 3	DONCASTER ROVERS	3-0	Wood	Dunn	Hair	Nightingale	Charlton	Kerfoot	Williams	Hutchinson 1	Charles 1	Vickers	Overfield 1
Dec 10	Blackburn Rovers	3-2	Wood	Dunn	Hair	Gibson	Charlton	Kerfoot	Williams	Hutchinson	Charles 2	Vickers	Overfield 1
Dec 17	BARNSLEY	3-1	Wood	Dunn	Hair	Gibson	Charlton	Kerfoot	Williams 1	Hutchinson 2	Charles	Vickers	Overfield
Dec 24	Middlesbrough	3-5	Wood	Dunn	Hair	Gibson	Charlton	Kerfoot	Overfield	Vickers 1	Charles 1	Hutchinson 1	Williams
Dec 26	NOTTS COUNTY	1-0	Wood	Dunn	Hair	Gibson	Charlton	Kerfoot	Hutchinson	Brook 1	Charles	Vickers	Overfield
Dec 27	Notts County	1-2	Wood	Dunn	Hair	Gibson	Charlton	Kerfoot	Hutchinson	Brook	Charles 1	Vickers	Overfield
Dec 31	BRISTOL CITY	2-1	Wood	Dunn	Hair	Gibson	Charlton	Kerfoot	Hutchinson 1	Brook 1	Charles	Vickers	Overfield
Jan 14	West Ham United	1-1	Wood	Dunn	Hair	Gibson	Charlton	Kerfoot	Hutchinson	Brook	Charles 1	Vickers	Overfield
Jan 21	PORT VALE	1-1	Wood	Dunn	Ashall	Gibson	Charlton	Kerfoot	Hutchinson	Vickers	Charles	Brook 1	Overfield
Feb 11	SWANSEA TOWN	2-2	Wood	Dunn	Ashall	Gibson	Charlton	Kerfoot	Meek	Nightingale 1	Charles 1	Ripley	Overfield
Feb 25	SHEFFIELD WEDNESDAY	2-1	Wood	Dunn	Ashall	Gibson	Charlton	Kerfoot	Meek	Charles 1	Forrest 1	Nightingale	Overfield
Feb 28	Liverpool	0-1	Wood	Dunn	Ashall	Gibson	Charlton	Kerfoot	Meek	Charles	Forrest	Nightingale	Overfield
Mar 3	Lincoln City	1-1	Wood	Dunn	Ashall	Gibson	Charlton	Kerfoot	Hutchinson	Charles 1	Forrest	Brook	Meek
Mar 10	BLACKBURN ROVERS	1-2	Wood	Dunn	Hair	Gibson	Charlton	Kerfoot	Hutchinson	Charles 1	Forrest	Brook	Overfield
Mar 17	Stoke City	1-2	Wood	Dunn	Hair	Gibson	Charlton	Kerfoot	Williams	Charles	Forrest	Brook 1	Overfield
Mar 24	PLYMOUTH ARGYLE	4-2	Wood	Dunn	Hair	Gibson	Charlton	Kerfoot	Williams	Charles 2	Brook 1	Nightingale 1	Meek
Mar 30	Fulham	2-1	Wood	Dunn	Hair	Gibson	Charlton	Kerfoot	Williams	Charles 1	Brook 1	Nightingale	Overfield
Mar 31	Nottingham Forest	0-2	Wood	Dunn	Hair	Gibson	Charlton	Kerfoot	Meek	Charles	Brook	Forrest	Overfield
Apr 2	FULHAM	6-1	Wood	Dunn	Hair	Gibson	Charlton	Kerfoot	Meek	Charles 3	Brook 1	Nightingale 2	Overfield
Apr 7	LEICESTER CITY	4-0	Wood	Dunn	Hair	Gibson	Charlton	Kerfoot	Meek	Charles 2	Brook 1	Nightingale	Overfield 1
Apr 14	Doncaster Rovers	2-1	Wood	Dunn	Hair	Ripley	Charlton	Kerfoot	Meek	Charles 1	Brook	Nightingale 1	Overfield
Apr 21	BRISTOL ROVERS	2-1	Wood	Dunn	Hair	Ripley	Charlton	Kerfoot	Meek	Charles 1	Brook	Nightingale	Overfield 1
Apr 23	Rotherham United	2-0	Wood	Dunn	Hair	Ripley	Charlton	Kerfoot	Meek	Charles	Brook	Nightingale 2	Overfield
Apr 28	Hull City	4-1	Wood	Dunn	Hair	Ripley	Charlton	Kerfoot	Meek	Charles 2	Brook 2	Nightingale	Overfield

F.A. CUP

Jan 7	CARDIFF CITY	1-2	Wood	Dunn	Hair	Gibson	Charles	Kerfoot	Williams	Brook 1	Charlton	Vickers	Overfield

DIVISION ONE 1956-57

Aug 18	EVERTON	5-1	Wood	Dunn	Hair	Gibson	Charlton	Kerfoot	Meek	Charles 1	Brook 3	Nightingale	Overfield 1
Aug 23	Charlton Athletic	2-1	Wood	Dunn	Hair	Gibson	Charlton	Kerfoot	Meek	Charles 2	Brook	Ripley	Overfield
Aug 25	Tottenham Hotspur	1-5	Wood	Dunn	Hair	Gibson	Charlton	Kerfoot	Meek	Charles	Brook	Ripley 1	Overfield
Aug 29	CHARLTON ATHLETIC	4-0	Wood	Dunn	Hair	Ripley	Charlton	Kerfoot	Meek	Charles 1	Brook 1	Forrest 2	Overfield
Sep 1	CHELSEA	0-0	Wood	Dunn	Hair	Ripley	Charlton	Kerfoot	Meek	Charles	Brook	Forrest	Overfield
Sep 5	Manchester City	0-1	Wood	Dunn	Hair	Gibson	Charlton	Kerfoot	Meek	Charles	Brook	Forrest	Overfield
Sep 8	BOLTON WANDERERS	3-2	Wood	Dunn	Hair	Gibson	Marsden	Kerfoot	Meek 1	Charles 1	Brook 1	Forrest	Overfield
Sep 12	MANCHESTER CITY	2-0	Wood	Dunn	Hair	Gibson	Marsden	Kerfoot	Meek	Charles 1	Brook 1	Forrest	Overfield
Sep 15	Wolverhampton Wans	2-1	Wood	Dunn	Hair	Gibson	Marsden	Kerfoot	Meek	Charles 2	Brook	Forrest	Overfield
Sep 22	ASTON VILLA	1-0	Wood	Dunn	Hair	Gibson	Marsden	Kerfoot	Meek	Charles 1	Brook	Forrest	Overfield
Sep 29	Luton Town	2-2	Wood	Dunn	Hair	Gibson	Marsden	Kerfoot	Meek	Charles 2	Brook	Forrest	Overfield
Oct 6	Cardiff City	1-4	Wood	Dunn	Hair	Gibson	Marsden	Kerfoot	Meek	Charles	Ripley	Forrest 1	Overfield

DIVISION ONE 1956-57 continued

Date	Opponent	Score	1	2	3	4	5	6	7	8	9	10	11
Oct 13	BIRMINGHAM CITY	1-1	Wood	Dunn	Hair	Gibson	Marsden	Kerfoot	Meek	Charles	Forrest	Ripley 1	Overfield
Oct 20	Burnley	0-0	Wood	Dunn	Hair	Gibson	Charlton	Kerfoot	Meek	Crowe	Forrest	Ripley	Overfield
Oct 27	PRESTON NORTH END	(o.g.) 1-2	Wood	Dunn	Hair	Gibson	Charlton	Kerfoot	Meek	Crowe	Forrest	Ripley	Overfield
Nov 3	Newcastle United	3-2	Wood	Dunn	Hair	Gibson	Charlton	Kerfoot	Meek	Charles 1	McKenna 2	Forrest	Overfield
Nov 10	SHEFFIELD WEDNESDAY	3-1	Wood	Dunn	Hair	Gibson	Charlton	Kerfoot	Meek	Charles 3	McKenna	Forrest	Overfield
Nov 17	Manchester United	2-3	Wood	Dunn	Hair	Gibson	Charlton	Kerfoot	Meek	Charles 1	McKenna 1	Forrest	Overfield
Nov 24	ARSENAL	3-3	Wood	Dunn	Hair	Gibson	Charlton	Kerfoot	Meek	Charles 2	McKenna	Forrest 1	Overfield
Dec 1	West Bromwich Albion	0-0	Wood	Dunn	Hair	Gibson	Charlton	Kerfoot	Meek	Charles	Brook	Forrest	Overfield
Dec 8	PORTSMOUTH	4-1	Wood	Dunn	Hair	Gibson	Charlton	Kerfoot	Meek	Charles 2	Ripley 2	Forrest	Overfield
Dec 15	Everton	1-2	Wood	Dunn	Hair	Gibson	Charlton	Kerfoot	Meek	Charles	Ripley 1	Forrest	Overfield
Dec 25	Blackpool	1-1	Wood	Dunn	Hair	Gibson	Charlton	Kerfoot	Meek	Charles	Brook 1	Forrest	Overfield
Dec 26	BLACKPOOL	5-0	Wood	Dunn	Hair	Gibson	Charlton	Kerfoot	Meek	Charles 2	Brook 3	Forrest	Overfield
Dec 29	Chelsea	(o.g.) 1-1	Wood	Dunn	Hair	Gibson	Charlton	Kerfoot	Meek	Charles	Brook	Forrest	Overfield
Jan 12	Bolton Wanderers	3-5	Wood	Dunn	Hair	Gibson	Marsden	Kerfoot	Meek 1	Charles 2	Brook	Crowe	Overfield
Jan 19	WOLVERHAMPTON WANS	0-0	Wood	Dunn	Hair	Gibson	Marsden	Kerfoot	Meek	Charles	Brook	Ripley	Overfield
Feb 2	Aston Villa	1-1	Wood	Dunn	Hair	Gibson	Marsden	Kerfoot	Meek	Charles	Brook	Crowe 1	Overfield
Feb 9	LUTON TOWN	1-2	Wood	Dunn	Hair	Gibson	Marsden	Kerfoot	Meek	Charles 1	Forrest	Crowe	Overfield
Feb 16	CARDIFF CITY	3-0	Wood	Dunn	Hair	Gibson	Marsden	Kerfoot	McKenna 1	Charles 1	Brook	Forrest 1	Overfield
Feb 23	Preston North End	0-3	Wood	Dunn	Hair	Gibson	Marsden	Kerfoot	McKenna	Charles	Brook	Crowe	Overfield
Mar 2	TOTTENHAM HOTSPUR	1-1	Wood	Dunn	Hair	Gibson	Marsden	Kerfoot	Meek	Charles 1	Brook	Forrest	Overfield
Mar 9	Portsmouth	5-2	Wood	Dunn	Hair	Gibson	Marsden	Kerfoot	Meek 1	Crowe 2	Charles 2	Brook	Overfield
Mar 11	BURNLEY	1-1	Wood	Dunn	Hair	Gibson	Marsden	Kerfoot	Meek	Crowe	Charles 1	Forrest	Overfield
Mar 16	NEWCASTLE UNITED	0-0	Wood	Dunn	Hair	Gibson	Marsden	Kerfoot	Meek	O'Brien	Charles	Brook	Overfield
Mar 26	Sheffield Wednesday	3-2	Wood	Dunn	Hair	Gibson	Charlton	Kerfoot	Meek	Crowe	Charles 3	O'Brien	Overfield
Mar 30	MANCHESTER UNITED	1-2	Wood	Dunn	Hair	Gibson	Charlton	Kerfoot	Meek	Crowe	Charles 1	O'Brien	Overfield
Apr 6	Arsenal	0-1	Wood	Dunn	Hair	Gibson	Charlton	Kerfoot	Meek	Crowe	Charles	O'Brien	Overfield
Apr 13	WEST BROMWICH ALBION	0-0	Wood	Dunn	Hair	Gibson	Marsden	Kerfoot	Meek	Crowe	Charles	O'Brien	Overfield
Apr 19	Sunderland	0-2	Wood	Dunn	Hair	Gibson	Marsden	Kerfoot	Meek	Brook	Charles	O'Brien	Overfield
Apr 20	Birmingham City	2-6	Wood	Dunn	Hair	Gibson	Marsden	Kerfoot	Meek	Crowe	Charles 2	O'Brien	Overfield
Apr 22	SUNDERLAND	3-1	Wood	Dunn	Hair	Gibson	Marsden	Kerfoot	Meek	Brook 1	Charles 2	O'Brien	Overfield

F.A. CUP

Date	Opponent	Score	1	2	3	4	5	6	7	8	9	10	11
Jan 5	CARDIFF CITY	1-2	Wood	Dunn	Hair	Gibson	Charlton	Kerfoot	Meek	Charles 1	Brook	Forrest	Overfield

DIVISION ONE 1957-58

Date	Opponent	Score	1	2	3	4	5	6	7	8	9	10	11
Aug 24	Blackpool	0-3	Wood	Dunn	Hair	Gibson	Charlton	Kerfoot	Crowe	O'Brien	Baird	Meek	Overfield
Aug 26	Aston Villa	0-2	Wood	Dunn	Hair	Gibson	Charlton	Kerfoot	Meek	O'Brien	Baird	Forrest	Overfield
Aug 31	LEICESTER CITY	2-1	Wood	Dunn	Hair	Gibson	Charlton	Kerfoot	Meek	O'Brien	Baird 1	Forrest	Overfield 1
Sep 4	ASTON VILLA	4-0	Wood	Dunn	Hair	Ripley	Charlton	Kerfoot	Meek	O'Brien 1	Baird 2	Brook 1	Overfield
Sep 7	Manchester United	0-5	Wood	Dunn	Hair	Ripley	Marsden	Kerfoot	Meek	O'Brien	Baird	Brook	Overfield
Sep 11	LUTON TOWN	0-2	Wood	Dunn	Charlton	Ripley	Marsden	Kerfoot	Meek	O'Brien	Baird	Brook	Overfield
Sep 14	NOTTINGHAM FOREST	1-2	Wood	Dunn	Ashall	Gibson	Charlton	Kerfoot	Meek	Forrest	Baird	Brook	Overfield 1
Sep 18	Luton Town	1-1	Wood	Dunn	Ashall	Gibson	Charlton	Kerfoot	Meek	Forrest	Baird	Brook	Overfield 1
Sep 21	BOLTON WANDERERS	2-1	Wood	Kerfoot	Ashall	Gibson	Charlton	Ripley	Meek 1	Crowe	Baird 1	Forrest	Overfield
Sep 25	SUNDERLAND	2-1	Wood	Marsden	Ashall	Gibson 1	Charlton	Kerfoot	Meek	Crowe	Baird 1	Forrest	Overfield
Sep 28	Arsenal	1-2	Wood	Kerfoot	Ashall	Gibson	Charlton	Ripley	Meek	Brook 1	Baird	Forrest	Overfield
Oct 5	WOLVERHAMPTON WANS	1-1	Wood	Kerfoot	Ashall	Gibson	Charlton	Ripley	Meek	Crowe	Baird 1	Forrest	Overfield
Oct 12	Portsmouth	2-1	Wood	Kerfoot	Ashall	Gibson	Charlton	Ripley	Meek	O'Brien	Baird 1	Brook 1	Overfield
Oct 19	WEST BROMWICH ALBION	1-1	Wood	Hair	Ashall	Kerfoot	Charlton	Ripley	Meek	Forrest 1	Baird	Brook	Overfield
Oct 26	Tottenham Hotspur	0-2	Wood	Hair	Ashall	Kerfoot	Charlton	Ripley	Meek	O'Brien	Baird	Brook	Overfield
Nov 2	PRESTON NORTH END	2-3	Wood	Dunn	Hair	Gibson	Charlton	Kerfoot	Meek	Ripley	Baird 2	O'Brien	Overfield
Nov 9	Sheffield Wednesday	2-3	Wood	Dunn	Hair	Gibson	Charlton	Kerfoot	Crowe	Baird	Ripley 1	Forrest 1	Meek
Nov 16	MANCHESTER CITY	2-4	Wood	Dunn	Hair	Kerfoot 1	Charlton	Cush	Crowe	Ripley	Baird 1	Forrest	Meek
Nov 23	Burnley	1-3	Wood	Dunn	Hair	Kerfoot	Charlton	Cush	Meek	Gibson	Baird 1	Crowe	Overfield
Nov 30	BIRMINGHAM CITY	1-1	Wood	Dunn	Hair	Gibson	Charlton	Kerfoot	Francis	Cush 1	Baird	Crowe	Meek
Dec 7	Chelsea	1-2	Wood	Dunn	Hair	Gibson	Charlton	Kerfoot	Meek	Cush	Baird 1	Crowe	Overfield
Dec 14	NEWCASTLE UNITED	3-0	Wood	Dunn	Hair	Gibson	Charlton	Kerfoot	Meek	Cush	Forrest 1	Crowe 1	Overfield 1
Dec 21	BLACKPOOL	2-1	Wood	Dunn	Hair	Gibson	Charlton	Kerfoot	Meek	Cush 1	Forrest 1	Crowe	Overfield
Dec 26	Sunderland	1-2	Wood	Dunn	Hair	Gibson	Charlton	Kerfoot	Meek	Cush	Forrest	Crowe 1	Overfield
Dec 28	Leicester City	0-3	Wood	Dunn	Hair	Gibson	Charlton	Kerfoot	Crowe	Cush	Baird	Forrest	Overfield
Jan 11	MANCHESTER UNITED	1-1	Wood	Dunn	Hair	Gibson	Charlton	Kerfoot	Meek	Cush	Baird 1	Forrest	Overfield
Jan 18	Nottingham Forest	1-1	Wood	Dunn	Hair	Gibson	Charlton	Kerfoot	Meek	Cush	Baird 1	Forrest	Overfield
Feb 1	Bolton Wanderers	2-0	Nimmo	Dunn	Hair	Cush 1	Charlton	Kerfoot	Meek	Peyton	Baird	Forrest	Overfield
Feb 19	Wolverhampton Wans	2-3	Wood	Dunn	Hair	Cush	Charlton	Kerfoot	Meek	Peyton 1	Baird	Forrest 1	Overfield
Feb 22	PORTSMOUTH	2-0	Wood	Dunn	Hair	Cush	Charlton	Kerfoot	Meek	Peyton	Baird 2	Forrest	Overfield
Mar 8	TOTTENHAM HOTSPUR	1-2	Wood	Dunn	Hair	Cush	Charlton	Kerfoot	Meek	Peyton	Baird 1	Forrest	Overfield
Mar 12	West Bromwich Albion	0-1	Wood	Dunn	Hair	Cush	Charlton	Kerfoot	Meek	Peyton	Baird	O'Brien	Overfield
Mar 15	Preston North End	0-3	Wood	Dunn	Hair	Cush	Charlton	Kerfoot	Meek	Peyton	Baird	Forrest	Overfield
Mar 19	ARSENAL	2-0	Wood	Dunn	Hair	Cush	Charlton	Kerfoot	Crowe	Peyton 1	Baird	O'Brien	Meek 1
Mar 22	BURNLEY	1-0	Wood	Dunn	Hair	Cush	Charlton	Kerfoot	Crowe	Peyton	Baird	O'Brien	Meek 1
Mar 29	Manchester City	0-1	Wood	Dunn	Hair	Gibson	Charlton	Kerfoot	Crowe	Peyton	Baird	O'Brien	Meek
Apr 4	Everton	1-0	Wood	Dunn	Hair	Gibson	Charlton	Kerfoot	Crowe	O'Brien	Baird 1	Forrest	Overfield
Apr 5	SHEFFIELD WEDNESDAY	2-2	Wood	Dunn	Hair	Gibson	Marsden	Kerfoot	Meek 1	Peyton	Baird 1	O'Brien	Overfield
Apr 7	EVERTON	1-0	Wood	Dunn	Hair	Cush	Charlton	Kerfoot	Meek	Forrest 1	Baird	O'Brien	Overfield
Apr 12	Birmingham City	1-1	Wood	Dunn	Hair	Cush	Charlton	Kerfoot	Meek	Crowe	Baird	O'Brien 1	Overfield
Apr 19	CHELSEA	0-0	Wood	Dunn	Hair	Cush	Charlton	Kerfoot	Meek	Crowe	Baird	O'Brien	Overfield
Apr 26	Newcastle United	2-1	Wood	Dunn	Hair	Gibson	Charlton	Kerfoot	Meek	Peyton	Baird 1	O'Brien 1	Overfield

F.A. CUP

Date	Opponent	Score	1	2	3	4	5	6	7	8	9	10	11
Jan 4	CARDIFF CITY	Rd 3 1-2	Wood	Dunn	Hair	Gibson	Charlton	Kerfoot	Meek	Cush	Forrest 1	Crowe	Overfield

DIVISION ONE 1958-59

Date	Opponent	Score	1	2	3	4	5	6	7	8	9	10	11
Aug 23	Bolton Wanderers	0-4	Wood	Dunn	Hair	Gibson	Charlton	Cush	Crowe	Peyton	Forrest	O'Brien	Overfield
Aug 26	LUTON TOWN	1-1	Wood	Dunn	Hair	Gibson	Charlton	Cush	Crowe 1	Peyton	Forrest	O'Brien	Overfield
Aug 30	BURNLEY	1-1	Wood	Ashall	Hair	Gibson	Charlton	Cush	Crowe	Peyton	Baird	Forrest 1	Overfield
Sep 3	Luton Town	1-1	Wood	Ashall	Hair	Gibson	Charlton	Kerfoot	Meek	Forrest	Baird 1	Cush	Overfield
Sep 6	Preston North End	2-1	Wood	Ashall	Hair	Gibson	Charlton	Kerfoot	Meek	Forrest	Baird 1	Cush	Overfield 1
Sep 10	BIRMINGHAM CITY	0-0	Wood	Ashall	Hair	Gibson	Charlton	Kerfoot	Meek	Forrest	Baird	Cush	Overfield
Sep 13	LEICESTER CITY	1-1	Wood	Ashall	Hair	Gibson	Charlton	Kerfoot	Meek 1	Forrest	Baird	Cush	Overfield
Sep 17	Birmingham City	1-4	Wood	Ashall	Hair	Gibson	Marsden	Cush	Meek	Crowe	Forrest 1	O'Brien	Overfield
Sep 20	Everton	2-3	Wood	Ashall	Hair	Gibson	Marsden	Cush 1	Meek	Crowe 1	Forrest	O'Brien	Overfield
Sep 27	ARSENAL	2-1	Wood	Ashall	Hair	Cush	Charlton	Gibson	Humphries	Crowe 1	Forrest	Peyton	Overfield 1
Oct 4	Manchester City	(o.g.) 1-2	Wood	Ashall	Hair	Gibson	Charlton	O'Brien	Humphries	Crowe	Baird	Peyton	Overfield
Oct 11	Portsmouth	0-2	Wood	Ashall	Hair	Gibson	Charlton	O'Brien	Humphries	Cush	Forrest	Crowe	Overfield
Oct 18	ASTON VILLA	0-0	Wood	Ashall	Hair	Cush	Charlton	Gibson	Humphries	Crowe	Forrest	O'Brien	Overfield
Oct 25	Tottenham Hotspur	3-2	Wood	Ashall	Hair	Cush 1	Charlton	Gibson	Humphries	Crowe	Forrest	O'Brien 1	Overfield 1
Nov 1	MANCHESTER UNITED	1-2	Wood	Ashall	Hair	Cush	Charlton	Gibson	Humphries	Crowe	Shackleton 1	O'Brien	Overfield
Nov 8	Chelsea	0-2	Wood	Ashall	Hair	Cush	Charlton	Gibson	Meek	Crowe	Shackleton	O'Brien	Overfield
Nov 15	BLACKPOOL	1-1	Wood	Ashall	Hair	Cush	Charlton	Gibson	Humphries	Crowe 1	Shackleton	Forrest	Overfield
Nov 22	Blackburn Rovers	4-2	Wood	Ashall	Hair	Cush	Charlton	Gibson	Humphries 1	Crowe	Shackleton 3	Forrest	Overfield
Nov 29	NEWCASTLE UNITED	(o.g.) 3-2	Wood	Ashall	Hair	Cush	Charlton	Gibson	Humphries	Crowe 1	Shackleton	Revie	Overfield 1
Dec 6	West Ham United	(o.g.) 3-2	Wood	Ashall	Hair	Cush	Charlton	Gibson	Humphries	Crowe 1	Shackleton	Revie	Overfield 1
Dec 13	NOTTINGHAM FOREST	1-0	Wood	Ashall	Hair	Cush	Charlton	Gibson	Humphries	Crowe 1	Shackleton	Revie	Overfield
Dec 20	BOLTON WANDERERS	3-4	Wood	Ashall	Dunn	McConnell	Charlton	Gibson 1	Humphries	Crowe 1	Shackleton 1	Revie	Overfield
Dec 26	West Bromwich Albion	2-1	Wood	Ashall	Hair	Cush	Charlton	Gibson	Humphries 1	Crowe 1	Shackleton	Revie	Overfield
Dec 27	WEST BROMWICH ALBION	0-1	Wood	Ashall	Hair	Cush	Charlton	Gibson	Humphries	Crowe	Shackleton	Revie	Overfield
Jan 3	Burnley	1-3	Wood	Ashall	Hair	Cush	Charlton	Gibson	Humphries	Crowe	Shackleton 1	Revie	Overfield
Jan 17	PRESTON NORTH END	1-3	Wood	Mitchell	Hair	Cush	Charlton	Gibson	Humphries	Revie 1	Shackleton	O'Brien	Meek
Jan 31	Leicester City	1-0	Burgin	Mitchell	Hair	Cush	Charlton	Kerfoot	Humphries	Crowe	Shackleton 1	Revie	Overfield
Feb 7	EVERTON	1-0	Burgin	Mitchell	Hair	Cush	Charlton	Kerfoot	Humphries	Crowe	Shackleton 1	Revie	Overfield
Feb 14	Wolverhampton Wans	2-6	Burgin	Mitchell	Hair	Kerfoot	Charlton	Cush	Humphries	Revie	Shackleton 1	O'Brien	Overfield 1
Feb 21	MANCHESTER CITY	0-4	Burgin	Ashall	Hair	Cush	Charlton	Hair	Humphries	Crowe	Shackleton	Revie	Kemp
Feb 24	Arsenal	0-1	Burgin	Ashall	Hair	Cush	Charlton	Hair	Humphries	Crowe	Shackleton	Revie	Overfield
Feb 28	PORTSMOUTH	1-1	Burgin	Ashall	Kilford	Revie	Charlton	Hair	Humphries	Cush 1	Shackleton	O'Brien	Meek
Mar 7	Aston Villa	1-2	Burgin	Dunn	Ashall	Kerfoot	Charlton	O'Brien	Meek	Crowe	Shackleton	Cush	Overfield 1
Mar 14	TOTTENHAM HOTSPUR	3-1	Burgin	Dunn	Ashall	Revie	Charlton	Kerfoot	Meek	Crowe 1	Shackleton 1	Cush	Overfield 1
Mar 21	Manchester United	0-4	Burgin	Dunn	Ashall	Revie	Charlton	Kerfoot	Meek	Crowe	Shackleton	Cush	Overfield
Mar 28	CHELSEA	4-0	Burgin	Ashall	Hair	Gibson	Charlton	Kerfoot	Meek	Crowe 1	Shackleton 1	O'Brien 2	Overfield
Mar 31	WOLVERHAMPTON WANS	1-3	Burgin	Ashall	Hair	Gibson	Charlton	Kerfoot	Meek	Crowe 1	Shackleton	O'Brien	Overfield

DIVISION ONE 1958-59 continued

			1	2	3	4	5	6	7	8	9	10	11
Apr 4	Blackpool	0-3	Burgin	Ashall	Hair	McConnell	Charlton	Kerfoot	Humphries	Crowe	Shackleton	O'Brien	Overfield
Apr 11	BLACKBURN ROVERS	2-1	Burgin	Dunn	Hair	McConnell	Charlton 1	Kerfoot	Crowe	Cush	Shackleton 1	Revie	Meek
Apr 18	Newcastle United	2-2	Burgin	Dunn	Hair	McConnell	Cush	Kerfoot	Crowe	Revie 1	Shackleton	Peyton	Meek
Apr 22	Nottingham Forest	3-0	Burgin	Dunn	Hair	McConnell	Charlton	Kerfoot	Crowe	Revie	Shackleton 3	Peyton	Meek
Apr 25	WEST HAM UNITED	1-0	Burgin	Dunn	Hair	McConnell	Charlton	Cush	Crowe	Revie	Shackleton 1	Peyton	Meek

F.A. CUP

Jan 10	Luton Town	1-5	Wood	Ashall	Hair	Cush	Charlton	Gibson	Humphries	Crowe	Shackleton	Revie	Overfield

DIVISION ONE 1959-60

Aug 22	BURNLEY	2-3	Burgin	Ashall	Hair	McConnell	Charlton 1	Cush 1	Humphries	Revie	Shackleton	Crowe	Meek
Aug 26	Leicester City	2-3	Burgin	Ashall	Hair	McConnell	Charlton	Cush 1	Meek	Revie	Shackleton	Crowe 1	Overfield
Aug 29	Luton Town	1-0	Burgin	Ashall	Hair	McConnell	Charlton	Cush	Meek	Cameron	Revie 1	Crowe	Overfield
Sep 2	LEICESTER CITY	1-1	Burgin	Ashall	Hair	McConnell	Charlton	Cush	Meek	Cameron	Revie	Crowe 1	Overfield
Sep 5	West Ham United	2-1	Burgin	Ashall	Hair	McConnell	Charlton	Cush	Meek	Cameron	Revie	Crowe 2	Overfield
Sep 9	Manchester United	0-6	Burgin	Ashall	Hair	Revie	Charlton	Cush	Francis	Meek	Cameron	Peyton	Overfield
Sep 12	CHELSEA	2-1	Burgin	Ashall	Kilford	Gibson	Charlton	Cush	Meek	Cameron	Revie	Crowe 2	Overfield
Sep 16	MANCHESTER UNITED	2-2	Burgin	Ashall	Kilford	Gibson	Charlton	Cush 1	Meek	Peyton	Revie	Crowe 1	Overfield
Sep 19	West Bromwich Albion	0-3	Burgin	Ashall	Hair	Gibson	Charlton	Cush	Meek	Cameron	McCole	Crowe	Overfield
Sep 26	NEWCASTLE UNITED	2-3	Wood	Ashall	Hair	Gibson	Charlton	Cush	Humphries	Revie 1	McCole 1	Crowe	Overfield
Oct 3	Birmingham City	0-2	Wood	Ashall	Hair	Gibson	Charlton	Cameron	Crowe	Revie	McCole	Peyton	Overfield
Oct 10	EVERTON	3-3	Wood	Ashall	Hair	Gibson	Charlton	Cush	Francis 1	Cameron	McCole 1	Crowe 1	Overfield
Oct 17	Blackpool	3-3	Burgin	Ashall	Hair	Gibson	Charlton	Cush	Francis 1	Revie	McCole 2	Crowe	Overfield
Oct 24	BLACKBURN ROVERS	0-1	Burgin	Ashall	Hair	Gibson	Charlton	Cush	Francis	Revie	McCole	Crowe	Overfield
Oct 31	Bolton Wanderers	1-1	Burgin	Ashall	Hair	Cameron	Charlton	Gibson	Francis	Revie	McCole 1	Peyton	Crowe
Nov 7	ARSENAL	3-2	Burgin	Ashall	Hair	Cameron	Charlton	Gibson	Francis	Revie	McCole 1	Peyton 2	Crowe
Nov 14	Wolverhampton Wans	2-4	Burgin	Ashall	Hair	Cameron	Charlton	McConnell	Crowe 1	Revie	McCole	Peyton 1	Meek
Nov 21	SHEFFIELD WEDNESDAY	1-3	Burgin	Ashall	Hair	Cameron	Charlton	Cush	Crowe	Revie	McCole 1	Peyton	Francis
Nov 28	Nottingham Forest	1-4	Burgin	Ashall	Hair	McConnell	Charlton	Gibson	Crowe	Revie 1	McCole	Cameron	Meek
Dec 5	FULHAM	1-4	Burgin	Caldwell	Hair	Cush	Charlton	Gibson	Meek	Revie	McCole 1	Crowe	Overfield
Dec 12	Manchester City	3-3	Burgin	Caldwell	Hair	Cush	Charlton	Gibson	Meek	Revie	McCole	Crowe	Overfield
Dec 19	Burnley	1-0	Burgin	Caldwell	Hair	Cush	Charlton	Gibson	Meek	Cameron	McCole	Crowe	Overfield
Dec 26	TOTTENHAM HOTSPUR	2-4	Burgin	Caldwell	Hair	Cush	Charlton	Gibson	Meek	Cameron	McCole	Crowe	Francis
Dec 28	Tottenham Hotspur	4-1	Burgin	Ashall	Hair	Cush	Charlton	Gibson	Crowe	Cameron	McCole	Peyton	Meek
Jan 2	LUTON TOWN	1-1	Burgin	Ashall	Hair	Cush	Charlton	Gibson	Crowe	Cameron	McCole 1	Peyton	Meek
Jan 16	WEST HAM UNITED	3-0	Wood	Ashall	Hair	Cush	Charlton	Gibson	Crowe 1	Revie	McCole 1	Peyton	Meek 1
Jan 23	Chelsea	3-1	Wood	Ashall	Hair	Cush	Charlton	Gibson	Bremner	Revie	McCole 2	Peyton 1	Meek
Feb 6	WEST BROMWICH ALBION	1-4	Wood	Ashall	Hair	Cush	Charlton	Gibson	Bremner	Revie	McCole 1	Peyton	Meek
Feb 13	Newcastle United	1-2	Wood	Ashall	Hair	Cush	Charlton	Gibson	Crowe	Revie 1	McCole	Peyton	Meek
Feb 27	Fulham	0-5	Humphreys	Ashall	Hair	Cush	Charlton	Gibson	Crowe	Revie	McCole	Peyton	Meek
Mar 5	BLACKPOOL	2-4	Humphreys	Ashall	Kilford	Cush	Charlton	Gibson	Bremner	Revie	McCole 1	Crowe	Meek 1
Mar 9	BIRMINGHAM CITY	3-3	Humphreys	Ashall	Kilford	McConnell	Cush	Gibson	Bremner 1	Revie 2	McCole	Peyton	Meek
Mar 19	MANCHESTER CITY	4-3	Burgin	Ashall	Hair	Gibson	Charlton	Goodwin	Bremner 1	Revie	McCole 2	Peyton 1	Meek
Mar 26	Arsenal	1-1	Burgin	Ashall	Hair	Gibson 1	Charlton	Goodwin	Bremner	Revie	McCole	Peyton	Meek
Apr 2	WOLVERHAMPTON WANS	0-3	Burgin	Ashall	Hair	Gibson	Charlton	Goodwin	Bremner	Revie	Cush	Peyton	Meek
Apr 9	Sheffield Wednesday	0-1	Burgin	Ashall	Hair	Gibson	Charlton	Goodwin	Bremner	Revie	McCole	Cameron	Meek
Apr 16	BOLTON WANDERERS	1-0	Burgin	Ashall	Caldwell	Gibson	Charlton 1	Goodwin	Bremner	Revie	McCole	Cameron	Meek
Apr 18	Preston North End	1-1	Burgin	Ashall	Caldwell	Gibson 1	Charlton	Goodwin	Francis	Revie	McCole	Cush	Meek
Apr 19	PRESTON NORTH END	2-1	Burgin	Ashall	Caldwell	Gibson	Charlton 1	Goodwin	Francis 1	Revie	McCole	Cush	Meek
Apr 23	Everton	0-1	Burgin	Ashall	Caldwell	Gibson	Charlton	Goodwin	Bremner	Revie	McCole	Cameron	Meek
Apr 27	Blackburn Rovers	2-3	Burgin	Ashall	Caldwell	Gibson	Charlton	Goodwin	Francis	Revie	McCole 1	Peyton	Meek 1
Apr 30	NOTTINGHAM FOREST	1-0	Burgin	Ashall	Caldwell	Gibson	Charlton	Goodwin	Bremner	Cameron	McCole 1	Peyton	Francis

F.A. CUP

Jan 9	Aston Villa	Rd 3 1-2	Wood	Ashall	Hair	Cush	Charlton	Gibson	Crowe	Cameron	McCole 1	Peyton	Meek

DIVISION TWO 1960-61

Aug 20	Liverpool	0-2	Burgin	Ashall	Jones	Smith	Charlton	Goodwin	Bremner	Revie	McCole	Fitzgerald	Grainger
Aug 24	BRISTOL ROVERS	1-1	Burgin	Jones	Hair	Smith	Charlton	Goodwin	Francis	Revie	McCole 1	Peyton	Grainger
Aug 27	ROTHERHAM UNITED	2-0	Burgin	Jones	Hair	Cameron	Charlton	Goodwin	Francis	Hawksby 1	McCole 1	Peyton	Grainger
Aug 29	Bristol Rovers	4-4	Burgin	Jones	Hair	Cameron	Charlton	Goodwin	Francis	Hawksby 1	McCole 1	Peyton 1	Grainger 1
Sep 3	Southampton	4-2	Burgin	Ashall	Hair	Cameron 1	Charlton	Goodwin	Francis 1	Murray	McCole 1	Peyton	Grainger 1
Sep 7	LEYTON ORIENT	1-3	Burgin	Ashall	Hair	Cameron 1	Charlton	Bell	Revie	McCole	Bremner	Peyton	Grainger
Sep 10	HUDDERSFIELD TOWN	1-4	Humphreys	Ashall	Hair	Cameron 1	Charlton	Goodwin	Murray	Revie	McCole	Peyton	Grainger
Sep 14	Leyton Orient	1-0	Burgin	Caldwell	Hair	Cameron	Charlton	Goodwin	Murray	Revie 1	McCole	Peyton	Grainger
Sep 17	MIDDLESBROUGH	(o.g.) 4-4	Burgin	Caldwell	Hair	Cameron 1	Charlton	Goodwin 1	Francis	Hawksby	McCole 1	Peyton	Grainger
Sep 24	Brighton	1-2	Burgin	Caldwell	Hair	Cameron	Charlton	Goodwin	Francis	Revie	McCole 1	Peyton	Grainger
Oct 1	IPSWICH TOWN	2-5	Burgin	McQuigan	Hair	Cameron	Charlton	Goodwin	Francis	Revie	McCole 2	Wright	Grainger
Oct 8	Sunderland	3-2	Humphreys	Caldwell	Hair	Cameron	Charlton	Goodwin	Francis 1	Revie	McCole 1	Peyton 1	Grainger
Oct 15	PLYMOUTH ARGYLE	2-1	Humphreys	Caldwell	Hair	Cameron	Charlton	Goodwin	Francis 1	Revie	McCole	Peyton	Grainger 1
Oct 22	Norwich City	2-3	Humphreys	Caldwell	Hair	Cameron	Charlton	Bell	Francis	Bremner 2	Fitzgerald	Peyton	Grainger
Oct 29	CHARLTON ATHLETIC	1-0	Humphreys	Caldwell	Hair	Cameron	Charlton	Goodwin	Francis	Bremner	Fitzgerald	Peyton	Grainger 1
Nov 5	Sheffield United	2-3	Humphreys	Caldwell	Hair	Cameron 1	Charlton	Goodwin	Francis 1	Bremner	McCole	Peyton	Grainger
Nov 12	STOKE CITY	0-1	Humphreys	Caldwell	Hair	Cameron	Charlton	Goodwin	Francis	Bremner	Fitzgerald	Revie	Grainger
Nov 19	Swansea Town	2-3	Humphreys	Caldwell	Hair	Cameron 1	Charlton	Goodwin	Francis	Bremner	McCole 1	Hawksby	Grainger
Dec 3	Lincoln City	3-2	Humphreys	Jones	Hair	Cameron	Charlton	Goodwin	Francis	Bremner 1	McCole 1	Peyton 1	Grainger
Dec 10	PORTSMOUTH	0-0	Humphreys	Jones	Hair	Cameron	Charlton	Goodwin	Murray	Bremner	McCole	Peyton	Grainger
Dec 17	LIVERPOOL	2-2	Humphreys	Jones	Hair	Revie	Charlton	Goodwin	Murray 1	Cameron	McCole	Bremner 1	Grainger
Dec 24	Derby County	3-2	Humphreys	Jones	Hair	Revie	Charlton	Goodwin	Murray	Francis	McCole 1	Bremner 2	Grainger
Dec 27	DERBY COUNTY	3-3	Humphreys	Jones	Hair	Revie	Charlton 1	Goodwin	Murray 1	Francis	McCole 1	Bremner	Grainger
Dec 31	Rotherham United	2 (o.g.) 3-1	Humphreys	Jones	Hair	Smith	Charlton	Goodwin	Francis	Cameron	McCole 1	Bremner	Grainger
Jan 14	SOUTHAMPTON	3-0	Humphreys	Jones	Hair	Cameron 1	Charlton	Goodwin	Francis 2	Revie	McCole	Bremner	Grainger
Jan 21	Huddersfield Town	1-0	Humphreys	Jones	Hair	Cameron	Charlton	Goodwin	Francis	Smith	McCole 1	Bremner	Grainger
Feb 4	Middlesbrough	0-3	Humphreys	Jones	Hair	Cameron	Charlton	Goodwin	Francis	Smith	McCole	Bremner	Grainger
Feb 10	BRIGHTON	3-2	Humphreys	Jones	Hair	Cameron	Charlton 1	Goodwin 1	Francis	Smith	McCole 1	Bremner	Grainger
Feb 18	Ipswich Town	0-4	Humphreys	Jones	Hair	Cameron	Charlton	Goodwin	Francis	Smith	McCole	Bremner	Hawksby
Feb 25	SUNDERLAND	2-4	Humphreys	Jones	Hair	Cameron	Charlton	Goodwin	Francis	Smith 1	McCole	Bremner 1	Grainger
Mar 4	Plymouth Argyle	1-3	Humphreys	Jones	Hair	Cameron	Charlton	Goodwin	Francis	Smith	McCole	Bremner	Grainger 1
Mar 8	LUTON TOWN	1-2	Humphreys	Jones	Hair	Cameron 1	Goodwin	McConnell	Francis	Bremner	McCole	Peyton	Grainger
Mar 11	NORWICH CITY	1-0	Humphreys	Jones	Kilford	Cameron	Charlton	McConnell	Fitzgerald	Smith 1	McCole	Bremner	Francis
Mar 18	Portsmouth	1-3	Humphreys	Jones	Kilford	Cameron	Goodwin	McConnell	Francis	Fitzgerald	Charlton 1	Bremner	Grainger
Mar 25	SHEFFIELD UNITED	(o.g.) 1-2	Humphreys	Hair	Kilford	Smith	Goodwin	McConnell	Francis	Bremner	Charlton	McCole	Grainger
Apr 1	Luton Town	1-1	Carling	Hair	Kilford	Smith	Goodwin	McConnell	Francis	Bremner 1	Charlton	McCole	Hawksby
Apr 3	Scunthorpe United	2-3	Carling	Hair	Kilford	Smith	Goodwin	McConnell	Fitzgerald	Bremner	Charlton 2	Peyton	Hawksby
Apr 8	SWANSEA TOWN	2-2	Humphreys	Hair	Kilford	Smith	Goodwin	McConnell	Fitzgerald	Bremner	Charlton 2	Peyton	Martin
Apr 15	Stoke City	0-0	Humphreys	Hair	Kilford	Smith	Charlton	McConnell	Bremner	Francis	McCole	Peyton	Martin
Apr 22	LINCOLN CITY	(o.g.) 7-0	Humphreys	Hair	Kilford	Smith	Charlton	Bell 1	Bremner 1	McConnell 1	McCole 2	Peyton 1	Martin
Apr 25	SCUNTHORPE UNITED	2-2	Carling	Hair	Kilford	Smith	Charlton	Bell	Bremner	McConnell	McCole 2	Peyton	Martin
Apr 29	Charlton Athletic	0-2	Carling	Hair	Kilford	Smith	Goodwin	Bell	Bremner	McConnell	Charlton	Peyton	Martin

LEAGUE CUP

Sep 28	BLACKPOOL	Rd 2 0-0	Burgin	Caldwell	Hair	Cameron	Charlton	Goodwin	Francis	Revie	McCole	Wright	Grainger
Oct 5	Blackpool	Rd 2 R 3-1 (AET)	Humphreys	Caldwell	Hair	Cameron	Charlton	Goodwin	Francis	Revie 1	McCole 1	Peyton	Grainger 1
Nov 23	Chesterfield	Rd 3 4-0	Carling	Jones	Hair	Cameron 1	Charlton	Goodwin	Bremner 1	Revie	McCole 1	Peyton 1	Martin
Dec 5	Southampton	Rd 4 4-5	Humphreys	Jones	Hair	Cameron 1	Charlton 1	Goodwin	Francis	Bremner	McCole 1	Peyton 1	Grainger

F.A. CUP

Jan 7	Sheffield Wednesday	Rd 3 0-2	Humphreys	Jones	Hair	Smith	Charlton	Goodwin	Francis	Cameron	McCole	Bremner	Grainger

DIVISION TWO 1961-62

Aug 19	CHARLTON ATHLETIC	1-0	Humphreys	Smith	Hair	Cameron	Charlton	Goodwin	Mayers	Bremner 1	McCole	Peyton	Johanneson
Aug 22	Brighton	3-1	Humphreys	Smith	Hair	McConnell	Charlton	Goodwin	Mayers 1	Bremner 1	McCole	Peyton 1	Johanneson
Aug 26	Liverpool	0-5	Humphreys	Smith	Hair	McConnell	Charlton	Goodwin	Mayers	Bremner	McCole	Peyton	Johanneson
Aug 30	BRIGHTON	1-1	Carling	Smith	Hair	Cameron	Charlton	Goodwin	Francis	McConnell	Bremner 1	Peyton	Johanneson
Sep 2	ROTHERHAM UNITED	1-3	Humphreys	Smith	Hair	Cameron	Charlton	Goodwin	Francis	Bremner	McCole 1	Peyton	Johanneson
Sep 6	Norwich City	0-2	Humphreys	Smith	Hair	Revie	Charlton	Goodwin	Mayers	Bremner	McCole	Peyton	Johanneson
Sep 9	Sunderland	1-2	Humphreys	Smith	Hair	Revie	Goodwin	Bell	Mayers	Bremner	McCole 1	Peyton	Johanneson
Sep 16	STOKE CITY	3-1	Humphreys	Hair	Bell	Smith	Charlton	Goodwin	Mayers	Bremner 1	McCole 1	Peyton 1	Hawksby

DIVISION TWO 1961-62 continued

			1	2	3	4	5	6	7	8	9	10	11
Sep 20	NORWICH CITY	0-1	Humphreys	Hair	Bell	Smith	Charlton	Goodwin	Mayers	Bremner	McCole	Peyton	Hawksby
Sep 23	Bristol Rovers	0-4	Humphreys	Hair	Bell	Smith	Charlton	Goodwin	Mayers	Francis	McCole	Peyton	Hawksby
Sep 30	PRESTON NORTH END	1-2	Younger	Jones	Bell	Smith	Charlton 1	Goodwin	Mayers	Francis	McCole	Peyton	Hawksby
Oct 7	Plymouth Argyle	1-1	Younger	Jones	Hair	Smith	Goodwin	Bell	Peyton	Bremner	Charlton	McConnell 1	Hawksby
Oct 14	HUDDERSFIELD TOWN	1-0	Younger	Hair	Kilford	Smith	Goodwin	Bell	Peyton	Bremner	Charlton 1	McConnell	Hawksby
Oct 21	Swansea Town	1-2	Younger	Hair	Kilford	Smith	Goodwin	Bell	Peyton	Revie	Charlton	McConnell 1	Hawksby
Oct 28	SOUTHAMPTON	1-1	Younger	Hair	Kilford	Smith	Goodwin	Bell	Bremner	Revie	Charlton	McConnell 1	Peyton
Nov 4	Luton Town	2-3	Younger	Hair	Kilford	Smith	Goodwin	Bell	Bremner 1	Revie 1	Charlton	McConnell	Peyton
Nov 11	LEYTON ORIENT	0-0	Younger	Hair	Bell	Smith	Goodwin	McConnell	Mayers	Bremner	Revie	Peyton	Hawksby
Nov 18	Middlesbrough	3-1	Younger	Hair	Bell	Smith	Goodwin	McConnell	Mayers 1	Bremner 1	Charlton 1	Peyton	Hawksby
Nov 25	WALSALL	4-1	Younger	Hair	Bell	Smith	Goodwin	McConnell	Mayers	Bremner 1	Charlton 2	Peyton 1	Hawksby
Dec 2	Derby County	2-2	Younger	Hair	Kilford	McConell	Goodwin	Bell 1	Mayers 1	Bremner	Charlton	Peyton 1	Hawksby
Dec 16	Charlton Athletic	3-3	Younger	Hair	Bell	Smith	Goodwin	McConnell	Mayers	Bremner 1	McAdams	Peyton	Hawksby
Dec 23	LIVERPOOL	1-0	Younger	Hair	Bell	Smith	Goodwin	McConnell	Bremner 1	McAdams	Charlton	Peyton	Mayers
Dec 26	SCUNTHORPE UNITED	1-4	Younger	Hair	Bell	Smith	Goodwin	McConnell	Bremner	McAdams	Charlton 1	Peyton	Mayers
Jan 12	Rotherham United	1-2	Younger	Smith	Kilford	Casey	Goodwin	McConnell	Mayers	Bremner	McAdams 1	Peyton	Hawksby
Jan 20	SUNDERLAND	1-0	Younger	Jones	Bell	Casey	Goodwin	McConnell	Bremner	Smith 1	McAdams	Peyton	Hawksby
Jan 27	NEWCASTLE UNITED	0-1	Younger	Jones	Bell	Casey	Goodwin	McConnell	Bremner	Smith	McAdams	Peyton	Johanneson
Feb 3	Stoke City	1-2	Younger	Hair	Bell	Smith	Goodwin	McConnell	Bremner	McAdams	Charlton	Peyton 1	Hawksby
Feb 10	BRISTOL ROVERS	0-0	Younger	Hair	Bell	Smith	Goodwin	McConnell	Mayers	Bremner	Charlton	Peyton	Hawksby
Feb 20	Scunthorpe United	1-2	Younger	Hair	Bell	Smith	Goodwin	McConnell	Mayers 1	Bremner	Charlton	Peyton	Hawksby
Feb 24	PLYMOUTH ARGYLE	2-3	Younger	Hair	Bell	Cameron	Goodwin	Smith	Mayers 1	Bremner	Charlton 1	McConnell	Hawksby
Mar 3	Huddersfield Town	1-2	Younger	Jones	Hair	Cameron	Goodwin	Smith	Bremner	Revie	Charlton 1	Lawson	Peyton
Mar 10	SWANSEA TOWN	2-0	Younger	Hair	Mason	Cameron	Goodwin	Smith	Bremner	Collins 1	McAdams 1	Lawson	Hawksby
Mar 17	Southampton	1-4	Sprake	Hair	Mason	Cameron	Goodwin	Smith	Bremner	Collins	McAdams	Lawson 1	Hawksby
Mar 24	LUTON TOWN	2-1	Younger	Hair	Mason	Goodwin	Charlton	Smith	Bremner 2	Collins	Lawson	Peyton	Hawksby
Mar 31	Leyton Orient	0-0	Younger	Hair	Mason	Goodwin	Charlton	Smith	Bremner	Collins	Lawson	Peyton	Hawksby
Apr 7	MIDDLESBROUGH	(o.g.) 2-0	Younger	Hair 1	Mason	Goodwin	Charlton	Smith	Bremner	Collins	Lawson	Peyton	Hawksby
Apr 9	Preston North End	(o.g.) 1-1	Younger	Hair	Mason	McConnell	Charlton	Smith	Bremner	Collins	Lawson	Peyton	Hawksby
Apr 14	Walsall	1-1	Younger	Hair	Mason	Goodwin	Charlton	Smith	Bremner	Collins	Lawson	Peyton	Johanneson 1
Apr 20	Bury	1-1	Younger	Hair	Mason	Goodwin	Charlton 1	Smith	Bremner	Collins	Lawson	Peyton	Johanneson
Apr 21	DERBY COUNTY	0-0	Younger	Hair	Mason	Goodwin	Charlton	Smith	Bremner	Collins	Lawson	Peyton	Johanneson
Apr 24	BURY	0-0	Younger	Hair	Mason	Goodwin	Charlton	Smith	Bremner	Collins	McAdams	Lawson	Johanneson
Apr 28	Newcastle United	(o.g.) 3-0	Younger	Hair	Mason	Goodwin	Charlton	Smith	Bremner	Collins	McAdams 1	Hawksby	Johanneson 1

LEAGUE CUP

Sep 13	BRENTFORD	Rd 1 4-1	Humphreys	Hair	Bell	Smith	Charlton	Goodwin	Mayers	Bremner	McCole 4	Peyton	Hawksby
Oct 4	HUDDERSFIELD TOWN	Rd 2 3-2	Younger	Hair	Kilford	Smith	Goodwin	Bell	Peyton	Bremner 1	Charlton 1	McConnell 1	Hawksby
	BYE	Rd 3											
Dec 12	Rotherham United	Rd 4 1-1	Younger	Hair	Bell	Casey	Goodwin	McConnell	Mayers	Bremner	Charlton 1	Peyton	Hawksby
Jan 15	ROTHERHAM UNITED	Rd 4 R 1-2	Younger	Jones	Kilford	Smith	Goodwin	McConnell	Bremner	Peyton	Addy	Hawksby	Johanneson 1

F.A. CUP

Jan 6	DERBY COUNTY	Rd 3 2-2	Younger	Hair	Bell	Smith	Goodwin	McConnell	Bremner	McAdams	Charlton 1	Peyton 1	Mayers
Jan 10	Derby County	Rd 3 R 1-3	Younger	Hair	Bell	Smith	Goodwin	McConnell	Bremner	McAdams 1	Charlton	Peyton	Mayers

DIVISION TWO 1962-63

Aug 18	Stoke City	1-0	Younger	Hair	Mason	Goodwin	Charlton	Smith	Bremner	Storrie 1	Charles	Collins	Johanneson
Aug 22	ROTHERHAM UNITED	3-4	Younger	Hair	Mason	Goodwin	Charlton	Smith	Bremner	Storrie 1	Charles 1	Collins	Johanneson 1
Aug 25	SUNDERLAND	1-0	Younger	Hair	Mason	Goodwin	Charlton	Bell	Bremner 1	Storrie	Charles	Collins	Johanneson
Aug 28	Rotherham United	1-2	Younger	Hair	Mason	Bremner	Charlton	Bell	Lawson	Storrie	Charles 1	Collins	Hawksby
Sep 1	Huddersfield Town	1-1	Younger	Hair	Mason	Smith	Charlton	Bell	Bremner	Storrie	Charles 1	Collins	Johanneson
Sep 5	BURY	1-2	Younger	Hair	Mason	Smith	Charlton	Bell	Bremner 1	Storrie	Charles	Collins	Johanneson
Sep 8	Swansea Town	2-0	Sprake	Reaney	Mason	Smith	Charlton	Hunter	Peyton	Bremner 1	Johnson 1	Collins	Johanneson
Sep 15	CHELSEA	2-0	Sprake	Reaney	Mason	Smith	Charlton	Hunter	Peyton	Bremner	Charles	Collins	Johanneson 2
Sep 18	Bury	1-3	Sprake	Reaney	Mason	Bremner	Charlton	Hunter	Peyton	Storrie 1	Charles	Collins	Johanneson
Sep 22	Luton Town	2-2	Sprake	Reaney	Mason	Addy	Charlton	Hunter	Johnson	Bremner	Storrie 1	Collins 1	Johanneson
Sep 29	SOUTHAMPTON	1-1	Sprake	Reaney	Mason	Addy	Charlton	Hunter	Lorimer	Storrie 1	Charles	Collins	Johanneson
Oct 6	MIDDLESBROUGH	2-3	Sprake	Reaney	Hair	Charles	Charlton	Hunter 1	Mason	Bremner 1	Storrie	Collins	Johanneson
Oct 13	Derby County	0-0	Sprake	Reaney	Mason	Bell	Charlton	Hunter	Hawksby	Storrie	Charles	Collins	Johanneson
Oct 20	NEWCASTLE UNITED	1-0	Sprake	Reaney	Mason	Bell	Charlton	Hunter	Hawksby	Peyton	Johnson	Collins	Johanneson 1
Oct 27	Walsall	1-1	Sprake	Reaney	Mason	Bell	Charlton	Hunter	Hawksby	Storrie	Johnson	Collins	Johanneson 1
Nov 3	NORWICH CITY	3-0	Sprake	Reaney	Mason	Bell 1	Goodwin	Hunter	Hawksby	Bremner	Storrie 1	Collins	Johanneson 1
Nov 10	Grimsby Town	1-1	Sprake	Reaney	Mason	Bell	Goodwin	Hunter	Henderson	Bremner	Storrie 1	Collins	Johanneson
Nov 17	PLYMOUTH ARGYLE	6-1	Sprake	Hair	Mason	Bell	Charlton	Hunter	Henderson	Bremner 1	Storrie 3	Collins 1	Johanneson 1
Nov 24	Preston North End	1-4	Sprake	Reaney	Mason	Bell 1	Charlton	Hunter	Henderson	Bremner	Storrie	Collins	Johanneson
Dec 1	PORTSMOUTH	3-3	Sprake	Reaney	Mason	Bell	Charlton	Hunter	Henderson	Bremner	Storrie 1	Collins 1	Johanneson 1
Dec 8	Cardiff City	0-0	Sprake	Reaney	Hair	Bell	Charlton	Hunter	Henderson	Peyton	Storrie	Collins	Johanneson
Dec 15	STOKE CITY	3-1	Sprake	Reaney	Hair	Bell	Charlton	Hunter	Henderson	Weston 3	Storrie	Collins	Johanneson
Dec 22	Sunderland	1-2	Sprake	Reaney	Hair	Bell	Charlton	Hunter	Henderson	Weston	Storrie	Bremner 1	Johanneson
Mar 2	DERBY COUNTY	3-1	Sprake	Reaney	Hair	Bell	Charlton 1	Hunter	Henderson	Weston 1	Storrie 1	Collins	Johanneson
Mar 9	Newcastle United	1-1	Sprake	Reaney	Hair	Bell	Charlton	Hunter	Henderson	Weston	Storrie 1	Collins	Johanneson
Mar 13	WALSALL	3-0	Sprake	Reaney	Hair	Bell	Charlton	Hunter	Henderson	Weston	Storrie 2	Collins	Johanneson 1
Mar 23	Norwich City	2-3	Sprake	Reaney	Hair	Bell	Charlton	Hunter	Weston	Bremner	Storrie	Collins 1	Johanneson 1
Mar 30	GRIMSBY TOWN	3-0	Williamson	Reaney	Hair	Bell	Charlton	Hunter	Weston	Bremner 1	Storrie	Collins 2	Johanneson
Apr 3	SCUNTHORPE UNITED	1-0	Williamson	Reaney	Hair	Bell	Charlton	Hunter	Weston	Bremner 1	Storrie	Collins	Johanneson
Apr 6	Plymouth Argyle	1-3	Williamson	Reaney	Hair	Bell	Charlton	Hunter	Weston	Bremner	Storrie 1	Collins	Johanneson
Apr 13	PRESTON NORTH END	4-1	Sprake	Reaney	Wright	Bell	Charlton	Hunter	Henderson	Bremner 2	Storrie 1	Collins 1	Johanneson
Apr 15	Charlton Athletic	2-1	Sprake	Reaney	Wright	Bell	Charlton 1	Hunter 1	Henderson	Bremner	Storrie	Collins	Johanneson
Apr 16	CHARLTON ATHLETIC	4-1	Sprake	Reaney	Wright	Bell	Charlton	Hunter	Henderson 1	Weston 1	Storrie 1	Collins	Johanneson 1
Apr 20	Porstmouth	0-3	Sprake	Reaney	Hair	Bell	Charlton	Hunter	Henderson	Peyton	Storrie	Collins	Johanneson
Apr 23	Scunthorpe United	2-0	Sprake	Reaney	Hair	Bell	Goodwin	Hunter	Henderson	Lawson 2	Storrie	Collins	Johanneson
Apr 27	CARDIFF CITY	3-0	Sprake	Reaney	Hair	Bell	Goodwin	Hunter	Henderson	Lawson	Storrie 3	Collins	Johanneson
Apr 30	Chelsea	2-2	Sprake	Reaney	Hair	Bell	Charlton	Hunter	Henderson	Lawson 2	Storrie	Collins	Johanneson
May 4	LUTON TOWN	3-0	Sprake	Reaney	Hair	Bell	Charlton	Hunter	Henderson	Weston 1	Storrie 2	Collins	Johanneson
May 6	Middlesbrough	1-2	Sprake	Reaney	Bell	Goodwin	Charlton	Hunter	Henderson	Weston	Storrie	Collins	Johanneson 1
May 11	HUDDERSFIELD TOWN	0-1	Sprake	Reaney	Hair	Bell	Charlton	Hunter	Henderson	Weston	Lawson	Collins	Johanneson
May 15	Southampton	1-3	Sprake	Reaney	Hair	Greenhoff	Charlton	Hunter	Weston 1	Bremner	Storrie	Collins	Johanneson
May 18	SWANSEA TOWN	5-0	Sprake	Reaney	Hair	Greenhoff	Charlton	Hunter	Weston	Lawson 1	Storrie 2	Collins 1	Johanneson 1

LEAGUE CUP

Sep 26	CRYSTAL PALACE	Rd 2 2-1	Sprake	Hair	Mason	Addy	Charlton 1	Hunter	Johnson	Storrie 1	Lawson	Peyton	Hawksby
Oct 17	Blackburn Rovers	Rd 3 0-4	Sprake	Reaney	Mason	Bell	Hallett	Hunter	Johnson	Storrie	Lawson	Peyton	Hawksby

F.A. CUP

Mar 6	STOKE CITY	Rd 3 3-1	Sprake	Reaney 1	Hair 1	Bell	Charlton 1	Hunter	Henderson	Weston	Storrie	Collins	Johanneson
Mar 16	Middlesbrough	Rd 4 2-0	Sprake	Reaney	Hair	Bell	Charlton	Hunter	Henderson	Weston	Storrie 1	Collins	Johanneson 1
Mar 19	Nottingham Forest	Rd 5 0-3	Sprake	Reaney	Hair	Bell	Charlton	Hunter	Henderson	Weston	Storrie	Collins	Johanneson

DIVISION TWO 1963-64

Aug 28	ROTHERHAM UNITED	1-0	Sprake	Reaney	Bell	Bremner	Charlton	Hunter	Weston 1	Lawson	Storrie	Collins	Johanneson
Aug 31	BURY	3-0	Sprake	Reaney	Bell	Bremner	Charlton	Hunter	Giles	Weston	Storrie 1	Collins 1	Johanneson 1
Sep 3	Rotherham United	2-2	Sprake	Reaney	Bell	Bremner	Charlton 1	Hunter	Giles	Weston	Storrie	Collins	Johanneson 1
Sep 7	Manchester City	2-3	Sprake	Reaney	Bell	Bremner	Charlton	Hunter	Giles	Weston	Storrie	Lawson 1	Johanneson 1
Sep 11	PORTSMOUTH	3-1	Sprake	Reaney	Hair	Bremner 1	Charlton	Hunter	Giles	Weston 1	Storrie 1	Collins	Johanneson
Sep 14	SWINDON TOWN	0-0	Sprake	Reaney	Hair	Bremner	Charlton	Hunter	Giles	Weston	Storrie	Collins	Johanneson
Sep 18	Portsmouth	1-1	Sprake	Reaney	Hair	Bremner	Charlton	Hunter	Giles	Weston	Storrie	Collins	Henderson 1
Sep 21	Cardiff City	0-0	Sprake	Reaney	Hair	Bremner	Charlton	Hunter	Giles	Weston	Storrie	Collins	Henderson
Sep 28	NORWICH CITY	4-2	Sprake	Reaney	Hair	Bremner	Goodwin	Hunter	Giles	Weston 2	Storrie	Collins 1	Johanneson 1
Oct 1	Northampton Town	3-0	Sprake	Reaney	Bell	Bremner	Goodwin	Hunter	Giles	Lawson 1	Weston 1	Collins 1	Johanneson
Oct 5	Scunthorpe United	1-0	Sprake	Reaney	Bell	Bremner	Goodwin	Hunter	Giles	Lawson 1	Weston	Collins	Johanneson
Oct 9	MIDDLESBROUGH	2-0	Sprake	Reaney	Bell	Bremner	Charlton	Hunter 1	Giles	Lawson	Weston	Collins 1	Johanneson
Oct 12	Huddersfield Town	2-0	Sprake	Reaney	Bell	Bremner	Charlton	Hunter	Giles 1	Lawson	Weston 1	Collins	Johanneson
Oct 19	DERBY COUNTY	2-2	Sprake	Reaney	Bell	Bremner	Charlton 1	Hunter	Giles	Lawson	Weston 1	Collins	Johanneson
Oct 26	Southampton	4-1	Sprake	Reaney	Bell	Bremner	Charlton	Hunter	Giles 1	Lawson 2	Weston	Collins	Johanneson 1
Nov 2	CHARLTON ATHLETIC	1-1	Sprake	Reaney	Bell	Bremner	Charlton 1	Hunter	Giles	Lawson	Weston	Collins	Johanneson
Nov 9	Grimsby Town	2-0	Sprake	Reaney	Bell	Bremner	Goodwin	Hunter	Giles	Lawson 1	Weston 1	Collins	Johanneson
Nov 16	PRESTON NORTH END	1-1	Sprake	Reaney	Bell	Bremner	Goodwin	Hunter	Giles	Lawson	Storrie	Collins	Johanneson 1
Nov 23	Leyton Orient	2-0	Sprake	Wright	Bell	Bremner	Goodwin	Hunter	Giles	Lawson	Weston	Collins 1	Johanneson 1
Nov 30	SWANSEA TOWN	2-1	Sprake	Reaney	Bell 1	Bremner	Goodwin	Hunter	Giles	Lawson	Weston	Collins	Johanneson 1

DIVISION TWO 1963-64 continued

			1	2	3	4	5	6	7	8	9	10	11
Dec 7	Plymouth Argyle	1-0	Sprake	Reaney	Bell	Bremner	Goodwin	Hunter	Giles	Weston	Storrie	Collins	Johanneson 1
Dec 14	NORTHAMPTON TOWN	0-0	Sprake	Reaney	Bell	Bremner	Goodwin	Hunter	Giles	Weston	Storrie	Collins	Johanneson
Dec 21	Bury	2-1	Sprake	Reaney	Bell	Bremner	Goodwin	Hunter	Giles	Weston 1	Lawson 1	Collins	Johanneson
Dec 26	SUNDERLAND	1-1	Sprake	Reaney	Bell	Bremner	Goodwin	Hunter	Giles	Weston	Lawson 1	Collins	Johanneson
Dec 28	Sunderland	0-2	Sprake	Reaney	Bell	Bremner	Goodwin	Hunter	Weston	Weston	Lawson	Collins	Giles
Jan 11	MANCHESTER CITY	1-0	Sprake	Reaney	Bell	Bremner	Madeley	Hunter	Giles	Weston 1	Lawson	Collins	Johanneson
Jan 18	Swindon Town	2-2	Williamson	Reaney	Bell	Bremner	Madeley	Hunter 1	Giles 1	Weston	Lawson	Collins	Johanneson
Feb 1	CARDIFF CITY	1-1	Sprake	Reaney	Wright	Bremner	Bell	Hunter	Giles	Weston	Lawson	Collins	Johanneson 1
Feb 8	Norwich City	2-2	Sprake	Reaney	Bell	Bremner	Madeley	Hunter	Giles	Weston 1	Peacock 1	Collins	Johanneson
Feb 15	SCUNTHORPE UNITED	1-0	Sprake	Reaney	Hair	Bremner	Madeley	Hunter	Giles	Weston	Peacock	Collins	Johanneson 1
Feb 22	HUDDERSFIELD TOWN	1-1	Sprake	Reaney	Hair	Bremner	Charlton	Hunter	Giles	Storrie 1	Peacock	Collins	Johanneson
Mar 3	Preston North End	0-2	Sprake	Reaney	Hair	Bell	Charlton	Hunter	Giles	Storrie	Peacock	Collins	Johanneson
Mar 7	SOUTHAMPTON	3-1	Sprake	Reaney	Bell	Greenhoff	Charlton	Hunter	Weston	Lawson 1	Peacock	Collins 1	Johanneson 1
Mar 14	Middlesbrough	3-1	Sprake	Reaney	Bell	Greenhoff	Charlton	Hunter	Giles 1	Lawson 1	Peacock 1	Collins	Johanneson
Mar 21	GRIMSBY TOWN	3-1	Sprake	Reaney	Bell	Bremner 1	Charlton	Hunter	Giles	Lawson 1	Peacock 1	Collins	Johanneson
Mar 27	Newcastle United	1-0	Sprake	Reaney	Bell	Bremner	Charlton	Hunter	Giles 1	Lawson	Peacock	Collins	Johanneson
Mar 28	Derby County	1-1	Sprake	Reaney	Bell	Bremner	Charlton	Hunter	Giles	Lawson	Peacock 1	Collins	Johanneson
Mar 30	NEWCASTLE UNITED	2-1	Sprake	Reaney	Bell	Bremner	Charlton	Hunter	Giles	Weston 1	Peacock	Collins	Johanneson 1
Apr 4	LEYTON ORIENT	2-1	Sprake	Reaney	Bell	Bremner	Charlton	Hunter	Giles 1	Weston 1	Peacock	Collins	Johanneson
Apr 11	Swansea Town	3-0	Sprake	Reaney	Bell	Bremner	Charlton	Hunter	Giles 1	Weston	Peacock 2	Collins	Cooper
Apr 18	PLYMOUTH ARGYLE	1-1	Sprake	Reaney	Bell 1	Bremner	Charlton	Hunter	Giles	Weston	Peacock	Collins	Johanneson
Apr 25	Charlton Athletic	2-0	Sprake	Reaney	Bell	Bremner	Charlton	Hunter	Giles	Weston	Peacock 2	Collins	Cooper

LEAGUE CUP

Sep 25	MANSFIELD TOWN	Rd 2 5-1	Sprake	Reaney	Hair	Bell 1	Charlton	Hunter	Henderson	Lawson 2	Weston	Collins	Johanneson 2
Oct 22	SWANSEA TOWN	Rd 3 2-0	Sprake	Reaney	Bell	Greenhoff	Charlton	Bremner	Giles	Lorimer 1	Storrie 1	Lawson	Johanneson
Nov 27	Manchester City	Rd 4 1-3	Sprake	Hair	Bell	Smith	Goodwin	Hunter	Henderson	Weston 1	Storrie	Giles	Hawksby

F.A. CUP

Jan 4	Cardiff City	Rd 3 1-0	Sprake	Reaney	Bell	Bremner 1	Goodwin	Hunter	Henderson	Weston	Lawson	Giles	Johanneson
Jan 25	EVERTON	Rd 4 1-1	Sprake	Reaney	Bell	Bremner	Madeley	Hunter	Henderson	Giles	Lawson 1	Collins	Johanneson
Jan 28	Everton	Rd 4 R 0-2	Sprake	Reaney	Bell	Bremner	Madeley	Hunter	Henderson	Giles	Lawson	Collins	Hawksby

DIVISION ONE 1964-65

Aug 22	Aston Villa	2-1	Sprake	Reaney	Bell	Bremner	Charlton 1	Hunter	Giles	Weston	Storrie	Collins	Johanneson 1
Aug 26	LIVERPOOL	(o.g.) 4-2	Sprake	Reaney	Bell	Bremner 1	Charlton	Hunter	Giles 1	Weston 1	Storrie	Collins	Johanneson
Aug 29	WOLVERHAMPTON WANS	3-2	Sprake	Reaney	Bell	Bremner	Charlton 1	Hunter	Giles	Weston	Storrie 2	Lawson	Johanneson
Sep 2	Liverpool	1-2	Sprake	Reaney	Bell	Bremner	Charlton	Hunter	Giles	Weston	Storrie	Collins 1	Johanneson
Sep 5	Sunderland	3-3	Sprake	Reaney	Bell 1	Bremner	Charlton	Hunter	Giles	Lawson	Storrie 1	Collins	Johanneson 1
Sep 7	Blackpool	0-4	Sprake	Reaney	Cooper	Bremner	Charlton	Hunter	Giles	Lawson	Storrie	Collins	Johanneson
Sep 12	LEICESTER CITY	3-2	Sprake	Reaney	Cooper	Greenhoff	Charlton	Hunter	Giles	Bremner 2	Storrie	Collins	Johanneson 1
Sep 16	BLACKPOOL	3-0	Sprake	Reaney	Cooper	Bremner	Charlton	Hunter 1	Giles	Weston	Storrie	Collins 2	Johanneson
Sep 19	Chelsea	0-2	Sprake	Reaney	Bell	Greenhoff	Charlton	Hunter	Giles	Bremner	Storrie	Collins	Johanneson
Sep 26	NOTTINGHAM FOREST	1-2	Sprake	Reaney	Bell	Bremner	Charlton	Hunter	Henderson	Storrie 1	Belfitt	Collins	Johanneson
Sep 30	FULHAM	2-2	Sprake	Reaney	Bell	Bremner	Charlton	Hunter	Greenhoff	Weston	Storrie 2	Collins	Johanneson
Oct 10	Stoke City	3-2	Sprake	Reaney	Madeley	Bremner	Charlton	Hunter	Greenhoff 1	Storrie 2	Bell	Collins	Johanneson
Oct 17	TOTTENHAM HOTSPUR	3-1	Sprake	Reaney	Bell 1	Bremner	Charlton	Hunter	Giles 1	Storrie	Belfitt 1	Collins	Johanneson
Oct 24	Burnley	1-0	Sprake	Reaney	Bell 1	Bremner	Madeley	Hunter	Giles	Storrie	Belfitt	Collins	Johanneson
Oct 31	SHEFFIELD UNITED	4-1	Sprake	Reaney	Bell	Bremner	Charlton	Hunter	Giles	Storrie 1	Belfitt 1	Collins 1	Johanneson 1
Nov 7	Everton	1-0	Sprake	Reaney	Bell 1	Bremner	Charlton	Hunter	Giles	Storrie	Belfitt	Collins	Johanneson
Nov 11	ARSENAL	3-1	Sprake	Reaney	Bell	Bremner	Charlton 1	Hunter	Giles	Storrie 1	Belfitt 1	Collins	Johanneson
Nov 14	BIRMINGHAM CITY	4-1	Sprake	Reaney	Bell	Bremner	Charlton 1	Hunter	Giles 1	Storrie 1	Belfitt	Collins 1	Johanneson
Nov 21	West Ham United	1-3	Sprake	Reaney	Bell	Bremner	Charlton	Hunter	Giles	Storrie	Belfitt 1	Collins	Henderson
Nov 28	WEST BROMWICH ALBION	1-0	Williamson	Reaney	Bell	Bremner	Charlton	Hunter	Giles	Storrie	Johnson 1	Collins	Cooper
Dec 5	Manchester United	1-0	Sprake	Reaney	Bell	Bremner	Charlton	Hunter	Giles	Johnson	Storrie	Collins 1	Cooper
Dec 12	ASTON VILLA	1-0	Sprake	Reaney	Bell	Bremner	Charlton	Hunter	Giles	Storrie	Johnson	Collins	Johanneson 1
Dec 19	Wolverhampton Wans	1-0	Sprake	Reaney	Cooper	Bremner	Charlton	Hunter	Giles	Storrie	Johnson 1	Collins	Johanneson
Dec 26	BLACKBURN ROVERS	1-1	Sprake	Reaney	Bell	Bremner	Charlton	Hunter	Giles	Storrie 1	Johnson	Collins	Johanneson
Dec 28	Blackburn Rovers	2-0	Sprake	Reaney	Cooper	Bremner	Madeley	Hunter	Giles	Storrie 1	Johnson	Collins	Johanneson 1
Jan 2	SUNDERLAND	2-1	Sprake	Reaney	Madeley	Bremner	Charlton 1	Hunter 1	Giles	Storrie	Johnson	Collins	Cooper
Jan 16	Leicester City	2-2	Sprake	Reaney	Bell	Bremner	Charlton 1	Hunter	Giles	Storrie	Johnson 1	Collins	Johanneson
Jan 23	CHELSEA	2-2	Sprake	Reaney	Bell	Bremner	Charlton	Hunter	Giles 1	Greenhoff	Storrie 1	Collins	Johanneson
Feb 6	Nottingham Forest	0-0	Sprake	Reaney	Bell	Bremner	Charlton	Hunter	Giles	Weston	Storrie	Collins	Cooper
Feb 13	Arsenal	2-1	Sprake	Reaney	Bell	Bremner	Charlton	Hunter	Giles 1	Weston 1	Storrie	Collins	Cooper
Feb 27	Tottenham Hotspur	0-0	Sprake	Reaney	Bell	Bremner	Charlton	Hunter	Giles	Storrie	Peacock	Collins	Johanneson
Mar 13	Fulham	2-2	Sprake	Reaney	Bell	Bremner	Charlton	Hunter	Giles	Weston	Peacock 1	Collins 1	Cooper
Mar 15	BURNLEY	5-1	Sprake	Reaney	Bell	Bremner	Charlton 2	Hunter	Giles	Storrie	Peacock	Collins 2	Johanneson 1
Mar 20	EVERTON	4-1	Sprake	Bell	Cooper	Bremner 1	Madeley	Hunter	Giles	Storrie	Peacock 1	Collins	Johanneson 2
Apr 3	WEST HAM UNITED	2-1	Sprake	Reaney	Bell	Bremner 1	Charlton	Hunter	Giles	Storrie	Peacock 1	Collins	Cooper
Apr 5	STOKE CITY	3-1	Sprake	Reaney	Bell	Bremner	Charlton	Greenhoff 1	Johnson	Weston 2	Peacock	Collins	Giles
Apr 12	West Bromwich Albion	2-1	Sprake	Reaney	Bell	Greenhoff	Charlton	Hunter	Giles	Weston	Peacock 2	Collins	Cooper
Apr 17	MANCHESTER UNITED	0-1	Sprake	Reaney	Bell	Greenhoff	Charlton	Hunter	Giles	Weston	Peacock	Collins	Cooper
Apr 19	Sheffield Wednesday	0-3	Sprake	Reaney	Bell	Madeley	Charlton	Hunter	Greenhoff	Bremner	Storrie	Weston	Giles
Apr 20	SHEFFIELD WEDNESDAY	2-0	Sprake	Reaney	Bell	Bremner	Charlton	Hunter	Giles 1	Lorimer	Storrie 1	Weston	Johanneson
Apr 24	Sheffield United	3-0	Sprake	Reaney	Bell	Bremner 1	Charlton	Hunter	Giles	Storrie 1	Peacock 1	Collins	Johanneson
Apr 26	Birmingham City	3-3	Sprake	Reaney 1	Cooper	Bremner	Charlton 1	Hunter	Giles 1	Weston	Peacock	Collins	Johanneson

LEAGUE CUP

Sep 23	HUDDERSFIELD TOWN	3-2	Williamson	Wright	Bell	Bremner	Charlton	Hunter 1	Henderson	Storrie 1	Belfitt 1	Johnson	Cooper
Oct 14	ASTON VILLA	2-3	Williamson	Wright	Bell	Madeley	Charlton	Hunter	Greenhoff	Henderson	Belffit	Collins 1	Johanneson 1

F.A. CUP

Jan 9	SOUTHPORT	Rd 3 3-0	Sprake	Reaney	Cooper	Bremner	Charlton	Hunter	Greenhoff 1	Storrie	Johnson 1	Collins	Johanneson 1
Jan 30	EVERTON	Rd 4 1-1	Sprake	Reaney	Bell	Bremner	Charlton	Hunter	Giles	Weston	Storrie 1	Collins	Johanneson
Feb 2	Everton	Rd 4 R 2-1	Sprake	Reaney	Bell	Bremner	Charlton 1	Hunter	Giles	Weston 1	Storrie	Collins	Cooper
Feb 20	SHREWSBURY TOWN	Rd 5 2-0	Sprake	Reaney	Bell	Bremner	Charlton	Hunter	Giles 1	Weston	Storrie	Collins	Johanneson 1
Mar 10	Crystal Palace	Rd 6 3-0	Sprake	Reaney	Bell	Bremner	Charlton	Hunter	Giles	Storrie 1	Peacock 2	Collins	Cooper
Mar 27	Manchester United (at Sheffield Wednesday)	SF 0-0	Sprake	Reaney	Bell	Bremner	Charlton	Hunter	Giles	Storrie	Peacock	Collins	Johanneson
Mar 31	Manchester United (at Nottingham Forest)	SF 1-0	Sprake	Reaney	Bell	Bremner 1	Charlton	Hunter	Giles	Storrie	Peacock	Collins	Cooper
May 1	Liverpool (at Wembley)	Final 1-2 (AET)	Sprake	Reaney	Bell	Bremner 1	Charlton	Hunter	Giles	Storrie	Peacock	Collins	Johanneson

DIVISION ONE 1965-66

Aug 21	SUNDERLAND	1-0	Sprake	Reaney	Bell	Bremner	Charlton	Hunter 1	Giles	Weston	Peacock	Collins	Cooper	
Aug 23	Aston Villa	2-0	Sprake	Reaney	Bell	Bremner	Charlton	Hunter	Giles	Weston	Peacock 1	Collins	Cooper 1	
Aug 28	West Ham United	1-2	Sprake	Reaney	Bell	Bremner	Charlton	Hunter	Weston	Lorimer	Peacock 1	Giles	Cooper	
Sep 1	ASTON VILLA	2-0	Sprake	Reaney	Bell	Bremner	Charlton*	Hunter	Giles	Lorimer	Peacock 2	Collins	Johanneson	Johnson*
Sep 4	NOTTINGHAM FOREST	2-1	Sprake	Reaney	Bell* 1	Bremner	Charlton	Hunter	Giles	Lorimer 1	Peacock	Collins	Johanneson	Cooper*
Sep 8	Tottenham Hotspur	(o.g.) 2-3	Sprake	Reaney	Cooper	Bremner	Charlton	Hunter	Giles	Lorimer 1	Peacock	Collins	Johanneson	
Sep 11	SHEFFIELD UNITED	2-2	Sprake	Reaney	Cooper	Bremner 1	Charlton	Hunter 1	Giles	Lorimer	Peacock	Collins	Johanneson*	Johnson*
Sep 15	TOTTENHAM HOTSPUR	2-0	Sprake	Reaney	Cooper	Bremner 1	Charlton 1	Hunter	Giles	Lorimer	Peacock	Collins	Johanneson*	Madeley*
Sep 18	Leicester City	3-3	Sprake	Reaney	Madeley 1	Bremner	Charlton	Hunter	Giles	Lorimer	Peacock 2	Collins	Cooper	
Sep 25	BLACKBURN ROVERS	3-0	Sprake	Reaney	Madeley	Bremner	Charlton	Hunter	Giles	Lorimer 2	Peacock	Collins	Cooper 1	
Oct 9	Sheffield Wednesday	0-0	Sprake	Reaney	Madeley	Bremner	Charlton	Hunter	Giles	Lorimer	Peacock	Johnson	Storrie	
Oct 16	NORTHAMPTON TOWN	6-1	Sprake	Reaney	Bell	Bremner 1	Charlton 1	Hunter	Storrie 1	Lorimer 2	Peacock 1	Giles	O'Grady	
Oct 23	Stoke City	2-1	Sprake	Reaney	Bell	Bremner	Charlton	Hunter	Storrie	Lorimer	Peacock 1	Giles	O'Grady 1	
Oct 30	BURNLEY	1-1	Sprake	Reaney	Bell	Bremner	Charlton	Hunter*	Storrie 1	Lorimer	Peacock	Giles	O'Grady	Madeley*
Nov 6	Chelsea	0-1	Sprake	Reaney	Bell	Bremner	Charlton	Hunter	Storrie	Lorimer	Peacock	Giles	Johnson	
Nov 13	ARSENAL	2-0	Sprake	Reaney	Madeley	Bremner 1	Charlton	Hunter	Storrie	Lorimer	Peacock*	Giles 1	O'Grady	Cooper*
Nov 20	Everton	0-0	Sprake	Reaney	Madeley	Bremner	Charlton	Hunter	Storrie	Lorimer	Bell	Giles	O'Grady	
Dec 11	WEST BROMWICH ALBION	4-0	Sprake	Reaney	Bell	Bremner	Charlton	Hunter	Storrie 1	Lorimer	Peacock	Giles 2	O'Grady 1	
Dec 27	Liverpool	1-0	Sprake	Reaney	Bell	Bremner	Charlton	Hunter	Storrie	Lorimer 1	Peacock	Giles*	O'Grady	Madeley*
Dec 28	LIVERPOOL	0-1	Sprake	Reaney	Bell	Madeley	Charlton	Hunter	Storrie	Lorimer	Peacock	Bremner	O'Grady	
Jan 1	SHEFFIELD WEDNESDAY	3-0	Sprake	Reaney	Bell	Bremner	Charlton	Hunter	Greenhoff	Storrie 1	Peacock 1	Gray 1	O'Grady	
Jan 8	West Bromwich Albion	2-1	Sprake	Reaney	Bell	Bremner	Charlton	Hunter	Greenhoff	Storrie	Peacock 1	Giles 1	O'Grady	
Jan 12	MANCHESTER UNITED	1-1	Sprake	Reaney	Bell	Bremner	Charlton	Hunter	Greenhoff	Storrie 1	Peacock	Giles	O'Grady	
Jan 15	STOKE CITY	2-2	Sprake	Reaney	Bell	Bremner	Charlton	Hunter	O'Grady 1	Storrie 1	Peacock	Giles	Johanneson	
Jan 29	Sunderland	0-2	Sprake	Reaney	Bell	Bremner	Madeley	Hunter	O'Grady	Lorimer	Peacock*	Giles	Johanneson	Johnson*

DIVISION ONE 1965-66 continued

Date	Opponent	Score	1	2	3	4	5	6	7	8	9	10	11	SUBS
Feb 5	WEST HAM UNITED	5-0	Sprake	Reaney*	Bell	Bremner 1	Charlton	Hunter 2	Storrie 1	Lorimer 1	Belfitt	Giles	O'Grady	Madeley*
Feb 19	Nottingham Forest	4-0	Sprake	Reaney	Bell	Bremner	Charlton	Hunter	Storrie	Lorimer 2	Madeley*	Giles 1	O'Grady	Hibbitt* 1
Feb 26	Sheffield United	1-1	Sprake	Reaney	Bell 1	Bremner	Charlton	Hunter	Storrie	O'Grady	Lorimer	Giles	Cooper	
Mar 5	Northampton Town	1-2	Sprake	Reaney	Bell	Bremner	Charlton	Hunter	O'Grady 1	Lorimer	Storrie	Giles	Cooper	
Mar 12	LEICESTER CITY	3-2	Sprake	Reaney	Cooper	Bremner	Charlton 2	Hunter 1	Greenhoff	Lorimer	Storrie	Giles	O'Grady	
Mar 19	Blackburn Rovers	3-2	Sprake	Reaney	Cooper	Bremner 1	Charlton	Hunter	Greenhoff	Lorimer 1	Storrie 1	Giles	O'Grady	
Mar 26	BLACKPOOL	1-2	Sprake	Reaney	Bell	Gray	Charlton 1	Hunter	O'Grady	Lorimer	Storrie	Giles	Cooper	
Mar 28	Blackpool	0-1	Sprake	Reaney	Bell	Bremner	Charlton	Hunter	Gray	Storrie	Belfitt	Giles	O'Grady	
Apr 4	CHELSEA	(o.g.) 2-0	Sprake	Reaney	Bell	Bremner 1	Charlton	Hunter	O'Grady	Lorimer	Madeley*	Giles	Johanneson	Greenhoff*
Apr 8	Fulham	3-1	Sprake	Reaney	Bell	Bremner 1	Charlton	Hunter	O'Grady	Lorimer	Storrie 1	Giles	Johanneson 1	
Apr 12	FULHAM	0-1	Harvey	Reaney	Bell	Bremner	Charlton	Hunter	O'Grady*	Lorimer	Storrie	Giles	Johanneson	Greenhoff*
Apr 16	EVERTON	4-1	Harvey	Bell	Cooper	Greenhoff	Charlton	Hunter	Lorimer	Bremner	Storrie	Giles*	Johanneson	Gray*
Apr 30	NEWCASTLE UNITED	(o.g.) 3-0	Sprake	Reaney	Bell	Bremner	Charlton	Hunter	Greenhoff	Lorimer 1	Storrie 1	Giles	O'Grady	
May 5	Arsenal	3-0	Sprake	Reaney	Bell	Bremner	Charlton	Hunter	Greenhoff 1	Lorimer	Storrie 2	Giles	O'Grady	
May 7	Burnley	(o.g.) 1-0	Sprake	Reaney	Bell	Bremner	Charlton	Hunter	Greenhoff*	Lorimer	Storrie	Giles	O'Grady	Cooper*
May 16	Newcastle United	0-2	Sprake	Reaney	Bell	Bremner	Charlton	Hunter	O'Grady	Lorimer	Storrie	Giles	Cooper	
May 19	Manchester United	1-1	Sprake	Reaney 1	Greenhoff	Bremner	Bell	O'Grady	Storrie	Giles	Belfitt	Collins	Johanneson	

LEAGUE CUP

Date	Opponent	Score	1	2	3	4	5	6	7	8	9	10	11	SUBS
Sep 22	HARTLEPOOL UNITED	Rd 2 4-2	Sprake	Reaney	Madeley	Johnson 1	Charlton	Hunter	Giles	Storrie 1	Belfitt 1	Bates	Cooper 1	
Oct 13	WEST BROMWICH ALBION	Rd 3 2-4	Harvey	Davey	Bell	Storrie	Madeley 1	Wright	Weston	Belfitt 1	Hawkins	Johnson	Cooper	

F.A. CUP

Date	Opponent	Score	1	2	3	4	5	6	7	8	9	10	11	SUBS
Jan 22	BURY	Rd 3 6-0	Williamson	Reaney 1	Bell	Bremner	Charlton	Hunter	Greenhoff 1	Lorimer 3	Peacock	Giles 1	Johanneson	
Feb 12	Chelsea	Rd 4 0-1	Sprake	Reaney	Bell	Bremner	Charlton	Hunter	Storrie	Lorimer	Madeley	Giles	O'Grady	

INTER-CITIES – FAIRS CUP

Date	Opponent	Score	1	2	3	4	5	6	7	8	9	10	11	SUBS
Sep 29	TORINO	Rd 1 2-1	Sprake	Reaney	Madeley	Bremner 1	Charlton	Hunter	Giles	Lorimer	Peacock 1	Collins	Cooper	
Oct 6	Torino	Rd 1 0-0	Sprake	Reaney	Madeley	Bremner	Charlton	Hunter	Giles	Lorimer	Peacock	Collins	Cooper	
Nov 24	S.C. Leipzig	Rd 2 2-1	Sprake	Reaney	Charlton	Bremner 1	Hunter	Storrie	Lorimer 1	Bell	Madeley	Giles	O'Grady	
Dec 1	S.C. LEIPZIG	Rd 2 0-0	Sprake	Reaney	Bell	Bremner	Charlton	Hunter	Storrie	Lorimer	Peacock	Giles	O'Grady	
Feb 2	VALENCIA	Rd 3 1-1	Sprake	Reaney	Bell	Bremner	Charlton	Hunter	Storrie	Lorimer	Belfitt	Giles	O'Grady	
Feb 16	Valencia	Rd 3 1-0	Sprake	Reaney	Bell	Bremner	Charlton	Hunter	Storrie	Lorimer	Madeley	Giles	O'Grady 1	
Mar 2	UJPEST DOZSA	Rd 4 4-1	Sprake	Reaney	Bell 1	Bremner 1	Charlton	Hunter	O'Grady	Lorimer	Storrie 1	Giles	Cooper 1	
Mar 9	Ujpest Dozsa	Rd 4 1-1	Sprake	Reaney	Bell	Bremner	Charlton	Hunter	O'Grady	Lorimer 1	Storrie	Giles	Cooper	
Apr 20	Real Zaragoza	S/F 0-1	Sprake	Reaney	Bell	Bremner	Charlton	Hunter	Greenhoff	E Gray	Storrie	Giles	Johanneson	
Apr 27	REAL ZARAGOZA	S/F 2-1	Sprake	Reaney	Bell	Bremner	Charlton 1	Hunter	Greenhoff	Gray	Storrie	Giles	Johanneson 1	
May 11	REAL ZARAGOZA	S/F R 1-3	Sprake	Reaney	Bell	Bremner	Charlton 1	Hunter	Greenhoff	Lorimer	Storrie	Giles	O'Grady	

DIVISION ONE 1966-67

Date	Opponent	Score	1	2	3	4	5	6	7	8	9	10	11	SUBS
Aug 20	Tottenham Hotspur	1-3	Sprake	Reaney	Bell	Bremner	Madeley	Hunter	Lorimer	Collins	Belfitt	Giles*1	Greenhoff	Cooper*
Aug 24	WEST BROMWICH ALBION	2-1	Sprake	Reaney	Bell 1	Bremner	Madeley	Hunter	Greenhoff	Collins*	Lorimer	Giles 1	Johanneson	Cooper*
Aug 27	MANCHESTER UNITED	3-1	Sprake	Reaney 1	Cooper	Bremner	Bell	Hunter	Lorimer 1	Gray	Madeley 1	Giles	Johanneson	
Aug 31	West Bromwich Albion	0-2	Sprake	Reaney	Bell	Bremner	Charlton	Hunter	Lorimer	Gray	Madeley	Giles	Greenhoff	
Sep 3	Burnley	1-1	Sprake	Reaney	Cooper	Bremner	Bell	Hunter	Lorimer	Bates	Madeley	Gray 1	Johanneson	
Sep 7	SUNDERLAND	2-1	Sprake	Reaney	Cooper	Bremner	Bell	Hunter	Lorimer	Gray	Madeley	Giles 1	Johanneson*1	Greenhoff*
Sep 10	NOTTINGHAM FOREST	1-1	Sprake	Reaney	Cooper	Bremner	Gray *1	Hunter	Lorimer	Bates	Madeley	Giles	Johanneson	Storrie*
Sep 17	Fulham	2-2	Sprake	Reaney	Bell	Bremner	Charlton	Hunter	Lorimer 1	Madeley	Belfitt	Giles	Johanneson 1	
Sep 24	EVERTON	1-1	Sprake	Reaney	Bell	Bremner	Charlton	Hunter	Lorimer	Gray	Peacock	Giles 1	Johanneson*	Madeley*
Oct 1	Stoke City	0-0	Sprake	Reaney	Bell	Bremner	Charlton	Madeley	Storrie	Gray	Peacock	Giles	Johanneson	
Oct 8	Aston Villa	0-3	Sprake	Reaney	Bell	Bremner	Charlton	Hunter*	Storrie	Madeley	Gray	Giles	Johanneson	Lorimer*
Oct 15	ARSENAL	3-1	Sprake	Reaney	Bell 1	Bremner	Charlton	Hunter	O'Grady	Greenhoff	Madeley 1	Giles 1	Johanneson	
Oct 29	SOUTHAMPTON	0-1	Harvey	Reaney	Bell	Bremner	Charlton	Hunter	Giles	Greenhoff	Madeley	Gray	Johanneson*	Lorimer*
Nov 5	Arsenal	1-0	Harvey	Reaney	Bell	Bremner	Charlton 1	Hunter	Madeley	Belfitt	Greenhoff	Giles	O'Grady	
Nov 12	LEICESTER CITY	3-1	Sprake	Reaney	Bell	Bremner	Charlton	Hunter	O'Grady	Gray	Greenhoff 1	Giles 2	Cooper	
Nov 19	Liverpool	0-5	Sprake	Reaney	Bell	Bremner	Charlton	Hunter	O'Grady	Madeley	Greenhoff	Giles	Cooper	
Nov 26	WEST HAM UNITED	2-1	Sprake	Reaney	Bell	Bremner	Charlton	Hunter	O'Grady	Lorimer	Greenhoff	Giles* 1	Johanneson 1	Storrie*
Dec 3	Sheffield Wednesday	0-0	Sprake	Reaney	Bell	Bremner	Charlton	Hunter*	O'Grady	Lorimer	Greenhoff	Collins	Johanneson	
Dec 10	BLACKPOOL	1-1	Sprake	Reaney	Bell	Bremner	Charlton	Hunter	Lorimer	Gray	Greenhoff 1	Collins	Johanneson	
Dec 17	TOTTENHAM HOTSPUR	3-2	Sprake	Reaney	Bell	Bremner	Charlton	Hunter	O'Grady	Gray 1	Greenhoff 2	Collins	Johanneson	
Dec 24	Newcastle United	2-1	Sprake	Reaney	Bell	Bremner	Charlton	Hunter	O'Grady 1	Gray	Greenhoff	Collins	Johanneson 1	
Dec 26	NEWCASTLE UNITED	5-0	Sprake	Reaney	Bell	Bremner	Charlton 1	Hunter	O'Grady	Lorimer 2	Storrie 1	Gray	Cooper 1	
Dec 31	Manchester United	0-0	Sprake	Reaney	Bell	Bremner	Charlton	Hunter	O'Grady	Lorimer	Greenhoff*	Gray	Johanneson	Cooper*
Jan 7	BURNLEY	3-1	Sprake	Reaney	Bell	Bremner	Charlton	Hunter	O'Grady	Lorimer	Greenhoff 1	Gray	Johanneson 2	
Jan 14	Nottingham Forest	0-1	Sprake	Reaney	Bell	Bremner	Charlton	Hunter	O'Grady	Lorimer	Greenhoff	Gray	Johanneson*	Cooper*
Jan 21	FULHAM	3-1	Sprake	Reaney	Cooper	Bremner	Madeley	Hunter	O'Grady	Giles 1	Greenhoff 1	Gray	Johanneson 1	
Feb 4	Everton	0-2	Sprake	Reaney	Bell	Bremner	Charlton	Hunter	Madeley	Giles	Lorimer	Gray	Cooper*	
Feb 11	STOKE CITY	3-0	Sprake	Madeley	Bell 1	Bremner	Charlton	Hunter	Collins	Lorimer 1	Belfitt 1	Gray	Johanneson*	Hibbitt*
Feb 25	ASTON VILLA	0-2	Sprake	Reaney	Bell	Madeley	Charlton	Hunter	Giles	Lorimer	Belfitt	Gray	Hibbitt*	Greenhoff*
Mar 4	Southampton	2-0	Sprake	Reaney	Bell	Bremner	Charlton 1	Hunter	Lorimer	Madeley	Greenhoff	Giles 1	Gray	Belfitt*
Mar 18	MANCHESTER CITY	0-0	Sprake	Reaney	Bell	Madeley	Charlton	Hunter	Johnson	Lorimer	Greenhoff	Bates	Hibbitt	
Mar 25	Blackpool	2-0	Sprake	Reaney	Bell	Bremner 1	Charlton 1	Hunter	Bates	Madeley	Peacock	Giles	Cooper	
Mar 27	Sheffield United	(o.g.) 4-1	Sprake	Reaney	Bell	Bremner 1	Charlton	Hunter	Bates	Madeley	Peacock 1	Giles 1	Cooper	
Mar 28	SHEFFIELD UNITED	2-0	Sprake	Reaney	Bell	Bremner	Charlton 1	Hunter	Greenhoff	Madeley	Peacock 1	Giles	Cooper	
Apr 1	CHELSEA	1-0	Sprake	Reaney	Bell	Bremner	Charlton	Hunter	Lorimer 1	Madeley	Greenhoff	Giles	Cooper	
Apr 10	Leicester City	0-0	Sprake	Reaney	Madeley	Bremner	Bell	Hunter	Giles	Belfitt	Greenhoff	Gray	Cooper	
Apr 22	West Ham United	1-0	Sprake	Reaney	Cooper	Bremner	Madeley	Hunter	Lorimer 1	Belfitt	Greenhoff	Gray	Johanneson*	Bates*
May 3	LIVERPOOL	2-1	Sprake	Reaney	Bell	Bremner	Hunter	Giles 1	Lorimer	Greenhoff 1	Cooper	Gray	Bates	
May 6	Chelsea	2-2	Sprake	Reaney	Bell	Greenhoff	Hunter	Gray	Bates	Lorimer 1	Belfitt 1	Giles	Cooper	
May 8	Manchester City	1-2	Sprake	Reaney	Cooper	Gray	Bell	Hunter	Johnson	Belfitt 1	Greenhoff	Giles	Lorimer	
May 13	Sunderland	2-0	Sprake	Reaney	Bell	Gray 1	Madeley	Hunter	O'Grady	Lorimer 1	Greenhoff*	Giles	Cooper	Belfitt*
May 15	SHEFFIELD WEDNESDAY	1-0	Harvey	Reaney	Cooper	Lumsden	Peacock	Gray*	Bates	Hawkins	Johnson	Belfitt	Hibbitt 1	Bremner*

LEAGUE CUP

Date	Opponent	Score	1	2	3	4	5	6	7	8	9	10	11	SUBS
Sep 13	NEWCASTLE UNITED	Rd 2 1-0	Harvey	Reaney	Bell	Bremner	Charlton	Hunter	Lorimer	Madeley	Peacock 1	Giles	Johanneson	
Oct 4	Preston North End	Rd 3 1-1	Sprake	Reaney	Bell	Bremner	Charlton	Madeley	Storrie 1	Gray	Peacock	Giles	Greenhoff	
Oct 12	PRESTON NORTH END	Rd 3 R 3-0	Sprake	Reaney	Bell	Bremner	Charlton	Hunter	O'Grady	Lorimer 2	Greenhoff 1	Madeley	Johanneson	
Nov 7	West Ham United	Rd 4 0-7	Harvey	Reaney	Bell	Bremner	Charlton	Hunter	Madeley	Belfitt	Greenhoff*	Giles	O'Grady	Bates*

F.A. CUP

Date	Opponent	Score	1	2	3	4	5	6	7	8	9	10	11	SUBS
Jan 28	CRYSTAL PALACE	Rd 3 3-0	Sprake	Reaney	Bell 1	Bremner	Charlton	Hunter	O'Grady 1	Giles	Greenhoff*	Gray	Johanneson 1	Madeley*
Feb 18	WEST BROMWICH ALBION	Rd 4 5-0	Sprake	Reaney	Bell	Madeley 1	Charlton	Hunter	Giles	Lorimer 2	Belfitt 2	Gray	O'Grady*	Bates*
Mar 11	Sunderland	Rd 5 1-1	Sprake	Reaney	Bell	Bremner	Charlton 1	Hunter	Madeley	Belfitt	Greenhoff	Giles	Lorimer	
Mar 15	SUNDERLAND	Rd 5 R (AET) 1-1	Sprake	Reaney	Bell	Bremner	Charlton	Hunter	Lorimer	Belfitt	Greenhoff	Giles 1	Johanneson*	Cooper*
Mar 20	Sunderland (At Hull City)	Rd 5 2R 2-1	Sprake	Reaney	Bell	Bremner	Charlton	Hunter	Lorimer	Belfitt 1	Greenhoff	Giles 1	Cooper	
Apr 8	MANCHESTER CITY	Rd 6 1-0	Sprake	Reaney	Bell	Bremner	Charlton 1	Hunter	Lorimer	Madeley	Peacock*	Giles	Gray	Greenhoff*
Apr 29	Chelsea (At Aston Villa)	S/F 0-1	Sprake	Reaney	Bell	Hunter	Madeley	Bremner	Giles	Belfitt*	Greenhoff	Gray	Cooper	Lorimer*

INTER-CITIES FAIRS CUP

Date	Opponent	Score	1	2	3	4	5	6	7	8	9	10	11	SUBS
Oct 18	DWS Amsterdam	Rd 2 3-1	Sprake	Reaney	Bell	Bremner 1	Charlton	Hunter	O'Grady	Greenhoff 1	Madeley	Giles	Johanneson 1	
Oct 26	DWS AMSTERDAM	Rd 2 5-1	Sprake	Reaney	Bell	Bremner	Charlton	Hunter	Storrie	Madeley 1	Greenhoff	Giles 1	Johanneson 3	
Jan 18	VALENCIA	Rd 3 1-1	Sprake	Reaney	Madeley	Bremner	Charlton	Hunter	Giles	Gray	Greenhoff 1	Collins	Cooper	
Feb 8	Valencia	Rd 3 2-0	Sprake	Madeley	Bell	Bremner	Charlton	Hunter	Giles 1	Lorimer 1	Belfitt	Gray	Hibbitt	
Mar 22	Bologna	Rd 4 0-1	Sprake	Reaney	Bell	Bremner	Charlton	Hunter	Lorimer	Belfitt	Madeley	Giles	Cooper	
Apr 19	BOLOGNA (Won on toss of coin)	Rd 4 1-0	Sprake	Reaney	Madeley	Bremner	Bell	Hunter	Giles 1	Belfitt	Greenhoff	Gray	Cooper	
May 19	KILMARNOCK	S/F 4-2	Sprake	Reaney	Bell	Bremner	Madeley	Hunter	O'Grady	Lorimer	Belfitt 3	Giles 1	Gray	
May 24	Kilmarnock	S/F 0-0	Sprake	Reaney	Bell	Bremner	Madeley	Hunter	Lorimer	Gray	Belfitt	Giles	Cooper	
Aug 30	Dinamo Zagreb	FINAL 0-2	Sprake	Reaney	Cooper	Bremner	Charlton	Hunter	Bates	Lorimer	Belfitt	Gray	O'Grady	
Sep 6	DINAMO ZAGREB	FINAL 0-0	Sprake	Bull	Cooper	Bremner	Charlton	Hunter	Reaney	Belfitt	Greenhoff	Giles	O'Grady	

GLASGOW CHARITY CUP

Date	Opponent	Score	1	2	3	4	5	6	7	8	9	10	11	SUBS
Aug 10	Glasgow Select XI (At Hampden Park)	1-1	Sprake	Reaney	Bell	Bremner	Charlton*	Hunter	Storrie	Collins	Lorimer	Giles 1	Gray	Madeley*

DIVISION ONE 1967-68

Date	Opponent	Score	1	2	3	4	5	6	7	8	9	10	11	SUBS
Aug 19	SUNDERLAND	1-1	Sprake	Reaney	Bell	Bremner	Charlton	Hunter	O'Grady	Madeley	Greenhoff 1	Gray	Johanneson	
Aug 23	Manchester United	0-1	Sprake	Reaney	Madeley	Bremner	Charlton	Hunter	O'Grady	Lorimer	Gray	Giles	Cooper	
Aug 26	Wolverhampton Wans	0-2	Sprake	Reaney	Cooper	Bremner	Charlton	Hunter	Lorimer	Greenhoff*	Belfitt	Gray	O'Grady	Bates*
Sep 2	FULHAM	2-0	Sprake	Reaney	Cooper	Bremner	Charlton	Hunter	Lorimer	Greenhoff	Belfitt 2	Gray	O'Grady	
Sep 9	Southampton	1-1	Sprake	Reaney	Bell	Bremner	Charlton	Hunter	Lorimer 1	Belfitt	Greenhoff	Gray	Cooper	

DIVISION ONE 1967-68 continued

			1	2	3	4	5	6	7	8	9	10	11	SUBS
Sep 16	Everton	1-0	Sprake	Reaney	Bell	Bremner	Charlton	Hunter	Lorimer	Gray 1	Giles	Cooper	O'Grady	
Sep 20	BURNLEY	2-1	Sprake	Reaney	Cooper	Bremner	Charlton	Hunter	Greenhoff*	Lorimer 2	Madeley	Gray	Hibbitt	Johnson*
Sep 23	LEICESTER CITY	3-2	Sprake	Madeley	Cooper	Bremner	Charlton	Hunter	Greenhoff 1	Lorimer 2	Jones	Gray*	Hibbitt	Reaney*
Sep 30	West Ham United	0-0	Sprake	Reaney	Cooper	Bremner	Charlton	Hunter	Greenhoff	Madeley	Jones	Gray	Lorimer	
Oct 7	CHELSEA	(o.g.) 7-0	Sprake	Reaney	Madeley	Bremner 1	Charlton 1	Hunter	Greenhoff 1	Lorimer 1	Jones*	Gray 1	Johanneson 1	Hibbitt*
Oct 14	West Bromwich Albion	0-2	Sprake	Reaney	Cooper	Madeley	Charlton	Hunter	Greenhoff*	Lorimer	Jones	Gray	Giles	Johanneson*
Oct 25	NEWCASTLE UNITED	2-0	Sprake	Reaney	Cooper	Madeley	Charlton	Hunter	Bates	Lorimer 1	Greenhoff	Gray	Johanneson 1	
Oct 28	Manchester City	0-1	Sprake	Reaney	Cooper	Madeley	Charlton	Hunter	Greenhoff	Lorimer	Jones	Gray	Johanneson	
Nov 4	ARSENAL	3-1	Sprake	Reaney	Cooper	Madeley	Charlton	Hunter	Greenhoff	Lorimer 1	Jones *1	Gray 1	Johanneson	Hibbitt*
Nov 8	MANCHESTER UNITED	1-0	Sprake	Reaney	Cooper	Bremner	Charlton	Hunter	Greenhoff 1	Lorimer	Madeley	Gray	Johanneson	
Nov 11	Sheffield United	0-1	Sprake	Reaney	Cooper	Bremner	Charlton*	Hunter	Greenhoff	Lorimer	Madeley	Gray	Johanneson	Hibbitt*
Nov 18	COVENTRY CITY	1-1	Sprake	Reaney	Cooper	Bremner	Madeley	Hunter	Greenhoff	Lorimer 1	Belfitt	Bates	Hibbitt	
Nov 25	Nottingham Forest	2-0	Harvey	Reaney	Cooper	Bremner	Madeley	Hunter	Greenhoff 1	Belfitt	Hawkins*	Bates	Hibbitt	Lorimer *1
Dec 2	STOKE CITY	2-0	Sprake	Reaney	Cooper	Bremner	Charlton	Hunter	Lorimer 1	Belfitt	Madeley 1	Gray	Hibbitt	
Dec 9	Liverpool	0-2	Sprake	Reaney	Cooper	Bremner	Charlton	Hunter	Greenhoff	Lorimer	Madeley	Belfitt	Gray	
Dec 16	Sunderland	2-2	Sprake	Reaney	Cooper	Bremner	Charlton	Hunter	Greenhoff 1	Lorimer	Madeley	Gray 1	Hibbitt	
Dec 23	WOLVERHAMPTON WANS	2-1	Sprake	Reaney	Cooper	Bremner	Charlton 1	Hunter	Greenhoff	Lorimer	Jones 1	Gray	Giles	Madeley*
Dec 26	Sheffield Wednesday	1-0	Sprake	Reaney	Cooper	Bremner	Charlton	Hunter	Greenhoff	Madeley	Jones	Giles 1	Gray	
Dec 30	SHEFFIELD WEDNESDAY	3-2	Sprake	Reaney	Cooper	Bremner	Charlton	Hunter 1	Greenhoff 1	Madeley	Jones	Giles	Gray 1	
Jan 6	Fulham	5-0	Sprake	Reaney	Cooper	Bremner	Charlton	Hunter	Greenhoff 3	Lorimer	Jones 2	Giles	Gray	
Jan 13	SOUTHAMPTON	5-0	Sprake	Reaney	Cooper	Bates	Madeley 2	Hunter	Greenhoff	Lorimer 1	Jones 1	Giles	Hibbitt 1	
Jan 20	EVERTON	2-0	Sprake	Reaney	Cooper	Bremner	Charlton	Hunter	Greenhoff	Lorimer	Jones 1	Giles 1	Johanneson	
Feb 3	Leicester City	2-2	Sprake	Reaney	Cooper	Bremner	Madeley 1	Hunter	Greenhoff	Lorimer	Jones	Giles 1	Johanneson	
Feb 10	WEST HAM UNITED	2-1	Sprake	Reaney	Cooper	Bremner	Madeley	Hunter	Greenhoff	Lorimer 2	Belfitt	Giles	Johanneson*	Hibbitt*
Mar 13	NOTTINGHAM FOREST	1-1	Sprake	Reaney	Cooper	Bremner 1	Charlton	Hunter	Greenhoff	Lorimer	Jones	Bates*	Hibbitt	Madeley*
Mar 16	Newcastle United	1-1	Sprake	Reaney	Madeley	Bremner	Charlton	Hunter 1	Greenhoff	Belfitt	Jones	Giles	O'Grady	
Mar 20	Chelsea	0-0	Sprake	Reaney	Cooper	Bremner	Charlton	Hunter	Greenhoff	Lorimer	Jones	Giles	Madeley	
Mar 23	MANCHESTER CITY	2-0	Sprake	Reaney	Cooper	Bremner	Charlton 1	Hunter	Greenhoff	Lorimer	Jones	Giles 1	Hibbitt*	Madeley*
Apr 6	SHEFFIELD UNITED	3-0	Sprake	Reaney	Cooper	Bremner	Charlton	Hunter	Greenhoff	Lorimer	Jones	Giles 2	Madeley 1	
Apr 12	Tottenham Hotspur	1-2	Harvey	Reaney	Cooper	Bremner	Charlton	Hunter	Greenhoff	Lorimer	Jones	Giles	Madeley 1	
Apr 13	Coventry City	1-0	Harvey	Reaney	Cooper	Bremner	Charlton	Hunter	Lorimer	Madeley	Jones	Giles*	Hibbitt 1	Belfitt*
Apr 17	TOTTENHAM HOTSPUR	1-0	Sprake	Reaney	Cooper	Bremner	Charlton	Hunter	Lorimer 1	Madeley	Jones	Giles*	Gray	Greenhoff*
Apr 20	WEST BROMWICH ALBION	3-1	Sprake	Reaney	Cooper	Bremner	Charlton 1	Hunter	Lorimer*	Madeley 1	Jones	Gray 1	Greenhoff	Belfitt*
Apr 23	Stoke City	2-3	Sprake	Reaney	Cooper	Bremner	Charlton 1	Hunter	Greenhoff 1	Lorimer	Jones	Madeley	Gray	
May 4	LIVERPOOL	1-2	Harvey	Reaney	Cooper*	Bremner	Madeley	Hunter	Greenhoff	Lorimer	Jones 1	Giles	Gray	Belfitt*
May 7	Arsenal	3-4	Harvey	Davey	Reaney	Bremner	Madeley	Gray	Lorimer 1	Belfitt*	Jones 1	Giles 1	Hibbitt	Greenhoff*
May 11	Burnley	0-3	Harvey	Sibbald	Davey	Yorath	Madeley	Gray	Lumsden	Bates	Belfitt	Hibbitt	Johanneson	

LEAGUE CUP

				1	2	3	4	5	6	7	8	9	10	11	SUBS
Sep 13	LUTON TOWN	Rd 2	3-1	Sprake	Reaney	Bell	Bremner	Charlton	Hunter	Lorimer 3	Belfitt*	Greenhoff	Gray	Cooper	Johnson*
Oct 11	BURY	Rd 3	3-0	Sprake	Reaney	Madeley	Gray	Charlton 1	Hunter	Greenhoff 1	Lorimer	Belfitt	Johnson	Johanneson 1	
Nov 15	Sunderland	Rd 4	2-0	Sprake	Reaney	Cooper	Bremner	Madeley	Hunter	Greenhoff 2	Belfitt	Hawkins*	Gray	Hibbitt	Bates*
Dec 13	STOKE CITY	Rd 5	2-0	Sprake	Reaney	Cooper	Bremner 1	Charlton	Hunter	Lorimer 1	Belfitt	Greenhoff	Gray*	Hibbitt	Bates*
Jan 17	Derby County	S/F	1-0	Sprake	Reaney	Cooper	Bremner	Charlton	Hunter	Greenhoff	Lorimer	Madeley	Giles 1	Gray	
Feb 7	DERBY COUNTY	S/F	3-2	Sprake	Reaney	Cooper	Bremner	Madeley	Hunter	Greenhoff	Lorimer	Belfitt 2	Giles	Gray* 1	Bates*
Mar 2	Arsenal (at Wembley)	Final	1-0	Sprake	Reaney	Cooper 1	Bremner	Charlton	Hunter	Greenhoff	Lorimer	Madeley	Giles	Gray*	Belfitt*

F.A. CUP

				1	2	3	4	5	6	7	8	9	10	11	SUBS
Jan 27	Derby County	Rd 3	2-0	Sprake	Reaney	Cooper	Bremner	Charlton *1	Hunter	Greenhoff	Lorimer 1	Jones	Giles	Gray	Madeley*
Feb 17	NOTTINGHAM FOREST	Rd 4	2-1	Sprake	Reaney	Cooper	Bremner	Madeley	Hunter	Greenhoff	Lorimer	Jones 1	Giles 1	Gray	
Mar 9	BRISTOL CITY	Rd 5	2-0	Sprake	Reaney	Cooper	Bremner	Charlton	Hunter	Greenhoff	Lorimer 1	Jones 1	Giles*	Hibbitt	Madeley*
Mar 30	SHEFFIELD UNITED	Rd 6	1-0	Sprake	Reaney	Cooper	Bremner	Charlton	Hunter	Lorimer	Madeley 1	Jones	Giles	O'Grady	
Apr 27	Everton (at Manchester United)	S/F	0-1	Sprake	Reaney	Cooper	Bremner	Charlton	Hunter	Lorimer	Madeley	Jones	Giles	Gray	

INTER-CITIES FAIRS CUP

				1	2	3	4	5	6	7	8	9	10	11	SUBS
Oct 3	Spora Luxemborg	Rd 1	9-0	Harvey	Reaney	Madeley 1	Bremner 1	Charlton	Hunter	Greenhoff 2	Lorimer 4	Jones 1	E Gray	Cooper	
Oct 17	SPORA LUXEMBORG	Rd 1	7-0	Sprake	Reaney	Cooper 1	Madeley*	Charlton	Hunter	Greenhoff 2	Lorimer 1	Belfitt	Hibbitt	Johanneson 3	Bates*
Nov 29	Partizan Belgrade	Rd 2	2-1	Harvey	Reaney	Cooper	Bremner	Charlton	Hunter	Greenhoff	Lorimer 1	Madeley	Belfitt 1	E Gray*	Bates*
Dec 6	PARTIZAN BELGRADE	Rd 2	1-1	Sprake	Reaney	Cooper	Bremner	Charlton	Hunter	Greenhoff	Lorimer 1	Madeley	E Gray	Hibbitt*	Johanneson*
Dec 20	HIBERNIAN	Rd 3	1-0	Sprake	Reaney*	Cooper	Bremner	Charlton	Hunter	Greenhoff	Lorimer	Jones	Gray	Giles	Madeley*
Jan 10	Hibernian	Rd 3	1-1	Sprake	Reaney	Cooper	Bremner	Charlton 1	Hunter	Greenhoff	Lorimer	Jones	Giles	Gray	
Mar 26	Rangers	Rd 4	0-0	Sprake	Reaney	Cooper	Bremner	Charlton	Hunter	Greenhoff *	Lorimer	Jones	Giles	Madeley	Belfitt *
Apr 9	RANGERS	Rd 4	2-0	Harvey	Reaney	Cooper	Bremner	Charlton	Hunter	Greenhoff	Madeley	Jones	Giles 1	Lorimer 1	
May 1	Dundee	S/F	1-1	Harvey	Reaney	Cooper	Bremner	Charlton	Hunter	Greenhoff	Lorimer	Madeley 1	Giles	Gray	
May 15	DUNDEE	S/F	1-0	Sprake	Reaney	Cooper	Bremner	Madeley	Hunter	Greenhoff	Lorimer	Jones	Giles	Gray 1	
Aug 7	FERENCVAROS	Final	1-0	Sprake	Reaney	Cooper	Bremner	Charlton	Hunter	Lorimer	Madeley	Jones *1	Giles*	Gray	Belfitt*, Greenhoff*
Sep 11	Ferencvaros	Final	0-0	Sprake	Reaney	Cooper	Bremner	Charlton	Hunter	O'Grady	Lorimer	Jones	Madeley	Hibbitt*	Bates*

DIVISION ONE 1968-69

			1	2	3	4	5	6	7	8	9	10	11	SUBS
Aug 10	Southampton	3-1	Sprake	Reaney	Madeley	Bremner	Charlton	Hunter	Lorimer *1	Greenhoff	Jones 1	Giles	Gray	Hibbitt* 1
Aug 14	QUEENS PARK RANGERS	4-1	Sprake	Reaney 1	Cooper	Bremner	Charlton	Hunter	Lorimer	Greenhoff	Jones 1	Giles 1	Hibbitt 1	
Aug 17	STOKE CITY	2-0	Sprake	Reaney	Cooper	Bremner	Charlton	Hunter	Belfitt	Greenhoff	Jones 1	Gray*	Hibbitt	Johanneson* 1
Aug 20	Ipswich Town	3-2	Sprake	Reaney	Cooper	Bremner	Charlton	Hunter	O'Grady 1	Belfitt 1	Jones	Gray	Hibbitt 1	
Aug 28	SUNDERLAND	1-1	Sprake	Reaney	Cooper	Bremner	Charlton	Hunter	O'Grady	Belfitt 1	Jones	Gray	Hibbitt	
Aug 31	LIVERPOOL	1-0	Sprake	Reaney	Cooper	Bremner	Charlton	Hunter	O'Grady	Lorimer	Jones 1	Belfitt*	Hibbitt	Bates*
Sep 7	WOLVERHAMPTON WANS	2-1	Sprake	Reaney	Cooper 1	Bremner	Charlton 1	Hunter	O'Grady	Lorimer	Jones	Madeley	Hibbitt	
Sep 14	Leicester City	1-1	Sprake	Reaney	Cooper	Bremner	Charlton	Hunter	O'Grady	Lorimer	Jones	Madeley 1	Hibbitt	
Sep 21	ARSENAL	2-0	Sprake	Reaney	Cooper	Bremner	Charlton 1	Hunter	O'Grady 1	Lorimer	Jones	Madeley	Hibbitt	
Sep 28	Manchester City	1-3	Sprake	Reaney*	Cooper	Bremner	Charlton	Hunter	O'Grady 1	Lorimer	Jones	Madeley	Hibbitt	Gray*
Oct 5	Newcastle United	1-0	Sprake	Reaney	Cooper	Bremner	Charlton 1	Hunter	O'Grady	Lorimer	Madeley	Giles	Gray	
Oct 9	Sunderland	1-0	Sprake	Reaney	Cooper	Bremner	Charlton	Hunter	O'Grady	Giles	Jones 1	Madeley	Gray	
Oct 12	WEST HAM UNITED	2-0	Sprake	Reaney	Cooper	Bremner	Charlton	Hunter	O'Grady	Giles 1	Jones	Madeley	Lorimer 1	
Oct 19	Burnley	1-5	Sprake	Reaney	Cooper*	Bremner 1	Charlton	Hunter	O'Grady	Giles	Jones	Madeley	Gray	Lorimer*
Oct 26	WEST BROMWICH ALBION	0-0	Sprake	Reaney	Madeley	Bremner	Charlton	Hunter	Lorimer	Gray	Jones	Bates	O'Grady	
Nov 2	Manchester United	0-0	Sprake	Reaney	Madeley	Bremner	Charlton	Hunter	Lorimer	Bates	Jones	Giles	O'Grady	
Nov 9	TOTTENHAM HOTSPUR	0-0	Sprake	Reaney	Cooper	Bremner	Charlton	Hunter	O'Grady	Madeley	Jones	Giles	Gray	
Nov 16	Coventry City	1-0	Sprake	Reaney	Cooper	Bremner	Charlton	Hunter	O'Grady	Madeley 1	Jones	Giles	Gray	
Nov 23	EVERTON	2-1	Sprake	Reaney	Cooper	Bremner	Charlton	Hunter	O'Grady	Madeley	Jones	Giles 1	Gray 1	
Nov 30	Chelsea	1-1	Sprake	Reaney	Cooper	Bremner	Charlton	Hunter	Lorimer	Madeley	Jones	Giles	O'Grady 1	
Dec 7	SHEFFIELD WEDNESDAY	2-0	Sprake	Reaney	Madeley	Bremner	Charlton	Hunter	O'Grady	Lorimer 2	Jones	Giles	Gray	
Dec 14	West Ham United	1-1	Sprake	Reaney	Madeley	Bremner	Charlton	Hunter	O'Grady	Lorimer	Jones	Giles	Gray 1	
Dec 21	BURNLEY	6-1	Sprake	Reaney	Madeley	Bremner 1	Charlton	Hunter	O'Grady	Lorimer 2	Jones 1	Giles 1	Gray 1	
Dec 26	NEWCASTLE UNITED	2-1	Sprake	Reaney	Madeley 1	Bremner	Charlton	Hunter	O'Grady	Lorimer 1	Jones	Giles*	Gray	Hibbitt*
Jan 11	MANCHESTER UNITED	2-1	Sprake	Reaney	Madeley	Bremner	Charlton	Hunter	O'Grady 1	Lorimer	Jones 1	Giles	Gray*	Cooper*
Jan 18	Tottenham Hotspur	0-0	Sprake	Reaney	Cooper	Bremner	Charlton	Hunter	O'Grady	Madeley	Jones	Giles	Gray	
Jan 24	Queens Park Rangers	1-0	Sprake	Reaney	Cooper	Bremner	Charlton	Hunter	Lorimer	Madeley	Jones 1	Giles*	Gray	Belfitt*
Feb 1	COVENTRY CITY	3-0	Sprake	Reaney	Cooper	Bremner 2	Charlton	Hunter	Lorimer	Madeley*	Jones	Gray	O'Grady 1	
Feb 12	IPSWICH TOWN	2-0	Sprake	Reaney	Cooper	Bremner	Charlton	Hunter	O'Grady	Belfitt 1	Jones 1	Giles	Gray	
Feb 15	CHELSEA	1-0	Sprake	Reaney	Cooper	Bremner	Charlton	Hunter	O'Grady	Lorimer 1	Jones*	Giles	Gray	Belfitt*
Feb 25	Nottingham Forest	2-0	Sprake	Reaney	Cooper	Bremner	Charlton	Hunter	O'Grady	Belfitt*	Jones 1	Giles	Gray	Lorimer* 1
Mar 1	SOUTHAMPTON	(o.g.) 3-2	Sprake	Reaney	Cooper	Bremner	Charlton	Hunter	O'Grady	Lorimer	Jones 1	Giles 1	Gray	
Mar 8	Stoke City	5-1	Sprake	Reaney	Cooper	Bremner 2	Charlton	Hunter	O'Grady 2	Madeley	Jones 1	Giles	Gray	
Mar 29	Wolverhampton Wans	0-0	Sprake	Reaney	Cooper	Bremner	Charlton	Hunter	O'Grady	Madeley*	Jones	Giles	Gray	Lorimer*
Apr 1	Sheffield Wednesday	0-0	Sprake	Reaney	Cooper	Bremner	Charlton	Hunter	O'Grady	Lorimer	Jones	Giles	Gray	
Apr 5	MANCHESTER CITY	1-0	Sprake	Reaney	Cooper	Bremner	Charlton	Hunter	O'Grady	Lorimer	Jones	Giles 1	Gray	
Apr 9	West Bromwich Albion	1-1	Sprake	Reaney	Cooper	Bremner	Charlton	Hunter	O'Grady	Madeley	Jones	Giles	Gray 1	
Apr 12	Arsenal	2-1	Sprake	Reaney	Cooper	Bremner	Madeley	Hunter	O'Grady*	Bates	Jones 1	Giles 1	Gray	Lorimer*
Apr 19	LEICESTER CITY	2-0	Sprake	Reaney	Cooper	Bremner	Charlton	Hunter	O'Grady	Madeley	Jones 1	Giles	Gray 1	
Apr 22	Everton	0-0	Sprake	Reaney	Cooper	Bremner	Charlton	Hunter	O'Grady	Madeley	Lorimer	Giles	Gray	
Apr 28	Liverpool	0-0	Sprake	Reaney	Cooper	Bremner	Charlton	Hunter	O'Grady	Madeley	Jones	Giles	Gray	
Apr 30	NOTTINGHAM FOREST	1-0	Sprake	Reaney	Cooper	Bremner	Charlton	Hunter	Lorimer	Madeley	Jones	Giles 1	O'Grady	

LEAGUE CUP

				1	2	3	4	5	6	7	8	9	10	11	SUBS
Sep 4	CHARLTON ATHLETIC	Rd 2	1-0	Sprake	Reaney	Cooper	Bremner	Charlton	Hunter	Lorimer	Belfitt*	Jones 1	Hibbitt	O'Grady	Bates*
Sep 25	BRISTOL CITY	Rd 3	2-1	Sprake	Reaney	Cooper	Bremner	Madeley	Gray	O'Grady	Lorimer	Jones 1	Giles	Johanneson 1	
Oct 16	Crystal Palace	Rd 4	1-2	Sprake	Reaney	Cooper	Gray	Charlton	Hunter	O'Grady	Giles	Jones	Madeley 1	Lorimer	

F.A. CUP

				1	2	3	4	5	6	7	8	9	10	11	SUBS
Jan 4	Sheffield Wednesday	Rd 3	1-1	Sprake	Reaney	Madeley	Bremner	Charlton	Hunter	O'Grady	Lorimer 1	Jones	Bates	Gray	
Jan 8	SHEFFIELD WEDNESDAY	Rd 3 R	1-3	Sprake	Reaney	Madeley	Bremner*	Charlton	Hunter	Gray	Lorimer	Jones	Bates	Johanneson 1	Belfitt*

DIVISION ONE 1968-69 continued

INTER-CITIES FAIRS CUP

Date	Opponent	Result	1	2	3	4	5	6	7	8	9	10	11	SUBS
Sep 18	Standard Liege	Rd 1 0-0	Sprake	Reaney	Cooper	Bremner	Charlton	Hunter	O'Grady	Lorimer	Jones	Madeley	Hibbitt	
Oct 23	STANDARD LIEGE	Rd 1 3-2	Sprake	Reaney	Cooper*	Bremner	Charlton	Hunter	O'Grady	Lorimer	Jones	Madeley	Hibbitt*	Bates*, E Gray*
Nov 13	NAPOLI	Rd 2 2-0	Sprake	Reaney	Madeley	Bremner	Charlton	Hunter	O'Grady	Jones	Belfitt	Giles	Lorimer	
Nov 27	Napoli	Rd 2 0-2	Sprake	Reaney	Cooper	Bremner	Charlton	Hunter	O'Grady	Madeley	Jones	Giles	Gray	
	(Won on toss of coin)													
Dec 18	HANNOVER 96	Rd 3 5-1	Sprake	Reaney	Madeley	Bremner	Charlton 1	Hunter 1	O'Grady 1	Lorimer 2	Jones	Gray	Giles	Hibbitt*
Feb 4	Hannover 96	Rd 3 2-1	Sprake	Reaney	Cooper	Bremner	Charlton	Hunter	O'Grady	Lorimer	Jones 1	Belfitt 1	Gray	
Mar 5	UJPEST DOZSA	S/F 0-1	Sprake	Reaney	Madeley	Bremner	Charlton	Hunter	O'Grady	Belfitt*	Jones	Giles	Gray	Lorimer*
Mar 19	Ujpest Dozsa	S/F 0-2	Sprake	Bates	Cooper	Bremner	Madeley	Hunter	Lorimer*	Belfitt	Jones*	Giles	Gray	Yorath*, Hibbitt*

DIVISION ONE 1969-70

Date	Opponent	Result	1	2	3	4	5	6	7	8	9	10	11	SUBS
Aug 9	TOTTENHAM HOTSPUR	3-1	Sprake	Reaney	Madeley	Bremner 1	Charlton	Hunter	O'Grady	Lorimer	Clarke 1	Giles 1	Gray	
Aug 13	ARSENAL	0-0	Sprake	Reaney	Cooper	Bremner	Madeley	Hunter	O'Grady	Lorimer	Clarke	Giles	Gray	
Aug 16	Nottingham Forest	4-1	Sprake	Reaney	Cooper	Bremner	Madeley	Hunter	Lorimer 1	Clarke 1	Jones	Giles 1	Gray 1	
Aug 19	Arsenal	1-1	Sprake	Reaney	Cooper	Bremner	Madeley	Hunter	Lorimer 1	Clarke	Jones	Giles	Gray	
Aug 23	NEWCASTLE UNITED	1-1	Sprake	Reaney	Cooper	Bremner	Madeley	Hunter	Lorimer	Clarke	Jones 1	Giles	Gray	
Aug 26	Burnley	1-1	Sprake	Reaney	Cooper	Bremner	Charlton	Hunter	Madeley	Clarke	Jones 1	Giles	Gray	
Aug 30	Everton	2-3	Sprake	Reaney	Cooper	Bremner 1	Charlton	Hunter	Madeley	Giles	Jones	Clarke 1	Gray*	Lorimer*
Sep 6	MANCHESTER UNITED	(o.g.) 2-2	Sprake	Reaney	Cooper	Bremner 1	Charlton	Hunter	Madeley	Lorimer	Jones	Giles	Gray*	O'Grady*
Sep 13	Sheffield Wednesday	2-1	Sprake	Reaney	Cooper	Bremner	Charlton	Hunter	Madeley	Clarke 1	Jones	Giles	Gray 1	
Sep 20	CHELSEA	2-0	Sprake	Reaney	Cooper	Bremner	Charlton*	Hunter	Madeley	Clarke	Jones	Giles 1	O'Grady	Lorimer* 1
Sep 27	Coventry City	2-1	Sprake	Reaney	Cooper	Bremner	Madeley	Hunter	Lorimer	Clarke 1	Jones	Giles	Gray 1	
Oct 4	STOKE CITY	2-1	Sprake	Reaney	Cooper	Bremner	Charlton	Hunter	Madeley	Clarke	Jones	Giles *2	Gray	Lorimer*
Oct 11	West Bromwich Albion	1-1	Sprake	Reaney	Cooper	Bremner	Charlton	Hunter	Lorimer	Madeley	Jones 1	Giles	Gray	Yorath*
Oct 18	Crystal Palace	1-1	Sprake	Reaney	Madeley	Bremner	Charlton	Hunter	Lorimer 1	Yorath*	Jones	Giles	Gray	Bates*
Oct 25	DERBY COUNTY	2-0	Sprake	Reaney	Madeley	Bremner	Charlton	Hunter	Lorimer	Clarke 2	Jones	Bates	Gray*	Hibbitt*
Oct 29	NOTTINGHAM FOREST	6-1	Sprake	Reaney	Madeley	Bremner	Charlton 1	Hunter	Lorimer 3	Clarke*	Jones	Bates 1	Gray	Hibbitt* 1
Nov 1	Sunderland	0-0	Sprake	Reaney	Madeley	Bremner	Charlton	Hunter	Lorimer	Belfitt	Jones	Bates	Gray	
Nov 8	IPSWICH TOWN	4-0	Sprake	Reaney	Madeley	Gray 1	Charlton	Hunter 1	Lorimer	Bates	Jones 1	Giles 1	Hibbitt*	Yorath*
Nov 15	Southampton	1-1	Sprake	Reaney	Madeley	Bremner	Charlton	Hunter	Lorimer	Bates	Jones 1	Giles	Hibbitt*	Yorath*
Nov 19	SUNDERLAND	2-0	Sprake	Reaney	Cooper	Bremner	Charlton	Hunter	Lorimer 1	Madeley	Jones 1	Bates*	Gray	Yorath*
Nov 22	LIVERPOOL	1-1	Sprake	Reaney	Cooper	Bremner	Charlton	Hunter	Lorimer	Madeley	Jones	Giles 1	Gray	
Nov 29	Manchester City	2-1	Sprake	Reaney	Cooper	Bremner	Charlton	Hunter	Lorimer	Madeley	Jones 1	Giles	Gray 1	
Dec 6	WOLVERHAMPTON WANS	(o.g.) 3-1	Sprake	Reaney	Cooper	Bremner	Charlton 1	Hunter	Lorimer	Clarke 1	Jones	Giles	Madeley	
Dec 13	SHEFFIELD WEDNESDAY	2-0	Sprake	Reaney	Cooper	Bremner	Charlton	Hunter	Lorimer	Clarke 2	Madeley	Giles	Hibbitt	
Dec 17	WEST HAM UNITED	4-1	Sprake	Reaney	Cooper	Bremner	Charlton	Hunter	Lorimer 2	Clarke 1	Jones	Giles 1	Madeley	
Dec 26	Newcastle United	1-2	Sprake	Reaney	Cooper	Bremner	Charlton	Hunter	Lorimer	Giles 1	Jones	Clarke	Madeley	
Dec 27	EVERTON	2-1	Sprake	Reaney	Cooper	Bremner	Charlton	Hunter	Lorimer	Clarke	Jones 2	Giles	Madeley	
Jan 10	Chelsea	5-2	Sprake	Reaney	Cooper 1	Bremner	Charlton	Hunter	Lorimer 1	Clarke* 1	Jones 1	Giles 1	Madeley	Bates*
Jan 17	COVENTRY CITY	3-1	Sprake	Reaney	Cooper	Bremner	Charlton* 1	Hunter	Lorimer	Clarke 2	Jones	Giles	Madeley	Bates*
Jan 26	Manchester United	2-2	Harvey	Reaney	Cooper	Bremner 1	Charlton	Hunter	Lorimer	Clarke	Jones 1	Giles	Madeley	
Jan 31	Stoke City	1-1	Sprake	Reaney	Cooper	Bremner	Charlton	Hunter	Lorimer	Clarke	Jones	Giles 1	Madeley	
Feb 10	WEST BROMWICH ALBION	5-1	Sprake	Reaney	Cooper	Bremner	Charlton	Hunter	Lorimer 1	Madeley	Jones 1	Giles 2	Gray 1	
Feb 14	Tottenham Hotspur	1-1	Sprake	Reaney	Cooper	Bremner	Charlton	Hunter	Lorimer 1	Madeley	Jones	Giles	Gray	
Feb 28	CRYSTAL PALACE	2-0	Sprake	Reaney	Madeley	Bremner	Charlton	Hunter	Lorimer	Clarke*	Jones 2	Giles	Gray	Cooper*
Mar 7	Liverpool	0-0	Sprake	Reaney	Cooper	Bremner	Charlton	Hunter	Lorimer	Clarke	Madeley	Giles	Gray	
Mar 21	Wolverhampton Wans	2-1	Sprake	Reaney	Cooper	Madeley	Charlton*	Yorath	Lorimer	Clarke 1	Jones 1	Bates	Gray	Belfitt*
Mar 28	SOUTHAMPTON	1-3	Sprake	Davey*	Madeley	Yorath	Charlton	Gray	Lorimer 1	Clarke	Belfitt	Bates	Hibbitt	Lumsden*
Mar 30	Derby County	1-4	Harvey	Davey	Peterson	Lumsden	Kennedy 1	Yorath	Galvin	Bates	Belfitt	Hibbitt	Johanneson	
Apr 2	West Ham United	2-2	Sprake	Reaney	Davey	Yorath	Madeley	Gray	Lorimer	Clarke 2	Belfitt*	Bates	Giles	Hibbitt*
Apr 4	BURNLEY	2-1	Harvey	Yorath	Peterson	Madeley	Faulkner	Gray 2	Lorimer	Bates	Johanneson	Galvin	Hibbitt	
Apr 18	MANCHESTER CITY	1-3	Harvey	Davey	Cooper	Bremner	Faulkner*	Gray	Lorimer	Clarke	Belfitt 1	Bates	Hibbitt	Peterson*
Apr 21	Ipswich Town	2-3	Harvey	Davey	Peterson	Yorath	Kennedy	Gray 1	Galvin	Lorimer	Belfitt	Bates	Hibbitt 1	

LEAGUE CUP

Date	Opponent	Result	1	2	3	4	5	6	7	8	9	10	11	SUBS
Sep 2	Fulham	Rd 2 1-0	Harvey	Reaney	Cooper	Madeley	Charlton 1	Gray	Lorimer	Bates	Jones	Belfitt	Hibbitt	
Sep 24	CHELSEA	Rd 3 1-1	Sprake	Reaney	Cooper	Bremner	Madeley 1	Hunter	Lorimer	Belfitt	Jones	Giles	Hibbitt*	Bates*
Oct 6	Chelsea	Rd 3 R 0-2	Harvey	Reaney	Cooper	Bremner	Charlton	Hunter	Lorimer	Belfitt	Jones	Madeley	Gray	

F.A. CUP

Date	Opponent	Result	1	2	3	4	5	6	7	8	9	10	11	SUBS
Jan 3	SWANSEA TOWN	Rd 3 2-1	Sprake	Reaney	Cooper	Bremner	Charlton	Hunter	Lorimer	Clarke	Jones 1	Giles 1	Madeley	
Jan 24	Sutton United	Rd 4 6-0	Harvey	Reaney	Cooper	Bremner	Charlton	Hunter	Lorimer 2	Clarke 4	Jones	Giles	Madeley	
Feb 7	MANSFIELD TOWN	Rd 5 2-0	Sprake	Reaney	Cooper	Bremner	Charlton	Hunter	Lorimer	Clarke 1	Jones	Giles 1	Gray	
Feb 21	Swindon Town	Rd 6 2-0	Sprake	Reaney	Cooper	Bremner	Charlton	Hunter	Madeley	Clarke 2	Jones	Giles	Gray	
Mar 14	Manchester United (at Sheffield Wednesday)	S/F 0-0	Sprake	Reaney	Cooper	Bremner	Charlton	Hunter	Lorimer*	Clarke	Jones	Giles	Madeley	Gray*
Mar 23	Manchester United (at Aston Villa)	S/F R 0-0 (AET)	Sprake	Reaney	Cooper*	Bremner	Charlton	Madeley	Lorimer	Clarke	Jones	Giles	Gray	Bates*
Mar 26	Manchester United (at Bolton Wanderers)	S/F 2R 1-0	Sprake	Reaney	Cooper	Bremner 1	Charlton	Madeley	Lorimer	Clarke	Jones	Giles	Gray	
Apr 11	Chelsea (at Wembley)	Final 2-2 (AET)	Sprake	Madeley	Cooper	Bremner	Charlton 1	Hunter	Lorimer	Clarke	Jones 1	Giles	Gray	
Apr 29	Chelsea (at Manchester United)	Final Replay 1-2 (AET)	Harvey	Madeley	Cooper	Bremner	Charlton	Hunter	Lorimer	Clarke	Jones 1	Giles	Gray	

EUROPEAN CUP

Date	Opponent	Result	1	2	3	4	5	6	7	8	9	10	11	SUBS
Sep 17	SK LYN OSLO	Rd 1 10-0	Sprake	Reaney	Cooper	Bremner 2	Charlton	Hunter	Madeley	Clarke 2	Jones 3	Giles* 2	O'Grady 1	Bates*
Oct 1	SK Lyn Oslo	Rd 1 6-0	Sprake	Reaney	Cooper	Bremner	Madeley	E Gray	Lorimer 1	Belfitt 2	Jones 1	Bates	Hibbitt 2	
Nov 12	FERENCVAROS	Rd 2 3-0	Sprake	Reaney	Madeley	Bremner	Charlton	Hunter	Lorimer	Bates	Jones 2	Giles 1	E Gray	
Nov 26	Ferencvaros	Rd 2 3-0	Sprake	Reaney	Cooper	Bremner	Charlton	Hunter	Lorimer 1	Madeley	Jones 2	Giles	E Gray*	Galvin*
Mar 4	Standard Liege	Rd 3 1-0	Sprake	Reaney	Cooper	Bremner	Charlton	Hunter	Lorimer 1	Clarke	Jones	Giles	Madeley	
Mar 18	STANDARD LIEGE	Rd 3 1-0	Sprake	Reaney	Cooper	Bremner	Charlton	Hunter	Lorimer	Clarke	Jones	Giles 1	Madeley	
Apr 1	CELTIC	S/F 0-1	Sprake	Reaney	Cooper	Bremner*	Charlton	Madeley	Lorimer	Clarke	Jones	Giles	E Gray	Bates*
Apr 15	Celtic	S/F 1-2	Sprake*	Madeley	Cooper	Bremner 1	Charlton	Hunter	Lorimer*	Clarke	Jones	Giles	E Gray	Harvey*, Bates*

F.A. CHARITY SHIELD

Date	Opponent	Result	1	2	3	4	5	6	7	8	9	10	11	SUBS
Aug 2	MANCHESTER CITY	2-1	Sprake	Reaney	Cooper	Bremner	Charlton 1	Hunter	Madeley	Clarke	Jones*	Giles	Gray 1	Lorimer*

DIVISION ONE 1970-71

Date	Opponent	Result	1	2	3	4	5	6	7	8	9	10	11	SUBS
Aug 15	Manchester United	1-0	Sprake	Madeley	Cooper	Bremner	Charlton	Hunter	Lorimer	Clarke	Jones 1	Giles	Gray	
Aug 19	Tottenham Hotspur	2-0	Sprake	Madeley	Cooper	Bremner	Charlton	Hunter	Lorimer	Clarke	Jones	Giles 1	Gray 1	
Aug 22	EVERTON	3-2	Sprake	Madeley	Cooper	Bremner 2	Charlton	Hunter	Lorimer	Clarke	Jones	Giles 1	Gray	
Aug 26	WEST HAM UNITED	3-0	Sprake	Madeley	Cooper	Bates	Charlton	Hunter	Lorimer	Clarke	Jones 1	Giles* 1	Gray	Belfitt* 1
Aug 29	Burnley	3-0	Sprake	Madeley	Cooper	Bremner	Charlton	Hunter	Lorimer	Clarke 2	Jones 1	Bates	Gray	
Sep 1	Arsenal	0-0	Sprake	Madeley	Cooper	Bremner	Charlton	Hunter	Lorimer	Clarke	Jones	Bates	Gray	
Sep 5	CHELSEA	1-0	Sprake	Madeley	Cooper	Bremner	Charlton	Hunter	Lorimer	Clarke 1	Jones	Bates	Gray	
Sep 12	Stoke City	0-3	Sprake	Madeley	Cooper	Bremner	Yorath	Hunter	Lorimer	Clarke	Jones	Bates	Gray	
Sep 19	SOUTHAMPTON	1-0	Sprake	Madeley	Cooper	Bremner	Charlton	Hunter	Lorimer	Clarke	Jones	Giles 1	Gray	
Sep 26	Nottingham Forest	0-0	Sprake	Madeley	Cooper	Bremner	Charlton	Hunter	Lorimer	Clarke	Jones	Giles	Gray	
Oct 3	HUDDERSFIELD TOWN	2-0	Sprake	Madeley	Cooper	Bremner	Charlton	Hunter	Lorimer 2	Clarke	Jones	Giles	Gray*	Hibbitt*
Oct 10	West Bromwich Albion	2-2	Sprake	Reaney	Cooper	Bremner	Charlton	Hunter	Lorimer	Clarke 1	Jones 1	Giles	Madeley	
Oct 17	MANCHESTER UNITED	2-2	Sprake	Reaney	Cooper	Bremner	Charlton 1	Hunter	Lorimer	Clarke	Belfitt 1	Bates*	Madeley	Hibbitt*
Oct 24	Derby County	2-0	Sprake	Davey	Cooper	Bremner	Charlton	Hunter	Lorimer 1	Clarke 1	Jones	Belfitt	Madeley	
Oct 31	COVENTRY CITY	2-0	Sprake	Davey	Cooper	Bremner	Charlton 1	Hunter	Lorimer	Clarke	Jones	Giles 1	Madeley	
Nov 7	Crystal Palace	1-1	Sprake	Davey	Cooper	Bates	Charlton	Hunter	Lorimer 1	Clarke	Jones	Giles	Madeley	
Nov 14	BLACKPOOL	3-1	Sprake	Madeley 1	Cooper	Bates	Charlton 1	Hunter	Lorimer	Clarke	Jones	Giles 1	Gray	
Nov 18	STOKE CITY	4-1	Sprake	Davey	Cooper	Bates	Charlton	Hunter	Lorimer 1	Clarke 1	Jones*	Giles 1	Madeley 1	Belfitt*
Nov 21	Wolverhampton Wans	(o.g.) 3-2	Sprake	Davey	Cooper	Madeley 1	Charlton	Hunter	Lorimer	Clarke 1	Jones*	Giles	Bates	Belfitt*
Nov 28	MANCHESTER CITY	1-0	Sprake	Madeley	Cooper	Bremner	Charlton	Hunter	Lorimer	Clarke 1	Bates	Giles	Gray	
Dec 5	Liverpool	1-1	Sprake	Madeley	Cooper	Bremner	Charlton	Hunter	Lorimer	Clarke	Jones	Giles	Gray*	Reaney*
Dec 12	IPSWICH TOWN	0-0	Sprake	Reaney	Cooper	Bremner	Charlton	Hunter	Lorimer	Clarke	Jones	Giles	Madeley	
Dec 19	Everton	1-0	Harvey	Reaney	Cooper	Bremner	Charlton 1	Hunter	Lorimer	Clarke*	Jones	Giles	Madeley	Bates*
Dec 26	NEWCASTLE UNITED	3-0	Sprake	Reaney	Cooper	Bremner	Charlton	Hunter	Lorimer	Clarke 1	Jones	Giles 2	Madeley	
Jan 9	TOTTENHAM HOTSPUR	1-2	Sprake	Reaney	Cooper	Bremner	Charlton	Hunter	Lorimer	Clarke 1	Jones	Giles	Madeley	
Jan 16	West Ham United	3-2	Sprake	Reaney	Cooper	Bates	Charlton	Hunter 1	Madeley	Clarke	Jones*	Giles 1	Yorath	Belfitt* 1
Jan 30	Manchester City	2-0	Sprake	Reaney	Cooper	Bates	Charlton* 1	Hunter	Madeley	Clarke 1	Jones	Giles	Yorath	Belfitt*
Feb 6	LIVERPOOL	0-1	Harvey	Reaney	Cooper	Bates	Charlton	Hunter	Lorimer	Clarke	Jones	Giles	Madeley	
Feb 20	WOLVERHAMPTON WANS	3-0	Harvey	Madeley 1	Cooper	Bremner	Charlton	Hunter	Lorimer	Clarke 1	Jones	Giles 1	Bates	
Feb 23	Ipswich Town	4-2	Harvey	Madeley	Cooper	Bremner*	Charlton	Hunter	Lorimer 1	Clarke 2	Jones	Giles 1	Bates	Belfitt*

DIVISION ONE 1970-71 continued

			1	2	3	4	5	6	7	8	9	10	11	SUBS
Feb 26	Coventry City	1-0	Harvey	Reaney*	Cooper	Bates	Charlton	Hunter	Lorimer 1	Clarke	Jones	Giles	Madeley	Hibbitt*
Mar 6	DERBY COUNTY	1-0	Harvey	Davey	Reaney	Bates	Charlton	Hunter	Lorimer 1	Belfitt	Jones	Giles	Madeley	
Mar 13	Blackpool	1-1	Harvey	Reaney	Cooper	Bates	Charlton	Hunter	Lorimer 1	Clarke	Jones	Giles	Madeley	
Mar 20	CRYSTAL PALACE	2-1	Harvey	Reaney	Cooper	Bates	Charlton	Hunter	Lorimer* 1	Clarke	Jones	Giles 1	Madeley	Belfitt*
Mar 27	Chelsea	1-3	Sprake	Reaney	Cooper 1	Bates	Charlton	Hunter	Lorimer	Clarke	Jones	Giles	Madeley	
Apr 3	BURNLEY	4-0	Sprake	Reaney	Cooper	Bates	Charlton	Hunter	Lorimer	Clarke 4	Jones*	Giles	Madeley	Belfitt*
Apr 10	Newcastle United	1-1	Sprake	Reaney	Cooper	Bates*	Charlton	Hunter	Lorimer 1	Clarke	Jones	Giles	Madeley	Belfitt*
Apr 12	Huddersfield Town	0-0	Sprake	Reaney	Cooper	Bates	Charlton	Hunter	Lorimer*	Clarke	Jones	Giles	Madeley	Belfitt*
Apr 17	WEST BROMWICH ALBION	1-2	Sprake	Reaney	Cooper	Bates*	Charlton	Hunter	Bremner	Clarke 1	Jones	Giles	Gray	Davey*
Apr 24	Southampton	(o.g.) 3-0	Sprake	Madeley	Cooper	Bremner	Charlton	Hunter	Bates	Clarke	Jones 2	Giles	Gray	
Apr 26	ARSENAL	1-0	Sprake	Madeley	Cooper	Bremner	Charlton 1	Hunter	Bates	Clarke	Jones	Giles	Gray	
May 1	NOTTINGHAM FOREST	2-0	Sprake	Madeley	Cooper	Bremner 1	Charlton	Hunter	Lorimer 1	Clarke	Jones	Giles	Gray	

LEAGUE CUP

Sep 8	Sheffield United	Rd 2 0-1	Sprake	Madeley	Cooper	Bremner	Charlton*	Hunter	Lorimer	Clarke	Jones	Bates	Gray	Belfitt*

F.A. CUP

Jan 11	Rotherham United	Rd 3 0-0	Sprake	Reaney	Cooper	Bremner	Charlton	Hunter	Lorimer	Clarke	Jones	Giles	Madeley	
Jan 18	ROTHERHAM UNITED	Rd 3 R 3-2	Sprake	Reaney	Cooper*	Bremner	Charlton	Hunter	Lorimer 2	Clarke	Belfitt	Giles 1	Madeley	Bates*
Jan 23	SWINDON TOWN	Rd 4 4-0	Sprake	Reaney	Davey	Bates	Charlton	Hunter	Lorimer*	Clarke 1	Jones 3	Giles	Madeley	Galvin*
Feb 13	Colchester United	Rd 5 2-3	Sprake	Reaney	Cooper	Bates	Charlton	Hunter 1	Lorimer	Clarke	Jones	Giles 1	Madeley	

INTER-CITIES FAIRS CUP

Sep 15	Sarpsborg	Rd 1 1-0	Sprake	Madeley	Cooper	Bremner	Kennedy	Gray	Lorimer 1	Belfitt	Jones	Bates	Hibbitt	
Sep 29	SARPSBORG	Rd 1 5-0	Sprake	Madeley	Cooper*	Bremner 2	Charlton 2	Hunter	Lorimer 1	Clarke	Belfitt	Bates	Gray	Reaney*
Oct 21	DYNAMO DRESDEN	Rd 2 1-0	Harvey	Davey	Cooper	Bremner	Charlton	Hunter	Lorimer 1	Clarke	Jones	Belfitt*	Galvin	Madeley*
Nov 4	Dynamo Dresden (Won on away goals)	Rd 2 1-2	Sprake	Davey	Madeley	Bremner	Charlton	Hunter	Lorimer	Clarke	Jones 1	Giles	Bates	
Dec 2	SPARTA PRAGUE	(o.g.) Rd 3 6-0	Sprake	Madeley	Cooper	Bremner 1	Charlton 1	Hunter	Lorimer	Clarke 1	Belfitt*	Giles	E Gray 2	Reaney*
Dec 9	Sparta Prague	Rd 3 3-2	Sprake*	Reaney	Cooper	Bremner	Madeley	Hunter *	Lorimer	Clarke 1	Belfitt 1	Bates	E Gray 1	Harvey*, Yorath*
Mar 10	VITORIA SETUBAL	Rd 4 2-1	Harvey	Davey*	Reaney	Bates	Charlton	Hunter	Lorimer 1	Belfitt	Jones*	Giles 1	Madeley	Yorath*, Jordan*
Mar 24	Vitoria Setubal	Rd 4 1-1	Harvey*	Reaney	Cooper	Bates	Charlton	Hunter	Lorimer 1	Clarke	Jones	Giles	Madeley	Sprake*
Apr 14	Liverpool	S/F 1-0	Sprake	Reaney*	Cooper	Bremner	Charlton	Hunter	Bates	Clarke	Jones	Giles	Madeley	Davey*
Apr 28	LIVERPOOL	S/F 0-0	Sprake	Madeley	Cooper	Bremner	Charlton	Hunter	Bates	Clarke*	Jones*	Giles	E Gray	Reaney*, Jordan*
May 28	Juventus	Final 2-2	Sprake	Reaney	Cooper	Bremner	Charlton	Hunter	Lorimer	Clarke	Jones*	Giles	Madeley 1	Bates• 1
Jun 2	JUVENTUS (Won on away goals)	Final 1-1	Sprake	Reaney	Cooper	Bremner	Charlton	Hunter	Lorimer	Clarke 1	Jones	Giles	Madeley*	Bates*

DIVISION ONE 1971-72

Aug 14	Manchester City	1-0	Sprake	Reaney	Cooper	Bremner	Charlton	Hunter	Lorimer 1	Clarke	Belfitt	Giles	Madeley	
Aug 17	Sheffield United	0-3	Sprake	Reaney	Madeley	Bremner	Charlton	Hunter	Lorimer	Clarke	Belfitt	Giles	Bates	
Aug 21	WOLVERHAMPTON WANS	0-0	Sprake	Reaney	Cooper	Bremner	Charlton	Hunter	Lorimer	Clarke	Jones	Giles*	Madeley	Bates*
Aug 25	TOTTENHAM HOTSPUR	1-1	Sprake	Reaney	Cooper	Bremner 1	Charlton	Hunter	Lorimer	Clarke	Jones	Bates	Madeley	
Aug 28	Ipswich Town	2-0	Sprake	Reaney	Cooper	Bremner	Charlton	Hunter	Lorimer 1	Clarke	Belfitt* 1	Bates	Madeley	Yorath*
Sep 1	NEWCASTLE UNITED	5-1	Sprake	Reaney	Cooper	Bremner	Charlton 1	Hunter	Lorimer 1	Clarke	Belfitt*	Giles 1	Madeley 1	Yorath* 1
Sep 4	CRYSTAL PALACE	2-0	Sprake	Reaney	Cooper	Bremner	Charlton	Hunter	Lorimer	Clarke	Belfitt	Giles 1	Madeley 1	
Sep 11	Arsenal	0-2	Harvey	Reaney	Yorath	Bremner	Charlton	Hunter	Lorimer	Clarke	Belfitt*	Giles	Madeley	Jordan*
Sep 18	LIVERPOOL	1-0	Sprake	Reaney	Cooper	Bremner	Charlton	Hunter	Lorimer 1	Galvin	Belfitt*	Giles	Madeley	Jordan*
Sep 25	Huddersfield Town	1-2	Sprake	Reaney*	Cooper	Bremner	Charlton 1	Hunter	Lorimer	Galvin	Belfitt	Giles	Madeley	Edwards*
Oct 2	WEST HAM UNITED	0-0	Sprake	Reaney	Cooper	Yorath	Charlton	Hunter	Lorimer	Mann*	Belfitt	Giles	Madeley	Galvin*
Oct 9	Coventry City	(o.g.) 1-3	Sprake	Reaney	Cooper	Bremner	Charlton	Hunter	Lorimer	Yorath*	Belfitt	Giles	Madeley	Jordan*
Oct 16	MANCHESTER CITY	3-0	Harvey	Reaney	Cooper	Bremner	Charlton	Hunter	Lorimer 1	Clarke* 1	Jones 1	Giles	Madeley	Jordan*
Oct 23	EVERTON	3-2	Sprake	Reaney	Cooper 1	Bremner	Charlton 1	Hunter	Lorimer 1	Jordan	Clarke	Giles*	Madeley	E Gray*
Oct 30	Manchester United	1-0	Sprake	Reaney	Cooper	Bremner	Charlton	Hunter	Lorimer 1	E Gray	Jordan*	Giles	Madeley	Belfitt*
Nov 6	LEICESTER CITY	2-1	Sprake	Reaney	Cooper	Bremner 1	Charlton	Hunter	Lorimer 1	E Gray	Jordan	Giles	Madeley	
Nov 13	Southampton	1-2	Sprake	Reaney	Cooper	Bremner	Charlton	Hunter	Lorimer	E Gray	Jordan	Giles 1	Madeley	
Nov 20	STOKE CITY	1-0	Sprake	Madeley	Cooper	Bremner	Charlton	Hunter	Lorimer 1	Clarke	Jones	Giles	E Gray	
Nov 27	Nottingham Forest	2-0	Sprake	Madeley	Cooper	Bremner	Charlton	Hunter	Lorimer 1	Clarke 1	Jones	Giles	E Gray	
Dec 4	WEST BROMWICH ALBION	3-0	Sprake	Madeley	Cooper	Bremner	Charlton	Hunter	Lorimer 1	Clarke	Jones	Giles 2	E Gray*	Reaney*
Dec 11	Chelsea	0-0	Sprake	Madeley	Cooper	Bremner	Charlton	Hunter	Lorimer	Clarke	Jones	Giles	E Gray	
Dec 18	Crystal Palace	1-1	Sprake	Madeley	Cooper	Bremner	Charlton	Hunter	Lorimer 1	Clarke	Jones	Giles	E Gray	
Dec 27	DERBY COUNTY	3-0	Sprake	Madeley	Cooper	Bremner	Charlton	Hunter	Lorimer 2	Clarke	Jones	Giles	E Gray 1	
Jan 1	Liverpool	2-0	Sprake	Reaney	Cooper	Bremner	Madeley	Hunter	Lorimer	Clarke 1	Jones 1	Giles	E Gray*	Bates*
Jan 8	IPSWICH TOWN	2-2	Sprake	Madeley	Cooper	Bremner 1	Charlton	Hunter	Lorimer	Clarke 1	Jones	Giles	E Gray	Reaney*
Jan 22	SHEFFIELD UNITED	1-0	Sprake	Madeley	Cooper	Bremner	Charlton	Hunter	Lorimer	Clarke 1	Jones	Giles	E Gray	
Jan 29	Tottenham Hotspur	0-1	Sprake	Madeley	Cooper	Bremner	Charlton	Hunter	Lorimer	Clarke	Jones	Giles	E Gray	
Feb 12	Everton	0-0	Sprake	Reaney*	Cooper	Bremner	Charlton	Hunter	Lorimer	Clarke	Madeley	Giles	E Gray	Jordan*
Feb 19	MANCHESTER UNITED	5-1	Sprake	Madeley	Cooper	Bremner	Charlton	Hunter	Lorimer 1	Clarke 1	Jones 3	Giles	E Gray	
Mar 4	SOUTHAMPTON	7-0	Sprake	Reaney	Madeley	Bremner	Charlton 1	Hunter	Lorimer 3	Clarke 2	Jones 1	Giles	E Gray	
Mar 11	COVENTRY CITY	1-0	Sprake	Reaney	Madeley	Bremner	Charlton 1	Hunter	Lorimer	Clarke	Jones	Giles	E Gray	
Mar 22	Leicester City	0-0	Sprake	Madeley	Cooper	Bremner	Charlton	Hunter	Lorimer	Clarke	Jones	Giles	E Gray	
Mar 25	ARSENAL	3-0	Sprake	Reaney	Cooper	Bremner	Charlton	Hunter	Lorimer 1	Clarke 1	Jones 1	Giles	Madeley	
Mar 27	NOTTINGHAM FOREST	6-1	Sprake	Reaney	Cooper	Bremner	Charlton	Hunter	Lorimer 2	Clarke 2	Jones*	E Gray 2	Madeley	Yorath*
Mar 31	West Ham United	2-2	Sprake	Reaney	Cooper	Bremner	Charlton	Hunter	Lorimer	Clarke	Jordan*	E Gray 2	Madeley	Bates*
Apr 1	Derby County	0-2	Sprake	Reaney	Cooper	Bremner	Charlton	Hunter	Lorimer	Clarke	Madeley	Giles	E Gray	
Apr 5	HUDDERSFIELD TOWN	3-1	Sprake	Madeley	Cooper	Bremner	Charlton	Hunter	Lorimer 1	Clarke*	Jones 1	Giles	E Gray 1	Reaney*
Apr 8	Stoke City	3-0	Harvey	Madeley	Cooper	Bremner	Charlton	Hunter	Lorimer 1	Clarke*	Jones 2	Giles	E Gray	Reaney*
Apr 19	Newcastle United	0-1	Harvey	Reaney	Madeley	Bremner	Charlton	Hunter	Lorimer	Clarke	Jones	Giles	E Gray	
Apr 22	West Bromwich Albion	1-0	Harvey	Reaney	Madeley	Bremner	Charlton	Hunter	Lorimer	Clarke*	Jones	Giles 1	Bates	Jordan*
May 1	CHELSEA	2-0	Harvey	Reaney	Madeley	Bremner 1	Charlton	Hunter	Lorimer	Clarke*	Jones 1	Giles	Bates	Jordan*
May 8	Wolverhampton Wans	1-2	Harvey	Reaney	Madeley	Bremner 1	Charlton	Hunter	Lorimer	Clarke*	Bates	Giles	E Gray	Yorath*

LEAGUE CUP

Sep 8	Derby County	Rd 2 0-0	Harvey	Reaney	Yorath	Bremner	Charlton	Hunter	Lorimer	Clarke	Belfitt	Giles	Madeley	
Sep 27	DERBY COUNTY	Rd 2 R 2-0	Sprake	Reaney	Cooper	Bremner*	Charlton	Hunter	Lorimer 2	Yorath	Belfitt	Giles	Madeley	Mann*
Oct 6	West Ham United	Rd 3 0-0	Sprake	Davey	Cooper	Bremner	Charlton	Hunter	Lorimer	Yorath	Belfitt	Giles	Madeley	
Oct 20	WEST HAM UNITED	Rd 3 R 0-1 (AET)	Harvey	Reaney	Cooper	Bremner	Charlton	Hunter	Lorimer	Clarke	Jones*	Giles	Madeley	E Gray*

F.A. CUP

Jan 15	BRISTOL ROVERS	Rd 3 4-1	Sprake	Reaney	Cooper	Bremner	Madeley	Hunter	Lorimer 2	Bates	Jordan*	Giles 2	E Gray	Galvin*
Feb 5	Liverpool	Rd 4 0-0	Sprake	Reaney	Cooper	Bremner	Madeley	Hunter	Lorimer	Clarke	Jones	Giles	Bates	
Feb 9	LIVERPOOL	Rd 4 R 2-0	Sprake	Reaney*	Cooper	Bremner	Charlton	Hunter	Lorimer	Clarke 2	Madeley	Giles	E Gray	Jordan*
Feb 26	Cardiff City	Rd 5 2-0	Sprake	Madeley	Cooper	Bremner	Charlton	Hunter	Lorimer	Clarke	Jones	Giles 2	E Gray	
Mar 18	TOTTENHAM HOTSPUR	Rd 6 2-1	Sprake	Madeley	Cooper*	Bremner	Charlton 1	Hunter	Lorimer	Clarke 1	Jones	Giles	E Gray	Reaney*
Apr 15	Birmingham City (at Sheffield Wednesday)	S/F 3-0	Harvey	Reaney	Madeley	Bremner	Charlton	Hunter	Lorimer 1	Clarke	Jones 2	Giles	E Gray	
May 6	Arsenal (at Wembley)	Final 1-0	Harvey	Reaney	Madeley	Bremner	Charlton	Hunter	Lorimer	Clarke 1	Jones	Giles	E Gray	

U.E.F.A. CUP

Sep 15	Lierse SK	Rd 1 2-0	Sprake	Reaney	Yorath	Bremner	Faulkner	Hunter	Lorimer 1	Galvin 1	Belfitt	Giles	Bates	
Sep 29	LIERSE SK	Rd 1 0-4	Shaw*	Reaney	Cooper	Yorath	Faulkner	Madeley	Lorimer	Mann*	Belfitt	Bates	Galvin	Sprake*, Hunter*

PLAY-OFF between first and last winners of the Inter-Cities Fairs Cup for retention of trophy

Sep 22	Barcelona	1-2	Sprake	Reaney	Davey	Bremner	Charlton	Hunter	Lorimer	Jordan 1	Belfitt	Giles	Galvin	

DIVISION ONE 1972-73

Aug 12	Chelsea	0-4	Harvey	Reaney	Cherry	Bremner	Ellam	Madeley	Lorimer	Bates	Jones*	Giles	E Gray	Yorath*
Aug 15	Sheffield United	(o.g.) 2-0	Harvey	Reaney	Cherry	Bremner	Charlton	Madeley	Lorimer	Bates	Jordan	Giles 1	E Gray	
Aug 19	WEST BROMWICH ALBION	2-0	Harvey	Reaney	Madeley	Bremner	Charlton	Hunter	Lorimer	Clarke 1	Jordan	Giles 1	Bates	
Aug 23	IPSWICH TOWN	3-3	Harvey	Reaney*	Madeley	Bremner	Charlton	Hunter	Lorimer	Clarke	Jordan 2	Giles 1	E Gray	Cherry*
Aug 26	Tottenham Hotspur	0-0	Harvey	Madeley	Cherry	Bremner	Charlton	Hunter	Lorimer	Clarke	Jordan	Giles	E Gray	
Aug 30	SOUTHAMPTON	1-0	Harvey	Reaney*	Cherry	Bremner 1	Charlton	Hunter	Lorimer	Bates	Jordan	Giles	Madeley	Yorath*
Sep 2	NORWICH CITY	2-0	Harvey	Reaney	Cherry	Bremner	Charlton 1	Hunter	Lorimer	Clarke	Jordan 1	Giles	E Gray	
Sep 9	Stoke City	2-2	Harvey	Madeley	Cherry	Bremner	Charlton	Hunter	Lorimer 1	Clarke 1	Jordan	Giles	E Gray	
Sep 16	LEICESTER CITY	3-1	Harvey	Madeley	Cherry	Bremner	Charlton	Hunter	Lorimer	Clarke 1	Jones* 1	Giles	Bates 1	Jordan*
Sep 23	Newcastle United	2-3	Harvey	Reaney	Cherry	Bremner	Charlton	Hunter	Lorimer	Clarke* 1	Jones 1	Giles	Bates	Jordan*
Sep 30	LIVERPOOL	1-2	Harvey	Madeley	Cherry	Bremner	Charlton	Hunter	Lorimer	Clarke	Jones 1	Giles	Bates	
Oct 7	DERBY COUNTY	5-0	Harvey	Madeley	Cherry	Bremner 1	Charlton	Hunter	Lorimer 1	Clarke 1	Jones	Giles* 2	E Gray	Bates*
Oct 14	Everton	2-1	Harvey	Madeley	Cherry	Bremner	Charlton	Hunter	Lorimer	Jordan 1	Jones 1	Bates	E Gray	
Oct 21	COVENTRY CITY	1-1	Harvey	Madeley	Cherry	Bremner	Charlton 1	Hunter	Lorimer	Clarke	Jones*	Giles	E Gray	Jordan*

DIVISION ONE 1972-73 continued

Date	Opponent	Rd	Score	1	2	3	4	5	6	7	8	9	10	11	SUBS
Oct 28	Wolverhampton Wans		2-0	Harvey	Madeley	Cherry	Bremner	Ellam	Hunter	Lorimer 1	Clarke	Yorath	Bates	E Gray 1	
Nov 4	Ipswich Town		2-2	Harvey	Madeley	Cherry	Bremner	Charlton 1	Hunter	Lorimer 1	Clarke	Jones	Bates	E Gray	
Nov 11	SHEFFIELD UNITED		2-1	Harvey	Reaney	Cherry	Bremner	Charlton	Hunter	Lorimer	Clarke 2	Jones	Giles	E Gray*	Bates*
Nov 18	Crystal Palace		2-2	Harvey	Reaney	Cherry	Bremner	Ellam	Hunter	Lorimer	Clarke	Jones 1	Giles 1	Bates*	Yorath*
Nov 25	MANCHESTER CITY		3-0	Harvey	Reaney	Cherry 1	Bremner	Madeley	Hunter	Lorimer 1	Clarke 1	Jones	Bates	Yorath	
Dec 2	Arsenal		1-2	Harvey	Reaney	Cherry	Bremner	Madeley	Hunter	Lorimer 1	Clarke	Jones*	Bates	Yorath	Jordan*
Dec 9	WEST HAM UNITED		1-0	Harvey	Reaney	Cherry	Bremner	Madeley	Hunter	Lorimer	Clarke	Jones 1	Bates	Yorath	
Dec 16	BIRMINGHAM CITY		4-0	Harvey	Reaney	Cherry	Bremner	Madeley	Yorath	Lorimer 1	Clarke 2	Jones 1	Giles	Bates	
Dec 23	Manchester United		1-1	Harvey	Reaney	Cherry	Yorath	Charlton	Madeley	Lorimer	Clarke 1	Jones	Giles	Bates	
Dec 26	NEWCASTLE UNITED		1-0	Harvey	Reaney	Cherry	Yorath	Madeley	Hunter	Lorimer	Clarke	Jones	Giles	Bates*	Jordan* 1
Jan 6	TOTTENHAM HOTSPUR		2-1	Harvey	Reaney	Cherry	Bremner	Madeley	Hunter*	Lorimer 1	Clarke	Jones 1	Giles	Bates	Yorath*
Jan 20	Norwich City		2-1	Harvey	Reaney	Cherry	Bremner	Madeley	Hunter	Lorimer	Clarke 1	Jordan 1	Giles	Bates	
Jan 27	STOKE CITY		1-0	Harvey	Reaney	Cherry	Bremner	Madeley	Hunter	Lorimer	Clarke 1	Jordan*	Giles	Bates	Yorath*
Feb 10	Leicester City		0-2	Harvey	Reaney	Cherry	Yorath	Madeley	Hunter	Lorimer	Clarke	Jones	Giles	Bates*	F Gray*
Feb 17	CHELSEA		1-1	Harvey	Reaney	Cherry	Bremner	Madeley	Hunter	Lorimer	Clarke	Jones 1	Giles	Bates	
Mar 3	Derby County		3-2	Harvey	Reaney*	Cherry	Bremner	Madeley	Hunter	Lorimer 2	Clarke	Jones	Giles	McQueen	Bates*
Mar 10	EVERTON		2-1	Harvey	Madeley	Cherry	Bremner	McQueen	Hunter	Lorimer 1	Clarke 1	Jordan	Giles	E Gray	
Mar 24	WOLVERHAMPTON WANS		0-0	Harvey	Reaney	Madeley	Bremner	McQueen	Hunter*	Lorimer	Jordan	Jones	Giles	E Gray	Yorath*
Mar 28	West Bromwich Albion		1-1	Harvey	Reaney	Cherry	Bremner	McQueen	Madeley	Lorimer	Clarke 1	Jones	Giles	E Gray*	Jordan*
Mar 31	Manchester City		0-1	Harvey	Reaney	Cherry	Bremner	McQueen	Madeley	Lorimer	Clarke	Jones	Giles	Yorath*	Jordan
Apr 2	Coventry City		1-0	Harvey	Reaney 1	Cherry	Bremner	Charlton	Madeley	Lorimer	Clarke	Jones	Giles	Yorath	
Apr 14	West Ham United		1-1	Harvey	Reaney	Cherry	Bremner	Yorath	Hunter	Lorimer	Clarke 1	Jones	Giles	Bates*	Jordan*
Apr 18	MANCHESTER UNITED		0-1	Harvey	Reaney	Cherry	Bremner	McQueen	Yorath	Lorimer	Clarke	Jones*	Giles	Bates	Jordan*
Apr 21	CRYSTAL PALACE		4-0	Harvey	Madeley	Cherry	Bremner* 1	Ellam	Yorath	Lorimer 1	Clarke 1	Jones	Giles	F Gray 1	Jordan*
Apr 23	Liverpool		0-2	Harvey	Reaney	Cherry	Bremner	Ellam	Hunter	Lorimer	Clarke	Jordan	Yorath	Madeley	
Apr 28	Southampton		1-3	Harvey	Cherry	Hampton	Bremner	Charlton*	Hunter 1	Bates	Clarke	Jordan	E Gray	F Gray	Ellam*
Apr 30	Birmingham City		1-2	Sprake	Galvin	Hampton	Yorath	Ellam*	F Gray	Liddell	Lorimer	Jordan 1	Mann	Bates	McGinley*
May 9	ARSENAL		6-1	Harvey	Reaney	Cherry	Bremner 1	Yorath	Hunter	Lorimer 3	Clarke*	Jordan 2	Giles	Madeley	Jones*

LEAGUE CUP

Date	Opponent	Rd	Score	1	2	3	4	5	6	7	8	9	10	11	SUBS
Sep 6	BURNLEY	Rd 2	4-0	Harvey	Reaney	Cherry 1	Bremner	Charlton	Hunter	Lorimer 2	Bates	Jordan	E Gray	Liddell*	Jones* 1
Oct 4	Aston Villa	Rd 3	1-1	Harvey	Madeley	Cherry	Bremner	Charlton 1	Hunter	Lorimer	Clarke	Jones	Bates	Yorath	
Oct 11	ASTON VILLA	(o.g.) Rd 3 R	2-0	Harvey	Madeley	Cherry	Bremner	Charlton*	Hunter	Lorimer	Clarke	Jones 1	Bates	E Gray	Yorath*
Oct 31	Liverpool	Rd 4	2-2	Harvey	Madeley	Cherry	Bremner	Ellam	Hunter	Lorimer 1	Clarke	Jones 1	Bates	E Gray	
Nov 22	LIVERPOOL	Rd 4 R	0-1	Harvey	Reaney	Cherry	Bremner	Charlton	Hunter	Lorimer	Clarke	Jones	Giles*	Madeley	Jordan*

F.A. CUP

Date	Opponent	Rd	Score	1	2	3	4	5	6	7	8	9	10	11	SUBS
Jan 13	Norwich City	Rd 3	1-1	Harvey	Reaney	Cherry	Bremner	Madeley	Hunter	Lorimer 1	Clarke	Jones	Giles	Bates	
Jan 17	NORWICH CITY	Rd 3 R	1-1 (AET)	Harvey	Reaney	Cherry	Bremner	Madeley	Hunter	Lorimer	Clarke	Jones	Giles 1	Bates	
Jan 29	Norwich City (at Aston Villa)	Rd 3 2R	5-0	Harvey	Reaney	Cherry	Bremner	Madeley	Hunter	Lorimer 1	Clarke* 3	Jones 1	Giles	Bates	Yorath*
Feb 3	PLYMOUTH ARGYLE	Rd 4	2-1	Harvey	Reaney	Cherry	Yorath	Madeley	Hunter	Lorimer	Clarke 1	Jones	Giles	Bates 1	
Feb 24	WEST BROMWICH ALBION	Rd 5	2-0	Harvey	Reaney	Cherry	Bremner	Madeley	Hunter	Lorimer	Clarke 2	Jones	Giles	E Gray	
Mar 17	Derby County	Rd 6	1-0	Harvey	Reaney	Cherry	Bremner*	Madeley	Hunter	Lorimer 1	Clarke	Jones	Giles	E Gray	Bates*
Apr 7	Wolverhampton Wans (at Manchester City)	S/F	1-0	Harvey	Reaney	Cherry	Bremner 1	Charlton*	Yorath	Lorimer	Clarke	Jones	Giles	Madeley	Jordan*
May 5	Sunderland (at Wembley)	Final	0-1	Harvey	Reaney	Cherry	Bremner	Madeley	Hunter	Lorimer	Clarke	Jones	Giles	E Gray*	Yorath*

CUP WINNERS CUP

Date	Opponent	Rd	Score	1	2	3	4	5	6	7	8	9	10	11	SUBS
Sep 13	Ankaragucu	Rd 1	1-1	Harvey	Reaney	Cherry	Bremner	Ellam	Hunter	Lorimer	Galvin*	Jordan 1	Giles	Madeley	Yorath*
Sep 27	ANKARAGUCU	Rd 1	1-0	Harvey	Reaney	Cherry	Bremner	Ellam	Hunter	Lorimer	Clarke	Jones 1	Giles	Bates	
Oct 25	Carl Zeiss Jena	Rd 2	0-0	Harvey	Reaney	Cherry	Bremner	Charlton	Hunter	Lorimer	Clarke	Jordan	Bates	E Gray	
Nov 8	CARL ZEISS JENA	Rd 2	2-0	Harvey	Reaney	Cherry 1	Bremner	Charlton	Hunter	Lorimer	Clarke	Jones 1	Bates*	Yorath	Giles*
Mar 7	RAPID BUCHAREST	Rd 3	5-0	Harvey	Reaney	Cherry	Bremner	McQueen*	Hunter	Lorimer 2	Clarke 1	Jordan 1	Giles 1	Madeley	Yorath*
Mar 21	Rapid Bucharest	Rd 3	3-1	Harvey	Reaney	E Gray	Madeley	McQueen	Hunter	Lorimer	Jordan 1	Jones 1	Giles*	Bates* 1	F Gray*, Yorath*
Apr 11	HAJDUK SPLIT	S/F	1-0	Harvey	Reaney	Cherry	Bremner	Yorath	Hunter	Lorimer	Clarke 1	Jones	Giles	Bates*	Jordan*
Apr 25	Hajduk Split	S/F	0-0	Harvey	Reaney	Cherry	Bremner	Yorath	Hunter	Lorimer	Jones	Jordan	Giles	Madeley	
May 16	A.C. Milan (at Salonika)	Final	0-1	Harvey	Reaney	Cherry	Bates	Yorath	Hunter	Lorimer	Jordan	Jones	F Gray*	Madeley	McQueen*

DIVISION ONE 1973-74

Date	Opponent	Rd	Score	1	2	3	4	5	6	7	8	9	10	11	SUBS
Aug 25	EVERTON		3-1	Harvey	Reaney	Madeley	Bremner 1	McQueen	Hunter	Lorimer	Clarke	Jones 1	Giles 1	E Gray	
Aug 28	Arsenal		2-1	Harvey	Reaney	Madeley 1	Bremner	McQueen	Hunter	Lorimer 1	Clarke	Jones	Giles	E Gray	
Sep 1	Tottenham Hotspur		3-0	Harvey	Reaney	Madeley	Bremner 2	McQueen	Hunter	Lorimer	Clarke* 1	Jones	Giles	E Gray	Cherry*
Sep 5	WOLVERHAMPTON WANS		4-1	Harvey	Reaney	Madeley	Bremner 1	McQueen	Hunter	Lorimer 2	Clarke	Jones 1	Giles	E Gray*	Jordan*
Sep 8	BIRMINGHAM CITY		3-0	Harvey	Reaney	Madeley	Bremner	McQueen	Hunter	Lorimer* 3	Clarke	Jones	Giles	E Gray	Jordan*
Sep 11	Wolverhampton Wans		2-0	Harvey	Cherry	Madeley	Bremner	McQueen	Hunter	Yorath	Clarke 1	Jones 1	Giles*	Jordan	Bates*
Sep 15	Southampton		2-1	Harvey	Reaney	Cherry	Bremner	McQueen	Hunter	Jordan	Clarke 2	Jones	Madeley	E Gray	
Sep 22	MANCHESTER UNITED		0-0	Harvey	Cherry	Madeley	Bremner	McQueen	Hunter	Jordan	Clarke	Jones	Giles	E Gray	
Sep 29	Norwich City		1-0	Harvey	Reaney	Madeley	Bremner	McQueen	Hunter	Jordan	Clarke	Jones	Giles 1	Madeley	
Oct 6	STOKE CITY		1-1	Harvey	Reaney	Cherry	Bremner	Madeley	Hunter	Lorimer*	Clarke	Jones 1	Giles	Bates	Yorath*
Oct 13	Leciester City		2-2	Harvey	Madeley	Cherry	Bremner 1	McQueen	Hunter	Lorimer	Clarke	Jones 1	Giles*	Bates	Jordan*
Oct 20	LIVERPOOL		1-0	Harvey	Cherry	Madeley	Bremner	McQueen	Hunter	Lorimer	Clarke	Jones 1	Bates	Yorath	
Oct 27	Manchester City		1-0	Harvey	Cherry	Madeley	Bremner	McQueen	Hunter	Lorimer	Clarke	Jones	Giles*	Bates 1	Jordan*
Nov 3	WEST HAM UNITED		4-1	Harvey	Reaney	Cherry	Bremner	McQueen	Hunter	Lorimer	Clarke 1	Jones 2	Bates 1	Madeley	
Nov 10	Burnley		0-0	Harvey	Reaney	Cherry	Bremner	McQueen	Hunter	Lorimer	Clarke	Jones	Bates*	Madeley	Jordan*
Nov 17	COVENTRY CITY		3-0	Harvey	Reaney	Cherry	Bremner	McQueen	Hunter	Lorimer*	Clarke	Jordan	Bates	Madeley	Yorath*
Nov 24	Derby County		0-0	Harvey	Reaney	Cherry	Bremner	McQueen	Hunter	Lorimer	Clarke	Jordan	Bates	Yorath	
Dec 1	QUEEN'S PARK RANGERS		2-2	Harvey	Reaney	Cherry	Bremner 1	McQueen	Hunter	Lorimer	Clarke	Jones 1	Bates*	Yorath	Jordan*
Dec 8	Ipswich Town		3-0	Harvey	Reaney	Cherry	Bremner	McQueen	Hunter	Lorimer	Clarke* 1	Jones 1	Yorath 1	Madeley	Jordan*
Dec 15	Chelsea		2-1	Harvey	Reaney	Cherry	Bremner	McQueen	Hunter	Lorimer	Jordan 1	Jones 1	Yorath	Madeley	
Dec 22	NORWICH CITY		1-0	Harvey	Reaney	Cherry	Bremner	McQueen	Hunter	Lorimer	Jordan	Jones	Yorath 1	Madeley	
Dec 26	Newcastle United		1-0	Harvey	Reaney	Cherry	Bremner	McQueen	Hunter	Lorimer	Jordan	Jones	Yorath	Madeley 1	
Dec 29	Birmingham City		1-1	Harvey	Reaney	Cherry	Bremner	McQueen	Hunter	Lorimer	Jordan 1	Jones	Yorath	Madeley	
Jan 1	TOTTENHAM HOTSPUR		1-1	Harvey	Reaney	Cherry	Bremner	McQueen	Hunter	Lorimer	Clarke*	Jones 1	Jordan	Madeley	Yorath*
Jan 12	SOUTHAMPTON		2-1	Harvey	Reaney	Cherry	Bremner	Madeley	Hunter	Lorimer	Jordan 1	Jones 1	Yorath	F Gray	
Jan 19	Everton		0-0	Harvey	Reaney	Cherry	Bremner	Madeley	Hunter	Lorimer	Jordan	Jones	Yorath	F Gray*	Ellam*
Feb 2	CHELSEA		1-1	Harvey	Reaney	Cherry 1	Bremner	McQueen	Hunter	Lorimer	Clarke	Jordan	Cooper*	Madeley	Yorath*
Feb 5	ARSENAL	(o.g.)	3-1	Harvey	Reaney	Cherry	Bremner	Ellam	Hunter	Lorimer	Clarke	Jordan 2	Yorath	Madeley	
Feb 9	Manchester United		2-0	Harvey	Reaney*	Cherry	Bremner	McQueen	Hunter	Lorimer	Clarke	Jones 1	Yorath	Madeley	Jordan* 1
Feb 23	Stoke City		2-3	Harvey	Yorath	Cherry	Bremner 1	Ellam	Hunter	Lorimer	Clarke 1	Jordan	Giles*	Madeley	Cooper*
Feb 26	LEICESTER CITY		1-1	Stewart	Reaney	Cherry	Bremner	Ellam	Hunter	Lorimer 1	Clarke	Jordan	Yorath*	Madeley	F Gray*
Mar 2	NEWCASTLE UNITED		1-1	Stewart	Reaney	Cherry	Bremner	McQueen	Hunter	Lorimer*	Clarke 1	Jordan	Yorath	F Gray	Liddell*
Mar 9	MANCHESTER CITY		1-0	Stewart	Reaney	Cherry	Bremner	McQueen	Hunter	Lorimer 1	Clarke	Jordan	Yorath	Madeley	
Mar 16	Liverpool		0-1	Harvey	Reaney	Cherry	Bremner	McQueen	Hunter	Lorimer*	Clarke	Jordan	Yorath	Madeley	Jones*
Mar 23	BURNLEY		1-4	Harvey	Reaney	Cherry	Bremner	McQueen	Hunter	Giles	Clarke 1	Jordan*	Yorath	Madeley	Jones*
Mar 30	West Ham United		1-3	Harvey	Reaney	Cherry	Bremner	McQueen	Hunter	Lorimer	Clarke 1	Jordan*	Yorath	Madeley	Jones*
Apr 6	DERBY COUNTY		2-0	Harvey	Reaney	Cherry	Bremner 1	McQueen	Hunter	Lorimer 1	Giles	Jordan	Yorath	Madeley	
Apr 13	Coventry City		0-0	Harvey	Reaney	Cherry	Bremner	McQueen	Hunter	Lorimer	Yorath	Jordan	Giles	Madeley	
Apr 15	SHEFFIELD UNITED		0-0	Harvey	Reaney	Cherry	Bremner	McQueen	Hunter	Lorimer	Clarke	Jones	Giles*	Madeley	F Gray*
Apr 16	Sheffield United		2-0	Harvey	Reaney	Cherry	Bremner	McQueen	Hunter	Lorimer 2	Clarke*	Jones	Yorath	Madeley	F Gray*
Apr 20	IPSWICH TOWN		3-2	Harvey	Reaney	Cherry	Bremner 1	McQueen	Hunter	Lorimer 1	Clarke 1	Jones	Madeley	E Gray	
Apr 27	Queen's Park Rangers		1-0	Harvey	Reaney*	Cherry	Bremner	McQueen	Hunter	Lorimer	Clarke 1	Jordan	Giles	Madeley	Yorath*

LEAGUE CUP

Date	Opponent	Rd	Score	1	2	3	4	5	6	7	8	9	10	11	SUBS
Oct 8	Ipswich Town	Rd 2	0-2	Harvey	Reaney*	Cherry	Bremner	Ellam	Hunter	Liddell	Yorath	Jones	Madeley	F Gray	O'Neill*

F.A. CUP

Date	Opponent	Rd	Score	1	2	3	4	5	6	7	8	9	10	11	SUBS
Jan 5	Wolverhampton Wans	Rd 3	1-1	Harvey	Reaney	Cherry	Bremner	McQueen	Hunter	Lorimer 1	Jordan	Jones	Yorath*	Madeley	F Gray*
Jan 9	WOLVERHAMPTON WANS	Rd 3 R	1-0	Stewart	Reaney	Cherry	Bremner	McQueen*	Hunter	Lorimer	Jordan	Jones 1	Clarke	Madeley	Yorath*
Jan 26	Peterborough United	Rd 4	4-1	Harvey	Reaney	Cooper	Bremner	Ellam	Hunter	Lorimer 1	Yorath 1	Jordan 2	Cherry	Madeley	
Feb 16	Bristol City	Rd 5	1-1	Harvey	Yorath	Cherry	Bremner 1	McQueen	Hunter	Lorimer	Jordan	Jones	Giles*	Madeley	Clarke*
Feb 19	BRISTOL CITY	Rd 5 R	0-1	Harvey	Cherry	Cooper	Bremner	Ellam	Hunter	Lorimer	Clarke	Jones	Giles*	Madeley	Jordan*

U.E.F.A. CUP

Date	Opponent	Rd	Score	1	2	3	4	5	6	7	8	9	10	11	SUBS
Sep 19	Strömgodset	Rd 1	1-1	Sprake	Madeley	Cherry	Yorath	McQueen	F Gray	Liddell	Clarke 1	Jones	Bates	E Gray	
Oct 3	STRÖMGODSET	Rd 1	6-1	Harvey	Reaney*	Cherry	Bremner	Ellam	Yorath	Lorimer	Clarke* 2	Jones 2	Bates 1	F Gray 1	O'Neill*, McGinley*
Oct 24	HIBERNIAN	Rd 2	0-0	Harvey	Cherry	Madeley	Bremner	Ellam	Yorath	Lorimer	Clarke	Jones*	Bates	F Gray*	Jordan*, O'Neill*
Nov 7	Hibernian (AET won 5-4 on penalties)	Rd 2	0-0	Shaw*	Reaney	Cherry	Bremner	Ellam	Yorath	Lorimer	Clarke	Jordan	Bates	F Gray	Letheran*
Nov 28	VITORIA SETUBAL	Rd 3	1-0	Harvey	Reaney*	Cherry 1	Bremner	McQueen	Hunter	Lorimer	Clarke	Jordan	Bates	Yorath*	Davey*, F Gray*
Dec 12	Vitoria Setubal	Rd 3	1-3	Harvey	Reaney	Cherry	Yorath	McQueen*	Ellam	Lorimer	Mann	Jordan	Hampton	F Gray	Liddell*1

DIVISION ONE 1974-75

			1	2	3	4	5	6	7	8	9	10	11	SUBS
Aug 17	Stoke City	0-3	Harvey	Reaney	Cooper	Bremner	McQueen	Cherry	Lorimer	Madeley	Jordan	Giles	McKenzie	
Aug 21	QUEEN'S PARK RANGERS	0-1	Harvey	Reaney	Cooper	Bates	McQueen	Cherry	Lorimer	Madeley	Jordan	Giles	McKenzie	
Aug 24	BIRMINGHAM CITY	1-0	Harvey	Reaney	Cherry	McGovern	McQueen	Hunter	Lorimer	Clarke 1	O'Hare	Giles	Madeley*	Jordan*
Aug 27	Queen's Park Rangers	1-1	Harvey	Reaney	Cherry	McGovern	McQueen	Hunter	Lorimer	Clarke	O'Hare	Giles	Yorath 1	
Aug 31	Manchester City	1-2	Harvey	Reaney	Cherry	McGovern	McQueen	Hunter	Lorimer	Clarke 1	O'Hare	Giles	Yorath*	Jordan*
Sep 7	LUTON TOWN	1-1	Harvey	Reaney	Cherry	McGovern	McQueen	Hunter	Lorimer	Clarke 1	O'Hare	Giles	Madeley	
Sep 14	Burnley	1-2	Harvey	Reaney	Cherry	Yorath	McQueen	Hunter	Lorimer 1	Clarke	Jordan	Giles	Madeley	
Sep 21	SHEFFIELD UNITED	5-1	Harvey	Reaney	Cherry	Yorath 1	McQueen 1	Hunter	Lorimer 1	Clarke 2	Jordan	Giles	Madeley	
Sep 28	Everton	2-3	Harvey	Reaney	Cherry	Yorath 1	Madeley	Hunter	Lorimer	Clarke 1	Jordan	Bates	F Gray	
Oct 5	ARSENAL	2-0	Harvey	Reaney	Cooper*	Yorath	McQueen	Hunter	Lorimer	McKenzie 2	Jordan	Giles	Madeley	Bates*
Oct 12	Ipswich Town	0-0	Harvey	Reaney	Cherry	Yorath	McQueen	Hunter	Lorimer	Clarke	Jordan	Giles	Cooper	
Oct 15	Birmingham City	0-1	Harvey	Reaney	Cherry	Yorath	McQueen	Hunter	Lorimer	Clarke	Jordan	Giles	Cooper	
Oct 19	WOLVERHAMPTON WANS	2-0	Harvey	Reaney	Cooper	Yorath*	McQueen	Hunter	Lorimer	Clarke 1	Jordan	McKenzie 1	Madeley	Giles*
Oct 26	Liverpool	0-1	Harvey	Reaney	Cooper	Yorath	McQueen	Hunter	Lorimer	McKenzie	Jordan	Giles*	Madeley	Clarke*
Nov 2	DERBY COUNTY	0-1	Harvey	Reaney	Cooper	Yorath	McQueen	Hunter	Lorimer *	Clarke	O'Hare	Giles	Madeley	McKenzie*
Nov 9	Coventry City	(o.g.) 3-1	Harvey	Reaney	Cherry	Bremner 1	McQueen	Yorath	Lorimer	Clarke	O'Hare 1	Madeley	Cooper	
Nov 16	MIDDLESBROUGH	2-2	Harvey	Reaney	Cooper	Bremner	McQueen	Yorath	McKenzie 2	Clarke	Jordan	Giles	Madeley	
Nov 23	Carlisle United	2-1	Harvey	Reaney	Cherry	Bremner	McQueen	Madeley	McKenzie 1	Clarke	Jordan 1	Giles	Yorath	
Nov 30	CHELSEA	2-0	Harvey	Reaney	Cherry 1	Bremner	McQueen	Madeley	McKenzie	Clarke 1	Jordan	Giles	Yorath	
Dec 4	TOTTENHAM HOTSPUR	2-1	Stewart	Reaney	Cherry	Bremner	McQueen	Madeley	McKenzie 1	Clarke	Jordan	Lorimer 1	Yorath	
Dec 7	West Ham United	1-2	Harvey	Reaney	Cherry	Bremner	McQueen	Madeley	McKenzie 1	Clarke	Jordan	Lorimer	Yorath	
Dec 14	STOKE CITY	3-1	Harvey	Reaney	Cherry	Bremner	McQueen 1	Madeley	McKenzie	Clarke	Jordan	Lorimer 1	Yorath* 1	Giles*
Dec 21	Newcastle United	0-3	Harvey	Reaney	Cherry	Bremner	McQueen	Madeley	McKenzie	Clarke	Jordan	Lorimer	Yorath	
Dec 26	BURNLEY	2-2	Harvey	Reaney	F Gray	Bremner	McQueen	Madeley*	McKenzie	Clarke	Jordan 1	Lorimer 1	Yorath	Giles*
Dec 28	Leicester City	2-0	Stewart	Reaney	F Gray 1	Bremner	McQueen	Madeley	McKenzie 1	Clarke	Lorimer	Giles	Yorath	
Jan 11	WEST HAM UNITED	2-1	Harvey	Reaney	F Gray	Bremner	McQueen	Madeley	McKenzie 1	Clarke 1	Lorimer	Giles	E Gray	
Jan 18	Chelsea	2-0	Harvey	Reaney	F Gray	Bremner	McQueen	Madeley	McKenzie 1	Clarke*	Lorimer	Giles	E Gray	Yorath* 1
Feb 1	COVENTRY CITY	0-0	Harvey	Reaney	F Gray	Bremner	McQueen	Madeley	Lorimer	Clarke	McKenzie	Yorath	E Gray	
Feb 8	Derby County	0-0	Harvey	Reaney	F Gray	Bremner	McQueen*	Madeley	Lorimer	Clarke	McKenzie	Yorath	E Gray	Cherry*
Feb 22	Middlesbrough	1-0	Stewart	Reaney	F Gray	Bremner	Madeley	Hunter	Lorimer	Clarke 1	Jordan	Giles	Cooper	
Feb 25	CARLISLE UNITED	3-1	Harvey	Reaney	F Gray	Bremner	Hunter	Madeley	Lorimer 1	Clarke 1	Jordan	Giles	E Gray 1	
Mar 1	MANCHESTER CITY	2-2	Harvey	Reaney*	F Gray	Bremner	Madeley	Hunter	Lorimer 2	Clarke	McKenzie	Yorath	E Gray	Jordan*
Mar 15	EVERTON	0-0	Stewart	Cherry	F Gray	Bremner	Madeley	Hunter	Lorimer	Clarke	McKenzie	Yorath	E Gray	
Mar 22	Luton Town	1-1	Stewart	Reaney	F Gray	Madeley	McQueen*	Hunter	McKenzie	Yorath	Jordan 1	Giles	E Gray	Cherry*
Mar 29	NEWCASTLE UNITED	1-1	Stewart	Reaney	Cherry*	Bremner	Madeley	Hunter	McKenzie	Clarke 1	Jordan	Giles	F Gray	Hampton*
Mar 31	LEICESTER CITY	2-2	Stewart	Reaney	F Gray	Bremner	Madeley	Hunter	McKenzie	Clarke* 1	Jordan	Giles 1	Yorath	Hampton*
Apr 1	Sheffield United	1-1	Stewart	Stevenson	F Gray	Bremner	Madeley 1	Hunter	Lorimer	Liddell	McKenzie	Yorath	E Gray	
Apr 5	LIVERPOOL	0-2	Stewart	Madeley	F Gray*	Bremner	McQueen	Hunter	Lorimer	McKenzie	Jordan	Yorath	E Gray	Cherry*
Apr 12	Arsenal	2-1	Stewart	Reaney	Cherry	Bremner	McQueen	Hunter 1	McKenzie*	Clarke 1	Jordan	Giles	Madeley	Lorimer*
Apr 19	IPSWICH TOWN	2-1	Letheran	Reaney	Cherry 1	Bremner	McQueen	Hunter	Lorimer	Madeley	Yorath	Giles*	E Gray	Harris* 1
Apr 26	Wolverhampton Wans	1-1	Stewart	Reaney	Cherry	Bremner	McQueen	Madeley	Lorimer	Clarke*	Harris	Yorath	F Gray 1	Thomas*
Apr 28	Tottenham Hotspur	2-4	Stewart	Reaney	Cherry	Bremner	Madeley*	Hunter	Lorimer 1	F Gray	Jordan 1	Yorath	E Gray	Harris*

LEAGUE CUP

Sep 10	Huddersfield Town	Rd 2 1-1	Harvey	Reaney	Cherry	Bates	McQueen	Hunter	Lorimer 1	Clarke	Jordan	Giles	Madeley	
Sep 24	HUDDERSFIELD TOWN	Rd 2 R 1-1 (AET)	Harvey	Reaney	Cherry	Yorath	Madeley	Hunter	Lorimer	Clarke 1	Jordan	Giles*	McKenzie	Bates*
Oct 7	HUDDERSFIELD TOWN	Rd 2 2R 2-1	Harvey	Reaney	Cherry	Yorath	McQueen	Hunter	Lorimer 1	McKenzie	O'Hare	Bates* 1	Madeley	F Gray*
Oct 9	Bury	Rd 3 2-1	Stewart	Reaney	Cherry 1	Bremner*	McQueen	Hunter	Lorimer 1	Cooper	Jordan	Yorath	McKenzie	Madeley*
Nov 13	Chester	Rd 4 0-3	Harvey	Reaney	Cooper	Yorath	McQueen	Cherry	Lorimer	Clarke	Jordan	Bremner*	Madeley	Bates*

F.A. CUP

Jan 4	CARDIFF CITY	Rd 3 4-1	Harvey	Reaney*	F Gray	Bremner	McQueen	Madeley	Lorimer	Clarke 2	McKenzie 1	Giles	E Gray 1	Cherry*
Jan 25	WIMBLEDON	Rd 4 0-0	Harvey	Reaney	F Gray	Bremner	McQueen	Madeley	McKenzie	Yorath	Lorimer	Giles	E Gray	
Feb 10	Wimbledon (at Crystal Palace)	(o.g.) Rd 4 R 1-0	Harvey	Reaney	F Gray	Bremner	Yorath	Madeley	McKenzie	Clarke	Jordan	Giles	E Gray	
Feb 18	Derby County	(o.g.) Rd 5 1-0	Stewart	Reaney	F Gray	Bremner	McQueen	Madeley	McKenzie	Clarke	Jordan	Yorath	E Gray	
Mar 8	Ipswich Town	Rd 6 0-0	Stewart	Madeley	F Gray	Bremner	McQueen	Hunter	Yorath	Clarke	Jordan	Giles	E Gray	
Mar 11	IPSWICH TOWN	Rd 6 R 1-1 (AET)	Stewart	Reaney*	F Gray	Bremner	Madeley	Hunter	Lorimer	Clarke	Jordan	Giles	Yorath	McKenzie* 1
Mar 25	Ipswich Town (at Leicester City)	Rd 6 2R 0-0 (AET)	Stewart	Reaney	F Gray	Bremner	Madeley	Hunter	Lorimer*	Clarke	Jordan	Giles	Yorath	McKenzie*
Mar 27	Ipswich Town (at Leicester City)	Rd 6 3R 2-3	Stewart	Reaney	F Gray	Bremner	Madeley	Hunter	E Gray	Clarke 1	Jordan	Giles 1	Yorath*	McKenzie*

EUROPEAN CUP

Sep 18	F.C. ZURICH	Rd 1 4-1	Harvey	Reaney	Cooper	Yorath	McQueen	Hunter	Lorimer 1	Clarke 2	Jordan 1	Giles	Madeley	
Oct 2	F.C. Zurich	Rd 1 1-2	Harvey	Reaney	Cherry	Yorath	Madeley	Hunter	Lorimer	Clarke 1	Jordan	Bates	F Gray*	Hampton*
Oct 23	Ujpest Dozsa	Rd 2 2-1	Harvey	Reaney	Cooper	Yorath	McQueen 1	Hunter	Lorimer 1	McKenzie	Jordan	Giles	Madeley	
Nov 6	UJPEST DOZSA	Rd 2 3-0	Harvey	Reaney	Cooper	Yorath	McQueen	Hunter*	Lorimer*	Clarke	Bremner	Giles	Madeley	Cherry*, Harris*
Mar 5	ANDERLECHT	Rd 3 3-0	Stewart	Madeley	F Gray	Bremner*	McQueen 1	Hunter	Lorimer 1	Clarke	Jordan 1	Giles	E Gray	Yorath*
Mar 19	Anderlecht	Rd 3 1-0	Stewart	Reaney	F Gray	Bremner 1	McQueen	Hunter	Lorimer	Clarke	Jordan	Yorath	Madeley	
Apr 9	BARCELONA	S/F 2-1	Stewart	Reaney	F Gray	Bremner 1	McQueen	Madeley	Yorath	Clarke 1	Jordan	Giles	E Gray	
Apr 23	Barcelona	S/F 1-1	Stewart	Cherry	F Gray	Bremner	McQueen	Hunter	Lorimer 1	Clarke	Jordan	Yorath	Madeley	
May 28	Bayern Munich (at Paris)	Final 0-2	Stewart	Reaney	F Gray	Bremner	Madeley	Hunter	Lorimer	Clarke	Jordan	Giles	Yorath*	E Gray*

CHARITY SHIELD

Aug 10	Liverpool (at Wembley Lost 6-5 on penalties)	1-1	Harvey	Reaney	Cherry 1	Bremner	McQueen	Hunter	Lorimer	Clarke*	Jordan	Giles	E Gray	McKenzie*

DIVISION ONE 1975-76

Aug 16	Aston Villa	2-1	Harvey	Reaney	F Gray	Bremner	McQueen	Cherry	Lorimer 2	Clarke	McKenzie	Yorath	Madeley	
Aug 20	Norwich City	1-1	Harvey	Reaney	F Gray	Bremner	McQueen	Cherry 1	Lorimer	Clarke	McKenzie	Yorath	Madeley	
Aug 23	IPSWICH TOWN	1-0	Harvey	Reaney	F Gray	Hunter	McQueen	Cherry	Lorimer 1	Clarke	McKenzie	Yorath	E Gray	
Aug 26	LIVERPOOL	0-3	Harvey	Reaney	F Gray	Bremner	McQueen	Cherry	Lorimer	Clarke	McKenzie	Yorath	Madeley	
Aug 30	Sheffield United	2-0	Harvey	Reaney	F Gray	Bremner	McQueen	Cherry	Lorimer	Clarke 1	McKenzie 1	Yorath	Madeley	
Sep 6	WOLVERHAMPTON WANS	3-0	Harvey	Reaney	F Gray	Bremner	McQueen 1	Cherry	Lorimer	Clarke 1	McKenzie* 1	Yorath	Madeley	Harris*
Sep 13	Stoke City	2-3	Harvey	Reaney	F Gray	Bremner	McQueen	Cherry	Lorimer 2	Clarke	McKenzie	Yorath	Madeley	
Sep 20	TOTTENHAM HOTSPUR	1-1	Harvey	Reaney	F Gray	Bremner	McQueen	Cherry	Lorimer * 1	Clarke	McKenzie	Yorath	Madeley	E Gray*
Sep 27	Burnley	1-0	Harvey	Reaney	F Gray	Hunter	Madeley	Cherry 1	Lorimer	Clarke	Bremner	Yorath	E Gray	
Oct 4	QUEEN'S PARK RANGERS	2-1	Harvey	Cherry	F Gray	Bremner	McQueen*	Hunter	Lorimer 1	Clarke 1	McKenzie	Yorath	Madeley	Reaney*
Oct 11	MANCHESTER UNITED	1-2	Stewart	Reaney	F Gray	Bremner	Madeley	Hunter	Cherry	Clarke 1	McKenzie*	Yorath	E Gray	Harris*
Oct 18	Birmingham City	2-2	Harvey	Reaney	F Gray	Bremner	Madeley	Hunter 1	Cherry 1	Clarke	McKenzie	Yorath	E Gray	
Oct 25	COVENTRY CITY	2-0	Harvey	Reaney	F Gray	Bremner	Madeley	Hunter	Lorimer	Clarke 1	McKenzie	Yorath 1	Cherry	
Nov 1	Derby County	2-3	Harvey	Reaney	F Gray	Bremner	Cherry 1	Hunter	Lorimer	Clarke	McKenzie 1	Yorath	Madeley	
Nov 8	NEWCASTLE UNITED	3-0	Harvey	Reaney	F Gray	Bremner	McQueen*	Madeley	Lorimer	Cherry	McKenzie 2	Yorath 1	E Gray	Harris*
Nov 15	Middlesbrough	0-0	Harvey	Reaney	F Gray	Bremner	Madeley	Cherry	Lorimer	Clarke	McKenzie	Yorath	E Gray	
Nov 22	BIRMINGHAM CITY	3-0	Harvey	Reaney	F Gray	Bremner 1	Madeley	Cherry	Lorimer	Clarke	McKenzie 2	Yorath	E Gray	
Nov 29	EVERTON	5-2	Harvey	Reaney	F Gray	Bremner	Madeley	Cherry	Lorimer 2	Clarke 2	McKenzie	Yorath*	E Gray 1	Jordan*
Dec 6	Arsenal	2-1	Harvey	Reaney	F Gray	Bremner	Madeley	Cherry	Lorimer	Clarke	McKenzie 2	Yorath	E Gray	
Dec 13	Ipswich Town	1-2	Harvey	Reaney	F Gray	Bremner	Madeley	Cherry	Lorimer	Clarke	McKenzie 1	Yorath	E Gray	
Dec 20	ASTON VILLA	1-0	Harvey	Reaney	F Gray	Bremner	Madeley	Cherry	Lorimer	Clarke 1	McKenzie	Yorath	E Gray	
Dec 26	Manchester City	1-0	Harvey	Reaney	F Gray	Bremner	Madeley 1	Cherry	Lorimer	Clarke	McKenzie	Yorath	E Gray	
Dec 27	LEICESTER CITY	4-0	Harvey	Reaney*	F Gray	Bremner	Madeley	Hunter	Lorimer 1	Clarke 1	McKenzie 2	Cherry	E Gray	Harris*
Jan 10	STOKE CITY	2-0	Harvey	Reaney	F Gray*	Bremner 1	Madeley	Hunter	Lorimer	Clarke	McKenzie 1	Yorath	Cherry	Harris*
Jan 17	Wolverhampton Wans	(o.g.) 1-1	Harvey	Reaney	F Gray	Bremner	Madeley	Hunter	Lorimer	Clarke	McKenzie	Yorath	Cherry	
Jan 31	NORWICH CITY	0-3	Harvey	Reaney	F Gray	Cherry	Madeley	Hunter	Lorimer*	Clarke	McKenzie	Yorath	E Gray	Jordan*
Feb 7	Liverpool	0-2	Harvey	Reaney*	F Gray	Lorimer	Madeley	Hunter	McKenzie	Clarke	Jordan	Yorath	E Gray	Stevenson*
Feb 21	MIDDLESBROUGH	0-2	Harvey	Reaney	F Gray	Lorimer*	Madeley	Hunter	McKenzie	Clarke	Jordan	Yorath	E Gray	Parkinson*
Feb 23	West Ham United	1-1	Harvey	Reaney	F Gray	Bates	Madeley	Hunter	McKenzie 1	Cherry	Jordan	Yorath	E Gray	
Feb 28	Coventry City	1-0	Harvey	Reaney	F Gray 1	Bates	Madeley	Hunter	McKenzie	Cherry	Jordan	Yorath	E Gray*	Clarke*
Mar 2	DERBY COUNTY	1-1	Harvey	Reaney	F Gray 1	Bates	Madeley	Hunter	McKenzie	Clarke	Jordan	Yorath	Cherry	
Mar 9	WEST HAM UNITED	1-1	Harvey	Reaney*	F Gray	Bates	Madeley	Hunter	McKenzie	Clarke	Jordan 1	Yorath	Cherry	E Gray*
Mar 13	Manchester United	2-3	Harvey	Cherry 1	F Gray	Bremner 1	Yorath	Hunter	McKenzie	Clarke	Jordan	Lorimer	E Gray	
Mar 20	Everton	3-1	Harvey	Cherry	F Gray	Bremner 1	Madeley	Hunter	Harris 1	Clarke	Jordan 1	Yorath	E Gray	
Mar 27	ARSENAL	3-0	Harvey	Reaney	F Gray	Bremner 1	Madeley	Hunter	Harris	Clarke 2	Jordan*	Cherry	E Gray	McKenzie*
Mar 31	Newcastle United	(o.g.) 3-2	Harvey	Reaney	F Gray	Bremner	Madeley	Hunter	Harris 1	Clarke	Jordan	Cherry 1	E Gray	
Apr 3	BURNLEY	2-1	Stewart	Reaney	F Gray	Bremner	Madeley	Hunter	Harris	McKenzie 1	Jordan	Cherry	Yorath*	Hampton* 1
Apr 10	Tottenham Hotspur	0-0	Harvey	Cherry	F Gray	Bremner	Parkinson	Hunter	Harris	Clarke	Jordan	McKenzie	E Gray	
Apr 14	SHEFFIELD UNITED	0-1	Harvey	Cherry	F Gray	Bremner	Parkinson	Hunter	Harris*	Clarke	McKenzie	Madeley	E Gray	Lorimer*
Apr 17	MANCHESTER CITY	2-1	Harvey	Cherry	F Gray	Bremner	Parkinson*	Hunter	Harris 1	Madeley	Jordan	McKenzie	E Gray	McNiven* 1
Apr 20	Leicester City	1-2	Harvey	Cherry	F Gray	Bremner	Madeley	Hunter	Harris	Yorath	Jordan	McKenzie 1	E Gray*	McNiven*
Apr 24	Queen's Park Rangers	0-2	Harvey	Reaney	F Gray*	Bremner	Madeley	Hunter	Harris	Cherry	Jordan	McKenzie	E Gray	Lorimer*

DIVISION ONE 1975-76 continued

LEAGUE CUP

Date	Opponent	Score	1	2	3	4	5	6	7	8	9	10	11	SUBS
Sep 9	IPSWICH TOWN	Rd 2 3-2	Harvey	Cherry	F Gray	Bremner	Madeley	Hunter	Lorimer 1	Clarke 1	McKenzie 1	Yorath	E Gray	
Oct 8	NOTTS COUNTY	Rd 3 0-1	Harvey	Reaney	Cherry	Bremner	Madeley	Hunter	Lorimer	McNiven*	McKenzie	F Gray	E Gray	Harris*

F.A. CUP

Date	Opponent	Score	1	2	3	4	5	6	7	8	9	10	11	SUBS
Jan 3	Notts County	Rd 3 1-0	Harvey	Reaney	F Gray	Bremner	Madeley	Cherry	Lorimer	Clarke 1	McKenzie	Hunter	Yorath	
Jan 24	CRYSTAL PALACE	Rd 4 0-1	Harvey	Reaney	F Gray	Bremner*	Madeley	Cherry	Lorimer	Clarke	McKenzie	Yorath	E Gray	Hunter*

DIVISION ONE 1976-77

Date	Opponent	Score	1	2	3	4	5	6	7	8	9	10	11	SUBS
Aug 21	WEST BROMWICH ALBION	2-2	Harvey	Reaney	F Gray	Cherry	Madeley	Hunter	Lorimer*	Clarke 1	McNiven	Currie	E Gray	Harris* 1
Aug 24	Birmingham City	0-0	Harvey	Reaney	F Gray	Cherry	Madeley	Hunter	Yorath	Clarke	McNiven	Currie	E Gray	
Aug 28	Coventry City	2-4	Harvey	Reaney	F Gray 1	Bremner	Madeley	Hunter	Cherry	Clarke	Jordan	Currie 1	E Gray	
Sep 4	DERBY COUNTY	2-0	Harvey	Reaney	F Gray	Bremner	Madeley	Hunter	Cherry 1	Clarke	McNiven	Currie	E Gray 1	
Sep 11	Tottenham Hotspur	0-1	Harvey	Reaney	F Gray	Bremner	Madeley	Hunter	Cherry	Clarke	McNiven	Currie	E Gray	
Sep 18	NEWCASTLE UNITED	2-2	Harvey	Reaney	F Gray	Bremner	Madeley	Hunter	Cherry	Clarke	McNiven 1	Currie*	E Gray	Harris* 1
Sep 25	Middlesbrough	0-1	Harvey	Reaney	F Gray	Lorimer	McQueen	Hunter	Cherry	Madeley	McNiven	Harris	E Gray*	Hampton*
Oct 2	MANCHESTER UNITED	0-2	Harvey	Reaney	F Gray	Madeley	McQueen	Hunter*	Cherry	Clarke	Jordan	Currie	E Gray	Lorimer*
Oct 6	West Ham United	3-1	Harvey	Reaney	Hampton	Madeley	McQueen	Hunter	Cherry	Lorimer 1	Jordan	F Gray	E Gray* 1	Harris* 1
Oct 16	Norwich City	2-1	Harvey	Reaney	Hampton	Madeley	McQueen	F Gray 1	Cherry	Lorimer	Jordan	Currie	E Gray 1	
Oct 23	LIVERPOOL	1-1	Harvey	Reaney	Hampton	Cherry	McQueen	Madeley	Lorimer	Currie	Jordan	F Gray*	E Gray	McNiven* 1
Oct 30	ARSENAL	2-1	Harvey	Reaney	Hampton	Madeley	McQueen	F Gray	Cherry 1	Lorimer*	Jordan 1	Currie	E Gray	McNiven*
Nov 6	Everton	2-0	Harvey	Reaney	Hampton	Madeley*	McQueen 1	F Gray	Cherry	Hankin	Jordan 1	Currie	E Gray	Harris*
Nov 10	STOKE CITY	1-1	Harvey	Reaney	Hampton	Cherry	McQueen	F Gray	Lorimer 1	Hankin	Jordan	Currie	E Gray	
Nov 20	Ipswich Town	1-1	Harvey	Reaney	Hampton	Cherry	McQueen 1	F Gray	Lorimer	Hankin	Jordan	Currie	E Gray	
Nov 27	LEICESTER CITY	2-2	Harvey	Reaney	Hampton	Cherry	McQueen	F Gray	Lorimer 1	Hankin	Jordan	Currie*	E Gray	McNiven* 1
Dec 11	ASTON VILLA	1-3	Harvey	Reaney	Hampton	Cherry	McQueen	F Gray	Lorimer	McNiven 1	Jordan	Stevenson	E Gray	
Dec 27	MANCHESTER CITY	0-2	Harvey	Reaney	Hampton	Cherry	McQueen	Madeley	Lorimer	Clarke	Jordan	F Gray	E Gray	
Dec 29	Sunderland	1-0	Harvey	Stevenson	Hampton	Madeley	McQueen	Cherry	Lorimer	Clarke	Jordan 1	F Gray	E Gray	
Jan 3	Arsenal	1-1	Harvey	Reaney	Hampton	Cherry*	McQueen	Madeley	F Gray	Clarke 1	Jordan	Currie	E Gray	Lorimer*
Jan 22	West Bromwich Albion	2-1	Harvey	Reaney	Hampton	Cherry*	McQueen 1	Madeley	F Gray	Clarke	Jordan	Currie	E Gray 1	Lorimer*
Feb 2	BIRMINGHAM CITY	1-0	Harvey	Reaney	Hampton	Cherry	McQueen 1	Madeley	F Gray	Clarke	Jordan	Currie	E Gray	
Feb 5	COVENTRY CITY	1-2	Harvey	Reaney	Hampton*	Cherry	McQueen	Madeley	F Gray	Clarke	Jordan 1	Lorimer	E Gray	Harris*
Feb 12	Derby County	1-0	Harvey	Reaney	Hampton	Cherry	McQueen	Madeley	F Gray	Clarke	Jordan 1	Currie	Lorimer	
Feb 19	TOTTENHAM HOTSPUR	2-1	Harvey	Reaney	Hampton	Cherry	McQueen	Madeley	F Gray	Clarke 1	Jordan 1	Currie	E Gray	
Mar 2	Newcastle United	0-3	Harvey	Reaney	Hampton	Cherry	McQueen	Madeley	F Gray	Clarke	Jordan	Currie*	E Gray	McNiven*
Mar 5	MIDDLESBROUGH	2-1	Stewart	Reaney	Hampton	Cherry*	McQueen 2	Madeley	F Gray	Clarke	Jordan	Currie	E Gray	Lorimer*
Mar 8	Queen's Park Rangers	0-0	Stewart	Reaney	Stevenson	Cherry	McQueen	Madeley	F Gray	Clarke*	Jordan	Lorimer	E Gray	Thomas*
Mar 12	Manchester United	0-1	Stewart	Reaney	Hampton	Cherry	McQueen	Madeley	F Gray	Lorimer	Jordan	Currie*	E Gray	McNiven*
Mar 23	NORWICH CITY	3-2	Stewart	Reaney 1	Hampton 1	Cherry	McQueen	Madeley	F Gray	Clarke	Jordan 1	Currie	E Gray*	Lorimer*
Apr 2	Liverpool	1-3	Stewart	Stevenson	Hampton	Madeley	McQueen 1	Cherry	F Gray	Lorimer*	Jordan	Currie	E Gray	Thomas*
Apr 8	Manchester City	1-2	Stewart	Reaney	Hampton	Cherry	McQueen	Madeley	F Gray	Lorimer	Jordan 1	Currie	E Gray	
Apr 9	SUNDERLAND	1-1	Stewart	Reaney	Hampton	Cherry 1	McQueen	Madeley	F Gray	Lorimer	Jordan	Currie	E Gray*	Harris*
Apr 12	Stoke City	1-2	Stewart	Reaney	Hampton	Cherry	McQueen	Madeley	F Gray	Lorimer	Jordan 1	Currie	Harris	
Apr 16	IPSWICH TOWN	2-1	Stewart	Reaney	F Gray	Cherry	McQueen	Madeley	Harris	Clarke 1	Jordan*	Currie	McGhie 1	Lorimer*
Apr 26	WEST HAM UNITED	1-1	Stewart	Stevenson	Hampton	Cherry	McQueen	Madeley	Harris	McNiven	Jordan 1	Currie	E Gray	
Apr 30	BRISTOL CITY	2-0	Stewart	Stevenson	F Gray	Cherry	McQueen	Madeley	Thomas 1	McGhie	Jordan*	Currie	E Gray 1	Harris*
May 4	EVERTON	0-0	Stewart	Stevenson	F Gray	Cherry	McQueen	Madeley	Thomas	McNiven	Harris	Currie	E Gray	
May 7	Aston Villa	1-2	Stewart	Stevenson	Hampton	Cherry	McQueen	Madeley	Thomas	F Gray	McNiven* 1	Currie	Harris	Whyte*
May 10	Bristol City	0-1	Stewart	Stevenson	Hampton	Cherry	McQueen	Madeley	Thomas*	McNiven	F Gray	Currie	E Gray	Harris*
May 14	QUEEN'S PARK RANGERS	0-1	Stewart	Stevenson	Hampton	Cherry	Whyte	Madeley	Jordan*	McNiven	F Gray	Currie	E Gray	Harris*
May 16	Leicester City	1-0	Stewart	Reaney	Hampton	Cherry	Lorimer	Madeley	Thomas	McNiven	F Gray 1	Currie	Harris	

LEAGUE CUP

Date	Opponent	Score	1	2	3	4	5	6	7	8	9	10	11	SUBS
Sep 1	Stoke City	Rd 2 1-2	Stewart	Reaney	F Gray	Bremner	Madeley	Hunter	Cherry	Clarke	Jordan	Currie 1	Harris	

F.A. CUP

Date	Opponent	Score	1	2	3	4	5	6	7	8	9	10	11	SUBS
Jan 8	NORWICH CITY	Rd 3 5-2	Harvey	Reaney 1	Hampton 1	F Gray	McQueen 1	Madeley	Lorimer	Clarke 1	Jordan 1	Currie	E Gray	
Jan 29	Birmingham City	Rd 4 2-1	Harvey	Reaney	Hampton	Cherry	McQueen	Madeley	F Gray	Clarke 1	Jordan 1	Currie	E Gray	
Feb 26	MANCHESTER CITY	Rd 5 1-0	Harvey	Reaney	Hampton	Cherry 1	McQueen	Madeley	F Gray	Clarke	Jordan	Currie	E Gray	
Mar 19	Wolverhampton Wans	Rd 6 1-0	Stewart	Reaney	Hampton	Cherry	McQueen	Madeley	F Gray	Clarke	Jordan	Currie	E Gray 1	
Apr 26	Manchester United (at Hillsborough)	S/F 1-2	Stewart	Reaney	Hampton	Cherry	McQueen	Madeley	F Gray*	Clarke 1	Jordan	Currie	E Gray	Lorimer*

DIVISION ONE 1977-78

Date	Opponent	Score	1	2	3	4	5	6	7	8	9	10	11	SUBS
Aug 20	Newcastle United	2-3	Stewart	Reaney	Cherry	Lorimer 1	McQueen	Madeley	E Gray	McNiven	Hankin* 1	Currie	Graham	F Gray*
Aug 24	WEST BROMWICH ALBION	2-2	Stewart	Reaney	Cherry	Lorimer	McQueen 1	Madeley	E Gray	McNiven	Jordan 1	Currie	Graham	
Aug 27	BIRMINGHAM CITY	1-0	Stewart	Reaney	Cherry	Lorimer	McQueen	Madeley	F Gray	Hankin 1	Jordan	Currie	Graham	
Sep 3	Coventry City	2-2	Stewart	Reaney*	Cherry	Lorimer	McQueen 1	Madeley	F Gray	Hankin 1	Jordan	Currie	Graham	Harris*
Sep 10	IPSWICH TOWN	2-1	Stewart	Cherry*	F Gray	Lorimer	McQueen	Madeley	E Gray	Hankin 2	Jordan	Currie	Graham	Stevenson*
Sep 17	Derby County	2-2	Stewart	Cherry	F Gray	Lorimer 1	McQueen	Madeley	E Gray	Hankin	Jordan	Currie	Graham 1	
Sep 24	MANCHESTER UNITED	1-1	Stewart	Cherry	F Gray	Lorimer	McQueen	Madeley	E Gray	Hankin 1	Jordan	Currie	Graham	
Oct 1	Chelsea	2-1	Stewart	Cherry	F Gray	Lorimer 1	McQueen	Madeley	E Gray	Hankin 1	Jordan	Currie	Graham	
Oct 5	ASTON VILLA	1-1	Stewart	Cherry	F Gray	Lorimer	McQueen 1	Madeley	E Gray	Hankin	Jordan	Currie	Graham	
Oct 8	Bristol City	2-3	Stewart	Cherry	F Gray	Lorimer	McQueen	Madeley	E Gray	Hankin 2	Jordan	Currie	Graham	
Oct 15	LIVERPOOL	1-2	Stewart	Stevenson	F Gray	Lorimer	McQueen	Cherry	E Gray	Hankin	Thomas 1	Currie	Graham*	Parkinson*
Oct 22	Middlesbrough	1-2	Harvey	Stevenson	F Gray	Lorimer	Parkinson	Madeley	Cherry	Hankin	Jordan	Currie	Harris 1	
Oct 29	Leicester City	0-0	Harvey	Cherry	F Gray	Lorimer	McQueen	Madeley	Graham	Currie	Jordan	E Gray	Harris	
Nov 5	NORWICH CITY	2-2	Harvey	Cherry	F Gray	Lorimer 2	McQueen	Madeley	E Gray*	Hankin	Jordan	Flynn	Graham	Harris*
Nov 12	Manchester City	3-2	Harvey	Cherry	F Gray	Lorimer	McQueen	Madeley	Harris	Hankin 1	Jordan 1	Flynn	Graham 1	
Nov 19	NOTTINGHAM FOREST	1-0	Harvey	Cherry	F Gray	Flynn	Madeley	Parkinson	Harris	Hankin 1	Jordan	Currie	Graham	
Nov 26	West Ham United	1-0	Harvey	Cherry	F Gray	Currie	Parkinson	Madeley	Harris	Hankin 1	Jordan	Flynn	Graham	
Dec 3	QUEEN'S PARK RANGERS	(o.g.) 3-0	Harvey	Reaney	F Gray	Currie 1	McQueen	Madeley	Harris	Cherry	Jordan	Flynn 1	Graham	
Dec 10	Arsenal	1-1	Harvey	Reaney	F Gray	Currie	McQueen 1	Madeley	Harris	Cherry	E Gray	Flynn	Graham	
Dec 17	MANCHESTER CITY	2-0	Harvey	Reaney	F Gray	Currie	McQueen 1	Madeley	Harris*	Cherry 1	Hankin	Flynn	Graham	E Gray*
Dec 26	Wolverhampton Wans	1-3	Harvey	Reaney*	F Gray	Cherry	McQueen	Madeley	Harris	Hankin	Jordan 1	Flynn	Graham	Lorimer*
Dec 27	EVERTON	3-1	Stewart	Cherry	F Gray	Lorimer 1	McQueen	Madeley	Harris	Hankin 2	Jordan	Flynn	Graham	
Dec 31	West Bromwich Albion	0-1	Stewart	Cherry	F Gray	Lorimer	McQueen	Madeley	Harris	Hankin	Jordan	Flynn	Graham	
Jan 2	NEWCASTLE UNITED	0-2	Stewart	Cherry	F Gray	Lorimer	McQueen	Madeley	Harris	Currie	Jordan	Flynn	Graham*	E Gray*
Jan 14	Birmingham City	3-2	Harvey	Reaney	F Gray	Lorimer	Parkinson	Cherry	E Gray	Currie	Hankin	Flynn	Graham 3	
Jan 21	COVENTRY CITY	2-0	Harvey	Reaney	F Gray	Lorimer	Parkinson	Madeley	Harris* 1	Hankin 1	Cherry	Currie	E Gray	Flynn*
Feb 4	Ipswich Town	1-0	Harvey	Cherry	F Gray	Lorimer	Madeley	E Gray 1	Parkinson	Hankin	Currie	Flynn	Graham	
Feb 25	CHELSEA	2-0	Stewart	Reaney	Hamton	Flynn	Cherry	Madeley	F Gray 1	Hankin	Currie 1	Clarke	Graham	
Mar 1	Manchester United	1-0	Harvey	Reaney	Hampton	Flynn	Cherry	Madeley	F Gray	Hankin	Currie	Clarke 1	Graham	
Mar 4	BRISTOL CITY	0-2	Harvey	Reaney*	Hampton	Flynn	Cherry	Madeley	F Gray	Thomas	Currie	Clarke	Graham	Parkinson*
Mar 11	Liverpool	0-2	Harvey	Stevenson	Hampton*	Flynn	Hart	Cherry	F Gray	Hankin	Currie	Clarke	Graham	Parker*
Mar 18	MIDDLESBROUGH	5-0	Harvey	Madeley	F Gray	Lorimer	Hart	Cherry*	Flynn	Hankin 1	Currie	Clarke 2	Graham 2	Harris*
Mar 25	Everton	0-2	Harvey	Madeley	F Gray	Flynn	Hart	Cherry	Lorimer	E Gray	Currie	Clarke*	Graham	Hampton*
Mar 27	WOLVERHAMPTON WANS	2-1	Harvey	Madeley	F Gray	Flynn	Hart	Cherry	Lorimer	Hankin 1	Currie	E Gray	Graham 1	
Mar 28	LEICESTER CITY	5-1	Harvey	Madeley*	Hampton	Flynn	Hart	Cherry	Harris	Hankin 1	E Gray 3	F Gray 1	Graham	Lorimer*
Apr 1	Norwich City	0-3	Harvey	Reaney	Hampton	Flynn*	Hart	Cherry	Harris	E Gray	Lorimer	F Gray	Graham	Thomas*
Apr 8	WEST HAM UNITED	1-2	Harvey	Reaney	F Gray	Flynn	Hart	Madeley	Lorimer	E Gray	Currie	Harris	Graham 1	
Apr 12	DERBY COUNTY	2-0	Harvey	Madeley	Hampton	Flynn	Hart	Cherry	F Gray	E Gray 1	Hankin 1	Currie	Graham	
Apr 15	Nottingham Forest	1-1	Stewart	Madeley	Hampton	Flynn	Hart	Cherry	F Gray 1	E Gray	Hankin	Currie	Graham	
Apr 22	ARSENAL	1-3	Stewart	Madeley	Hampton	Flynn	Hart	Cherry	F Gray	Hankin	E Gray*	Currie 1	Graham	Clarke*
Apr 26	Aston Villa	1-3	Harvey	Madeley	Hampton*	Flynn	Hart	Cherry	F Gray	Hankin 1	Currie	Clarke	Graham	E Gray*
Apr 29	Queen's Park Rangers	0-0	Harvey	Madeley	F Gray	Flynn	Hart	Cherry	E Gray	Hankin	Clarke	Currie	Graham	

LEAGUE CUP

Date	Opponent	Score	1	2	3	4	5	6	7	8	9	10	11	SUBS
Aug 31	Rochdale	Rd 2 3-0	Stewart	Reaney	F Gray	Madeley	McQueen	Cherry 1	Lorimer	Hankin	Jordan 1	Currie	Graham*	Harris* 1
Oct 26	COLCHESTER UNITED	Rd 3 4-0	Harvey	Cherry	F Gray	Lorimer 1	Parkinson	Madeley	Graham 1	Hankin 1	Jordan 1	E Gray	Harris	
Nov 30	Bolton Wanderers	Rd 4 3-1	Harvey	Reaney	F Gray 1	Currie	Parkinson	Madeley	Harris	Hankin*	Jordan 1	Cherry	Graham 1	Hampton*
Jan 18	EVERTON	Rd 5 4-1	Harvey	Reaney	F Gray	Lorimer 2	Parkinson	Madeley	Cherry	Hankin	Currie 1	E Gray 1	Graham	
Feb 8	NOTTINGHAM FOREST	S/F 1-3	Harvey	Reaney	F Gray	Lorimer*	Parkinson	Madeley	Cherry	Hankin	Currie	E Gray 1	Graham	Harris*
Feb 22	Nottingham Forest	S/F 2-4	Stewart	Reaney	Hampton	Cherry	F Gray 1	Madeley	E Gray	Hankin	Currie	Clarke	Graham 1	

F.A. CUP

Date	Opponent	Score	1	2	3	4	5	6	7	8	9	10	11	SUBS
Jan 7	MANCHESTER CITY	Rd 3 1-2	Harvey	Reaney*	F Gray 1	Cherry	McQueen	Madeley	Harris	Hankin	Currie	Flynn	Graham	Clarke*

DIVISION ONE 1978-79

			1	2	3	4	5	6	7	8	9	10	11	SUBS
Aug 19	Arsenal	2-2	Harvey	Madeley	F Gray	Flynn	Hart	Cherry 1	Harris	E Gray	Hawley	Currie 1	Graham	
Aug 23	MANCHESTER UNITED	2-3	Harvey	Stevenson	F Gray 1	Flynn	Hart 1	Madeley	Harris	Hankin	E Gray	Currie	Graham	
Aug 26	WOLVERHAMPTON WANS	3-0	Stewart	Stevenson	F Gray 1	Flynn	Hart	Madeley	Harris*	E Gray	Hankin 1	Currie 1	Graham	Hawley*
Sep 2	Chelsea	3-0	Stewart	Stevenson	F Gray	Flynn	Hart	Madeley	Hampton	Hankin	Hawley 2	Currie	Graham 1	
Sep 9	Manchester City	0-3	Stewart	Stevenson	F Gray*	Flynn	Hart	Madeley	Cherry	Hankin	Hawley	Hampton	Graham	Harris*
Sep 16	TOTTENHAM HOTSPUR	1-2	Harvey	Stevenson	F Gray	Flynn	Hart	Madeley	Harris	Hankin	Lorimer	Cherry	Graham 1	
Sep 23	Coventry City	0-0	Harvey	Stevenson	F Gray	Flynn	Hart	Madeley	Harris	Hankin	Lorimer	Cherry	Graham	
Sep 30	BIRMINGHAM CITY	3-0	Harvey	Stevenson	Cherry	Flynn 1	Hart	Madeley	Harris	Hankin 1	Lorimer*	F Gray 1	Graham	Thomas*
Oct 7	Bolton Wanderers	1-3	Harvey	Stevenson	Cherry	Flynn	Hart	Madeley	Harris	Hankin	E Gray	F Gray	Graham 1	
Oct 14	WEST BROMWICH ALBION	1-3	Harvey	Stevenson 1	Cherry	Flynn	Hart	Madeley	E Gray	Hankin	F Gray	Currie	Graham	
Oct 21	Norwich City	2-2	Harvey	Cherry	F Gray 1	Flynn	Hart	Madeley	E Gray	Hankin	Hawley 1	Currie	Graham	
Oct 28	DERBY COUNTY	4-0	Harvey	Cherry	F Gray	Flynn 1	Hart 1	Madeley	E Gray	Hankin 1	Hawley 1	Currie	Graham	
Nov 4	Liverpool	1-1	Harvey	Cherry	F Gray	Flynn	Hart	Madeley	E Gray	Hankin	Hawley	Currie	Graham	
Nov 11	ARSENAL	0-1	Harvey	Cherry	F Gray	Flynn	Hart	Madeley	Harris	Hankin	Hawley 1	Currie	Graham	
Nov 18	Wolverhampton Wans	1-1	Harvey	Cherry	F Gray	Flynn	Hart	Madeley	E Gray	Hankin	Hawley	Currie 1	Graham	
Nov 22	CHELSEA	2-1	Harvey	Cherry	F Gray	Flynn	Hart	Madeley	E Gray	Hankin 1	Hawley	Currie	Graham 1	
Nov 25	SOUTHAMPTON	(o.g.) 4-0	Harvey	Cherry	F Gray	Flynn	Hart	Madeley 1	E Gray	Hankin	Hawley	Currie 1	Graham 1	
Dec 2	Ipswich Town	3-2	Harvey	Cherry 1	F Gray	Flynn	Hart	Madeley	E Gray	Hankin 1	Hawley	Currie	Harris 1	
Dec 9	BRISTOL CITY	1-1	Harvey	Cherry	F Gray	Flynn 1	Hart	Madeley	E Gray	Hankin	Thomas	Currie	Harris	
Dec 16	Everton	1-1	Harvey	Cherry	F Gray	Flynn	Hart	Madeley	E Gray	Hankin	Hawley 1	Currie	Harris	
Dec 23	MIDDLESBROUGH	3-1	Harvey	Cherry	F Gray	Flynn	Hart	Madeley	Harris	E Gray 1	Hawley 1	Currie 1	Graham	
Dec 26	Aston Villa	2-2	Harvey	Cherry	F Gray	Flynn	Hart	Madeley	E Gray 2	Harris	Hawley	Currie	Graham	
Dec 30	Queen's Park Rangers	4-1	Harvey	Cherry	F Gray*	Flynn	Hart	Madeley	E Gray 1	Graham	Hawley 2	Currie	Harris 1	Parkinson*
Jan 13	MANCHESTER CITY	1-1	Harvey	Cherry	F Gray	Flynn	Hart	Madeley	E Gray	Graham	Hawley 1	Currie	Harris	
Jan 20	Tottenham Hotspur	2-1	Harvey	Stevenson	F Gray	Flynn	Hart 1	Parkinson	Hankin 1	Graham	Hawley	Currie	Harris	
Feb 3	COVENTRY CITY	1-0	Harvey	Cherry	Stevenson	Flynn	Parkinson	Madeley	F Gray	Hankin	Harris	Currie 1	Graham	
Feb 10	Birmingham City	1-0	Harvey	Cherry	Stevenson	Flynn	Hart	Madeley	F Gray 1	Harris*	Hawley	Currie	Graham	E Gray*
Feb 24	West Bromwich Albion	2-1	Harvey	Cherry	Stevenson	Flynn	Hart	Madeley	Harris*	Graham 2	Hawley	Currie	F Gray	Parkinson*
Mar 3	NORWICH CITY	2-2	Harvey	Cherry	F Gray	Flynn	Parkinson	Madeley	Harris	Hird	Hawley 2	Currie	Graham	
Mar 10	Derby County	1-0	Harvey	Cherry	F Gray	Flynn	Hart	Madeley*	Harris	Hird	Hawley 1	Currie	Graham	E Gray*
Mar 24	Manchester United	1-4	Harvey	Hird	Cherry	Flynn	Hart	E Gray	Harris	F Gray*	Hawley	Currie	Graham	Hankin* 1
Mar 31	Southampton	2-2	Harvey	Hird	F Gray	Flynn	Hart	Cherry	E Gray	Hankin	Hawley 2	Currie	Graham	
Apr 7	IPSWICH TOWN	1-1	Harvey	Cherry 1	F Gray	Flynn	Hart	Madeley	E Gray	Hankin	Hawley	Currie*	Graham	Hird*
Apr 10	Middlesbrough	0-1	Harvey	Hird	F Gray	Flynn	Hart	Cherry	E Gray	Hankin*	Hawley	Madeley	Graham	Stevenson*
Apr 14	ASTON VILLA	1-0	Harvey	Cherry	F Gray	Flynn	Hart 1	Madeley	E Gray*	Hankin	Hawley	Hird	Graham	Harris*
Apr 16	Nottingham Forest	0-0	Harvey	Hird	F Gray	Flynn	Hart	Cherry	Harris	Hampton	Hawley	Madeley	Graham	
Apr 21	EVERTON	1-0	Harvey	Hird	F Gray	Flynn	Hart	Cherry	Harris	Hankin	Madeley	Currie 1	Graham	
Apr 25	BOLTON WANDERERS	5-1	Harvey	Hird	F Gray 1	Flynn	Hart 1	Madeley	Harris 1	Cherry 1	Hankin*	Currie	Graham	Hawley* 1
Apr 28	Bristol City	0-0	Harvey	Hird	F Gray	Cherry	Hart	Madeley	Harris	Hampton	Hankin	E Gray	Graham	
May 4	QUEEN'S PARK RANGERS	4-3	Harvey	Hird	F Gray	Flynn	Hart	Madeley	Harris	Cherry 1	Hankin 2	Currie	Graham* 1	Hawley*
May 15	NOTTINGHAM FOREST	1-2	Harvey	Hird	F Gray	Flynn	Hart	Madeley	Harris	Cherry 1	Hawley	Currie	Graham	E Gray*
May 17	LIVERPOOL	0-3	Harvey	Hird	F Gray	Flynn	Hart	Madeley	Harris	Cherry	Hawley	E Gray	Graham	

LEAGUE CUP

			1	2	3	4	5	6	7	8	9	10	11	SUBS
Aug 29	West Bromwich Albion	Rd 2 0-0	Stewart	Madeley	F Gray	Flynn	Hart	Stevenson	Hampton	Hankin	Hawley	Currie	Graham	
Sep 6	WEST BROM ALB	Rd 2 R 0-0 (AET)	Stewart	Stevenson	F Gray	Flynn	Hart	Madeley	Cherry	Hankin	Hawley	Currie*	Graham	E Gray*
Oct 2	West Brom Alb (At Manchester City)	Rd 2 2R 1-0	Harvey	Stevenson	Cherry	Flynn	Hart 1	Madeley	Thomas*	Hankin	E Gray	F Gray	Graham	Lorimer*
Oct 10	Sheffield United	Rd 3 4-1	Harvey	Stevenson	Cherry	Flynn	Hart	Hampton	E Gray 2	Hankin	F Gray 1	Currie 1	Graham	
Nov 7	Queen's Park Rangers	Rd 4 2-0	Harvey	Cherry	F Gray	Flynn	Hart	Madeley	E Gray	Hankin 1	Hawley 1	Currie	Graham	
Dec 3	LUTON TOWN	Rd 5 4-1	Harvey	Cherry 1	F Gray 1	Flynn	Hart	Madeley	E Gray 1	Hankin	Hawley	Currie 1	Harris	
Jan 24	SOUTHAMPTON	S/F 2-2	Harvey	Cherry	F Gray	Flynn	Hart	Madeley	E Gray	Hankin 1	Hawley	Currie 1	Graham*	Harris*
Jan 30	Southampton	S/F 0-1	Harvey	Cherry	F Gray	Flynn	Hart	Madeley	E Gray	Hankin	Hawley	Currie	Graham	Harris*

F.A. CUP

			1	2	3	4	5	6	7	8	9	10	11	SUBS
Jan 18	Hartlepool United	Rd 3 6-2	Harvey	Cherry	F Gray 1	Flynn	Hart 1	Madeley	E Gray 2	Graham 1	Hawley	Currie	Harris 1	
Feb 26	WEST BROM ALB (At W.B.A.)	Rd 4 3-3	Harvey	Cherry	F Gray 1	Flynn	Hart	Madeley	Harris 1	Stevenson	Hawley	Currie	Graham 1	
Mar 1	West Brom Alb	Rd 4 R 0-2 (AET)	Harvey	Cherry	F Gray	Flynn	Parkinson	Madeley	Harris	Stevenson*	Hawley	Currie	Graham*	Thomas*

DIVISION ONE 1979-80

			1	2	3	4	5	6	7	8	9	10	11	SUBS
Aug 18	Bristol City	2-2	Harvey	Hird	Stevenson	Flynn	Parkinson	Hampton	Curtis 2	Cherry	Hankin	Harris	Graham	
Aug 22	EVERTON	2-0	Harvey	Hird 1	Hampton	Flynn	Hart	Stevenson	Harris 1	Cherry	Hankin	Curtis	Graham	
Aug 25	Norwich City	1-2	Harvey	Hird	Hampton*	Flynn	Hart 1	Stevenson	Harris	Cherry	Hankin	Curtis	Graham	Parkinson*
Sep 1	ARSENAL	1-1	Harvey	Hird	Stevenson	Flynn	Hart 1	Parkinson	Greenhoff	Cherry	Hawley	Curtis	Graham	
Sep 8	Nottingham Forest	0-0	Harvey	Hird	Hampton	Flynn	Hart	Madeley	E Gray	Cherry	Hankin	Curtis	Graham	
Sep 15	LIVERPOOL	1-1	Harvey	Hird	Hampton	Flynn	Hart	Madeley	E Gray	Cherry	Hankin	Curtis 1	Graham	
Sep 22	Bolton Wanderers	1-1	Harvey	Hird	Hampton	Flynn	Hart	Madeley	E Gray* 1	Cherry	Hankin	Curtis	Graham	Greenhoff*
Sep 29	MANCHESTER CITY	1-2	Harvey	Hird	Hampton	Greenhoff	Hart	Madeley*	Harris	Cherry	Hankin 1	Curtis	Graham	Chandler*
Oct 6	IPSWICH TOWN	2-1	Harvey	Hird 1	Hampton	Flynn	Greenhoff	Parkinson	Hamson	Cherry 1	Hankin	Curtis	Graham	
Oct 13	Brighton	0-0	Lukic	Hird	Hampton	Flynn	Stevenson	Parkinson	Hamson	Cherry	Hankin	Curtis	Graham	
Oct 20	TOTTENHAM HOTSPUR	1-2	Lukic	Hird	Hampton	Flynn	Greenhoff*	Madeley	E Gray	Cherry	Hankin 1	Curtis	Entwistle	Chandler*
Oct 27	Southampton	2-1	Lukic	Stevenson	Hampton	Chandler	Parkinson	Madeley	E Gray	Cherry	Hankin	Curtis 1	Entwistle 1	
Nov 3	BRISTOL CITY	1-3	Lukic	Cherry	Stevenson	Hampton*	Hart	Madeley	Chandler	Entwistle	Hankin	Curtis	E Gray 1	Harris*
Nov 10	Coventry City	0-3	Lukic	Cherry	Stevenson	Flynn*	Hart	Madeley	Hird	Greenhoff	Hankin	Curtis	E Gray	Entwistle*
Nov 13	Everton	1-5	Lukic	Cherry	Stevenson	Greenhoff	Hart	Madeley	Hird 1	Entwistle	Hamson	Curtis	E Gray	
Nov 17	WEST BROMWICH ALBION	1-0	Lukic	Cherry	Stevenson	Hird	Hart	Madeley*	E Gray	Hamson	Entwistle	Curtis	Harris	Connor* 1
Nov 24	Aston Villa	0-0	Lukic	Cherry	Stevenson	Hamson	Hart	Greenhoff	Hird	Graham	Connor	Curtis	E Gray	
Dec 1	CRYSTAL PALACE	1-0	Lukic	Cherry	Stevenson	Hamson	Hart	Greenhoff	E Gray	Hird 1	Connor	Curtis	Graham	
Dec 8	Manchester United	1-1	Lukic	Cherry	Stevenson	Hamson*	Hart	Greenhoff	E Gray	Hird	Connor 1	Curtis	Graham	Harris*
Dec 15	WOLVERHAMPTON WANDERERS	3-0	Lukic	Cherry	Stevenson	Hamson 1	Hart	Greenhoff	E Gray	Hird	Connor 1	Curtis	Graham 1	
Dec 21	Stoke City	2-0	Lukic	Cherry	Stevenson	Hamson	Hart	Greenhoff	E Gray	Hird	Connor 1	Curtis	Harris 1	Entwistle*
Dec 26	Middlesbrough	1-3	Lukic	Cherry	Stevenson	Hamson	Hart	Greenhoff*	E Gray	Hird 1	Connor	Curtis	Harris	Entwistle* 1
Dec 29	NORWICH CITY	2-2	Lukic	Cherry	Stevenson	Hamson	Hart	Madeley	E Gray	Hird 1	Connor	Hankin 1	Harris	
Jan 1	DERBY COUNTY	1-0	Lukic	Cherry	Stevenson	Hamson	Hart	Madeley	E Gray	Hird 1	Connor	Hankin	Harris	
Jan 12	Arsenal	1-0	Lukic	Cherry	Stevenson	Hamson	Greenhoff	Madeley	E Gray	Hird	Connor 1	Entwistle	Hampton	
Jan 19	NOTTINGHAM FOREST	1-2	Lukic	Cherry	Stevenson	Hamson	Greenhoff	Madeley	E Gray	Hird	Connor 1	Entwistle*	Hampton	Graham*
Feb 9	BOLTON WANDERERS	2-2	Lukic	Cherry	Hampton	Flynn	Greenhoff	Madeley	Hankin	Hird 1	Connor	Hamson	Graham 1	
Feb 16	Manchester City	1-1	Lukic	Cherry	Hampton	Flynn	Greenhoff	Madeley	E Gray	Hird	Connor	Firm	Graham 1	
Feb 23	BRIGHTON	1-1	Lukic	Stevenson	Cherry	Flynn 1	Firm	Greenhoff*	E Gray	Hird	Connor	Hampton	Graham	
Mar 1	Tottenham Hotspur	1-2	Lukic	Cherry*	Stevenson	Flynn	Hart	Firm	E Gray	Chandler 1	Connor	Hamson	Graham	Entwistle*
Mar 8	SOUTHAMPTON	2-0	Lukic	Hird	Parkinson	Flynn	Hart 1	Madeley	E Gray	Chandler	Connor	Parlane 1	Graham	
Mar 14	Ipswich Town	0-1	Lukic	Cherry	Parkinson	Flynn	Hart	Madeley	E Gray*	Hird	Connor	Parlane	Graham	Chandler*
Mar 19	Liverpool	0-3	Lukic	Cherry	Parkinson	Flynn	Hart	Madeley	Parlane	Hird	Connor	Hamson	Graham*	Chandler*
Mar 22	COVENTRY CITY	0-0	Lukic	Hird	Parkinson	Chandler	Hart	Madeley	Hamson	Cherry	Connor	Parlane	Graham	
Mar 29	West Bromwich Albion	1-2	Lukic	Hird	Parkinson*	Flynn	Hart	Madeley	Cherry	E Gray	Chandler 1	Parlane	Graham	Greenhoff*
Apr 2	MIDDLESBROUGH	2-0	Lukic	Hird	Greenhoff	Flynn	Hart	Dickinson	E Gray	Cherry	Chandler	Parlane	Graham	
Apr 5	Derby County	0-2	Lukic	Hird	Cherry 1	Flynn 1	Hart	Greenhoff	E Gray	Thomas	Chandler	Parlane	Graham*	Connor*
Apr 8	STOKE CITY	3-0	Lukic	Hird	Cherry	Flynn	Hart	Madeley	E Gray	Chandler	Harris 2	Parlane 1	Dickinson	
Apr 12	Crystal Palace	0-1	Lukic	Hird	Stevenson	Dickinson	Hart	Madeley	E Gray	Chandler	Connor	Thomas	Harris	
Apr 19	ASTON VILLA	0-0	Lukic	Hird	Stevenson	Dickinson	Hart*	Greenhoff	E Gray	Chandler	Parlane	Thomas	Harris	Connor*
Apr 26	Wolverhampton Wanderers	1-3	Lukic	Hird	Greenhoff	Flynn 1	Dickinson*	Madeley	Chandler	Cherry	Parlane	Connor	Thomas	Stevenson*
May 3	MANCHESTER UNITED	2-0	Lukic	Hird 1	Cherry	Flynn	Greenhoff	Madeley	Harris	Chandler	Parlane 1	Stevenson*	Graham	

LEAGUE CUP

			1	2	3	4	5	6	7	8	9	10	11	SUBS
Aug 29	ARSENAL	Rd 2 1-1	Harvey	Hird	Hampton	Flynn	Hart	Stevenson 1	Harris	Cherry	Greenhoff	Curtis	Graham	
Sep 4	Arsenal	Rd 2 0-7	Harvey	Hird	Hampton	Flynn	Hart	Stevenson	Hankin	Cherry	Greenhoff*	Curtis	Graham	Harris*

F.A. CUP

			1	2	3	4	5	6	7	8	9	10	11	SUBS
Jan 5	NOTTINGHAM FOREST	o.g. Rd 3 1-4	Lukic	Cherry	Stevenson	Hamson	Hart	Madeley	E Gray	Hird	Connor	Curtis*	Harris	Entwistle*

UEFA CUP

			1	2	3	4	5	6	7	8	9	10	11	SUBS
Sep 19	Valetta	Rd 1 4-0	Harvey	Hird	Hampton	Flynn	Hart 1	Madeley	E Gray	Cherry	Hankin	Curtis	Graham* 3	Harris*
Oct 3	VALETTA	Rd 1 3-0	Lukic	Hird	Hampton	Flynn	Hart 1	Parkinson	Hamson	Cherry	Hankin 1	Curtis 1	Graham	
Oct 24	Universitatea Craiova	Rd 2 0-2	Lukic	Hird	Stevenson	Flynn	Hart	Madeley	Harris*	Cherry	Hankin	Curtis	E Gray	Hamson*
Nov 7	UNIVERSITATEA CRAIOVA	Rd 2 0-2	Lukic	Cherry	Stevenson	Flynn	Hart	Madeley	E Gray	Parkinson*	Hankin	Curtis	Graham	Harris*

DIVISION ONE 1980-81

			1	2	3	4	5	6	7	8	9	10	11	SUBS
Aug 16	ASTON VILLA	1-2	Lukic	Cherry	Stevenson 1	Flynn	Hart	Greenhoff	E Gray*	Harris	Curtis	Sabella	Graham	Parlane*
Aug 19	Middlesbrough	0-3	Lukic	Cherry	Stevenson	Flynn	Hart	Greenhoff	E. Gray	Connor*	Curtis	Chandler	Graham	Parlane*

DIVISION ONE 1980-81 continued

			1	2	3	4	5	6	7	8	9	10	11	SUBS
Aug 23	Norwich City	3-2	Lukic	Cherry	Greenhoff	Flynn	Hart 1	Madeley	Chandler	Hamson*	Connor 1	Sabella	Graham 1	Thomas*
Aug 30	LEICESTER CITY	1-2	Lukic	Cherry	Greenhoff	Flynn	Hart 1	Madeley	Chandler	Hamson	Connor	Sabella	Graham	
Sep 6	Stoke City	0-3	Lukic	Cherry	Greenhoff	Flynn	Hart	Madeley*	Parlane	Hamson	Connor	Sabella	Graham	Harris*
Sep 13	TOTTENHAM HOTSPUR	0-0	Lukic	Hird	Stevenson	Cherry	Hart	Firm	Chandler	Parlane	Connor*	Sabella	Graham	Hamson*
Sep 20	MANCHESTER UNITED	0-0	Lukic	Hird	Stevenson	Flynn	Hart	Firm	Cherry	Connor	Parlane	E Gray	Graham	
Sep 27	Sunderland	1-4	Lukic	Hird	Stevenson	Flynn	Hart	Firm*	Cherry	Connor	Parlane 1	E Gray	Graham	Harris*
Oct 4	Ipswich Town	1-1	Lukic	Greenhoff	E Gray	Flynn	Hart	Cherry	Harris	Curtis	Parlane	Sabella 1	Graham	
Oct 8	MANCHESTER CITY	1-0	Lukic	Greenhoff	E Gray	Flynn	Hart	Cherry	Harris 1	Curtis	Parlane*	Sabella	Graham	Hamson*
Oct 11	EVERTON	1-0	Lukic	Greenhoff	E Gray	Flynn	Hart	Cherry	Harris	Curtis 1	Hamson	Sabella	Graham	
Oct 18	Wolverhampton Wanderers	1-2	Lukic	Greenhoff	E Gray*	Flynn	Hart	Cherry	Harris	Curtis	Hamson	Sabella	Connor 1	Hird*
Oct 22	Nottingham Forest	1-2	Lukic	Greenhoff	E Gray	Flynn	Hart	Cherry	Harris* 1	Hird	Connor	Sabella	Chandler	Thomas*
Oct 25	CRYSTAL PALACE	1-0	Lukic	Greenhoff	Madeley	Flynn	Hart	Cherry	Harris	Hird	Connor 1	E Gray	Graham	
Nov 1	Coventry City	1-2	Lukic	Greenhoff	Madeley	Flynn	Hart	Cherry	Harris	Hird	Connor 1	E Gray	Graham	
Nov 8	ARSENAL	0-5	Lukic	Greenhoff	Madeley*	Flynn	Hart	Cherry	Parlane	Hird	Connor	E Gray	Graham	Harris*
Nov 12	MIDDLESBROUGH	2-1	Lukic	Greenhoff	E Gray	Flynn	Hart	Cherry	Harris	Hird 2	Connor	Sabella	Graham	
Nov 15	Aston Villa	1-1	Lukic	Greenhoff	E Gray	Flynn	Hart	Cherry	Harris	Hird	Connor*	Sabella 1	Graham	Hamson*
Nov 22	Southampton	1-2	Lukic	Greenhoff	E Gray	Flynn	Hart	Cherry	Harris	Hird	Hamson	Sabella	Graham 1	
Nov 29	BRIGHTON	1-0	Lukic	Greenhoff	E Gray	Flynn	Hart	Cherry	Harris 1	Hird	Connor	Sabella	Graham	
Dec 6	West Bromwich Albion	2-1	Lukic	Greenhoff	E Gray	Flynn	Hart	Cherry	Harris 1	Hird	Connor	Sabella	Graham 1	
Dec 13	NOTTINGHAM FOREST	1-0	Lukic	Greenhoff 1	E Gray	Flynn	Hart	Cherry	Harris	Hird	Connor*	Sabella	Graham	Parlane*
Dec 20	Manchester City	0-1	Lukic	Greenhoff	E Gray	Flynn	Hart	Cherry	Harris	Hird	Connor	Sabella	Graham	
Dec 26	BIRMINGHAM CITY	0-0	Lukic	Greenhoff	E Gray	Flynn	Hart	Cherry	Harris	Hird	Connor	Sabella	Graham*	Parlane*
Dec 27	Liverpool	0-0	Lukic	Hird	E Gray	Flynn	Hart	Cherry	Harris	Parlane	Connor*	Sabella	Graham	Hamson*
Jan 10	SOUTHAMPTON	0-3	Lukic	Hird	E Gray	Flynn	Hart	Cherry	Parlane*	Hamson	Chandler	Sabella	Graham	Harris*
Jan 17	Leicester City	1-0	Lukic	Greenhoff	E Gray	Flynn	Hart 1	Cherry	Harris	Hird	Connor	Sabella*	Graham	Chandler*
Jan 31	NORWICH CITY	1-0	Lukic	Greenhoff	E Gray	Flynn	Hart	Cherry	Harris 1	Hird	Connor	Sabella	Graham	
Feb 7	Tottenham Hotspur	1-1	Lukic	Greenhoff	E Gray	Flynn	Hart	Cherry	Harris 1	Hird	Connor	Chandler*	Graham	Stevenson*
Feb 14	STOKE CITY	1-3	Lukic	Greenhoff	E Gray	Flynn 1	Hart	Cherry	Harris	Hird	Connor*	Parlane	Graham	Sabella*
Feb 21	SUNDERLAND	1-0	Lukic	Greenhoff	E Gray	Flynn	Hart	Cherry	Harris 1	Hird	Parlane	Stevenson	Graham	
Feb 28	Manchester United	1-0	Lukic	Greenhoff	E Gray	Flynn 1	Hart	Cherry	Harris	Hird	Parlane	Stevenson	Graham	
Mar 14	Everton	2-1	Lukic	Greenhoff	E Gray	Flynn	Parkinson	Cherry	Harris 1	Hird	Parlane 1	Stevenson	Graham	
Mar 21	WOLVERHAMPTON WANDERERS	1-3	Lukic	Greenhoff	E Gray	Flynn	Parkinson	Cherry	Harris 1	Chandler*	Parlane	Stevenson	Graham	Connor*
Mar 28	Crystal Palace	1-0	Lukic	Parkinson	E Gray	Flynn	Hart	Cherry	Hird	Harris	Parlane 1	Stevenson	Graham	
Mar 31	IPSWICH TOWN	3-0	Lukic	Greenhoff	E Gray	Flynn	Hart 1	Cherry	Harris 1	Hird 1	Parlane	Stevenson	Graham	
Apr 4	COVENTRY CITY	3-0	Lukic	Greenhoff	E Gray	Flynn 1	Hart	Firm	Harris	Hird	Parlane* 1	Stevenson 1	Graham	Butterworth*
Apr 11	Arsenal	0-0	Lukic	Greenhoff	E Gray	Flynn	Hart	Cherry	Harris	Hird	Parlane	Stevenson	Graham	
Apr 18	LIVERPOOL	0-0	Lukic	Greenhoff	E Gray	Flynn	Hart	Cherry	Harris	Hird	Parlane	Stevenson	Graham	
Apr 21	Birmingham City	2-0	Lukic	Greenhoff	E Gray	Flynn	Hart*	Cherry	Harris	Hird 1	Parlane 1	Stevenson	Graham	Firm*
May 2	Brighton	0-2	Lukic	Greenhoff	E Gray	Flynn	Firm	Cherry	Harris*	Hird	Parlane	Stevenson	Graham	Connor*
May 6	WEST BROMWICH ALBION	0-0	Lukic	Greenhoff	E Gray	Flynn	Connor	Cherry	Harris	Hird	Parlane	Stevenson*	Graham	Dickinson*

LEAGUE CUP

Aug 27	Aston Villa	Rd 2 0-1	Lukic	Cherry	Greenhoff	Flynn	Hart	Madeley	Thomas	Chandler	Connor	Sabella	Graham	
Sep 3	ASTON VILLA	Rd 2 1-3	Lukic	Cherry	Greenhoff	Flynn	Hart	Madeley	Parlane	Hamson*	Connor	Sabella	Graham 1	Harris*

F.A. CUP

Jan 3	COVENTRY CITY	Rd 3 1-1	Lukic	Greenhoff*	E Gray	Flynn	Hart	Cherry	Parlane	Hird 1	Connor	Sabella	Graham	Hamson*
Jan 6	Coventry City	Rd 3 R 0-1	Lukic	E Gray	Hird	Flynn	Hart	Cherry	Parlane	Chandler	Hamson	Sabella	Graham	

DIVISION ONE 1981-82

Aug 29	Swansea City	1-5	Lukic	Hird	F Gray	Flynn	Hart	Cherry	Harris	Graham	Parlane 1	E Gray	Barnes	
Sep 2	EVERTON	1-1	Lukic	Greenhoff	E Gray	Flynn	Hart	Cherry	Harris	Graham 1	Parlane	Stevenson	Barnes	
Sep 5	WOLVERHAMPTON WANDERERS	3-0	Lukic	Greenhoff*	E Gray	Flynn	Firm	Cherry	Harris	Graham 3	Parlane	Stevenson	Barnes	Hird*
Sep 12	Coventry City	0-4	Lukic	Greenhoff	E Gray	Flynn	Firm	Cherry	Harris*	Graham	Connor	Stevenson	Barnes	Hird*
Sep 19	ARSENAL	0-0	Lukic	Greenhoff	E Gray	Flynn	F Gray	Cherry	Harris	Graham	Connor	Stevenson	Barnes	
Sep 23	Manchester City	0-4	Lukic	Greenhoff	E Gray*	Flynn	F Gray	Cherry	Harris	Hird	Connor	Stevenson	Barnes	Hamson*
Sep 26	Ipswich Town	1-2	Lukic	Greenhoff*	F Gray	Flynn	Stevenson	Cherry	Harris	Graham	Aspin	Hird	Barnes 1	Thomas*
Sep 30	Manchester United	0-1	Lukic	Hird	F Gray	Flynn*	Stevenson	Cherry	Harris	Graham	Aspin	Hamson	Barnes	Connor*
Oct 3	ASTON VILLA	1-1	Lukic	Stevenson	F Gray	Hird	Hart	Cherry	Harris	Graham	Balcombe 1	Hamson	Barnes	
Oct 10	Liverpool	0-3	Lukic	Hird	F Gray	Hamson*	Hart	Cherry	Harris	Graham	Aspin	E Gray	Barnes	Stevenson*
Oct 17	WEST BROMWICH ALBION	3-1	Lukic	Cherry 1	F Gray	Hird	Hart	Burns	Harris*	Graham 1	Connor 1	Hamson	Barnes	Greenhoff*
Oct 24	SUNDERLAND	1-0	Lukic	Cherry	F Gray	Hird	Hart	Burns	E Gray 1	Graham	Connor	Hamson	Barnes	
Oct 31	Nottingham Forest	1-2	Lukic	Cherry	F Gray	Hird	Hart	Burns	E Gray	Graham	Butterworth 1	Hamson	Stevenson	
Nov 7	NOTTS COUNTY	1-0	Lukic	Hird	F Gray	Stevenson	Hart	Cherry	E Gray	Graham	Butterworth 1	Hamson	Barnes	
Nov 21	Southampton	0-4	Lukic	Cherry	F Gray	Flynn	Hart	Burns	Stevenson	Graham	Butterworth	Hamson	Barnes	
Nov 28	WEST HAM UNITED	3-3	Lukic	Cherry 1	F Gray	Stevenson	Hart	Burns	Harris	Graham 1	Butterworth	Hamson	Hird 1	
Dec 5	Stoke City	2-1	Lukic	Cherry	F Gray	Stevenson	Hart	Burns	Harris	Graham 1	Butterworth	Hamson 1	Hird	
Dec 12	TOTTENHAM HOTSPUR	0-0	Lukic	Cherry	F Gray	Stevenson	Hart	Burns	Harris	Graham	Butterworth*	Hamson	Hird	Connor*
Jan 16	SWANSEA CITY	2-0	Lukic	Cherry	F Gray	Stevenson 1	Hart	Burns	E Gray	Graham*	Butterworth 1	Hamson	Hird	Greenhoff*
Jan 30	Arsenal	0-1	Lukic	Cherry	F Gray	Stevenson	Hart	Burns	E Gray	Graham	Butterworth	Hamson	Hird*	Harris*
Feb 6	COVENTRY CITY	0-0	Lukic	Cherry	F Gray	Flynn	Hart	Firm	E Gray	Graham	Parlane	Hamson	Hird	
Feb 20	IPSWICH TOWN	0-2	Lukic	Hird	F Gray	Stevenson	Hart	Burns	Butterworth	Graham	Parlane	E Gray	Barnes	
Feb 27	LIVERPOOL	0-2	Lukic	Cherry	F Gray	Stevenson	Hart	Burns	Hird	Graham	Butterworth	E Gray*	Barnes	Connor*
Mar 2	Brighton	0-1	Lukic	Cherry	F Gray	Greenhoff	Hart*	Burns	Harris	Graham	Butterworth	Connor	Hird	Flynn*
Mar 10	MANCHESTER CITY	0-1	Lukic	Greenhoff	E Gray	Hird	Burns	Cherry	Butterworth	Aspin	Worthington	Connor	Barnes	
Mar 13	Sunderland	1-0	Lukic	Greenhoff	E Gray	Hird	Cherry	Burns	Parlane	Aspin	Worthington 1	Connor	F Gray	
Mar 16	Wolverhampton Wanderers	0-1	Lukic	Greenhoff*	E Gray	Hird	Cherry	Burns	Parlane	Aspin	Worthington	Connor	F Gray	Harris*
Mar 20	NOTTINGHAM FOREST	1-1	Lukic	Hird	E Gray	F Gray	Cherry	Burns	Parlane*	Graham	Worthington 1	Connor	Barnes	Aspin*
Mar 27	Notts County	1-2	Lukic	Hird	E Gray	Graham	Hart	Cherry	Connor	Aspin	Worthington 1	F Gray	Barnes	
Apr 3	MANCHESTER UNITED	0-0	Lukic	Hird	E Gray	F Gray	Hart	Cherry	Aspin	Graham	Worthington	Hamson	Barnes	
Apr 6	Middlesbrough	0-0	Lukic	Cherry	F Gray	Hird	Hart	Burns	Aspin	Graham	Worthington	Hamson	Parlane	
Apr 10	Birmingham City	1-0	Lukic	Hird	E Gray	Aspin	Hart 1	Burns	Parlane	Graham	Worthington	Hamson	Barnes	
Apr 13	MIDDLESBROUGH	1-1	Lukic	Hird*	F Gray	Aspin	Hart	Burns	Parlane 1	Graham	Worthington	Connor	Barnes	Butterworth*
Apr 17	SOUTHAMPTON	1-3	Lukic	Hird	E Gray*	Hamson	Hart	Burns	Parlane	Graham	Worthington 1	Connor	Barnes	Harris*
Apr 24	West Ham United	3-4	Lukic	Hird	F Gray	Flynn 1	Hart	Cherry	E Gray	Graham 1	Worthington	Butterworth*	Barnes	Connor* 1
Apr 28	Aston Villa	4-1	Lukic	Hird	F Gray	Flynn	Hart	Cherry	E Gray	Graham 1	Worthington 2	Connor 1	Barnes	
May 1	STOKE CITY	0-0	Lukic	Hird*	F Gray	Flynn	Hart	Cherry	E Gray	Graham	Worthington	Connor	Barnes	Burns*
May 4	Everton	0-1	Lukic	Cherry	F Gray	Flynn	Hart	Burns	E Gray	Graham	Worthington	Connor	Barnes	
May 8	Tottenham Hotspur	1-2	Lukic	Cherry	F Gray	Flynn	Hart	Burns*	E Gray	Graham	Worthington 1	Connor	Barnes	Hird*
May 12	BIRMINGHAM CITY	3-3	Lukic	Hird	F Gray	Flynn*	Hart	Cherry	E Gray	Graham	Worthington 2	Connor 1	Barnes	Aspin*
May 15	BRIGHTON	2-1	Lukic	Hird 1	Hamson 1	Aspin	Hart	Cherry	E Gray	Graham	Worthington	Connor	Barnes	
May 18	West Bromwich Albion	0-2	Lukic	Hird	Burns	Aspin	Hart	Cherry	E Gray	Graham	Hamson	Connor	Barnes	

LEAGUE CUP

Oct 7	IPSWICH TOWN	Rd 2 0-1	Lukic	Stevenson	F Gray	Hird	Hart	Cherry	Harris	Graham	Burns	E Gray	Barnes	
Oct 27	Ipswich Town	Rd 2 0-3	Lukic	Greenhoff	F Gray	Hird*	Hart	E Gray	Harris	Graham	Connor	Hamson	Barnes	Stevenson*

F.A. CUP

Jan 2	Wolverhampton Wanderers	Rd 3 3-1	Lukic	Cherry	F Gray	Stevenson	Hart	Burns	E Gray 1	Graham	Butterworth	Hamson 1	Hird 1	
Jan 28	Tottenham Hotspur	Rd 4 0-1	Lukic	Cherry	F Gray	Stevenson*	Hart	Burns	E Gray	Graham	Butterworth	Hamson	Hird	Flynn*

DIVISION TWO 1982-83

Aug 28	Grimsby Town	1-1	Lukic	Hird	E Gray	Dickinson	Hart	Thomas	Connor 1	Butterworth	Worthington	F Gray	Graham	
Sep 4	WOLVERHAMPTON WANDERERS	0-0	Lukic	Hird	E Gray	Dickinson	Hart	Thomas	Connor*	Butterworth	Worthington	F Gray	Graham	Cherry*
Sep 8	Leicester City	1-0	Lukic	Cherry	E Gray	Dickinson	Hart	Thomas	Hird	Butterworth 1	Worthington	F Gray	Graham	
Sep 11	Sheffield Wednesday	3-2	Lukic	Cherry	E Gray*	Dickinson	Hart	Thomas	Hird	Butterworth 1	Worthington 2	F Gray	Graham	Connor*
Sep 18	DERBY COUNTY	2-1	Lukic	Cherry	E Gray	Dickinson	Hart	Thomas	Hird*	Butterworth	Worthington 1	F Gray 1	Graham	Parlane*
Sep 25	Fulham	2-3	Lukic	Cherry	E Gray*	Dickinson	Hart	Thomas 1	Hird	Butterworth	Worthington	F Gray	Graham 1	Burns*
Oct 2	CAMBRIDGE UNITED	2-1	Lukic	Dickinson*	Cherry	Burns	Hart	Thomas	Hird 1	Butterworth 1	Worthington	F Gray	Graham	Gavin*
Oct 9	Chelsea	0-0	Lukic	Cherry	E Gray	Burns	Hart	Thomas	Hird	Butterworth	Worthington	F Gray	Graham	
Oct 16	CARLISLE UNITED	1-1	Lukic	Cherry	E Gray	Flynn	Hart 1	Thomas	Hird	Butterworth	Worthington	F Gray*	Graham	Connor*
Oct 20	BURNLEY	3-1	Lukic	Cherry	E Gray	Burns	Hart	Thomas	Hird 1	Butterworth 1	Worthington 1	F Gray	Graham	
Oct 23	Blackburn Rovers	0-0	Lukic	Cherry	E Gray	Burns	Hart	Thomas	Hird	Butterworth	Worthington	F Gray	Graham	
Oct 30	NEWCASTLE UNITED	3-1	Lukic	Cherry	E Gray	Burns 1	Dickinson	Thomas	Hird*	Butterworth 1	Worthington 1	F Gray	Graham	Connor*
Nov 6	CHARLTON ATHLETIC	1-2	Lukic	Cherry*	E Gray	Burns	Dickinson	Thomas	Hird	Butterworth	Worthington	F Gray	Graham	Connor* 1
Nov 13	Crystal Palace	1-1	Lukic	Cherry	F Gray	Flynn	Hart	Burns	Hird	Connor 1	Worthington	Thomas	Graham	
Nov 20	MIDDLESBROUGH	0-0	Lukic	Cherry	F Gray	Sheridan	Hart	Burns	Hird	Connor	Worthington*	Thomas	Graham	Butterworth*
Nov 27	Barnsley	1-2	Lukic	Cherry	F Gray	Sheridan	Hart	Burns	Hird	Connor	Butterworth 1	Thomas	Graham	
Dec 4	QUEEN'S PARK RANGERS	0-1	Lukic	Dickinson	F Gray	Sheridan	Hart	Burns	Aspin	Gavin*	Butterworth	Cherry	Graham	Hird*
Dec 11	Rotherham United	1-0	Lukic	Dickinson	F Gray	Sheridan	Hart	Burns	Hird	Gavin 1	Butterworth	Thomas	Graham	

DIVISION TWO 1982-83 continued

			1	2	3	4	5	6	7	8	9	10	11	SUBS
Dec 18	SHREWSBURY TOWN	1-1	Lukic	Thomas	F Gray	Dickinson	Hart	Burns	Hird 1	Sheridan	Butterworth	McNab	Gavin	
Dec 26	Oldham Athletic	2-2	Lukic	Dickinson	F Gray	Sheridan 1	Hart	Burns 1	Hird	McNab	Butterworth	Thomas	Graham	
Dec 28	BOLTON WANDERERS	1-1	Lukic	Dickinson*	F Gray	Sheridan	Hart	Burns	Hird	Butterworth	Aspin	Thomas	Graham 1	Gavin*
Jan 1	Middlesbrough	0-0	Lukic	Aspin	F Gray	Sheridan	Hart	Burns	McNab	Connor	Butterworth	Thomas	Graham	
Jan 3	Wolverhampton Wanderers	0-3	Lukic	Aspin	F Gray*	Sheridan	Hart	Burns	McNab	Connor	Butterworth	Thomas	Graham	Hird*
Jan 15	GRIMSBY TOWN	1-0	Lukic	Aspin	E Gray*	Sheridan	Hart	Burns	McNab	Connor	Butterworth 1	F Gray	Graham	Hird*
Jan 22	Derby County	3-3	Lukic	Aspin	E Gray	Sheridan	Hart 1	Burns	Thomas*	Connor	Butterworth	F Gray	Graham 2	Hird*
Feb 12	Cambridge United	0-0	Lukic	Aspin	E Gray	Sheridan	Hart	Dickinson*	Thomas	Connor	Butterworth	F Gray	Graham	Hird*
Feb 19	CHELSEA	3-3	Lukic	Aspin	E Gray	Sheridan	Hart	Dickinson	Thomas*	Connor	Butterworth 1	F Gray 1	Graham 1	Hird*
Feb 26	Carlisle United	2-2	Lukic	Aspin	E Gray	Sheridan*	Hart	Dickinson	Thomas	Butterworth 1	Connor 1	F Gray	Graham	Hird*
Mar 5	BLACKBURN ROVERS	2-1	Lukic	Aspin	F Gray 1	Sheridan	Hart	Dickinson	Thomas*	Butterworth	Connor	Donnelly	Graham	Hird 1
Mar 12	Newcastle United	1-2	Harvey	Aspin*	F Gray	Sheridan	Hart	Dickinson	Hird	Butterworth	Connor 1	Burns	Graham	Donnelly*
Mar 19	Charlton Athletic	1-0	Harvey	Thomas	F Gray	Sheridan 1	Hart	Dickinson	Hird	Butterworth	Connor	Donnelly	Graham	
Mar 26	CRYSTAL PALACE	2-1	Harvey	Thomas	F Gray 1	Sheridan	Hart	Dickinson	Hird	Butterworth	Ritchie 1	Donnelly	Graham	
Apr 2	Bolton Wanderers	2-1	Harvey	Thomas	F Gray	Sheridan	Hart 1	Dickinson	Hird	Butterworth 1	Ritchie	Donnelly	Graham	
Apr 5	OLDHAM ATHLETIC	0-0	Harvey	Thomas	F Gray	Sheridan	Hart	Dickinson	Hird	Butterworth*	Ritchie	Donnelly	Graham	E Gray*
Apr 9	Burnley	(o.g.) 2-1	Harvey	Thomas	F Gray	Sheridan	Hart	Dickinson	Hird	E Gray	Ritchie 1	Donnelly	Graham	
Apr 16	FULHAM	1-1	Harvey	Thomas	F Gray	Sheridan	Hart	Dickinson	Hird	E Gray	Wright* 1	Donnelly	Graham	Aspin*
Apr 23	Queen's Park Rangers	0-1	Harvey	Thomas	F Gray	Sheridan	Hart	Dickinson	Hird	E Gray	Ritchie	Donnelly*	Graham	Gavin*
Apr 27	SHEFFIELD WEDNESDAY	1-2	Harvey	Thomas*	F Gray	Sheridan	Hart	Dickinson	Hird	Butterworth	Ritchie 1	Donnelly	Graham	Gavin*
Apr 30	BARNSLEY	0-0	Harvey	Thomas	F Gray	Sheridan	Hart	Dickinson	Hird	Butterworth	Ritchie	Donnelly	Graham	
May 2	LEICESTER CITY	(o.g). 2-2	Harvey	Aspin	F Gray 1	Sheridan	Brown	Dickinson	Thomas	Butterworth	Ritchie	Donnelly	Wright	
May 7	Shrewsbury Town	0-0	Harvey	Aspin	F Gray	Sheridan	Hart	Dickinson	Thomas	Butterworth*	Ritchie	Donnelly	Sellars	Wright*
May 14	ROTHERHAM UNITED	2-2	Harvey	Aspin	F Gray	Wright	Hart	Dickinson	Thomas	Butterworth 1	Ritchie	Donnelly 1	Graham*	Hird*

LEAGUE CUP

			1	2	3	4	5	6	7	8	9	10	11	SUBS
Oct 6	NEWCASTLE UNITED Rd 2	0-1	Lukic	Cherry*	E Gray	Burns	Hart	Thomas	Hird	Butterworth	Worthington	F Gray	Graham	Connor*
Oct 27	Newcastle United o.g. Rd 2 AET	4-1	Lukic	Cherry	E Gray*	Burns	Hart	Thomas	Hird	Butterworth 1	Worthington 1	F Gray	Graham	Connor* 1
Nov 10	HUDDERSFIELD TOWN Rd 3	0-1	Lukic	Cherry	E Gray*	Burns	Hart	Thomas	Connor	Butterworth	Worthington	F Gray	Graham	Hird*

F.A. CUP

			1	2	3	4	5	6	7	8	9	10	11	SUBS
Jan 8	PRESTON NORTH END Rd 3	3-0	Lukic	Aspin	E Gray	Sheridian* 1	Hart	Burns	Aspin	Connor 1	Butterworth	Thomas	Graham 1	Hird*
Jan 29	Arsenal (o.g). Rd 4	1-1	Lukic	Aspin	E Gray	Thomas	Hart	Dickinson	Hamson*	Connor	Butterworth	F Gray	Graham	Hird*
Feb 2	ARSENAL Rd 4 R AET	1-1	Lukic	Aspin	E Gray	Thomas	Hart	Dickinson	Hird	Butterworth 1	Connor	F Gray	Graham	
Feb 9	Arsenal Rd 4 2nd R	1-2	Lukic	Aspin	E Gray	Sheridan	Hart	Dickinson	Thomas	Butterworth	Connor 1	F Gray	Graham	

DIVISION TWO 1983-84

			1	2	3	4	5	6	7	8	9	10	11	SUBS
Aug 27	NEWCASTLE UNITED	0-1	Harvey	Thomas	F Gray	Sheridan	Brown	Dickinson	Watson*	McCluskey	Ritchie	Donnelly	Barnes	Butterworth*
Aug 29	BRIGHTON	3-2	Harvey	Thomas	F Gray 1	Sheridan 1	Brown	Dickinson	Watson 1	McCluskey	Ritchie	Hamson*	Barnes	Butterworth
Sep 3	Middlesbrough	2-2	Harvey	Aspin	F Gray 1	Watson	Brown	Dickinson	Sheridan	McCluskey 1	Ritchie	Thomas	Barnes*	Donnelly*
Sep 6	Grimsby Town	0-2	Harvey	Aspin*	F Gray	Watson	Brown	Dickinson	Sheridan	McCluskey	Butterworth	Thomas	Gavin	Donnelly*
Sep 10	CARDIFF CITY	1-0	Hughes	Thomas	F Gray	Watson	Brown	Dickinson	E Gray	McCluskey 1	Ritchie*	Sheridan	Gavin	Butterworth*
Sep 17	Fulham	1-2	Hughes	Thomas	F Gray	Watson	Brown	Dickinson	E Gray	McCluskey*	Ritchie 1	Sheridan	Gavin	Butterworth*
Sep 24	MANCHESTER CITY	1-2	Harvey	Thomas	F Gray	Burns	Brown	Dickinson	Sheridan	McCluskey*	Ritchie 1	Donnelly	Gavin	Wright*
Oct 1	Shrewsbury Town	1-5	Harvey	Thomas	F Gray	Burns	Brown*	Dickinson	Sheridan	McCluskey	Ritchie 1	Donnelly	Gavin	Watson*
Oct 8	Sheffield Wednesday	1-3	Harvey	Hird	F Gray 1	Watson*	Burns	Dickinson	Sheridan	McCluskey	Ritchie	Donnelly	Thomas	Barnes*
Oct 14	CAMBRIDGE UNITED	3-1	Harvey	Hird 1	F Gray	Watson 1	Burns	Dickinson	Sheridan	McCluskey	Ritchie	Donnelly 1	Thomas	
Oct 22	Barnsley	2-0	Harvey	Hird	F Gray	Watson	Burns	Dickinson	Sheridan*	McCluskey	Ritchie	Donnelly 1	Thomas	Barnes* 1
Oct 29	PORTSMOUTH	2-1	Harvey	Aspin	F Gray	Watson	Burns	Brown	Thomas	McCluskey	Ritchie	Donnelly 1	Barnes 1	
Nov 5	CRYSTAL PALACE	1-1	Harvey	Aspin	F Gray	Watson*	Burns	Dickinson	Thomas	McCluskey 1	Ritchie	Donnelly	Barnes	Butterworth*
Nov 12	Blackburn Rovers	1-1	Harvey	Aspin	F Gray	Watson	Burns	Dickinson	Wright	McCluskey	Ritchie	Donnelly 1	Barnes	
Nov 19	Derby County	1-1	Harvey	McGoldrick	F Gray	Watson	Burns	Dickinson	Thomas	McCluskey	Ritchie 1	Donnelly	Barnes	
Nov 26	CHELSEA	1-1	Harvey	McGoldrick	F Gray	Watson	Burns	Dickinson	Thomas	McCluskey 1	Ritchie	Donnelly	Barnes	
Dec 3	Carlisle United	0-1	Harvey	Dickinson	F Gray	Watson	Burns	Brown	Thomas*	McCluskey	Ritchie	Donnelly	Barnes	Hamson*
Dec 15	Charlton Athletic	0-2	Harvey	McGoldrick	F Gray	Watson*	Burns	Dickinson	Wright	McCluskey	Ritchie	Donnelly	Barnes	Hamson*
Dec 26	HUDDERSFIELD TOWN	1-2	Harvey	McGoldrick	F Gray	Hamson	Burns	Dickinson	Wright 1	McCluskey	Ritchie	Donnelly*	Sellars	Hird*
Dec 27	Oldham Athletic	2-3	Harvey	McGoldrick	F Gray 1	Hamson	Aspin	Dickinson	Wright 1	McCluskey*	Ritchie	Donnelly	Sellars	Hird*
Dec 31	MIDDLESBROUGH	4-1	Harvey	McGoldrick	F Gray	Hamson	Aspin	Dickinson	Wright 1	McCluskey* 2	Ritchie	Donnelly	Sellars 1	Lorimer*
Jan 2	Manchester City	(o.g). 1-1	Harvey	McGoldrick	F Gray	Hamson	Aspin	Dickinson	Wright	McCluskey*	Ritchie	Donnelly	Sellars	Lorimer*
Jan 21	FULHAM	1-0	Harvey	Hird	Hamson	Watson 1	Aspin	Irwin	Wright	Sellars	Ritchie	Lorimer	Barnes	
Feb 4	SHREWSBURY TOWN	3-0	Harvey	Hird	Hamson	Watson 2	Brown 1	Dickinson	Wright	Sellars*	Ritchie	Lorimer	Barnes	McCluskey*
Feb 11	Cardiff City	1-0	Harvey	Hird	Hamson	Watson	Brown	Dickinson	Wright	Sellars	Ritchie	Lorimer	Barnes*	McCluskey* 1
Feb 15	SWANSEA CITY	1-0	Harvey	Hird	Hamson	Watson	Brown	Dickinson	Wright	Sellars	Ritchie	Lorimer 1	Barnes*	McCluskey*
Feb 18	Portsmouth	3-2	Harvey	Hird	Hamson	Watson 1	Brown*	Dickinson	Wright 1	Sellars	Ritchie	Lorimer 1	Barnes	McCluskey*
Feb 25	BARNSLEY	1-2	Harvey	Hird	Hamson	Watson	Brown	F Gray	Wright 1	Sellars	McCluskey*	Lorimer	Barnes	Gavin*
Mar 3	Crystal Palace	0-0	Harvey	Hird	E Gray*	Watson	Brown	Irwin	Wright	Sellars	Gavin	Lorimer	Barnes	Thomas*
Mar 10	BLACKBURN ROVERS	1-0	Harvey	Hird	Hamson	Watson*	Aspin	Dickinson	Wright	Sellars	Ritchie	Lorimer	Barnes	Butterworth* 1
Mar 17	GRIMSBY TOWN	2-1	Harvey	Hird	Hamson	Aspin 1	Brown	Dickinson	Wright	Sellars 1	Ritchie	Lorimer	Barnes	
Mar 24	Brighton	0-3	Harvey	Hird	F Gray*	Aspin	Brown	Dickinson	Wright	Sellars	Ritchie	Lorimer	Barnes	Butterworth*
Mar 28	Newcastle United	0-1	Harvey	Hird	Hamson	Irwin	Aspin	Dickinson	Butterworth	Sellars	Ritchie	Lorimer	Barnes	
Mar 31	SHEFFIELD WEDNESDAY	1-1	Harvey	Hird	Hamson	Irwin	Aspin	Dickinson	Butterworth	Sellars	Ritchie 1	Lorimer	Barnes	
Apr 7	Cambridge United	2-2	Harvey	Hird*	Hamson	Irwin	Aspin	Brown	Butterworth	Sellars 1	Ritchie	Lorimer	Barnes 1	Wright*
Apr 14	DERBY COUNTY	0-0	Harvey	Irwin	Hamson	Donnelly*	Aspin	Dickinson	Wright	Sellars	Ritchie	Lorimer	Barnes	Gavin*
Apr 21	Huddersfield Town	2-2	Harvey	Irwin	Hamson	Watson	Aspin	Dickinson	Wright 1	Lorimer	Ritchie	Donnelly*	Barnes 1	McCluskey*
Apr 24	OLDHAM ATHLETIC	2-0	Harvey	Irwin	Hamson	Watson	Aspin	Dickinson	Wright	Donnelly	Ritchie 1	Lorimer 1	Gavin	
Apr 28	Chelsea	0-5	Harvey	Irwin	Hamson	Watson	Aspin	Dickinson	Wright	Sellars*	Ritchie	Lorimer	Gavin	McCluskey*
May 5	CARLISLE UNITED	3-0	Harvey	Irwin	Hamson	Watson	Aspin	Brown	Wright	Donnelly	Ritchie* 1	Lorimer	Gavin 1	McCluskey* 1
May 7	Swansea City	2-2	Harvey	Irwin	Hamson	Watson	Thompson	Brown	Wright 1	Donnelly	Ritchie*	Lorimer 1	Gavin	McCluskey*
May 12	CHARLTON ATHLETIC	1-0	Harvey	Irwin	Hamson	Watson	Aspin	Brown	Wright 1	Donnelly	McCluskey	Lorimer	E Gray	

LEAGUE CUP

			1	2	3	4	5	6	7	8	9	10	11	SUBS
Oct 5	CHESTER CITY Rd 2	0-1	Harvey	McGoldrick	F Gray	Watson	Burns	Dickinson	Hird	Butterworth	Ritchie	Thomas	Gavin*	McCluskey*
Oct 26	Chester City Rd 2	4-1	Harvey	Aspin	F Gray	Watson	Burns 1	Dickinson	Thomas	McCluskey	Ritchie 2	Donnelly	Barnes 1	
Nov 9	OXFORD UNITED Rd 3	1-1	Harvey	Aspin	F Gray	Watson	Burns	Dickinson	Thomas	McCluskey 1	Ritchie*	Donnelly	Barnes	Gavin*
Nov 23	Oxford United Rd 3 R	1-4	Harvey	McGoldrick*	F Gray	Watson	Burns 1	Dickinson	Thomas	McCluskey	Ritchie	Donnelly	Barnes	Wright*

F.A. CUP

			1	2	3	4	5	6	7	8	9	10	11	SUBS
Jan 7	SCUNTHORPE UNITED Rd 3	1-1	Harvey	McGoldrick	F Gray*	Hamson	Aspin	Dickinson	Wright 1	McCluskey	Ritchie	Donnelly	Barnes	Lorimer*
Jan 10	Scunthorpe United Rd 3 R AET	1-1	Harvey	McGoldrick	Hamson	Watson	Aspin	Dickinson	Wright 1	McCluskey	Ritchie	Lorimer	Sellars	
Jan 16	Scunthorpe United Rd 3 2nd R	2-4	Harvey	McGoldrick	Hamson	F Gray	Aspin	Irwin	Wright 1	McCluskey	Ritchie 1	Lorimer	Sellars	

DIVISION TWO 1984-85

			1	2	3	4	5	6	7	8	9	10	11	SUBS
Aug 25	Notts County	2-1	Harvey	Irwin	Hamson*	Watson	Linighan	Aspin	Wright 2	Sheridan	McCluskey	Lorimer	F Gray	Gavein*
Aug 27	FULHAM	2-0	Harvey	Irwin	F Gray	Watson	Linighan	Aspin	Wright 1	Sheridan	McCluskey 1	Lorimer	Sellars	
Sep 1	WOLVERHAMPTON WANDERERS	3-2	Harvey	Irwin	F Gray	Watson	Linighan	Aspin	Wright 2	Sheridan	McCluskey	Lorimer 1	Sellars	
Sep 8	Grimsby Town	2-0	Harvey	Irwin	F Gray	Watson	Linighan	Aspin	Wright	Sheridan	McCluskey 1	Lorimer 1	Sellars	
Sep 12	Cardiff City	1-2	Harvey	Irwin	F Gray	Watson*	Linighan	Aspin	Wright	Sheridan	McCluskey	Lorimer	Sellars 1	Gavin*
Sep 15	PORTSMOUTH	0-1	Harvey	Irwin	F Gray	Watson	Linighan	Aspin	Wright	Sheridan	McCluskey*	Lorimer	Sellars	Ritchie*
Sep 22	Crystal Palace	1-3	Harvey	Irwin	F Gray	Watson	Linighan	Aspin	Wright	Sheridan*	Ritchie	Lorimer	Sellars 1	Gavin*
Sep 29	OLDHAM ATHLETIC	6-0	Harvey	Irwin	F Gray	Sellars	Linighan 1	Dickinson	Wright 1	Sheridan 1	Ritchie 3	Lorimer	Gavin	
Oct 6	SHEFFIELD UNITED	1-1	Harvey	Irwin	F Gray	Sellars	Linighan	Dickinson	Wright	Sheridan	Ritchie	Lorimer 1	Gavin	
Oct 13	Barnsley	0-1	Harvey	Irwin	F Gray	Sellars	Linighan	Dickinson	Wright	Sheridan	Ritchie	Lorimer	Gavin*	McCluskey*
Oct 20	Huddersfield Town	0-1	Harvey	Irwin	F Gray	Sellars	Linighan	Dickinson	Wright	Sheridan*	Ritchie	Lorimer	Gavin	Donnelly*
Oct 27	MIDDLESBROUGH	2-0	Harvey	Irwin	F Gray	Sellars	Linighan	Dickinson	Wright	Sheridan	Ritchie 1	Lorimer 1	Gavin	
Nov 3	Charlton Athletic	3-2	Harvey	Aspin	Hamson	Sellars	Linighan	Dickinson	Wright	Sheridan 1	McCluskey 1	Lorimer	Gavin 1	
Nov 10	CARLISLE UNITED	1-1	Harvey	Irwin	Hamson	Sellars	Linighan	Dickinson 1	Wright	Sheridan	McCluskey*	Lorimer	Gavin	Ritchie*
Nov 17	BRIGHTON	1-0	Harvey	Irwin	Hamson	Sellars	Linighan	Dickinson	Wright	Sheridan	Ritchie 1	Lorimer	F Gray	
Nov 24	Oxford United	2-5	Harvey	Irwin	Hamson	Sellars*	Linighan	Dickinson	Wright 1	Sheridan	Ritchie	Lorimer 1	F Gray	Gavin*
Dec 1	WIMBLEDON	5-2	Harvey	Irwin	Hamson	Sellars 1	Linighan	Aspin	Wright 1	Sheridan	Ritchie 3	Lorimer*	F Gray	Eli*
Dec 8	Shrewsbury Town	3-2	Harvey	Irwin	Hamson	Sellars	Linighan 1	Aspin	Wright	Sheridan	Ritchie 2	Dickinson	F Gray	
Dec 15	BIRMINGHAM CITY	0-1	Harvey	Irwin	Hamson	Sellars	Linighan	Aspin	Wright	Sheridan	Ritchie	Dickinson	F Gray	
Dec 22	Wolverhampton Wanderers	2-0	Hughes	Irwin	Hamson	Sellars	Linighan	Aspin	Wright	Sheridan	McCluskey 1	Lorimer	F Gray 1	
Dec 26	Blackburn Rovers	1-2	Hughes	Irwin	Hamson	Sellars	Linighan	Aspin	Wright	Sheridan	McCluskey 1	Lorimer	F Gray	
Dec 29	CARDIFF CITY	1-1	Harvey	Irwin	Hamson	Sellars	Linighan	Aspin	Wright	Sheridan	McCluskey	Lorimer 1	F Gray	
Jan 1	MANCHESTER CITY	1-1	Hughes	Irwin	Hamson	Sellars	Linighan	Aspin	Wright	Sheridan	Ritchie* 1	Lorimer	F Gray	McCluskey*
Jan 19	NOTTS COUNTY	5-0	Hughes	Irwin 1	Hamson	Sellars	Linighan	Aspin	Wright 3	Sheridan 1	Ritchie	Lorimer	F Gray*	McCluskey*
Feb 2	Oldham Athletic	1-1	Day	Irwin	Hamson	Sellars	Linighan	Aspin	Wright	Sheridan	Ritchie	Lorimer 1	F Gray	
Feb 9	GRIMSBY TOWN	0-0	Day	Irwin	Hamson	Sellars*	Linighan	Aspin	Wright	Sheridan	Ritchie	Lorimer	F Gray	McCluskey*
Feb 23	CHARLTON ATHLETIC	1-0	Day	Irwin	Hamson	Sellars*	Linighan	Aspin	Wright	Sheridan	Ritchie	Lorimer 1	F Gray	McCluskey*
Feb 26	Carlisle United	2-2	Day	Irwin	Hamson	McCluskey	Linighan	Aspin 1	Wright 1	Sheridan	Ritchie	Lorimer	F Gray	

DIVISION TWO 1984-85 continued

			1	2	3	4	5	6	7	8	9	10	11	SUBS
Mar 2	Middlesbrough	0-0	Day	Irwin	Hamson	Stiles	Linighan	Aspin	Wright	Sheridan	Ritchie	Lorimer	F Gray	
Mar 9	HUDDERSFIELD TOWN	0-0	Day	Irwin	Hamson	Sellars	Linighan	Aspin	Wright	Sheridan	Ritchie	Lorimer	F Gray	
Mar 12	Portsmouth	1-3	Day	Irwin	Hamson*	Sellars	Linighan	Brown	Baird	Sheridan 1	Ritchie	Lorimer	F Gray	Wright*
Mar 16	BARNSLEY	2-0	Day	Irwin	Hamson	Sellars 1	Linighan	Dickinson	Wright	Sheridan	Baird	Lorimer 1	F Gray	
Mar 23	Sheffield United	1-2	Day	Irwin*	Hamson	Sellars	Linighan	Aspin	Wright	Sheridan	Baird	Lorimer	F Gray	Ritchie* 1
Mar 30	Fulham	2-0	Day	Irwin	Hamson	Sellars	Linighan	Aspin	Wright 2	Sheridan	Ritchie	Lorimer	F Gray*	McCluskey*
Apr 6	BLACKBURN ROVERS	0-0	Day	Irwin	Hamson	Sellars	Linighan	Aspin	Wright	Sheridan	Ritchie	Lorimer	McCluskey*	Simmonds*
Apr 8	Manchester City	2-1	Day	Irwin	Hamson	Sellars 1	Linighan	Aspin	Wright	Sheridan	Baird 1	Lorimer	F Gray	
Apr 13	CRYSTAL PALACE	4-1	Day	Irwin	Hamson	Sellars 1	Linighan	Aspin	Wright	Sheridan 2	Baird 1	Lorimer	F Gray	
Apr 20	Brighton	1-1	Day	Irwin	Hamson	Sellars 1	Linighan	Aspin	Wright	Sheridan	Baird	Lorimer	F Gray	
Apr 27	OXFORD UNITED	1-0	Day	Irwin	Hamson	Sellars	Linighan	Aspin	Wright	Sheridan	Baird 1	Lorimer	F Gray	
May 4	Wimbledon	2-2	Day	Irwin	Hamson	Sellars	Linighan	Aspin	Wright	Sheridan	Baird 2	Lorimer*	F Gray	Ritchie*
May 6	SHREWSBURY TOWN	1-0	Day	Irwin	Hamson	Sellars	Linighan	Aspin	Wright*	Sheridan	Baird 1	Lorimer	F Gray	Ritchie*
May 11	Birmingham City	0-1	Day	Irwin	Hamson	Sellars	Linighan	Aspin*	Wright	Sheridan	Baird	Lorimer	F Gray	Ritchie*

LEAGUE CUP

			1	2	3	4	5	6	7	8	9	10	11	SUBS
Sep 25	Gillingham	Rd 2 2-1	Day	Irwin	F Gray	Sellars	Linighan	Dickinson	Wright 1	Sheridan	Ritchie 1	Lorimer	Gavin	
Oct 10	GILLINGHAM	Rd 2 3-2	Day	Irwin	F Gray	Sellars 1	Linighan	Dickinson	Wright	Sheridan	Ritchie	Lorimer 1	Gavin 1	
Oct 31	WATFORD	Rd 3 0-4	Day	Irwin	F Gray	Sellars*	Linighan	Dickinson	Wright	Sheridan	Ritchie	Lorimer	Gavin	McCluskey*

F.A. CUP

			1	2	3	4	5	6	7	8	9	10	11	SUBS
Jan 4	EVERTON	Rd 3 0-2	Hughes	Irwin	Hamson	Sellars	Linighan	Aspin	Wright	Sheridan	McCluskey*	Lorimer	F Gray	Gavin*

DIVISION TWO 1985-86

			1	2	3	4	5	6	7	8	9	10	11	SUBS
Aug 17	Fulham	1-3	Day	Irwin	Hamson	Snodin	Linighan	Aspin	McCluskey	Sheridan	Baird	Lorimer 1	Sellars	
Aug 21	WIMBLEDON	0-0	Day	Irwin	Hamson	Snodin	Linighan	Aspin	McCluskey	Sheridan	Baird	Lorimer	Sellars	
Aug 24	HULL CITY	1-1	Day	Irwin	Hamson	Snodin	Linighan	Aspin	McCluskey	Sheridan	Baird 1	Lorimer*	Sellars	Wright*
Aug 26	Stoke City	2-6	Day	Irwin	Hamson	Snodin 1	Linighan	Aspin 1	McCluskey*	Sheridan	Baird	Lorimer	Sellars	Wright*
Aug 31	CHARLTON ATHLETIC	1-2	Day	Irwin	Hamson	Snodin	Linighan	Aspin	Wright	Sheridan	Baird*	Lorimer 1	Sellars	McCluskey*
Sep 4	Brighton	1-0	Day	Irwin	Hamson	Snodin	Linighan	Aspin	Wright	Sheridan	McCluskey 1	Lorimer	Dickenson	
Sep 7	Shrewsbury Town	3-1	Day	Irwin	Phelan	Snodin	Linighan	Aspin	Wright 1	Sheridan	McCluskey 1	Lorimer	Dickenson*	Baird* 1
Sep 14	SUNDERLAND	1-1	Day	Irwin	Phelan	Snodin	Linighan	Aspin	Wright*	Sheridan 1	Baird	Lorimer	McCluskey	Sellars*
Sep 21	BRADFORD CITY	2-1	Day	Irwin	Phelan	Snodin	Linighan	Aspin	McCluskey	Sheridan	Baird	Lorimer 1	Sellars 1	Wright*
Sep 28	SHEFFIELD UNITED	1-1	Day	Irwin	Phelan	Snodin	Linighan	Dickenson	Wright	Sheridan	Baird 1	Lorimer	Sellars	
Oct 5	Huddersfield Town	1-3	Day	Irwin	Phelan	Snodin	Linighan	Dickenson*	Wright	Sheridan	Baird 1	Lorimer	Sellars	McCluskey*
Oct 12	MIDDLESBROUGH	1-0	Day	Irwin	Phelan	Hamson	Linighan	Aspin	McCluskey	Sheridan	Baird	Lorimer 1	Ritchie*	Wright*
Oct 19	GRIMSBY TOWN	1-1	Day	Swinbourne	Phelan	Hamson	Linighan	Aspin	McCluskey	Dickinson	Baird 1	Lorimer	Ritchie	
Oct 27	Barnsley	0-3	Day	Dickenson	Phelan	Snodin	Linighan	Aspin	McCluskey	Hamson	Baird	Lorimer	Ritchie	
Nov 2	PORTSMOUTH	2-1	Day	Irwin	Phelan	McGregor	Linighan	Aspin	Ritchie	Sheridan	Baird	Hamson	Simmonds 2	
Nov 9	Millwall	1-3	Day	Dickenson	Phelan	McGregor	Linighan	Aspin	Ritchie 1	Sheridan	Baird	McCluskey	Hamson	
Nov 16	CRYSTAL PALACE	1-3	Day	McGregor	Phelan	Snodin	Linighan*	Aspin	Ritchie	Sheridan	McCluskey 1	Hamson	Simmonds	Dickinson*
Nov 23	Carlisle United	2-1	Day	Caswell	Robinson	Snodin	Linighan 1	McGregor	Ritchie 1	Sheridan	McCluskey	Hamson	Dickinson	
Nov 30	NORWICH CITY	0-2	Day	Swinbourne	Caswell	Robinson*	Snodin	Linighan	McGregor	Ritchie	Sheridan	McCluskey	Hamson	Dickinson	Simmonds*
Dec 7	Wimbledon	3-0	Day	Caswell	Robinson	Snodin 1	Linighan	Aspin	Ritchie	Stiles	Baird 1	Hamson	Dickinson 1	
Dec 14	FULHAM	1-0	Day	Irwin	Robinson	Snodin	Aspin	Linighan	Ritchie	Sheridan 1	Baird	Hamson	Dickinson	
Dec 22	Hull City	1-2	Day	Caswell	Robinson	Snodin	Linighan	Aspin	Ritchie	Sheridan 1	McCluskey*	Hamson	Dickinson	Phelan*
Dec 26	Blackburn Rovers	0-2	Day	Caswell	Phelan	Snodin	Aspin	Linighan*	Ritchie	Sheridan	McCluskey	Hamson	Dickinson	Sellars*
Dec 28	BRIGHTON	2-3	Day	Irwin	Thompson	Snodin 1	Aspin	Eli*	Ritchie	Sheridan	Baird 1	Hamson	Dickinson	Sellars*
Jan 1	OLDHAM ATHLETIC	3-1	Day	Irwin	Sellars	Snodin	Aspin	Swan	Ritchie 1	Harle	Baird 2	Snodin	Dickinson	
Jan 11	Sunderland	2-4	Day	Irwin	Hamson	Snodin	Linighan	Aspin	Ritchie	Harle	Baird 1	Sheridan 1	Dickinson	
Jan 18	Charlton Athletic	0-4	Day	Irwin	Caswell	Snodin	Dickinson	Aspin	Ritchie	Rennie	Baird	Sheridan	Hamson	
Feb 1	STOKE CITY	4-0	Day	Caswell	Robinson	Snodin	Aspin	Rennie	Ritchie	Swan 2	Baird 1	Hamson	Stiles 1	
Feb 8	Grimsby Town	0-1	Day	Caswell*	Robinson	Snodin	Aspin	Rennie	Ritchie	Swan	Baird	Hamson	Stiles	Dickinson*
Feb 15	BARNSLEY	0-2	Day	Stiles	Robinson	Snodin	Aspin	Rennie	Ritchie	Swan	Baird	Hamson	Harle*	Phelan*
Mar 8	HUDDERSFIELD TOWN	2-0	Day	Aspin	Robinson	Snodin 1	Ormsby 1	Rennie	Simmonds	Sheridan	Baird	Swan	Stiles	
Mar 15	Middlesbrough	2-2	Day	Aspin	Robinson*	Snodin	Ormsby	Rennie 1	Simmonds 1	Sheridan	Baird	Swan	Stiles	Ritchie*
Mar 22	SHREWSBURY TOWN	1-1	Day	Aspin	Hamson	Snodin	Ormsby	Rennie 1	Simmonds	Sheridan	Baird	Swan	Stiles	
Mar 28	Oldham Athletic	1-3	Day	Aspin	Hamson	Snodin	Ormsby	Rennie	Simmonds	Sheridan	Baird	Swan	Ritchie 1	
Mar 31	BLACKBURN ROVERS	1-1	Day	Aspin	Hamson	Snodin	Ormsby	Rennie	McCluskey	Sheridan	Baird	Swan	Ritchie 1	
Apr 5	Portsmouth	3-2	Day	Aspin	Robinson	Snodin	Ormsby	Rennie	McCluskey	Sheridan	Baird 1	Swan	Ritchie 2	
Apr 9	Bradford City	1-0	Day	Aspin 1	Robinson	Snodin	Ormsby	Rennie	McCluskey*	Sheridan	Baird	Swan	Ritchie	Stiles*
Apr 12	MILLWALL	3-1	Day	Aspin	Robinson	Snodin	Ormsby	Rennie	Sellars* 1	Stiles	Ritchie 1	Swan 1	Taylor	Simmonds*
Apr 19	Crystal Palace	0-3	Day	Aspin	Robinson	Snodin	Ormsby	Rennie	Taylor	Sheridan	Baird	Swan	Ritchie	Sellars*
Apr 22	Sheffield United	2-3	Day	Aspin	Robinson	Snodin 1	Ormsby	Rennie	Stiles	Sellars	Baird	Swan	Ritchie 1	
Apr 26	CARLISLE UNITED	2-0	Day	Aspin	Hamson	Snodin*	Ormsby	Rennie	Ritchie 2	Sellars	Baird	Swan	Stiles	Sheridan*
May 3	Norwich City	0-4	Day	Aspin	Hamson	Robinson	Ormsby	Rennie	Ritchie	Sellars	Baird	Swan	Stiles	

MILK CUP

			1	2	3	4	5	6	7	8	9	10	11	SUBS
Sep 25	WALSALL	Rd 2 0-0	Day	Irwin	Phelan	Snodin	Linighan	Dickenson	McCluskey*	Sheridan	Baird	Lorimer	Sellars	Wright*
Oct 8	Walsall	Rd 2 3-0	Day	Irwin	Phelan	Snodin 2	Linighan 1	Dickenson*	Ritchie	Sheridan	Baird	Lorimer	Hamson	McCluskey*
Oct 30	ASTON VILLA	Rd 3 0-3	Day	Dickinson	Phelan	Snodin	Linighan	Aspin	Ritchie	Sheridan	Baird	McCluskey	Hamson	

FULL MEMBERS CUP

			1	2	3	4	5	6	7	8	9	10	11	SUBS
Oct 14	Manchester City	Grp 1 1-6	Day	Irwin	Phelan	Hamson	Linighan*	Aspin	McCluskey*	Sheridan	Baird	Lorimer 1	Sellars	Swam*, Simmonds*
Oct 16	SHEFFIELD UNITED	Grp 1 1-1	Day	Irwin*	Phelan	Sellars 1	Linighan	Aspin*	Simmonds	Sheridan	Baird	Lorimer	Thompson	Swan*, Stiles*

F.A. CUP

			1	2	3	4	5	6	7	8	9	10	11	SUBS
Jan 4	Peterborough United	Rd 3 0-1	Day	Irwin	Sellars	Snodin	Aspin	Linighan	Ritchie	Swan*	Baird	Hamson	Dickinson	Sheridan*

DIVISION TWO 1986-87

			1	2	3	4	5	6	7	8	9	10	11	SUBS
Aug 23	Blackburn Rovers	1-2	Sinclair	Haddock	Caswell	Snodin	Ormsby*	Rennie	Ritchie 1	Stiles	Baird	Edwards	Ashurst	Swan*
Aug 25	STOKE CITY	2-1	Sinclair	Aspin	Thompson	Snodin	Ashurst	Rennie	Stiles	Sheridan 1	Baird 1	Edwards	Ritchie	
Aug 30	SHEFFIELD UNITED	0-1	Sinclair	Aspin	Haddock	Snodin	Ashurst	Rennie	Stiles	Sheridan	Baird	Edwards	Ritchie	
Sep 2	Barnsley	1-0	Sinclair	Aspin	Haddock	Snodin	Ashurst	Rennie	Stiles	Sheridan	Baird 1	Edwards	Ritchie	
Sep 6	Huddersfield Town	1-1	Sinclair	Aspin	Haddock	Swan	Ashurst	Rennie	Stiles*	Sheridan 1	Baird	Edwards	Ritchie	Buckley*
Sep 13	READING	3-2	Sinclair	Aspin	Haddock	Swan*	Ashurst	Rennie	Stiles	Sheridan	Baird	Edwards 1	Ritchie 1	Buckley* 1
Sep 20	Bradford City	0-2	Sinclair	Aspin	Haddock	Snodin*	Ashurst	Rennie	Stiles	Sheridan	Buckley	Edwards	Ritchie	Swan*
Sep 27	HULL CITY	3-0	Day	Aspin	Haddock	Ormsby 1	Ashurst	Rennie	Stiles	Sheridan	Baird 1	Edwards	Ritchie 1	
Oct 4	Plymouth Argyle	1-1	Day	Aspin	Haddock	Ormsby	Ashurst	Rennie	Stiles	Sheridan	Baird 1	Edwards	Ritchie	
Oct 11	CRYSTAL PALACE	3-0	Day	Aspin	Robinson	Ormsby 1	Ashurst	Rennie	Stiles	Sheridan 1	Baird	Edwards 1	Ritchie	
Oct 18	PORTSMOUTH	3-1	Day	Aspin	Robinson	Ormsby	Ashurst	Rennie	Stiles	Sheridan 1	Baird 1	Edwards	Ritchie 1	
Oct 25	Grimsby Town	0-0	Day	Aspin	Robinson	Ormsby	Ashurst	Rennie	Stiles*	Sheridan	Baird	Edwards	Ritchie	Thompson*
Nov 1	SHREWSBURY	1-0	Sinclair	Aspin 1	Robinson	Ormsby	Ashurst	Rennie	Haddock*	Sheridan	Baird	Edwards	Ritchie	Buckley*
Nov 8	Millwall	0-1	Day	Aspin	Robinson	Snodin	Ashurst	Ormsby	Rennie*	Sheridan	Baird	Edwards	Ritchie	
Nov 15	OLDHAM ATHLETIC	0-2	Day	Aspin	Robinson	Snodin	Ashurst	Ormsby	Buckley	Sheridan	Baird	Taylor	Ritchie	
Nov 21	Birmingham City	1-2	Day	Aspin	Robinson	Snodin	Ashurst	Ormsby	Thompson	Sheridan 1	Baird	Edwards	Taylor	
Nov 29	DERBY COUNTY	2-0	Day	Aspin	Robinson	Snodin	Ashurst	Ormsby	Stiles	Sheridan* 1	Baird	Edwards 1	Ritchie	Doig*
Dec 6	West Bromwich Albion	0-3	Day	Aspin	Robinson	Snodin	Ashurst	Ormsby	Stiles	Sheridan	Baird	Edwards	Rennie*	Ritchie*
Dec 13	BRIGHTON	3-1	Day	Aspin	Robinson	Snodin 1	Ashurst	Ormsby	Doig*	Sheridan 1	Baird 1	Edwards	Rennie	Stiles*
Dec 21	Stoke City	2-7	Day	Aspin	Robinson*	Thompson	Ashurst	Swan	Doig	Sheridan 1	Baird 1	Edwards	Rennie	Ritchie*
Dec 26	SUNDERLAND	(o.g.) 1-1	Day	Aspin	Rennie	Thompson	Ashurst	Swan	Buckley	Sheridan	Baird	Edwards	Ritchie	
Dec 27	Oldham Athletic	1-0	Day	Aspin	Stiles	Snodin	Swan	Ormsby	Buckley	Sheridan	Baird	Ritchie 1	Rennie	
Jan 1	Ipswich Town	0-2	Day	Aspin	Stiles	Snodin	Ashurst	Ormsby	Buckley*	Sheridan	Baird	Ritchie	Rennie	Edwards*
Jan 3	HUDDERSFIELD TOWN	1-1	Day	Aspin	Stiles	Snodin	Ashurst	Ormsby	Ritchie	Sheridan	Baird 1	Edwards	Rennie	
Jan 24	BLACKBURN ROVERS	0-0	Day	Aspin	Adams	Stiles	Ashurst	Ormsby	Ritchie	Rennie	Pearson	Baird	Buckley*	Doig*
Feb 7	Sheffield United	0-0	Day	Aspin	McDonald	Aizlewood	Ashurst	Ormsby	Stiles	Sheridan	Pearson	Baird	Adams	
Feb 14	BARNSLEY	2-2	Day	Aspin	McDonald	Aizlewood	Ashurst	Ormsby	Stiles*	Sheridan 1	Pearson	Baird 1	Adams	Edwards*
Feb 28	BRADFORD CITY	1-0	Day	Aspin	McDonald	Aizlewood	Ashurst	Ormsby	Ritchie	Sheridan	Pearson	Baird	Stiles*	Edwards* 1
Mar 7	GRIMSBY TOWN	2-0	Day	Aspin	McDonald	Aizlewood	Ashurst	Rennie	Ritchie 1	Sheridan 1	Pearson	Edwards	Adams	
Mar 10	Portsmouth	1-1	Day	Aspin	McDonald	Aizlewood	Ashurst	Ormsby	Stiles	Sheridan	Pearson	Baird	Adams 1	
Mar 21	Crystal Palace	0-1	Day	Aspin	McDonald	Aizlewood	Ashurst	Ormsby	Stiles	Sheridan	Pearson	Baird	Adams	
Mar 28	PLYMOUTH ARGYLE	4-0	Day	Aspin	McDonald	Aizlewood	Ashurst	Ormsby	Ritchie	Sheridan* 1	Pearson	Baird 3	Adams	Edwards*
Apr 4	MILLWALL	2-0	Day	Aspin	McDonald	Aizlewood	Ashurst	Ormsby	Ritchie 1	Sheridan	Pearson	Baird 1	Adams	
Apr 8	Hull City	0-0	Day	Aspin	McDonald	Aizlewood*	Ashurst	Ormsby	Ritchie	Sheridan	Pearson	Baird	Adams	Stiles*
Apr 14	Shrewsbury Town	2-0	Day	Aspin	McDonald	Aizlewood	Ashurst	Ormsby	Ritchie	Sheridan 1	Pearson 1	Baird	Adams	
Apr 18	IPSWICH TOWN	3-2	Day	Aspin	McDonald 1	Aizlewood	Ashurst	Ormsby 1	Ritchie	Sheridan 1	Pearson	Baird	Adams	
Apr 20	Sunderland	1-1	Day	Aspin	McDonald	Aizlewood	Ashurst	Ormsby	Ritchie*	Sheridan	Pearson 1	Baird	Adams	Stiles*
Apr 22	Reading	1-2	Day	Aspin	McDonald	Aizlewood	Ashurst	Ormsby	Edwards	Sheridan	Pearson 1	Baird	Adams	
Apr 25	BIRMINGHAM CITY	4-0	Day	Aspin	McDonald	Aizlewood	Ashurst	Ormsby	Edwards 1	Sheridan 1	Pearson	Baird 2	Adams	
May 2	Derby County	1-2	Day	Aspin	McDonald	Rennie*	Ashurst 1	Ormsby	Stiles	Sheridan	Pearson	Baird	Adams	Edwards*

DIVISION TWO 1986-87 continued

Date	Team	Result	1	2	3	4	5	6	7	8	9	10	11	SUBS
May 4	WEST BROMWICH ALBION	3-2	Day	Aspin	McDonald	Aizlewood	Ashurst	Ormsby 1	Stiles	Sheridan 1	Pearson 1	Baird	Adams	
May 9	Brighton	1-0	Day	Aspin	McDonald	Haddock	Ashurst	Ormsby	Stiles	Sheridan	Pearson*	Baird	Adams	Edwards* 1

LEAGUE PLAY-OFFS

Date	Team	Result	1	2	3	4	5	6	7	8	9	10	11	SUBS
May 14	Oldham Athletic	S/F 1 1-0	Day	Aspin	McDonald	Aizlewood	Ashurst	Ormsby	Ritchie*	Sheridan	Pearson	Baird	Adams	Edwards* 1
May 17	Oldham Athletic	S/F 2 1-2	Day	Aspin	McDonald	Aizlewood	Ashurst	Ormsby	Stiles*	Sheridan	Pearson	Baird	Adams	Edwards* 1
	Won on Away Goal													
May 23	Charlton Athletic	F 1 0-1	Day	Aspin	McDonald	Aizlewood	Ashurst	Ormsby	Edwards	Sheridan	Pearson*	Baird	Adams	Ritchie*
May 25	CHARLTON ATHLETIC	F 2 1-0	Day	Aspin	McDonald	Aizlewood	Ashurst	Ormsby 1	Ritchie*	Sheridan	Taylor	Baird	Adams	Edwards*
May 29	Charlton Athletic	FR AET 1-2	Day	Aspin	McDonald	Aizlewood	Ashurst	Ormsby*	Stiles	Sheridan 1	Pearson	Baird	Adams	Edwards*
	at Birmingham City													

LITTLEWOODS CUP

Date	Team	Result	1	2	3	4	5	6	7	8	9	10	11	SUBS
Sep 23	Oldham Athletic	Rd 2 2-3	Sinclair	Aspin 1	Thompson	Stiles	Ashurst	Rennie	Taylor* 1	Sheridan	Edwards	Swan	Ritchie	Wright*
Oct 8	OLDHAM ATHLETIC	Rd 2 0-1	Day	Aspin	Thompson	Ormsby	Ashurst	Rennie	Stiles*	Sheridan	Baird	Edwards	Ritchie	Taylor*

FULL MEMBERS CUP

Date	Team	Result	1	2	3	4	5	6	7	8	9	10	11	SUBS
Oct 1	BRADFORD CITY	Rd 1 0-1	Day	Thompson	Haddock	Rennie*	Swan	Ritchie	Baird	Buckley	Wright	Ashurst	Taylor*	Robinson*, Sheridan*

F.A. CUP

Date	Team	Result	1	2	3	4	5	6	7	8	9	10	11	SUBS
Jan 11	Telford United at WBA	Rd 3 2-1	Day	Aspin	Stiles	Rennie	Ashurst	Ormsby	Ritchie	Sheridan	Baird 2	Edwards	Doig	
Feb 3	Swindon Town (o.g.)	Rd 4 2-1	Day	Aspin	Adams	Stiles*	Ashurst	Ormsby	Ritchie	Sheridan	Pearson	Baird 1	Rennie	Edwards*
Feb 21	Queens Park Rangers	Rd 5 2-1	Day	Aspin	Adams	Rennie*	Ashurst	Ormsby 1	Stiles*	Sheridan	Pearson	Baird 1	Ritchie	Edwards*, Buckley*
Mar 15	Wigan Athletic	Rd 6 2-0	Day	Aspin	Adams 1	Stiles 1	Ashurst	Rennie	Ritchie	Sheridan	Pearson	Baird	Swan	
Apr 12	Coventry City	S/F AET 2-3	Day	Aspin	Adams*	Stiles*	Ashurst	Ormsby	Ritchie	Sheridan	Pearson	Baird	Rennie 1	Edwards*1, Haddock*
	at Hillsborough													

DIVISION TWO 1987-88

Date	Team	Result	1	2	3	4	5	6	7	8	9	10	11	SUBS
Aug 16	Barnsley	1-1	Day	Aspin	Adams	Aizlewood	Ashurst	Rennie	Williams	Sheridan	Pearson	Taylor* 1	Snodin	Edwards*, Haddock*
Aug 19	LEICESTER CITY	1-0	Day	Aspin	Adams	Aizlewood	Ashurst	Rennie	Williams	Sheridan 1	Pearson	Taylor*	Snodin*	Edwards*, Haddock*
Aug 22	READING	0-0	Day	Aspin	Adams*	Aizlewood	Ashurst	Rennie	Williams	Sheridan	Pearson*	Edwards	Haddock	Buckley*
Aug 29	Bradford City	0-0	Day	Aspin	Adams	Aizlewood	Ashurst	Rennie	Williams	Sheridan	Pearson	Taylor	Haddock	
Aug 31	WEST BROMWICH ALBION	1-0	Day	Aspin	Adams	Aizlewood	Ashurst	Rennie	Williams*	Sheridan 1	Edwards 1	Taylor*	Haddock	Doig*, Pearson*
Sep 5	Ipswich Town	0-1	Day	Aspin	Adams	Aizlewood	Ashurst	Rennie	Williams	Sheridan	Edwards	Taylor*	Haddock	Pearson*
Sep 12	HULL CITY	0-2	Day	Aspin	Adams	Aizlewood*	Ashurst	Rennie	Stiles	Sheridan	Pearson	Edwards	Snodin	Haddock*
Sep 15	Huddersfield Town	0-0	Day	Aspin	Adams	Grayson*	Ashurst	Rennie	Snodin*	Sheridan	Pearson	Mumby	Haddock	Stiles*, Edwards*
Sep 19	Middlesbrough	0-2	Day	Aspin	Adams	Haddock*	Ashurst	Rennie	Mumby	Sheridan	Pearson	Taylor*	Snodin	Stiles*, Edwards*
Sep 26	MANCHESTER CITY	2-0	Day	Aspin	Adams	Haddock	Ashurst	Rennie*	De Mange 1	Sheridan	Melrose*	Taylor	Snodin 1	Mumby*, Pearson*
Sep 30	STOKE CITY	0-0	Day	Aspin	Adams	Haddock	Ashurst	Rennie	De Mange	Sheridan	Melrose*	Taylor	Snodin	Pearson*
Oct 3	Blackburn Rovers	1-1	Day	Aspin	Adams	Haddock	Ashurst	Rennie	De Mange	Sheridan	Melrose*	Perason	Snodin	Taylor* 1
Oct 10	ASTON VILLA	1-3	Day	Haddock	Adams	Stiles*	Ashurst	Rennie	De Mange	Sheridan	Taylor* 1	Mumby	Snodin	Aspin*, Melrose*
Oct 17	Plymouth Argyle	3-6	Day	Aspin	Adams*	Haddock	Ashurst	Williams	De Mange	Sheridan	Taylor 1	Pearson*	Snodin 2	Stiles*, Swan*
Oct 20	Oldham Athletic	1-1	Day	Aspin	Adams	Stiles	Ashurst	Haddock	De Mange	Williams	Taylor	Pearson*	Snodin	Swan* 1
Oct 24	BOURNEMOUTH	3-2	Day	Haddock	Adams	Williams	Ashurst	Rennie 1	De Mange	Sheridan	Taylor 1	Swan 1	Snodin 1	
Oct 31	Sheffield United	2-2	Day	Williams	Aspin	De Mange	Ashurst	Haddock	Doig	Sheridan	Taylor	Swan 1	Snodin 1	
Nov 7	SHREWSBURY TOWN	2-1	Day	Williams	McDonald	De Mange	Ashurst	Haddock	Rennie	Stiles 1	Taylor 1	Swan	Snodin	
Nov 14	Millwall	(o.g.) 1-3	Day	Williams	Rennie	De Mange	Ashurst	Haddock	Pearson	Stiles	Taylor	Swan	Snodin	
Nov 21	SWINDON TOWN	4-2	Day	Williams*	Adams	De Mange	Ashurst	Haddock 1	Batty	Rennie 1	Taylor 1	Davison 1	Snodin	Stiles*
Nov 28	Crystal Palace	0-3	Day	Williams	Adams	De Mange	Ashurst	Haddock	Batty	Rennie*	Taylor	Davison	Snodin	Swan*
Dec 5	BIRMINGHAM CITY	4-1	Day	Aspin	Adams	Williams	Ashurst	Haddock	Batty	Sheridan 1	Taylor 1	Davison* 1	Snodin	Swan* 1
Dec 12	Reading	1-0	Day	Aspin	Adams	De Mange	Ashurst	Haddock	Batty	Sheridan 1	Taylor	Davison	Swan	
Dec 19	HUDDERSFIELD TOWN	3-0	Day	Aspin	Adams	Williams	Ashurst	Haddock	Batty	Sheridan 2	Taylor	Davison 1	Swan	
Dec 26	Manchester City	(o.g.) 2-1	Day	Aspin	Adams	Williams	Ashurst	Haddock	Batty	Sheridan	Swan	Davison 1	Snodin*	Stiles*
Dec 28	MIDDLESBROUGH	2-0	Day	Aspin	Adams	Williams	Ashurst	Haddock	Batty	Sheridan	Swan 1	Davison	Snodin 1	
Jan 1	BRADFORD CITY	2-0	Day	Aspin	Adams	Williams 1	Ashurst	Haddock	Batty	Sheridan	Swan 1	Davison	Snodin*	Stiles*, Taylor*
Jan 3	Hull City	1-3	Day	Aspin	Adams	Williams	Ashurst	Haddock	Batty*	Sheridan*	Taylor*	Davison	Swan	De Mange*, Mumby*
Jan 16	BARNSLEY	0-2	Day	Aspin	Adams	Williams	Ashurst	Haddock	De Mange	Sheridan 1	Pearson 1	Davison 1	Rennie*	Taylor*
Jan 30	West Bromwich Albion	4-1	Day	Aspin	Adams	Williams 1	Ashurst	Haddock	Rennie	Sheridan	Pearson 1	Davison	Snodin	
Feb 6	IPSWICH TOWN	1-0	Day	Aspin	Adams	Williams	Ashurst	Haddock	Rennie	Sheridan 1	Pearson	Davison	Snodin	
Feb 13	Leicester City	2-3	Day	Aspin	Adams	Williams 1	Ashurst	Haddock*	Rennie	Sheridan 1	Pearson	Davison	Batty	Taylor*
Feb 23	Stoke City	1-2	Day	Williams	Adams	Aizlewood	Ashurst	Haddock	Batty	Sheridan	Pearson 1	Davison	Snodin	
Feb 27	BLACKBURN ROVERS	2-2	Day	Williams	Adams	Aizlewood	Ashurst	Haddock*	Batty	Sheridan 1	Pearson	Taylor	Snodin 1	Rennie*
Mar 5	PLYMOUTH ARGYLE	1-0	Day	Williams*	Adams	Aizlewood	Ashurst	Swan	Batty	Sheridan	Baird 1	Pearson	Snodin	Rennie*
Mar 12	Aston Villa	2-1	Day	Williams	Haddock	Aizlewood*	Ashurst	Swan 1	Batty	Taylor 1	Baird	Pearson	Snodin	Rennie*
Mar 19	SHEFFIELD UNITED	5-0	Day	Williams	Haddock	Aizlewood*	Ashurst	Swan 1	Batty	Taylor	Baird	Pearson 3	Snodin	Sheridan* 1
Mar 26	Bournemouth	0-0	Day	Williams	Adams	Aizlewood	Ashurst	Swan	Batty	Haddock*	Baird	Pearson	Snodin*	Sheridan*, Davison*
Apr 2	Shrewsbury Town	0-1	Day	Williams*	Adams	Aizlewood	Ashurst	Swan	Batty	Sheridan	Baird	Pearson*	Taylor	Batty*, Snodin*
Apr 6	Millwall	1-2	Day	Haddock	Adams	Aizlewood	Ashurst	Swan	Batty	Sheridan 1	Baird	Davison*	Taylor*	Snodin*, Pearson*
Apr 23	OLDHAM ATHLETIC	1-1	Day	Haddock	Adams	Aizlewood	Ashurst	Swan*	Batty	Sheridan	Baird	Rennie	Snodin 1	Taylor*
Apr 30	Swindon Town	2-1	Day	Haddock	Adams	Stiles	Swan	Rennie	Batty	Sheridan	Baird 2	Taylor*	Snodin	Pearson*
May 2	CRYSTAL PALACE	1-0	Day	Brockie	Adams	Stiles*	Swan	Rennie	Batty	Sheridan 1	Baird	Maguire	Snodin*	Pearson*, Aizlewood*
May 6	Birmingham City	0-0	Day	Brockie	Adams*	Grayson	Swan	Rennie	Batty	Sheridan	Baird	Maguire	Snodin	Noteman*

LITTLEWOODS CUP

Date	Team	Result	1	2	3	4	5	6	7	8	9	10	11	SUBS
Sep 23	YORK CITY	Rd 2 1-1	Day	Aspin	Adams	Stiles	Ashurst	Rennie	Williams*	Sheridan	Pearson*	Taylor	Snodin 1	Doig*, Mumby*
Oct 6	York City	Rd 2 4-0	Day	Haddock	Ashurst	Rennie	Adams	Stiles	De Mange	Sheridan 2	Snodin*	Taylor 1	Pearson*	Doig*, Mumby* 1
Oct 28	OLDHAM ATHLETIC	Rd 3 2-2	Day	Aspin*	Adams	Williams	Ashurst	Haddock	De Mange	Sheridan	Taylor	Swan 2	Snodin	Stiles*
Nov 4	Oldham Athletic	Rd 3 R AET 2-4	Day	Williams	McDonald	De Mange	Ashurst	Haddock	Doig*	Sheridan	Taylor 1	Swan*	Snodin 1	Melrose*, Stiles*

SIMOD CUP

Date	Team	Result	1	2	3	4	5	6	7	8	9	10	11	SUBS
Nov 25	SHEFFIELD UNITED	Rd 1 3-0	Day	Grayson	Adams	De Mange	Ashurst	Haddock	Batty	Rennie 1	Taylor 1	Davison	Noteman 1	
Dec 8	Millwall	Rd 2 0-2	Day	Aspin	Swan	De Mange	Ashurst	Haddock*	Batty	Sheridan	Taylor	Davison	Snodin	Stiles*, Pearson*

F.A. CUP

Date	Team	Result	1	2	3	4	5	6	7	8	9	10	11	SUBS
Jan 9	ASTON VILLA	Rd 3 1-2	Day	Aspin	Adams	Williams	Ashurst	Haddock	Batty	Sheridan	Taylor	Davison 1	Snodin*	Melrose*

DIVISION TWO 1988-89

Date	Team	Result	1	2	3	4	5	6	7	8	9	10	11	SUBS
Aug 27	OXFORD UNITED	1-1	Day	Haddock	Adams	Aizlewood	Blake	Ashurst	Stiles*	Hilaire	Baird	Pearson	Snodin 1	Rennie* Davison*
Sep 3	Portsmouth	0-4	Day	Haddock	Adams	Aizlewood	Blake*	Ashurst	Taylor	Stiles	Baird	Pearson	Hilaire	Davison*, Aspin
Sep 10	MANCHESTER CITY	1-1	Day	G Williams	Adams*	Aizlewood	Blake 1	Ashurst	Batty	Sheridan	Baird	Davison*	Hilaire	Aspin*, Pearson*
Sep 17	Bournemouth	0-0	Day	G Williams	Adams	Aizlewood	Blake	Ashurst	Batty	Sheridan*	Taylor*	Davison	Hilaire	Haddock*, Pearson*
Sep 21	BARNSLEY	2-0	Day	G Williams	Adams	Aizlewood*	Blake	Ashurst	Batty	Sheridan	Baird	Davison 1	Hilaire 1	Haddock*, Pearson
Sep 24	CHELSEA	0-2	Day	G Williams	Adams	Haddock*	Blake	Ashurst	Batty	Sheridan	Baird*	Davison	Hilaire	Snodin*, Pearson*
Oct 1	Brighton	1-2	Day	G Williams	Adams	Aizlewood*	Blake	Rennie	Batty	Snodin	Baird 1	Pearson	Hilaire	Sheridan*, Haddock
Oct 3	Sunderland	1-2	Day	Haddock*	Adams	Stiles	Blake	Rennie	Batty	Sheridan	Baird*	Davison 1	Hilaire	Aspin*, Pearson*
Oct 8	WATFORD	0-1	Day	Aspin	Adams	Stiles*	Blake	Rennie	Batty	Sheridan	Baird	Davison*	Hilaire	Snodin*, Pearson*
Oct 16	Swindon Town	0-0	Day	Aspin	Snodin	Aizlewood	Blake	Rennie	Batty*	Sheridan	Baird	Davison*	Hilaire 1	Ashurst*, Pearson*
Oct 22	LEICESTER CITY	1-1	Day	Aspin	Snodin	Aizlewood	Blake	Rennie	Batty*	Sheridan	Baird*	Davison 1	Hilaire 1	Stiles*, Pearson*
Oct 26	Bradford City	1-1	Day	Aspin	Snodin	Aizlewood	Blake	Rennie	Batty	Sheridan*	Baird*	Davison 1	Hilaire	Stiles*, Pearson*
Oct 29	HULL CITY	2-1	Day	Aspin	Snodin	Aizlewood	Blake	Rennie	Batty	Sheridan 1	Baird 1	Davison 1	Hilaire	Stiles*, Pearson*
Nov 5	Ipswich Town	1-0	Day	Aspin	Snodin	Aizlewood	Blake	Rennie	Batty	Sheridan* 1	Baird	Davison*	Hilaire	Stiles*, Pearson*
Nov 12	WEST BROMWICH ALBION	2-1	Day	Aspin	Snodin*	Aizlewood 1	Blake	Rennie	Batty	Sheridan	Baird 1	Davison*	Hilaire	A Williams*, Pearson*
Nov 19	Oldham Athletic	2-2	Day	Aspin	Snodin	Aizlewood	Blake	Rennie	Batty*	Sheridan	Baird	Davison* 2	Hilaire	A Williams*, Pearson*
Nov 22	Birmingham City	0-0	Day	Aspin	Snodin	Aizlewood	Blake	Rennie	A Williams*	Sheridan	Baird	Davison*	Hilaire	Haddock*, Taylor*
Nov 26	STOKE CITY	4-0	Day	Aspin	Snodin	Aizlewood	Blake	Rennie	Whitlow	Sheridan* 1	Baird 2	Davison 1	Hilaire	Batty*, Taylor
Dec 3	Walsall	3-0	Day	Aspin	Snodin	Aizlewood	Blake	Rennie	Whitlow 1	Sheridan	Baird	Davison 2	Hilaire	A Williams*, Taylor
Dec 10	SHREWSBURY TOWN	2-3	Day	Aspin	Snodin	Aizlewood	Blake	Rennie	Whitlow	Sheridan 1	Baird*	Davison 1	Hilaire	Taylor*, A Williams*
Dec 17	Crystal Palace	1-2	Andrews	Aspin	Snodin	Aizlewood	Blake	Rennie	Whitlow	Sheridan	Baird	Davison 1	Hilaire	Taylor*, A Williams*
Dec 26	BLACKBURN ROVERS	2-0	Day	Aspin	Snodin	Aizlewood	Blake	Rennie	Whitlow	Sheridan	Baird 1	Davison* 1	Hilaire	Pearson*, A Williams
Dec 31	PLYMOUTH ARGYLE	2-0	Day	Aspin	Snodin 1	Aizlewood	Blake	Rennie	Whitlow	Sheridan	Baird*	Davison*	Hilaire	Pearson*, A Williams
Jan 2	Manchester City	0-0	Day	Aspin	Snodin	Aizlewood	Blake	Rennie	Whitlow	A Williams	Baird	Davison	Hilaire	Pearson*, Batty*
Jan 14	BIRMINGHAM CITY	1-0	Day	Aspin	Snodin	Aizlewood	Blake	Rennie	Whitlow	Sheridan	Baird	Davison	Hilaire 1	Pearson*, Swann
Jan 21	Oxford United	2-3	Day	Aspin	Snodin	Aizlewood	Blake 1	Rennie	Whitlow*	Sheridan	Baird	Davison	Hilaire	A Williams*, Pearson*
Feb 4	SUNDERLAND	2-0	Day	Aspin	Snodin	Adams	Blake	Rennie	Batty	Sheridan 1	Baird	Davison 1	Hilaire	Pearson, A Williams
Feb 11	Watford	1-1	Day	Aspin*	Snodin	Adams	Blake	Rennie	Batty	Sheridan	Baird	Davison 1	Hilaire	Pearson* 1, A Williams*
Feb 18	Leicester City	2-1	Day	Aspin	Snodin 1	Adams	Blake	Rennie	Batty	Sheridan	Baird*	Davison 1	Hilaire	Pearson*, Aizlewood*
Feb 25	SWINDON TOWN	0-0	Day	Aspin	Snodin*	Adams	Blake	Rennie	Batty	Sheridan	Baird*	Davison	Hilaire	Pearson*, Aizlewood*
Mar 1	BRADFORD CITY	3-3	Day	Aspin	Snodin	Adams*	Blake 1	Rennie	Batty	Sheridan	Baird 1	Davison	Hilaire	Aizlewood*, Pearson
Mar 5	West Bromwich Albion	1-2	Day	G Williams	Snodin	Adams* 1	Blake	Rennie	Batty	Sheridan	Baird	Davison*	Hilaire	Aizlewood*, Pearson
Mar 11	IPSWICH TOWN	2-4	Day	G Williams	Snodin	Aizlewood	Blake 1	Rennie*	Batty	Sheridan	Baird	Davison* 1	Hilaire 1	Whitlow*, Pearson*
Mar 14	Hull City	2-1	Day	G Williams	Snodin	Aizlewood	Swann	Aspin	Batty	Sheridan	Baird 1	Davison* 1	Hilaire	Whitlow*, Pearson*

193

DIVISION TWO 1988-89 continued

			1	2	3	4	5	6	7	8	9	10	11	SUBS
Mar 19	Barnsley	2-2	Day	Haddock	Snodin	Aizlewood 1	Blake	Aspin	Whitlow	Sheridan 1	Pearson	Davison*	Hilaire*	Taylor*, A Williams*
Mar 25	PORTSMOUTH	1-0	Day	Aspin	Snodin	Aizlewood	Blake	Fairclough	Strachan	Sheridan*	Baird 1	Davison*	Hilaire	Pearson*, A Williams*
Mar 27	Blackburn Rovers	0-2	Day	Aspin	Snodin	Aizlewood	Blake	Fairclough	Strachan	Sheridan*	Baird	Davison*	Hilaire	Batty*, Williams*
Apr 1	BOURNEMOUTH	3-0	Day	Aspin	Snodin*	Aizlewood	Blake	Fairclough	Strachan	Sheridan	Baird	Shutt 3	Whitlow	A Williams*, Pearson
Apr 5	CRYSTAL PALACE	1-2	Day	Aspin	Snodin	Aizlewood	Rennie	Fairclough	Strachan	Sheridan	Baird	Shutt 1	Hilaire*	Pearson*, A Williams
Apr 9	Plymouth Argyle	0-1	Day	Aspin	Snodin*	A Williams	Blake	Fairclough	Strachan	Batty	Baird	Shutt*	Whitlow	Rennie*, Pearson*
Apr 15	BRIGHTON	1-0	Day	Haddock*	Aizlewood	A Williams 1	Blake	Fairclough	Strachan	Sheridan	Pearson	Davison	Whitlow*	Rennie*, Kerr*
Apr 22	Chelsea	0-1	Day	Aspin*	Kerr*	Aizlewood	Blake	Fairclough	Strachan	A Williams	Baird	Davison	Whitlow	Pearson*, Sheridan*
Apr 29	Stoke City	2-3	Day	A Williams	Whitlow	Aizlewood*	Blake	Fairclough	Strachan 1	Sheridan 1	Baird*	Davison 1	Hilaire	Haddock*, Batty*
May 1	WALSALL	1-0	Day	A Williams	Whitlow	Aizlewood* 1	Blake	Fairclough	Strachan	Sheridan	Baird	Davison*	Hilaire	Batty*, Haddock*
May 6	OLDHAM ATHLETIC	0-0	Day	Haddock	Whitlow	Rennie*	Blake	Fairclough	Strachan	Batty	Baird	Speed	Hilaire*	Stiles*, Mumby*
May 13	Shrewsbury Town	3-3	Day	Haddock	Whitlow	Ormsby	Blake	Fairclough	Strachan 2	Batty	Baird*	Rennie 1	Hilarie	Stiles*, Kerr*

LITTLEWOODS CUP

Sep 27	Peterborough United	Rd 2 2-1	Day	G Williams*	Adams	Aizlewood	Blake	Rennie	Batty	Snodin 1	Baird 1	Pearson	Hilaire	Haddock*, Davison
Oct 12	PETERBOROUGH UNITED	Rd 2 3-1	Day	Aspin	Snodin	Aizlewood	Blake	Rennie	Batty	Sheridan 1	Baird	Davison* 1	Hilaire 1	Pearson*, Stiles
Nov 2	LUTON TOWN	Rd 3 0-2	Day	Aspin	Snodin	Aizlewood	Blake	Rennie	Batty	Sheridan	Baird	Davison	Hilaire	Stiles, Pearson

SIMOD CUP

Nov 9	SHREWSBURY TOWN	Rd 1 3-1	Day	Aspin	Whitlow	Aizlewood 1	Blake	Rennie	Batty	Sheridan	Baird*	Davison 2	Hilaire	A Williams, Grayson
Nov 29	Millwall	Rd 2 0-2	Day	Aspin	Snodin	Aizlewood	Blake	Rennie	Whitlow*	Sheridan	Baird*	Davison	Hilaire	Haddock*, Pearson*

F.A. CUP

Jan 6	Brighton	Rd 3 2-1	Day	Aspin	Snodin	Aizlewood	Blake	Rennie	A Williams*	Sheridan	Baird 2	Davison*	Hilaire	Haddock*, Pearson*
Jan 28	Nottingham Forest	Rd 4 0-2	Day	Aspin	Snodin	Swann	Blake	Rennie*	Batty	Sheridan	Baird	Adams	Hilaire	G Williams*, Davison*

DIVISION TWO 1989-90

Aug 19	Newcastle United	2-5	Day	Sterland	Beglin	Thomas*	McClelland	Haddock	Strachan	Batty	Baird 1	Davison* 1	Hendrie	Whitlow*, Shutt*
Aug 23	MIDDLESBROUGH	(o.g.) 2-1	Day	Sterland	Whitlow	Thomas*	Fairclough	Haddock	Strachan	Batty	Baird*	Davison 1	Hendrie	Shutt*, Jones*
Aug 26	BLACKBURN ROVERS	1-1	Day	Sterland	Whitlow	Thomas*	Fairclough 1	Haddock	Strachan	Batty	Baird	Davison*	Hendrie	Jones*, Speed*
Sep 2	Stoke City	1-1	Day	Sterland	Whitlow	Jones	Fairclough	Haddock	Strachan 1	Batty	Baird	Davison*	Hendrie	Speed*, Pearson
Sep 9	IPSWICH TOWN	1-1	Day	Sterland	Whitlow	Jones 1	Fairclough	Haddock	Strachan	Batty	Baird	Davison	Hendrie*	Speed*, Williams
Sep 16	Hull City	1-0	Day	Sterland	Whitlow	Jones	Blake	Fairclough	Strachan	Batty	Baird	Davison 1	Hendrie*	Williams*, Haddock
Aug 23	SWINDON TOWN	4-0	Day	Sterland	Whitlow	Jones	Blake	Haddock	Strachan 3	Batty	Baird	Davison 1	Hendrie*	Williams*, Shutt
Sep 27	OXFORD UNITED	2-1	Day	Sterland 1	Whitlow	Jones*	Blake	Haddock	Strachan	Batty	Baird	Davison 1	Hendrie	Williams*, Shutt
Sep 30	Port Vale	0-0	Day	Sterland	Whitlow	Jones*	Blake	Haddock	Strachan	Batty	Baird	Davison*	Williams	Speed*, Shutt*
Oct 7	West Ham United	0-0	Day	Sterland	Whitlow	Jones 1	Fairclough	Haddock	Strachan	Batty	Baird	Davison*	Williams	Shutt*, Speed
Oct 14	SUNDERLAND	2-0	Day	Sterland	Whitlow	Jones	Fairclough 1	Haddock	Strachan	Batty	Baird	Davison 1	Williams	Shutt, Speed
Oct 17	Portsmouth	3-3	Day	Sterland 1	Whitlow 1	Jones	Fairclough	Haddock	Strachan	Batty	Baird	Davison 1	Williams	Blake, Speed
Oct 21	WOLVERHAMPTON W.	1-0	Day	Sterland	Whitlow	Jones	Fairclough	Haddock	Strachan*	Batty	Baird	Davison 1	Williams*	Speed*, Shutt*
Oct 28	Bradford City	1-0	Day	Sterland	Whitlow	Jones	Fairclough	Haddock	Strachan	Batty	Baird	Davison 1	Williams*	Shutt*, Speed
Nov 1	PLYMOUTH ARGYLE	2-1	Day	Sterland	Whitlow	Jones*	Fairclough	Haddock	Strachan 1	Batty	Baird	Davison 1	Williams	Speed*, Shutt
Nov 4	BOURNEMOUTH	3-0	Day	Sterland	Whitlow	Jones	Fairclough 1	Haddock	Strachan 1	Batty	Baird 1	Davison	Williams*	Speed*, Shutt
Nov 11	Leicester City	3-4	Day*	Sterland	Whitlow	Jones	Fairclough	Haddock	Strachan 1	Batty	Baird 1	Davison	Williams 1	Shutt*, Speed
Nov 18	WATFORD	2-1	Turner	Sterland	Whitlow	Jones	Fairclough 1	Haddock	Strachan	Batty	Baird	Davison*	Williams 1	Shutt, Speed
Nov 25	West Bromwich Albion	1-2	Turner	Sterland	Whitlow	Jones*	Fairclough 1	Haddock	Strachan	Batty	Baird	Davison	Williams*	Shutt*, Speed*
Dec 2	NEWCASTLE UNITED	1-0	Day	Sterland	Whitlow	Jones	Fairclough	Blake	Strachan	Batty	Baird 1	Davison	Williams*	Shutt*, Kerr
Dec 9	Middlesbrough	2-0	Day	Sterland	Whitlow	Jones	Fairclough 1	Blake	Strachan	Batty	Pearson	Shutt 1	Williams	Speed, Haddock
Dec 16	BRIGHTON	3-0	Day	Sterland	Whitlow	Jones 1	Fairclough	Haddock	Strachan 1	Batty	Pearson	Shutt*	Hendrie* 1	Baird*, Speed*
Dec 26	Sheffield United	2-2	Day	Sterland 1	Whitlow	Jones	Fairclough	Blake	Strachan	Batty	Baird	Shutt 1	Hendrie	Pearson, Haddock
Dec 30	Barnsley	0-1	Day	Sterland	Whitlow*	Jones	Fairclough	Haddock	Strachan	Batty	Baird	Shutt	Hendrie*	Pearson*, Kerr*
Jan 1	OLDHAM ATHLETIC	1-1	Day	Sterland	Kerr	Jones	Fairclough	Haddock	Strachan	Batty	Baird*	Shutt*	Hendrie 1	Pearson*, Snodin*
Jan 13	Blackburn Rovers	2-1	Day	Sterland*	Whitlow	Jones	Fairclough	Haddock	Strachan 1	Batty	Chapman 1	Davison	Hendrie	Beglin*, Baird
Jan 20	STOKE CITY	2-0	Day	Beglin	Whitlow	Jones	Fairclough	Haddock	Strachan 1	Batty	Chapman	Davison*	Hendrie 1*	Pearson*, Kerr*
Feb 4	Swindon Town	2-3	Day	Beglin	Whitlow*	Jones	Fairclough	Haddock	Strachan 1	Batty	Chapman	Kerr	Hendrie 1	Pearson*, Speed*
Feb 10	HULL CITY	4-3	Day	Kamara	Beglin*	Jones 1	Fairclough	Haddock	Strachan 1	Batty	Chapman*	Varadi 1	Hendrie 1	Hilaire*, O'Donell*
Feb 17	Ipswich Town	2-2	Day	Kamara	Beglin	Jones	Fairclough	Haddock	Strachan	Batty	Chapman 2	Varadi	Hendrie*	Hilaire*, Speed
Feb 24	WEST BROMWICH ALBION	2-2	Day	Kamara 1	Beglin	Jones	Fairclough	Haddock	Strachan	Batty	Chapman 1	Varadi*	Hendrie	Sterland*, Speed
Mar 3	Watford	0-1	Day	Sterland	Beglin	Jones	Fairclough	Haddock	Strachan	Batty	Chapman	Varadi*	Kamara*	Hendrie*, Speed*
Mar 7	PORT VALE	0-0	Day	Sterland	Beglin	Jones	Fairclough	Haddock	Strachan	Batty	Chapman	Varadi	Hendrie*	Speed*, Kamara
Mar 10	Oxford United	4-2	Day	Sterland	Beglin*	Jones	Fairclough 1	Haddock	Strachan	Speed*	Chapman 2	Varadi 1	Snodin	Hendrie*, Kerr*
Mar 17	WEST HAM UNITED	3-2	Day	Sterland	Snodin	Jones	Fairclough	Haddock	Strachan 1	Speed	Chapman 2	Varadi*	Hendrie	Shutt*, Kerr
Mar 20	Sunderland	1-0	Day	Sterland 1	Snodin*	Jones	Fairclough	Haddock	Strachan	Batty	Chapman	Varadi*	Speed	Davison*, Hendrie*
Mar 24	PORTSMOUTH	2-0	Day	Sterland	Beglin	Jones 1	Fairclough	Haddock	Strachan*	Batty	Chapman 1	Varadi*	Speed	Hendrie*, Whitlow*
Mar 31	Wolverhampton Wanderers	0-1	Day	Sterland	Whitlow	Jones	Fairclough	Haddock	Strachan	Batty	Chapman	Varadi*	Speed*	Hendrie*, Kamara*
Apr 8	BRADFORD CITY	1-1	Day	Sterland	Beglin	Jones	Fairclough	Haddock	Strachan	Batty	Chapman	Hendrie*	Speed 1	Davison*, Kamara
Apr 10	Plymouth Argyle	1-1	Day	Sterland	Beglin	Jones	Fairclough	Haddock	Strachan	Batty	Chapman	Hendrie*	Speed	Davison*, Kamara
Apr 13	Oldham Athletic	1-3	Day	Sterland	Beglin	Jones	Fairclough	Haddock*	Strachan	Batty	Chapman	Varadi	Kamara*	Davison*1, Speed*
Apr 16	SHEFFIELD UNITED	4-0	Day	Sterland	Beglin	Jones	Fairclough	McClelland	Strachan 2	Kamara	Chapman 1	Davison*	Speed 1	Shutt*, Batty
Apr 21	Brighton	(o.g.) 2-2	Day	Sterland	Beglin	Jones	Fairclough	McClelland	Strachan	Kamara*	Chapman	Varadi*	Speed 1	Batty*, Shutt*
Apr 25	BARNSLEY	1-2	Day	Sterland	Beglin	Jones	Fairclough 1	McClelland	Strachan	Kamara	Chapman	Shutt*	Speed	Pearson*, Batty
Apr 28	LEICESTER CITY	2-1	Day	Sterland 1	Beglin	Jones*	Fairclough	Haddock	Strachan 1	Kamara	Chapman	Davison*	Speed	Batty*, Varadi*
May 5	Bournemouth	1-0	Day	Sterland	Beglin	Jones	Fairclough	Haddock	Strachan	Kamara	Chapman 1	Davison*	Speed	Shutt*, Batty*

LITTLEWOODS CUP

Sep 19	Oldham Athletic	Rd 2 1-2	Day	Sterland	Whitlow	Jones	Fairclough*	Haddock	Strachan 1	Batty	Baird	Davison*	Hendrie	Blake*, Williams*
Oct 3	OLDHAM ATHLETIC	Rd 2 1-2	Day	Sterland	Whitlow	Jones	Blake*	Haddock	Strachan	Batty	Baird	Davison	Williams	Fairclough1*, Speed*

ZENITH DATA CUP

Nov 7	BLACKBURN ROVERS	Rd 1 1-0	Day	Sterland*	Whitlow	Jones	Fairclough	Haddock	Strachan	Batty	Baird	Davison 1	Williams	Speed*, Shutt
Nov 28	Barnsley	Rd 2 2-1	Edwards	Sterland	Whitlow	Jones	Fairclough	Haddock*	Strachan 1	Batty	Baird	Davison*	Williams 1	Kerr*, Shutt
Dec 19	Stoke City	Rd 3 2-2 AET 5-4 on Pens	Day	Sterland	Whitlow*	Jones	Blake	Haddock	Strachan	Batty	Pearson*	Baird	Hendrie	Shutt 2, Kerr*
Jan 17	Aston Villa	NTH/SF 0-2	Day	Beglin*	Whitlow	Jones	Fairclough	Haddock	Strachan	Batty	Baird	Blake	Hendrie*	Pearson*, Kerr*

F.A. CUP

Jan 6	IPSWICH TOWN	Rd 3 0-1	Day	Sterland	Kerr	Jones	Fairclough	Haddock	Strachan	Batty	Baird*	Shutt*	Hendrie	Speed*, Snodin*

DIVISION ONE 1990-91

Aug 25	Everton	3-2	Lukic	Sterland	Snodin	Batty	Fairclough 1	Whyte	Strachan	Varadi* 1	Chapman	McAllister	Speed* 1	Haddock*, Kamara*
Aug 28	MANCHESTER UNITED	0-0	Lukic	Sterland	Haddock	Batty	Fairclough	Whyte	Strachan	Varadi	Chapman	McAllister	Speed*	Snodin*, Kamara
Sep 1	NORWICH CITY	3-0	Lukic	Sterland	Snodin*	Batty	Fairclough	Whyte	Strachan	Varadi 1	Chapman 2	McAllister*	Speed	Haddock*, Whitlow*
Sep 8	Luton Town	0-1	Lukic	Sterland	Snodin*	Batty	Haddock	Whyte	Strachan	Jones*	Chapman	McAllister	Whitlow	Speed*, Varadi*
Sep 15	TOTTENHAM HOTSPUR	0-2	Lukic	Sterland	Whitlow*	Batty	Fairclough	Whyte	Strachan	Varadi	Chapman	McAllister	Speed*	Haddock*, Snodin*
Sep 23	Sheffield United	2-0	Lukic	Sterland	Haddock	Batty	Fairclough	Whyte	Strachan 1	Varadi*	Chapman	McAllister	Speed	Pearson* 1, Whitlow
Sep 29	ARSENAL	2-2	Lukic	Sterland	Haddock	Batty	Fairclough	Whyte	Strachan 1	Pearson	Chapman 1	McAllister	Snodin*	Speed*, Kamara
Oct 6	Crystal Palace	1-1	Lukic	Sterland	Haddock	Batty	Fairclough	Whyte	Strachan	Pearson	Chapman	McAllister	Speed 1	Kamara, Shutt
Oct 20	QUEEN'S PARK RANGERS	2-3	Lukic	Sterland	Snodin	Batty	Fairclough	Whyte1	Strachan	Pearson*	Chapman 1	McAllister	Speed	Kamara*, Shutt*
Oct 27	Aston Villa	0-0	Lukic	Sterland	Kamara	Batty	Fairclough	Whyte	Strachan	Pearson	Chapman	McAllister	Speed	Varadi, Snodin
Nov 3	NOTTINGHAM FOREST	3-1	Lukic	Sterland	Kamara	Batty	Fairclough	Whyte	Strachan 1	Shutt*	Chapman 1	McAllister 1	Speed	Snodin*, Varadi
Nov 11	Manchester City	3-2	Lukic	Sterland	Kamara	Batty	Fairclough	Whyte	Strachan 1	Shutt* 1	Chapman 1	McAllister	Speed	Pearson*, Snodin
Nov 17	DERBY COUNTY	3-0	Lukic	Sterland	Kamara	Batty	Fairclough	Whyte	Strachan 1	Shutt	Chapman 1	McAllister	Speed 1	Pearson, Snodin
Nov 24	Coventry City	1-1	Lukic	Sterland	Kamara*	Batty	Fairclough	Whyte	Strachan	Shutt*	Chapman 1	McAllister	Speed	Haddock*, Pearson*
Dec 1	SOUTHAMPTON	2-1	Lukic	Sterland	Haddock	Batty	Fairclough 1	Whyte	Strachan	Shutt 1	Chapman*	McAllister*	Speed	Pearson*, Williams*
Dec 8	Manchester United	1-1	Lukic	Sterland 1	Haddock	Batty	Fairclough	Whyte	Strachan	Shutt	Chapman	McAllister	Speed	Pearson, Williams
Dec 16	EVERTON	2-0	Lukic	Sterland 1	Haddock*	Batty	Fairclough	Whyte	Strachan 1	Shutt 1	Chapman	McAllister	Speed	Snodin*, Pearson
Dec 23	Sunderland	1-0	Lukic	Sterland 1	Haddock*	Batty	Fairclough	Whyte	Strachan	Shutt	Chapman	McAllister	Speed	Snodin*, Pearson
Dec 26	CHELSEA	4-1	Lukic	Sterland 1	Snodin	Batty	Fairclough	Whyte	Strachan	Shutt	Chapman 2	McAllister	Speed*	Whitlow*1, Pearson
Dec 29	WIMBLEDON	3-0	Lukic	Sterland 1	Snodin*	Batty	Fairclough	Whyte	Strachan	Shutt*	Chapman 1	McAllister	Speed 1	Whitlow*, Pearson*
Jan 1	Liverpool	0-3	Lukic	Sterland	Snodin*	Batty	Fairclough	Whyte	Strachan	Shutt*	Chapman	McAllister	Speed	Whitlow*, Pearson*
Jan 12	Norwich City	0-2	Lukic	Sterland	Snodin	Batty	Fairclough	Whyte	Strachan	Shutt*	Chapman	McAllister	Whitlow*	Speed*, Pearson*
Jan 19	LUTON TOWN	2-1	Lukic	Sterland	Snodin*	Batty	Fairclough 1	Whyte	Strachan 1	Shutt	Chapman	McAllister	Speed	Haddock*, Varadi
Feb 2	Tottenham Hotspur	0-0	Lukic	Sterland	Haddock	Whitlow	Fairclough	Whyte	Strachan	Williams	Chapman*	McAllister	Speed	Pearson*, Snodin
Mar 2	Southampton	0-2	Lukic	Sterland	Whitlow	Batty	Fairclough	Whyte	Williams*	Shutt	Chapman	McAllister	Speed	Davison*, McClelland
Mar 9	COVENTRY CITY	2-0	Lukic	Sterland	Whitlow	Batty	Fairclough	Whyte1	Strachan	Davison* 1	Chapman	McAllister	Speed	Shutt*, Beglin
Mar 17	Arsenal	0-2	Lukic	Sterland	Whitlow	Batty	Fairclough	Whyte	Strachan	Davison*	Chapman	McAllister	Speed	Shutt*, McClelland
Mar 23	CRYSTAL PALACE	1-2	Lukic	Sterland	Whitlow	Batty	Fairclough	Whyte	Strachan	Shutt*	Chapman	McAllister*	Speed 1	Williams*, Pearson*
Mar 30	Chelsea	2-1	Lukic	Sterland	Whitlow	Batty	Fairclough 1	Whyte	Strachan*	Shutt 1	Chapman	McAllister	Speed	Williams*, Varadi
Apr 2	Sunderland	5-0	Lukic	Sterland	Whitlow	Batty	McClelland	Whyte	Strachan	Shutt 1	Chapman 2	McAllister	Speed 2	Williams, Varadi
Apr 6	Wimbledon	1-0	Lukic	Sterland	Whitlow	Batty	McClelland	Whyte	Strachan	Shutt*	Chapman 1	McAllister	Speed	Williams*, Fairclough
Apr 10	MANCHESTER CITY	1-2	Lukic	Sterland	Whitlow	Batty	McClelland	Whyte	Williams*	Shutt	Chapman	McAllister 1	Speed	Davison*, Fairclough

DIVISION ONE 1990-91 continued

Date	Opponent	Score	1	2	3	4	5	6	7	8	9	10	11	SUBS
Apr 13	LIVERPOOL	4-5	Lukic	Sterland	Whitlow	Batty	Fairclough	Whyte	Strachan	Shutt 1	Chapman 3	McAllister	Speed	Williams, Davison
Apr 17	Queen's Park Rangers	0-2	Lukic	Sterland	Whitlow*	Batty	Fairclough	Whyte	Strachan	Shutt	Chapman	McAllister	Speed	Williams*, Davison
Apr 23	Derby County	1-0	Lukic	Sterland	Snodin*	Batty	Fairclough	Whyte	Strachan	Shutt 1	Chapman	McAllister	Speed	Williams*, Davison
May 4	ASTON VILLA	(o.g). 5-2	Lukic	Sterland	Snodin	Batty	Fairclough	Whyte1	Williams*	Shutt 1	Chapman 2	McAllister	Speed	Davison*, Kerr
May 8	SHEFFIELD UNITED	2-1	Lukic 1	Sterland	Snodin	Batty	Fairclough	Whyte	Williams	Shutt 1	Chapman	McAllister	Speed	Davison, Kerr
May 11	Nottingham Forest	3-4	Lukic	Sterland	Snodin	Batty	Fairclough	Whyte	Strachan*	Shutt 1	Chapman 2	McAllister	Speed	Williams*, Davison

RUMBELOWS CUP

Date	Opponent	Score	1	2	3	4	5	6	7	8	9	10	11	SUBS
Sep 26	Leicester City	Rd 2 0-1	Lukic	Sterland	Whitlow*	Batty	Fairclough	Whyte	Strachan	Varadi*	Chapman	McAllister	Speed	Pearson*, Williams*
Oct 10	LEICESTER CITY	(o.g). Rd 2 3-0	Day	Sterland	Haddock	Batty	Fairclough	Whyte	Strachan 1	Pearson*	Chapman*	McAllister	Speed 1	Shutt*, Kamara*
Oct 31	OLDHAM ATHLETIC	Rd 3 2-0	Lukic	Kamara	Snodin	Batty	Fairclough	Whyte	Strachan	Pearson	Chapman 1	McAllister	Speed 1	Williams, Shutt
Nov 27	Queen's Park Rangers	Rd 4 3-0	Lukic	Sterland	Haddock	Batty	Fairclough 1	Whyte	Strachan*	Shutt	Chapman 1	McAllister 1	Speed	Snodin*, Pearson
Jan 16	ASTON VILLA	Rd 5 4-1	Lukic	Sterland	Snodin*	Batty	Fairclough	Whyte	Strachan	Shutt*	Chapman 2	McAllister 1	Speed 1	Pearson*, Haddock*
Feb 10	Manchester United	S/F 1-2	Lukic	Sterland	Haddock	Whitlow	Fairclough	Whyte 1	Strachan	Williams	Chapman	McAllister	Speed	Pearson, Snodin
Feb 24	MANCHESTER UNITED	S/F 0-1	Lukic	Sterland	Haddock*	Batty	Fairclough	Whyte	Strachan*	Shutt	Chapman	McAllister	Speed	Whitlow*, Pearson*

ZENITH DATA CUP

Date	Opponent	Score	1	2	3	4	5	6	7	8	9	10	11	SUBS
Dec 19	Wolverhampton Wans.	Rd 2 2-1	Day	Sterland	Haddock	Snodin	Fairclough	Beglin	Strachan*	McAllister 1	Veradi* 1	Pearson	Speed	Williams*, Kerr*
Jan 22	DERBY COUNTY	Rd 3 2-1	Lukic	Sterland	Snodin	Batty	Haddock	Whyte	Strachan	Shutt*	Chapman	Williams	Speed	Varadi*, Whitlow
Feb 20	MANCHESTER CITY	NTH/SF AET 2-0	Lukic	Sterland	Whitlow	Batty	Fairclough	Whyte	Strachan	Shutt	Chapman	McAllister*	Speed*	Williams* 1, Davison*
Mar 19	EVERTON	NTH/F 3-3	Lukic	Sterland 1	Whitlow	Batty	Fairclough	Whyte	Strachan	Davison*	Chapman 2	McAllister	Williams*	Shutt*, Speed*
Mar 21	EVERTON	N/F AET 1-3	Lukic	Sterland 1	Whitlow	Batty	Fairclough	Whyte	Strachan	Shutt*	Chapman	McAllister*	Williams	Davison*, Speed*

F.A. CUP

Date	Opponent	Score	1	2	3	4	5	6	7	8	9	10	11	SUBS
Ja.n5	Barnsley	Rd 3 1-1	Lukic	Sterland 1	Snodin	Batty	Fairclough	McClelland	Strachan	Shutt*	Chapman	McAllister	Speed*	Pearson*, Whitlow*
Jan 8	BARNSLEY	(o.g). Rd 3R 4-0	Lukic	Sterland	Snodin	Batty	Fairclough	McClelland	Strachan 1	Shutt	Chapman* 1	McAllister 1	Speed*	Pearson*, Whitlow*
Jan 27	Arsenal	Rd 4 0-0	Lukic	Sterland	Haddock	Batty	Fairclough	Whyte	Strachan	Shutt*	Chapman	McAllister	Speed	Pearson*, Snodin
Jan 30	ARSENAL	Rd 4R AET 1-1	Lukic	Sterland*	Haddock	Batty	Fairclough	Whyte	Strachan	Pearson	Chapman 1	McAllister	Speed	Varadi, Snodin*
Feb 13	Arsenal	Rd 4 2R AET 0-0	Lukic	Sterland	Haddock*	Batty	Fairclough	Whyte	Strachan	Shutt*	Chapman	McAllister	Speed	Whitlow*, McClelland*
Feb 16	ARSENAL	Rd 4 3R 1-2	Lukic	Sterland	Whitlow	Batty	Fairclough	Whyte	Strachan	Shutt*	Chapman	McAllister	Speed	McClelland*, Snodin

DIVISION ONE 1991-92

Date	Opponent	Score	1	2	3	4	5	6	7	8	9	10	11	SUBS
Aug 20	NOTTINGHAM FOREST	1-0	Lukic	McClelland	Dorigo	Batty	Fairclough	Whyte	Strachan	Wallace	Chapman	McAllister 1	Speed	Sterland, Hodge
Aug 24	SHEFFIELD WEDS	1-1	Lukic	McClelland*	Dorigo	Batty	Fairclough	Whyte	Strachan	Wallace	Chapman	McAllister	Speed*	Sterland*, Hodge* 1
Aug 28	Southampton	4-0	Lukic	McClelland	Dorigo	Batty	Fairclough*	Whyte	Strachan 2	Wallace	Chapman	McAllister*	Speed 2	Sterland*, Hodge*
Aug 31	Manchester United	1-1	Lukic	Sterland*	Dorigo*	Batty	McClelland	Whyte	Strachan	Wallace	Chapman 1	McAllister	Speed	Hodge*, Wetherall*
Sep 3	ARSENAL	2-2	Lukic	Sterland*	Dorigo*	Batty	McClelland	Whyte	Strachan 1	Wallace	Chapman 1	McAllister	Speed	Hodge*, Wetherall*
Sep 7	MANCHESTER CITY	3-0	Lukic	Sterland	Dorigo 1	Batty 1	McClelland	Whyte	Strachan	Wallace*	Chapman	McAllister	Speed	Hodge*, Wetherall
Sep 14	Chelsea	1-0	Lukic	Sterland	Dorigo	Batty	McClelland	Whyte	Strachan*	Shutt 1	Chapman	McAllister	Speed	Hodge*, Wetherall
Sep 18	Coventry City	0-0	Lukic	Sterland	Dorigo	Batty	McClelland	Whyte	Strachan	Shutt*	Chapman	McAllister	Speed	Hodge*, Wetherall
Sep 21	LIVERPOOL	1-0	Lukic	Sterland	Dorigo	Batty	McClelland	Whyte	Strachan	Hodge 1	Chapman	McAllister	Speed*	Shutt*, Wetherall
Sep 28	Norwich City	2-2	Lukic	Sterland	Dorigo 1	Batty	McClelland	Whyte	Varadi *	Hodge*	Chapman	McAllister	Speed 1	Shutt*, Whitlow*
Oct 1	Crystal Palace	0-1	Lukic	Sterland	Dorigo	Batty	McClelland	Whyte	Varadi*	Hodge	Chapman	McAllister*	Speed	Shutt*, Whitlow*
Oct 5	SHEFFIELD UNITED	4-3	Lukic	Sterland* 2	Dorigo	Batty	McClelland	Whyte	Hodge 2	Shutt	Chapman	McAllister*	Speed	Fairclough*, Whitlow*
Oct 19	Notts County	4-2	Lukic	Sterland	Dorigo	Batty	Fairclough	Whyte 1	Strachan	Shutt	Chapman 1	Hodge 1	Speed	McAllister* 1, Kamara*
Oct 26	OLDHAM ATHLETIC	(o.g). 1-0	Lukic	Sterland	Dorigo	Batty	Fairclough	Whyte	Strachan*	Wallace	Chapman	McAllister	Speed*	Shutt*, Kamara*
Nov 2	Wimbledon	0-0	Lukic	Sterland	Dorigo	Shutt	Fairclough	Whyte	Strachan	Wallace*	Chapman	McAllister	Speed	Newsome, Snodin
Nov 16	QUEEN'S PARK RANGERS	2-0	Lukic	Sterland 1	Dorigo	Batty	Fairclough	Whyte	Strachan	Wallace 1	Chapman	McAllister	Speed*	Varadi*, McClelland
Nov 24	Aston Villa	4-1	Lukic	Sterland 1	Dorigo	Batty	Fairclough	Whyte	Strachan	Wallace 1	Chapman 2	McAllister	McClelland	Hodge, Shutt
Nov 30	EVERTON	1-0	Lukic	Sterland	Dorigo	Batty	Fairclough	Whyte	Strachan	Wallace 1	Chapman	McAllister	Speed*	Hodge*, McClelland*
Dec 7	Luton Town	2-0	Lukic	Sterland	Dorigo	Batty	Fairclough	Whyte	Strachan	Wallace 1	Chapman	McAllister	Speed 1	Hodge, McClelland
Dec 14	TOTTENHAM HOTSPUR	1-1	Lukic	Sterland	Dorigo	Batty	McClelland	Whyte	Strachan	Wallace	Chapman	McAllister	Speed 1	Hodge, Shutt
Dec 22	Nottingham Forest	0-0	Lukic	Sterland	Dorigo	Batty	McClelland	Whyte	Strachan*	Wallace	Chapman	McAllister	Speed	Kelly*, Hodge
Dec 26	SOUTHAMPTON	3-3	Lukic	Sterland	Dorigo	Batty	McClelland	Whyte	Hodge 2	Wallace	Chapman	McAllister	Speed 1	Kelly, Newsome
Dec 29	MANCHESTER UNITED	1-1	Lukic	Sterland 1	Dorigo	Batty*	Fairclough	Whyte	Strachan	Wallace	Chapman	McAllister	Speed*	Hodge*, McClelland
Jan 1	West Ham United	3-1	Lukic	Sterland	Dorigo	Batty	Fairclough	Whyte	Strachan	Wallace	Chapman 2	McAllister 1	Speed	Hodge, Shutt
Jan 12	Sheffield Weds	6-1	Lukic	Sterland	Dorigo 1	Hodge*	Fairclough	Whyte	Shutt*	Wallace 1	Chapman 3	McAllister	Speed	Whitlow* 1, Davison*
Jan 18	CRYSTAL PALACE	1-1	Lukic	Sterland	Dorigo	Batty	Fairclough 1	Whyte	Strachan	Wallace	Hodge*	McAllister*	Speed	Whitlow*, Davison*
Feb 1	NOTTS COUNTY	3-0	Lukic	Sterland* 1	Dorigo	Batty 1	Fairclough	Whyte	Strachan*	Wallace 1	Hodge	McAllister	Speed	Whitlow*, Kelly*
Feb 8	Oldham Athletic	0-2	Lukic	Sterland*	Dorigo	Batty	Fairclough	Whyte	Strachan	Wallace	Hodge*	McAllister	Speed	Whitlow*, Cantona*
Feb 23	Everton	1-1	Lukic	Sterland	Dorigo	Batty	Fairclough	Whyte	Strachan	Wallace*	Cantona	McAllister	Speed	Shutt* 1, McClelland
Nov 29	LUTON TOWN	2-0	Lukic	Sterland	Dorigo*	Batty	Fairclough	Whyte	Strachan	Wallace*	Chapman 1	McAllister	Speed*	Cantona* 1, Agana*
Mar 3	ASTON VILLA	0-0	Lukic	Sterland	Whitlow	Batty	Fairclough*	Whyte	Strachan	Agana*	Chapman	McAllister	Speed	McClelland*, Cantona*
Mar 7	Tottenham Hotspur	3-1	Lukic	Sterland*	Whitlow*	Batty	Fairclough	Whyte	Strachan	Wallace 1	Chapman	McAllister 1	Speed	Newsome* 1, Cantona*
Mar 11	Queen's Park. Rangers	1-4	Lukic	Newsome	Whitlow	Batty	Fairclough	Whyte	Strachan	Wallace	Chapman	McAllister*	Speed 1	Cantona*, Grayson
Mar 14	WIMBLEDON	5-1	Lukic	Newsome	Cantona 1	Batty	Fairclough	Whyte	Strachan*	Wallace 1	Chapman 3	McAllister	Speed	Shutt*, Mauchlen
Mar 22	Arsenal	1-1	Lukic	Cantona	Dorigo	Batty	Fairclough	Whyte	Strachan	Wallace	Chapman 1	McAllister	Speed	Hodge, Newsome
Mar 28	WEST HAM UNITED	0-0	Lukic	Cantona	Dorigo	Batty	Fairclough	Newsome	Strachan	Wallace*	Chapman	McAllister	Speed	Hodge*, Mauchlen
Apr 4	Manchester City	0-4	Lukic	Cantona	Dorigo	Batty	Fairclough	Whyte	Strachan	Wallace	Chapman	McAllister	Speed	Hodge, Newsome
Apr 11	CHELSEA	3-0	Lukic	Hodge*	Dorigo	Batty	Fairclough	Whyte	Strachan	Wallace* 1	Chapman 1	McAllister	Speed	Newsome*, Cantona* 1
Apr 18	Liverpool	0-0	Lukic	Newsome	Dorigo	Batty	Fairclough	Whyte	Hodge*	Wallace*	Chapman	McAllister	Speed	Shutt*, Cantona*
Apr 20	COVENTRY CITY	2-0	Lukic	Newsome	Dorigo	Batty	Fairclough 1	Whyte	Strachan*	Wallace	Chapman	McAllister* 1	Speed	Shutt*, Cantona*
Apr 26	Sheffield United	(o.g). 3-2	Lukic	Newsome 1	Dorigo	Batty	Fairclough	Whyte	Strachan*	Wallace 1	Chapman	McAllister*	Speed	Shutt*, Cantona*
May 2	NORWICH CITY	1-0	Lukic	Newsome	Dorigo	Batty	Fairclough	Whyte	Cantona*	Wallace 1	Chapman*	McAllister	Speed	Hodge*, Strachan*

RUMBELOWS CUP

Date	Opponent	Score	1	2	3	4	5	6	7	8	9	10	11	SUBS
Sep 24	Scunthorpe United	Rd 2 0-0	Lukic	Sterland	Dorigo	Batty	McClelland	Whyte	Strachan*	Hodge	Chapman	McAllister	Speed	Shutt*, Whitlow
Oct 8	SCUNTHORPE UNITED	Rd 2 3-0	Lukic	Sterland 1	Dorigo	Batty	McClelland	Whyte	Hodge	Shutt*	Chapman 1	Williams*	Speed 1	Fairclough*, Kelly*
Oct 29	TRANMERE ROVERS	Rd 3 3-1	Lukic	Sterland	Dorigo	Hodge*	Fairclough	Whyte	Strachan	Shutt 1	Chapman 2	McAllister	Wallace*	Kamara*, Williams*
Dec 4	Eveerton	Rd 4 4-1	Lukic	Sterland	Dorigo	Batty	Fairclough	Whyte	Strachan*	Wallace	Chapman	McAllister	Speed	Hodge*, McClelland
Jan 8	MANCHESTER UNITED	Rd 5 1-3	Lukic	Sterland	Dorigo*	Batty	Fairclough	Whyte	Strachan	Wallace	Chapman*	McAllister	Speed 1	Hodge*, McClelland*

ZENITH DATA SYSTEMS CUP

Date	Opponent	Score	1	2	3	4	5	6	7	8	9	10	11	SUBS
Oct 22	NOTTINGHAM FOREST	Rd 2 1-3	Lukic	Sterland*	Dorigo	Batty	Fairclough	Whyte	Newsome*	Shutt	Snodin	Kamara	Speed	Wallace* 1, Grayson*

F.A. CUP

Date	Opponent	Score	1	2	3	4	5	6	7	8	9	10	11	SUBS
Jan 15	MANCHESTER UNITED	Rd 3 0-1	Lukic	Sterland	Dorigo	Hodge*	Fairclough	Whyte	Williams*	Wallace	Chapman	McAllister	Speed	Davison*, Whitlow*

PREMIER LEAGUE 1992-93

Date	Opponent	Score	1	2	3	4	5	6	7	8	9	10	11	SUBS
Aug 15	WIMBLEDON	2-1	Lukic	Newsome*	Dorigo	Batty*	Fairclough	Whyte	Cantona	Rd Wallace	Chapman 2	McAllister	Speed	Strachan*, Hodge*, Day
Aug 19	Aston Villa	1-1	Lukic	Newsome	Dorigo	Batty•	Fairclough	Whyte	Cantona*	Rd Wallace	Chapman	McAllister	Speed 1	Strachan*, Hodge*, Day
Aug 22	Middlesbrough	1-4	Lukic	Newsome*	Dorigo	Batty*	Fairclough	Whyte	Cantona 1	Rd Wallace	Chapman	McAllister	Speed	Strachan*, Hodge*, Day
Aug 25	TOTTENHAM HOTSPUR	5-0	Lukic	Newsome	Dorigo	Batty	Fairclough	Whyte	Cantona 3	Rd Wallace 1	Chapman 1	McAllister	Speed	Strachan, Hodge, Day
Aug 29	LIVERPOOL	2-2	Lukic	Newsome	Dorigo	Batty*	Fairclough*	Whyte	Cantona	Rd Wallace	Chapman 1	McAllister 1	Speed	Strachan*, Hodge*, Day
Sep 1	Oldham Athletic	2-2	Lukic	Newsome	Dorigo	Batty	Fairclough	Whyte	Cantona 2*	Rd Wallace	Chapman	McAllister	Speed	Strachan, Hodge*, Day
Sep 6	Manchester United	0-2	Lukic	Newsome*	Dorigo	Batty	Fairclough	Whyte	Cantona	Rd Wallace *	Chapman	McAllister	Speed	Strachan*, Hodge*, Day
Sep 13	ASTON VILLA	1-1	Lukic	Newsome*	Sellars	Batty	Fairclough	Whyte	Cantona	Strachan	Chapman	McAllister	Speed	Hodge* 1, Rocastle, Day
Sep 19	Southampton	1-1	Lukic	Weatherall*	Dorigo	Batty	Fairclough	Whyte	Strachan	Hodge*	Chapman	McAllister	Speed 1	Sellars*, Shutt*, Day
Sep 26	EVERTON	2-0	Lukic	Sellars*	Dorigo	Batty	Fairclough	Whyte	Strachan	Cantona	Chapman 1	McAllister 1	Speed	Shutt*, Newsome, Day
Oct 3	Ipswich Town	2-4	Lukic	Sellars*	Dorigo	Batty	Fairclough	Whyte	Strachan	Cantona	Chapman 1	McAllister	Speed 1	Rocastle*, Newsome, Day
Oct 17	SHEFFIELD UNITED	3-1	Lukic	Newsome	Dorigo	Batty	Fairclough	Whyte 1	Strachan	Cantona*	Chapman 1	McAllister	Speed 1	Shutt*, Sellars, Day
Oct 24	Queen's Park Rangers	1-2	Lukic	Newsome	Dorigo	Batty	Fairclough	Whyte	Strachan 1	Rd Wallace	Chapman	McAllister	Speed	Shutt*, Rocastle*, Day
Oct 31	COVENTRY CITY	2-2	Lukic	Newsome	Dorigo	Batty*	Fairclough 1	Whyte	Strachan	Rd Wallace*	Chapman 1	McAllister	Speed	Rocastle*, Cantona*, Day
Nov 7	Manchester City	0-4	Day	Newsome	Wetherall	Hodge*	Fairclough	Whyte	Strachan	Cantona	Rd Wallace	McAllister	Speed	Chapman*, Rocastle, Pettinger
Nov 21	ARSENAL	3-0	Lukic	Newsome	Dorigo	Rocastle	Fairclough 1	Whyte	Strachan	Rd Wallace*	Chapman	McAllister 1	Speed	Shutt*, Ray Wallace, Day
Nov 29	Chelsea	0-1	Lukic	Newsome	Dorigo	Rocastle	Fairclough	Whyte	Strachan	Rd Wallace	Chapman	McAllister	Speed	Shutt*, Ray Wallace, Day
Dec 5	NOTTINGHAM FOREST	1-4	Lukic	Newsome	Dorigo	Rocastle*	Fairclough	Rd.Wallace	Strachan	Rd Wallace*	Chapman	McAllister	Speed 1	Hodge*, Shutt*, Day
Dec 12	SHEFFIELD WEDNESDAY	3-1	Lukic	Newsome	Dorigo	Rocastle*	Fairclough	Whyte	Strachan	Rd Wallace*	Chapman 1	McAllister	Speed 1	Varadi* 1, Hodge*, Day
Dec 20	Crystal Palace	0-1	Lukic	Newsome	Dorigo	Rocastle	Fairclough	Whyte*	Strachan	Rd Wallace*	Chapman	McAllister	Speed	Varadi*, Hodge*, Day
Dec 26	Blackburn Rovers	1-3	Lukic	Sterland*	Dorigo	Batty	Fairclough	Whyte	Strachan	Varadi	Chapman	McAllister	Speed 1	Newsome*, Shutt, Day
Dec 28	NORWICH CITY	0-0	Lukic	Sterland	Dorigo	Batty	Fairclough	Wetherall*	Strachan	Varadi	Chapman	McAllister	Speed	Newsome*, Rd Wallace, Day
Jan 9	SOUTHAMPTON	2-1	Lukic	Sterland*	Dorigo	Rd Wallace	Fairclough 1	Wetherall	Strachan*	Shutt	Chapman	McAllister	Speed	Newsome*, Rocastle*, Day
Jan 16	Everton	0-2	Day	Newsome*	Dorigo	Batty	Wetherall	Whyte	Strachan*	Shutt	Chapman	McAllister	Speed	Fairclough*, Rd Wallace*, Lukic
Jan 30	MIDDLESBROUGH	3-0	Lukic	Wetherall	Dorigo	Batty 1	Fairclough 1	Whyte	Strachan	Shutt*	Rd Wallace*	McAllister	Speed	Rocastle*, Strandli* 1, Day
Feb 6	Wimbledon	0-1	Lukic	Sellars	Dorigo	Batty	Newsome	Whyte	Rocastle	Strandli*	Chapman *	McAllister	Speed	Shutt*, Bowman*, Day
Feb 8	MANCHESTER UNITED	0-0	Lukic	Sellars*	Dorigo	Batty	Newsome	Whyte	Bowman	Shutt*	Chapman	McAllister	Speed	Hodge*, Strandli*, Day
Feb 13	OLDHAM ATHLETIC	2-0	Lukic	Sellars*	Dorigo	Batty	Newsome	Whyte	Bowman	Rd Wallace*	Chapman 1	McAllister 1	Speed	Hodge*, Shutt*, Day
Feb 20	Tottenham Hotspur	0-4	Lukic	Bowman	Dorigo	Batty	Newsome	Whyte	Hodge	Rd Wallace*	Chapman*	McAllister	Speed	Rocastle*, Strandli*, Day
Feb 24	Arsenal	0-0	Lukic	Fairclough	Dorigo	Batty	Wetherall	Whyte	Strachan*	Rd Wallace	Strandli	McAllister *	Speed	Chapman*, Newsome*, Day
Feb 27	IPSWICH TOWN	1-0	Lukic	Newsome	Dorigo 1	Batty	Fairclough	Wetherall	Strachan	Rd Wallace	Strandli	Ray Wallace	Speed	Chapman*, Rocastle, Day
Mar 13	MANCHESTER CITY	1-0	Lukic	Kerslake	Dorigo	Batty	Fairclough*	Wetherall	Rocastle 1	Rd Wallace	Strandli*	Hodge	Speed	Newsome*, Chapman*, Day

PREMIER LEAGUE 1992-93 continued

				1	2	3	4	5	6	7	8	9	10	11	SUBS
Mar 21	Nottingham Forest		1-1	Lukic	Kerslake	Dorigo	Batty	Wetherall	Newsome	Rocastle	Rd Wallace* 1	Chapman	Hodge	Speed	Forrester*, Tinkler, Day
Mar 24	CHELSEA		1-1	Lukic	Kerslake	Dorigo*	Batty	Wetherall 1	Newsome	Rocastle	Rd Wallace	Chapman*	Hodge	Speed	Strachan*, Strandli*, Day
Apr 6	Sheffield United		1-2	Lukic	Kerslake	Kerr	Tinkler	Wetherall	Whyte	Strachan	Forrester	Strandli 1	McAllister*	Speed	Hodge*, Shutt, Day
Apr 10	BLACKBURN ROVERS		5-2	Lukic	Kerslake	Kerr	Tinkler	Fairclough	Whyte	Strachan 3	Rd Wallace 1	Chapman 1	Forrester*	Speed	Newsome*, Hodge, Day
Apr 14	Norwich City		2-4	Lukic	Kerslake	Kerr	Tinkler*	Fairclough*	Whyte	Strachan	Rd Wallace 1	Chapman 1	Forrester	Speed	Newsome*, Hodge*, Day
Apr 17	CRYSTAL PALACE		0-0	Lukic	Kerslake	Sharp	Forrester	Wetherall	Newsome	Strachan	Rd Wallace	Chapman	McAllister*	Speed	Tinkler*, Whyte, Day
Apr 21	Liverpool		0-2	Lukic	Kerslake*	Sharp	Rocastle	Newsome	Whyte	Strachan	Rd Wallace	Chapman	Shutt	Speed	Ray Walker*, Tinkler, Day
May 1	QUEEN'S PARK RANGERS		1-1	Lukic	Ray Wallace	Sharp	Batty	Newsome	Whyte	Rocastle*	Rd Wallace	Chapman	Hodge	Forrester*	Tinkler*, Strandli*, Day
May 4	Sheffield Wednesday		1-1	Lukic	Ray Wallace	Sharp*	Batty	Newsome	Whyte	Whelan	Rd Wallace	Chapman 1	Hodge	Tinkler	Kerr*, Wetherall, Day
May 8	Coventry City		3-3	Beeney	Ray Wallace	Dorigo	Batty	Newsome	Whyte	Shutt*	Rd Wallace 3	Chapman	Hodge	Tinkler*	Kerr*, Rocastle*, Lukic

CHARITY SHIELD

Aug 8	LIVERPOOL Wembley		4-3	Lukic	Newsome*	Dorigo 1	Batty	Fairclough	Whyte	Cantona 3	Rd Wallace	Chapman*	McAllister	Speed	Strachan*, Rocastle, Hodge*, Wetherall, Day

EUROPEAN CUP

Sep 16	Vfb Stuttgart	Rd 1	0-3	Lukic	Rocastle*	Dorigo	Batty	Fairclough	Whyte	Cantona*	Strachan	Chapman	McAllister	Speed	Hodge*, Newsome, Shutt*, Sellars, Day
Sep 30	Vfb STUTTGART	Rd 1	4-1	Lukic	Sellars	Dorigo	Batty	Fairclough	Whyte	Strachan	Cantona 1	Chapman 1	McAllister 1	Speed 1	Newsome, Rocastle, Hodge, Shutt, Day
Oct 9	Vfb Stuttgart Barcelona	Rd 1 R	2-1	Lukic	Newsome	Dorigo	Batty	Fairclough	Whyte	Strachan 1	Cantona*	Chapman	McAllister	Speed	Shutt* 1, Rocastle, Sellars, Ray Wallace, Day
Oct 21	Glasgow Rangers	Rd 2	1-2	Lukic	Newsome	Dorigo	Batty	Fairclough	Whyte	Strachan*	Cantona*	Chapman	McAllister 1	Speed	Rd Wallace*, Wetherall, Rocastle*, Shutt, Day
Nov 4	GLASGOW RANGERS	Rd 2	1-2	Lukic	Newsome	Dorigo	Rocastle	Fairclough*	Whyte	Strachan	Cantona	Chapman	McAllister	Speed	Rd Wallace*, Wetherall, Hodge*, Shutt, Day

COCA-Cola CUP

Sep 22	SCUNTHORPE UNITED	Rd 2	4-1	Lukic	Wetherall	Dorigo*	Batty	Sellars*	Whyte	Strachan 1	Shutt 1	Chapman 1	McAllister	Speed 1	Hodge*, Rocastle*
Oct 27	Scunthorpe United	Rd 2	2-2	Lukic	Newsome	Kerr	Batty	Fairclough	Wetherall	Strachan*	Rd Wallace 1	Chapman 1	McAllister	Speed	Sellars*, Whyte*
Nov 10	Watford	Rd 3	1-2	Lukic	Newsome*	Kerr	Rd Wallace	Fairclough	Whyte	Strachan	Cantona	Chapman	McAllister 1	Speed	Rocastle*, Sellars

F.A. CUP

Jan 2	CHARLTON ATHLETIC	Rd 3	1-1	Lukic	Sterland*	Dorigo	Batty*	Fairclough	Wetherall	Strachan	Shutt	Chapman	McAllister	Speed 1	Newsome*, Rd Wallace*
Jan 13	Charlton Athletic	(o.g.) Rd 3 R	3-1	Day	Sterland*	Dorigo	Rd Wallace*	Wetherall	Whyte	Strachan	Shutt	Chapman	McAllister 1	Speed 1	Fairclough*, Rocastle*
Jan 25	Arsenal	Rd 4	2-2	Lukic	Wetherall	Dorigo	Batty	Fairclough	Whyte	Strachan	Shutt	Chapman* 1	McAllister*	Speed 1	Rocastle*, Rd Wallace
Feb 3	ARSENAL	Rd 4 R AET	2-3	Lukic	Wetherall	Dorigo	Batty	Fairclough*	Whyte	Strachan*	Shutt	Chapman	McAllister	Speed	Rocastle*, Rd Wallace*

PREMIER LEAGUE 1993-94

Aug 14	Manchester City		1-1	Lukic	Kelly	Dorigo	Batty	Fairclough	O'Leary	Strachan*	Whelan	Deane 1	McAllister	Speed	Rd Wallace*, Newsome, Beeney
Aug 17	WEST HAM UNITED		1-0	Lukic	Kelly	Dorigo	Batty	Fairclough	O'Leary	Strachan*	Whelan*	Deane	McAllister	Speed	Rd Wallace*, Newsome, Beeney
Aug 21	NORWICH CITY		0-4	Lukic	Kelly	Dorigo	Batty	Fairclough	O'Leary*	Strachan	Whelan	Deane	McAllister	Speed	Rd Wallace*, Newsome*, Beeney
Aug 24	Arsenal		1-2	Lukic	Kelly	Dorigo	Batty	Fairclough	Newsome	Strachan 1	Whelan*	Deane	McAllister	Speed	Rd Wallace*, Wetherall, Beeney
Aug 28	Liverpool		0-2	Lukic	Kelly	Dorigo	Batty	Fairclough	Newsome	Strachan	Rd Wallace*	Deane	McAllister	Speed	Whelan*, Tinkler, Beeney
Aug 30	OLDHAM ATHLETIC		1-0	Beeney	Kelly	Dorigo	Batty	Wetherall	Newsome	Strachan 1	Rd Wallace	Deane	McAllister	Speed	Hodge, Forrester, Lukic
Sep 11	Southampton		2-0	Beeney	Kelly	Dorigo	Batty	Wetherall	Newsome	Strachan	Rd Wallace*	Deane 1	McAllister	Speed 1	Strandli*, Fairclough, Lukic
Sep 18	SHEFFIELD UNITED		2-1	Beeney	Kelly	Dorigo	Batty	Fairclough	Wetherall	Strachan 1	Rd Wallace*	Deane	McAllister 1	Speed	Strandli*, Hodge, Lukic
Sep 25	Coventry City		2-0	Beeney	Kelly	Dorigo	Newsome	Fairclough	Wetherall	Strachan	Rd Wallace 2	Deane	McAllister	Speed	Strandli, Rocastle, Lukic
Oct 2	WIMBLEDON		4-0	Beeney	Kelly	Dorigo	Fairclough	Newsome	Wetherall	Strachan	Rd Wallace*	Deane	McAllister 2	Speed 2	Strandli*, Rocastle, Lukic
Oct 17	Ipswich Town		0-0	Beeney	Kelly	Dorigo	Fairclough	Newsome	Wetherall	Rocastle*	Rd Wallace	Deane	McAllister	Speed	Strandli*, Batty, Lukic
Oct 23	BLACKBURN ROVERS		3-3	Beeney	Kelly	Dorigo	Fairclough	Newsome 1	Wetherall*	Rocastle*	Rd Wallace	Deane	McAllister 2	Speed	Whelan*, Batty*, Lukic
Oct 30	Sheffield Wednesday		3-3	Beeney	Kelly	Dorigo	Fairclough 1	Newsome	Wetherall	Rocastle*	Rd Wallace 1	Deane	McAllister	Speed 1	Hodge*, Strandli, Lukic
Nov 6	CHELSEA		4-1	Beeney	Kelly	Dorigo	Fairclough	Newsome	Wetherall	Rocastle 1	Rd Wallace 2	Deane 1	McAllister	Speed	Hodge, Forrester, Lukic
Nov 20	Tottenham Hotspur		1-1	Beeney	Kelly	Dorigo	Fairclough	Pemberton	Wetherall	Rocastle*	Rd Wallace	Deane 1	McAllister	Speed	Whelan*, Hodge, Lukic
Nov 23	Everton		1-1	Beeney	Kelly	Dorigo	Fairclough	Pemberton	Wetherall	Rocastle*	Rd Wallace 1	Deane	McAllister	Speed	Whelan*, Hodge, Lukic
Nov 27	SWINDON TOWN		3-0	Beeney	Kelly	Dorigo	Fairclough	Pemberton*	Wetherall	Strachan	Rd Wallace 1	Deane 1	McAllister	Speed 1	Forrester*, Hodge, Lukic
Dec 4	MANCHESTER CITY		3-2	Beeney	Kelly	Dorigo	Fairclough	Sharp*	Wetherall	Strachan	Rd Wallace* 1	Deane 1	McAllister	Speed 1	Whelan*, Ray Wallace, Lukic
Dec 8	West Ham United		1-0	Beeney	Kelly	Dorigo	Fairclough	Sharp	Wetherall	Strachan	Rd Wallace 1	Deane	McAllister	Speed*	Whelan, Pemberton*, Lukic
Dec 13	Norwich City		1-2	Beeney	Kelly	Dorigo	Fairclough	Sharp*	Wetherall	Strachan	Rd Wallace 1	Deane	McAllister	Hodge	Whelan*, Newsome, Lukic
Dec 18	ARSENAL	(o.g.)	2-1	Beeney	Kelly	Dorigo	Fairclough	Newsome	Wetherall	Strachan*	Rd Wallace	Deane	McAllister 1	Hodge	Rocastle*, Sharp, Lukic
Dec 22	Newcastle United		1-1	Beeney	Kelly	Dorigo	Fairclough 1	Newsome	Pemberton	Whelan*	Rd Wallace	Deane	McAllister	Hodge	Sharp*, Wetherall, Lukic
Dec 29	QUEEN'S PARK RANGERS		1-1	Beeney	Kelly	Dorigo	Fairclough	Newsome	White	Strachan	Rd Wallace*	Deane	McAllister	Hodge 1	Sharp*, Pemberton, Lukic
Jan 1	Manchester United		0-0	Beeney	Kelly	Dorigo	Fairclough	Newsome	Pemberton	Strachan	White	Deane	McAllister	Hodge*	Sharp*, Wetherall, Lukic
Jan 15	IPSWICH TOWN		0-0	Beeney	Kelly	Dorigo	Fairclough	Newsome	Forrester*	Strachan	White*	Deane	McAllister	Hodge	Speed*, Wetherall*, Lukic
Jan 23	Blackburn Rovers		1-2	Beeney	Kelly	Dorigo	Fairclough	Newsome	Forrester*	Strachan	White*	Deane	McAllister	Speed 1	Pemberton*, Whelan*, Lukic
Feb 6	Aston Villa		0-1	Beeney	Kelly	Dorigo	Fairclough	Newsome	Hodge	Strachan	White*	Deane	McAllister	Speed	Whelan*, Pemberton, Lukic
Feb 19	LIVERPOOL		2-0	Lukic	Kelly	Dorigo	Fairclough	O'Leary*	Wetherall 1	Strachan	Rd Wallace*	Deane	McAllister 1	Speed	White*, Newsome*, Beeney
Feb 28	Oldham Athletic		1-1	Lukic	Kelly	Dorigo	Fairclough	Newsome	Wetherall	Strachan	Rd Wallace	Deane	McAllister 1	Speed	White, Pemberton, Beeney
Mar 5	SOUTHAMPTON		0-0	Lukic	Kelly	Dorigo	Fairclough	O'Leary	Wetherall	Strachan	Rd Wallace	Deane*	McAllister	Speed	White*, Newsome, Beeney
Mar 13	Sheffield United		2-2	Lukic	Kelly	Dorigo	Fairclough	O'Leary	Wetherall	Strachan	Rd Wallace	Deane 1	McAllister	Speed 1	Whelan, Newsome, Beeney
Mar 16	ASTON VILLA		2-0	Lukic	Kelly	Dorigo	Fairclough	O'Leary*	Wetherall	Strachan	Rd Wallace 1	Deane 1	McAllister	Speed	Newsome*, Whelan, Beeney
Mar 19	COVENTRY CITY		1-0	Lukic	Kelly	Dorigo	Fairclough	Newsome	Wetherall	Strachan	Rd Wallace 1	Deane	McAllister	Speed	White, Pemberton, Beeney
Mar 26	Wimbledon		0-1	Lukic	Kelly	Dorigo	Fairclough	Newsome*	Wetherall	Strachan	Rd Wallace	Deane	McAllister	Speed	White*, Tinkler, Beeney
Apr 1	NEWCASTLE UNITED		1-1	Lukic	Kelly	Dorigo	Fairclough 1	Newsome	Wetherall*	Strachan	Rd Wallace	Deane	McAllister	Speed	White*, Tinkler, Beeney
Apr 4	Queen's Park Rangers		4-0	Lukic	Kelly	Dorigo*	Fairclough	Newsome	Wetherall	White 2	Rd Wallace 1	Deane 1	McAllister	Speed	Whelan, Tinkler*, Beeney
Apr 17	TOTTENHAM HOTSPUR		2-0	Lukic	Kelly	Sharp	Fairclough	Newsome	Wetherall	White	Rd Wallace 2	Deane	McAllister	Speed	Tinkler, Strachan, Beeney
Apr 23	Chelsea		1-1	Lukic	Kelly	Sharp	Fairclough	Newsome	Wetherall	White*	Rd Wallace	Deane	McAllister	Speed 1	Strachan*, Tinkler, Beeney
Apr 27	MANCHESTER UNITED		0-2	Lukic	Kelly	Dorigo*	Fairclough	Newsome	Wetherall*	Strachan	Rd Wallace	Deane	McAllister	Speed	Whelan*, Pemberton*, Beeney
Apr 30	EVERTON	(o.g.)	3-0	Lukic	Kelly	Sharp	Fairclough	O'Leary	Wetherall	Strachan	Rd Wallace*	Whelan*	McAllister 1	Speed	White*1, Tinkler*, Beeney
May 3	SHEFFIELD WEDNESDAY		2-2	Lukic	Kelly	Sharp*	Fairclough	O'Leary	Wetherall	Strachan	Rd Wallace 1	Deane	McAllister	Speed*	Tinkler*, White* 1, Beeney
May 7	Swindon Town		5-0	Lukic	Kelly	Pemberton	Fairclough 1	O'Leary	Wetherall	Strachan*	Rd Wallace 1	Deane 2	McAllister	White* 1	Whelan*, Ford*, Beeney

COCA-Cola CUP

Sep 21	Sunderland	Rd 2	1-2	Beeney	Kelly	Dorigo	Fairclough	Hodge	Wetherall	Strachan	Rd Wallace	Deane	McAllister	Speed 1	Rocastle, Sharp, Lukic
Oct 6	Sunderland	Rd 2	1-2	Beeney	Kelly	Dorigo	Fairclough	Newsome	Wetherall*	Strachan*	Whelan 1	Deane	McAllister	Speed	Rocastle*, Strandli*, Lukic

F.A. CUP

Jan 8	CREWE ALEXANDRA	Rd 3	3-1	Beeney	Kelly	Dorigo	Fairclough	Newsome	Hodge	Strachan	Forrester 2	Deane	McAllister	White	Sharp, Pemberton, Lukic
Jan 29	Oxford United	Rd 4	2-2	Beeney	Kelly	Dorigo	Fairclough	Newsome*	White	Strachan	Rd Wallace*	Deane	McAllister	Speed 1	Hodge*, Wetherall* 1, Lukic
Feb 9	OXFORD UNITED	Rd 4 R AET	2-3	Beeney	Kelly	Dorigo	Fairclough	Newsome	White 1	Strachan 1	Strandli*	Deane*	McAllister	Speed	Forrester*, Wetherall*, Lukic

PREMIER LEAGUE 1994-95

Aug 20	West Ham United		0-0	Lukic	Kelly	Worthington	Palmer	Wetherall	White	Strachan	Wallace*	Deane	McAllister	Speed	Masinga*, Fairclough, Beeney
Aug 23	ARSENAL		1-0	Lukic	Kelly	Worthington	Palmer	Wetherall	White	Strachan*	Wallace	Masinga	McAllister	Speed	Pemberton, Whelan* 1, Beeney
Aug 27	CHELSEA		2-3	Lukic	Kelly	Worthington	Palmer	Wetherall	White	Wallace	Whelan 1	Masinga 1	McAllister	Speed	Pemberton, Tinkler, Beeney
Aug 30	Crystal Palace		2-1	Lukic	Kelly	Worthington	Palmer	Wetherall	White 1	Wallace	Whelan 1	Masinga*	McAllister	Speed	Strachan, Fairclough*, Beeney
Sep 11	MANCHESTER UNITED		2-1	Lukic	Kelly	Worthington	Palmer	Wetherall 1	White*	Wallace	Whelan	Masinga*	McAllister	Speed	Deane*1, Fairclough*, Beeney
Sep 17	Coventry City		1-2	Lukic	Kelly	Worthington	Palmer	Wetherall*	Strachan	Wallace	Whelan	Masinga*	McAllister	Speed 1	Fairclough*, Pemberton*, Beeney
Sep 26	Sheffield Wednesday		1-1	Lukic	Kelly	Worthington	Palmer	Wetherall	Tinkler*	Wallace	Deane	Masinga*	McAllister 1	Speed	Whelan*, Radebe*, Beeney
Oct 1	MANCHESTER CITY		2-0	Lukic	Kelly	Worthington	Palmer	Wetherall	Fairclough	Wallace	Whelan 2	Deane*	McAllister	Speed	Pemberton*, Radebe, Beeney
Oct 8	Norwich City		1-2	Lukic	Kelly	Worthington*	Palmer	Wetherall	Dorigo	Wallace 1	Whelan*	Deane	McAllister	Speed	Fairclough*, Pemberton*, Beeney
Oct 15	TOTTENHAM HOTSPUR		1-1	Lukic	Kelly*	Worthington	Palmer	Wetherall	Dorigo	Wallace	Whelan	Deane 1	McAllister	Speed	Pemberton*, Tinkler, Beeney
Oct 24	LEICESTER CITY		2-1	Lukic	Kelly	Worthington	Palmer	Wetherall	Dorigo	Wallace	Whelan 1	Deane	McAllister 1	Speed	Pemberton, Masinga, Beeney
Oct 29	Southampton	(o.g.)	3-1	Lukic	Kelly	Worthington	Palmer	Wetherall	Dorigo*	Wallace 2	Whelan	Deane	McAllister	Speed	Radebe*, White, Beeney
Nov 1	Ipswich Town		0-2	Lukic	Kelly	Worthington	Palmer	Wetherall	White*	Wallace	Whelan	Deane	McAllister	Speed	Masinga*, Radebe, Beeney
Nov 5	WIMBLEDON		3-1	Lukic	Kelly	Worthington	Palmer	Wetherall 1	White* 1	Wallace	Whelan	Deane*	McAllister	Speed 1	Masinga*, Radebe*, Beeney
Nov 19	Queens Park Rangers	(o.g.)	2-3	Lukic	Kelly	Worthington	Palmer	Wetherall	Radebe*	Wallace	Whelan	Deane 1	McAllister	Speed	White*, Pemberton, Beeney
Nov 26	NOTTINGHAM FOREST		1-0	Lukic	Kelly	Dorigo	Palmer	Wetherall	White	Wallace*	Whelan* 1	Deane	McAllister	Speed	Masinga*, Pemberton*, Beeney
Dec 5	Everton		0-3	Lukic	Kelly	Dorigo	Palmer	Wetherall	White	Wallace	Whelan	Deane	McAllister	Speed	Masinga, Radebe, Beeney
Dec 10	WEST HAM UNITED		2-2	Lukic	Kelly	Dorigo	Palmer	Wetherall	Tinkler	Strachan	Whelan	Deane 1	McAllister	Worthington* 1	White*, Radebe, Beeney
Dec 17	Arsenal		3-1	Lukic	Kelly	Dorigo	Palmer	Wetherall	Radebe	Pemberton	Whelan*	Deane 1	Masinga 2	Speed	White*, Worthington, Beeney
Dec 26	NEWCASTLE UNITED		0-0	Lukic	Kelly	Dorigo	Palmer	Wetherall*	Pemberton	White	Whelan	Masinga*	McAllister	Speed	Strachan*, Worthington*, Beeney
Dec 31	LIVERPOOL		0-2	Lukic	Kelly	Dorigo*	Radebe	Wetherall	Pemberton	Strachan*	Whelan	Masinga	McAllister	Speed	Worthington*, White*, Beeney
Jan 2	Aston Villa		0-0	Lukic	Kelly	Worthington	Radebe	Wetherall	Pemberton	White	Masinga*	Deane	McAllister	Speed	Wallace*, Tinkler, Beeney
Jan 14	SOUTHAMPTON		0-0	Lukic	Kelly	Worthington	Palmer	Wetherall	Pemberton	White*	Radebe*	Deane	McAllister	Speed	Masinga*, Wallace*, Beeney
Jan 24	QUEENS PARK RANGERS		4-0	Lukic	Kelly	Worthington	Palmer	Wetherall	Pemberton	White 1	Masinga 2	Deane 1	McAllister	Speed	Yeboah*, Radebe, Beeney
Feb 1	Blackburn Rovers		1-1	Lukic	Kelly	Dorigo	Palmer	Radebe*	Pemberton	White	Masinga*	Deane	McAllister 1	Speed	Yeboah*, Worthington*, Beeney
Feb 4	Wimbledon		0-0	Lukic	Kelly	Dorigo	Palmer	Radebe	Pemberton	White	Masinga	Deane	McAllister	Worthington	Yeboah, Whelan, Beeney
Feb 22	EVERTON		1-0	Lukic	Kelly	Dorigo	Radebe*	Wetherall	Pemberton	White	Yeboah 1	Masinga	McAllister	Speed	Worthington*, Whelan, Beeney
Feb 25	Manchester City		0-0	Lukic	Kelly	Dorigo	Palmer	Wetherall	Worthington	White	Yeboah*	Masinga	McAllister	Speed	Deane*, Radebe, Beeney
Mar 4	SHEFFIELD WEDNESDAY		0-1	Lukic	Kelly	Dorigo	Palmer	Wetherall	Pemberton	Wallace*	Yeboah	Deane	McAllister	Speed	Masinga*, Radebe, Beeney

PREMIER LEAGUE 1994-95 continued

			1	2	3	4	5	6	7	8	9	10	11	SUBS
Mar 11	Chelsea	3-0	Lukic	Kelly	Dorigo	Palmer	Wetherall	Pemberton	Wallace*	Yeboah 2	Deane	McAllister 1	Speed	Masinga*, Tinkler, Beeney
Mar 15	Leicester City	3-1	Lukic	Kelly	Dorigo	Palmer 1	Wetherall	Pemberton	Wallace	Yeboah 2	Deane	McAllister	Speed	Radebe, Tinkler, Beeney
Mar 18	COVENTRY CITY	(o.g.) 3-1	Lukic	Kelly	Dorigo	Palmer	Radebe*	Tinkler	Wallace 1	Yeboah 1	Deane	McAllister	Speed	Cozens*, White, Beeney
Mar 22	Nottingham Forest	0-3	Lukic	Kelly*	Dorigo	Palmer	Couzens	Pemberton	Wallace	Yeboah	Deane	McAllister	Speed	White*, Worthington, Beeney
Apr 2	Manchester United	0-0	Lukic	Kelly	Dorigo	Palmer	Wetherall	Pemberton	Wallace*	Yeboah	Deane*	McAllister	Couzens	Whelan*, Worthington*, Beeney
Apr 5	IPSWICH TOWN	4-0	Lukic	Kelly*	Dorigo	Palmer	Wetherall	Pemberton	Wallace	Yeboah 3	Deane	McAllister	Speed 1	Couzens*, Whelan, Beeney
Apr 9	Liverpool	1-0	Lukic	Kelly	Dorigo	Palmer	Wetherall	Pemberton	Wallace	Yeboah	Deane 1	McAllister	Speed	Worthington, Whelan, Beeney
Apr 15	BLACKBURN ROVERS	1-1	Lukic	Kelly	Dorigo	Palmer	Wetherall	Pemberton	Wallace*	Yeboah	Deane 1	McAllister	Speed	Whelan*, Worthington, Beeney
Apr 17	Newcastle United	2-1	Lukic	Kelly	Dorigo	Palmer	Wetherall	Pemberton	White*	Yeboah* 1	Deane	McAllister 1	Speed	Masinga*, Worthington*, Beeney
Apr 29	ASTON VILLA	1-0	Lukic	Kelly	Dorigo	Palmer 1	Wetherall	Pemberton	Wallace	Yeboah	Deane	McAllister	Speed	Whelan, Worthington, Beeney
May 6	NORWICH CITY	2-1	Lukic	Kelly	Dorigo	Palmer 1	Wetherall	Pemberton	Wallace*	Yeboah*	Deane	McAllister	Speed	Whelan*, Sharp*, Beeney
May 9	CRYSTAL PALACE	3-1	Lukic	Kelly	Dorigo	Palmer	Wetherall	Pemberton	Wallace	Yeboah	Deane	McAllister	Speed	Couzens, Sharp, Beeney
May 14	Tottenham Hotspur	1-1	Lukic	Kelly	Dorigo	Palmer	Wetherall	Pemberton	Wallace*	Yeboah	Deane	McAllister	Speed	Sharp*, Fairclough, Beeney

COCA-Cola CUP

Sep 21	MANSFIELD TOWN	Rd 2 0-1	Lukic	Kelly	Worthington	Palmer	Fairclough	Strachan*	Wallace	Whelan	Masinga*	McAllister	Speed	Deane*, Radebe*, Beeney
Oct 4	Mansfield Town	Rd 2 0-0	Lukic	Kelly	Worthington	Palmer	Wetherall	Fairclough*	Wallace*	Whelan	Deane	McAllister	Speed	Dorigo*, Pemberton*, Beeney

F.A. CUP

Jan 7	Walsall	Rd 3 1-1	Lukic	Kelly	Worthington	Palmer	Wetherall 1	Pemberton	White*	Radebe	Deane	McAllister	Speed	Masinga*, Wallace*, Beeney
Jan 17	WALSALL	Rd 3 R AET 5-2	Lukic	Kelly	Worthington	Palmer	Wetherall 1	Pemberton	Wallace	Whelan	Deane 1	McAllister	Speed	Masinga* 3, Radebe*, Beeney
Jan 28	OLDHAM ATHLETIC	Rd 4 3-2	Lukic	Kelly	Worthington	Palmer 1	Wetherall	Pemberton	White 1	Masinga* 1	Deane	McAllister	Speed	Yeboah*, Radebe, Beeney
Feb 19	Manchester United	Rd 5 1-3	Lukic	Kelly	Dorigo	Whelan	Wetherall	Pemberton	White	Wallace*	Masinga*	McAllister	Speed	Yeboah* 1, Worthington*, Beeney

PREMIER LEAGUE 1995-96

			1	2	3	4	5	6	7	8	9	10	11	SUBS
Aug 19	West Ham United	2-1	Lukic	Kelly	Dorigo*	Palmer*	Wetherall	Pemberton	Wallace*	Yeboah 2	Deane	McAllister	Speed	Beeseley*, Whelan*, Worthington*
Aug 21	LIVERPOOL	1-0	Lukic	Kelly	Dorigo	Palmer	Wetherall	Pemberton	Wallace*	Yeboah 1	Deane	McAllister	Speed	Beesley, Whelan*, Beeney
Aug 26	ASTON VILLA	2-0	Lukic	Kelly	Dorigo	Palmer	Wetherall	Pemberton	Wallace*	Yeboah	Deane	McAllister	Speed 1	White* 1, Beesley, Beeney
Aug 30	Southampton	1-1	Lukic	Kelly	Dorigo 1	Palmer	Wetherall	Pemberton	Wallace*	Yeboah*	Deane	McAllister	Speed	White*, Worthington*, Beesley
Sep 9	Tottenham Hotspur	1-2	Lukic	Kelly	Dorigo	Palmer	Wetherall	Pemberton	White*	Yeboah 1	Deane	McAllister	Speed	Whelan*, Beesley, Beeney
Sep 16	QUEEN'S PARK RANGERS	1-3	Lukic	Kelly	Worthington*	Palmer	Wetherall 1	Pemberton	Whelan*	Yeboah	Deane	McAllister	Speed	White*, Beesley*, Pettinger
Sep 23	Wimbledon	4-2	Lukic	Kelly	Beesley	Palmer 1	Wetherall	Pemberton	Masinga*	Yeboah 3	Deane	McAllister	Speed	Tinkler*, Worthington, Pettinger
Sep 30	SHEFFIELD WEDNESDAY	2-0	Lukic	Kelly	Beesley	Palmer	Wetherall	Tinkler	Couzens	Yeboah 1	Masinga*	McAllister	Speed	Deane*, Bowman, Beeney
Oct 14	ARSENAL	0-3	Lukic	Kelly	Dorigo	Palmer	Wetherall	Pemberton	Couzens	Yeboah	Deane	Tinkler*	Speed	Wallace*, Whelan, Beesley
Oct 21	Manchester City	0-0	Lukic	Kelly	Worthington	Palmer	Wetherall	Pemberton	Wallace*	Yeboah	Deane	McAllister	Couzens	Whelan*, Beesley*, Tinkler
Oct 28	COVENTRY CITY	3-1	Lukic	Kelly	Jobson	Palmer	Wetherall	Pemberton	Whelan*	Yeboah	Deane*	McAllister 3	Speed	Sharp*, Couzens*, Worthington
Nov 4	Middlesbrough	1-1	Lukic	Kelly	Jobson	Palmer	Wetherall	Pemberton	Whelan	Yeboah	Deane 1	McAllister	Worthington	Masinga, Couzens, Ford
Nov 18	CHELSEA	1-0	Lukic	Kelly	Dorigo	Palmer	Wetherall	Jobson	Couzens*	Yeboah 1	Deane	McAllister	Speed	Wallace*, Worthington, Beeney
Nov 25	Newcastle United	1-2	Lukic	Kelly	Dorigo*	Palmer	Wetherall	Jobson	Ford*	Yeboah	Deane 1	McAllister	Speed	Bowman*, Brolin*, Whelan
Dec 2	MANCHESTER CITY	0-1	Lukic	Kelly	Dorigo	Palmer	Wetherall	Jobson	Brolin*	Yeboah	Deane	McAllister	Ford*	Whelan*, Pemberton*, Worthington
Dec 9	WIMBLEDON	1-1	Lukic	Pemberton	Dorigo	Palmer	Wetherall	Jobson 1	Brolin	Yeboah	Deane*	McAllister	Speed	Wallace*, Couzens, Beeney
Dec 16	Sheffield Wednesday	2-6	Lukic	Kelly*	Dorigo	Palmer	Wetherall	Jobson	Brolin 1	Yeboah*	Couzens	McAllister	Speed	Wallace* 1, Deane*, Worthington
Dec 24	MANCHESTER UNITED	3-1	Beeney	Kelly	Dorigo	Palmer	Wetherall	Jobson	Brolin	Yeboah* 1	Deane 1	McAllister 1	Speed	Wallace*, Radebe, Worthington
Dec 27	Bolton Wanderers	2-0	Beeney	Kelly	Dorigo	Ford	Wetherall 1	Jobson	Brolin* 1	Yeboah	Deane	McAllister	Speed	Radebe*, Wallace, Couzens
Dec 30	Everton	0-2	Beeney	Kelly	Dorigo*	Ford	Wetherall	Jobson	Brolin	Masinga*	Deane	McAllister	Speed	Worthington*,Wallace*, Radebe
Jan 1	BLACKBURN ROVERS	0-0	Beeney	Kelly	Worthington	Palmer	Ford	Jobson	Brolin*	Yeboah	Deane	McAllister	Speed	Wallace*, Wetherall, Couzens
Jan 13	WEST HAM UNITED	2-0	Beeney	Kelly	Dorigo*	Palmer	Wetherall	Ford	Brolin* 2	Wallace*	Chapman	McAllister	Speed	Couzens*, Harte*, Gray*
Jan 20	Liverpool	0-5	Beeney	Kelly	Worthington	Palmer	Wetherall	Ford	Brolin*	Wallace	Chapman*	McAllister	Speed	Deane*, Couzens*, Beesley
Jan 31	Nottingham Forest	1-2	Beeney	Kelly	Dorigo*	Palmer 1	Jobson	Couzens*	Brolin*	Wallace	Deane	McAllister	Speed	Bowman*, Tinkler* Gray*
Feb 3	Aston Villa	0-3	Beeney	Maybury*	Dorigo	Palmer	Bowman	Pemberton*	Wallace	Couzens	Deane	McAllister	Speed	Tinkler*, Worthington*, Gray*
Mar 2	BOLTON WANDERERS	0-1	Lukic	Radebe*	Worthington*	Palmer	Wetherall	Beesley	Wallace	Yeboah	Deane	McAllister	Brolin	Gray*, Couzens*, Ford
Mar 6	Queen's Park Rangers	2-1	Lukic	Radebe	Worthington	Palmer	Wetherall	Beesley	Gray	Yeboah 2	Brolin*	McAllister	Ford	Masinga*, Bowman, Tinkler
Mar 13	Blackburn Rovers	0-1	Lukic	Kelly	Worthington	Palmer	Wetherall	Beesley*	Radebe	Wallace	Deane	McAllister	Gray	Brolin*, Masinga, Pemberton
Mar 17	EVERTON	2-2	Lukic	Kelly	Pemberton	Palmer	Radebe	Tinkler	Couzens*	Brolin*	Deane 2	Ford	Gray	Wallace*, Masinga*, Beesley
Mar 30	MIDDLESBROUGH	0-1	Lukic*	Kelly	Radebe	Palmer	Wetherall	Pemberton*	Gray	Kewell*	Deane	McAllister	Speed	Blunt*, Wallace*, Jackson*
Apr 3	SOUTHAMPTON	1-0	Lukic	Kelly	Kewell*	Palmer	Wetherall	Radebe	Gray	Blunt	Brolin*	McAllister	Speed	Deane* 1, Wallace*, Tinkler
Apr 6	Arsenal	1-2	Lukic	Kelly	Harte	Palmer	Wetherall	Radebe	Gray	Brolin	Deane 1	McAllister	Speed	Tinkler, Pemberton, Wallace
Apr 8	NOTTINGHAM FOREST	1-3	Lukic	Kelly	Radebe*	Palmer	Wetherall 1	Blunt	Gray	Brolin*	Deane	McAllister	Speed	Harte*, Wallace*, Pemberton
Apr 13	Chelsea	0-4	Lukic	Kelly	Harte	Palmer	Wetherall	Pemberton*	Gray	Brolin	Deane	McAllister	Speed	Radebe*, Wallace, Worthington
Apr 17	Manchester United	0-1	Beeney	Kelly	Worthington	Palmer	Wetherall	Beesley	Gray	Ford	Deane	McAllister	Speed	Radebe*, Tinkler*, Masinga*
Apr 29	NEWCASTLE UNITED	0-1	Beeney	Kelly	Worthington	Ford*	Wetherall	Beesley	Speed*	Radebe	Deane*	McAllister	Gray*	Masinga*, Wallace*, Tinkler
May 2	TOTTENHAM HOTSPUR	1-3	Lukic	Kelly	Worthington	Palmer	Wetherall 1	Beesley	Ford*	Tinkler	Masinga	McAllister	Gray	Couzens*, Radebe, Bowman
May 5	Coventry City	0-0	Lukic	Kelly	Worthington	Palmer	Wetherall	Tinkler	Wallace	Radebe	Masinga	McAllister	Gray*	Couzens*, Beesley, Ford

COCA-Cola CUP

Sep 19	NOTTS COUNTY	Rd 2 0-0	Lukic	Kelly	Worthington*	Palmer	Wetherall	Pemberton	White*	Yeboah	Deane	McAllister	Speed	Beesley*, Gray*, Pettinger
Oct 3	Notts County	Rd 2 3-2	Lukic	Kelly	Couzens 1	Palmer	Wetherall	Beesley	Tinkler*	Yeboah	Deane	McAllister* 1	Speed 1	Worthington*, Wallace, Masinga
Oct 25	Derby County	Rd 3 1-0	Lukic	Kelly	Worthington	Palmer	Wetherall	Pemberton	Beesley	Yeboah*	Deane	McAllister	Speed 1	Whelan*, Couzens, Beeney
Nov 29	BLACKBURN ROVERS	Rd 4 2-1	Lukic	Kelly	Dorigo*	Palmer	Wetherall	Ford	Brolin*	Yeboah 1	Deane 1	McAllister	Speed*	Whelan*, Bowman*, Beeney
Jan 10	READING	Rd 5 2-1	Beeney	Kelly	Dorigo	Palmer	Wetherall	Ford	Brolin	Wallace*	Masinga* 1	McAllister	Speed 1	Couzens*, Harte*, Lukic
Feb 11	Birmingham City	(o.g.) SF 2-1	Lukic	Kelly	Dorigo	Palmer	Wetherall	Beesley	Wallace*	Yeboah 1	Ford*	McAllister	Speed	Deane*, Radebe*, Beeney
Feb 25	BIRMINGHAM CITY	SF 3-0	Lukic	Kelly	Dorigo*	Palmer	Wetherall	Beesley	Wallace	Yeboah 1	Deane 1	McAllister	Masinga* 1	Radebe*, Brolin*, Beeney
Mar 24	Aston Villa (at Wembley)	0-3	Lukic	Kelly	Radebe*	Palmer	Wetherall	Pemberton	Ford*	Yeboah	Gray	McAllister	Speed	Deane*, Brolin*, Worthington

F.A. CUP

Jan 7	Derby County	Rd 3 4-2	Beeney	Kelly	Dorigo	Palmer	Wetherall*	Jobson	Ford	Yeboah 1	Deane 1	McAllister 1	Speed 1	Wallace*, Couzens, Lukic
Feb 14	Bolton Wanderers	Rd 4 1-0	Lukic	Kelly	Dorigo	Palmer	Wetherall	Beesley	Wallace* 1	Yeboah*	Ford	McAllister	Speed	Deane*, Radebe, Beeney
Feb 21	PORT VALE	Rd 5 0-0	Lukic	Kelly	Dorigo	Palmer	Wetherall	Beesley	Wallace	Yeboah	Ford	McAllister	Speed*	Deane*, Radebe, Beeney
Feb 27	Port Vale	Rd 5 R 2-1	Lukic	Radebe	Worthington	Palmer	Wetherall	Beesley	Wallace*	Yeboah	Deane	McAllister 2	Masinga*	Brolin*, Gray*, Bowman
Mar 10	LIVERPOOL	Rd 6 0-0	Lukic	Kelly	Worthington	Palmer	Wetherall	Beesley	Radebe	Yeboah	Brolin*	McAllister	Ford*	Deane*, Pemberton*, Gray
Mar 20	Liverpool	Rd 6 R 0-3	Lukic	Kelly	Worthington	Palmer	Radebe	Pemberton	Ford*	Yeboah	Deane	McAllister	Speed	Gray*, Beesley, Brolin

U.E.F.A. CUP

Sep 12	A.S. Monaco	Rd 1 3-0	Lukic	Kelly	Dorigo*	Palmer	Wetherall	Pemberton	Whelan	Yeboah 3	Deane	McAllister	Speed	Beesley*, White, Tinkler, Beeney, Couzens
Sep 25	A.S. MONACO	Rd 1 0-1	Lukic	Kelly	Beesley	Palmer	Wetherall	Pemberton*	White*	Yeboah	Deane	McAllister	Speed	Tinkler*, Sharp, Couzens*, Ford, Beeney
Oct 17	P.S.V. EINDHOVEN	Rd 2 3-5	Lukic	Kelly	Dorigo*	Palmer 1	Wetherall	Pemberton	Whelan*	Yeboah	Deane	McAllister 1	Speed* 1	Couzens*, Wallace*, Beesley*, Tinkler, Beeney
Oct 31	P.S.V. Eindhoven	Rd 2 0-3	Lukic	Kelly	Beesley*	Palmer	Wetherall	Pemberton	Whelan*	Yeboah	Bowman	McAllister	Speed*	Sharp*, Ford*, White*, Deane, Beeney

PREMIER LEAGUE 1996-97

Aug 17	Derby County	(o.g) 3-3	Martyn	Kelly	Sharpe	Palmer	Radebe*	Jobson	Couzens*	Ford	Rush	Deane*	Bowyer 1	Beeney, Wetherall*, Harte*, Tinkler*, Wallace
Aug 17	SHEFFIELD WEDNESDAY	0-2	Martyn	Kelly	Sharpe	Palmer	Radebe*	Jobson	Harte	Ford*	Rush	Hately*	Bowyer	Beeney, Wetherall*, Gray*, Tinkler*, Wallace
Aug 26	WIMBLEDON	1-0	Martyn	Couzens*	Sharpe 1	Palmer	Wetherall	Jobson	Tinkler*	Harte	Rush	Hately*	Bowyer	Beeney, Kelly*, Radede*, Kewell, Wallace
Sep 4	Blackburn Rovers	1-0	Martyn	Kelly	Sharpe	Palmer	Wetherall	Jobson	Harte 1	Ford*	Rush	Wallace*	Bowyer*	Beeney, Gray*, Radede*, Couzens, Hateley
Sep 7	Manchester United	0-4	Martyn	Kelly	Sharpe	Palmer	Wetherall	Jobson	Harte	Ford*	Rush	Wallace*	Bowyer*	Beeney, Radebe*, Gray*, Couzens, Hateley*
Sep 14	Coventry City	1-2	Martyn	Kelly	Harte	Palmer	Wetherall	Jobson	Gray*	Hateley	Rush	Wallace	Couzens*1	Beeney,Radebe, Jackson, Blunt*, Ford*
Sep 21	NEWCASTLE UNITED	0-1	Martyn	Kelly	Harte	Palmer	Wetherall	Jobson	Couzens*	Ford	Rush*	Wallace	Sharpe	Beeney, Radebe, Jackson*, Blunt, Boyle*
Sep 28	Leicester City	0-1	Martyn	Kelly	Harte	Palmer	Wetherall	Jobson	Couzens*	Ford	Jackson	Wallace	Sharpe	Beeney, Radebe*, Kewell, Blunt, Boyle
Oct 12	Nottingham Forest	2-0	Martyn	Kelly	Couzens*	Radebe	Wetherall	Jobson	Ford	Hateley	Rush*	Wallace 2	Sharpe	Beeney, Dorigo*, Harte, Jackson, Beesley
Oct 19	Aston Villa	0-2	Martyn	Kelly	Radebe	Palmer*	Wetherall*	Jobson	Ford	Hateley	Rush	Wallace	Sharpe	Beeney, Harte, Couzens*, Beesley*, Jackson
Oct 26	Arsenal	0-3	Martyn	Kelly	Couzens*	Palmer*	Radebe	Beesley	Ford	Harte	Rush	Shepherd	Sharpe	Beeney, Deane*, Wetherall, Tinkler, Jackson
Nov 2	SUNDERLAND	3-0	Martyn	Kelly	Beesley	Ford 1	Radebe	Wetherall	Bowyer*	Wallace	Rush	Deane 1	Sharpe	Beeney, Couzens*, Kewell, Hart, Jackson
Nov 16	LIVERPOOL	0-2	Martyn	Kelly	Ford	Palmer	Radebe	Beesley	Bowyer*	Wallace*	Rush	Deane	Sharpe	Beeney, Harte, Couzens, Jackson*, Wetherall
Nov 23	Southampton	2-0	Martyn	Kelly 1	Ford*	Palmer	Radebe	Beesley	Bowyer	Jackson	Rush	Deane	Sharpe 1	Beeney, Kewell, Harte, Wetherall*, Couzens

Date	Opponent	Score	GK	2	3	4	5	6	7	8	9	10	11	Subs
Dec 1	CHELSEA	2-0	Martyn	Kelly	Beesley	Palmer	Radebe	Wetherall	Bowyer	Ford	Rush 1	Deane 1	Sharpe	Beeney, Wallace, Harte, Yeboah, Jackson
Dec 7	Middesbrough	0-0	Martyn	Kelly	Beesley	Palmer	Radebe	Wetherall	Bowyer	Ford*	Rush	Deane	Sharpe	Beeney, Jackson*, Harte, Yeboah, Couzens
Dec 14	Tottenhan Hotspur	0-0	Martyn	Kelly	Beesley	Palmer	Radebe	Halle	Bowyer	Wallace*	Rush	Deane	Ford*	Beeney, Wetherall, Kewell*, Jackson, Harte
Dec 21	Everton	0-0	Martyn	Kelly	Beesley	Palmer	Radebe*	Wetherall	Bowyer	Halle	Rush	Deane	Sharpe*	Beeney, Wallace, Yeboah, Ford, Jackson*
Dec 26	COVENTRY CITY	1-3	Martyn	Kelly	Beesley*	Palmer	Radebe*	Wetherall*	Bowyer	Jackson	Rush	Deane 1	Halle	Beeney, Dorigo*, Yeboah*, Ford, Harte
Dec 28	Manchester United	0-1	Martyn	Kelly	Dorigo	Palmer	Radebe*	Jackson	Bowyer	Yeboah	Rush	Deane	Halle	Beeney, Gray*, Beesley, Ford, Harte
Jan 1	Newcastle United	0-1	Martyn	Kelly*	Dorigo	Palmer	Radebe*	Wetherall	Bowyer	Jackson	Rush*	Deane	Beesley	Beeney, Wallace*, Gray*, Ford, Harte
Jan 11	LEICESTER CITY	3-0	Martyn	Kelly	Dorigo	Beesley	Molenaar	Wetherall	Bowyer 1	Wallace	Rush 2	Deane	Jackson	Beeney, Gray, Sharpe, Ford, Harte
Jan 20	West Ham United	2-0	Martyn	Kelly 1	Radebe	Palmer	Molenaar	Wetherall	Bowyer 1	Jackson	Rush	Deane	Halle	Beeney, Wallace, Beesley, Ford, Harte
Jan 29	DERBY COUNTY	0-0	Beeney	Kelly	Dorigo	Palmer	Molenaar	Radebe	Bowyer	Wallace	Jackson*	Deane	Halle	Evans, Rush*, Beesley, Ford, Harte
Feb 1	ARSENAL	0-0	Martyn	Kelly	Dorigo	Halle	Molenaar	Radebe	Bowyer	Wallace	Rush	Deane*	Jackson	Beeney, Wetherall, Gray*, Ford, Harte
Feb 19	Liverpool	0-4	Martyn	Kelly	Dorigo	Palmer	Molenaar	Radebe	Bowyer	Jackson*	Wallace*	Deane	Halle	Beeney, Wetherall, Rush*, Harte*, Yeboah
Mar 1	West Ham United	1-0	Martyn	Halle	Harte	Wetherall	Molenaar	Radebe	Bowyer*	Yeboah	Rush	Deane	Sharpe 1	Beeney, Palmer*, Gray, Jackson, Ford
Mar 8	EVERTON	1-0	Martyn	Halle	Harte	Palmer	Molenaar 1	Wetherall	Bowyer	Yeboah	Rush	Deane	Sharpe	Beeney, Wallace, Gray, Jackson, Ford
Mar 12	SOUTHAMPTION	0-0	Martyn	Kelly	Halle	Palmer	Molenaar	Wetherall	Bowyer	Yeboah	Rush	Deane	Sharpe*	Beeney, Dorigo*, Harte, Jackson, Ford
Mar 15	Tottenham Hotspur	0-1	Martyn	Kelly	Dorigo	Halle	Molenaar	Radebe	Bowyer	Yeboah*	Rush	Deane	Sharpe	Beeney, Harte, Wetherall, Jackson, Ford
Mar 22	Sheffield Wednesday	2-2	Martyn	Kelly*	Dorigo	Halle	Molenaar	Radebe	Bowyer	Wallace 1	Rush	Deane	Sharpe 1	Beeney, Wetherall*, Gray, Jackson, Harte
Apr 7	BLACKBURN ROVERS	0-0	Martyn	Kelly	Dorigo	Jackson	Wetherall	Halle	Bowyer	Wallace*	Rush	Deane	Sharpe*	Beeney, Laurent*, Lilley*, Ford, Harte
Apr 16	Wimbledon	0-2	Martyn	Halle	Dorigo	Molenaar	Radebe	Wetherall*	Bowyer	Wallace	Rush	Deane*	Sharpe*	Beeney, Kelly*, Lilley*, Laurent*, Harte
Apr 19	Nottingham Forest	1-1	Martyn	Kelly	Dorigo	Halle	Radebe	Wetherall	Bowyer	Laurent	Lilley	Deane 1*	Sharpe*	Beeney, Palmer*, Wallace*, Molenaar, Harte
Apr 22	Aston Villa	1-1	Martyn	Kelly	Dorigo	Palmer	Radebe	Wetherall	Bowyer	Laurent*	Lilley	Rush	Halle	Beeney, Sharpe, Harte, Molenaar, Wallace*
May 3	Chelsea	0-0	Martyn	Kelly	Dorigo	Palmer	Radebe	Wetherall	Bowyer	Lilley	Deane	Rush	Halle	Beeney, Sharpe, Laurent, Molenaar, Wallace
May 11	MIDDLESBROUGH	1-1	Martyn	Halle	Dorigo	Radebe	Kelly	Wetherall	Bowyer	Lilley	Deane 1	Rush*	Sharpe	Beeney, Wallace*,Jackson, Molenaar, Laurent

COCA-COLA CUP

Date	Opponent	Round	Score	GK	2	3	4	5	6	7	8	9	10	11	Subs
Sep 18	Darlington	Rd2 Leg1	2-2	Martyn	Kelly	Harte	Ford	Wetherall	Jackson	Gray*	Wallace 2	Rush	Couzens		Sharpe, Beeney, Radebe, Blunt*
Sep 25	Darlington	Rd2 Leg2	2-0	Martyn	Kelly	Harte 1	Palmer	Wetherall	Jackson	Gray	Wallace 1	Rush	Couzens		Sharpe, Beeney, Jackson, Boyle,
		Won	4-2 Agg												
Oct 23	ASTON VILLA	Rd3	1-2	Martyn	Kelly	Beesley*	Palmer	Radebe*	Jackson	Ford	Wallace	Rush	Couzens		Sharpe, Beeney, Wetherall, Harte

F.A. CUP

Date	Opponent	Round	Score	GK	2	3	4	5	6	7	8	9	10	11	Subs
Jan 14	Crystal Palace	Rd3 o.g	2-2	Martyn	Kelly	Dorigo*	Jackson	Radebe	Wetherall	Bowyer	Wallace	Rush	Deane 1		Beesley, Beeney, Sharpe*, Harte
Jan 25	Crystal Palace	Rd3 rep	1-0	Martyn	Kelly	Dorigo	Palmer	Radebe	Halle	Bowyer	Wallace 1	Rush	Deane		Jackson, Beeney, Ford, Beesley
Feb 4	Arsenal	Rd4	1-0	Martyn	Kelly	Dorigo	Palmer	Molenaar	Halle	Bowyer*	Jackson	Wallace* 1	Deane		Harte, Beeney, Wetheralll*, Rush*
Feb 15	Portsmouth	Rd5	2-3	Martyn	Kelly	Dorigo	Palmer	Molenaar	Radebe	Bowyer 2	Jackson*	Wallace	Deane		Halle, Beeney, Rush*, Wetheralll

Index Page numbers in bold indicate a photograph.